D1155015

DATE DUE

THURGOOD MARSHALL

The Library of Black America

THURGOOD MARSHALL

His Speeches, Writings, Arguments, Opinions, and Reminiscences

Edited by Mark V. Tushnet

Foreword by Randall Kennedy

Lawrence Hill Books

Library of Congress Cataloging-in-Publication Data

Marshall, Thurgood, 1908–1993.
Thurgood Marshall : his speeches, writings, arguments, opinions, and reminiscences /
edited by Mark Tushnet; foreword by Randall Kennedy.
p. cm. — (Library of Black America)
Includes index.
ISBN 1-55652-385-8 (cloth) — ISBN 1-55652-386-6 (pbk.)
1. Marshall, Thurgood, 1908–1993. 2. United States. Supreme Court—Biography. 3.
Judges—United States—Biography. I. Tushnet, Mark V., 1945– II. Title. III. Series.

KF8745.M34 A4 2001
347.73'2634—dc21
[B]

2001016793

Cover image: Copy photograph of the official portrait of Justice Thurgood Marshall,
painted c. 1991–1992. Artist: Symmie Knox. Collection of the Supreme Court of the
United States.

Cover design: Joan Sommers Design
Interior design: Hendrickson Creative Communications

Published by Lawrence Hill Books, an imprint of Chicago Review Press, Incorporated
814 North Franklin Street
Chicago, Illinois 60610
ISBN 1-55652-385-8 (cloth)
ISBN 1-55652-386-6 (paper)
Printed in the United States of America
5 4 3 2 1

Contents

PART III

WRITINGS AS A JUDGE 171

PART IV

JUDICIAL OPINIONS   303

PART V

REMINISCENCES 411

Foreword

This tremendously useful collection of writings and statements by Thurgood Marshall permits readers to go behind the symbolism that encases Marshall's reputation to see concretely what he wrote and thought over the course of his distinguished career. Many people know that Thurgood Marshall was an important African American "first"—the first black judge to sit on the United States Court of Appeals for the Second Circuit, the first black solicitor general, and the first black Supreme Court justice. Many people also know that before he began to be appointed to high government posts in the 1960s, Marshall served as the chief attorney for the NAACP and in that capacity directed an extraordinary campaign of litigation that advanced the legal rights of African Americans (and by extension all racial minorities). Largely missing from public understanding, however, is detailed knowledge about the work he produced. In the following pages, one can study firsthand various facets of that work. One can read briefs and oral arguments in which Marshall attempted to elicit favorable responses from judges, speeches and articles in which he attempted to set agendas for fellow jurists, essays in which he attempted to influence lay audiences, and opinions in which, as a justice, he applied his interpretation of the law to specific disputes. Also in the pages that follow is a transcript of an extensive, intimate interview with Justice Marshall that has never before been published. By bringing materials out of hard-to-reach research libraries and making them broadly accessible, Professor Mark Tushnet permits readers to make up their own minds on an informed basis about Marshall's strengths and weaknesses.

Chief among the strengths was an unflagging persistence directed at exposing massive defects in American democracy. From the oldest article in the collection ("Equal Justice Under Law," written in 1939 for *The Crisis*) to the most recent ("A Tribute to Justice William J. Brennan," written in 1990 for the *Harvard Law Review*), Thurgood Marshall single-mindedly identified socially destructive practices, policies, and habits of mind: lynching, segregation, torture, capital punishment, complacency in the presence of brutality, indifference toward poverty. He was the lawyer as muckraker: exposing injustice, shaming apathy, demanding intelligent response.

Some of the evils against which Marshall railed are safely interred in American history. One of these is the ghastly phenomenon of lynching—murder perpetrated by a group to punish people for perceived violations of law or custom. Between the 1880s and the 1930s, particularly in the South, white supremacists deployed lynching as a weapon of racial intimidation. During that period at least 4,700 people were lynched, 70 percent of whom were black. Among the most sobering of the pages that follow are those in which Marshall excoriates the failure of states and the federal government to protect African Americans from racist, vigilante violence. In an article for the *Lawyers Guild Review* in 1942 (coauthored with William H. Hastie, the first black federal judge), Marshall devotes an entire section to "lynchings and mob violence." He notes that in the aftermath of a lynching that occurred at Sikeston, Missouri, on January 25, 1942, a federal grand jury that declined to indict any of the suspected lynchers evinced considerably more hostility toward the victim of the mob than the mob itself.

Although the days are past when white supremacists could, with impunity, murder blacks accused of violating Jim Crow racial etiquette, there are other evils Marshall battled that remain all too evident. One is racist police misconduct. Because of racial profiling, routine humiliating mistreatment, and racially selective resorts to excessive violence, many blacks harbor intense resentment and distrust toward the criminal justice system, particularly police authorities. Several of the documents in this volume highlight the deep-rootedness of this problem. Marshall's brief in *Lyons v. Oklahoma* (1944) details a case in which law enforcement officials beat a confession out of a suspect. His article "Negro Discrimination and the Need for Federal Action" (1942) notes the beating of an African American army nurse by a policeman in Montgomery, Alabama, "because she refused to vacate the rear seat of a bus so that white passengers might be seated"—a remarkable neglected fact in light of the landmark Montgomery Bus Boycott of 1954–1955 that was sparked by a similar incident involving the legendary Rosa Parks. Another article, "The Gestapo in Detroit," relates how police in that city effectively sided with white thugs who terrorized blacks during disturbances that erupted during the summer of 1943. According to Marshall's carefully substantiated account,

> The trouble reached riot proportions because the police . . . enforced law with an unequal hand. They used "persuasion" rather than firm action with white rioters, while against Negroes they used the ultimate in force: nightsticks, revolvers, riot guns, sub-machine guns, and deer guns. As a result, 25 of the 34 persons killed were Negroes. Of the latter, 17 were killed by police. . . . The entire record . . . reads like the story of the Nazi Gestapo.

* * *

Many commentators have remarked that Marshall's career as an attorney was more impressive than his career as a justice. This is probably true. In making this assessment, however, one must recognize that the first act of Marshall's career was so extraordinary that following acts, though impressive by normal standards, were bound to be anticlimactic. After all, the campaign that he led to delegitimate segregation, the campaign whose great landmark is *Brown v. Board of Education*, is probably the most effective and influential campaign of social reform litigation in American history. Events, moreover, conspired to limit Marshall's reach as a justice. When he took his seat on the Court in 1967, he joined a slim liberal majority. By 1972, however, because of personnel changes, the Court was dominated by conservatives. Instead of writing opinions for the Court in major contested cases of constitutional law, Marshall was increasingly consigned to writing dissents.

Still, it is wrong to portray Marshall, as some do, as a second- or third-rate justice. To the contrary, in important respects, his record was exemplary. No justice has more consistently tried to bring judicial practice into line with the noblest sentiments expressed in the foundational documents of American democracy—the Declaration of Independence and the Constitution.

He wrote a number of pioneering decisions for the Court. Several are included in this collection, including *Stanley v. Georgia* (1969) and *Police Department of the City of Chicago v. Mosley* (1972). In a key decision that reinforces individuals' rights to privacy, the Court ruled in *Stanley* that states cannot criminalize mere private possession of obscene material within one's lodgings. "Whatever may be the justifications for . . . statutes regulating obscenity," Marshall averred, "we do not think they reach into the privacy of one's own home. If the First Amendment means anything, it means that a State has no business telling a man, sitting alone in his own house, what books he may read or what films he may watch. Our whole constitutional heritage rebels at the thought of giving government the power to control men's minds."

In *Mosley*, the Court struck down a city ordinance that generally forbade picketing within 150 feet of a public school but exempted peaceful labor picketing from this restriction. In an oft-cited passage that elevates equality of treatment to a central position in the jurisprudence of freedom of expression, Marshall declared that the ordinance violated the federal constitution because

> [A]bove all else, the First Amendment means that government has no power to restrict expression because of its message, its ideas, its subject matter, or its content. To permit the continued building of our politics and culture, and to assure self-fulfillment for each individual, our people are guaranteed the right to express any thought, free from government censorship. The essence of this forbidden censorship is content control. Any restriction on expressive activity because of its content would completely undercut the "profound national commitment to the principle that debate on public issues should be uninhibited, robust, and wide-open."

There is a bit of wishful thinking in Marshall's assertion. His portrayal of the law is more libertarian than the actual state of the jurisprudence. But it vividly captures one of Marshall's abiding passions: freeing people from wrongful government censorship, including people with whom Marshall himself frequently disagreed.

Marshall succeeded on occasion in obtaining Court majorities in the teeth of circumstances that would have discouraged and silenced a lesser jurist. His role in *Ake v. Oklahoma* is indicative of Marshall's efforts to change the minds of colleagues. In that case, a defendant charged with capital murder pleaded not guilty by reason of insanity. When his court-appointed attorney sought funds to pay for a psychiatrist, state authorities balked, claiming that the defendant was entitled to a lawyer at public expense but nothing more. Meanwhile, the state used psychiatrists in its prosecution and obtained a conviction and sentence of death. When the defendant appealed to the Supreme Court, it initially refused to hear his case. Marshall, however, wrote a lengthy dissent from the Court's action that convinced several of the other justices that the case at least merited a full hearing on the merits. A year later, after full briefing and oral argument, a majority sided with Marshall, who wrote an opinion establishing that, at least in certain circumstances, the due process clause of the federal constitution imposes an affirmative obligation on states to provide criminal defendants with resources beyond the mere provision of an attorney.

Marshall's greatest contribution to the Supreme Court, however, consisted not in his majority opinions but in his forceful dissents, an array of which are featured here. After the Court permitted states to begin anew to execute defendants convicted of aggravated murder, Marshall (along with Justice Brennan) dissented in every case in which the justices affirmed a death sentence because he believed that capital punishment, no matter how carefully administered, violated the federal constitution in *all* circumstances. Objecting to what he termed the "emasculation" of federally guaranteed equal protection of the laws, Marshall dissented vociferously when the Supreme Court held in *Milliken v. Bradley* (1974) that "innocent" suburban school districts could not be used to help dilute the racial isolation of predominantly black inner-city school districts even if a state had participated in purposefully segregating the inner-city schools. Evoking his special relationship to the history of desegregation in public schooling, Marshall observed that

> desegregation is not and was never expected to be an easy task. Racial attitudes ingrained in our Nation's childhood and adolescence are not quickly thrown aside in its middle years. But just as the inconvenience of some cannot be allowed to stand in the way of the rights of others, so public opposition, no matter how strident, cannot be permitted to divert this Court from the enforcement of the constitutional principles at issue. . . . Today's holding, I fear, is more a reflection of a perceived public mood that we have gone far enough in enforcing the Constitution's guarantee of equal justice than it is the product of neutral principles of law. In the short run, it may seem to be the easier course to allow our great metropolitan areas to be divided up into two cities—one white, the other black—but it is a course, I predict, our people will ultimately regret.

Similarly harsh was Marshall's dissent in *Regents of the University of California v. Bakke* (1978), the Court's first full-fledged battle over affirmative action. Though the Court narrowly affirmed the authority of public universities to take race into account to assist racial minorities in competition for admission, it did so on an exceedingly narrow basis that did not support the affirmative action program at issue in the case. Arguing in favor of a legal standard that would have given broad leeway to public institutions to engage in affirmative discrimination on behalf of African Americans (and perhaps other historically oppressed racial minorities), Marshall insisted that it was essential to remember that "during most of the past 200 years, the Constitution as interpreted by this Court, did not prohibit the most ingenious and pervasive forms of discrimination against the Negro." Now, he declared, "when a State acts to remedy the effects of that legacy of discrimination, I cannot believe that this same Constitution stands as a barrier."

What Marshall perceived as mistreatment of the poor also provoked strong dissents. Except in a few sharply defined circumstances, Marshall's colleagues declined to order officials to accommodate the disabilities imposed by impoverishment. Marshall, by contrast, believed that the egalitarian ethos of the Constitution required much more in terms of relieving people of the burdens of poverty. In *United States v. Kras* (1973), for example, a citizen sought exemption from a rule that required petitioners for bankruptcy to pay a $50 filing fee. Unemployed, with children, including one who suffered from cystic fibrosis, Robert William Kras claimed that day-to-day living expenses made it impossible for him to pay the filing fee, even on an installment plan that the government offered. In such circumstances, he argued, it violated the federal constitution to prohibit him from taking advantage of bankruptcy protection simply because he was too poor to pay the filing fee. The Court majority upheld the constitutionality of the filing fee requirement, even as applied to Kras. In the course of doing so, the Court noted that the weekly installments would amount to a sum "less than the price of a movie and a little more than the cost of a pack or two of cigarettes." Marshall objected to the majority's reading of doctrine. But even more he objected to the Court's chastising lecture regarding what it perceived as Kras's irresponsible spending habits. In a Dickensian rebuke to the Court's smugness, Marshall wrote:

I cannot agree with the majority that it is so easy for the desperately poor to save $1.92 each week over the course of six months. The 1970 Census found that over 800,000 families in the Nation had annual incomes of less than $1,000, or $19.23 a week. I see no reason to require that families in such straits sacrifice over 5% of their annual income as a prerequisite to getting a discharge in bankruptcy.

It may be easy for some people to think that weekly savings of less than $2 are no burden. But no one who has had close contact with poor people can fail to understand how close to the margin of survival many of them are. . . . A pack or two of cigarettes may be, for them, not a routine purchase but a luxury indulged in only rarely. The desperately poor almost never go to see a movie, which the majority seems to believe is an almost weekly activity. They have more important things to do with what little money they have—like attempting to provide some comforts for a gravely ill child, as Kras must do.

It is perfectly proper for judges to disagree about what the Constitution requires. But it is disgraceful for an interpretation of the Constitution to be premised upon unfounded assumptions about how people live.

* * *

In addition to allowing readers to appreciate the strengths demonstrated by Marshall's writings, this collection also offers an opportunity to consider certain problems.

One difficulty in evaluating Marshall is the problem of authorship. Most of the items attributed to Marshall were, in reality, written in collaboration with others—subordinates at the NAACP or the solicitors general's office and law clerks at the court of appeals and Supreme Court. That being so, to what extent can a given item be relied upon as a reflection of the substance and style of Marshall's own thinking? This question has relevance, of course, that extends far beyond Marshall. Thomas Jefferson wrote George Washington's farewell address. Walter Lippman penned Woodrow Wilson's Fourteen Points. Theodore Sorenson wrote John F. Kennedy's *Profiles in Courage*. Peggy Noonan wrote President George H. Bush's "Thousand Points of Light" speech. Anonymous law clerks only two or three years removed from law school write much, if not most, of what appears under the names of the justices—addresses, law review articles, and the published opinions that constitute the federal judicial law of the land. Still, the question remains: to what extent did others write Marshall's work and to what extent, then, can that work be relied upon as evidence about Marshall's qualities as a thinker? Although a comprehensive answer is beyond the bounds of this essay and the available record, I shall hazard a few speculative generalizations. It is likely that Marshall played a larger role in the crafting of documents when he had fewer assistants to rely upon, a narrower scope of responsibilities, and greater stores of personal energy. From published accounts, reliable gossip, and my own observations, it seems that at least during the final decade of Marshall's tenure on the Court, almost all of the justice's writing was produced by law clerks. This is by no means peculiar to Marshall. The same can be said of many of the justices, especially as they age. Marshall, moreover, directed the law clerks as to substance and tone and was very willing and able to intervene editorially when he perceived a clerk to be advancing his or her pet theory as opposed to advancing a Marshallian perspective on the dispute at hand. That the writings of the Marshall Chambers, albeit penned by various hands, bear internal consistency and distinctive markings reflects, in substantial degree, the justice's supervision of the products that bear his imprimatur. Still, the public should know that when a justice is said to "write" an opinion, the relationship of his or her labor to the actual words on the page is often complex and sometimes tenuous.

Another problematic facet of Marshall's career is his relationship to the black bar in particular and to black communities in general. Early in his career, he contributed articles to publications based within the black intelligentsia. In this collection, readers will see some of these writings, pieces that appeared in *The Crisis*, *The Journal of Negro History*, and the *Journal of Negro Education*. Marshall, moreover, socialized with, encouraged, and utilized fellow black attorneys during the 1930s, 1940s, and 1950s when he toured the country tirelessly representing clients in civil and criminal cases at all levels—state and federal, trial courts and appellate tribunals. One of the most revealing and rare documents in this collection is the transcript of remarks that Marshall offered on November 25, 1951, at a testimonial dinner honoring Raymond Pace Alexander, a prominent black attorney in Philadelphia who handled scores of highly publicized criminal and civil rights cases. Lauding Alexander, Marshall acknowledged the racial difficulties that black lawyers faced. "Negro lawyers," he observed, "have had a tough time." After all, they suffer too from debilitating racist stereotypes—the notion, for example, that "all Negroes are thieves and cannot be trusted." Marshall insisted, however, that these obstacles could be overcome, and joined in the hard work of erasing prejudices by, among other things, strengthening the black bar's collective presence.

Unfortunately, as Marshall attained prominence among whites as well as blacks, and especially after he entered the government, he became detached from the black bar, black politics, and black institutional life. This probably stemmed in large part from Marshall's strict insistence upon doing nothing that could be said to impair the reality or appearance of his impartiality as a justice. But whatever the motivation, the fact is that, until his retirement from the bench, Marshall rather self-consciously distanced himself from activities organized to advance African American interests.

Marshall hired more black law clerks than did his colleagues. But he still hired relatively few, and *none* from his alma mater, the Howard University School of Law. Howard would undoubtedly have benefited from more attention from Marshall. And it is possible that Marshall and his work would have benefited from a deeper engagement with the contentious universe of black activist thought that emerged in the aftermath of the civil rights revolution of the 1960s. Marshall fought hard all of his life for praiseworthy ends. But by the 1970s and 1980s, his fund of ideas about how best to extend the boundaries of social justice was largely depleted. Indeed, during the final two decades of his public career he often resorted to a course of defensive legalism that appears uninspiring and unpersuasive even to the sympathetic observer.

An illustration is provided by his dissent in *Payne v. Tennessee* (1991), a decision handed down the very day that Marshall announced his retirement from the Court. In *Payne*, the Court decided that a state did not violate the federal constitution if it permitted a jury to consider "victim impact statements" in deciding whether to impose a death sentence. Prosecutors use victim impact statements to apprise a jury of the loss generated by a murder. Often such statements will emphasize the virtues of homicide victims and the agonies that murder has foisted upon friends and families. In the five years prior to *Payne*, a sharply divided Supreme Court twice held that the federal constitution prohibited the use of victim impact statements on the grounds that they would impermissibly inject into trials a high risk of unfairness insofar as juries might be swayed to punish more harshly the killers of sympathetic as opposed to unsympathetic victims. In *Payne*, however, a still sharply divided Court reversed itself, ruling that victim impact statements are permissible. Justice Marshall responded with one of the angriest dissents of his career. "Power, not reason," he charged, "is the new currency of this Court's decision making." Neither the law nor the facts supporting the earlier decisions had undergone any change, Marshall observed. "Only the personnel of this Court did." Here he was referring to the retirement of William F. Brennan, who had voted against the permissibility of victim impact statements, and his replacement by David Souter, who voted in favor of their permissibility. As Marshall described the situation, the Court's majority was renouncing a "historical commitment to a conception of 'the judiciary as a source of impersonal and reasoned judgments,'" and declaring itself free "to discard any principle of constitutional liberty . . . with which five or more Justices now disagree." Marshall insisted, "The implications of this radical new exception to the doctrine of *stare decisis* are staggering. The majority today sends a clear signal that scores of established constitutional liberties are now ripe for reconsideration, thereby inviting the very type of open defiance of our precedents that the majority rewards in this case."

In his dissent, Marshall spent some space discussing the *substantive* merits of his disagreement with the Court over the wisdom of permitting victim impact statements. But most of the opinion, including its impassioned flourishes, was devoted to the *procedural* question of whether it was proper for the Court to overrule precedents that had only recently been established. On this point, Marshall, ironically, adopted the stance of a conservative, emphasizing the benefits of continuity, stability, tradition. It was an awkward, ill-fitting stance. Marshall, after all, had spent much of his storied career figuring out ways to topple precedent. Moreover, as noted above, Marshall never felt himself bound by the Court's judgment regarding capital punishment. There is—or should be—nothing sacred about precedent in and of itself. In the face of uncertainty or evenly balanced merits, it makes sense to defer to tradition. But otherwise what should be decisive is the content of the precedent in question. If the precedent is good, it should be defended. If it is bad, it should be erased. That Marshall spent so little space and effort advancing the positive case in favor of the content of the conclusion he favored, reflects, I think, a regrettable feature of his thought and conduct—a formalistic and legalistic strain of liberalism—that has, thus far, attracted insufficient attention.

Thurgood Marshall's greatness can withstand critical attention. Indeed the impressiveness of his steady, unflamboyant, but unflinching campaign against social inequities becomes more impressive the closer one examines his efforts, career, and the forces against which he battled. The hostility he weathered and the inertia he somehow overcame would surely have crushed lesser spirits. He was a major presence in American life throughout much of the twentieth century, and the best features of his career will hopefully be widely emulated by Americans of all sorts in the years to come.

RANDALL KENNEDY
Harvard Law School
January 2001

Introduction

"Mr. Civil Rights" to African Americans in the 1950s; the first African American justice of the United States Supreme Court; one of the few justices who would appear in history books even if he had not been appointed to the Supreme Court; the last Warren Court liberal on the Supreme Court; one of the most important American lawyers in the twentieth century. All these phrases describe Thurgood Marshall.

Marshall's career centered on the contradiction between the Constitution's promises and its reality. He was passionately devoted to the Constitution, and yet he always recognized that the real world did not fulfill the Constitution's commitments, and might never do so. In a formulation he repeated often, Marshall said, "the goal of a true democracy such as ours . . . is that any baby born in the United States, even if he is born to the blackest, most illiterate, most unprivileged Negro in Mississippi, is, merely by being born and drawing his first breath in this democracy, endowed with the exact same rights as a child born to a Rockefeller. Of course it's not true. Of course it never will be true. But I challenge anybody to tell me that it isn't the type of goal we should try to get to as fast as we can."

Born in Baltimore, Maryland, in 1908, Marshall was raised in segregation, and always thought of himself as a Southerner; when President Richard Nixon was reportedly seeking a Southerner to name to the Supreme Court, Marshall jocularly but pointedly commented that as far as he was concerned there already was a Southerner on the Court. But he was of course an African American Southerner, shaped by the experience of segregation. Even as the son of reasonably well-established parents, his mother a school teacher and his father the head of the serving staff at an elite white country club, Marshall felt the sting of segregation as he grew up. One of his most vivid memories was of having to rush home to find a bathroom he could use, being unable to locate one open to a black child in downtown Baltimore. Segregation could not dampen Marshall's spirit, however, and he recalled a number of fights provoked by his reaction to being treated as a second-class citizen.

Initially intending to become a dentist like his brother William, Marshall attended Lincoln University in Pennsylvania, but he encountered trouble in his science classes and changed his aspirations. Excluded by state law from the University of Maryland Law School, Marshall attended Howard University Law School. The Howard experience transformed his life. Marshall went to Howard just as it was undergoing a dramatic reorientation under the leadership of Charles Hamilton Houston, a charismatic graduate of Amherst College and Harvard Law School. Houston changed Howard Law School from a second-rate night school to what he called a school for "social engineers." Houston was a demanding teacher, who inspired his students to do the best work they could and to put their talents to the service of their community.

Marshall commuted from Baltimore to Washington to go to law school. In his second year he took a job at the law school's library, and came under Houston's wing. Marshall assisted Houston with legal research as Houston defended George Crawford, an African American accused of murder in Virginia's hunt country. Houston and Marshall counted it as a victory when Crawford did not receive the death penalty upon conviction, and Marshall's observation of Houston at work— the hours spent in legal and factual research—shaped his own understanding of what it meant to be a lawyer for the African American community.

After graduation in 1933, Marshall opened a private practice in Baltimore. The economic opportunities for an individual practitioner in the African American community during the Depression were limited, and Marshall was hard-pressed to make a living. Out of conviction, and to spread his name in the community, Marshall became active in the local branch of the National Association for the Advancement of Colored People (NAACP). Recalling his own inability to attend the state law school, Marshall leaped at the chance to represent Donald Murray, an Amherst graduate who wanted to sue the state to force it to desegregate the university's law school. Counseled by Houston, Marshall won the first court decision requiring a previously segregated state university to admit African Americans.

Meanwhile, Houston had moved to New York to develop the NAACP's legal department. From its founding in 1909, the NAACP had sporadically engaged in constitutional litigation. In the late 1920s a number of NAACP leaders began to think about developing a more systematic litigation campaign. They negotiated with the American Fund for Public Service, also known as the Garland Fund, to obtain a substantial grant to prepare a plan for such litigation. That report, written by Nathan Margold, became something of an icon in the NAACP's legal thought. Margold proposed litigation aimed at segregation in education and housing. More of an academic than a trial lawyer, Margold had an overly ambitious vision of what the NAACP's small staff could accomplish. When Margold left the NAACP to join the Roosevelt administration, Houston came on board and refocused the litigation campaign.

Houston decided to bring cases like Donald Murray's, involving graduate and professional education, and lawsuits seeking to bring the salaries of African American school teachers up to the level of white teachers. Both branches of Houston's strategy were based on the Supreme Court's decision in *Plessy v. Ferguson* (1896), which held that segregated facilities were constitutional if they were "separate but equal." As Houston saw things, the salaries were plainly unequal, and no Southern state provided *any* graduate and professional education for African Americans. In both branches, then, the legal theory was a simple one: if "separate but equal" was the law, insist that states comply with it.

Houston found an enthusiastic follower in Marshall. In addition to Murray's suit, Marshall filed a number of lawsuits in Maryland's counties seeking to equalize teacher salaries. After overcoming a number of procedural obstacles, in 1939 and 1940 Marshall won the first major decisions requiring salary equalization. By then,

Marshall had relocated from Baltimore to New York, where in 1936 he joined Houston on the NAACP's staff. Houston returned to his Washington law practice in 1938, in part because his father wanted him to come back home and in part because he thought that civil rights lawyers would be out of business when they succeeded in their legal challenges to segregation. Marshall became the NAACP's chief lawyer in 1938, a position he held until he left the organization in 1961.

Houston's tutelage and Marshall's own impressive talents made him a superb trial lawyer and appellate advocate. Always respectful (at least in public) of his adversaries, Marshall worked tirelessly to investigate cases involving civil rights violations. Marshall's attention to detail and his ability to get along with adversaries made him an effective investigator of major race-relations events, including the Detroit race riot in 1943 and discrimination against African Americans in courts-martial during the Korean War. His effusive personality made him a speaker sought out by nearly all the NAACP's local branches around the country, and his talks and travels provided important moral support to the local lawyers and their clients, who had to face the assaults of the Jim Crow system daily. Marshall thought of himself primarily as a trial lawyer, adept not so much at cutting cross-examination (a tactic unlikely to help his clients in the South) but rather at carefully compiling a record that would maximize the chance that some appeals court would reverse the adverse trial court decisions that were to be expected. As an oral advocate, Marshall was a master as well. A great raconteur, Marshall developed the capacity to speak in the different voices of the characters in his anecdotes; and he used that capacity as well as an oral advocate, shifting from a careful legal analysis to sharper tones as the occasion demanded. Having immersed himself in civil rights law and procedure, Marshall was usually in full control of oral arguments, meeting skeptical objections to his positions with a tenacious insistence that he asked for only what the law required, slipping only when he was forced on to unfamiliar terrain.

In 1939 the legal staff was formally split off from the NAACP for tax-related reasons. The NAACP engaged in political lobbying, which meant that donations to it were not deductible as charitable contributions. The new NAACP Legal Defense and Educational Fund, Inc., known as the Inc Fund, was a tax-exempt organization. Marshall continued to play a large role in general NAACP affairs, however.[1]

Marshall pursued Houston's litigation plans for about a decade. Salary equalization suits throughout the South were initially successful, providing greater income for important members of local African American communities and enhancing the NAACP's stature (and increasing its membership as grateful teachers signed up). University lawsuits were more difficult. Houston and Marshall achieved a major victory in 1938 when the United States Supreme Court accepted their argument in

---

[1] Under pressure from Southern senators in the mid-1950s, the Internal Revenue Service then forced a sharper division of lines between the NAACP and the Inc Fund. The separation had long-term effects on the litigation program, but they had not become important before Marshall left the organization.

Missouri ex rel. Gaines v. Canada that the state of Missouri had to provide its African American citizens with a law school education in Missouri, either by admitting them to the existing state law school or by creating a new law school for African Americans. The case had a more disappointing outcome on the ground, however, when Lloyd Gaines, the plaintiff, disappeared. Organizing other university challenges was difficult, and became even harder during World War II, when many potential plaintiffs went into the armed forces.

Marshall renewed the university challenges at the end of the war. Conditions had changed in important ways. Wartime experiences had made many African Americans even more willing to stand up to segregation. A legal theory that accepted the "separate but equal" doctrine was far more troublesome in 1945 than it had been in 1935. Marshall found himself pressed by his colleagues, particularly by his principal deputy Robert Carter, to develop a more radical direct attack on segregation. Marshall thought that the legal landscape had to change before such a direct attack had any reasonable prospect of success. He temporized by bringing a series of challenges to segregated university education in which the main theory was the one the Court had accepted in *Gaines*, that states had to provide equal educational opportunities for whites and blacks either by desegregation or by creating new segregated programs. Marshall gave a new twist to that theory, though. Relying on a cadre of academic supporters, both black and white, Marshall developed records showing that the educational opportunities offered by new segregated programs were not, and could not be, equal to those provided in long-established programs.

The Supreme Court accepted this new theory in *Sweatt v. Painter* (1950), a case involving legal education in Texas. In response to an NAACP lawsuit, the Texas legislature created a law school for African Americans. Initially housed in an office building in downtown Austin, the state capital, the law school was soon transferred to a segregated university in Houston. The state contended that the new law school would provide education in law substantially equal to that provided by the University of Texas Law School. When *Sweatt v. Painter* reached the Supreme Court, Texan Tom Clark was the key figure in casting the state's claims in their true light. Clark pointed out to his colleagues that the University of Texas Law School was a central institution in the state's legal and political culture. Its students developed lifetime friendships and relationships that made them more effective lawyers. In rejecting the state's case, *Sweatt v. Painter* emphasized that equal educational opportunities had to be measured by more than the material facilities—the "bricks and mortar" of schools—but included important intangible qualities of association as well.[2]

---

[2] Another case decided on the same day, *McLaurin v. Oklahoma State Regents*, held that the state denied equal opportunities to a graduate student who was forced to sit in a carrel at the side of his classrooms, in a segregated area of the library, and in a segregated portion of the school cafeteria.

Marshall immediately grasped the importance of this decision, saying that it provided a roadmap for the direct attack on school segregation at all levels of education. Parents and students throughout the South were eager to challenge segregation, both to improve the quality of the segregated schools by enforcing the "equal" part of "separate but equal" and to eliminate segregation entirely through a direct attack. Marshall coordinated the NAACP legal staff's lawsuits in four states—Kansas, Delaware, Virginia, and South Carolina.[3]

Marshall conducted the trial himself in the South Carolina case, *Briggs v. Elliott.* There governor James Byrnes responded to the lawsuit by getting the state legislature to enact a bond issue that would devote substantial funds to improving the material aspects of the segregated black schools. Marshall did not oppose this building program, and indeed it smoothed the way for the direct attack: the new investments in black schools made it more plausible for the state to claim that it was offering separate education that really was equal. As he developed his case, Marshall relied on testimony from social psychologist Kenneth Clark, who interviewed African American students in the elementary grades in Clarendon County, South Carolina, the site of the lawsuit. Clark administered psychological tests to the students, and concluded that the students' self-image was impaired by the fact that they were forced to attend segregated schools. Prodded by Robert Carter, Marshall relied on Clark's testimony to establish that segregation itself harmed African American students, whether or not they were attending schools that were in a bricks-and-mortar sense equal to the schools for whites.

The segregation cases, under the name of *Brown v. Board of Education* after the Kansas case, reached the Supreme Court in 1952. At the time the Supreme Court was quite divided over finding segregated education unconstitutional. A majority probably favored that course, but Chief Justice Fred Vinson, himself brought up in segregated Kentucky, was unable to provide significant leadership to the Court. As a result, the Court asked the parties to argue the case again. Vinson died before the reargument occurred, and his replacement, Earl Warren, was a dedicated opponent of segregation. Warren led the Court to its unanimous decision on May 17, 1954, finding segregation unconstitutional.

Marshall hoped that the Court's decision would lead to rapid desegregation. Responses in the upper South and border states such as Delaware and Maryland were encouraging. Farther South, though, resistance to desegregation was strong. *Brown* gave ambitious politicians an opportunity to develop strong constituencies among whites opposed to desegregation. School boards were recalcitrant, at best proposing only the most modest steps in the direction of desegregation. Sporadically, violent resistance to desegregation broke out. When Arkansas governor Orval Faubus sent the state National Guard to help those objecting to desegregation in Little

---

[3] The NAACP monitored a fifth case, in the District of Columbia, where the legal theory was slightly different.

Rock, a national crisis occurred. President Dwight Eisenhower took control of the state National Guard and dispatched federal troops to ensure that Little Rock's Central High School remained open and desegregated. A challenge to the Little Rock desegregation order reached the Supreme Court in *Cooper v. Aaron* (1958), in which the Court dramatically reaffirmed its holding in *Brown* after an emergency session called to ensure that the schools would reopen in the fall of 1958 on a desegregated basis.

Southern defenders of segregation mounted a sustained challenge to the NAACP and its lawyers, which occupied much of Marshall's time in the late 1950s. State attorneys charged that the NAACP lawyers had violated ethical rules against stirring up litigation and soliciting clients. State legislatures investigated NAACP branches for alleged Communist influence. Eventually the Supreme Court found all these attacks unconstitutional, but they diverted the legal staff's effort away from desegregation litigation and into self-defense.

The pressures of work severely limited the amount of other writing Marshall could do. Not only did he have clients to represent at trial and speeches to give to NAACP branches, he also had to manage the operations of a small law firm—the NAACP's legal staff. Marshall did produce articles for the NAACP's magazine *The Crisis*, seeking to educate the NAACP's members about civil rights law and the NAACP's legal program. Sometimes he extended his audience to the academy, but what he wrote tended to summarize the NAACP's cases and its program. His writings as a lawyer did not venture bold new theories, largely because he did not have the time to do so. Sometimes, however, he used the investigations he conducted to present vivid accounts of the realities of discrimination.

Marshall found the work he was doing in the late 1950s personally unsatisfying. He had become a major figure in the civil rights community (although he resented somewhat the rise of Martin Luther King, Jr., as a leader) but his professional and personal lives were no longer providing him the rewards he wanted. He had married Vivian "Buster" Marshall after graduating from college. Although they both wanted children, Buster had a number of miscarriages. Marshall's travels throughout the country further strained the marriage. Buster died of lung cancer in April 1955. Marshall married Cecilia Suyatt, a secretary in the NAACP's office, in December. By the end of the 1950s, they had two young sons, and Marshall wanted to spend more time in New York with his family.

His opportunity arose when President John F. Kennedy nominated him to a position on the federal court of appeals in New York, at the time probably the second most important federal court in the country after the Supreme Court. Southern senators delayed Marshall's confirmation for nearly a year, but eventually he was approved and took his seat on the Second Circuit in 1961, where he served until 1965. Then President Lyndon Johnson asked him to step down from his lifetime position as a judge to become solicitor general, the government's chief lawyer and advocate before the Supreme Court. Johnson almost certainly intended to use Marshall's service as solicitor general as a prelude to his nomination to the Supreme Court, and Marshall almost certainly understood Johnson's intention, although no records or other evidence exists to confirm these judgments. Marshall accepted Johnson's offer, in part because he felt that Johnson, a fellow Southerner, was truly devoted to civil rights.

Marshall had been a great oral advocate when he was arguing NAACP cases. He had an intuitive grasp of what the justices were concerned about, and was able to respond to their concerns quickly and in ways that accommodated their concerns to the legal positions he was advancing. As solicitor general, Marshall was somewhat less successful. He argued cases in areas that he was less familiar with, and sometimes he was defending government positions in cases where the Warren Court was inclined to rule against the government. Marshall argued a federal companion case to *Miranda v. Arizona* (1966), for example, and defended the warnings the Federal Bureau of Investigation gave suspects, warnings the Court found too limited.

After Marshall had served two years as solicitor general, Johnson maneuvered Tom Clark into retiring by naming his son Ramsey as attorney general, and then nominated Marshall to the Supreme Court. The political situation in 1967 was different from that in 1961, and Marshall was easily confirmed as the nation's first African American justice of the Supreme Court.

Marshall joined the Court when it was thoroughly dominated by New Deal–Great Society liberals. Chief Justice Earl Warren and Associate Justice William J. Brennan gave the Court administrative and intellectual leadership. William O. Douglas, appointed to the Court by Franklin D. Roosevelt, remained a strong voice for liberalism. Abe Fortas, a long-time Johnson crony, was the fifth member of a solidly liberal majority. They were joined on some issues by Hugo Black, a New Deal liberal whose constitutional commitments made him seem more conservative in the Warren Court era, and on others by Byron White, a Kennedy appointee who was conservative on criminal law issues but liberal on race ones. The Court's only conservatives were John Marshall Harlan and Potter Stewart, and even they represented the more liberal wing of the Republican party.

Marshall surely expected to contribute to the further expansion of the Warren Court's liberal constitutional agenda, but his expectations were defeated by a rapid change in the Court's composition. Earl Warren announced his retirement in June 1968, and Republicans, sensing that they might regain the presidency in that year's election, refused to confirm a successor. After Richard Nixon's victory, Warren departed, replaced by the far more conservative Warren Burger. Burger was also less adept than Warren at personal relations, which made Marshall's time on the Court even more uncomfortable as Burger occasionally blundered in his treatment of Marshall as a person. Then Republicans forced Abe Fortas to resign. Fortas's replacement was Harry Blackmun, a reliable conservative in his first years on the Court who gradually became more liberal. In 1971 Justices Black and Harlan both retired for reasons of health. When Lewis F. Powell and William Rehnquist joined the Court in early 1972, the solid Warren Court liberal majority of which Marshall was a part became a solid moderately conservative majority, from which Marshall consistently dissented.

The Court's changing composition severely limited Marshall. Significantly, he wrote more dissents and separate concurring opinions than he did opinions for the Court; and many of the majority opinions he wrote were in technical and statutory areas, not in constitutional ones. Marshall's most enduring contribution to constitutional law was probably his theory of the equal protection clause, which would have required the courts to balance the importance of a regulation's impact on a group, the nature of that impact, and the goals the state was seeking to achieve by singling out that group for regulation. This theory made more sense of the Court's decisions than the Court's own articulation of its doctrine. In addition, along with Brennan, Marshall was the Court's most consistent opponent of the death penalty. He was the only member of the Court who had represented criminal defendants facing the death penalty, and he drew on his experience in his opinions and extrajudicial comments to emphasize the impossibility of administering the death penalty fairly.

Beyond his contributions to doctrine, Marshall gave the Court a unique perspective. As its only African American member, Marshall brought to the conversations among the justices a distinctive range of experience. He was also the only justice with substantial experience as a trial lawyer and as a criminal defense lawyer, and his colleagues regularly noted the ways in which Marshall invoked experience, often to chastise them for ignoring the real world in which constitutional rules operated. Within his chambers, Marshall was frequently grumpy about the directions in which the Court was moving, and he expressed his dissatisfaction in a number of his extrajudicial writings and talks. To his colleagues, Marshall expressed his disagreement as a raconteur who came up with an anecdote that pointed out what was wrong with what they were doing.

For most of his time on the Court, Marshall was a "quick study," who could understand the central point of a legal argument by reading the lawyers' briefs. He relied on his law clerks to draft opinions, but not to outline the cases for him. As he aged, Marshall found the Court's work increasingly taxing. His law clerks began to draft more extensive memoranda for him before the Court heard cases argued. His close friend William Brennan retired for health reasons in 1990. Marshall had not been in good health for many years, and Brennan's departure, coupled with Marshall's own health problems, led Marshall to retire in 1991. He died in 1993.

* * *

This book presents a selection of Marshall's writings as a lawyer and advocate, and a small selection of edited excerpts from his most important Supreme Court opinions. Footnotes have been added to identify cases and names to which Marshall referred; footnotes appearing in the original are specifically identified.

Part I provides a glimpse of Marshall at work as a lawyer. It includes the brief he filed in the first major case he argued before the Supreme Court and the brief in his most important Supreme Court case, *Brown v. Board of Education*. Marshall's greatest talent lay in his ability to present a persuasive oral argument, and Part I contains edited excerpts from the transcripts of his oral arguments in *Brown* and *Cooper v. Aaron*, the Little Rock school desegregation case. Readers will find in these materials a demonstration of Marshall's eloquence and his tenacity in defending his positions against strong challenges.

Part II presents most of the articles Marshall published while he was a practicing lawyer. They are arranged chronologically and, taken as a group, give a good overview of the legal work of the NAACP and the Legal Defense Fund from 1909 to the mid-1950s.

Part III contains nearly all of the speeches and articles Marshall gave while he was a member of the Supreme Court. It is divided into two sections. The first section collects the talks Marshall gave at the annual meetings of the judges of the Court of Appeals for the Second Circuit and the lawyers who appeared before that court. Brief descriptive titles have been added to the transcriptions and otherwise untitled texts Marshall prepared. Marshall usually offered candid comments on the Court's work in these speeches, and they provide important insights into the generally skeptical view Marshall took of the Court's work after Warren Burger became chief justice. The second section of Part III includes Marshall's published articles and some previously unpublished speeches. These are arranged chronologically, with a few departures to ensure that speeches and articles that are thematically linked can be read together.

Part IV, the selections from Marshall's Supreme Court opinions, is arranged thematically. It begins with three cases dealing with Marshall's approach to interpreting the equal protection clause, followed by two of his dissents in affirmative action cases. The next cases deal with questions related to the way constitutional law deals with indigents, a matter clearly related to (but sometimes doctrinally distinct from) equal protection law. The final sections deal with Marshall's decisions in free speech and criminal justice cases, concluding with his final opinion as a justice, a dissent in a death penalty case in which Marshall insisted on the importance of adherence to precedent and chastised his colleagues for making "[p]ower, not reason . . . the currency" of the Court's action. These excerpts provide an introduction to Marshall's constitutional jurisprudence. Readers seeking additional material on that topic can use the Appendix as a guide to some of Marshall's other major decisions.

Part V is a transcript of an extensive oral history interview Marshall gave in 1977. Full of the anecdotes Marshall loved to tell, his reminiscences give readers a feel for Marshall's personality, as well as his own overview of the events in his life.

PART I

LEGAL BRIEFS AND ORAL ARGUMENTS

Insisting that good lawyers had to master the facts of the cases they brought or defended, Charles Hamilton Houston trained Marshall as a trial lawyer. Marshall's own abilities made him a great appellate lawyer. Both in trial courts and before appellate courts, Marshall had a sure instinct for the facts that mattered, and an ability to present his case in the way his audience—sometimes a jury, sometimes one or more judges, and sometimes the African American community—would understand best.

Marshall's work as a trial lawyer is contained in the transcripts of the cases he handled. The most effective trial lawyers do not fit the television image of an attorney cross-examining a hostile witness who ultimately confesses after having been exposed. Rather, these trial lawyers patiently compile a factual record to support their motions asking a judge to find in favor of their clients. Marshall frequently told of learning how to be a trial lawyer by riding in the backseat of Houston's car, balancing a typewriter on his knees while pounding out a motion to exclude evidence. Later, Marshall learned how to coordinate the presentation of facts from expert witnesses, an ability he used to great effect in the school desegregation lawsuits.

When Marshall headed the Legal Defense Fund, he was more a coordinator of other lawyers' work than an initial drafter of legal documents like briefs. By the late 1940s, the Legal Defense Fund's legal briefs were highly collaborative works, incorporating ideas from many members of the Fund staff and its outside advisers.

1

Marshall's oral advocacy, in contrast, was his alone. He was a master at striking the right tone: sometimes engaged in what seemed to be a simple conversation with the justices about how they all should handle a difficult legal problem, sometimes a sarcastic critic of his opponents' position, and sometimes the eloquent orator whose words went to the heart of the moral case for his clients.

What follows are two of Marshall's appellate briefs and transcripts of several of his oral arguments before the Supreme Court. The first brief is from *Lyons v. Oklahoma*, the second case Marshall argued before the Supreme Court.[1] The brief shows Marshall's instinct as a trial lawyer for presenting the facts of a case in a way that should incline the reader to agree with the conclusions Marshall wants the Court to draw. Although an appellate brief,[2] it illustrates some of Marshall's talents as a trial lawyer as well. The second is the initial brief in *Brown v. Board of Education*. This brief is notable for its brevity and for the straightforward manner in which it presents the argument that school segregation is unconstitutional. Marshall's oral arguments in the school desegregation cases were the most important in his career. The cases were argued three times, and this collection includes transcripts of all three of Marshall's arguments. Several years later, the Little Rock school crisis erupted. The Supreme Court scheduled two emergency arguments. The first dealt with some highly technical aspects of the case's procedural posture and, although it shows Marshall's facility in dealing with a complex legal problem on equal terms with the justices, it is omitted here in favor of the argument on the merits.[3]

---

[1] The first, *Adams v. United States*, arose out of a racially charged incident near an Army base in Louisiana. The Court disposed of the case on a highly technical ground that Marshall and his colleagues discovered late in the litigation.

[2] An *appellate brief* is the written presentation of the arguments a lawyer makes to an appeals court.

[3] Legal arguments can deal with preliminary technicalities, such as whether the case was filed in the proper court, or with the merits, that is, with the basic issue fundamentally dividing the parties.

1. *Lyons v. Oklahoma* (1944)

The issue in *Lyons* was whether a defendant's constitutional rights were violated when his confession to murder was admitted in his trial. Lyons first confessed after being beaten; he then repeated his confession. The first confession was not admitted against him, but the second one was. Long-standing state rules of criminal procedure barred the admission of coerced confessions. It was not until 1936, however, that the Supreme Court held that admitting a coerced confession into evidence at a criminal trial violated a defendant's right to due process of law. (Today we would say that admitting such a confession violated the defendant's rights under the Fifth Amendment not to be compelled to testify against himself, but the Supreme Court did not hold that the self-incrimination clause limited state governments until 1964.) The issue of police brutality and so-called "third degree" tactics attracted a great deal of attention from the public and legal academics in the 1930s,[1] which amplified a more focused concern by some that police officers were particularly harsh in dealing with African Americans suspected of crimes against whites. Marshall's brief in *Lyons* was written to evoke these concerns without specifically mentioning them.

W. D. LYONS V. STATE OF OKLAHOMA
Brief on Behalf of Petitioner.
Statement of Facts.

Late on the night of December 31, 1939, Elmer Rogers, his wife and one son were brutally murdered in their home near Fort Towson, Oklahoma. Another son, James Glenn Rogers, escaped with his smaller brother, Billie Don. Both Mr. and Mrs. Rogers were shot with a shotgun and the house set afire, burning both of them and one of the young boys.

The crime aroused the entire community and there was much newspaper publicity. Shortly thereafter several white prisoners from a nearby prison camp were arrested for the crime. This brought about additional publicity condemning the Oklahoma State Prison System. Warden Jesse Dunn of the State Prison System was sent to Fort Towson and began a personal investigation of the situation, and shortly thereafter made a change in officials in charge of the prison camp.

Vernon Cheatwood, special investigator for the Governor of Oklahoma, was sent to Fort Towson after the convicts from the nearby prison camp had been arrested for the crime. Vernon Cheatwood had been a special investigator for six or seven years and had much experience in obtaining confessions. During his investigation the prisoners arrested for the crime were released and W. D. Lyons, a young Negro, was arrested in Hugo, Oklahoma.

---

[1] Police interrogators who use violence and severe verbal intimidation to obtain a confession are said to be employing the "third degree."

The "Arrest".

On the night of January 11, 1940, W. D. Lyons left his mother-in-law's home to get a drink of illegal whiskey hidden in the woods and on his way back met Ennis Aikens. Aikens, a witness for the State of Oklahoma, testified that he and Lyons saw several cars of police officers drive up to the home of Lyons' mother-in-law and that Lyons requested him to go down to the house and ask his wife "what the trouble was down there." Shortly thereafter Lyons returned to the house and was met by two men with drawn revolvers. Reasor Cain and Oscar Bearden made the "arrest." Reasor Cain at that time was a special officer for the Frisco Railroad but is no longer employed by the Frisco. The employment of Oscar Bearden does not appear in the record. These two men promptly seized Lyons and since they did not have handcuffs they bound his arms behind his back with his belt. The men then started toward the jail with Lyons.

About three blocks from the court house and jail Reasor Cain broke off a piece of one-inch board lying on the street and Oscar Bearden struck Lyons on the head with this board. He then kicked Lyons and threatened his life by telling him they were going to burn him and kill him by degrees unless he "confessed." About a block from the jail they bumped Lyons' head against a tree. When they reached the jail the jailor, Leonard Holmes, greeted Lyons by striking him in the mouth with the jail keys which weighed about five pounds.

Events Leading Up To The Confessions.

Bearden then told Cain and Holmes to "get some more officers, and we will drag him through 'colored town' and let the rest of the Negroes learn a lesson." Harvey Hawkins returned and reported there were no more officers around at that time. The jailor and Deputy Sheriff Floyd Brown then carried Lyons to the top floor of the women's side of the jail where Floyd Brown kicked him and knocked him down with his fist. While on the floor Lyons was kicked in the stomach and ribs by Brown. Lyons was then placed in a cell.

After about five minutes Lyons was carried downstairs to a small room adjoining the sheriff's office. In this room at the time were the sheriff, two deputy sheriffs, the state ballistic expert, two highway patrolmen, and the state investigator. Roy Harmon, sheriff and state's witness, admitted there were at least three or four men in the room besides Lyons.

These officers beat Lyons again and bumped his head against the wall. One of the officers made Lyons stand against a wall with his hands stretched above his head while the officer, with cowboy boots on, kicked the skin off the shins of Lyons' legs. An investigator kicked him in the stomach and blacked Lyons' eye. The local constable also beat him and threatened him in an effort to make him confess. The sheriff questioned Lyons for about thirty minutes and then the beatings were resumed until the sheriff stopped them again and had Lyons carried upstairs to a cell.

Although the officers denied beating or threatening Lyons, one witness sub-poenaed by the State, corroborates Lyons' testimony. She testified that she saw him in the jail at Hugo and noticed that his eye was blackened, his arms were bruised. She testified further that he could hardly walk.

First Confession.

Eleven days later, about six-thirty in the evening, one of the highway patrolmen and Floyd Brown took Lyons from his cell to the office of the county prosecutor. On the way the highway patrolman struck Lyons on the head with a blackjack. Cheatwood met them in the hall and told the officer not to hit Lyons on the head because "I know how to get it out of him when we get him up here." He was then carried to the county prosecutor's office in the court house.

Sheriff Roy Harmon testified the room was about 14 or 16 feet square. According to the testimony of witnesses for the State of Oklahoma, from time to time during the night there were at least twelve men in that room. They were the following:

1. Floyd Brown.
2. Roy Harmon.
3. Van Raulston.
4. Vernon Cheatwood.
5. Harvey Hawkins.
6. Other highway patrolman.
7. County Prosecutor Norman Horton.
8. Assistant Prosecutor.
9. Reasor Cain.
10. Howard Rorie.
11. "Mr. Holmes."
12. Jess Faulkner.

Lyons was handcuffed and put in a chair while Vernon Cheatwood with a black-jack in his hands sat in a chair directly in from of Lyons and about eight or ten inch-es from him. One of the highway patrolmen was sitting on one side of Lyons with Reasor Cain standing behind him. The County Prosecutor was asking the questions.

During the questioning Vernon Cheatwood was beating Lyons on the knees, hands, arms and legs with a blackjack. This weapon was described by Lyons as "about two inches wide and about three-fourths of an inch thick on the end, and about a foot and a half long, and every time he hit me with it something in it would rat-tle like buck shot or steel balls." Every now and then Reasor Cain would strike Lyons with his fist. Lyons also testified that "when Mr. Reasor Cain got tired the highway patrolmen would take it awhile, about an hour and a half to two hours each, and they beat me that way all night and yelling questions . . . they would say, 'You killed those people, didn't you? You goddamned black son-of-a-bitch, you are going to tell me before we turn you loose'. . . . He said I was going to sing a different song before forty-eight hours from now."

Cheatwood, Cain and now and then the highway patrolmen, would take Lyons out of the chair and bend him across a table while Cheatwood beat him on the back of the head with the blackjack. Then they would put Lyons back in the chair and start beating him on the legs and arms again. Cheatwood also threatened "to stick red-hot irons" to Lyons to make him confess.

About two-thirty in the morning the officers brought in a pan of bones and placed them in Lyons' lap. The use of the bones from the bodies of dead people was freely admitted by officers of the State of Oklahoma. The effect of this on Lyons was explained by him in the following testimony: "They said they was the bones of Mrs. Rogers, Mr. Rogers and the baby, and I had never seen any bones of a dead person before, had I ever seen dead people before, and was I afraid of those bones on my lap in the pan. Mr. Cheatwood would lay the bones on my hands, such as teeth and body bones, and make me hold it and look at it, wouldn't let me turn my head away, and beat me on the hands and knees." These officers continued to question and beat Lyons until about four-thirty the next morning. At about this time Lyons made a "confession" because they "beat me and beat me until I couldn't stand no more, until I gave in to them and answered the questions that they demanded." Even then he denied killing Elmer Rogers but later answered the question "yes" because "I was forced to . . . I was beat with a blackjack, tortured all night long— because I feared I would get some more torture."

Then Lyons was lifted from the chair and led downstairs and over to the jail where he remained about five minutes after which time three of the officers brought him back to the sheriff's office. He was held there while the officers ate their breakfast and was then carried to the scene of the crime in Fort Towson.

In the car with Lyons were one of the highway patrolmen, Floyd Brown, the assistant prosecuting attorney and Vernon Cheatwood. During the trip to Fort Towson the highway patrolman and Cheatwood threatened Lyons. Cheatwood told Lyons they were taking him to Fort Towson to kill him and he should say his prayers.

At the scene of the crime Floyd Brown and Harvey Hawkins threatened to burn him and beat him with a pick hammer if he did not do as they told him. Lyons was standing facing a fire that had been built and with his back to the officers Brown and Hawkins. When he turned around Hawkins had an axe in his hand saying that Lyons knew something about it. They threatened to torture him again if he did not say he had had the axe.

In the meantime Cheatwood and the assistant prosecutor went to the home of the family of Mrs. Rogers. E. O. Colclasure, father of Mrs. Rogers, testified that Cheatwood showed him a blackjack and told him "I beat that boy last night for, I think, six—either six or seven hours . . . I haven't even got to go to bed last night."

Mrs. Vernon Colclasure, sister-in-law of Mrs. Rogers testified that Cheatwood showed her the blackjack also and stated he beat Lyons "from his knees on down."

Cheatwood and the assistant prosecutor returned to the scene of the crime with Vernon Colclasure. In the presence of these people Harvey Hawkins asked Lyons if he had not hidden the axe where it was found. Lyons denied that he knew about the axe.

Cheatwood asked Lyons to show him where he had been hunting on the day prior to the murder. Lyons took them about a half a mile southeast from the scene of the murder and showed them where he had been shooting while hunting and also showed them where he had discarded some empty shells from his shotgun.

Lyons was returned to the jail around 8:30 in the morning and he was again placed in the women's side of the jail. At this time his eye was still closed, his lip broken and his nose was bleeding. At about 2 o'clock in the same afternoon the assistant county attorney, a Mr. Haskell, with two highway patrolmen and Vernon Cheatwood brought Lyons a paper to be signed. Lyons asked what the paper was and Cheatwood said, "never mind", whereupon Lyons signed the paper. During this entire period Lyons did not have a lawyer to consult nor had any lawyer been appointed to defend him or to protect his rights.

Second Confession.

About fifteen minutes later Cheatwood and the Sheriff carried Lyons to the front of the jail where pictures were taken. Immediately thereafter, on the same day, Reasor Cain and Floyd Brown placed Lyons in an automobile and carried him to the Antlers, Oklahoma, jail where they arrived at about 4 o'clock in the afternoon.

Cheatwood, the Governor's special investigator, returned to the Webb Hotel in Hugo and in the presence of people sitting in the lobby told the porter to "go up to my room and get me my nigger beater." The porter went to the room and brought back a blackjack. Whereupon Cheatwood stated: "This is what I beat the nigger boy's head with." Cheatwood also described the blackjack to the clerk of the Webb Hotel. On the night prior to the trial in this case Cheatwood suggested to the clerk that he forget what he had said to him about the blackjack.

About sundown Deputy Sheriff Van Raulston and Roy Marshall took Lyons from the jail at Antlers and carried him to the penitentiary at McAlester, Oklahoma. During the trip Deputy Sheriff Van Raulston continued to threaten Lyons and stated "We ought to hang and bury him right here." Van Raulston also explained that they could tell the courts Lyons had attempted to run away and nobody would do anything about it.

As soon as they arrived at the penitentiary Warden Jesse Dunn was summoned and Lyons was carried to the Warden's office. This was about 10 or 10:30 the night of the same day Lyons made his "confession" at Hugo. Warden Dunn asked Van Raulston whether "that is the nigger that did the shooting." Van Raulston replied, "He has already admitted some in the confession in the jail house." When Warden

Dunn asked Lyons about the murders and Lyons told him he did not know anything about them both Warden Dunn and Deputy Sheriff Van Raulston questioned Lyons for about two hours and Lyons continued to deny that he knew anything about the murders. Whereupon Deputy Sheriff Van Raulston said, "I will make him talk." Van Raulston took a blackjack out of a desk and started beating Lyons on his knees, hands, legs and shoulders. He continued to beat Lyons and threatened him for about an hour and a half or two hours.

After this continued beating Lyons answered the questions as he was instructed to answer them. Lyons made these statements "Because I couldn't stand any more of the beating." A stenographer was called in who took down the alleged statement. Warden Dunn and Deputy Sheriff Van Raulston talked in a mumbling, low tone to the stenographer while Lyons merely nodded his head. Lyons had been without drinking water since about 12 noon of the same day and asked the Warden for water. After this was completed Lyons was taken to the kitchen to eat. Lyons was returned to the Warden's office where the "confession" was signed. The Warden then told one of the guards to take Lyons to the basement. He was then placed in a cell about 15 feet from the electric chair. Prior to this time Warden Dunn had threatened Lyons by telling him how many men he had sent to death in the electric chair during the time he was Warden. Lyons spent the entire night in the death cell. On the next day they carried him up to the fourth floor of the penitentiary where he remained until the preliminary hearing. During this time Lyons did not have an attorney to represent him.

During the time Lyons was confined to the penitentiary Cheatwood visited him several times.

Two or three days after Lyons was placed in the penitentiary Sheriff Cap Duncan, who at that time was a sergeant of the Guard at the penitentiary talked to Lyons in his cell and it is alleged that Lyons admitted to him that he and Van Bizzell killed the Rogers family.

On Saturday, January 27, Reasor Cain, Van Raulston and Vernon Cheatwood carried Lyons into the Warden's office with two penitentiary guards. Cheatwood placed handcuffs on Lyons and asked him whether or not he was going to get on the stand at his preliminary hearing and swear that he and Van Bizzell killed the Rogers family. When Lyons told him he would not do this Cheatwood began beating him again with a blackjack until Lyons stated he would get on the stand and admit the murders. Lyons was then carried back to Hugo for preliminary hearing.

Sheriff Roy Harmon told Lyons that they were afraid of mob action and that the National Guard had been called out for the preliminary hearing. At the preliminary hearing two local attorneys appointed by the Court to defend Lyons refused to act and were excused by the court. Nevertheless, W. D. Lyons, without representation by counsel, was subjected to a preliminary hearing and was returned to the State Penitentiary.

With the exception of the confessions the only evidence produced by the State was that : (a) Lyons was carrying a 12-gauge shot gun wrapped in a newspaper in the colored section of Fort Towson on the day of the murder; (b) that he purchased six number-4 shot gun shells from the local store on the day of the murder; (c) that Mr. and Mrs. Rogers were killed with number-4 shot from a 12-gauge shot gun; (d) officers testified that on the morning of the confession Lyons pointed out a spot at the scene of the crime where an axe was buried.

Lyons admitted he had borrowed a 12-gauge shot gun on that day for the purpose of hunting and that he purchased some shells. Lyons had bought shells at the same store several times before. He carried the gun wrapped in newspaper while in town because he did not have a hunting license.

On the day following the murders Lyons went hunting about a half-mile from where the Rogers home had been. Lyons shot twice at a rabbit and missed. He left the empty shells on the ground. The gun Lyons borrowed was broken and the trigger would not stay cocked so that the hammer had to be released at the same time the trigger was pulled.

Lyons denied that he pointed out the spot where the axe was supposed to have been buried. Clarence Keyes, who was a deputy sheriff at the time of the crime, testified that immediately after the crime was committed the grounds were carefully raked in search of the axe used in the murder and that no axe was on the ground at that time nor at any place under the soil close enough to be reached by the rake. . . .

Argument.

I.

The conviction of petitioner by means of confessions obtained by coercion and other illegal methods was a denial of due process within the meaning of the Fourteenth Amendment to the Constitution of the United States.[2]

The entire case of the State of Oklahoma against the petitioner rested upon an alleged confession and an alleged admission while at the State Penitentiary. The only material evidence other than the confessions is that the petitioner borrowed a shot gun, purchased some shells and was hunting with a 12-gauge shot gun near the scene of the crime on the morning preceding the killing. This was freely admitted by the petitioner as well as the fact that he was also hunting in the same vicinity on the day after the crime was committed. The other evidence is that the deceased was killed by shot from a 12-gauge shot gun.[3] Empty shells admittedly dropped by petitioner during his hunting were fired from the same gun used by petitioner while

---

[2] The Fourteenth Amendment provides in part, "No State shall . . . deprive any person of life, liberty, or property, without due process of law."

[3] It was obviously impossible to connect the shot which killed the deceased with the gun carried by the defendant. [footnote in original]

hunting. The testimony that petitioner on the morning of the confession pointed out to state officials where he hid the axe was denied by petitioner. The former deputy sheriff of Choctaw County testified that shortly after the crime had been committed, all of the ground was raked in search of an axe and that no axe had been found on the scene at that time.

It is apparent from the record in this case that there were two confessions. One made at Hugo, Oklahoma, at about 4:30 in the morning of January 23, 1940, hereinafter referred to as the "first confession"; the other at the penitentiary at McAlester some time before 11:00 o'clock on the night of the same day, hereinafter referred to as "second confession." The prosecution, realizing the clear inadmissibility of the first confession, sought to introduce in evidence the second confession. Objection to the introduction of this confession was promptly made and the jury excluded. After hearing evidence on the admissibility of the confession the trial judge refused to admit the first confession in evidence on the ground that: "The defendant may have been frightened into making the confession that was made here in the court house, by long hours of questioning and by placing bones of the purported bodies of the deceased persons in his lap during the questioning."

The Court, however, admitted into evidence the second confession over the objection of the petitioner. The prejudicial error of the Court's ruling admitting the second confession is apparent from the statement of the judge, made later in the trial in commenting upon the second confession: "They were permitted to bring it out for this purpose: They contended that the defendant was still scared when we went to Oklahoma City. *The Court was of the opinion that several days had elapsed.* At the time, it was not made clear to the Court that both confessions were made on the same day, as I get it now." (Italics ours).[4]

First Confession.

The participation of the state of Oklahoma in the denial of due process to the petitioner is clearer in this record than in many similar cases. As a result of tremendous newspaper publicity brought about by the arrest of certain convicts of a nearby prison camp, Warden Jesse Dunn was rushed to the scene. The Governor sent one of his best investigators to the scene at about the same time. After the arrival of the Governor's investigator, Vernon Cheatwood, the prisoners from the convict camp were released and W. D. Lyons was arrested. Cheatwood remained in the case until after the conviction of Lyons.

It is admitted that the first confession was secured in the court house itself and it is also admitted that officials of the State of Oklahoma brought in the bones of the deceased persons who had been dead for twenty-two days, and placed them in the lap of the petitioner while he was being questioned over a long period of time

---

[4] Errors made during a trial sometimes do not affect the jury's decision; they are called harmless errors. Errors that affect the outcome are prejudicial.

in the court house. This action on the part of officials of the State of Oklahoma, admitted by them to be true, will forever remain a disgrace to law enforcement in the United States. Such action is in direct violation of the principle established by this Court in the case of *Brown v. Mississippi* [1936]: " . . . The rack and torture chamber may not be substituted for the witness stand . . . "

The petitioner testified as to the threats, coercion and beating he received at the hands of the officials of the State of Oklahoma prior to his confession. Although all of the witnesses for the prosecution denied any beating of the petitioner, the county prosecutor in his opening statement admitted: "and that after this defendant, W. D. Lyons, was questioned for long hours about this transaction, he finally admitted that he and Van Bizzell killed those people . . . ." During the examination of Lyons by the county prosecutor the following admissions were made:

"Q. I wasn't there in the office until six thirty was I, when they beat you? Isn't it true that Vernon Cheatwood had a strap of leather, and was tapping you like that, and because you refused to answer questions they put to you?

"By Mr. Belden: We object to the attempt to intimidate the witness.

"By the Court: Don't intimidate the witness, just the ordinary tone of voice.

"A. That blackjack he had was loaded.

"Q. How do you know it was loaded? You were insolent to the officers, and sat and sulked when I asked you questions, isn't that true?

"A. No sir.

"Q. You say they kept you in the office until four-thirty the next morning?

"A. That is right.

"Q. And beat you?

"A. That is right.

"Q. Isn't it true that you refused to answer, and they struck you on the knee with a piece of leather?

"A. They struck me all night. I didn't rest any."

Mr. Horton also made the following statement during the same cross-examination:

"Isn't it true that after they got through hitting you, as you say, with a strap of leather, and you refused to answer any questions at all times, that I made them stop whipping you, and told them to get out of the room, and I asked you if you wouldn't talk to me alone? Is that right?"

Second Confession.

Deputy Sheriff Van Raulston was one of two men who carried the petitioner to the State Penitentiary where the second confession was obtained on the same night. Van Raulston admitted that he was present in the county attorney's office during part of the time preceding the obtaining of the first confession and during the time petitioner was being questioned. Petitioner testified that Van Raulston beat him prior to the making of the second confession.

Petitioner had no sleep between Sunday night and Tuesday night, the night of the second confession. Lyons testified:

"He beat me awhile longer, until I couldn't stand any more, I was already hurting from—already hurting from that last night beating. I hadn't had any sleep since that Sunday night. It was Tuesday night then. Mr. Van Raulston asked me was I ready to answer his questions? and I told him yes, and Mr. Dunn and Mr. Van Raulston was telling me how the crime happened".

In an effort to bolster the second confession, Van Raulston testified that he had recently been in an automobile accident and was physically unable to beat petitioner. If it were true that Van Raulston was unable physically to beat petitioner or to protect himself, it is unbelievable that such an officer would be entrusted with the duty of transporting a man charged with a triple murder from one county into another county in an automobile.

It should also be noted that the Chaplain of the State Penitentiary, who was a witness to the second confession and who was the only completely disinterested person present, was not produced at the trial.

Admission to Sheriff Duncan.

Sheriff Duncan, at that time a sergeant at the Oklahoma State Penitentiary, a few days after the second confession, testified that he secured from Lyons an admission that Lyons had killed the deceased. This alleged admission was made while the petitioner was still under the influence of prior intimidation, coercion and beating, which intimidation continued up to the time of the arraignment.[5] No further effort was made by the prosecution to show that the influence prior to the first and second confessions had been removed at this time, two or four days thereafter.

Petitioner testified as to the long period of questioning, threatening, and beatings on the night of January 22 and morning of January 23 prior to the first confession. According to the testimony of witnesses for the prosecution there were at least twelve officers and individuals in the room during this period. The prosecution only called four of these persons. Each of these men testified that they were not in the room during the entire time Lyons was there and therefore they could only testify as to what happened while they were in the room. It seems that the only person present the entire time, which the exception of Lyons, was Vernon Cheatwood and it is significant that he was not called to the witness stand by the prosecution during the time the question of the admissibility of the confession was being considered.

Aside from the beatings during the hours preceding the confession, the act of placing the bones from Mr. and Mrs. Rogers' bodies on Lyons' lap and forcing him

---

[5] On the morning of the preliminary hearing Cheatwood again beat Lyons demanding that he plead guilty. [footnote in original]

to pick them up was sufficient not only to frighten Lyons into a "confession" but also to have a sufficient lasting effect to carry over to subsequent "confessions." This act was admitted by all of the witnesses for the prosecution who were present on the morning of the first confession.

No effort was made by the prosecution to explain how the bones of Mr. and Mrs. Rogers were obtained. It must be noted, however, that these bones were produced twenty-two days after these people were dead and certainly past the time when the bodies should have been buried.

Diligent research has revealed no case as gruesome as this one. The nearest case on this point is *State v. Ellis*, where the accused was taken to the morgue and forced to put his hand on the deceased. In the *Ellis* case, as in the instant case, the prosecution made no effort to introduce the first confession but introduced a second confession made to the warden of the jail on the next day. The admission of the second confession was held to be error and the conviction reversed by an opinion, part of which stated:

> "A prisoner, who had been thus subjected to such rigid inquiry with violence to his person; who had witnessed the gruesome and uncanny scenes mentioned and to whom food and sleep had been denied for so long, would not immediately thereafter be freed from the dominating influences of his experience, and a confession shortly after such treatment had ceased would, in the absence of proof to the contrary, be adjudged involuntary."

The prosecution at no time during the trial of this case made any effort whatsoever to overcome the presumption that the influences which brought about the first confession continued up to the time the second confession was made at McAlester, the statements were made to Sheriff Duncan, and the preliminary arraignment.

Although Deputy Sheriff Van Raulston, who was present when the first confession was obtained, and Roy Marshall, who accompanied Van Raulston on the trip to McAlester with Lyons, denied beating Lyons or threatening him prior to the second confession, no effort was made by either of them to give any affirmative evidence to overcome the presumption of the continuation of the influences which brought about the first confession.

Warden Jesse Dunn, who is alleged to have taken the confession at McAlester, was not placed on the witness stand at this time. It is peculiarly significant that the only completely disinterested witness to this confession, the Chaplain at the penitentiary, was at no time called to the witness stand by the prosecution.

This Court has repeatedly set aside convictions based upon confessions secured by protracted and repeated questioning as well as instances of brutality similar to the instant case. In an effort to circumvent this line of decisions the State of Oklahoma, while refusing to introduce in evidence the first confession, introduced a second confession and an alleged admission made subsequent to the first confession.

Many years ago the principle was established that where a confession is obtained by such methods as to make it involuntary, all subsequent confessions made while the accused is under the operation of the same influences are likewise involuntary.

"When a prisoner has been once induced to confess upon a promise or threat, it is a common practice to reject any subsequent confession of the same or like facts, though at a subsequent time."

In the United States a long line of decisions of state courts has firmly established the same principle as to subsequent confessions where the first is involuntary. There are two cases in which the facts are peculiarly close to the facts in the instant case.

In a Mississippi case there was evidence of brutality in securing a confession by use of "the water cure". The court excluded the confession made to the officer who administered "the water cure" but admitted other confessions and statements made after the first confession was made. The Mississippi Court reversed this conviction stating:

"It clearly appears in the case before us that the original confession in the jail was secured by force and in violation of the law. . . . It is impossible for the reasoning mind to ignore the force and effect that these proceedings had upon these negroes. It would be vain and idle to indulge the hope that the effect was removed from their minds before the confessions were repeated to the state's witness."

The facts in the case of *Reason v. State* are very similar to the facts in the instant case. In that case Reason, charged with murder, made a confession at the local jail as the result of threats that unless he did so he would be hanged as soon as he reached Holly Springs. This confession was not admitted, but the Court permitted the State, over appellant's objection, to introduce in evidence a second confession made as soon as the prisoner reached Holly Springs. The conviction was reversed because of the introduction into evidence of the second confession. The opinion stated in part:

". . . It is too plain for argument that this reiterated confession was induced by the same cause that underlay the first confession, since the danger of immediate death at Holly Springs could, in the opinion of the prisoner be averted only by adhering to his story. . . . "

The Criminal Court of Appeals in its opinion in the instant case had no doubt that the circumstances surrounding the first confession made it clearly inadmissible. The opinion stated: "If we were dealing with the first confession in the instant case, as heretofore stated, we would unhesitatingly apply the rule as announced in the *Chambers* case and immediately reverse this case. . . . " The opinion also stated: "We again emphasize that if the State in the instant case had introduced in evidence confession number one, and relied upon the same following the opinion in the *Chambers* case, we would unhesitatingly reverse this case."

The Criminal Court of Appeals of Oklahoma, however, ruled that the second confession *made on the same day as the first confession*, was admissible. Such an interpretation of the rule of due process of law will permit law enforcement officials to circumvent the rulings of this Court on the admissibility of confessions by following the procedure in the instant case of extorting a confession by force, violence, threats and long periods of questioning and then transferring the prisoner to another place and securing a second confession on the same day. Such procedure if upheld will nullify the long line of decisions of this Court.

This Court in the case of *Canty v. Alabama* reversed the decision of the Supreme Court of Alabama in a case where effort was made to substantiate a subsequent confession made under changed circumstances without relying upon the first confession which was obviously extorted by force and violence.

Petitioner requested the trial court to instruct the jury that: "You are instructed that if you find that at the time the confession was obtained at McAlester, that the defendant was still suffering from the treatment that he had received in the County Attorney's office or elsewhere by the officers that had him in custody or was induced to sign the confession by reason of fear as a result of the conduct of the officers that had him in custody and that by reason thereof said confession was not a free and voluntary confession, you are not to consider the confession, or any of the evidence therein contained." This instruction was refused. The refusal of the trial court to give this instruction was a denial to the petitioner of due process of law as guaranteed by the Fourteenth Amendment to the United States Constitution. The dissenting opinion of Judge Doyle of the Criminal Court of Appeals of Oklahoma pointed out that this instruction should have been given, stating: "The well established rule is that, if a confession has once been obtained through illegal influence, it must be clearly shown that such influence has been removed before a subsequent confession can be received in evidence." . . .

Conclusion.

The active participation of the State of Oklahoma, acting through its officials, in denying to the petitioner due process of law and the flagrant disregard for . . . the decisions of this Court interpreting the Fourteenth Amendment to the United States Constitution, requires a reversal of the judgment in this case. . . .

> The Supreme Court affirmed Lyons's conviction. Writing for the majority, Justice Stanley Reed said:
>
> > Involuntary confessions, of course, may be given either simultaneously with or subsequently to unlawful pressures, force or threats. The question of whether those confessions subsequently given are themselves voluntary depends on the inferences as to the continuing effect of the

coercive practices which may fairly be drawn from the surrounding circumstances. . . .

The admissibility of the later confession depends upon the same test—is it voluntary. Of course the fact that the earlier statement was obtained from the prisoner by coercion is to be considered in appraising the character of the later confession. The effect of earlier abuse may be so clear as to forbid any other inference than that it dominated the mind of the accused to such an extent that the later confession is involuntary. If the relation between the earlier and later confession is not so close that one must say the facts of one control the character of the other, the inference is one for the triers of fact and their conclusion, in such an uncertain situation, that the confession should be admitted as voluntary, cannot be a denial of due process. . . .

In our view, the earlier events at Hugo do not lead unescapably to the conclusion that the later McAlester confession was brought about by the earlier mistreatments. The McAlester confession was separated from the early morning statement by a full twelve hours. It followed the prisoner's transfer from the control of the sheriff's force to that of the warden. One person who had been present during a part of the time while the Hugo interrogation was in progress was present at McAlester, it is true, but he was not among those charged with abusing Lyons during the questioning at Hugo. There was evidence from others present that Lyons readily confessed without any show of force or threats within a very short time of his surrender to Warden Dunn and after being warned by Dunn that anything he might say would be used against him and that he should not "make a statement unless he voluntarily wanted to." Lyons, as a former inmate of the institution, was acquainted with the warden. The petitioner testified to nothing in the past that would indicate any reason for him to fear mistreatment there. The fact that Lyons, a few days later, frankly admitted the killings to a sergeant of the prison guard, a former acquaintance from his own locality, under circumstances free of coercion suggests strongly that the petitioner had concluded that it was wise to make a clean breast of his guilt and that his confession to Dunn was voluntary. The answers to the warden's questions, as transcribed by a prison stenographer, contain statements correcting and supplementing the questioner's information and do not appear to be mere supine attempts to give the desired response to leading questions. . . .

We cannot say that an inference of guilt based in part upon Lyons' McAlester confession is so illogical and unreasonable as to deny the petitioner a fair trial.

Justice Frank Murphy wrote the only dissent, although Justice Wiley Rutledge dissented without writing an opinion. According to Justice Murphy,

Even though approximately twelve hours intervened between the two confessions and even assuming that there was no violence surrounding the second confession, it is inconceivable under these circumstances that the second confession was free from the coercive atmosphere that admittedly impregnated the first one. The whole confession technique used here constituted one single, continuing transaction. To conclude that the brutality inflicted at the time of the first confession suddenly lost all of its effect in the short space of twelve hours is to close one's eyes to the realities of human nature. An individual does not that easily forget the type of torture that accompanied petitioner's previous refusal to confess, nor does a person like petitioner so quickly recover from the gruesome effects of having had a pan of human bones placed on his knees in order to force incriminating testimony from him. Cf. *State v. Ellis, Reason v. State*.[6]

---

[6] "Cf." introduces citations of cases that are similar to but not precisely the same as the case the court is dealing with.

2. *Brown v. Board of Education* (1952)

Marshall collaborated with his colleagues in drafting the briefs in *Brown v. Board of Education* and the four cases accompanying it—*Briggs v. Elliott* (South Carolina), *Davis v. Prince Edward County School Board* (Virginia), *Bolling v. Sharpe* (District of Columbia), and *Gebhart v. Belton* (Delaware). They knew that the cases' great significance meant that considerations of high politics would play a much larger role than any detailed legal arguments in guiding the Court to its decision. That probably accounts for the cursory treatment questions of great importance received in their opening brief. The brief is notable for three things. First, it emphasizes that racial discrimination is "unreasonable." Constitutional doctrine in the early 1950s remained influenced by the Supreme Court's transformation during the New Deal. After aggressively enforcing the Fourteenth Amendment's due process clause to limit the states' ability to regulate economic matters, the Supreme Court retreated. It adopted the rule that the Constitution was violated only when the government applied unreasonable regulations. An important 1938 decision suggested, however, that the standard of review might be higher when questions of discrimination against what the Court called "discrete and insular minorities" was involved. The Court's 1944 decision upholding the internment of Japanese American citizens during World War II said that "all legal restrictions which curtail the civil rights of a single racial group are immediately suspect" and must be given "the most rigid scrutiny." Later cases established that racial classifications required what the Court came to call "strict scrutiny," but in the early 1950s that doctrine had not been fully developed. Marshall and his colleagues believed that they could succeed even with the standard of reasonableness, apparently more generous to the states.

Second, the brief emphasizes the harm segregation does to African American school children. Marshall's principal deputy, Robert Carter, was a strong proponent of including evidence from social scientists about the harms of segregation in the trial records. Although some members of the legal team were skeptical about the value of this testimony, the opening brief did refer to it. The legal case for doing so was strengthened by the fact that the trial court, while upholding segregation, made a factual finding (quoted in the brief) that segregation had adverse psychological effects on African American children.

Finally, the brief does not argue that *Plessy v. Ferguson*, the case establishing the constitutionality of the Jim Crow regime in the South, should be overruled. It argues instead that *Plessy v. Ferguson* is irrelevant, because it involved segregated transportation while *Brown* and its companion cases involved segregated education; that the Court had in fact never upheld segregation in education; and that recent Court decisions dealing with education had established that segregated education was constitutionally questionable.

BROWN V. BOARD OF EDUCATION
(INITIAL BRIEF, 1952)
Statement of the Case

Appellants are of Negro origin and are citizens of the United States and of the State of Kansas.[1] Infant appellants are children eligible to attend and are now attending elementary schools in Topeka, Kansas, a city of the first class within the meaning of Chapter 72-1724, General Statutes of Kansas, 1949, hereinafter referred to as the statute. Adult appellants are parents of minor appellants and are required by law to send their respective children to public schools designated by appellees. Appellees are state officers empowered by state law to maintain and operate the public schools of Topeka, Kansas.

For elementary school purposes, the City of Topeka is divided into 18 geographical divisions designated as territories. In each of these territories one elementary school services white children exclusively. In addition, four schools are maintained for the use of Negro children exclusively. These racial distinctions are enforced pursuant to the statute. In accordance with the terms of the statute there is no segregation of Negro and white children in junior and senior high schools.

On March 22, 1951, appellants instituted the instant action seeking to restrain the enforcement, operation and execution of the statute on the ground that it deprived them of equal educational opportunities within the meaning of the Fourteenth Amendment. In their answer, appellees admitted that they acted pursuant to the statute, and that infant appellants were not eligible to attend any of the 18 white elementary schools solely because of their race and color. The Attorney General of the State of Kansas filed a separate answer for the specific purpose of defending the constitutional validity of the statute in question.

Thereupon, the court below was convened in accordance with Title 28, United States Code, § 2284.[2] On June 25–26, a trial on the merits took place. On August 3, 1951, the court below filed its opinion, its findings of fact, and conclusions of law, and entered a final judgment and decree in appellees' favor denying the injunctive relief sought.[3]

Specifications of Error
The District Court erred:

1. In refusing to grant appellants' application for a permanent injunction to restrain appellees from acting pursuant to the statute under which they

---

[1] Appellants are the parties bringing the case to the Supreme Court; ordinarily they are the parties who lost in the lower courts.

[2] This statutory provision required special trial courts composed of three judges to hear cases challenging the constitutionality of state statutes.

[3] An injunction, or injunctive relief, orders people to refrain from acting in a specified way.

are maintaining separate public elementary schools for Negro children solely because of their race and color.

2. In refusing to hold that the State of Kansas is without authority to promulgate the statute because it enforces a classification based upon race and color which is violative of the Constitution of the United States.

3. In refusing to enter judgment in favor of appellants after finding that enforced attendance at racially segregated elementary schools was detrimental and deprived them of educational opportunities equal to those available to white children.

Summary of Argument

The Fourteenth Amendment precludes a state from imposing distinctions or classifications based upon race and color alone. The State of Kansas has no power thereunder to use race as a factor in affording educational opportunities to its citizens.

Racial segregation in public schools reduces the benefits of public education to one group solely on the basis of race and color and is a constitutionally proscribed distinction. Even assuming that the segregated schools attended by appellants are not inferior to other elementary schools in Topeka with respect to physical facilities, instruction and courses of study, unconstitutional inequality inheres in the retardation of intellectual development and distortion of personality which Negro children suffer as a result of enforced isolation in school from the general public school population. Such injury and inequality are established as facts on this appeal by the uncontested findings of the District Court.

The District Court reasoned that it could not rectify the inequality that it had found because of this Court's decisions in *Plessy v. Ferguson*, and *Gong Lum v. Rice*. This Court has already decided that the *Plessy* case is not in point. Reliance upon *Gong Lum v. Rice* is mistaken since the basic assumption of that case is the existence of equality while no such assumption can be made here in the face of the established facts. Moreover, more recent decisions of this Court, most notably *Sweatt v. Painter* and *McLaurin v. Board of Regents* clearly show that such hurtful consequences of segregated schools as appear here constitute a denial of equal educational opportunities in violation of the Fourteenth Amendment. Therefore, the court below erred in denying the relief prayed by appellants.

Argument

I

The State of Kansas in affording opportunities for elementary education to its citizens has no power under the Constitution of the United States to impose racial restrictions and distinctions.

While the State of Kansas has undoubted power to confer benefits or impose disabilities upon selected groups of citizens in the normal execution of governmental functions, it must conform to constitutional standards in the exercise of this authority. These standards may be generally characterized as a requirement that the state's action be reasonable. Reasonableness in a constitutional sense is determined by examining the action of the state to discover whether the distinctions or restrictions in issue are in fact based upon real differences pertinent to a lawful legislative objective.

When the distinctions imposed are based upon race and color alone, the state's action is patently the epitome of that arbitrariness and capriciousness constitutionally impermissive under our system of government. A racial criterion is a constitutional irrelevance, and is not saved from condemnation even though dictated by a sincere desire to avoid the possibility of violence or race friction. Only because it was a war measure designed to cope with a grave national emergency was the federal government permitted to level restrictions against persons of enemy descent. This action, "odious", and "suspect", even in times of national peril, must cease as soon as that peril is past.

This Court has found violation of the equal protection clause in racial distinctions and restrictions imposed by the states in selection for jury service, ownership and occupancy of real property, gainful employment, voting, and graduate and professional education. The commerce clause in proscribing the imposition of racial distinctions and restrictions in the field of interstate travel is a further limitation of state power in this regard.

Since 1940, in an unbroken line of decisions, this Court has clearly enunciated the doctrine that the state may not validly impose distinctions and restrictions among its citizens based upon race or color alone in each field of governmental activity where question has been raised. On the other hand, when the state has sought to protect its citizenry against racial discrimination and prejudice, its action has been consistently upheld, even though taken in the field of foreign commerce.

It follows, therefore, that under this doctrine, the State of Kansas which by statutory sanctions seeks to subject appellants, in their pursuit of elementary education, to distinctions based upon race or color alone, is here attempting to exceed the constitutional limits to its authority. For that racial distinction which has been held arbitrary in so many other areas of governmental activity is no more appropriate and can be no more reasonable in public education.

II

The court below, having found that appellants were denied equal educational opportunities by virtue of the segregated school system, erred in denying the relief prayed.

The court below made the following finding of fact:

Segregation of white and colored children in public schools has a detrimental effect upon the colored children. The impact is greater when it has the sanction of the law; for the policy of separating the races is usually interpreted as denoting the inferiority of the negro group. A sense of inferiority affects the motivation of a child to learn. Segregation with the sanction of law, therefore, has a tendency to retard the educational and mental development of negro children and to deprive them of some of the benefits they would receive in a racially integrated school system.

This finding is based upon uncontradicted testimony that conclusively demonstrates that racial segregation injures infant appellants in denying them the opportunity available to all other racial groups to learn to live, work and cooperate with children representative of approximately 90% of the population of the society in which they live; to develop citizenship skills; and to adjust themselves personally and socially in a setting comprising a cross-section of the dominant population. The testimony further developed the fact that the enforcement of segregation under law denies to the Negro status, power and privilege; interferes with his motivation for learning; and instills in him a feeling of inferiority resulting in a personal insecurity, confusion and frustration that condemns him to an ineffective role as a citizen and member of society. Moreover, it was demonstrated that racial segregation is supported by the myth of the Negro's inferiority, and where, as here, the state enforces segregation, the community at large is supported in or converted to the belief that this myth has substance in fact. It was testified that because of the peculiar educational system in Kansas that requires segregation only in the lower grades, there is an additional injury in that segregation occurring at an early age is greater in its impact and more permanent in its effects even though there is a change to integrated schools at the upper levels.

That these conclusions are the consensus of social scientists is evidenced by the appendix filed herewith. Indeed, the findings of the court that segregation constitutes discrimination are supported on the face of the statute itself where it states that: "[N]o discrimination on account of color shall be made in high schools *except as provided herein*" (emphasis supplied).

Under the Fourteenth Amendment equality of educational opportunities necessitates an evaluation of all factors affecting the educational process. Applying this yardstick, any restrictions or distinction based upon race or color that places the Negro at a disadvantage in relation to other racial groups in his pursuit of educational opportunities is violative of the equal protection clause.

In the instant case, the court found as a fact that appellants were placed at such a disadvantage and were denied educational opportunities equal to those available to white students. It necessarily follows, therefore, that the court should have concluded as a matter of law that appellants were deprived of their right to equal educational opportunities in violation of the equal protection clause of the Fourteenth Amendment.

Under the mistaken notion that *Plessy v. Ferguson* and *Gong Lum v. Rice* were controlling with respect to the validity of racial distinctions in elementary education, the trial court refused to conclude that appellants were here denied equal educational opportunities in violation of their constitutional rights. Thus, notwithstanding that it had found inequality in educational opportunity as a fact, the court concluded as a matter of law that such inequality did not constitute a denial of constitutional rights, saying:

> *Plessy v. Ferguson* and *Gong Lum v. Rice* uphold the constitutionality of a legally segregated school system in the lower grades and no denial of due process results from the maintenance of such a segregated system of schools absent discrimination in the maintenance of the segregated schools. We conclude that the above-cited cases have not been overruled by the later case of *McLaurin v. Oklahoma,* and *Sweatt v. Painter.*

Plessy v. Ferguson is not applicable. Whatever doubts may once have existed in this respect were removed by this Court in *Sweatt v. Painter.*

Gong Lum v. Rice is irrelevant to the issues in this case. There, a child of Chinese parentage was denied admission to a school maintained exclusively for white children and ordered to attend a school for Negro children. The power of the state to make racial distinctions in its school system was not in issue. Petitioner contended that she had a constitutional right to go to school with white children, and that in being compelled to attend schools with Negroes, the state had deprived her of the equal protection of the laws.

Further, there was no showing that her educational opportunities had been diminished as a result of the state's compulsion, and it was assumed by the Court that equality in fact existed. There the petitioner was not inveighing against the system, but that its application resulted in her classification as a Negro rather than as a white person, and indeed by so much conceded the propriety of the system itself. Were this not true, this Court would not have found basis for holding that the issue raised was one "which has been many times decided to be within the constitutional power of the state" and, therefore, did not "call for very full argument and consideration."

In short, she raised no issue with respect to the state's power to enforce racial classifications, as do appellants here. Rather, her objection went only to her treatment under the classification. This case, therefore, cannot be pointed to as a controlling precedent covering the instant case in which the constitutionality of the system itself is the basis for attack and in which it is shown the inequality in fact exists.

In any event the assumptions in the *Gong Lum* case have since been rejected by this Court. In the *Gong Lum* case, without "full argument and consideration," the Court assumed the state had power to make racial distinctions in its public schools without violating the equal protection clause of the Fourteenth Amendment and assumed the state and lower federal court cases cited in support of this assumed state power had been correctly decided. Language in *Plessy v. Ferguson* was cited in support of these assumptions. These assumptions upon full argument and consideration were rejected in the *McLaurin* and *Sweatt* cases in relation to racial distinctions in state graduate and professional education. And, according to those cases, *Plessy v. Ferguson*, is not controlling for the purpose of determining the state's power to enforce racial segregation in public schools.

Thus, the very basis of the decision in the *Gong Lum* case has been destroyed. We submit, therefore, that this Court has considered the basic issue involved here only in those cases dealing with racial distinctions in education at the graduate and professional levels.

In the *McLaurin* and *Sweatt* cases, this Court measured the effect of racial restrictions upon the educational development of the individual affected, and took into account the community's actual evaluation of the schools involved. In the instant case, the court below found as a fact that racial segregation in elementary education denoted the inferiority of Negro children and retarded their educational development. Thus the same factors which led to the result reached in the *McLaurin* and *Sweatt* cases are present. Their underlying principles, based upon sound analyses, control the instant case.

Conclusion

In light of the foregoing, we respectfully submit that appellants have been denied their rights to equal educational opportunities within the meaning of the Fourteenth Amendment and that the judgment of the court below should be reversed.

The Supreme Court heard argument in *Brown* and its companion cases in 1952 but ordered further argument, directing the attorneys to address several specific questions dealing with the original understanding of the Fourteenth Amendment with respect to school segregation and with the possible structure of a remedy if the Court found segregation unconstitutional. After reargument the Court struck down school segregation in a short opinion by Chief Justice Earl Warren for a unanimous Court. After stressing "the inconclusive nature of the [Fourteenth] Amendment's history," the Chief Justice's opinion referred to the social scientific evidence in the cases: "To separate [elementary school children] from others of similar age and qualifications solely because of their race generates a feeling of inferiority as to their status in the community that may affect their hearts and minds in a way unlikely ever to be undone." Here the Chief Justice quoted the lower court's finding of fact, which Marshall had included in the opening brief. The opinion also inserted a footnote referring to other social scientific material. This "Footnote 11" became a focus of great controversy once the decision was announced, with critics suggesting that it showed that the Court's decision rested not on law but on policy grounds.

3. The School Desegregation Arguments

A. THE INITIAL ARGUMENT

The Legal Defense Fund staff divided up the arguments in the five desegregation cases, but initially the lawyer who handled the case at trial presented the oral argument to the Supreme Court. Marshall was the trial lawyer in *Briggs v. Elliott*, the South Carolina desegregation case. As the transcripts indicate, Marshall sometimes referred to questions that had arisen in the preceding arguments. His argument began by focusing on a question that arose only in South Carolina, where the legislature had appropriated substantial amounts to improve the physical conditions of the segregated schools for African Americans. The trial court found that the new appropriations would provide substantial equality in physical facilities, and Marshall had to establish that doing so would not eliminate the constitutional problem of segregation itself. The most important exchange in the initial argument, presented here, concerned the status of *Plessy v. Ferguson*. Marshall sought to minimize *Plessy*'s relevance to school segregation so that he would not have to ask the Supreme Court formally to overrule *Plessy*. Justice Frankfurter in particular thought that Marshall's effort was misguided. To Frankfurter, *Plessy* was the foundation of segregation in all forms, and he thought it disingenuous of Marshall to try to steer clear of that decision. Frankfurter also stressed the deep roots of segregation in white Southern life, and wanted Marshall to acknowledge that eliminating school segregation would be a major step for the courts to take. Marshall politely resisted Frankfurter's urging, believing that he could do better as an oral advocate if he treated the case as involving a simple question of law and left concern about social significance to the justices themselves. Finally, Frankfurter and Marshall discussed the question of the appropriate remedy if the Court held segregation unconstitutional. Here Frankfurter's concern was to avoid issuing a sweeping order that would involve the Supreme Court in detailed supervision of desegregation throughout the South. As the case developed, the issue of remedy came to play an increasingly large role.

BRIGGS V. ELLIOTT
(DECEMBER 9–10, 1952)

Mr. Marshall: [On] both the Fourteenth Amendment and the Fifteenth Amendment, this Court has repeatedly said that these distinctions on a racial basis or on a basis of ancestry are odious and invidious, and those decisions, I think, are entitled to just as much weight as *Plessy v. Ferguson* or *Gong Lum v. Rice*.

The Chief Justice: Mr. Marshall, in *Plessy v. Ferguson*, in the Harlan dissent—

Mr. Marshall: Yes, sir.

The Chief Justice [Vinson]: Do you attach any significance when he is dealing with illustrations of the absence of education?

Mr. Marshall: Yes, sir. I do not know, sir. I tried to study his opinions all along. But I think that he was trying to take the position of the narrow issue involved in this case, and not touch on schools, because of the fact that at that time—and this is pure speculation—at that time the public school system was in such bad shape, when

25

people were fighting compulsory attendance laws, they were fighting the money to be put in schools, and it was in a state of flux, but on the other hand, in the majority opinion, the significant thing, the case that they relied on, was the Roberts case, which was decided before the Fourteenth Amendment was even passed.[1]

Justice Frankfurter: But that does not do away with a consideration of the Roberts case, does it?

Mr. Marshall: No, sir, it does not.

Justice Frankfurter: The significance of the Roberts case is that that should be considered by the Supreme Court at a time when that issue was rampant in the United States.

Mr. Marshall: Well, sir, I do not know about those days. But I can not conceive of the Roberts case being good for anything except that the legislatures of the states at those times were trying to work out their problems as they best could understand. And it could be that up in Massachusetts at that time they thought that Negroes—some of them were escaping from slavery, and all—but I still say that the considerations for the passage of any legislation before the Civil War and up to 1900, certainly, could not apply at the present time. I think that every race has made progress, but I do not believe that those considerations have any bearing at this time. The question today is—

Justice Frankfurter: They do not study these cases. But may I call your attention to what Mr. Justice Holmes said about the Fourteenth Amendment?

The Fourteenth Amendment itself as an historical product did not destroy history for the state and substitute mechanical departments of law . . .

Mr. Marshall: I agree, sir.

Justice Frankfurter: Then you have to face the fact that this is not a question to be decided by an abstract starting point of natural law, that you cannot have segregation. If we start with that, of course, we will end with that.

Mr. Marshall: I do not know of any other proposition, sir, that we could consider that would say that because a person who is as white as snow with blue eyes and blond hair has to be set aside.

Justice Frankfurter: Do you think that is the case?

Mr. Marshall: Yes, sir. The law of South Carolina applies that way.

Justice Frankfurter: Do you think that this law was passed for the same reason that a law would be passed prohibiting blue-eyed children from attending public schools? You would permit all blue-eyed children to go to separate schools? You think that this is the case?

Mr. Marshall: No, sir, because the blue-eyed people in the United States never had the badge of slavery which was perpetuated in the statutes.

---

[1] *Roberts v. City of Boston* (1850) was a decision by the Massachusetts Supreme Court upholding racial segregation of Boston's public schools. Five years later the city ended that segregation.

Justice Frankfurter: If it is perpetuated as slavery, then the Thirteenth Amendment would apply.

Mr. Marshall: But at the time—

Justice Frankfurter: Do you really think it helps us not to recognize that behind this are certain facts of life, and the question is whether a legislature can address itself to those facts of life in despite of or within the Fourteenth Amendment, or whether, whatever the facts of life might be, where there is a vast congregation of Negro population as against the states where there is not, whether that is an irrelevant consideration? Can you escape facing those sociological facts, Mr. Marshall?

Mr. Marshall: No, I cannot escape it. But if I did fail to escape it, I would have to throw completely aside the personal and present rights of those individuals.

Justice Frankfurter: No, you would not. It does not follow because you cannot make certain classifications, you cannot make some classifications.

Mr. Marshall: But the personal and present right that I have to be considered like any other citizen of Clarendon County, South Carolina, is a right that has been recognized by this Court over and over again. And so far as the appellants in this case are concerned, I cannot consider it sufficient to be relegated to the legislature of South Carolina where the record in this Court shows their consideration of Negroes, and I speak specifically of the primary cases.

Justice Frankfurter: If you would refer to the record of the case, there they said that the doctrine of classification is not excluded by the Fourteenth Amendment, but its employment by state legislatures has no justifiable foundation.

Mr. Marshall: I think that when an attack is made on a statute on the ground that it is an unreasonable classification, and competent, recognized testimony is produced, I think then the least that the state has to do is to produce something to defend their statutes.

Justice Frankfurter: I follow you when you talk that way.

Mr. Marshall: That is part of the argument, sir.

Justice Frankfurter: But when you start, as I say, with the conclusion that you cannot have segregation, then there is no problem. If you start with the conclusion of a problem, there is no problem.

Mr. Marshall: But Mr. Justice Frankfurter, I was trying to make three different points. I said that the first one was peculiarly narrow, under the McLaurin and the Sweatt decisions.

The second point was that on a classification basis, these statutes were bad.

The third point was the broader point, that racial distinctions in and of themselves are invidious. I consider it as a three-pronged attack. Any one of the three would be sufficient for reversal.

Justice Frankfurter: You may recall that this Court not so many years ago decided that the legislature of Louisiana could restrict the calling of pilots on the Mississippi to the question of who your father was.

Mr. Marshall: Yes, sir.

Justice Frankfurter: And there were those of us who sustained that legislation, not because we thought it was admirable or because we thought it comported with human notions or because we believed in primogeniture, but for different reasons, that it was so imbedded in the conflict of the history of that problem in Louisiana that we thought on the whole that was an allowable justification.

Mr. Marshall: I say, sir, that I do not think—

Justice Frankfurter: I am not taking that beside this case. I am not meaning to intimate any of that, as you well know, on this subject. I am just saying how the subjects are to be dealt with.

Mr. Marshall: But Mr. Justice Frankfurter, I do not think that segregation in public schools is any more ingrained in the South than segregation in transportation, and this Court upset it in the Morgan case.[2] I do not think it is any more ingrained.

Justice Frankfurter: It upset it in the Morgan case on the ground that it was none of the business of the state; it was an interstate problem.

Mr. Marshall: That is a different problem. But a minute ago the very question was raised that we have to deal with realities, and it did upset that. Take the primary case. There is no more ingrained rule than there were in the cases of McLaurin and Sweatt, the graduate school cases.

Justice Frankfurter: I am willing to suggest that this problem is more complicated that the simple recognition of an absolute *non possumus*.[3]

Mr. Marshall: I agree that it is not only complicated. I agree that it is a tough problem. But I think that it is a problem that has to be faced.

Justice Frankfurter: That is why we are here.

Mr. Marshall: That is what I appreciate, Your Honor. But I say, sir, that most of my time is spent down in the South, and despite all these predictions as to what might happen, I do not think that anything is going to happen any more except on the graduate and professional level. And this Court can take notice of the reports that have been in papers such as *The New York Times*. But it seems to me on that question, this Court should go back to the case of *Buchanan v. Warley*, where on the question as to whether or not there was this great problem, this Court in *Buchanan v. Warley* said:

> That there exists a serious and difficult problem arising from a feeling of race hostility which the law is powerless to control, and for which it must give a measure of consideration, may be freely admitted. But its solution cannot be promoted by depriving citizens of their constitutional rights and privileges.[4]

---

[2] *Morgan v. Virginia* (1946) invalidated a state law requiring segregation of the races on interstate buses, as a violation of the Constitution's ban on unjustified interferences with interstate commerce.

[3] Literally, "we are not able." In context, it refers to Frankfurter's belief that Marshall was urging complete and immediate desegregation throughout the South.

[4] *Buchanan v. Warley* (1917) invalidated a Louisville zoning ordinance that required racial segregation in every neighborhood.

In this case, granting that there is a feeling of race hostility in South Carolina, if there be such a thing, or granting that there is that problem, that we cannot have the individual rights subjected to this consideration of what the groups might do, for example, it was even argued that it will be better for both the Negro and the so-called white group. This record is not quite clear as to who is in the white group, because the superintendent of schools said that he did not know; all he knew was that Negroes were excluded. So I imagine that the other schools take in everybody.

So it seems to me that insofar as this case is concerned, whereas in the Kansas case there was a finding of fact that was favorable to the appellants—in this case the opinion of the court mentions the fact that the findings are embodied in the opinion, and the court in that case decided that the only issue would be these facilities, the curriculum, transportation, et cetera.

In the brief for the appellees in this case and the argument in the lower court, I have yet to hear any one say that they denied that these children are harmed by reason of this segregation. Nobody denies that, at least up to now. So there is a grant, I should assume, that segregation in and of itself harms these children.

Now, the argument is made that because we are drawn into a broader problem down in South Carolina, because of a situation down there, that this statute should be upheld.

So there we have a direct cleavage from one side to the other side. I do not think any of that is significant. As a matter of fact, I think all of that argument is made without foundation. I do not believe that in the case of the sworn testimony of the witnesses, statements and briefs and quotations from magazine articles will counteract what is actually in the brief.

So what do we have in the record? We have testimony of physical inequality. It is admitted. We have the testimony of experts as to the exact harm which is inherent in segregation wherever it occurs. That I would assume is too broad for the immediate decision, because after all, the only point before this Court is the statute as it was applied in Clarendon County. But if this Court would reverse and the case would be sent back, we are not asking for affirmative relief. That will not put anybody in any school. The only thing that we ask for is that the state-imposed racial segregation be taken off, and to leave the county school board, the county people, the district people, to work out their own solution of the problem to assign children on any reasonable basis they want to assign them on.

Justice Frankfurter: You mean, if we reverse, it will not entitle every mother to have her child go to a non-segregated school in Clarendon County?

Mr. Marshall: No, sir.

Justice Frankfurter: What will it do? Would you mind spelling this out? What would happen?

Mr. Marshall: Yes, sir. The school board, I assume, would find some other method of distributing the children, a recognizable method, by drawing district lines.

Justice Frankfurter: What would that mean?

Mr. Marshall: The usual procedure—

Justice Frankfurter: You mean that geographically the colored people all live in one district?

Mr. Marshall: No, sir, they do not. They are mixed up somewhat.

Justice Frankfurter: Then why would not the children be mixed?

Mr. Marshall: If they are in the district, they would be. But there might possibly be areas—

Justice Frankfurter: You means we would have gerrymandering of school districts?

Mr. Marshall: Not gerrymandering, sir. The lines could be equal.

Justice Frankfurter: I think that nothing would be worse than for this Court— I am expressing my own opinion—nothing would be worse, from my point of view, than for this Court to make an abstract declaration that segregation is bad and then have it evaded by tricks.

Mr. Marshall: No, sir. As a matter of fact, sir, we have had cases where we have taken care of that. But the point is that it is my assumption that where this is done, it will work out, if I might leave the record, by statute in some states.

Justice Frankfurter: It would be more important information, in my mind, to have you spell out in concrete what would happen if this Court reverses and the case goes back to the district court for the entry of a decree.

Mr. Marshall: I think, sir, that the decree would be entered which would enjoin the school officials from, one, enforcing the statute; two, from segregating on the basis of race or color. Then I think what ever district lines they draw, if it can be shown that those lines are drawn on the basis of race or color, then I think they would violate the injunction. If the lines are drawn on a natural basis, without regard to race or color, then I think that nobody would have any complaint.

For example, the colored child that is over here in this school would not be able to go to that school. But the only thing that would come down would be the decision that whatever rule you set in, if you set in, it shall not be on race, either actually or by any other way. It would violate the injunction, in my opinion.

Justice Frankfurter: There is a thing that I do not understand. Why would not that inevitably involve—unless you have Negro ghettoes, or if you find that language offensive, unless you have concentrations of Negroes, so that only Negro children would go there, and there would be no white children mixed with them, or vice versa—why would it not involve Negro children saying, "I want to go to this school instead of that school"?

Mr. Marshall: That is the interesting thing in this procedure. They could move over into that district, if necessary. Even if you get stuck in one district, there is always an out, as long as this statute is gone.

There are several ways that can be done. But we have instances, if I might, sir, where they have been able to draw a line and to enclose—this is in the North—to enclose the Negroes, and in New York those lines have on every occasion been declared unreasonably drawn, because it is obvious that they were drawn for that purpose.

Justice Frankfurter: Gerrymandering?

Mr. Marshall: Yes, sir. As a matter of fact, they used the word "gerrymander."

So in South Carolina, if the decree was entered as we have requested, then the school district would have to decide a means other than race, and if it ended up that the Negroes were all in one school, because of race, they would be violating the injunction just as bad as they are by violating what we consider to be the Fourteenth Amendment now.

Justice Frankfurter: Now, I think it is important to know, before one starts, where he is going. As to available schools, how would that cut across this problem? If everything was done that you wanted done, would there be physical facilities within such drawing of lines as you would regard as not evasive of the decree?

Mr. Marshall: Most of the school buildings are now assigned to Negroes, so that the Negro buildings are scattered around in that county. Now, as to whether or not lines could be properly drawn, I say quite frankly, sir, I do not know. But I do know that in most of the southern areas—it might be news to the Court—there are very few areas that are predominantly one race or the other.

Justice Frankfurter: Are you going to argue the District of Columbia case?

Mr. Marshall: No, sir.

If you have any questions, I would try, but I cannot bind the other side.

Justice Frankfurter: I just wondered, in regard to this question that we are discussing, how what you are indicating or contemplating would work out in the District if tomorrow there were the requirement that must be mixed groups.

Mr. Marshall: Most of the schools in the District of Columbia would be integrated. There might possibly be some in the concentrated areas up in the northwest section. There might be. But I doubt it. But I think the question as to what would happen if such decree was entered—I again point out that it is actually a matter that is for the school authorities to decide, and it is not a matter for us, it seems to me, as lawyers, to recommend except where there is racial discrimination or discrimination on one side or the other.

But my emphasis is that all we are asking for is to take off this state-imposed segregation. It is the state-imposed part of it that affects the individual children. And the testimony in many instances is along that line.

So in South Carolina, if the district court issued a decree—and I hasten to add that in the second hearing when we were prevented from arguing segregation, the argument was made that on the basis of the fact that the schools were still unequal, we should get relief on the basis of the Sipuel decision—the court said in that case, no, that the only relief we could get would be this relief as of September, and in that case the court took the position that it would be impossible to break into the middle of the year.[5] If I might anticipate a question on that, the point would come up as to, if a decree in this case should happen to be issued by the district court, or in a case similar to this, as to whether or not there would be a time given for the actual enrollment of the children, et cetera, and changing of children from school to school. It would be my position in a case like that, which is very much in answer to the brief filed by the United States in this case—it would be my position that the important thing is to get the principle established, and if a decree were entered saying that facilities are declared to be unequal and that the appellants are entitled to an injunction, and then the district court issues the injunction, it would seem to me that it would go without saying that the local school board had the time to do it. But obviously it could not do it over night, and it might take six months to do it one place and two months to do it another place.

Again, I say it is not a matter of judicial determination. That would be a matter for legislative determination.

Rebuttal Argument

Mr. Marshall: May it please the Court, so far as the appellants are concerned in this case, at this point it seems to me that the significant factor running through all these arguments up to this point is that for some reason, which is still unexplained, Negroes are taken out of the main stream of American life in these states.

There is nothing involved in this case other than race and color, and I do not need to go to the background of the statutes or anything else. I just read the statutes, and they say, "White and colored."

While we are talking about the feeling of the people in South Carolina, I think we must once again emphasize that under our form of government, these individual rights of minority people are not to be left to even the most mature judgment of the majority of the people, and that the only testing ground as to whether or not individual rights are concerned is in this Court.

If I might digress just for a moment, on this question of the will of the people of South Carolina, if Ralph Bunche were assigned to South Carolina, his children would have to go to a Jim Crow school. No matter how great anyone becomes, if he happens to have been born a Negro, regardless of his color, he is relegated to that school. . . .

Justice Frankfurter: . . . If it is in the Constitution, I do not care about what they say. But the question is, is it in the Constitution?

Mr. Marshall: This Court has said just that on other occasions. They said it in the Fifth Amendment cases, and they also said it in some of the Fourteenth Amendment cases, going back to Mr. Justice Holmes in the first primary case in

---

[5] *Sipuel v. Oklahoma State Regents* (1948) ordered the state university to admit an African American applicant to its law school "as soon as it does for applicants of any other group."

Nixon v. Herndon.[6] And I also think—I have no doubt in my mind—that this Court has said that these rights are present, and if all of the people in the State of South Carolina and most of the Negroes still wanted segregated schools, I understand the decision of this Court to be that any individual Negro has a right, if it is a constitutional right, to assert it, and he has a right to relief at the time he asserts that right.

Justice Frankfurter: Certainly. Any single individual, just one, if his constitutional rights are interfered with, can come to the bar of this Court and claim it.

Mr. Marshall: Yes, sir.

Justice Frankfurter: But what we are considering and what you are considering is a question that is here for the very first time.

Mr. Marshall: I agree, sir. And I think that the only issue is to consider as to whether or not that individual or small group, as we have here, of appellants, that their constitutionally protected rights have to be weighed over against what is considered to be the public policy of the state of South Carolina, and if what is considered to be the public policy of the state of South Carolina runs contrary to the rights of that individual, then the public policy of South Carolina, this Court, reluctantly or otherwise is obliged to say that this policy has run up against the Fourteenth Amendment, and for that reason his rights have to be affirmed.

But I for one think—and the record shows, and there is some material cited in some of the amicus briefs in the Kansas case—that all of these predictions of things that were going to happen, they have never happened.[7] And I for one do not believe that the people in South Carolina or those southern states are lawless people.

Every single time that this Court has ruled, they have obeyed it, and I for one believe that rank and file people in the South will support whatever decision in this case is handed down.

Justice Frankfurter: I have not heard that the bar of this case has suggested that South Carolina or Kansas will not obey whatever decree this Court hands down.

Mr. Marshall: There was only one witness, and he was corrected by Judge Parker.[8] That was in this particular case. So it seems to me, and I in closing would like to emphasize to the Court, if I may, that this question, the ultimate question of segregation at the elementary and high school levels, has come to this Court through the logical procedure of case after case, going all the way back to the Gaines case, and coming up to the present time.

---

[6] *Nixon v. Herndon* (1927) invalidated a Texas statute allowing only whites to vote in primary elections.

[7] An *amicus curiae* is a "friend of the court," who obtains permission to present arguments that it believes will help the court reach the correct decision; Marshall here refers to the briefs filed by these amici.

[8] Judge John J. Parker was the chief judge of the federal Court of Appeals for the Fourth Circuit, which includes Maryland, Virginia, West Virginia, and North and South Carolina. He presided over the hearing in *Briggs v. Elliott*. President Herbert Hoover nominated him for the Supreme Court in 1930, but the nomination failed after the NAACP and labor unions mounted a major campaign against his confirmation.

We had hoped that we had put in the evidence into the record, the type of evidence which we considered this Court to have considered in the Sweatt and McLaurin cases, to demonstrate that at the elementary and high school levels, the same resulting evil which was struck down in the Sweatt and McLaurin cases exists, for the same reason, at the elementary and high school levels, and I say at this moment that none of that has been disputed.

The only thing put up against it is a legislative argument which would ultimately relegate the Negro appellants in this case to plead with the legislature of South Carolina to do what they have never done in the past, to recognize their pleas.

We therefore respectfully urge that the judgment of the United States District Court be reversed. . . .

Justice Reed: In the legislatures, I suppose there is a group of people, at least in the South, who would say that segregation in the schools was to avoid racial friction.

Mr. Marshall: Yes, sir. Until today, there is a good-sized body of opinion that would say that, and I would say respectable public opinion.

Justice Reed: Even in that situation, assuming, then, that there is a disadvantage to the segregated group, the Negro group, does the legislature have to weigh as between the disadvantage of the segregated group and the advantage of the maintenance of law and order?

Mr. Marshall: I think that the legislature should, sir. But I think, considering the legislatures, that we have to bear in mind that I know of no Negro legislator in any of these States, and I do not know whether they consider the Negro's side or not. It is just a fact. But I assume that there are people who will say that it was and is necessary, and my answer to that is, even if the concession is made that it was necessary in 1895, it is not necessary now because people have grown up and understand each other.

They are fighting together and living together. For example, today they are working together in other places. As a result of the ruling of this Court, they are going together on the higher level. Just how far it goes—I think when we predict what might happen, I know in the South where I spent most of my time, you will see white and colored kids going down the road together to school. They separate and go to different schools, and they come out and they play together. I do not see why there would necessarily be any trouble if they went to school together.

Justice Reed: I am not thinking of trouble. I am thinking of whether it is a problem of legislation or of the judiciary.

Mr. Marshall: I think, sir, that the ultimate authority for the asserted right by an individual in a minority group is in a body set aside to interpret our Constitution, which is our Court.

Justice Reed: Undoubtedly that passes on the litigation.

Mr. Marshall: Yes, sir.

Justice Reed: But where there are disadvantages and advantages, to be weighed, I take it that it is a legislative problem.

Mr. Marshall: In so far as the State is concerned, in so far as the majority of the people are concerned. But in so far as the minority—

Justice Reed: The states have the right to weigh the advantages and the disadvantages of segregation, and to require equality of employment, for instance?

Mr. Marshall: Yes, sir.

Justice Reed: I think that each state has been given that authority by decisions of this Court.

Mr. Marshall: And some states have, and others have not. I think that is the main point in this case, as to what is best for the majority of the people in the states. I have no doubt—I think I am correct—that that is a legislative policy for the state legislature.

But the rights of the minorities, as has been our whole form of government, have been protected by our Constitution, and the ultimate authority for determining that is this Court. I think that is the real difference.

As to whether or not I, as an individual, am being deprived of my right is not legislative, but judicial.

The Chief Justice: Thank you.

Mr. Marshall: Thank you, sir.

The Court found itself divided over the desegregation cases. Chief Justice Vinson and Justice Stanley Reed, both Southerners, were ambivalent at best about overturning school segregation. Justice Robert Jackson, from New York, had no doubt that segregation was unwise policy, but he was uncertain that the Court had a constitutional basis for ruling against segregation. Justice Frankfurter was concerned primarily about the way a decision against segregation could be enforced. At Frankfurter's urging, the Court set the case for reargument. It directed the lawyers to answer five questions, sometimes referred to by number in the materials that follow. Three questions dealt with the original understanding of the Fourteenth Amendment: did its adopters think that it made school segregation unconstitutional automatically? Did they think that it authorized Congress or the courts in the future to hold segregation unconstitutional? Whatever the original understanding, did the courts have the power to hold segregation unconstitutional? The other two questions dealt with the issue of remedy: would desegregation have to occur immediately? What sort of remedial order should the Supreme Court order? Before the reargument took place, Chief Justice Vinson died and was replaced by Earl Warren.

B. THE REARGUMENT

Marshall struggled with the reargument, largely because he was not particularly interested in or familiar with the detailed history of the Fourteenth Amendment's adoption on which the briefs requested by the Court focused. He tried to turn the Court's attention to its own cases, arguing as best he could that the cases illuminated the original understanding. Later in the argument Justice Frankfurter pressed him about the Delaware case, where the lower courts had held segregation in Delaware unconstitutional because the physical facilities at the segregated schools for African Americans were in fact inferior to those at the schools for whites. Frankfurter insisted that Marshall could not accept that basis for the decision, because Marshall was arguing that segregation was unconstitutional without regard to equality in physical facilities. Frankfurter then extended his position to claim that Marshall had to repudiate the NAACP's prior cases successfully challenging segregation in higher education, where the theory was that the states had not provided substantially equal facilities for African Americans. This exchange was largely a diversion from the main issues in *Brown*, and appears to have had no effect on the outcome.

Marshall opened his rebuttal argument, presented here, responding to Justice Frankfurter's questions about remedy. He stated the position that he would develop in more detail when the case was argued for the third time, which was that the Court should direct that desegregation occur immediately, and that the only reasons for delay would be minor administrative questions dealing with such issues as drawing district lines. He then directly rebutted assertions made by his opponents, many of which were invocations of the concerns of white Southerners, sometimes in the form of veiled threats that the South would disregard a decision invalidating segregation. He concluded with an eloquent attack on the irrationality of race discrimination.

BRIGGS V. ELLIOTT
(DECEMBER 7, 1953)
Rebuttal Argument

Mr. Marshall: May it please the Court, there are several points I would like to clear up preliminarily, and then I would like to make sure that our position is correctly stated, and as it relates to statements made by counsel on the other side.

Justice Frankfurter: Mr. Marshall, I do not want to interrupt your closing argument, but I hope before you sit down you will state to the Court whether you have anything more to say on the question of remedies.

Mr. Marshall: Yes, sir.

Justice Frankfurter: In case you should prevail, more than is contained in your brief.

Mr. Marshall: Yes, sir, I would be glad to get to that first, Mr. Justice Frankfurter.

In our brief we found ourselves, after having given as much research as we could, in a position where we intelligently could not put forth a plan. We find that in the briefs of the other side they recognized there would be certain administrative problems involved, and anything else that they mentioned we, of course—well, not of course—we do not recognize as being valid for this Court to consider.

On the other hand, we spent as much time as we could during the time of filing and the present time on the United States government's suggestion as to the decree; and so far as we are concerned, it appears to us that there are administrative problems, there would be administrative problems, and that the decree of this Court could very well instruct the lower court to take into consideration that factor, and if necessary give to the State involved a sufficient time to meet the administrative problems, with the understanding so far as we are concerned that I do not agree with the last part of the government: that if it isn't done within a school year, that they could get more time for this reason, sir.

I can conceive of nothing administrative-wise that would take longer than a year. If they don't have staff enough to do these administrative things, the sovereign states can hire more people to do it.

So for that reason I don't think it should take more than a year for them to adequately handle the administrative techniques, and I submit that a longer period of time would get the lower court into the legislative field as to whether to not to do it this way or that way.

Specifically, I am a firm believer that, especially insofar as the federal courts are concerned, their duty and responsibility ends with telling the state, in this field at least, what you can't do.

And I don't think anybody is recommending to this Court that this Court take over the administrative job. Obviously, that is not recommended by anyone. So with that, I think that is our position.

We said in the opening brief that if any plans were put forth, we would be obliged to do it, we wanted to do it, and that is our position on the limited point.

It gets me, if it please the Court, to one of the points that runs throughout the argument in the brief on the other side, and that is that they deny that there is any race prejudice involved in these cases. They deny that there is any intention to discriminate.

But throughout the brief and throughout the argument they not only recognize that there is a race problem involved, but they emphasize that that is the whole problem. And for the life of me, you can't read the debates, even the sections they rely on, without an understanding that the Fourteenth Amendment took away from the states the power to use race.

As I understand their position, their only justification for this being a reasonable classification is, one, that they got together and decided that it is best for the races to be separated and, two, that it has existed for over a century.

Neither argument, to my mind, is any good. The answer to the first argument is in two places, if I may for a moment address myself to it. This one that Mr. Davis and Mr. Moore both relied on,[9] these horrible census figures, the horrible number of Negroes in the South—and I thought at some stage it would be recognized by them

---

[9] John W. Davis, who served as President Woodrow Wilson's solicitor general and was the Democratic candidate for the presidency in 1924, was his generation's leading Supreme Court advocate, and argued South Carolina's case in the Supreme Court. T. Justin Moore, a member of a major Richmond law firm, argued the case for Virginia.

that it shows that, in truth and in fact, in this country that high percentage of Negroes they talk about can be used to demonstrate to the world that, insofar as this country is concerned, two-thirds of the Negroes are compelled to submit to segregation.

They say that is the reason for it. The best answer is in the record in the Clarendon County case, where the only witness the other side put on this point— and a reading of it will show he was put on for the express purpose—he is a school administrator—of explaining how the school system would be operated under the new bill that was going to tax people, but they dragged this other point in and made him an expert in race relations and everything else.

He emphasized—well, the best way to do it is this way on page 119 of the record in the Briggs case:

> What I was saying is that the problem of the mixed groups and racial tensions is less in communities where the minority population is small. That has been true of the testimony that I have heard . . .

Then the question, "Well, Mr. Crow"—incidentally, that was his name—"Mr. Crow, assuming that in Clarendon County, especially in School District Number 22, the population was 95 percent white and 5 percent Negro, would that change your opinion?"

Answer. No.

Question. Then that is not really the basis of your opinion, is it?

Answer. The question that you have asked me is in my opinion, will the elimination of segregation be fraught with undesirable results, and I have said that I thought it would. That may not be stating your question exactly, but that is still my answer.

Question. As a matter of fact, Mr. Crow, isn't your opinion based on the fact that you have all of your life believed in segregation of the races? Isn't that the reason, the real reason, the basis of your opinion?

Answer. That wouldn't be all.

Question. But it is a part of it?

Answer. I suppose it is.

And that answers all of those arguments about this large number of people involved. They are all American citizens who, by accident of birth, are a different color; and it makes no difference one way or another insofar as this Court is concerned.

Then, in that same vein, Attorney General Almond gets to the name-calling stage about these state conventions.[10] Well, let's go up to the later convention in his state of Virginia. I don't believe that the man I am now going to quote can be characterized as anything but a respected former senator of the United States; and in debating the section in the latter constitution of Virginia, not the one in this period

---

[10] J. Lindsay Almond was Virginia's attorney general, and presented the state's case to the Supreme Court along with T. Justin Moore.

but the later one, Senator Carter Glass, who was a delegate to the Convention, spoke thusly in the debates:

> Discrimination, that is precisely what we propose. That exactly is what this Convention was elected for, to discriminate to the very extremity of permissible action under the limitations of the Federal Constitution.

That is quoted in the statement of jurisdiction in the Virginia case on page eleven. And another answer I submit is quoted in our reply brief involving the University of North Carolina Law School case which was decided adversely to the Negro applicants in the district court; and on appeal to the Fourth Circuit Court of Appeals, the very circuit that is involved here, in an opinion by Judge Soper of Maryland met this question of what we are doing is for the benefit of the white and Negro people alike, saying:

> —the defense seeks in part to avoid the charge of inequality by the paternal suggestion that it would be beneficial to the colored race in North Carolina as a whole, and to the individual plaintiffs in particular, if they would cooperate in promoting the policy adopted by the State rather than seek the best legal education which the State provides. The duty of the Federal Courts, however, is clear. We must give first place to the rights of the individual citizens, and when and where he seeks only equality of treatment before the law, his suit must prevail. It is for him to decide in which direction his advantage lies."[11]

As to this time of how long segregation has been in existence in the South, the same argument has been made in every case that has come up to this Court, the argument of *stare decisis*, that you should leave this because it has been long standing, the separate but equal doctrine, and that there are so many states involved, was made in even more detailed fashion in the Sweatt brief filed by Attorney General Price Daniel;[12] and as an aside, it is significant that in the Virginia brief on the last page they go out of their way to pay acknowledgment to that brief filed by the attorney general, which was obviously discarded by this Court.

There is not one new item that has been produced in all of these cases. And we come to the question as to whether or not the wishes of these states shall prevail, as to whether or not our Constitution shall prevail.

And over against the public policy of the state of Virginia and the state of South Carolina is an amendment that was put in the Constitution after one of the worst wars that was ever fought; and around that constitutional provision we say that the public policy of the United States does not look to the state policy, but looks to our government.

---

[11] Morris Soper was a judge on the Court of Appeals for the Fourth Circuit.

[12] Attorney General of Texas from 1946–53, and later U.S. senator and the state's governor.

And in the brief we have filed, in our reply brief, we quote from a document which just came out, at least we just got ahold of it a couple of weeks ago, a monograph, which we cite in our brief from the selective service of our government, and we have some quotes in our brief.

I don't emphasize or urge the quotes as such, but a reading of that monograph will convince anyone that the discriminatory segregation policies, education and otherwise, in the South almost caused us to lose one war, and I gather from the recommendations made in there that unless it is corrected, we will lose another.

Now that is the policy that I understand them to say that it is just a little feeling on the part of Negroes, they don't like segregation. As Mr. Davis said yesterday, the only thing the Negroes are trying to get is prestige.

Exactly correct. Ever since the Emancipation Proclamation, the Negro has been trying to get what was recognized in *Strauder v. West Virginia*, which is the same status as anybody else regardless of race.[13]

I can't, for the life of me—it seems to me they recommend to us what we should do. It seems to me they should show some effort on their part to conform their States to the clear intent of past decisions.

For example, the argument was made in McLaurin and Sweatt of what would happen if these decisions were granted, and indeed the brief, joint brief, filed by the attorneys general of all the states (and if I remember correctly it was signed by General Almond) said that if this Court broke down exclusion and segregation in the graduate and professional schools, or maybe it was the law schools—I know exactly what they said—the schools would have to close up and go out of business.

And the truth of the matter—and we cite in our record the figures that show that since that decision there are now fifteen hundred Negroes in graduate and professional schools in heretofore all white universities, fifteen hundred at least in twelve states, one of the states significantly out of the group being South Carolina.

It is also pointed out in our brief a very long list of private schools in the South, which as a result, with no legal binding upon them at all, do so.

It is also significant that in states like Arkansas—I could name four or five— without any lawsuit, segregation was broken down. The truth of the matter is that I, for one, have more confidence in the people of the South, white and colored, than the lawyers on the other side. I am convinced they are just as lawful as anybody else, and once the law is laid down, that is all there is to it.

In their argument on the congressional debate, they do a job too well. They say no education was intended to be covered by the Fourteenth Amendment.

Obviously, that is not correct, because even their pet case, *Plessy v. Ferguson*, recognized that education was under the Fourteenth Amendment.

---

[13] *Strauder v. West Virginia* (1880) struck down a statute barring African Americans from serving on juries.

Then Mr. Moore goes to great detail to point out that the Fourteenth Amendment could go no further than the Civil Rights Act; and he emphasized yesterday and he emphasized today that, in addition to that, there were some rights that were deliberately excluded.

His language is clearly eliminated, and then he says, "Suffrage was clearly not intended to be included."

And how anyone can stand in this Court, having read the opinion of Mr. Justice Holmes in the first Texas primary case, and take that position is beyond me; because that decision, in the language of Mr. Justice Holmes, said specifically that they urged the Fourteenth and Fifteenth Amendments but we don't have to get to the Fifteenth Amendment, because the Fourteenth Amendment said that the states can do a lot of classifying which we, speaking as a Court, can't seem to understand, but it is clear that race cannot be used in suffrage. So I don't see the purport of any of that argument.

Justice Frankfurter: Do you think the Fifteenth Amendment was redundant, superfluous?

Mr. Marshall: No, sir, definitely not.

Justice Frankfurter: So if it had not been there, it would have been included in the Fourteenth?

Mr. Marshall: I think definitely, under the reasoning of Mr. Justice Holmes, it would have been.

Justice Frankfurter: That is superfluous, then it is an extra.

Mr. Marshall: It is an extra.

Justice Frankfurter: An extra.

Mr. Marshall: I just—maybe it is timidity, but I just can't say a constitutional amendment is superfluous; but if you are asking me if I think Mr. Justice Holmes was absolutely correct, definitely, yes, sir.

That brings me to the other point which I want to make clear. It involves the questions yesterday about our position as to the McLaurin case, and I am a little worried in thinking of what I said yesterday as to whether the position was absolutely clear. And it is suggested today that the position we take in this case is a negation of the McLaurin case, and as to whether or not the McLaurin case is a negation of the separate-but-equal doctrine, and it is argued that McLaurin had a constitutional grievance because he was denied equality; but in the McLaurin case the answer is that the only inequality which he suffered is that which is inherent, emphasis on "inherent" if you please, in segregation itself.

He had the same schools, same everything else; but he had this segregation, so that is inherent. And if McLaurin won because he was denied equality, it is also true and much more important that he suffered constitutional inequality in the enjoyment of these identical offerings.

And it follows that with education, this Court has made segregation and inequality equivalent concepts. They have equal rating, equal footing; and if segregation thus necessarily imports inequality, it makes no great difference whether we say that the Negro is wronged because he is segregated, or that he is wronged because he received unequal treatment.

We believe that what we really ask this Court is to make it explicit what they think was inevitably implicit in the McLaurin case, that the two are together. But most certainly I do not agree, and I want to make it clear, that the McLaurin case is under the one-way, and I think that with understanding, the Court has no difficulty in our position at least.

And finally I would like to say that each lawyer on the other side has made it clear as to what the position of the State was on this, and it would be all right possibly but for the fact that this is so crucial. There is no way you can repay lost school years.

These children in these cases are guaranteed by the states some twelve years of education in varying degrees; and this idea, if I understand it, to leave it to the states until they work it out—and I think that is a most ingenious argument—you leave it to the states, they say, and then they say that the states haven't done anything about it in a hundred years, so for that reason this Court doesn't touch it.

The argument of judicial restraint has no application in this case. There is a relationship between federal and state, but there is no corollary or relationship as to the Fourteenth Amendment.

The duty of enforcing, the duty of following the Fourteenth Amendment is placed upon the states. The duty of enforcing the Fourteenth Amendment is placed upon this Court, and the argument that they make over and over again to my mind is the same type of argument they charge us with making, the same argument Charles Sumner made. Possibly so.

And we hereby charge them with making the same argument that was made before the Civil War, the same argument that was made during the period between the ratification of the Fourteenth Amendment and the *Plessy v. Ferguson* case.

And I think it makes no progress for us to find out who made what argument. It is our position that, whether or not you base this case solely on the intent of Congress or whether you base it on the logical extension of the doctrine as set forth in the McLaurin case, on either basis the same conclusion is required, which is that this Court makes it clear to all of these states that in administering their governmental functions, at least those that are vital not to the life of the state alone, not to the country alone, but vital to the world in general, that little pet feelings of race, little pet feelings of custom—I got the feeling on hearing the discussion yesterday that when you put a white child in a school with a whole lot of colored children, the child would fall apart or something. Everybody knows that is not true.

Those same kids in Virginia and South Carolina—and I have seen them do it—they play in the streets together, they play on their farms together, they go down the road together, they separate to go to school, they come out of school and play ball together. They have to be separated in school.

There is some magic to it. You can have them voting together, you can have them not restricted because of law in the houses they live in. You can have them going to the same state university and the same college; but if they go to elementary and high school, the world will fall apart. And it is the exact same argument that has been made to this Court over and over again, and we submit that when they charge us with making a legislative argument, it is in truth they who are making the legislative argument.

They can't take race out of this case. From the day this case was filed until this moment, nobody has in any form or fashion, despite the fact I made it clear in the opening argument that I was relying on it, done anything to distinguish this statute from the Black Codes, which they must admit, because nobody can dispute, say anything anybody wants to say, one way or the other, the Fourteenth Amendment was intended to deprive the states of power to enforce Black Codes or anything else like it.

We charge that they are Black Codes. They obviously are Black Codes if you read them. They haven't denied that they are Black Codes, so if the Court wants to very narrowly decide this case, they can decide it on that point.

So whichever way it is done, the only way that this Court can decide this case in opposition to our position, is that there must be some reason which gives the State the right to make a classification that they can make in regard to nothing else in regard to Negroes; and we submit the only way to arrive at that decision is to find that for some reason Negroes are inferior to all other human beings.

Nobody will stand in the Court and urge that, and in order to arrive at the decision that they want us to arrive at, there would have to be some recognition of a reason why of all of the multitudinous groups of people in this country you have to single out Negroes and give them this separate treatment.

It can't be because of slavery in the past, because there are very few groups in this country that haven't had slavery some place back in the history of their groups. It can't be color because there are Negroes as white as the drifted snow, with blue eyes, and they are just as segregated as the colored man.

The only thing can be is an inherent determination that the people who were formerly in slavery, regardless of anything else, shall be kept as near that stage as is possible; and now is the time, we submit, that this Court should make it clear that that is not what our Constitution stands for.

Thank you, sir.

On May 17, 1954, the Supreme Court held segregation unconstitutional, and entered an order directing the parties to brief and argue the case a third time, now focusing solely on the question of remedy.

C. THE THIRD ARGUMENT, ON REMEDY

The justices had several concerns about the appropriate remedial order they should enter. Should the Supreme Court simply say that segregation was unconstitutional and leave it to trial judges throughout the South to develop acceptable plans to desegregate schools in their area? Should the Court prescribe detailed rules for the trial judges to follow? Should a schedule for desegregation be set, and if so, what should that schedule be? Underlying all these questions was a deeper concern about whether the Court could secure compliance with its decision. In the argument that follows, these latent concerns are occasionally expressed in terms of demographic differences between the deep South and the border states.

Marshall's position was unequivocal. The right to attend a nonsegregated school was, in legal terms, "personal and present." It was a right held by each individual African American child, and each child was entitled to assert his or her right immediately. That meant that desegregation should occur "forthwith." Marshall conceded that school districts might face rather minor administrative problems; they would have to assign children to new schools, redraw district lines (since each school would take in both white and African American children), assign teachers to schools, and the like. These problems might vary slightly from district to district, but Marshall insisted that every district could overcome these administrative difficulties within a year.

Marshall was clearly correct if desegregation meant simply reassigning children to schools, but the Court and Marshall knew that desegregation meant more than that. Justice Frankfurter pressed Marshall to concede that desegregation would work large changes in Southern society, and that the remedial decree should take that into account. Marshall refused to do so, attempting to hold the Court to its word in the initial desegregation decision. His aim was not to persuade the justices to issue a "forthwith" decree, but to demonstrate to them how difficult it would be for them to justify anything else. He repeatedly mentioned statements from prominent white Southerners expressing their resistance to the May 17 decision, and his rebuttal argument spent a fair amount of time stressing how his opponents had told the Court, in effect, that the justices should not expect the South to comply with that decision.

BROWN V. BOARD OF EDUCATION
(April 12, 1955)

Mr. Marshall: May it please the Court, as was pointed out in argument yesterday by Mr. Robinson,[14] it is our opinion that in answering specifically the questions propounded by this Court that the Court should issue a forthwith decree, and I say on that when we use "forthwith decree" in our briefs and argument as explained in the brief for this case, we actually are urging, not tomorrow or as of whatever day the opinion comes

---

14 Spottswood Robinson III was a member of the NAACP's legal team; he was appointed by President Lyndon Johnson to the Court of Appeals for the District of Columbia Circuit in 1966.

down in this case, but we are arguing as of the September school term being this year of the next school term, and as I use "forthwith" that was what we were urging.

I am just using it as a shorthand way of saying September, 1955.

Justice Frankfurter: You do not want that word in the decree, then?

Mr. Marshall: It came about this way, Mr. Justice Frankfurter: We took the position that in any decree issued that says "forthwith," that normal administrative details always come into consideration, so as far as we are concerned, if the decree says "September of 1955," that will be exactly what we want.

Justice Frankfurter: I am sure you will agree in this kind of litigation, it is of the utmost importance to use language of fastidious accuracy?

Mr. Marshall: Absolutely, we agree with you fully. That is why we would rather have it say September of 1955.

The other specific point is that we believe that the appellants in these cases, those of high school age from Prince Edward County and those of elementary and high school age of District One which includes Clarendon County, should be admitted as of September, 1955, and the entire class that they represent.

Justice Harlan: Mr. Marshall, on page twenty-nine of your joint brief—

Mr. Marshall: Yes, sir.

Justice Harlan: —as I read it, you suggest as an alternative date, September 1, 1956.

Mr. Marshall: Yes, sir.

Justice Harlan: You indicate that that would be acceptable?

Mr. Marshall: Yes, sir.

Justice Harlan: Have you receded from that view?

Mr. Marshall: No, sir. I was going to limit the argument to two sections, and as I understand it, the two questions can be divided. We say that we are entitled to forthwith action as of September. We felt obliged by the wording of Question Five to, at that stage of our argument, assume that this Court had then agreed that forthwith was not proper, and in answering that in good faith to the Court, we took the position that, if we cannot have forthwith, the least this Court should do would be to put a date certain and put certain other safeguards. And we most certainly do not recede from that position. . . .

I say, in all deference to the attorneys general, they get paid for the handling of problems. It is not just the consideration of one side of this, but the large number of Negroes in the South who have, for years—since 1870—been suffering the denial of rights which this Court said on May 17, that they have been injured in a way that there is only one way to correct. And I think that it is our job to constantly urge to this Court that in taking all of this into consideration it take that, too, into consideration. And on these difficult problems, whenever our government faces them, the history of our government shows that it is the inherent faith in our democratic process that gets us through, the faith that the people in the South are no different from anybody else as to being law-abiding. And in that connection, you will find that in our brief, we set out in a footnote the several studies that have shown by people who take polls—not the takers, but the brains behind the taking—that it is almost impossible to predict from one person's opinion, what he will actually do. You just cannot do that. You get his opinion. He would not like to go to school with the Negro, he would not like to have his children to go to school with the Negro, but that is not saying he won't, and that is not saying that he would prefer for his child to grow up and be an imbecile as to going with the Negroes. It does not say that. It says that in the context of an area where segregation has not only been considered lawful but it has been considered on a very high level, to ask somebody as to whether or not you want to destroy my present system, his answer would be no.

Automatically people do that. And I cannot see the basis for any statement that gradual, indeterminate delay of relief in this case will do anything. It is significant. I think it would be a better position if somebody came before this Court from Carolina and Virginia and said, if you give us five years or four years, we can work it out. They don't say that. And they are taking no step to say it. As a matter of fact, in the brief filed by the state of Virginia, their reply brief, the whole brief relies upon the initial statement that it is this commission that has been appointed, that is working on the May 17 decision. And it is very interesting what they are working on, which appears at page three of the appendix, the final paragraph of this official state commission:

> That in view of the foregoing, I have been directed to report that the Commission, working with its counsel, will explore avenues towards formulation of a program within the framework of law designed to prevent enforced integration of the races in the public schools of Virginia.

That is what they are working on. And they are coming to this Court, asking to be given time to work on that, and I submit that when you consider the decision of May 17 and Questions Four and Five, it was obvious that the average state official involved would be obliged to first make it clear to the general public in his state that the state segregation statutes requiring segregation in public education by order of this Court, is unconstitutional. . . .

And now, once having done that, I find it very difficult to draw an exception as to enforcement so that—if this is referred to the district courts and I use that advisedly, I mean I know technically, but the effect would be to say to all the district courts of the states, the several states could decide in their own minds as to how much time was necessary—then the Negro in this country would be in a horrible shape. He, as a matter of fact, would be as bad, if not worse off than under the separate but equal doctrine for this reason. When they produce reasons for delay, they are up in the air, they are pretty hard to pin down.

And, as a lawyer, it is difficult to meet that type of presentation. In separate but equal, we could count the number of books, the number of bricks, the number of teachers and find out whether the school was physically equal or not. But now, enforcement of this will be left to the judgment of the district court with practically no safeguards, and that, most certainly, we submit, would not be in keeping with the principle of our Constitution at first, and as it is today. It is a national Constitution. There is no place for local option in our Constitution. And we would have, as far north as southern Illinois—whereas of today there are some segregated schools— that in Illinois, the district judge there, if he wanted to, could say, because unlimited time was given by the Supreme Court in South Carolina and Virginia, "I can give undetermined time in Illinois."

And it would apply all over the country. . . .

Justice Frankfurter: If I am to take any stock in what the chief justice of Delaware said, he pointed out the complexities of the various school districts in that state?

Mr. Marshall: Yes.

Justice Frankfurter: I do not know whether it is so or not but I assume it would be so, if he said so.

Mr. Marshall: But Mr. Justice Frankfurter, granting the complexity and assuming throughout each of these states there are terrific complexities, the only thing that this Court is dealing with, this Court is not dealing with the complexities, this Court is dealing with whether or not race can be used. That is the only thing that is before this Court.

Justice Frankfurter: But the physical situation in the different districts may make the result not because of race, but because of those physical differences.

Mr. Marshall: No, sir, physically, Mr. Justice Frankfurter, I submit it will have to be further attended to by the people who are working on it.

Justice Frankfurter: Yes, sir.

Mr. Marshall: But this Court cannot do it.

Justice Frankfurter: I do not imagine this Court is going to work out the details of all the states of the Union.

Mr. Marshall: I certainly would not want to be a party to thinking about it. But that is why, it seems to me, that the real basic issue as I said in the beginning, is that what we want from this Court is the striking down of race.

Now, whatever other plan they want to work out, the question is made about the educational level of children. That has been an administrative detail since we have had public schools.

They give tests to grade children so what do we think is the solution? Simple. Put the dumb colored children in with the dumb white children, and put the smart colored children with the smart white children—that is no problem.

Justice Frankfurter: I hope you will not swallow whole that science can tell us that that is a great certainty any more than polls can tell us about these things.

Mr. Marshall: The proof is that in my own profession some of the greatest lawyers—they had difficulty in getting out of law school—but they turned out to be the greatest lawyers in the country. I think there is no question about it. But the point is that all of these problems that they urge are problems which are peculiar in administrative detail and have no merit in either the constitutional issue involved, or the question of decree in this case, if for no other reason that you cannot sell it.

Justice Frankfurter: In the northern states where there is not a problem of race at all, at least in some of them, there are problems of districting schools which are of the same nature as those that involve southern states, is that right?

Mr. Marshall: Yes, sir.

Justice Frankfurter: Not because of race, but because of the inherent problems?

Mr. Marshall: And they should be solved in the north, without regard to race.

Justice Frankfurter: But that may take an amount of time that is not definitively determined by the authority of this Court.

Mr. Marshall: Then we get to our suggestion of the September of 1956 point. We say that we believe that, if we do not get immediate relief, then the least—

Justice Frankfurter: Well, we should not use "immediately enforce." I thought that we agreed that we would not use words like "immediately" or "forthwith" except the declaration that this Court has made on May 17, 1954 that you can not make distinction because of race.

Mr. Marshall: Yes, sir. If we cannot get that, then we say that the least that would do us any good at all would be a decree which included four items: (1) that this Court make the clearest declaration that not only those statutes but others are in violation of the Fourteenth Amendment. We think it is necessary for that to be put in the decree. (2) that they start immediately to desegregate; (3) file reports; (4) that it must end at a day certain, and that, we take the position, is the minimum that we should expect if we cannot get the decree which will say that as of the next school term—

Justice Frankfurter: What you are saying is that the decision of this Court on May 17, 1954 was not empty words, that was a declaration of unconstitutionality of everything that made a differential on the ground of race.

What you want is a manifestation clear and unequivocal on that, that states, the counties, the cities and the schools—all are affected because we have specific cases and not the world at large?

Mr. Marshall: Yes, sir.

Justice Frankfurter: That, in good faith, this declaration should be carried into action?

Mr. Marshall: That is what we would like to have, because we take the position that this Court could have ordered this done immediately after the May 17 decision, could it not?

Justice Frankfurter: It could have. It might as well say some physical thing that can be done should be done in the next five minutes.

Mr. Marshall: No, sir.

Justice Frankfurter: There are certain unalterable facts of life that cannot be changed even by this Court. I am not talking about the feelings of people. I am talking about districting the accommodations, the arrangement of personnel, and all the complexities that go with the administering of schools.

Mr. Marshall: What I would say, Mr. Justice Frankfurter, is that it should be done as of the school term which is September, 1955. I am getting to using words again.

And now we take the position that the Court should do it. That is the fundamental place we are now. It is whether or not the Court should do it. And we take the position that having done this, having gone into answering the broad equity powers, there is no question about the gradual and effective—we say it can never be effective and that having answered those, we then say that we come back to the point that this Court at this time should enter that type of decree, that is the substance of our position. . . .

In conclusion, in so far as this particular, as our side is concerned—I am trying to leave some time for rebuttal—in summing up, while we still believe that we are entitled to this type of decree that would come under the answer to [Question] Four (a), and we are convinced that any other form of gradual adjustment would not meet the words of the question of this Court which is effective gradual adjustment. We say only at that stage that assuming that that is done, then we believe that the least we should expect is that protection be given to these cases. For example, the children in these cases and the class that they represent.

They are graduating every day. That is the one narrow issue involved in this case. When we go from the narrow issue of the individual named plaintiffs involved and get to the class, the class is limited to children of school age. Your school age is something you cannot control and any delay in that is costly. The Court has said that that segregation system could very well be harming these children personally. On the other hand, we have this effort to—these plans to protect people's rights against these theories, these predictions of what cannot be done. And even if this Court should take that position, we believe that a deadline date is the only thing that will prevent our arriving at the position in the attorney general of Virginia's reply brief where on the last page he says, the only thing that would do him any good is an interminable period of desegregation and, as between that and what we think we are clearly entitled to, we say that the only thing that will protect us is a deadline because we hope that the court will recognize that there is practically no way under the sun that a lawyer seeking relief under any other decree could show that the delay was not one way or the other; and that in this effort to solve this very difficult problem, it seems to us that the answer should be that this is not a matter for local option. This is not a matter that shall be geared down to the local mores and customs of each community in the country, to the extent that not the Constitution but the mores and customs of some people in some community will determine what are and how they shall be enforced insofar as constitutional rights are concerned.

Justice Reed: Mr. Marshall, I gather from your argument that "gradual" has no place in your thinking as far as the decree is concerned?

Mr. Marshall: I would say pretty well, yes. I would say gradual is involved in this case as of now because Virginia and South Carolina and the other states have had from May 17 until now, which is almost a year. . . .

Rebuttal Argument

Mr. Marshall: May it please the Court, I had hoped as I saw the issues in this case, that by now I would be discussing the one point I think is still before the Court. That is, assuming that the Court decides to consider effective gradual adjustment, that by now somebody representing one of the two states would have been able to give the Court some idea as to when that could be done under any circumstances.

And to hear from the lawyer Almond, not in his lifetime, some other place, it was so for hundreds of years, I say on that point—which as I understand is limited to the decision being effective—there is nothing before this Court that can show any justification for giving this interminable gradual adjustment. I am particularly shocked at arguments of the impotency of our government to enforce its Constitution. I am shocked that anybody would put the right of the Negro child to participate in education, which this Court has said is the most important function, on a nonsegregated basis. I am shocked that anybody classes that right to take a drink of whiskey involved in prohibition with the right of a Negro child to participate in education.

We are not talking about the same thing. There is nothing in anything that shows that there is any connection. The point was made that in South Carolina they have had segregated schools for such a long time, and it would not be wise to get rid of them expeditiously. I remind this court that in two cases where *certiorari* was applied for here and denied, the two primary cases from South Carolina, *Elmore* and *Baskins*,[15] Negroes have been denied the right to vote in South Carolina since, if I remember correctly, before the turn of the century, but yet when the district court issues a temporary injunction or preliminary—I have forgotten which, but before ultimate decision, Judge Waring (now retired) ruled that Negroes could not be excluded from the primary election in South Carolina in the very state he is talking about, they had to re-open their books which they did and register some sixty or eighty thousand Negroes within ten days of the decision.[16]

They say, well, education has been here for a long time. And once again these general phrases of time and its significance at this step. I know I was correct in the beginning of trying to make clear the issues in this case.

Everybody on the other side takes the position that we are obliged to show that effective gradual adjustment will not work.

---

[15] *Elmore v. Rice* (1947) and *Brown v. Baskin* (1949) struck down South Carolina's efforts to maintain a primary election open only to white voters.

[16] J. Waties Waring was a federal trial judge in South Carolina, whose rulings in favor of African Americans led to his social ostracism in Charleston.

As I read these questions they are obliged to show that it will work. It is said constantly that we have not shown anything. We have shown our right to immediate relief. And this is a court of equity. And although I, of course, recognize that the burden of proof never shifts in a case but the burden of going forward shifts back and forward, in this, a court of equity, it is unbelievable that at this late day and age the argument would be made that calls for consideration and that the person arguing it should be given advantage brought out by their own wrongdoing.

Both attorneys in the Virginia case say that all of these things they talk about, they admit frankly, are because of the denial of the rights to these people involved. They mention these educational tests. There again, we have use of figures that can be used any way. They use figures on a percentage basis. They leave out the fact that in each one of those percentages, there are Negro children that run the gamut in each one of those twenty-five figures, but they try to give the impression that all the Negro children are below all the white children when that is not true.

There are geniuses in both groups and there are lower ones in both groups, and it has no bearing. No right of an individual can be conditioned as to any average of other people in his racial group or any other group.

Now these health theories, and again we have figures that you can go any way you want. I did not check them because I think they are so completely immaterial, unless the state of Virginia either has no public health service in its schools or they do not know how to use it.

It has always been interesting to me, if the Court please, from the Morgan case involving transportation, that, well, whenever Negroes are separated from other people because of race, they always make an exception as to the Negro servants.

In Virginia, it is interesting to me that the very people that argue for this side, that would object to sending their white children to school with Negroes, are eating food that has been prepared, served, and almost put in their mouths by the mothers of those children; and they do it day in and day out, but they cannot have the child go to school. That is not the point involved in this case. The point is as to whether or not, at this late date, with emphasis, this government can any longer tolerate this extreme difference based upon race or color.

Not one man has stood before this Court yet representing the other side, and shown concretely what they have done in support of the May 17 decision. They have not even started to begin to think about desegregating.

Rather, their emphasis is based on the hope—without any foundation that I can imagine—that this Court will buy the idea of turning this over for a period of an indeterminate number of years. They say I do not have faith in the district courts.

That is untrue. My argument was that I was sure the district courts in these cases would do absolutely right and follow the ruling of the Court; but in this governmental protection of these rights and the governmental leadership in this so-called educational process, this changing-of-attitudes process can be brought about more effectively, and I submit anything else would be of no effect, than for this Court to issue the strongest type of a decree which will arm the district judge and the court of appeals judge will these necessary high level decrees so that they can operate from then on.

That is why we think that the instruction from this Court, we all agree—I do not know why there was so much argument about it—there should be this evidence given in the lower court.

That is in our proceedings. We say you can present it to the lower court, you can show all of these difficulties. We agree on that. The only thing we do not agree on is they want no time limit, and I do not believe that anybody in good faith could listen to these four arguments and not be certain that when they go to any court they are going to argue the same thing they are arguing here, which is never.

So I say, with a strong, forthright decree from this Court, all of the district courts in the country can solve this problem. To my mind—again I come back to it–despite the criticism that has been made of what I say, that we can not continue to exist with this division in our country, whether it is on sectional lines or areawise.

This local option business, the question there is always a twofold score, that we cannot integrate Negroes because we have got so many in this country.

However, the reason we cannot integrate them is because we have to listen to what the people in that county want. Well, obviously, that is what they mean. They mean the ten percent of the white people. They mean specifically that the enforcement of our constitutional rights, recognized in this Court's decision on May 17, must be geared down to the point, as one of the lawyers said, you not only bring in people in the community, you bring in experts.

This district court would be a legislative body, and after listening to all the people in the community, there would be the decision as to when this could come about.

The opposite of orderly procedure. And we would have, for example, as was raised by Mr. Justice Reed, the number in Clarendon County, I do not think it is probable but you could have three different time limits in Clarendon County, one for each district. Obviously that is not what is intended. Obviously, I do not believe that our Constitution, that this Court—and I most certainly do not believe that Questions four and five were either—intended to put the right of the children in these cases to be subjected to what the will of the majority of the people in that community want.

Finally, one thing that to my mind is completely without any semblance of legal authority is that, if you do not give me what I want, I will close up the public schools. It is quoted in the *Southern News* and in this very state of South Carolina in one of these hearings on these bills to abolish the public school system in South Carolina, they are already working on it, to be ready. And one leader, who happened to be a white leader who is not in favor of integration, made the statement that "I do not know what the solution to this problem is, but as to foreclosing these schools, one thing I do know: we will not solve the problem by increasing ignorance."

Now that is something I just do not believe, and proof is right in South Carolina, and immediately after this May 17 decision Governor Byrnes stopped the building of all schools under the equalization program.[17]

A month or so later, he started the program again. So, sure, there will be noise here and there, but we have got to continue, if the Court please. I cannot overemphasize that the problem is tough and we have faith in our government and not the belief that our government is not enforcing its Constitution in South Carolina and Virginia, just as it is anyplace else.

So far as I am concerned, the arguments that are made to the contrary, in addition to the arguments made in their briefs, they have shown only one point insofar as the legal argument is concerned.

That is, that they should have an opportunity to have time to make certain adjustments. We agree on that, and they should present them to the district court; but we want a time limitation, a time limit. We believe we are entitled to our rights as of the next school term, and if we cannot get that type of decree in the judgment of this Court, then what is going to happen? They are making all the threats as to what will happen if they do not get the decree, putting that aside if this Court in its wisdom decides that you will not, in this case, issue a decree which will require admission of these students by September.

The only thing that will give us anything at the end of this lawsuit would be a decree which would do the four things I say. It is important to start that immediately, to report to the district court step by step, and to end it at a date certain. Otherwise, we will have in the State of Virginia and in the county involved, the State of South Carolina, and throughout the country the continuation of what has been branded as an unlawful procedure, what has been branded by this Court as unconstitutional.

It is not the question of having my constitutional right to day-by-day variations in county by county determined one way or the other according to the local option.

In my county they say my child will go to school, schools will be desegregated in five years. I move over into the next county, hoping that he will go in one year and they make it six years. I will be traveling all around the country trying to get my constitutional rights.

It makes no difference under this Constitution of the United States that your child is born in one state or one county or the other. You have the exact same rights in South Carolina and Virginia, insofar as the Constitution is concerned, as you have in New York or any place else.

Therefore, insofar as these cases are concerned, we believe that the first decree is the one we are entitled to; and if we are not entitled to that, in your judgment, at

---

[17] South Carolina governor James F. Byrnes had served briefly on the Supreme Court, in the cabinet, and as director of war mobilization efforts in World War II.

least, we get the second decree so that our plaintiffs in these cases and other Negroes will at least have some protection.

Without a decree, providing for a time limit, there will be no protection whatsoever for the decision of this Court rendered on May 17.

Thank you very much.

Second Rebuttal Argument
Justice Frankfurter: If it would not interfere with the course of the argument you ultimately have in mind, would you care to sketch what you see to be the sequence of steps of events if there were a decree in terms, say, that not one of these four hundred-odd, whatever the number may be in the school districts, including the ones in Clarendon County, not one of these children should be excluded from any high school in that district for reason of color.

Suppose that were the decree, what do you see or contemplate as the consequence of that decree?

Mr. Marshall: If that decree were filed with nothing more then I would be almost certain that the school board through its lawyers would come into the district court either before—this is a possibility that I have to put two on.

If they don't admit them and we file a suggestion of contempt with the district court—

Justice Frankfurter: Before you get to contempt there must be some action which would be the basis of contempt. What do you think it would involve as the consequence?

Mr. Marshall: They refuse.

Justice Frankfurter: That is that the hundred, or four hundred students would knock at the door of the white schools.

Mr. Marshall: Oh, oh, that, no, sir, not necessarily because there is not room for them.

Justice Frankfurter: I should like to have you spell out with particularity just what would happen in that school district.

Mr. Marshall: Well, I would say, sir, that the school board would sit down and take this position with its staff, administrative staff, superintendents, supervisors, et cetera. They would say "The present policy of admission based on race, that is now gone. Now we have to find some other one." The first thing would be to use the maps that they already have, show the population, the school population, then I would assume they would draw district lines without the idea of race but district lines circled around the schools like they did in the District of Columbia.

That would be problem number one.

Problem number two would then be "What are we going to do about reassigning teachers?"

Now that there is no restricting about white and Negro it might be that we will shift teachers here or shift teachers there.

Third would be the problem of bus transportation. We have two buses going down the same road, one taking Negroes, one taking whites.

So we might still do it that way or we might do it another way.

Justice Frankfurter: Throughout all this period, I wouldn't know how long that would be, there would be no actual change in the actual intake of students, is that right?

Mr. Marshall: I would say so, yes, sir.

Justice Frankfurter: All right.

Mr. Marshall: I would say so. That was the point I was going to get to.

And assuming that they are doing that and the time is going on, they might come into the district court and ask for further relief, which would be to say "We are working in good conscience on this. We just can't do it within a reasonable time," or we would go into court and say they are not proceeding in good faith; either way the district court would at that stage decide as to whether or not they were proceeding in good faith, at which stage the district court would have the exact same leeway that has been argued for all along.

Justice Frankfurter: Now as to primary schools, that is if that is what they are called.

Mr. Marshall: Yes, sir.

Justice Frankfurter: The problem would be a little different because the number makes a difference.

Mr. Marshall: Well, it would be different because of numbers. The figure shift would be the shifting of the children.

Justice Frankfurter: I am assuming that under the responsibilities of the law officers in various states, there would be a conscious desire to meet the order of this Court. I am assuming that this process which you outlined would proceed, wouldn't that be a process in each one of these school districts?

Mr. Marshall: That would be and I think that that is the type of problem. The only thing is, we are now on this do-it-right-away point.

Justice Frankfurter: Your analysis shows that do-it-right-away merely means show that you are doing it right away, beginning to do it right away.

Mr. Marshall: I take the position, Mr. Justice Frankfurter, this has been in the back of our minds since Question Four (a) and the others all along, as to whether or not we will be required to answer this in the context which we have been answering this, or whether it was not the question of contempt, that it would never come up except on contempt.

Justice Frankfurter: That is the way it would come up.

Mr. Marshall: The way you put it.

Justice Frankfurter: The school authorities would say we have not got the room, or we have not got the teachers, or the teachers have resigned, or a thousand and one reasons or twenty thousand reasons that develop from a problem of that sort; you couldn't possibly proceed in contempt, could you?

Mr. Marshall: I doubt that we would even move for contempt.

Justice Frankfurter: Except there might be different difficulties of interpretation as to the reasons for delay.

Mr. Marshall: And, for example, we would not recognize as reason for delay the waiting for these attitudes to catch up with us. We would not recognize that.

Justice Frankfurter: Well, an attitude might depend on the nonavailability of teachers. That might be an attitude.

Mr. Marshall: There would always be availability of competent capable Negro teachers, always.

There is no shortage. And I think it is very significant in New York—

Justice Frankfurter: I am not sure why you say that with such confidence. In different localities established as you well know, better than I—

Mr. Marshall: Yes, sir.

Justice Frankfurter: Why do you make such a statement?

Mr. Marshall: Well, there are so many that are in areas that don't want to leave because of home ties or what have you, and because they are so well trained there are school boards that won't hire them because they don't want them, and those are very available, I mean well-qualified teachers, sir.

North Carolina, they take a most interesting position: They say the Negro teachers have more experience, more college training.

Justice Frankfurter: You have heard that the bar of this Court with considerable pride stated those standards of Negro teachers.

Mr. Marshall: Yes, sir, and it was followed by the fact that they would deprive the white children of the benefit of superior teachers and fire the Negro teachers.

Justice Frankfurter: I merely suggested, in the areas of education that I know something about, a plethora of well-equipped teachers is not there.

Mr. Marshall: Well, it is on the broad general figures, Mr. Justice Frankfurter, but on the Negro side we are producing them and—in all frankness as the attorney general of North Carolina, Mr. Lake, said—in the South that is about one of the few places they can get work.

And you have masters, M.A's, that are unemployed.

The other point that I would like to come back to is to continue this class point as I see it affects these cases.

The named plaintiffs, I think there is no question they are entitled to relief. And on some of the questions it seems to me that if the named plaintiffs in such a small number are admitted, I would not have the real physical difficulties if you only admitted, if the school board only admitted those named plaintiffs.

However, it seems to me we have to be realistic, and most certainly by the time the case, before the case gets to judgment, many if not all of the other Negroes will have intervened when they find that they are not protected and the only way they can get protected is to intervene.

I would imagine with considerable reliance that they would intervene.

The only thing it seems to me is this, that it is going to be difficult to consider this in the narrow named-plaintiff category without the understanding that the whole class will eventually be in it.

That brings me to the next point, which is that I hope the Court will bear in mind the need for this time limit, which I come back to because in normal judicial proceedings in these and other cases, there will be so much time lost anyhow.

We have to go before the local school board, we have to exhaust our remedies before we can go into court, there is no question about that.

Then we get into court and then, unless we have this time limit, we most certainly will have this terrific long extended argument and testimony as to all of these reasons for delay, which I or any lawyer would be powerless to stop.

It would depend of course on the district judge.

But as of this time, the only valid reasons that have been set up have been the reasons set up relating to the physical adjustments and not a single appellant, appellee, and not a single attorney general has said one thing to this Court in regard to physical difficulties which could not be met within a year.

I come back to our original position as to why we picked a year.

We picked a year because we talked with administrators, school officials and we just could not find anything longer than a year. I submit that the American Tobacco Trust case, which we have on about the next to the last page of our brief, which involved a dissolution of this trust, this Court said that because of the involved situation and everything, a time limit had to be set, and this Court set a six months' time limit and told the district court that you can give them an extension of sixty days if they show valid reasons.

However, if you are convinced that they can do it in less than six months, see that they do it in less than six months. Now that is at least one case in which this Court did do it on the basis of whatever material was before them, and the material you have before this Court at this time shows that we certainly have a right, if nothing else was shown, we would have a right to this immediate action, the time to take care of these administrative details, and that you have nothing else to go on.

The other side has not produced anything except attitudes, opinion polls, et cetera.

On the basis of that, it seems to me we get back to the normal procedure which would the type of judgment from this Court that would require them to be admitted at, let us say, the next school term; and the contempt side, as I mentioned before.

Or what I consider to be the more realistic approach, which would be to let the other states involved know and the other areas know that it will not do you any good, if there were no time limit fixed the school officials in the other states that will follow whatever this Court will say, if they knew that they had a chance, just a chance of getting interminable delay from the district court after the lawsuit was filed, then I would imagine that they would not begin action until after the lawsuit was filed.

However, if they knew that if a lawsuit was filed they would have to either desegregate immediately or would get no more than a year, they would start working.

So it seems to me that if I am correct in that, then this time limit gets so involved with this constitutional right that—so far as not the plaintiffs in these cases are concerned but insofar as precedent, effect, and so forth in the country is concerned— that now this time limit is involved with the constitutional right and that the statement on time should be just as forthright as the statement was made on the constitutional position taken in the May 17 decision; and so we submit to the Court that on behalf of the appellants and petitioners we have been appreciative of all of this time that has been given.

The last thing that I could possibly say is what I said in the beginning. That in considering problems as tough as these, and they are tough, that what I said before is apropos now. It is the faith in our democratic processes that gets us over these, and that is why in these cases we believe that this Court, in the time provision, it must be forthright and say that it shall not under any circumstances take longer than a year.

And once having done that, the whole country knows that this May 17 decision means that the protection of the rights here involved of any person in the category, any Negro, will get prompt action in the Court.

Once that is done, then we leave the local communities to work their way out of it, but to work their way out of it within the framework of a clear and precise statement that not only are these rights constitutionally protected, but that you cannot delay enforcement of it.

Thank you very much.

The Supreme Court held that trial courts should develop appropriate remedial plans, guided by "a practical flexibility." Referring to the holding that segregation was unconstitutional, Chief Justice Warren's opinion said that "the vitality of these constitutional principles cannot be allowed to yield simply because of disagreement with them." Trial courts should require the school districts to "make a prompt and reasonable start toward full compliance." The defendants could ask for additional time, but they had the burden of showing that more time was "necessary in the public interest, and is consistent with good-faith compliance at the earliest practicable date." Courts could "consider problems related to administration, arising from the physical conditions of the school plant, the school transportation system, personnel, revision of school districts and attendance zones into compact units to achieve a system of determining admission to the public schools on a nonracial basis, and revision of local laws and regulations which may be necessary in solving the foregoing problems." In the opinion's most famous phrase, Chief Justice Warren wrote that the trial courts should enter orders "to admit to public schools on a racially nondiscriminatory basis with all deliberate speed the parties to these cases."

4. *Cooper v. Aaron* (1958)

The decision on the remedy in *Brown* may have embodied the Court's hope that desegregation would begin promptly and proceed smoothly. If so, that hope was soon defeated. Although desegregation was accomplished with relative ease in some border states, the deep South resisted desegregation fiercely. At best, Southern political and educational leaders proposed plans for extremely gradual desegregation, in which one grade per year would be desegregated—meaning that full desegregation would take twelve years. At worst, they developed disingenuous "freedom of choice" plans and student assignment laws that were expected to (and did) produce school systems in which the students remained completely segregated.

The Court first confronted Southern resistance in *Cooper v. Aaron*, dealing with the desegregation of the schools in Little Rock, Arkansas. The city's school board, led by superintendent Virgil Blossom, adopted a desegregation plan for Central High School. Nine African American children were admitted to Central High in the fall of 1957. Arkansas Governor Orval Faubus attempted to thwart desegregation by using the state's National Guard units to block their entry to Central High. After Faubus seemed to have backed down by withdrawing the National Guard, crowds opposed to desegregation forced the African American students to withdraw. President Dwight Eisenhower then dispatched military units to ensure that the nine students could attend Central High. Angry crowds frequently surrounded the school, creating an atmosphere of violent resistance. In February 1958 the school board went to the federal district court for permission to suspend the desegregation process because of the turmoil at Central High. Judge Harry Lemley granted the request, but the court of appeals reversed, thus reinstating the desegregation plan. However, the court of appeals delayed the force of its decision. The effect of that stay would have been to ensure that Central High would open in the fall of 1958 without any desegregation. The parents of the African American children asked the Supreme Court for a prompt decision that would affirm the court of appeals and guarantee that Central High would open in September with African American students in attendance. The Court convened in an emergency session in August to consider that request.

The procedural posture of the case before the Supreme Court was quite complex, and the first part of the argument (not printed here) dealt with these procedural complexities. Once those were resolved, the Court turned to the merits of the lower courts' actions. The argument that follows deals with that part of the case.

COOPER V. AARON
(SEPTEMBER 11, 1958)

Mr. Marshall: May it please the Court, there are one or two preliminary points, and then I think the argument for respondents can be rather brief, because I think the issues are so clear.

The first one—I hate to start at the end in answering an argument—I take the flat position that this "battle between the sovereignties" was decided by the Constitution when it was adopted. That was settled some years ago.

This leads into the second point. I think it is one thing for a politician in a state to argue, or a political officer in a state to argue, the disagreement with the Supreme Court of the United States, or the doubt as to the power of authority of the Supreme Court. It is another thing for a lawyer to stand in this Court and argue that there is any doubt about it. And I think that is where we are in this case. For example, the reason to hold up this for these other laws. Mr. Butler said he was not too sure what was in it.[1] Here is one batch of laws passed by the legislature in Arkansas, the general assembly giving the governor his authority, and here is what has come about.

Since Judge Lemley's order, as a result of Judge Lemley's order, this is the action we can expect to be amplified for two and a half or more years. This is S.B. 2— Senate Bill Number Two—introduced by Beardon. It says: "It has been found, and it is hereby declared by the general assembly, that a large majority of the people of this State are opposed to the forcible integration of, or mixing of, the races in the public schools of the State; that practically all of the people of this State are opposed to the use of federal troops in aid of such integration; that the people of this State are opposed to the use of any federal power to enforce the integration of the races in the public schools; that it is now threatened that Negro children will be forcibly enrolled and permitted to attend some of the public schools of this State formerly attended only by white children; that the President of the United States has indicated that federal troops may be used to enforce the orders of the district court respecting enrollment and attendance of Negro pupils in schools formerly attended only by white children; and that the forcible operation of a public school in this State attended by both Negro and White children will inevitably result in violence in and about the school and throughout the district involved, endangering the safety of buildings and other property and lives; that the State, or the feeling of the great majority of the people of this State, is such that the forcible mixing of races in public schools will seriously impair the operation of a suitable and efficient school" and on and so on.

That exact same section is quoted in every one of this batch of bills which gives to the governor the right to close the schools, take away the money, use it for private schools—to give the State money to private schools, providing they are operated on a segregated basis—and other means of relief.

The other batch of bills are bills that are aimed at—and I hope, despite references that have been made to counsel on this side, they did not mention who this bill was directed to—this is an act entitled "An Act to prohibit the fomenting and agitation and litigation that interferes with the orderly administration of public schools and institutions of higher learning, and to prohibit the solicitation, receipt, or donation of funds for the purpose of filing or prosecuting lawsuits to define, maintain, and provide penalties," and so forth. A statute similar to the one in Virginia which a three-judge court in an exhaustive opinion by Judge Soper declared to be unconstitutional, and which bills are now before this Court.

---

[1] Richard Butler represented the Little Rock school board.

If time is given it is obvious from this that in two and a half years the law will be so crystalized in Little Rock—I mean Arkansas—that there will be no litigation, and they are protected by making sure that there will be no lawyers to litigate. And that is the reason that the plea is made for time.

Whether or not the school board believes as they do, time is time. I don't believe, if it please the Court, that ever before has an effort been made to get a watering down of constitutional rights without any basis. And although it was brought out in questioning, as of right now these petitioners in this case have given not the slightest idea of doing anything. And that is what gets me to the point that they say that we agree that we should balance equity. I never have agreed, as a lawyer, that we should balance personal equity against constitutional rights.

But even if you go into the so-called, what the petitioners call, equities, with all of the problems that the children went through in that school, and the faculties—democracy is tough. There is always going to be a measure of difficulty and problems. The school board is so worried because they get threatening telephone calls and letters. I don't believe anybody ever in public office who is worth his salt, who would make a decision one way or another, didn't get telephone calls and letters. That is a part of service to democracy. I don't welcome it, but I recognize it.

But I think we have to think about these children and their parents, these Negro children that went through this every day and their parents that stayed at home wondering what was happening to their children, listening to the radio about the bomb threats and all of that business. I don't see how anybody under the sun could say, after those children and those families went through that for a year, to tell them, "All you have done is gone. You fought for what you considered democracy and you lost. Go back to the segregated school from which you came." I just don't believe it.

And I don't believe you can balance those rights. There is no question here of the right of one group of children against another.

The other side constantly talks, and indeed Judge Lemley talks, about the injury to education. It is according to what type of education we are talking about. In our brief—I think it starts at around page eight—we quoted from the decision in the Brown case, and *West Virginia v. Barnette*, and the argument of the solicitor general two weeks ago, as to what education is. Education is not the teaching of the three Rs. Education is the teaching of the overall citizenship, to learn to live together with fellow citizens, and above all to learn to obey the law. We talk about public education. We think from those three quotations there it is clear that is what we mean. And the danger to the education in Arkansas and in Little Rock and in Central High comes about through the order of Judge Lemley which says that not only the school board and the state can and should submit to mob violence and threats of mob violence, but that the federal judiciary likewise should do so.

I do not know of any more horrible destruction of principle of citizenship than to tell young children that those of you who withdrew, rather than to go to school with Negroes, those of you who were punished last year, the few that the school board did punish, "Come back, all is forgiven, you win."

Therefore, I am not worried about Negro children in these states. I don't believe they are in this case as such. I worry about the white children in Little Rock who are told, as young people, that the way to get your rights is to violate the law and defy the lawful authorities. I am worried about their future. I don't worry about the Negro kids' future. They have been struggling with democracy long enough. They know about it.

This is actually, laid bare, the State of Arkansas, with the governor holding these bills, refusing to sign them, and saying publicly that he holds them to see what this Court is going to do. Maybe it has happened before, but I don't know of any other instance where the governor of a state has tried to hold something over this Court. And I think that this Court has to recognize that, not to consider this case as counsel for the school board would say, as to whether or not the children in Little Rock lost some education last year.

The evidence in the record is in complete conflict. They say there is great feeling of having troops in the school. The record shows that the president is responsible for sending the troops to Little Rock, but the record shows—I think it is page 269—that they were put in the school at the request of Superintendent Blossom. He is the one who put them inside of the school. The president didn't. And he is now complaining about it.

And to show this horrible effect in the record in this case, about the effect of troops being in the school, there is also a witness who is a band director, who has his band class and everything up on the fifth floor, a round thing on top. Obviously, the sound goes up and they won't disturb them. There are no Negroes in the band class. There are not even any Negroes on that floor, and he said he couldn't teach because of the effect of Negroes being down on the first floor, that affected him teaching up on the fifth floor. That is stretching a little, in my imagination. That is moving a little too far.

And I think that that is the type of testimony in this record and there is just no basis for it. And I would not urge that this Court make this effort to balance the harm to one or harm to the other.

The next point I would like to make is that in the Deep South today there are three sets of school boards. There is one set that is working along and working it out, either with or without court orders, and working it out on a procedural basis and ranging over periods of years, varying with each school district.

There are other school boards that say we just won't move at all.

Then, there is a third group that says that the only way to move is over a very gradual period of years. And in this case we have as gradual a plan as you can find. There was no ultimate time limit on it. It would just go on and on. And it was approved by the district court, affirmed by the court of appeals, and not brought to this Court. We went back down to see it work out. And now they say that the most gradual of gradual plans can't work.

Then, that group has joined the other group which says it just can't work anyhow. And so the Brown decision means nothing except in the areas where the people voluntarily accept it.

And in their brief they argue, in one particular place—it is on page 29 of their brief—they argue this, after two and a half years they say: "If in the nature of things there will never be any protection, operation should be suspended until such time as the people by processes of time are taught to respect court decisions and to be willing on patriotic grounds to subdue the passions which now control their thinking."

If constitutional rights are to wait for that period, I submit you don't need the Constitution and you don't need this Court, if everybody is going to voluntarily do right. But it is interesting on this time element. This two and a half years must be measured with three different groups of students—Negro. The seven now in, the record shows, will be graduated within two and a half years. They will be gone. Now, when the argument is made that rights are not being destroyed, certainly the argument cannot be made that those children's rights aren't through, they are out, they are out of school.

The second group are those that are eligible, under the plan, to come in this year.

And the third group are the others in the class which are farther down the line in the high school on down to the elementary school.

And so we took the position from the beginning of this hearing that these three all fell into one package and you couldn't strike one without striking the other. Constantly their argument is understandably aimed at only the seven children, and to me that is the most dangerous argument that can be made. It is one thing to say that we need time to put a plan into action. It is another thing to say that a plan, once in performance, should be suspended, stopped, or halted.

We have argued in our brief, and we have argued from the beginning of this, that any application for time is based on the same principle as those set out in the Brown decision where they asked for time originally. There is no difference. Certainly public opposition is not sufficient.

The most interesting argument I get from the state—I mean from the school board—is that two partners come in in a case and say, "I am not responsible for nonperformance because my partner stopped me from performing." I don't see a bit of difference. The state is a unit. The Fourteenth Amendment is aimed against the state.[2] And all of this panoply of state action from the governor on down is made against them, and in that line I have to comment on the continued resentment of the school board at any suggestions that they seek relief in Hoxie or the Clinton, Tennessee relief.

---

[2] This refers to the "state action" doctrine, which holds that, because it begins with the words, "No State shall," the Fourteenth Amendment applies only to action taken by public officials.

They say, for example, it is not their job to go into court and get an injunction. They don't have to go into court and get an injunction. All they have to do is to go into court and say to the court, "I suggest that your injunction and decree is being violated." That is all they have to do. And in Clinton the judge called in the United States Department of Justice, through the attorney general's office. But there is no action yet. They stood here this afternoon and complained that they have been tied in litigation in this case for three months. They could very well have been tied there three months in seeing what could be done there. And indeed Judge Lemley could have done so. But from the beginning to the end of this case the record will show that whenever there was a move against integration of Central High School, each step, each step the school board made a move to get the Negro kids out of there, each step of the way. And they are still at this late date arguing the same point against public violence.

Finally, if it please the Court, although we are respondents, the question of relief is important. In our brief we requested that the Court affirm the court of appeals, and that the Court set aside Judge Lemley's order and reinstate Judge Davies' orders and Judge Mills' order.[3] But after thinking about it, we would like permission of the Court to amend the request to the Court, that if the Court should decide to affirm the Court of Appeals of the Eighth Circuit, that even to order the mandate to issue forthwith would not meet the realities of the situation because school opens on Monday, and there is a matter of mandate issuing. We would respectfully suggest that if the Court does decide to affirm, that the Court rule that Judge Lemley's order be set aside and these other orders reinstated as of the entry of the judgment in this Court. We think that that would give the type of relief, and on that I understand that both sides of the counsel table are in agreement as to this Court clarifying the situation. The only question is about time. And I submit that the decision, the clarification cannot be made and time given at the same time.

There is one other point I forgot to mention, if it please the Court. On the last appearance the Court questioned about Judge Davies' original orders. We have with us certified copies of each of his two original orders. With permission of the Court I would like to deposit them in the clerk's office in case anyone would desire to see them.

If there are no further questions, we would submit, on the ground that the one single issue in this case, with the case stripped down, is the issue as to whether or not a federal district court can delay an integration plan—desegregation plan— already in progress, solely because of violence and threats of violence. It is a narrow question, and I believe it is the only question in this case.

We, therefore, submit that the decision of the court of appeals is eminently correct and that it should be affirmed. It should be affirmed in such fashion as to make it clear even to the politicians in Arkansas that Article VI of the Constitution means what it says.

---

[3] The orders directing desegregation of the schools.

The Supreme Court unanimously affirmed the court of appeals, with a decision announced on September 12. The heading of the opinion listed all nine justices as authors, stressing the extraordinary nature of the decision and the Court's unanimity. The Court held that "the constitutional rights of [the children] are not to be sacrificed or yielded to the violence and disorder which have followed upon the actions of the Governor and Legislature." It continued, "Law and order are not here to be preserved by depriving the Negro children of their constitutional rights." Responding to Governor Faubus's assertion that he was not bound to comply with the implications of the Court's decision in *Brown*, the Court declared that "the federal judiciary is supreme in the exposition of the law of the Constitution," and that "the interpretation of the Fourteenth Amendment enunciated by this Court in the *Brown* case is the supreme law of the land."

PART II

WRITINGS AND SPEECHES
AS A LAWYER

arshall wrote several articles while he headed the Legal Defense Fund, and gave many speeches, only a few of which were transcribed. The articles and speeches were generally aimed at educating the audience about the NAACP's legal challenges to segregation, recent Supreme Court decisions, and related matters. Audiences varied, but Marshall directed most of his talks and articles at nonspecialists. The articles published in the NAACP's official magazine *The Crisis* were, of course, directed at the NAACP's membership. *The Journal of Negro Education*, published at Howard University, was an important resource for African American professionals, particularly (but not exclusively) teachers and educators. The articles and speeches conveyed information, but they also were designed to rally support for the NAACP's efforts.

Marshall was primarily a trial and appellate lawyer, not an academic writer or publicist. He educated the public more through his work in the courtroom and in informal comments after losing or (more often) winning important cases. The early articles are particularly dry, providing summaries of court cases, but others report on Marshall's investigations and the NAACP's wartime concerns. Only a few (such as selection 11, a journalistic account of Marshall's investigation of court-martial proceedings against African American soldiers during the Korean War) convey some flashes of the eloquence and wit Marshall brought to his courtroom performance. The articles are significant documents even so, because taken as a group they give a reasonably good overview of the Legal Defense Fund's activities from the late 1930s through the mid-1950s.

Selection 5 summarizes the NAACP's activities in the Supreme Court from its founding to 1939. Selections 6 and 8 offer overviews of civil rights enforcement efforts in the early 1940s, while selection 9 frames Marshall's interpretation of developments later in that decade through a tribute to liberal justice Frank Murphy. Selection 7 provides Marshall's account of the Detroit race riot of 1943. Selections 10, 13, and 14 summarize the NAACP's attack on segregation and the Supreme Court's response, through the 1955 decision on remedy in *Brown v. Board of Education*. Selection 12, a transcription of remarks Marshall made at a ceremonial dinner, captures some of the spontaneity of his informal talks, and provides his comment on the challenges faced by civil rights lawyers. Finally, selection 15 returns to an earlier stage in the NAACP's legal activities and reflects on the importance of its victories in securing the right to vote.

5. "Equal Justice Under Law"
The Crisis, July 1939

The Oklahoma franchise case, *Lane v. Wilson*, decided on May 22, 1939, marks the twelfth favorable decision from the United States Supreme Court in cases handled by the N.A.A.C.P. Over a period of twenty-four years the association has been successful in twelve out of thirteen cases before the highest court of the land.

These decisions have served as guide posts in a sustained fight for full citizenship rights for Negroes. They have broadened the scope of protection guaranteed by the Thirteenth, Fourteenth, and Fifteenth amendments to the Constitution in the fields of the right to register and vote, equal justice before the law, Negroes on juries, segregation, and equal educational opportunities.[1] These precedents have been cited more than sixty-five times in the highest courts in the land and have been of benefit to all citizens, both Negro and white. It is significant that the last case is a follow-up of the very first N.A.A.C.P. case.

REGISTRATION AND VOTING

The first *cause celebre* has become known as the "Grandfather Clause Case," *Guinn and Beale v. United States* decided in June, 1915. In 1910 the constitution of Oklahoma was amended restricting the right to register and vote to persons who could read and write. However, the clause also provided that persons who either voted prior to 1866 or whose lineal descendants were eligible to vote prior to 1866 were exempt from the test. Since Negroes were not eligible to vote before 1866, the law actually disfranchised most Negroes.

Maryland and other states had passed similar statutes in an effort to disfranchise colored people. The N.A.A.C.P. began a campaign to have these laws declared unconstitutional. Certain election officials in Oklahoma were indicted for violation of federal statutes by refusing Negroes the right to vote because of the grandfather clause. When the case reached the U.S. supreme court, the N.A.A.C.P. filed briefs *amicus curiae* in the case setting forth arguments on the unconstitutionality of the grandfather clause of the Oklahoma constitution.

The provisions were declared unconstitutional by the supreme court in an opinion which clarified the Fifteenth amendment and declared that its provisions were self-executing and destroyed all types of discrimination in voting. The precedent established by this case was used to strike down similar provisions in other states and pointed the way for Negroes to have a fuller realization of their citizenship rights. Mr. Chief Justice White, in construing the Fifteenth amendment declared:

---

[1] The Thirteenth Amendment, adopted in 1865, abolished slavery; the Fifteenth, adopted in 1870, provided that the right to vote could not be denied on the basis of race.

"But it is equally beyond the possibility of question that the amendment
in express terms restricts the power of the United States or the state to
abridge or deny the right of a citizen of the United States to vote on account
of race, color or previous condition of servitude. The restriction is coinci-
dent with the power and prevents its exertion in disregard of the command
of the amendment."

In an effort to circumvent the decision in the Guinn case the state of Oklahoma
passed a statute requiring all persons eligible to register to do so within twelve
days or to be barred from registering thereafter. However, the statute also provided that all those who voted in 1914 were automatically registered. Since Negroes
were disfranchised by the grandfather clause in 1914 they were disfranchised by
the new act.

When I. W. Lane was refused registration in Wagoner county, in 1934, the
N.A.A.C.P. started a case in the local federal courts to declare this new law unconstitutional. The case eventually reached the supreme court where lawyers for the association maintained that the new law, although not expressly discriminatory on its
face, was actually aimed at disfranchising a large group of Negroes.

On May 22, 1939, Mr. Associate Justice Frankfurter rendered the opinion of the
supreme court declaring the new act unconstitutional. The opinion also broadened
the scope of the interpretation of the Fifteenth amendment by stating:

"The amendment nullifies sophisticated as well as simple minded modes
of discrimination. It hits onerous procedural requirements which effectively handicap exercise of the franchise by the colored race although the
abstract right to vote may remain unrestricted as to race."

THE TEXAS CASES

After the grandfather clause case outlawed the attempts to disfranchise Negroes
by preventing them from registering, several states immediately began to devise other
schemes. Texas passed a statute which provided that "in no event shall a Negro be
eligible to participate in a democratic party primary election held in the State of
Texas." The N.A.A.C.P. immediately challenged the constitutionality of this statute
when Dr. L. A. Nixon was refused the right to vote in a primary election in El Paso.
A suit for damages was instituted and this case was carried to the supreme court after
it was dismissed in the lower court.

The supreme court, in what has become known as the "First Texas Primary
Case", *Nixon v. Herndon*, in March, 1927, reversed the lower court and declared the
statute unconstitutional. Mr. Associate Justice Holmes stated:

"The statute of Texas in the teeth of the prohibition referred to assumes to
forbid Negroes to take part in a primary election the importance of which
we have indicated, discriminating against them by the distinction of color

alone. States may do a good deal of classifying that it is difficult to believe rational, but there are limits, and it is too clear for extended argument that color cannot be made the basis of a statutory classification affecting the right set up in this case."

The state of Texas, however, was not willing to give up so it attempted to evade the prohibitions of the Fourteenth and Fifteenth amendments against state action by passing an act empowering the state Democratic committee to set up its own limitations on its primary. The committee immediately passed a resolution restricting the primary to white electors.

Dr. Nixon was again refused the right to vote in the primary and an action for damages was started which was dismissed and carried to the supreme court. This case, decided in May, 1932, has become known as the "Second Texas Primary Case". The supreme court declared the new act unconstitutional in an opinion by Mr. Associate Justice Cardozo which declared:

"With the problem thus laid bare and its essentials exposed to view, the case is seen to be ruled by *Nixon v. Herndon, supra*. . . . The Fourteenth amendment, adopted as it was with special solicitude for the equal protection of members of the Negro race, lays down a duty upon the court to level by its judgment these barriers of color."

EQUAL JUSTICE IN THE COURTS
The campaign to secure equal justice in the courts has brought about several precedents which have been of value to all defendants in criminal cases, both Negro and white. Criminal cases handled by the N.A.A.C.P. are limited to cases where the particular defendant is about to be denied due process of law because of his race or color and where the case will establish a precedent for the benefit of others.

One of the most far reaching decisions on the question of equal justice came in the "Elaine, Arkansas, Cases," *Moore v. Dempsey*, decided in February, 1923. These cases were the result of an armed clash at Elaine, Arkansas, in October, 1919. Negro farmers in Phillips county, Arkansas, were holding a meeting to decide on the best method of obtaining a better price for their cotton. The colored church where they were gathered was fired into by a group of whites and a pitched battle resulted when the Negroes fought back. Twelve Negroes were sentenced to death and sixty-seven to long prison terms as a result of the riot.

Shortly after the arrest a mob marched to the jail for the purpose of lynching the men, but were prevented from doing so by the presence of United States troops and a promise by a local committee "that if the mob would refrain, they [would] execute those found guilty in the form of law." Negro witnesses in the trial were whipped until they agreed to testify against the men.

The defendants were tried by a jury of whites in the presence of a mob which threatened lynching and mob violence if there were no convictions. Court appointed counsel was afraid to ask for a change of venue,[2] called no witnesses, and did not put the defendants on the stand. The entire trial lasted three quarters of an hour and in less than five minutes the jury brought in a verdict of guilty of murder. The case was appealed to the Arkansas supreme court and lost.

Attorneys for the N.A.A.C.P. applied for a writ of habeas corpus in the federal courts which was refused and the case was appealed to the U.S. supreme court.[3] The defense was made that habeas corpus was limited by a former case, *Frank v. Magnum*, and would not lie in this case for errors in the trial which were not properly objected to at trial. The supreme court, however, held that the Frank opinion did not control the case and Mr. Associate Justice Holmes in the majority opinion, in commenting on the Frank case, stated:

> But if the case is that the whole proceeding is a mask—that counsel, jury and judge were swept to the fatal end by an irresistible wave of public passion, and that the state courts failed to correct the wrong, neither perfection in the machinery for correction nor the possibility that the trial court and counsel saw no other way of avoiding an immediate outbreak of the mob can prevent this court from securing to the petitioners their constitutional rights.

This decision establishing the principle that a trial dominated by a mob is not due process of law has become the guide post and has replaced the Frank case. It has been cited numerous times in important cases, including the famous Scottsboro cases, and has outlawed trials by mob violence.

A precedent extending the requirements of due process of law to the question of a confession secured by violence was established in the "Brown, Ellington and Shields Cases", *Brown v. Mississippi*, decided in February, 1936. Three Negro farm laborers, Ed Brown, Henry Shields and Yank Ellington, were convicted of murder in DeKalb county, Mississippi, in 1934. The only evidence against them were confessions obtained by force and violence. When arrested Ellington was hanged to a tree in an effort to make him "confess", which he eventually did. The marks of the rope were still on Ellington's neck at the trial and the deputy sheriff admitted his part in the torture. In response to an inquiry as to how severely he beat Ellington, he stated: "Not too much for a Negro; not as much as I would have done if it were

---

[2] "Venue" refers to the place of trial, and a motion for a change of venue is a request that the trial's location be changed.

[3] The writ of habeas corpus is the traditional method by which a person convicted of a crime in a state court challenges the lawfulness of his conviction in a lower federal court; it is an alternative to "direct" review by the Supreme Court for federal court consideration of constitutional challenges to criminal convictions. The conditions for obtaining the writ, that is, for allowing the lower federal courts to consider constitutional challenges to convictions, were quite restricted until the early 1960s.

left to me." Two others also admitted the beatings—not a single witness denied beating the men.

The conviction was affirmed by the Mississippi supreme court and a petition for certiorari was granted by the U.S. supreme court where the conviction was reversed and a new trial granted.[4] Mr. Chief Justice Hughes in the opinion for the court declared:

> The rack and torture chamber may not be substituted for the witness stand. . . . The duty of maintaining the constitutional rights of a person on trial for his life rises above mere rules of procedure and whenever the court is clearly satisfied that such violations exist, it will refuse to sanction such violations and will apply the corrective.

JURY SERVICE

The association has also challenged the exclusion of Negroes from grand and petit juries. Precedents have been re-established enforcing the principle that the trial and conviction of a Negro by a jury of whites, upon an indictment found and returned by a grand jury of white persons, from both of which juries all qualified Negroes have been excluded solely on account of race or color, is a denial of the equal protection of the laws guaranteed by the Fourteenth amendment to the Constitution.[5]

The point was raised in the Elaine, Ark., cases and was again raised in *Hollins v. Oklahoma* decided by the supreme court in 1935 in a memorandum opinion. Jess Hollins was convicted in Sapula, Okla., in 1931, of rape and sentenced to die. He had no lawyer and no lawyer was appointed for him. Three days before his execution the N.A.A.C.P. was called into the case and secured a stay of execution.[6] An appeal was taken to the supreme court of Arkansas [*sic*] where a reversal was secured on the ground that qualified Negroes were excluded from the jury which tried Hollins.

The next case on jury exclusion was *Hale v. Kentucky*, decided in April, 1938. Joe Hale was indicted for murder in McCracken county, Kentucky. His lawyers moved to set aside the indictment on the ground that the jury commissioners had excluded Negroes from the jury lists. He offered evidence that no Negroes had been on the juries in that county from 1906 to 1936, and that they were systematically excluded.

---

[4] A petition for certiorari is the procedure by which a party who has lost in a lower court asks the Supreme Court to review the lower court's decision; the Court has complete discretion whether to grant or deny these petitions.

[5] The Fourteenth Amendment provides, "No State shall . . . deny to any person within its jurisdiction the equal protection of the laws."

[6] A stay of execution is a temporary delay of an already scheduled execution, to allow the courts to consider the legal challenges to the conviction.

Hale was convicted and sentenced to die. His conviction was affirmed by the court of appeals of Kentucky and the case was carried to the U.S. supreme court by the N.A.A.C.P. The decision was reversed in a per curiam opinion[7] which stated:

"We are of the opinion that the affidavits, which by the stipulation of the state were to be taken as proof, and were uncontradicted, sufficed to show a systematic and arbitrary exclusion of Negroes from the jury lists because of their race or color, constituting a denial of the equal protection of the laws guaranteed to petitioner by the Fourteenth amendment."

SEGREGATION ORDINANCES

Commencing about 1910, a wave of residential segregation laws swept the country. City after city in the southern and border states passed ordinances, the purpose and effect of which were to keep colored people from invading the areas which hitherto had been restricted to white residents. All of these ordinances prohibited whites from living in colored districts and on their face purported to protect colored people as well as white, but, of course, no one for a moment believed that they were anything but the initial step in an attempt to create Negro ghettos throughout the United States. Ghettos mean crowding, poor lighting and worse sanitation, and the resultant higher delinquency and crime rates, greater infant morality and higher death rates from tuberculosis and the other infectious and contagious diseases.

More than a dozen cities, among them Baltimore, Md.; Dallas, Tex.; Asheville, N.C.; Richmond, Va.; St. Louis, Mo.; and Louisville, Ky., within a year passed such ordinances; these differed in detail, but all aimed at the same result. The constitutionality of a number of these were tested and generally were upheld by the state courts.

The National Association for the Advancement of Colored People, convinced of their unconstitutionality and illegality, made a careful test of the ordinance passed in Louisville, Ky., and carried the case to the supreme court of the United States. This case became known as the "Louisville Segregation Case", *Buchanan v. Warley*, decided November, 1917.

Buchanan brought an action for specific performance of a contract for the sale of certain real estate in the City of Louisville. The defendant by way of answer set forth that he was a Negro and by virtue of an ordinance of Louisville would be unable to occupy the land in a white block. The plaintiff alleged that the ordinance was in conflict with the Fourteenth amendment of the United States Constitution. The court of appeals of Kentucky held the ordinance valid.

The ordinance prohibited whites from living in Negro districts and Negroes from living in white districts. Violation of the ordinance was made a criminal offense.

---

[7] A *per curiam* opinion is a very brief, usually unanimous court decision rendered without elaborate discussion and without identifying a particular justice as its author.

The U.S. supreme court reversed the decision of the Kentucky court of appeals and held the ordinance unconstitutional. Mr. Associate Justice Day, in the opinion for the court stated:

". . . it is said that such acquisitions by colored people depreciate property owned in the neighborhood by white persons. But property may be acquired by undesirable white neighbors or put to disagreeable though lawful uses with like results. . . . We think this attempt to prevent alienation of the property in question to a person of color was not a legitimate exercise of the police power of the state, and is in direct violation of the fundamental law enacted in the Fourteenth amendment. . . ."

This precedent struck down these ordinances, but several cities continued to enforce them until it became necessary to carry two more cases to the supreme court. The "New Orleans Segregation Case", *Harmon v. Tyler*, decided in 1926, was disposed of by the court with the short memorandum: "Reversed on the authority of *Buchanan v. Warley*, 245 U.S. 60." The "Richmond Segregation Case", *City of Richmond v. Deans*, was likewise disposed of by the supreme court in 1930 by affirming a decision of the lower court declaring the Richmond ordinance unconstitutional.

These cases have clearly established the principle that segregation ordinances by municipalities are "state action" within the meaning of the Fourteenth amendment and are therefore a denial of the equal protection of the laws and unconstitutional and void. However, it has been held that property owners' covenants by individuals against transfer of property to Negroes in certain neighborhoods is not "state action" and therefore is not controlled by the Fourteenth amendment.[8]

In the case of *Corrigan v. Buckley*, decided by the supreme court in May, 1926, an appeal to the court from the Court of Appeals of the District of Columbia was dismissed for want of jurisdiction.[9] The case was a suit in equity to enjoin the conveyance of certain property in Washington to a Negro because thirty white owners of the property in that neighborhood had made mutual covenants not to sell their property to Negroes.[10] The property in question was included in the mutual covenants.

The defendants alleged that the covenants were unconstitutional and violated the Fifth, Thirteenth and Fourteenth amendments. The Court of Appeals of the District of Columbia denied that the covenants were void. The supreme court held that the covenants did not violate these amendments to the Constitution and therefore dismissed the appeal for want of jurisdiction.

---

[8] Covenants are agreements by a group of property owners that restrict each owner's ability to use its own property.

[9] That is, on the ground that the statutes regulating the Supreme Court did not allow an appeal in a case of this sort.

[10] That is, a suit seeking to bar the home-owner from selling the property to the prospective buyers.

EDUCATIONAL OPPORTUNITIES

For several years the N.A.A.C.P. has been maintaining an active campaign to secure the ultimate goal of equality of educational opportunities for Negro youth along with other citizens of the United States. The first clear statement of the law by the U.S. supreme court on this question was established in the "University of Missouri Case," *Missouri ex rel Gaines v. Canada et al*, decided December 12, 1938.

Lloyd Gaines, a qualified Negro, was refused admission to the University of Missouri law school solely because of his race or color. Asserting that this refusal constituted a denial by the state of Missouri of the equal protection of the laws in violation of the Fourteenth amendment, he brought an action for mandamus to compel the university to admit him.[11]

The registrar urged him to accept a scholarship by the state to a law school outside the state of Missouri. Gaines refused to do so. The University of Missouri defended the mandamus action on the ground that eventually Lincoln university (the Negro college of Missouri) would offer a law school and in the meantime scholarships for Negroes to law schools outside the state would offer equal educational opportunities. The petition for mandamus was dismissed and this ruling was affirmed by the supreme court of Missouri.

A petition for writ of certiorari was granted by the U.S. supreme court and the case was argued. The case was reversed by the supreme court in a memorable decision. Mr. Chief Justice Hughes, in the majority opinion, declared:

> ". . . The admissibility of laws separating the races in the enjoyment of privileges afforded by the State rests wholly upon the equality of the privileges which the laws give to the separated groups within the State. The question here is not of a duty of the State to supply legal training, or of the quality of the training which it does supply, but of its duty when it provides such training to furnish it to the residents of the State upon the basis of an equality of right. . . ."

This precedent establishes the test for all educational facilities in the country and applies to nineteen states and the District of Columbia maintaining separate schools for the races in the section of the country where almost 80% of the Negroes live.

The opinions in these cases define the constitutional rights of the Negro as a citizen. In addition, they broaden the interpretation of constitutional rights for all citizens and extend civil liberties for whites as well as Negroes.

The activity of lawyers acting for the N.A.A.C.P. has added to the body of law on civil rights for all Americans. The association, by pressing these cases, has

---

[11] An action for mandamus seeks to obtain an order directing an official to take some action, such as admitting Gaines to the university. In the 1930s and 1940s, injunctions directed officials to *stop* doing something, while mandamus orders directed them to *do* something.

brought nearer to realization the ideal embodied in the quotation engraved over the Supreme Court building in Washington, D.C.: "Equal Justice Under Law."

While it may be true that laws and constitutions do not act to right wrong and overturn established folkways overnight, it is also true that the reaffirmation of these principles of democracy build a body of public opinion in which rights and privileges of citizenship may be enjoyed, and in which the more brazen as well as the more sophisticated attempts at deprivation may be halted.

6. Negro Discrimination and the Need for Federal Action
William H. Hastie and Thurgood Marshall
Lawyers Guild Review, November 1942

This article was a report on the activities of the federal government during the early years of World War II. It was published in the journal of the National Lawyers Guild, an association of leftist lawyers.

No effort is made in this report to cover the entire field of discrimination against Negroes as spotlighted and accentuated during the present war emergency. This is merely an effort to pick the most critical situations as examples of the types of discrimination now present which lead to the tension in the South today. It should be recognized at the outset that while other Americans are taking steps to protect their basic civil rights, Negro Americans are faced with a two fold problem: namely, to obtain basic civil rights which have been denied them in the past and to protect such few rights as have heretofore been accorded them.

The actions and speeches of the Dixons of Alabama, the Talmadges of Georgia, the Connallys of Texas, and the Bilbos of Mississippi demonstrate clearly that there are too many people in this country willing to defeat the war effort if they believe it to be necessary in order to protect the un-American doctrine of "white supremacy." There is an ever-growing breach between these elements and the rest of the country. A show down is inevitable. The question confronting us at this time is whether or not the people of the country and the Federal Government will surrender to these undemocratic elements as was done in the United States Senate in the recent surrender to the filibusterers against the anti-poll tax bill. The following examples are particularly acute.

I LYNCHINGS AND MOB VIOLENCE
There have been at least six lynchings this year in the United States. Thus the effective intimidation of the Negro population in the South continues. Until this ever present threat of violence is removed, there can never be any civil liberties in the South. Constitutional guarantees and laws guaranteeing civil rights are worthless scraps of paper to the people who are prevented from exercising these rights by the constant threat of mob violence. The recent outbreaks of mob violence again emphasize the fact that only Federal action will free us from lynchings and the threat of lynching. It is significant that lynchings have increased and decreased as the enactment of Federal legislation has seemed remote or imminent.

A. Anti-Lynching Legislation.
Congressman Joseph A. Gavagan of New York and several other Congressmen introduced anti-lynching bills in the present Congress during January, 1941. The

recent outbreak of lynchings came at a time when it was apparent that no action was to be taken on these bills.

Anti-lynching bills will be reintroduced in the next Congress and steps must be taken to secure passage of an adequate anti-lynching bill. No realistic approach to the enactment of this legislation is possible without considering the tactics whereby a small determined reactionary minority of the United States Senate can use the archaic rules of the Senate to prevent action upon anti-poll tax legislation, anti-lynching legislation, and prospectively all legislation looking forward to a democratic and economically sound post war era. Thus the first step towards enactment of this legislation as well as all other liberal legislation must be a revision of the Senate rules so that it will be impossible for a small group of Senators to prevent the Senate from voting on a bill which they dislike.

B. Criminal Prosecution.

In the states with the worst lynching records, criminal prosecutions of the members of the mob never go further than a perfunctory investigation by either a coroner's jury or by a grand jury, ending with the decision that a person lynched "came to his death at the hands of parties unknown."

During the past year the U.S. Department of Justice for the first time has been investigating several of the lynchings. The lynching at Sikeston, Missouri, January 25th, 1942, was investigated by the United States Department of Justice and presented to the U.S. Grand Jury, which refused to indict either the members of the mob or the state officials involved. Due credit should be given to the present United States Department of Justice for this much. It is quite evident that more vigorous action must be taken by the members of the Department of Justice presenting these cases to the Grand Jury. The report of the Grand Jury on the Sikeston lynching includes a statement that begins with a rehearsal of evidence presented to it of the crime alleged to have been committed by the victim of the mob and then proceeds to find the victim guilty of the crime for which he was charged, by stating that "in this instance a brutal criminal was denied due process." This was of course beyond the scope of the Grand Jury investigation and was unnecessary, uncalled for and indeed is contrary to the facts revealed by other investigations. The worst feature of the report was that it found as a matter of law that the state officials who were apparently guilty of wilful "inaction" to say the least, were not within the purview of federal statutes. This statement notifies all sheriffs and police officers that they can continue in the dereliction of their duty and if they escape state prosecution they cannot be prosecuted by any other authorities. Since this finding was a matter of law, it is difficult to conceive that this legal conclusion would have been reached by the grand jury if the Special Assistant Attorney General had properly and forcefully advised them that wilful inaction is legal equivalent of affirmative action in such a case arising under the Fourteenth amendment and the civil rights statutes.

In view of the fact that the U.S. Department of Justice is now investigating the three recent lynchings in Mississippi, it is to be hoped that when and if these matters are presented to Grand Jury, the Special Assistant Attorney General will take a firm stand in the Grand Jury room as to the law in the case and insist that failure of state officials to protect their prisoners is a violation of the conspiracy statutes.

II VIOLENCE AGAINST NEGROES IN UNIFORM BY CIVILIANS AND STATE OFFICIALS

An attack on a Negro soldier or sailor in uniform is a direct attack on our government. Unless the federal government is willing to protect its soldiers and sailors on leave and while on duty, it is impossible to maintain the proper morale among Negro soldiers and sailors and their families, and the authority of government itself is seriously undermined. It is impossible to develop combat efficiency in Negro soldiers and sailors while denying them basic civil rights during the period of their training.

One of the most serious consequences of congestion on segregated public carriers is the almost daily conflict between colored soldiers and white fellow passengers. Whether traveling on duty or on furlough the colored soldier experiences the indignity of segregation. Moreover, he is often ordered to move from seats customarily set aside for Negro passengers so that white persons may be seated. With increasing frequency he is denied accommodations altogether when there are sufficient white persons waiting to fill the entire vehicle.

In October in Montgomery, Alabama, a Negro Army nurse was beaten and her nose broken by city policemen because she refused to vacate the rear seat of a bus so that white passengers might be seated. At about the same time in Norfolk, Virginia, two Negro sergeants were beaten and jailed for a similar offense. In some large camps a short furlough may be worthless to the Negro soldier because local transportation officials will prevent him from boarding trains or bus so that space may be available for white passengers.

It is imperative that the Office of Defense Transportation or such other agency as the President may designate institute effective controls over passenger traffic to the end that Negro soldiers and sailors have equal access with all other passengers to public carriers.

There have been many cases of assaults upon Negro soldiers while on active duty. The most recent case of this type involved the death of Raymond Carr, a Negro military policeman, while on duty in Alexandria, Louisiana, on November 1st. Carr was killed by a Louisiana state policeman because he refused to submit to an unlawful arrest and removal from his post of duty in disobedience of military orders.

The only action by state authorities has been to suspend the state policeman for a day. The state authorities have told the U.S. Army authorities in effect that they did not intend to recognize the authority of the United States Army where Negro soldiers were involved. The killing of this Negro soldier while on duty is a clear violation of Sections 51 and 52 of Title 18 of the United States Code as well as Section 54 which provides:

> "If two or more persons in any State, Territory, or District conspire to prevent, by force, intimidation, or threat, any person from accepting or holding any office, trust, or place of confidence under the United States, or from discharging any duties thereof; or to induce by like means any officer of the United States to leave any State, Territory, District, or place, where his duties as an officer are required to be performed, or to injure him in his person or property on account of his lawful discharge thereof, or to injure his property so as to molest, interrupt, hinder, or impede him in the discharge of his official duties, each of such persons shall be fined not more than $5,000 or imprisoned not more than six years, or both."

Unless the U.S. Department of Justice immediately begins investigation and prosecution of this state policeman who has killed a Negro soldier who refused to disobey his army regulations, then there is very little hope that Negroes can have of expecting protection from their government. The only way to prevent further occurrences is by positive and uncompromising action by the U.S. War Department and the Department of Justice.

III VIOLENCE AGAINST DEFENSE WORKERS
It is certainly agreed that American citizens have a right to go about their work without molestation by either civilians or state authorities. There are several incidents where white workers incited by bigots have refused to work with Negro workers and in some cases have even committed assaults upon Negro workers. In some plants in the state of Alabama, white and colored workers are going to work armed in anticipation of racial outbreaks.

Now that the Ku Klux Klan is under indictment by the federal government, smaller organizations, such as Vigilantes, Inc., have come into existence. It is the duty of the federal government to ferret out the leaders of these subversive elements aimed to prevent Negroes from working in defense plants.

IV THE RIGHT OF FRANCHISE
The Poll Tax issue in eight southern states prevents large numbers of Negro and white citizens from qualifying as voters.[1] Negroes in several of these states and in other southern states without Poll Tax provisions are prevented from voting by being

---

[1] Unless a person paid a poll tax, usually amounting to a few dollars but sometimes adding up to substantial sums, he or she would not be allowed to vote.

excluded from voting in primary elections. The system of "white primary" is prevalent throughout the deep South. It is an admitted fact that in these same states nomination at the Democratic primary is tantamount to election at the regular elections. The refusal to permit Negroes to vote at this stage of the election process excludes Negroes from voting at the only stage that their votes would have any effect.

Last year the United States Department of Justice on its own initiative started criminal proceedings in Louisiana against Democratic primary election officials who had tampered with the ballots in the primary. This case now known as the Classic Case, was instituted, and argued by the U.S. Department of Justice and resulted in a decision by the U.S. Supreme Court, that primary elections which constitute an integral part of the election machinery of a state are within the protection of the U.S. Constitution.

Despite this precedent, Negroes are still barred from primary elections in the deep South, solely because of their race or color. A civil suit started in the federal court in Houston, Texas, by Negroes against Democratic primary election officials following the theory in the Classic Case has been argued and is now pending in the United States Circuit Court of Appeals for the Fifth Circuit. The U.S. Department of Justice refused to file a brief *amicus* in this case but promised to reconsider the matter when and if the case reaches the United States Supreme Court. However, the National Lawyers Guild and the American Civil Liberties Union filed briefs which were accepted by the court.

There are on file with the U.S. Department of Justice numerous affidavits from qualified Negroes in the states of Texas, Alabama, Arkansas, and South Carolina, who were refused the right to vote in the 1942 Democratic primary elections, in these states solely because of their race or color. Several of these complaints were presented to the United States Grand Jury in Dallas and were "whitewashed." The United States Department of Justice has not only declined to participate in the Houston Case, but it is evident that it now refuses to proceed criminally on any of the affidavits presented to it.

It is up to the U.S. Department of Justice to institute criminal proceedings against the officials who refuse to permit qualified Negroes to vote in primary elections solely because of their race or color. To do otherwise is to permit these officials to continue to deny to qualified Negroes the very fundamental civil rights to which they are entitled. Instead of helping in the civil case now pending and also brining criminal procedure in these cases, the U.S. Department of Justice at the present time seems to be doing nothing on this question.

V PEONAGE

The U.S. Department of Justice is maintaining a vigorous campaign against peonage which has resulted in several successful prosecutions. There are many now pending. The Department should be commended for this.

7. The Gestapo in Detroit
The Crisis, August 1943

On June 20 and 21, 1943, a "race riot" occurred in Detroit, after a fight between a white and an African American man at a popular amusement park. Rumors spread among African Americans that an African American woman and her child had been thrown into the Detroit River. Whites traveling through an African American neighborhood—the Hastings Street area to which Marshall refers—were attacked, and many stores were looted. Later African Americans leaving movie theaters on Woodward Avenue in downtown Detroit were set upon by whites. In the ensuing riot, twenty-five African Americans and nine whites died, and property worth more than $2 million was damaged.

Riots are usually the result of many underlying causes, yet no single factor is more important than the attitude and efficiency of the police. When disorder starts, it is either stopped quickly or permitted to spread into serious proportions, depending upon the actions of the local police.

Much of the blood spilled in the Detroit riot is on the hands of the Detroit police department. In the past the Detroit police have been guilty of both inefficiency and an attitude of prejudice against Negroes. Of course, there are several individual exceptions.

The citizens of Detroit, white and Negro, are familiar with the attitude of the police as demonstrated during the trouble in 1942 surrounding the Sojourner Truth housing project.[1] At that time a mob of white persons armed with rocks, sticks and other weapons attacked Negro tenants who were attempting to move into the project. Police were called to the scene. Instead of dispersing the mob which was unlawfully on property belonging to the federal government and leased to Negroes, they directed their efforts toward dispersing the Negroes who were attempting to get into their own homes. All Negroes approaching the project were searched and their automobiles likewise searched. White people were neither searched nor disarmed by the police. This incident is typical of the one-sided law enforcement practiced by the Detroit police. White hoodlums were justified in their belief that the police would act the same way in any further disturbances.

In the June riot of this year, the police ran true to form. The trouble reached riot proportions because the police once again enforced the law with an unequal hand. They used "persuasion" rather than firm action with white rioters, while against Negroes they used the ultimate in force: night sticks, revolvers, riot guns, sub-

---

[1] A housing project built by the federal government intended to house African American defense workers, and located on the border between white and African American neighborhoods.

machine guns, and deer guns. As a result, 25 of the 34 persons killed were Negroes. Of the latter, 17 were killed by police.

The excuse of the police department for the disproportionate number of Negroes killed is that the majority of them were shot while committing felonies: namely, the looting of stores on Hastings street. On the other hand, the crimes of arson and felonious assaults are also felonies. It is true that some Negroes were looting stores and were shot while committing these crimes. It is equally true that white persons were turning over and burning automobiles on Woodward avenue. This is arson. Others were beating Negroes with iron pipes, clubs, and rocks. This is felonious assault. Several Negroes were stabbed. This is assault with intent to murder.

All these crimes are matters of record; many were committed in the presence of police officers, several on the pavement around the City Hall. Yet the record remains: Negroes killed by police—17; white persons killed by police—none. The entire record, both of the riot killings and of previous disturbances, reads like the story of the Nazi Gestapo.

Evidence of tension in Detroit has been apparent for months. The *Detroit Free Press* sent a reporter to the police department. When Commissioner Witherspoon was asked how he was handling the situation he told the reporter: "We have given orders to handle it with kid gloves. The policemen have taken insults to keep trouble from breaking out. I doubt if you or I could have put up with it." This weak-kneed policy of the police commissioner coupled with the anti-Negro attitude of many members of the force have helped to make a riot inevitable.

SUNDAY NIGHT ON BELLE ISLE
Belle Isle is a municipal recreation park where thousands of white and Negro war workers and their families go on Sundays for their outings. There had been isolated instances of racial friction in the past. On Sunday night, June 20, there was trouble between a group of white and Negro people. The disturbance was under control by midnight. During the time of the disturbance and after it was under control, the police searched the automobiles of all Negroes and searched the Negroes as well. They did not search the white people. One Negro who was to be inducted into the army the following week was arrested because another person in the car had a small pen knife. This youth was later sentenced to 90 days in jail before his family could locate him. Many Negroes were arrested during this period and rushed to local police stations. At the very beginning the police demonstrated that they would continue to handle racial disorders by searching, beating and arresting Negroes while using mere persuasion on white people.

THE RIOT SPREADS
A short time after midnight disorder broke out in a white neighborhood near the Roxy theatre on Woodward avenue. The Roxy is an all-night theatre attended by white and Negro patrons. Several Negroes were beaten and others were forced to remain

in the theatre for lack of police protection. The rumor spread among the white people that a Negro had raped a white woman on Belle Island and that the Negroes were rioting.

At about the same time a rumor spread around Hastings and Adams streets in the Negro area that white sailors had thrown a Negro woman and her baby into the lake at Belle Isle and that the police were beating Negroes. The rumor was also repeated by an unidentified Negro at one of the night spots. Some Negroes began to attack white persons in the area. The police immediately began to use their sticks and revolvers against them. The Negroes began to break out the windows of stores of white merchants on Hastings street.

The interesting thing is that when the windows in the stores on Hastings street were first broken, there was no looting. An officer of the Merchants' Association walked the length of Hastings street, starting 7 o'clock Monday morning and noticed that none of the stores with broken windows had been looted. It is thus clear that the original breaking of windows was not for the purpose of looting.

Throughout Monday, the police, instead of placing men in front of the stores to protect them from looting, contented themselves with driving up and down Hastings street from time to time, stopping in front of the stores. The usual procedure was to jump out of the squad cars with drawn revolvers and riot guns to shoot whoever might be in the store. The policemen would then tell the Negro bystanders to "run and not look back." On several occasions, persons running were shot in the back. In other instances, bystanders were clubbed by police. To the police, all Negroes on Hastings street were "looters." This included war workers returning from work. There is no question that many Negroes were guilty of looting, just as there is always looting during earthquakes or as there was when English towns were bombed by the Germans.

CARS DETOURED INTO MOBS

Woodward avenue is one of the main thoroughfares of the city of Detroit. Small groups of white people began to rove up and down Woodward, beating Negroes, stoning cars containing Negroes, stopping street cars and yanking Negroes from them, and stabbing and shooting Negroes. In no case did the police do more than try to "reason" with these mobs, many of which were, at this stage, quite small. The police did not draw their revolvers or riot guns, and never used any force to disperse these mobs. As a result of this, the mobs got larger and bolder and even attacked Negroes on the pavement of the City Hall in demonstration not only of their contempt for Negroes, but of their contempt for law and order as represented by the municipal government.

During this time, Mayor Jeffries was in his office in the City Hall with the door locked and the window shade drawn. The use of night sticks or the drawing of revolvers would have dispersed these white groups and saved the lives of many Negroes. It would not have been necessary to shoot, but it would have been sufficient to threaten to shoot into the white mobs. The use of a fire hose would have dispersed many of the groups. None of these things was done and the disorder took on the proportions of a major riot. The responsibility rests with the Detroit police.

At the height of the disorder on Woodward avenue, Negroes driving north on Brush street (a Negro street) were stopped at Vernor Highway by a policeman who forced them to detour to Woodward avenue. Many of these cars are automobiles which appeared in the pictures released by several newspapers showing them overturned and burned on Woodward avenue.

While investigating the riot, we obtained many affidavits from Negroes concerning police brutality during the riot. It is impossible to include the facts of all of these affidavits. However, typical instances may be cited. A Negro soldier in uniform who had recently been released from the army with a medical discharge was on his way down Brush street Monday morning toward a theatre on Woodward avenue. This soldier was not aware of the fact that the riot was still going on. While in the Negro neighborhood on Brush street, he reached a corner where a squad car drove up and discharged several policemen with drawn revolvers, who announced to a small group on the corner to run and not look back. Several of the Negroes who did not move quite fast enough for the police were struck with night sticks and revolvers. The soldier was yanked from behind by one policeman and struck in the head with a blunt instrument and knocked to the ground, where he remained in a stupor. The police then returned to their squad car and drove off. A Negro woman in the block noticed the entire incident from her window, and she rushed out with a cold, damp towel to bind the soldier's head. She then hailed two Negro postal employees who carried the soldier to a hospital where his life was saved.

There are many additional affidavits of similar occurrences involving obviously innocent civilians throughout many Negro sections in Detroit where there had been no rioting at all. It was characteristic of these cases that the policemen would drive up to a corner, jump out with drawn revolvers, striking at Negroes indiscriminately, ofttimes shooting at them, and in all cases forcing them to run. At the same time on Woodward avenue, white civilians were seizing Negroes and telling them to "run, nigger, run." At least two Negroes, "shot while looting," were innocent persons who happened to be in the area at that time.

One Negro who had been an employee of a bank in Detroit for the past eighteen years was on his way to work on a Woodward avenue street car when he was seized by one of the white mobs. In the presence of at least four policemen, he was beaten and stabbed in the side. He also heard several shots fired from the back of the mob. He managed to run to two of the policemen who proceeded to "protect" him from the mob. The two policemen, followed by two mounted policemen, proceeded down Woodward avenue. While he was being escorted by these policemen, the man was struck in the face by at least eight of the mob, and at no time was any effort made to prevent him from being struck. After a short distance this man noticed a squad car parked on the other side of the street. In sheer desperation, he broke away from the two policemen who claimed to be protecting him and ran to the squad car, begging for protection. The officer in the squad car put him in the back seat and drove off, thereby saving his life.

During all this time, the fact that the man was either shot or stabbed was evident because of the fact that blood was spurting from his side. Despite this obvious felony, committed in the presence of at least four policemen, no effort was made at that time either to protect the victim or to arrest the persons guilty of the felony.

In addition to the many cases of one-sided enforcement of the law by the police, there are two glaring examples of criminal aggression against innocent Negro citizens and workers by members of the Michigan state police and Detroit police.

SHOOTING IN YMCA

On the night of June 22 at about 10 o'clock, some of the residents of the St. Antoine Branch of the Y.M.C.A. were returning to the dormitory. Several were on their way home from the Y.W.C.A. across the street. State police were searching some other Negroes on the pavement of the Y.M.C.A. when two of the Y.M.C.A. residents were stopped and searched for weapons. After none was found they were allowed to proceed to the building. Just as the last of the Y.M.C.A. men was about to enter the building, he heard someone behind him yell what sounded to him like, "Hi, Ridley." (Ridley is also a resident of the Y.) Another resident said he heard someone yell what sounded to him like "Heil, Hitler."

A state policeman, Ted Anders, jumped from his car with his revolver drawn, ran to the steps of the Y.M.C.A., put one foot on the bottom step and fired through the outside door. Immediately after firing the shot he entered the building. Other officers followed. Julian Witherspoon, who had just entered the building, was lying on the floor, shot in the side by the bullet that was fired through the outside door. There had been no show of violence or weapons of any kind by anyone in or around the Y.M.C.A.

The officers with drawn revolvers ordered all those residents of the Y.M.C.A. who were in the lobby of their building, to raise their hands in the air and line up against the wall like criminals. During all this time these men were called "black b— and monkeys," and other vile names by the officers. At least one man was struck, another was forced to throw his lunch on the floor. All the men in the lobby were searched.

The desk clerk was also forced to line up. The officers then went behind the desk and into the private offices and searched everything. The officers also made the clerk open all locked drawers, threatening to shoot him if he did not do so.

Witherspoon was later removed to the hospital and has subsequently been released.

VERNOR APARTMENT SIEGE

On the night of June 21 at about eight o'clock, a Detroit policeman was shot in the two hundred block of Vernor Highway, and his assailant, who was in the vacant lot, was, in turn, killed by another policeman. State and city policemen then began to attack the apartment building at 290 E. Vernor Highway, which was fully occupied by tenants. Searchlights were thrown on the building and machine guns, revolvers, rifles, and deer guns were fired indiscriminately into all of the occupied apartments facing the outside. Tenants of the building were forced to fall to the floor and remain there in order to save their lives. Later slugs from machine guns, revolvers, rifles, and deer guns were dug from the inside walls of many of the apartments. Tear gas was shot into the building and all the tenants were forced out into the streets with their hands up in the air at the point of drawn guns.

State and city policemen went into the building and forced out all the tenants who were not driven out by tear gas. The tenants were all lined up against the walls, men and women alike, and forced to remain in this position for some time. The men were searched for weapons. During this time these people were called every type of vile name and men and women were cursed and threatened. Many men were struck by policemen.

While the tenants were lined up in the street, the apartments were forcibly entered. Locks and doors were broken. All the apartments were ransacked. Clothing and other articles were thrown around on the floor. All of these acts were committed by policemen. Most of the tenants reported that money, jewelry, whiskey, and other items of personal property were missing when they were permitted to return to their apartments after midnight. State and city police had been in possession of the building in the meantime.

Many of these apartments were visited shortly after these events. They resembled part of a battlefield. Affidavits from most of the tenants and lists of property destroyed and missing are available.

Although a white man was seen on the roof of an apartment house up the street from the Vernor apartments with a rifle in his hand, no effort was made to search either that building or its occupants. After the raid on the Vernor apartments, the police used as their excuse the statement that policeman Lawrence A. Adams had been shot by a sniper from the Vernor apartments, and that for that reason, they attacked the building and its occupants. However, in a story released by the police department on July 2 after the death of Patrolman Lawrence A. Adams, it was reported that "The shot that felled Adams was fired by Homer Edison, 28 years old, of 502 Montcalm, from the shadows of a parking lot. Edison, armed with a shot gun, was shot to death by Adams' partner." This is merely another example of the clumsy and obvious subterfuges used by the police department in an effort to cover up their total disregard for the rights of Negroes.

Justification for our belief that the Detroit police could have prevented the trouble from reaching riot proportions is evidenced in at least two recent instances.

During the last month in the town of Atlanta, Georgia, several white youths organized a gang to beat up Negroes. They first encountered a young Negro boy on a bicycle and threw him to the ground. However, before they could beat this lone Negro, a squad car drove up. The police promptly arrested several of the white boys, and dispersed the group immediately, thus effectively forestalling and preventing what might have resulted in a riot. On the Sunday preceding the Detroit riot, Sheriff Baird, of Wayne County, Michigan, with jurisdiction over the area just outside Detroit, suppressed a potential riot in a nearby town. A large group of Negroes and a large group of white people were opposing each other and mob violence was threatened. The sheriff and his deputies got between the two groups and told them that in case of any violence, the guilty parties would be handled and that the law enforcement officers would do everything possible to prevent the riot. Because of this firm stand, the members of both groups dispersed.

If similar affirmative action had been taken by the Detroit police when the small groups were running up and down Woodward avenue beating, cutting and shooting Negroes, the trouble never would have reached the bloody and destructive magnitude which has shocked the nation.

This record by the Detroit police demonstrates once more what all Negroes know only too well: that nearly all police departments limit their conception of checking racial disorders to surrounding, arresting, maltreating, and shooting Negroes. Little attempt is made to check the activities of whites.

The certainty of Negroes that they will not be protected by police, but instead will be attacked by them, is a contributing factor to racial tensions leading to overt acts. The first item on the agenda of any group seeking to prevent rioting would seem to be a critical study of the police department of the community, its record in handling Negroes, something of the background of its personnel, and the plans of its chief officers for meeting possible racial disorders.

8. The Legal Attack to Secure Civil Rights
Speech at the NAACP Wartime Conference, 1944

Marshall here presents an overview of antidiscrimination law to an audience of
NAACP members, few of whom were lawyers. The speech outlines the remedies
available for various forms of discrimination, and stresses the important role that
nonlawyers—including members of the NAACP's branches—play in guaranteeing that rights formally protected by law are actually protected in reality. Marshall
describes the actions NAACP members can take to support litigation by bringing
complaints to the lawyers' attention, and to place pressure on federal officials to
enforce the law.

On last night we heard a clear statement of some of the problems facing us today.
My job tonight is to point out a part of the general program to secure full citizenship rights.

The struggle for full citizenship rights can be speeded by enforcement of existing statutory provisions protecting our civil rights. The attack on discrimination by
use of legal machinery has only scratched the surface. An understanding of the
existing statutes protecting our civil rights is necessary if we are to work toward
enforcement of these statutes.

The titles "civil rights" and "civil liberties" have grown to include large numbers of subjects, some of which are properly included under these titles and others
which should not be included. One legal treatise has defined the subject of civil rights
as follows: "In its broadest sense, the term *civil rights* includes those rights which
are the outgrowth of civilization, the existence and exercise of which necessarily
follow from the rights that repose in the subjects of a country exercising self-government."

The Fourteenth and Fifteenth Amendments to the Constitution are prohibitions
against action by the states and state officers violating civil rights. In addition to these
provisions of the United States Constitution and a few others, there are several
statutes of the United States which also attempt to protect the rights of individual
citizens against private persons as well as public officers. Whether these provisions
are included under the title of "civil rights" or "civil liberties" or any other subject
is more or less unimportant as long as we bear in mind the provisions themselves.

All of the statutes, both federal and state, which protect the individual rights
of Americans are important to Negroes as well as other citizens. Many of these
provisions, however, are of peculiar significance to Negroes because of the fact
that in many instances these statutes are the only protection to which Negroes can
look for redress. It should also be pointed out that many officials of both state and
federal governments are reluctant to protect the rights of Negroes. It is often diffi-

90

cult to enforce our rights when they are perfectly clear. It is practically impossible to secure enforcement of any of our rights if there is any doubt whatsoever as to whether or not a particular statute applies to the particular state of facts.

As to law enforcement itself, the rule as to most American citizens is that if there is any way possible to prosecute individuals who have willfully interfered with the rights of other individuals such prosecution is attempted. However, when the complaining party is a Negro, the rule is usually to look for any possible grounds for *not* prosecuting. It is therefore imperative that Negroes be thoroughly familiar with the rights guaranteed them by law in order that they may be in a position to insist that all of their fundamental rights as American citizens be protected.

The Thirteenth Amendment to the Constitution, abolishing slavery, the Fourteenth Amendment, prohibiting any action of state officials denying due process or the equal protection of its laws, and the Fifteenth Amendment, prohibiting discrimination by the states in voting, are well-known to all of us. In addition to these provisions of the Constitution, there are the so-called Federal "Civil Rights Statutes" which include several Acts of Congress such as the Civil Rights Act and other statutes which have been amended from time to time and are now grouped together in several sections of the United States Code. The original Civil Rights Act was passed in Congress in 1866, but was vetoed by President Andrew Johnson the same year. It was, however, passed over the veto. It was reintroduced and passed in 1870 because there was some doubt as to its constitutionality, having been passed before the Fourteenth Amendment was ratified. The second bill has been construed several times and has been held constitutional by the United States Supreme Court, which in one case stated that "the plain objects of these statutes, as of the Constitution which authorized them, was to place the colored race, in respect to civil rights, upon a level with the whites. They made the rights and responsibilities, civil and criminal, of the two races exactly the same."

The Thirteenth and Fourteenth and Fifteenth Amendments, along with the civil rights statutes, protect the following rights:

1. Slavery is abolished and peonage is punishable as a federal crime. (13th amendment)
2. All persons born or naturalized in the U.S. are citizens and no state shall make or enforce any law abridging their privileges and immunities, or deny them equal protection of the law. (14th Amendment)
3. The right of citizens to vote cannot be abridged by the United States or by any state on account of race or color. (15th Amendment)
4. All persons within the jurisdiction of the United States shall have the same right to enforce contracts, or sue, be parties, give evidence, and to the full and equal benefit of all laws and proceedings as is enjoyed by white citizens.

5. All persons shall be subject to like punishment, pains, penalties, taxes, licenses, and extractions of every kind, and to no other.

6. All citizens shall have the same right in every state and territory, as is enjoyed by white citizens to inherit, purchase, lease, sell, hold and convey property.

7. Every person who, under color of statutes, custom or usage, subjects any citizen of the United States or person within the jurisdiction thereof to the deprivation of any rights, privileges, or immunities secured by the Constitution and laws is liable in an action at law, suit in equity, or other proper proceedings for redress.

8. Citizens possessing all other qualifications may not be disqualified from jury service in federal or state courts on account of race or color; any officer charged with the duty of selection or summoning of jurors who shall exclude citizens for reasons of race or color shall be guilty of a misdemeanor.

9. A conspiracy of two or more persons to deprive any person or class of persons of any rights guaranteed by Constitution and laws is punishable as a crime and the conspirators are also liable in damages.

Most of these provisions only protect the citizen against wrong-doing by public officials, although the peonage statutes and one or two others protect against wrongs by private persons.[1]

Despite the purposes of these Acts which the United States Supreme Court insisted in 1879 "made the rights and responsibilities, civil and criminal, of the two races exactly the same," the experience of all of us points to the fact that this purpose has not as yet been accomplished. There are several reasons for this. In the first place, in certain sections of this country, especially in the deep South, judges, prosecutors and members of grand and petit juries, have simply refused to follow the letter or spirit of these provisions. Very often it happens that although the judge and prosecutor are anxious to enforce the laws, members of the jury are reluctant to protect the rights of Negroes. A third reason is that many Negroes themselves for one reason or another hesitate to avail themselves of the protection afforded by the United States Constitution and statutes.

These statutes protecting our civil rights in several instances provide for both criminal and civil redress. Some are criminal only and others are for civil action only. Criminal prosecution for violation of the federal statutes can be obtained only through the United States Department of Justice.

---

[1] Anti-peonage statutes made it illegal to execute labor contracts that effectively kept workers in slavery because of their agreement to work under conditions that made it impossible for them ever to leave the employer.

Up through and including the administration of Attorney General Homer S. Cummings, Negroes were unable to persuade the U.S. Department of Justice to enforce any of the civil rights statutes where Negroes were the complaining parties. The NAACP and its staff made repeated requests and in many instances filed detailed statements and briefs requesting prosecution for lynch mobs, persons guilty of peonage and other apparent violations of the federal statutes. It was not until the administration of Attorney General Frank Murphy that any substantial efforts were made to enforce the civil rights statutes as they apply to Negroes. Attorney General Murphy established a Civil Rights Section in the Department of Justice.

During the present administration of Attorney General Francis Biddle there have been several instances of prosecution of members of lynch mobs for the first time in the history of the United States Department of Justice. There have also been numerous successful prosecutions of persons guilty of peonage and slavery. However, other cases involving the question of beating and killing of Negro soldiers by local police officers, the case involving the action of Sheriff Tip Hunter, of Brownsville, Tennessee, who killed at least one Negro citizen and forced several others to leave town, the several cases of refusal to permit qualified Negroes to vote, as well as other cases, have received the attention of the Department of Justice only to the extent of "investigating." Our civil rights as guaranteed by the federal statutes will never become a reality until the U.S. Department of Justice decides that it represents the entire United States and is not required to fear offending any section of the country which believes that it has the God-given right to be above the laws of the United States and the United States Supreme Court.

One interesting example of the apparent failure to enforce the criminal statutes is that although the statute making it a crime to exclude persons from jury service because of race or color was declared unconstitutional [sic] by the Supreme Court in 1879, and is still on the statute books, there have been no prosecutions by the Department of Justice in recent years for the obvious violations of these statutes. The Department of Justice has most certainly on several occasions been put on notice as to these violations by the many cases carried to the Supreme Court by the NAACP and in which cases the Supreme Court has reversed the convictions on the ground that Negroes were systematically excluded from jury service. One whole-hearted prosecution of a judge or other official for excluding Negroes from jury service because of their race would do more to make that particular law a reality than dozens of other cases merely reversing the conviction of individual defendants.

There are, however, certain bright spots in the enforcement of the federal statutes. In addition to the lynching and peonage cases handled by the Washington office of the Department of Justice, there have been a few instances of courageous United States Attorneys in such places as Georgia who have vigorously prosecuted police officers who have used the power of their office as a cloak for beating up Negro citizens.

As a result of the recent decision in the Texas primary case, it is possible to use an example of criminal prosecution under the civil rights statutes by taking a typical case of the refusal to permit the Negroes to vote in the Democratic Primary elections. Let us see how a prosecution is started: In Waycross, Georgia, for example, we will suppose a Negro elector on July 4, 1944, went to the polls with his tax receipt and demanded to vote in the Democratic Primary. He should, of course, have witnesses with him. Let us also assume that the election officials refused to let him vote solely because of his race or color.

As a matter of law, the election officials violated a federal criminal law and are subject to fine and imprisonment. But how should the voter or the organized Negro citizens, or the local NAACP branch go about trying to get the machinery of criminal justice in motion? Of course, the details of what happens must be put in writing and sworn to by the person who tried to vote and also by his witnesses. Then the matter must be placed before the United States Attorney. This is the *federal* district attorney.

I wonder how many of the delegates here know who is the United States Attorney for their district, or even where his office is. Every branch should know the United States Attorney for that area, even if a delegation goes in just to get acquainted and let him know that we expect him to enforce the civil rights laws with the same vigor as used in enforcing other criminal statutes.

But back to the voting case. The affidavits must be presented to the United States Attorney with a demand that he investigate and place the evidence before the Federal Grand Jury. At the same time copies of the affidavits and statements in the case should be sent to the National Office. We will see that they get to the Attorney General in Washington. I wish that I could guarantee [to] you that the Attorney General would put pressure on local United States Attorneys who seem reluctant to prosecute. At least we can assure you that we will give the Attorney General no rest unless he gets behind these reluctant United States attorneys throughout the South.

There is no reason why a hundred clear cases of this sort should not be placed before the United States Attorneys and the Attorney General every year until the election officials discover that it is both wiser and safer to follow the United States laws than to violate them. It is up to us to see that these officials of the Department of Justice are called upon to act again and again wherever there are violations of the civil rights statutes. Unfortunately, there are plenty of such cases. It is equally unfortunate that there are not enough individuals and groups presenting these cases and demanding action.

The responsibility for enforcement of the civil provisions of the civil rights statutes rests solely with the individual. In the past we have neglected to make full use of these statutes. Although they have been on the books since 1870, there were very few cases under these statutes until recent years. Whereas in the field of general law there are many, many precedents for all other types of action, there are very few precedents for the protection of civil liberties.

The most important of the civil rights provisions is the one which provides that "every person who, under color of any statute, ordinance, regulation, custom or usage of any state or territory subjects or causes to be subjected any citizen of the United States or person within the jurisdiction thereof to the deprivation of any rights, privileges, or immunities secured by the Constitution and laws shall be liable to the party injured in an action at law, suit in equity or other proper proceeding for redress." Under this statute any officer of a state, county or municipality who while acting in an official capacity, denies to any citizen or person within the state any of the rights guaranteed by the Constitution or laws is subject to a civil action. This statute has been used to equalize teachers' salaries and to obtain bus transportation for Negro school children. It can be used to attack *every* form of discrimination against Negroes by public school systems.

The statute has also been used to enjoin municipalities from refusing to permit Negroes to take certain civil service examinations and to attack segregation ordinances of municipalities. It can likewise be used to attack all types of discrimination against Negroes by municipalities as well as by states themselves.

This statute, along with other of the civil rights statutes, can be used to enforce the right to register and vote throughout the country. The threats of many of the bigots in the South to disregard the ruling of the Supreme Court of the United States in the recent Texas Primary decision has not intimidated a single person. The United States Supreme Court remains the highest court in this land. Election officials in states affected by this decision will either let Negroes vote in the Democratic Primaries, or they will be subjected to both criminal and civil prosecution under the civil rights statutes. In every state in the deep South Negroes have this year attempted to vote in the primary elections. Affidavits concerning the refusal to permit them to vote in Alabama, Florida and Georgia have already been sent to the United States Department of Justice. We will insist that these election officials be prosecuted and will also file civil suits against the guilty officials.

It can be seen from these examples that we have just begun to scratch the surface in the fight for full enforcement of these statutes. The NAACP can move no faster than the individuals who have been discriminated against. We only take up cases where we are requested to do so by persons who have been discriminated against.

Another crucial problem is the ever-present problem of segregation. Whereas the principle has been established by cases handled by the NAACP that neither states nor municipalities can pass ordinances segregating residences by race, the growing problem today is the problem of segregation by means of restrictive covenants, whereby private owners band together to prevent Negro occupancy of particular neighborhoods. Although this problem is particularly acute in Chicago, it is at the same time growing in intensity throughout the country. It has the full support of the real estate boards in the several cities, as well as most of the banks and other leading agencies. The legal attack on this problem has met with spotty success. In several instances restrictive covenants have been declared invalid because the neighborhood has changed, or for other reasons. Other cases have been lost. However, the NAACP is in the process of preparing a detailed memorandum and will establish procedure which will lead to an all-out legal attack on restrictive covenants. Whether or not this attack will be successful cannot be determined at this time.

The National Housing Agency and the Federal Public Housing Authority have established a policy of segregation in federal public housing projects. A test case has been filed in Detroit, Michigan, and is still pending in the local federal courts. The Detroit situation is the same as in other sections of the country. Despite the fact that the Housing Authority and other agencies insist that they will maintain separate but equal facilities, it never develops that the separate facilities are equal in all respects. In Detroit separate projects were built and it developed that by the first of this year every single white family in the area eligible for public housing had been accommodated and there were still some 800 "white" units vacant with "no takers." At the same time there were some 45,000 Negroes inadequately housed and with no units open to them. This is the inevitable result of "separate but equal" treatment.

I understand that in Chicago a public housing project to be principally occupied by Negroes is being opposed by other Negroes on the ground that it will depreciate their property. It is almost unbelievable that Negroes would oppose public housing for the same reason used by real estate boards and other interests who are determined to keep Negroes in slum areas so that they may be further exploited. The NAACP is in favor of public housing and works toward that end every day. It will continue to do so despite real estate boards and other selfish interests opposing public housing whether they be white or Negro. The NAACP is, of course, opposed to segregation in public housing and will continue to fight segregation in public housing.

We should also be mindful of the several so-called civil rights statutes in the several states. There are civil rights acts in at least 18 states, all of which are in the North and Middle West. These statutes are in California, Colorado, Connecticut, Illinois, Indiana, Iowa, Kansas, Massachusetts, Michigan, Minnesota, Nebraska, New Jersey, New York, Ohio, Pennsylvania, Rhode Island, and Washington. California provides only for civil action. Illinois, Kansas, Minnesota, New York, and Ohio have both civil and criminal provisions. In New Jersey the only action is a criminal action, or an action for penalty in the name of the state, the amount of the penalty going to the state.

In those states not having civil rights statutes it is necessary that every effort be made to secure passage of one. In states having weak civil rights statutes efforts should be made to have them strengthened. In states with reasonably strong civil rights statutes, like Illinois and New York, it is necessary that every effort be made to enforce them.

The Chicago branch has the record of more successful prosecutions for violation of the local civil rights statute than any other branch of the NAACP. In New York City resort to the enforcement of the criminal provisions has greatly lessened the number of cases. Outside of New York City there are very few successful cases against the civil rights statutes because of the fact that members of the jury are usually reluctant to enforce the statutes. I understand the same is true for Illinois. The only method of counteracting this vicious practice is by means of educating the general public, from which juries are chosen, to the plight of the Negro.

It should also be pointed out that many of our friends of other races are not as loud and vociferous as the enemies of our race. In Northern and Mid-Western cities it repeatedly happens that a prejudiced Southerner on entering a hotel or restaurant, seeing Negroes present makes an immediate and loud protest to the manager. It is very seldom that any of our friends go to the managers of places where Negroes are excluded and complain to them of this fact. Quite a job can be done if our friends of other races will only realize the importance of this problem and get up from their comfortable chairs and actually go to work on the problem.

Thus it seems clear that although it is necessary and vital to all of us that we continue our program for additional legislation to guarantee and enforce certain of our rights, at the same time we must continue with ever-increasing vigor to enforce those few statutes, both federal and state, which are now on the statute books. We must not be delayed by people who say "the time is not ripe," nor should we proceed with caution for fear of destroying the "status quo." Persons who deny to us our civil rights should be brought to justice now. Many people believe the time is always "ripe" to discriminate against Negroes. All right then—the time is always "ripe" to bring them to justice. The responsibility for the enforcement of these statutes rests with every American citizen regardless of race or color. However, the real job has to be done by the Negro population with whatever friends of the other races are willing to join us.

9. Mr. Justice Murphy and Civil Rights
Michigan Law Review, 1950

This article is part of a collection of tributes to Justice Frank Murphy, a former governor of Michigan, published in the Michigan Law Review shortly after Murphy's death. Here the audience consists of legal specialists, and Marshall pays closer attention to legal detail than in his articles for a more general audience. Marshall's survey of Murphy's decisions in the area of civil rights and civil liberties begins with a fairly detailed examination of Murphy's decisions regarding general civil liberties, including criminal procedure. In describing Justice Murphy's dissent in the Lyons case (selection 1), Marshall argues that the Supreme Court later accepted the analysis adopted by Murphy. Only at the conclusion does Marshall turn to Murphy's decisions dealing with discrimination, the field we now call civil rights. The effect of this structure is to suggest that civil liberties and civil rights are a single topic, and that those who are devoted to one ought to be, and frequently are, devoted to both.

There is constant danger that the unpopularity of an individual, or of the group of which he is a member, will be reflected in dealings with his rights by his neighbors or by the organized community. In America today this bias is most likely to stem from differences of race, origin, nationality, or religious or political belief. Prejudice may victimize an entire group or any of its members. Any charge of shocking or anti-social conduct against one who is already thus unpopular increases the likelihood of unfair treatment. Not only private citizens, but legislators, judges and administrative officers of government are prone to such prejudicial attitudes and behavior.

To secure those thus disadvantaged against imposition is a major function of the Constitution and of the Supreme Court as the final exponent and enforcer of fundamental law and its supremacy.

Certainly no Justice who sat with Mr. Justice Murphy would disagree with what has been said in these introductory paragraphs. None of Mr. Justice Murphy's brethren would concede himself to have a less genuine devotion to the equalitarian principles of our fundamental law or a less sincere desire that those principles be translated into specific precept and strictly enforced.

But, in the field of civil rights, Mr. Justice Murphy was a zealot. To him, the primacy of civil rights and human equality in our law and their entitlement to every possible protection in each case, regardless of competing considerations, was a fighting faith. Among his brethren were those who might on occasion accept a substantial abridgement of free speech for the better vindication of other interests of social importance. Considered limitations of expediency upon efforts to enforce very high standards of fairness in state courts might appear controlling to others. Still others might defer to legislative judgment in close cases of interference with basic individual rights. But Mr. Justice Murphy's orientation in matters of civil liberties was fixed. His sense of values was unchanging. He followed wherever his abiding conviction of the primacy of civil rights might lead. Of him one writer has said:

> "Mr. Justice Murphy was a great judge because of three qualities. The first was simplicity; the second was courage; the third was insight into the substance of the problems of the changing times in which he lived."

It was most particularly in the field now under discussion that these qualities were demonstrated.

Mr. Justice Murphy came to the Supreme Court with a background of complete support for individual rights and a determination to oppose vigorously discriminatory governmental action as well as hostile action of individuals. His earlier judicial experience was highlighted by the trial of the famous Sweet case in Recorders Court in Detroit, Michigan. That case involved the acquittal of Negro Americans charged with murder in the killing of a member of a mob which threatened the family and friends of Dr. Sweet who had moved into a so-called white neighborhood. This trial will always be remembered for the brilliant defense conducted by Clarence Darrow and the complete fairness of Judge Frank Murphy.

While mayor of the City of Detroit during the depression, he demonstrated a determination to use all of the resources of the city for the welfare of the large group of its unemployed residents. As Governor of the State of Michigan, he refused to remove the sit-down strikers at the automobile plants on the grounds that to do so would bring about bloodshed on both sides. As Attorney General of the United States, he will always be remembered for having set up and put into motion the Civil Rights Division of the Department of Justice for the purposes of enforcing the civil rights statutes of the United States and of protecting the civil rights of Americans throughout the country. This varied experience developed his keen insight for the problems which he was to face in his tenure on the Supreme Court.

A consideration of the major cases involving fundamental issues affecting the civil rights of unpopular minorities will clearly demonstrate Justice Murphy's contribution to the basic law of the land.

In his majority opinions, Mr. Justice Murphy consistently insisted upon the fullest protection of individual rights. Regardless of the other issues involved he always felt that the proper approach was to consider all other problems in the light of the constitutional right being asserted. Even in cases where the asserted right was not sustained, his approach made it necessary for the majority of the Court to consider and pass upon its merits.

One of the first opinions of Mr. Justice Murphy was written in the case of *Thornhill v. Alabama*. In considering the claimed right involved, Mr. Justice Murphy, after reviewing prior decisions to the effect that freedom of speech and press secured by the First Amendment are fundamental rights and liberties guaranteed all persons under the Fourteenth Amendment against abridgements by a state, said:

> "It is imperative that, when the effective exercise of these rights is claimed to be abridged, the courts should 'weigh the circumstances' and 'appraise the substantiality of the reasons advanced' in support of the challenged regulations."

After reviewing the State of Alabama's claim that the anti-picketing statute was necessary to prevent the evils arising from industrial dispute, Murphy exposed the illogic of this statement. The State, he held, could not for this reason impair the effective exercise of the freedom to discuss matters of public concern such as industrial relations, for the same argument could likewise be used to support abridgement of freedom of speech and of the press concerning almost every such matter of general public concern and importance. The State claimed that the restrictive statute was necessary to prevent peaceful picketing from influencing persons to refrain from doing business with the "picketed" business. Justice Murphy recognized that every expression of opinion on matters important to society had the potentiality of inducing action or interest of one rather than another group in society. In weighing the two claims he concluded:

> "Abridgement of the liberty of such discussion can be justified only where the clear danger of substantive evils arises under circumstances affording no opportunity to test the merits of ideas by competition for acceptance in the market of public opinion. We hold that the danger of injury to an industrial concern is neither so serious nor so imminent as to justify the sweeping proscription of freedom of discussion embodied in § 3448."

In the *Carlson* case, decided the same day, Murphy restated the rule in the *Thornhill* case as giving affirmative protection to the right of peaceful picketing as follows:

> " . . . publicizing the facts of a labor dispute in a peaceful way through appropriate means, whether by pamphlet, by word of mouth or by banner, must now be regarded as within that liberty of communication which is secured to every person by the Fourteenth Amendment against abridgement by a State."

The opinion in the *Thornhill* case has had a far-reaching impact on labor–management relations throughout the country. The decision has been cited more than three hundred times in published reports. It has given substantial and important protection to organized labor in its never-ending struggle for better working conditions. Both as to the number of persons affected and the problem involved, it is in many respects, one of the most important decisions of the Supreme Court.

On the question of freedom of the press, in concurring opinions in *Pennekamp v. Florida* and *Craig v. Harney*, Murphy recognized that the freedom of the press covered something more than the right merely to approve and condone insofar as the judiciary is concerned; it included the right to criticize and disparage the judicial process free from the threat of a contempt citation. The rule as advanced by Murphy was that:

"Judges should be foremost in their vigilance to protect the freedom of others to rebuke and castigate the bench and in their refusal to be influenced by unfair or misinformed censure. Otherwise freedom may rest upon the precarious base of judicial sensitiveness and caprice. And a chain reaction may be set up, resulting in countless restrictions and limitations upon liberty."

The answer suggested by Murphy to the problem involved is that:

"Silence and a steady devotion to duty are the best answers to irresponsible criticism; and those judges who feel the need for giving a more visible demonstration of their feelings may take advantage of various laws passed for that purpose which do not impinge upon a free press. The liberties guaranteed by the First Amendment, however, are too highly prized to be subjected to the hazards of summary contempt procedure."

One of the opinions by Mr. Justice Murphy during his last term again emphasizes his position as to judicial restraint in contempt action. In the case of *Fisher v. Pace*, Murphy, in dissenting from affirmance of a contempt order against an attorney who had objected in open court to what he considered unfair conduct of the trial judge, pointed out that there had been no substantial interference with the trial itself and that the action of the trial judge was a denial of due process.

He stated that the record of petty disagreements in the pending case did not approach the serious interference of judicial process which justifies the use of contempt proceedings and concluded: "The contempt power is an extraordinary remedy, an exception to our tradition of fair and complete hearings. Its use should be carefully restricted to cases of actual obstruction."

In criminal cases, Murphy was most insistent that the Supreme Court exercise its supervisory and review jurisdiction in such a manner as to give the fullest protection to individual rights. His zeal and determination have been evident in majority, dissenting and concurring opinions. These opinions have been intended as guide posts for state and federal courts.

Speaking for the majority of the Court in *Glasser v. United States*, Murphy stated:

"In all cases the constitutional safeguards are to be jealously preserved for the benefit of the accused, but especially is this true where the scales of justice may be delicately poised between guilt and innocence. Then error, which under some circumstances would not be ground for reversal, cannot be brushed aside as immaterial, since there is a real chance that it might have provided the slight impetus which swung the scales toward guilt."

This opinion gave a clearer meaning to the constitutional guarantee of right of counsel in criminal cases. Even where the defendant himself was a lawyer and the record did not show a clear preservation of the objection to having appointed counsel represent conflicting interests of two defendants, Murphy placed the duty upon the trial judge of seeing that the trial was conducted with solicitude for the essential rights of the accused. He refused to permit this right of counsel to be nullified by technical distinctions:

"To determine the precise degree of prejudice sustained by Glasser as a result of the court's appointment of Stewart as counsel for Kretske is at once difficult and unnecessary. The right to have the assistance of counsel is too fundamental and absolute to allow courts to indulge in nice calculations as to the amount of prejudice arising from its denial."

Again in one of the dissenting opinions in *Carter v. Illinois*, Murphy demonstrated his deep conviction that legal technicalities should not prevent the Supreme Court from enforcing constitutional guarantees:

"Legal technicalities doubtless afford justification for our pretense of ignoring plain facts before us, facts upon which a man's very life or liberty conceivably could depend. Moreover, there probably is legal warrant for our not remanding the case to the Supreme Court of Illinois to allow those facts to be incorporated in the formal record before it and to reconsider its decision in light thereof. But the result certainly does not enhance the high traditions of the judicial process."

After noting that the defendant, "an uneducated, bewildered layman," was called upon to read and interpret a five-page indictment and to plead guilty or not guilty, Murphy gave expression to his concern for the security of the protective cloak provided for even the illiterate or uneducated by the due process clause of the Constitution and his conviction as to the Court's function in this regard when he stated:

"He was compelled to weigh the factors involved in a guilty plea against those resulting from the submission of his case to a jury. He was forced to judge the chances of setting up a successful defense. These are all complicated matters that only a man versed in the legal lore could hope to comprehend and to decide intelligently. Petitioner obviously was not of that type. Yet at this crucial juncture petitioner lacked the aid and guidance of such a person. In my view, it is a gross miscarriage of justice to condemn a man to death or to life imprisonment in such a manner."

Since the adoption of the Fourteenth Amendment the Supreme Court has always insisted that Negroes may not be systematically excluded from jury service. However, Mr. Justice Murphy insisted that a broader view be taken to prevent exclusion of any class of people from jury service:

"The American tradition of trial by jury, considered in connection with either criminal or civil proceedings, necessarily contemplates an impartial jury drawn from a cross-section of the community. . . . This does not mean, of course, that every jury must contain representatives of all the economic, social, religious, racial, political and geographical groups of the community; frequently such complete representation would be impossible. But it does mean that prospective jurors shall be selected by court officials without systematic and intentional exclusion of any of these groups. Recognition must be given to the fact that those eligible for jury service are to be found in every stratum of society. Jury competence is an individual rather than a group or class matter. That fact lies at the very heart of the jury system. To disregard it is to open the door to class distinctions and discriminations which are abhorrent to the democratic ideals of trial by jury."

Murphy consistently expressed his view that race, religion and class were irrelevant factors which may not be constitutionally considered in selecting juries. He clearly indicated his view that the issue to be considered was broader than mere exclusion:

"Racial limitation no less than racial exclusion in the formation of juries is an evil condemned by the equal protection clause. . . .

"If a jury is to be fairly chosen from a cross section of the community it must be done without limiting the number of persons of a particular color, racial background or faith—all of which are irrelevant factors in setting qualifications for jury service. This may in a particular instance result in the selection of one, six, twelve or even no Negroes on a jury panel. The important point, however, is that the selections must in no way be limited or restricted by such irrelevant factors."

In his dissent in the "blue ribbon" jury case, Murphy again urged the Court to insist upon juries drawn from a cross-section of the community. He disagreed with the majority opinion mainly because he believed that the fact that it was difficult to prove that the petitioners in the case were prejudiced thereby, should not preclude the Court from declaring "blue ribbon" juries invalid. To Murphy the protection of our jury system was more important than procedural difficulties of the particular case. He believed that it was impossible to measure accurately the prejudice in a particular case by the exclusion of certain types of qualified people from juries. Murphy pointed out that prejudice may be absent in one case and present in another, and that "it may gradually and silently erode the jury system before it becomes evident." He concluded: "If the constitutional right to a jury impartially drawn from a cross-section of the community has been violated, we should vindicate that right even though the effect of the violation has not yet put in a tangible appearance. Otherwise that right may be irretrievably lost in a welter of evidentiary rules."

In the opinions which Murphy either wrote or joined concerning the validity of convictions based upon coerced confessions, his clear perception of realism is consistent. In *Lyons v. Oklahoma* the petitioner admittedly had been coerced into signing a confession of murder. The majority found that the long and oppressive coercion and intimidation which led up to such a confession need not necessarily have influenced the subsequent confession admitted at petitioner's trial. Murphy, in dissenting, did away with the niceties involved in attempting to weigh the effect of earlier brutality upon the subsequent admitted confession, saying: "To conclude that the brutality inflicted at the time of the first confession suddenly lost all of its effect in the short space of twelve hours is to close one's eyes to the realities of human nature."

Six years later, majority opinions in three confession cases show that Murphy had won over a majority of the Court to his realistic approach to a consideration of the facts and circumstances in alleged coerced confessions. Mr. Justice Frankfurter's opinion in the *Watts* case stated in part: "We would have to shut our minds to plain significance of what here transpired to deny that this was a calculated endeavor to secure a confession through the pressure of unrelenting interrogation."

Mr. Justice Douglas' concurring opinion in the *Watts* case indicates that, in the interim since *Lyons v. Oklahoma* wherein he had joined the majority, he has adopted the views of Mr. Justice Murphy. In the *Watts* case, after reviewing the factual situation obtaining prior to the confession, Douglas said: "It would have been naive to think that this protective custody was less than the Inquisition."

Mr. Justice Murphy played an important role in opposing efforts to limit the use of habeas corpus proceedings in state and federal courts. Prisoners convicted of various crimes have in most instances found themselves with court records in which federal questions have not been properly raised, and in many cases these prisoners have been without funds to employ lawyers. In many such instances there have been federal questions which, if properly raised, would have brought about reversals. Cases of this type have consistently resulted in a clear division of the Court. One group has insisted upon rigid application of all procedural rules concerning habeas corpus, exhaustion of state remedies, clear presentation of the federal question and the authority of local, state and federal courts to dismiss petitions for habeas corpus without hearings on the federal questions presented.[1] In contrast,

---

[1] Various procedural requirements had to be satisfied before a federal court could use the mechanism of habeas corpus to consider whether a person's constitutional rights had been violated. One requirement was that the defendant ask every available state court to overturn the conviction (the "exhaustion" requirement), in a way clearly indicating the federal constitutional claims made by the defendant (the "clear presentation" requirement).

Murphy and others have insisted that the petition for a writ of habeas corpus should not be limited by rigid procedural rules and that while orderly procedure requires certain rules, they should not be used to circumvent the basic purpose of the writ to inquire into the legality of the prisoner's incarceration. Consistently, in such cases, Murphy has demonstrated his willingness to cut through procedural red tape to get to the basic question of the petitioner's constitutional rights.

In recent years the Court has recognized the increasing number of petitions for writs of habeas corpus filed in federal courts. There have also been several instances in which the same prisoner has filed several petitions for a writ of habeas corpus. The combination of these two situations brought about a 5–4 decision. In *Price v. Johnston*, four successive petitions for writs of habeas corpus were filed in the District Court for the Northern District of California. Price, who was not a lawyer, had filed them pro se.[2] All four petitions had been denied without hearing.

The last petition alleged in general language that petitioner had been denied a fair and impartial trial. After an order to show cause was issued, the petition was amended to allege "that the government knowingly employed false testimony on the trial, to obtain the conviction." The Government's return did not deny this allegation nor did it question the sufficiency of the allegations of facts. It did incorporate by reference the records of the three prior proceedings and urged the court to dismiss the petition on the basis of these prior rulings. The district court denied this fourth petition without a hearing and without opinion.

On appeal, the Ninth Circuit ordered up the original files in the three previous cases and directed that the petitioner be brought before the court for the argument of his appeal. After argument, the case was set for reargument before the court en banc.[3] Petitioner's motion for permission to appear personally for the reargument was denied. In the majority of the Ninth Circuit it was concluded that the court was without power to order the production of a prisoner for argument of his appeal in person. One judge believed that the court had such power but should not have exercised it in this case. Two judges dissented on the ground that there was power to grant the requested relief. The court then considered the appeal on the briefs filed by petitioner and respondents and oral argument by the Government. Petitioner was not represented at the oral argument. The judgment of the district court was affirmed with two judges dissenting.

In speaking for the majority of the Court, Mr. Justice Murphy reviewed the history of the writ of habeas corpus as the judicial method for lifting undue restraint upon personal liberty but noted that in recent years many procedural problems had arisen especially in federal courts.

---

[2] *Pro se* means "for himself" or "on his own behalf."

[3] The federal courts of appeals have several judges. Usually a panel of three judges heard a case, but in exceptional cases, all the judges on the court would sit en banc to hear the case.

In this particular case, Murphy held that the question of whether or not petitioner should be granted the right to argue his appeal in person was within the power of the Court of Appeals and that this right was within the meaning of section 262 of the Judicial Code providing that the Supreme Court and courts of appeals as well as the district courts shall have power to issue all writs not specifically provided for by statute, "which may be necessary for the exercise of their respective jurisdictions, and agreeable to the usages and principles of law."

He pointed out that the rule that habeas corpus could be used only where necessary to appellate jurisdiction must be considered in the light of the proviso that such writ "is available in those exceptional cases 'where, because of special circumstances, its use as an aid to an appeal over which the court has jurisdiction may fairly be said to be reasonably necessary in the interest of justice.'"

It was clear to the majority of the Court that this case came within the rule concerning the exceptional cases. After a careful review of the common law in regard to habeas corpus, Murphy concluded: "In short, we do not read § 262 as an ossification of the practice and procedure of more than a century and a half ago. Rather it is a legislatively approved source of procedural instruments designed to achieve the 'rational ends of law' . . . . We accordingly look to the usages and principles which have attached themselves to the writ of *habeas corpus* down through the years to the present time."

The majority opinion then stated that it must be emphasized that the power of a court of appeals to issue such a writ is discretionary, and its discretion must be examined "with the best interests of both the prisoner and the government in mind. . . . Section 262, in other words, does not justify an indiscriminate opening of the prison gates to allow all those who so desire to argue their own appeals."

The Ninth Circuit was found to have been in error in deciding that it was without power to issue the writ. Finally, it was emphasized that:

> "We are not unaware of the many problems caused by the numerous and successive *habeas corpus* petitions filed by prisoners. But the answer is not to be found in repeated denials of petitions without leave to amend or without the prisoners having an opportunity to defend against their alleged abuses of the writ. That only encourages the filing of more futile petitions. The very least that can and should be done is to make *habeas corpus* proceedings in district courts more meaningful and decisive, making clear just what issues are determined and for what reasons."

As to the amendment to the fourth petition alleging that the Government knowingly used false testimony at the trial, Murphy pointed out that, although the Government argued in the Supreme Court that it was a mere allegation of law unsupported by facts, this question had not been passed upon by the lower courts but that the petition had been dismissed on the ground of the petitioner's alleged abuse of the writ of habeas corpus by filing four successive petitions. It was pointed out that petitioner had made every effort to raise the due process issue set forth in *Mooney v. Holohan* and that there had been no proper occasion prior to the fourth petition for the District Court to have passed upon this question. Whether or not petitioner had any evidence on this point was not before the District Court because the petition was dismissed without hearing. The majority of the Supreme Court held that petitioner was entitled either to be heard on the present pleadings or permitted to amend and clarify his petition in the District Court, and that "appellate courts cannot make factual determinations which may be decisive of vital rights where the crucial facts have not been developed."

Finally, it was pointed out that prisoners who are unfamiliar with the law and complicated rules of pleading are very often forced to act in their own behalf and that the courts cannot impose on them the same high standards of the legal art which are placed on members of the legal profession, and that "especially is this true in a case like this where the imposition of those standards would have a retroactive and prejudicial effect on the prisoner's inartistically drawn petition."

The dissenting opinion by Mr. Justice Frankfurter, in which Mr. Chief Justice Vinson and Justices Reed and Jackson concurred, as well as the dissenting opinion of Justice Jackson, urged that a consideration of the three prior petitions along with the fourth demonstrated that the latter petition was without merit and could have merit only if petitioner had stated in his pleadings that there was newly discovered matter or that there were circumstances which could satisfactorily explain the reason for not raising such matters in the previous petitions.

Mr. Justice Frankfurter, while not agreeing with Mr. Justice Jackson that the Court of Appeals was without power to issue the necessary writ to bring petitioner before it, nevertheless disagreed with the majority opinion that the writ should be used to bring a prisoner before the Court for the purpose of arguing his own case.

During the same term, the Court again divided 5–4 on the availability of habeas corpus as a remedy in the federal courts. In the case of *Wade v. Mayo* petitioner had been convicted of the charge of breaking and entering, and the conviction was affirmed on appeal to the Supreme Court of Florida. A petition for habeas corpus had been filed in the trial court and appealed to the Supreme Court of Florida in order to exhaust state remedies. Thereafter, a petition for writ of habeas corpus was filed in the United States District Court for the Southern District of Florida alleging that the refusal to appoint counsel at the trial deprived petitioner of his constitutional right to due process of law. Petitioner pointed out that this particular point had not been raised in the appeal from the conviction because two Florida cases had previously ruled that the Supreme Court of Florida was without power to reverse for failure to appoint counsel except in capital cases.

The District Court granted the writ; a hearing was held and a ruling was made that the conviction was in violation of the due process clause of the Fourteenth Amendment. However, the Fifth Circuit reversed on the grounds that the Fourteenth Amendment did not require the appointment of counsel in non-capital cases unless the state law so required. Subsequent to these decisions the Florida Supreme Court for certiorari decided that the question of non-appointment of counsel could be raised by means of habeas corpus proceedings.

Mr. Justice Murphy approached the problem by examining the rule requiring the exhaustion of state remedies. After procedure in state courts has been exhausted there is a choice between applying for certiorari in the Supreme Court or habeas corpus in a federal district court. And prompt and orderly procedure will often require that the prisoner must first seek review in the Supreme Court and where this is not done it may be a relevant consideration for a district court in determining whether to entertain a petition for habeas corpus. But Mr. Justice Murphy pointed out that application to the Supreme Court is not in any real sense a part of the state procedure but "is an invocation of federal authority growing out of the supremacy of the Federal Constitution and the necessity of giving effect to that supremacy if the state processes have failed to do so."

Mr. Justice Murphy once again showed a determination not to permit the writ of habeas corpus to be limited by rigid procedural rules. His opinion recognized that writs of certiorari are matters of grace. This discretion frequently results in writs being denied without consideration of the merits, and "good judicial administration is not furthered by insistence on futile procedure."

In the dissenting opinion, Mr. Justice Reed took the position that the principle of exhausting state remedies required application for certiorari to the United States Supreme Court pointing out that: "Where there is a denial of constitutional rights by the highest court of a state, a remedy exists by direct review in this Court." On the other hand, Murphy insisted that "the flexible nature of the writ of *habeas corpus* counsels against erecting a rigid procedural rule that has the effect of imposing a new jurisdictional limitation on the writ."

Although the majority increased from 5–4 in *Price v. Johnston* to 6–3 in *Wade v. Mayo*, the split became more apparent in *Taylor v. Alabama* and *Taylor v. Dennis*. Taylor had been convicted of rape and sentenced to death by the Circuit Court of Mobile County, Alabama. His conviction was affirmed on appeal to the Supreme Court of Alabama. Shortly thereafter he told an attorney, who had been called into the case after the appeal, that the confession used to convict him was secured by force and duress and that because of fear he had been afraid to tell this to this court-appointed lawyer. Affidavits were secured from Taylor and from three men who were prisoners in the local jail at the time the confession was obtained.

In conformance with Alabama procedure, a petition was filed with the Supreme Court of Alabama requesting permission to file a petition for coram nobis in the trial court.[4] The State filed a motion to dismiss and, at the hearing on this motion,

---

[4] The petition for *coram nobis* is a now obsolete method of obtaining review in a criminal case after the usual time for an appeal has expired. Some state court systems used the writ of *coram nobis* instead of the writ of habeas corpus as a vehicle for obtaining postconviction review.

produced photographs of the body of the petitioner alleged to have been taken shortly after the beatings were alleged to have occurred. The Supreme Court of Alabama, by a vote of 6–1, refused to permit the petition for writ of error coram nobis to be filed.

The Supreme Court split 4–1–3 on this case with the majority opinion by Mr. Justice Burton upholding the action of the Supreme Court of Alabama in denying the petition as not being a denial of due process of law. The majority held that the Alabama Supreme Court was correct in not considering the case as if it had been submitted on demurrer but rather that the court was justified in examining the record in the trial itself and other materials to determine the reasonableness of the allegations.[5]

Mr. Justice Frankfurter, in a concurring opinion, made it clear that he agreed with the decision of the lower court in deciding that the allegations of the petition were beyond belief. However, he pointed out: "There is not now before us any right that the petitioner may have under the Judicial Code to bring an independent *habeas corpus* proceeding in the District Court of the United States."

Murphy, in a dissenting opinion, once again made his position clear. Instead of looking first to technical procedural matters of state corrective machinery, he examined the constitutional principle that no conviction in a state court is valid which is based in whole or in part upon an involuntary confession.

> "This principle reflects the common abhorrence of compelling any man, innocent or guilty, to give testimony against himself in a criminal proceeding. It is a principle which was written into the Constitution because of the belief that to torture and coerce an individual into confessing a crime, even though that individual be guilty, is to endanger the rights and liberties of all persons accused of crime. History has shown that once tyrannical methods of law enforcement are permitted as to one man such methods are invariably used as to others. Brutality knows no distinction between the innocent and the guilty. And those who suffer most from these inquisitorial processes are the friendless, the ignorant, the poor and the despised. *Chambers v. Florida*, 309 U.S. 227, 237–238. To guard against this evil, therefore, the Constitution requires that a conviction be set aside whenever it appears that a confession introduced at the trial is involuntary in nature."

This approach to the problem involved made it clear to the minority of the Court that the case should have been reversed because the petitioner had in fact not had a hearing on his allegations of denial of constitutional rights.

> "The problem in this case is whether the petitioner, having been found guilty of rape and sentenced to death, is now entitled to a hearing on his

---

[5] If a case is submitted on demurrer, the court is required to assume that all the factual allegations made by the plaintiff or petitioner are true, and may not go beyond those allegations to examine other materials, such as the defendant's response or, in this case, the trial record.

allegation that the confession introduced at the trial was obtained by coercive methods. The Supreme Court of Alabama refused to allow a hearing on the theory that the allegation was unreasonable. In affirming that refusal, however, this Court relies upon considerations which are either irrelevant, inconclusive or contrary to the constitutional principle just discussed."

If petitioner's allegations were in fact true his conviction and death sentence were in violation of the Constitution. The effect of the rule as laid down in the majority opinion is that these allegations can never be proved. Under the rule urged by Murphy, the petitioner would be given an opportunity to prove these allegations. In one case the quality of justice by the Alabama courts remains in doubt. In the other the doubt would be resolved one way or the other.

The serious effect of the rule of the majority in *Taylor v. Alabama*, supra, is demonstrated in *Taylor v. Dennis*, supra, where the Court, by an even division, upheld the denial of a petition for writ of habeas corpus by the District Court for the Middle District of Alabama. The District Court had dismissed the petition without a hearing on the merits on the basis of the prior state proceedings.

This decision temporarily at least impairs the effectiveness of the prior decisions of Murphy and other Justices who have consistently opposed efforts to limit the availability of the writ of habeas corpus in federal courts.

Mr. Justice Murphy's impassioned dissent in the *Yamashita* case is not only a fine example of his important contribution to judicial writing and to the development of the Court in these confusing times; it serves also to demonstrate that ever present strain of his humane conviction and sincere devotion to concepts of natural justice, which are the basis of the professional criticism of his judicial craftsmanship. Murphy might not have had Holmes' genius for logical exegesis, which could destroy a generation of fuzzy thinking with a single sentence. But Murphy did have a profound feeling for the social problems of his day, and for the people whose lives were to be affected by his decisions. He could and did write forcefully, simply, and when the emotional pitch demanded, eloquently. And to reach the right result uniformly, he could select and marshal the judicial precedents in a clear and workmanlike manner.

In his *Yamashita* dissent he began with an obviously difficult task; he had been Governor General of the Philippines and felt a strong emotional tie with the unfortunate people who, at the hands of the Japanese, had been the victims of unspeakable war atrocities. But his devotion to eternal constitutional principles of due process and his belief that the guarantee of a fair trial superseded all motives of vengeance and retaliation evoked all the fire and eloquence of the zealot.

The first long section of his dissenting opinion is devoted to the proposition that the Fifth Amendment should be applicable to all crimes committed within the federal orbit. This is followed by the argument that the scope of judicial review should be enlarged on habeas corpus petitions, especially in review of military cases. At this point, however, Justice Murphy, after having devoted several pages to an analysis of what the Fifth Amendment should do, recapitulates and says: "But for the purposes of this case I accept the scope of review recognized by the Court at this time." Then he launches into the specific problems raised by the petition, and, together with his brother Rutledge, makes out a highly plausible, technical argument to support the proposition which his fundamental judicial feelings dictated.

The decision of the Supreme Court on application for habeas corpus, prohibition and certiorari cannot be properly evaluated without a thorough consideration of the powerful and impassioned dissents of Justices Murphy and Rutledge. The Court had nothing before it but a question of jurisdiction. As precedent, *In re Yamashita* is significant in that it indicates how much latitude will be given to the military in the trial of war crimes in time of war.

Purely as a matter of statutory construction, Mr. Justice Rutledge might have seemed to have the better of the argument as to the applicability of Article of War 25 which by its language prohibits the use of depositions in capital cases before military commissions. Murphy's attack upon the vagueness of the charge, however, is also highly persuasive; a finding of guilty was possible without proof of any connection between Yamashita and the unspeakable acts of the troops in Manila other than the fact of nominal command. Yet the majority opinion has been plausibly defended as having reached a desirable result from the point of view of the necessities of military jurisdiction in time of war. Of course in evaluating the result in the case, it must be remembered that the Court was not concerned with the guilt or innocence of the petitioner. The central issue was whether the petitioner could invalidate his conviction by the military tribunal on the ground that it had failed to afford him the procedural safeguards which the Constitution provides.

Murphy's introduction and peroration in the *Yamashita* case may not add to legal scholarship, but it is judicial forensic literature of the highest order:

"That there were brutal atrocities inflicted upon the helpless Filipino people, to whom tyranny is no stranger, by Japanese armed forces under the petitioner's command is undeniable. Starvation, execution or massacre without trial, torture, rape, murder and wanton destruction of property were foremost among the outright violations of the laws of war and of the conscience of a civilized world. That just punishment should be meted out to all those responsible for criminal acts of this nature is also beyond dispute. But these factors do not answer the problem in this case. They do not justify the abandonment of our devotion to justice in dealing with a fallen enemy commander. To conclude otherwise is to admit that the enemy has lost the battle but has destroyed our ideals.

"War breeds atrocities. From the earliest conflicts of recorded history to the global struggles of modern times inhumanities, lust and pillage have been the inevitable by-products of man's resort to force and arms.

Unfortunately, such despicable acts have a dangerous tendency to call forth primitive impulses of vengeance and retaliation among the victimized peoples. The satisfaction of such impulses in turn breeds resentment and fresh tension. Thus does the spiral of cruelty and hatred grow."

Murphy made a great contribution toward meaningful enforcement of the constitutional prohibition against unlawful searches and seizures. In *Harris v. United States* it appeared that Harris was arrested by federal officers and his home ransacked without a search warrant until an envelope was found in a bedroom containing evidence of another crime. The conviction for the crime involving this evidence was sustained by a five to four decision.

Murphy, in a vigorous dissenting opinion, pointed out that such a decision permitting unlimited searching of premises where a valid arrest is made would destroy the constitutional right involved:

"Under today's decision, a warrant of arrest for a particular crime authorizes an unlimited search of one's home from cellar to attic for evidence of 'anything' that might come to light, whether bearing on the crime charged or any other crime. A search warrant is not only unnecessary; it is a hindrance."

On the other hand, Murphy insisted that "the mere fact that a man has been validly arrested does not give the arresting officers untrammeled freedom to search every cranny and nook for anything that might have some relation to the alleged crime or, indeed, to any crime whatsoever."

In the *Trupiano* case Murphy, in the majority opinion, while distinguishing the *Harris* case, nevertheless succeeded in clarifying a portion of the rule in the *Harris* case as follows:

"A search or seizure without a warrant as an incident to a lawful arrest has always been considered to be a strictly limited right. It grows out of the inherent necessities of the situation at the time of the arrest. But there must be something more in the way of necessity than merely a lawful arrest. The mere fact that there is a valid arrest does not *ipso facto* legalize a search or seizure without a warrant. *Carroll v. United States, supra,* . . . [267 U.S. 132, 45 S.Ct. 280 (1925)]. Otherwise the exception swallows the general principle, making a search warrant completely unnecessary wherever there is a lawful arrest. And so there must be some other factor in the situation that would make it unreasonable or impracticable to require the arresting officer to equip himself with a search warrant. In the case before us, however, no reason whatever has been shown why the arresting officers could not have armed themselves during all the weeks of their surveillance of the locus with a duly obtained search warrant—no reason, that is, except indifference to the legal process for search and seizure which the Constitution contemplated."

In *Wolf v. Colorado* the dissenting opinion of Mr. Justice Murphy again demonstrated his keen determination to require governmental officials to recognize individual rights. The majority opinion decided that the Fourteenth Amendment prohibited states from making unreasonable searches and seizures, but that the rule that such evidence seized in violation of the Fourth Amendment could not be used in federal courts did not prevent the use of such evidence in violation of the Fourteenth Amendment from being used in state courts.

Murphy's position was clear. The constitutional protection had to be given real meaning. He pointed out:

"The conclusion is inescapable that but one remedy exists to deter violations of the search and seizure clause. That is the rule which excludes illegally obtained evidence. Only by exclusion can we impress upon the zealous prosecutor that violation of the Constitution will do him no good. And only when that point is driven home can the prosecutor be expected to emphasize the importance of observing constitutional demands in his instructions to the police."

Once again, in the *Schneiderman* case, Murphy demonstrated his determination to protect individual rights and to marshal legal support for them. Twelve years after Schneiderman was naturalized the Government sought to denaturalize him. The minority of the Court believed that in the review of denaturalization proceedings the same issues would be present as in a review of a naturalization proceeding.

On the other hand, Murphy looked to the rights of the naturalized citizen and his right to freedom of thought and expression. He then set forth the rules which should be followed in such hearings and said that the statute governing such proceedings should not be so construed as to "circumscribe liberty of political thought." He cautioned that:

"Were the law otherwise, valuable rights would rest upon a slender reed, and the security of the status of our naturalized citizens might depend in considerable degree upon the political temper of majority thought and the stresses of the times. Those are consequences foreign to the best traditions of this nation and the characteristics of our institutions."

In dissenting in the case of *Baumgartner v. United States* Murphy made it clear that his views were even broader than those expressed in the *Schneiderman* case:

"American citizenship is not a right granted on a condition subsequent that the naturalized citizen refrain in the future from uttering any remark or adopting an attitude favorable to his original homeland or those there in power, no matter how distasteful such conduct may be to most of us. He is not required to imprison himself in an intellectual or spiritual strait-jacket; nor is he obliged to retain a static mental attitude. Moreover, he does not lose the precious right of citizenship because he subsequently dares to criticize his adopted government in vituperative or defamatory terms."

Mr. Justice Murphy's contributions to the law of the land as to the validity of distinctions based on race or ancestry are unique. In this field his experience as Governor-General of the Philippine Islands and his part as judge in the famous *Sweet* trial in Detroit gave him the necessary first-hand knowledge of the extent to which racial hostility could defeat the ends of justice. This background along with Murphy's deep-rooted sense of justice gave to the Supreme Court a man determined to oppose every governmental act which was tainted in whole or in part by racial considerations.

Although there were not many cases specifically involving the rights of Negroes during Murphy's term, his record was consistently in favor of freedom of the individual and in opposition to all types of governmental oppression. In both the white primary case, and the restrictive covenant cases, Murphy joined the Court in invalidating governmentally imposed racial restrictions.

In the case of *Screws v. United States*, there were four opinions with the majority reversing the conviction of a peace officer of Georgia who had clubbed a Negro to death through malice. However, Murphy, in his dissenting opinion, set forth his belief that the Federal Government should intervene in cases of this type, because it was clear that the Negro who had been killed had been denied his life without due process and under color of state law. In doing so, he pointed out: "Too often unpopular minorities, such as Negroes, are unable to find effective refuge from the cruelties of bigoted and ruthless authority. States are undoubtedly capable of punishing their officers who commit such outrages. But where, as here, the states are unwilling for some reason to prosecute such crimes the Federal Government must step in unless constitutional guarantees are to become atrophied."

In the case of *Steele v. Louisville & Nashville R.R. Co.* the Court declared invalid the practice of railroad brotherhoods in discriminating against Negro firemen. Once again, Mr. Justice Murphy felt it necessary to restate in a concurring opinion his belief as to the relative position of the right of minority groups to be free from oppression. To him, the important point was that "the utter disregard of the dignity and the well-being of colored citizens shown by this record is so pronounced as to demand the invocation of constitutional condemnation." He therefore objected to the opinion in the case which analyzed the statute "solely upon the basis of legal niceties," without considering the more basic right involved.

In the cases concerning the treatment of Japanese-Americans during the last war, Murphy, in concurring with the majority in the *Hirabayashi* case made it clear that "distinctions based on color and ancestry are utterly inconsistent with our traditions and ideals." At the same time, he made it clear that while he concurred with the decision in this case, he believed that the action in approving the curfew for Japanese-Americans during the period of extreme emergency went "to the very brink of constitutional power."

This case was followed by the *Korematsu* case and *Ex parte Endo*. In these cases, Murphy dissented in the first and concurred in the second on the grounds that the action complained of was beyond "the very brink of constitutional power and falls into the ugly abyss of racism." In his dissenting opinion in the *Korematsu* case, Murphy in most vigorous terms set forth his resentment against governmental action in subjecting individuals to oppression because of the disloyal action of other members of the group. The warning set forth by Mr. Justice Murphy in the *Korematsu* case will no doubt be quoted over and over again:

"I dissent, therefore, from this legalization of racism. Racial discrimination in any form and in any degree has no justifiable part whatever in our democratic way of life. It is unattractive in any setting but it is utterly revolting among a free people who have embraced the principles set forth in the Constitution of the United States. All residents of this nation are kin in some way by blood or culture to a foreign land. Yet they are primarily and necessarily a part of the new and distinct civilization of the United States. They must accordingly be treated at all times as the heirs of the American experiment and as entitled to all the rights and freedoms guaranteed by the Constitution."

CONCLUSION

In many respects, Mr. Justice Murphy represented the trend of the present day Supreme Court toward giving further recognition to the rights of individuals. On many occasions he joined with the majority in upholding these rights, in many other instances he joined in dissenting opinions which state that these rights be upheld. Mr. Justice Murphy will be remembered for his consistency in insisting, and his determination, that the rights of individuals be free from oppression. Although Murphy did not succeed in all of these efforts, he did succeed in placing individual rights in such perspective as to require the consideration of these rights by the majority in cases where he found himself in the minority.

Whereas there have been others who have had the zeal for protecting individual rights and whereas there have been others who have demonstrated their ability as judges, Mr. Justice Murphy stands out as one who had a firm conviction that the Constitution and laws of this country demanded the protection of individual rights. His ability to place individual rights within the orthodox legal framework of our country is a contribution for which we will forever be indebted.

10. The Supreme Court as Protector of Civil Rights: Equal Protection of the Laws

Annals of the American Academy of Political and Social Sciences, vol. 275 (May 1951)

By 1951 the Supreme Court had developed a substantial body of doctrine dealing with unconstitutional discrimination. Many, but not all, of the cases had been brought to the Court by the NAACP. In this article, Marshall provides an educated audience with an overview of the Court's work, emphasizing recent decisions and the degree of protection these decisions afforded minority groups. He concludes with a plea that the Court overrule *Plessy v. Ferguson*, a course he was already urging on the courts in the cases that eventually reached the Court as *Brown v. Board of Education.*

Although almost a century has elapsed since the Civil War and the abolition of slavery as an American institution, the transition of the Negro from a slave-chattel to a full-fledged free American citizen has been painfully retarded. The Fourteenth Amendment was adopted to assure that this change from slave status to citizenship would take place, and, in fact, to protect all persons against discrimination based on race, religion, color, blood, or national origin.

That many of the vestiges of slavery remain and that racial discrimination still is practiced in all sections of the United States is to a considerable extent the responsibility of the United States Supreme Court which spelled out the meaning of this new constitutional provision. The Court's narrow, cautious, and often rigid interpretation of the amendment's reach and thrust in the past gave constitutional sanction to practices of racial discrimination and prejudice. Such practices have been permitted to become a part of the pattern of contemporary American society, in effective nullification of the constitutional mandate.

Prime examples of this narrow and corrosive limitation of the amendment's effect are the *Civil Rights Cases*, in which a federal civil rights act was declared unconstitutional on the ground that the Fourteenth Amendment could not affect the activities of private persons; *Plessy v. Ferguson*, which condoned enforced racial segregation under the "separate but equal" formula; and *Pace v. Alabama*, which upheld the constitutionality of a legislative proscription of intermarriage between Negroes and white persons.

CHANGE IN TREND

The harm which these decisions have done to the cause of civil rights, however, has been somewhat repaired in subsequent cases, for we are now reaching the point where it is possible to view it as likely that the constitutional interdiction against racial and color discrimination will be given the high evaluation it deserves.

Many years after the passage of the Fourteenth Amendment, its mandate of equal protection of the laws was neglected, as the Court forged and sharpened the concept of due process into a formidable constitutional weapon to cut away governmental interference with private property and with the liberty of corporations. With the appointment of what has become popularly known as the "Roosevelt Court,"[1] this weapon was laid aside, and the due process clause, as a constitutional deterrent to governmental action, now seems to be of significance only in that area where the right being asserted is fundamental to and implicit in our concept of liberty.

While now deferring to the legislative judgment in economic matters, however, the Court has begun to look upon the protection of personal liberty as one of its primary functions. The requirement that equal protection of the laws be accorded, expressly required by the Fourteenth Amendment and read into the Fifth Amendment by the Court itself, is increasingly furnishing the means through which protection of a very vital phase of personal liberty may be realized—the right to be free from differences of treatment because of race, color, blood, or national origin.

In this special field the Supreme Court in the past decade has evidenced an increasing awareness of the brutal realities of racial discrimination and its contradiction of constitutional guarantees. A real effort is now being made to require that members of an unpopular color or racial minority be accorded the same treatment as anyone else.

NOT UNIFORMITY BUT IMPARTIALITY

The obligation to furnish equal protection of the laws does not establish an abstract uniformity applicable alike to all persons without regard to circumstances or conditions. Equal protection requires that all persons be fairly treated in their relations with the state. But the concept makes allowance for dissimilarity of circumstances in order that legislation may fall with evenhandedness upon all persons. Special burdens and duties may be imposed upon a particular group or class for the benefit of the public as a whole. Arbitrary discrimination alone is prohibited.

If control or regulation of a particular group is undertaken, the classification or distinction upon which such legislation is founded must be based upon a real or substantial difference which has pertinence to the legislative objective. This is an extremely flexible formula, and a classification's reasonableness is largely dependent upon the peculiar needs, the special difficulties, and the particular requirements of the local situation. Here again the Court must necessarily give great weight to legislative judgment in view of the necessity for familiarity with local conditions.

---

[1] After failing to persuade Congress in 1937 to adopt his proposal that would have allowed him to appoint up to six new members of the Supreme Court, President Franklin D. Roosevelt nonetheless transformed the Court over the next few years by appointing a total of nine new justices.

Where the legislature, however, attempts to single out persons because of their particular race, color, or national origin in order to subject them to discriminatory penalties, then a determination of the unreasonableness of these penalties within the purview of the Constitution is not precluded by lack of any special or specific familiarity with local conditions or needs. The Supreme Court of the United States, far removed from the stresses which keep racial animosity alive, is best able to determine whether the state in fact provides equal protection of the laws as required by the Constitution.

This was recognized in *United States v. Carolene Products Company*, where Justice Stone stated:

> There may be narrower scope for operation of the presumption of constitutionality when legislation appears on its face to be within a specific prohibition of the Constitution, such as those of the first ten amendments, which are deemed equally specific when held to be embraced within the Fourteenth. . . .
>
> Nor need we inquire whether similar conditions enter into the review of statutes directed at particular religions . . . , or national . . . , or racial minorities . . . ; whether prejudice against discrete and insular minorities may be a special condition, which tends seriously to curtail the operation of those political processes ordinarily to be relied upon to protect minorities, and which may call for a correspondingly more searching judicial inquiry.

It is sometimes said that there is a presumption of unconstitutionality running against governmental action based upon race or color. This may be an overstatement of fact, but certainly this type of governmental action in terms of motivation, purpose, and effect is now subjected to a more searching scrutiny than is ordinarily the case with other kinds of state activity. Here the Supreme Court now retains for itself the final word as to whether the state has violated constitutional standards of conduct, and therefore functions as the ultimate guardian of civil rights.

THE EXCLUSION CASES

In giving effect to the equality requirement of the Fourteenth Amendment, the Supreme Court has had little difficulty in successfully dealing with total deprivation of rights or exclusion based on race and color. Since 1879 in *Strauder v. West Virginia*, it has been enforcing the equal protection of the laws in this area with vigor and strength. There it said:

> [The equal protection clause of the Fourteenth Amendment] was designed to assure to the colored race the enjoyment of all civil rights that under the law are enjoyed by white persons, and to give to that race the protection of the General Government, in that enjoyment, whenever it should be denied by the States. . . .

... What is this but declaring ... that all persons, whether colored or white, shall stand equal before the laws of the States, and, in regard to the colored race, for whose protection the amendment was primarily designed, that no discrimination shall be made against them by law because of their color?

Thus, exclusion of Negroes from jury service, total deprivation of a right to educational opportunities furnished by the state, or exclusion of Negroes from certain residential areas have all been held to be a denial of equal protection.

A glaring exception is the Japanese cases, in which legal sanction was given to the governmental exclusion of American citizens of Japanese origin from the West Coast during World War II,[2] although it seems evident that the Court recognized this action as going to the brink of constitutional power. This sweeping military interference with individual freedom was justified under the compulsion of a national emergency. Yet we unquestionably invite disaster if there are times when it is considered permissible to ignore or thrust aside constitutional guarantees and prohibitions.

Now, after the danger has passed, the United States Court of Appeals for the Ninth Circuit, in a sober and biting analysis of the military treatment of the Japanese, finds that their exclusion from the West Coast did not derive from any real apprehension of danger by sabotage, but was based upon General De Witt's belief in disloyalty by blood. It is to be hoped that if the future poses a similar problem, the Court will have learned that in determining the permissible reach of constitutional safeguards with respect to civil rights, military judgment must be subjected to as searching an analysis as any other type of governmental interference.

Except for these cases, however, a total deprivation of rights or exclusion based upon race or color has been struck down with vigor and directness. Where, however, the infringement has been more subtly camouflaged, or where the Court has not considered the restriction a total deprivation or exclusion, its role as protector of civil rights has left, on the whole, much to be desired. In four recent cases, however, which we will examine here, we see signs of the Court's growing maturity in its handling of civil rights problems.

RIGHT TO A GAINFUL OCCUPATION

In 1948 in *Takahashi v. Fish and Game Commission*, the Court, in a 7–2 decision, held a California fish and game statute unconstitutional which prohibited the issuance of a license for commercial fishing to any person ineligible for citizenship. Controversy between Torao Takahashi and the state centered upon the purpose of

---

[2] *Hirabayashi v. United States* (1943) upheld a military order imposing a curfew on Japanese Americans living on the West Coast; *Korematsu v. United States* (1944) upheld a military order directing that all Japanese Americans be relocated from the West Coast to inland camps.

the statute. The former asserted that the statute was the outgrowth of racial animosity. The latter's claimed purpose was the conservation of fish. Of course, if racial antagonism was the statute's motivation, then it was illegal in its objective. If, on the other hand, the state was legitimately attempting to conserve its fish resources, classification of alien Japanese as ineligible for commercial fishing licenses bore no reasonable relation to the statute's objective. Hence the classification was invalid whatever its purpose.

The Court, however, refused to meet these issues, but chose to base decision upon an unconstitutional conflict between state and federal power with respect to the regulation of immigration; upon the state's obligation under the Fourteenth Amendment and federal laws passed thereunder to furnish equal protection of the laws to all persons in lawful residence within its jurisdiction; and upon an absence of a sufficient state interest to enact such legislation in any event.

Although the Court refused to repudiate the power of the state to deal with aliens exclusively as a class, it stated that this power must be held to narrow limits. This case can be distinguished from *Clarke v. Deckenbach*, in which prohibition of operation of billiard and pool halls by aliens was upheld on the ground that the special social problems incident to these establishments justified the state in excluding aliens as a class. It cannot be squared with *Heim v. McCall*, however, in which the prohibition of employment of aliens in public works was permitted, or with *Patsone v. Pennsylvania*, in which a statute prohibiting aliens from hunting wild game was held to meet the requirements of equal protection of the laws. Nor is it correct to view the decision as merely the application of *Truax v. Raich*, since the statute there was struck down because of its sweeping and indiscriminate effect upon all aliens and all businesses of more than a certain number of employees.

The decision can be explained only as a drastic restriction of state authority to discriminate against aliens as a class. If the rationale of *Takahashi v. Fish and Game Commission* is taken as a guide to future Court decisions, it is apparent that the state will have to prove the purity and the legitimacy of its motives, and show that there is a reasonable relationship between the classification on the basis of alienage and the statute's objectives, before the burdens imposed will be allowed to stand. If these formidable prerequisites are required in the future, the rights of aliens, lawfully in residence, to freedom from discrimination by the state because of their origin will be assured.

RIGHT TO REAL PROPERTY

The decisions in *Oyama v. California* and *Shelley v. Kraemer* treat of different phases of the same problem—the right of a citizen to the ownership, use, and occupancy of real property. In *Oyama v. California* the issue before the Court was the validity of California's statutory presumption that a conveyance of land to a citizen or to an alien eligible to take title by an ineligible alien, who had paid consideration for the land, was prima facie evidence[3] of an evasion of the state's Alien Land Law, and the land would escheat to the state.[4] The Court in a rather strange division refused to decide the basic constitutional problem—the validity of the Alien Land Law which prohibited aliens ineligible for citizenship from taking title to real property in California—but rested decision on the narrow ground that an American citizen of Japanese origin is denied the equal protection of the laws when a gift of land to him from his father, ineligible to citizenship, is presumed to be an evasion of the law, no such presumption being operative when the parent is a citizen or is eligible for citizenship. Thus the citizen son was denied the equal protection of the laws in that the state took away his property because his father was an alien.

Although the narrow limitations of the majority opinion seem basically untenable, the effect of the decision was to protect the parties involved against the impact of the statute. Yet the reason for the Court's refusal to hold the Alien Land Law unconstitutional, as it would be required to do under the rationale of the *Takahashi* case, is extremely difficult to understand. The only plausible explanation seems to lie in Chief Justice Vinson and Justice Frankfurter's insistence that constitutional questions be decided only within the narrow limits of the facts before the Court. Adherence to that principle in this case, however, has caused the Court to reach a decision via a tortuous and circuitous route, whereas the more simple path of holding the Alien Land Law unconstitutional seems sounder and more inviting. If the state must now do all that we understand the subsequent decision in *Takahashi v. Fish and Game Commission* to mean that it must, before its subjection of aliens to special burdens will meet the test of constitutionality, the narrowness of the decision in the *Oyama* case seems particularly unnecessary.

In *Shelley v. Kraemer*, on the other hand, the Court met a much more difficult constitutional problem with unusual directness. Although enforced segregation in residential areas by legislative fiat had been held a denial of equal protection of the laws in *Buchanan v. Warley*, private restrictive agreements which accomplished the same result through judicial enforcement had in effect been sustained in *Corrigan v. Buckley*. Then for approximately twenty years the Supreme Court refused to meet this issue in subsequent cases. In 1948, however, the Court felt that the question was ripe for decision, granted certiorari in Shelley v. Kraemer and its companion cases, and held that racial restrictive covenants, although valid as between private persons, when enforced by the state courts constituted a denial of the equal protection of the laws.

Concept of state action

As we have seen, the guarantees of the Fourteenth Amendment can be infringed only through state machinery. Between the *Civil Rights Cases* and *Shelley v. Kraemer*,

---

[3] *Prima facie evidence* is evidence that is sufficient to justify a particular conclusion unless it is disbelieved or contradicted by other evidence.

[4] That is to say, the land would be forfeited and become the state's property.

the concept of state action underwent considerable expansion. State action was found in the acts of legislature, judiciary, executive, administrative agencies, and political subdivisions of the state; in the action of government officials clothed with state power, even though their action may not have been sanctioned by the state; in the refusal of a state to act where a duty required it to do so; in attempts to effect discrimination by the delegation of what is normally a state function to private agencies; in the discriminatory acts of a labor union granted sole bargaining rights under Congressional mandate; and in the action of a private company maintaining a company-owned town. To reach judicial enforcement of restrictive covenants, however, the Court had to expand the concept of state action to new limits.

In *Shelley v. Kraemer*, moreover, there apparently was no insistence upon narrowly limiting decision in order to avoid deciding a broader constitutional issue than the facts required. Had this been a consideration, it would seem that decision could have rested on public policy without reaching the state-action question, on the ground that private agreements which restrict use of property to persons because of race or color are at war with national policy evidenced in the Fourteenth Amendment, and no person can use the judicial machinery to enforce agreements so directly contrary to national policy. Yet the Court chose to find a specific denial of the equal protection of the laws in the enforcement of such agreements, and the Shelley v. Kraemer decision is a broad prohibition against any use of the state's judicial process to give effect to these agreements.

The decision is unquestionably one of the most important in the whole field of civil rights. With judicial enforcement of restrictive covenants now held to be a denial of the equal protection of the laws, it becomes possible for colored minorities to break out of crowded ghettos into unsegregated areas, with consequent opportunity of acceptance as members of an integrated community. Thus increased opportunity is given for eventual solution of racial problems in this country.

RIGHT TO AN EDUCATION

In *Sweatt v. Painter* and *McLaurin v. Oklahoma State Regents for Higher Education et al.,* effort was made to have the Court re-examine and overrule *Plessy v. Ferguson* and declare its "separate but equal" formula, under which racial segregation has flourished, to be violative of the constitutional requirement of equality of treatment. In all the education cases decided by the Court for more than half a century after *Plessy v. Ferguson*, the "separate but equal" doctrine seemed at least tacitly accepted as a correct statement of the law. Yet in no case did the Court actually decide that the segregated facility was in fact equal.

In *Sweatt v. Painter* the state urged that a segregated law school for Negroes was substantially equal to the law school of the University of Texas, and therefore met the requirements of equal protection of the laws under the "separate but equal" formula. The Court measured the law school for Negroes against the University of Texas and found in terms of number of the faculty, variety of courses and opportunity for specialization, size of the student body, scope of the library, availability of law review and similar activities, the University of Texas Law School was superior. . . . The law school, the proving ground for legal learning and practice, cannot be effective in isolation from the individuals and institutions with which the law interacts. Few students and no one who has practiced law would choose to study in an academic vacuum, removed from the interplay of ideas and the exchange of views with which the law is concerned.

Sweatt's admission to the University of Texas Law School was therefore ordered.

In *McLaurin v. Oklahoma* State Regents, although McLaurin was admitted to the state university, he was subjected to special rules and regulations, because of his color, not applicable to other students. The Court held that the state had overreached the limits of its power in treating him differently from other students, and that the equal protection of the laws required that McLaurin be admitted subject only to the same terms and conditions as all other students.

Educational segregation defeated

The Court was content to solve only the specific problem presented, and explicitly refused to re-examine or reaffirm *Plessy v. Ferguson.* In its restricted context of constitutional protection as applied to state graduate and professional schools, however, it has set standards so high and so rigid that it seems highly improbable that racial segregation at these educational levels can successfully meet the test of constitutionality. Indeed, a careful reading of these two opinions forces the conclusion that *Plessy v. Ferguson*'s "separate but equal" doctrine is now totally without significance at the professional and graduate school levels of state universities.

An indication of inequality was found in Sweatt's isolation from the ruling majority. Since it would seem that integration is of equal if not greater importance at the elementary, high school, and college levels, the whole structure of segregation in public education seems to have been dealt a shattering blow.

The Court, even in deciding the question presented in what seems to have been the "separate but equal" format, did break free from that philosophy in finding the enforced segregation of Negroes in a separate law school in the *Sweatt* case an inequality and in recognizing that McLaurin was denied equal treatment by virtue of the mental and psychological burdens he was forced to undergo in being required to conform to segregational practices within the classroom, the library, and the cafeteria at the University of Oklahoma. In that respect certainly these two decisions stand for the proposition that racial segregation in a state's educational system is a denial of the equal protection of the laws.

As a direct or indirect result of these decisions, Negroes are now attending graduate and professional schools in Arkansas, Texas, Maryland, Delaware, Kentucky, Oklahoma, Virginia, West Virginia, and Louisiana. North Carolina,

Tennessee, and Georgia have refused to accede to the inevitable, but it is doubtful that even the most rabid racist in those states does not now realize that the admission of Negroes into the state universities must soon take place. As far as we know, no effort has been made to test the issue in Alabama or Mississippi, and the situation in Florida is beclouded. On the whole, more than a thousand Negroes, heretofore denied opportunity for graduate and professional training, have already been accepted for that training along with other students. Thus a major modification in the pattern of American life is in the making.

SOME REMAINING PROBLEMS

Constitutional protection against freedom from distinctions based upon race or color is still far from secure. The authority of the state to enforce segregation in theaters and other places of public amusement, restaurants, intrastate carriers, and recreational facilities, and in colleges and elementary and high schools, remains directly untouched. There also remains the question as to whether corporations which undertake to build huge housing developments and are thereby given certain governmental rights and concessions are still acting in a private capacity, so that exclusion of Negroes from these developments cannot be prohibited by the Constitution. Yet, authority to practice discrimination in these areas should fall, if subjected to the same analysis which the Court applied to the *Sweatt* and *McLaurin* cases.

The fact that the Court did not decide segregation to be unconstitutional per se or in all areas is not fatal. The *Sweatt* and *McLaurin* cases indicate the Supreme Court's conviction that segregation is a denial of equality, and these decisions are potent weapons with which to continue the fight against segregation. The Court's present strategy may be to breach the pattern of segregation area by area by dealing with specific problems as they are presented. It may feel that in whittling away the legal foundation upon which segregation is based, in that fashion, the protection afforded to civil rights may be more palatable to the community and hence more lasting.

Surely segregation remains as the chief problem with which a civil rights attorney must deal, and our job would have been nearer conclusion had it been possible to convince the Court that it should overrule *Plessy v. Ferguson*. But having failed in that objective in the *Sweatt* and *McLaurin* cases, the Court must now be convinced as each new issue arises that the time is ripe for the "separate but equal" doctrine to be further delimited. The problem is carefully to marshal overwhelming evidence of the inequalities inherent in segregation in the particular areas involved, and thereby demonstrate that an extension of the principles of the *Sweatt* and *McLaurin* cases is timely. With each succeeding case, the Court must also be urged to overrule *Plessy v. Ferguson* and to break completely with the "separate but equal" philosophy.

CONCLUSION

Any fair assessment of the Court's role in the past decade compels the conclusion that it has done considerably more than any other arm of the federal government to secure, preserve, and extend civil rights. Although its approach has been undeniably cautious, the Court seems to be making a real effort to deal effectively with our most disturbing problem with practical wisdom and insight. If it continues along the path blazed by its recent decisions, the Constitution's mandate of equal protection of the laws will eventually accomplish the objective its framers intended—that of prohibiting all forms of community discriminatory action based upon race or color.

11. Summary Justice—The Negro GI in Korea
The Crisis, vol. 58 (May 1951)

Marshall reports on his trip to Korea to investigate claims that African American soldiers were being subjected to unfair treatment in the military's court-martial process.

Thirty-nine Negro American soldiers convicted and sentenced by courts-martial held in Korea asked the NAACP to represent them. All, beginning with Lt. Leon A. Gilbert, who received sentence of death on September 6, had pleaded "not Guilty." When we examined records of the trials, we knew something was very wrong.

These soldiers were members of the 24th Infantry Regiment. This Regiment won the first notable United Nations' victory in retaking the rail and highway city of Yechon on July 28 after a bloody sixteen hour battle. At Bloody Peak, its Third Battalion fought its way up and down the mountain several times in the face of superior enemy fighting power, with whole companies being wiped out. Despite staggering casualties, these infantry-men fought on until they took Bloody Peak and held it.

And yet, we were faced with a large number of courts-martial cases involving Negroes, with conviction for cowardice, for desertion, for misbehavior in the presence of the enemy and other serious offenses. It seemed hard to believe that these men could change over from heroes to cowards, all within a few days, even under the violent pressure of warfare.

Letters from the men insisted they had been treated unfairly. In most cases there was no dispute between the prosecution and defense on points of law, but versions of the facts given by witnesses varied widely.

We needed facts. It would do little good to submit appeals for review of these trials unless we found out everything we could about each individual case. And the place to get the facts was across the Pacific.

At first, General MacArthur refused permission for me to go to Tokyo, where the prisoners were. He sent a cable which read:

Not the slightest evidence exists here of discrimination as alleged. As I think you know in this command there is no slightest bias of its various members because of race, color or other distinguishing characteristics. Every soldier in this command is measured on a completely uniform basis with the sole criteria his efficiency and his character. Nevertheless, on receipt of your message I at once ordered the Inspector General to make thorough investigation of your charges and will be glad to have you forward here any evidence in your possession bearing upon the matter.

In any individual trial a soldier can obtain special counsel to defend him if he so desires. In such individual trial there would of course be no objection to Thurgood Marshall representing the accused and coming to this command for such purpose. You understand of course that courts martial are convened by the Major Subordinate Commander in Korea and the hearings are conducted there.

DECISION NO HELP

This decision of MacArthur's was certainly no help to the men who had already been condemned, and we were continuing to receive requests from others who had been convicted under questionable circumstances. We did not hear of these trials until long after they took place, so the General's willingness to have me represent men who might be accused in the future was not encouraging. That same afternoon Walter White, the executive secretary of the NAACP, sent another cable to MacArthur, urging reconsideration of its decision, and said:

> Examination of courts martial records indicates many convicted under circumstances making impartial justice improbable.

He also forwarded a memorandum of twenty-three cases of individual soldiers, and requested a conference between General MacArthur, the Inspector General, and myself. On December 24, MacArthur cabled that there was "no objection" to such a conference.

Immediately after my arrival in Tokyo on January 14, General MacArthur ordered that I be given the fullest cooperation from everyone under his command. My work was to be carried on through the office of the Inspector General. The most complete cooperation possible was forthcoming throughout my stay.

I must emphasize that every consideration was shown me. But it helped reveal how little consideration had been given to men who had risked their lives for their country.

All the condemned men were confined in a stockade outside Tokyo. I was permitted to see every man I wanted to, as many times as I liked, and with complete privacy. Altogether, I saw about eighty men. I talked to Lt. Gilbert half a dozen times, and to some of the others several times. It was possible to get each man's story, as he wanted to tell it, asking him to explain any questionable or obscure details. All the information which had been lacking in the courts-martial records became available for checking—names of witnesses, dates, times of day, places—everything a defense lawyer should have when a man's life is at stake.

FURTHER INVESTIGATION

Each day a list of all points which warranted further investigation was submitted to the Inspector General. Inquiry into these detailed points would begin that very day, so that this checking process moved along only a few days behind my questioning.

I then went back and did my own checking on stories that did not quite fit together. In this way it was possible to separate hearsay from facts. It helped distinguish exaggerated statements from the facts, and to document these facts whenever possible.

In many cases, charges were made or strengthened by officers whose statements in the records of the trials called for extremely careful checking. It wasn't possible for some of the things they said to be true. And yet, to find out where they now were required use of the Locator File in the huge six-story Dai Ichi building which was MacArthur's Far East Command headquarters. I hate to think how many times it turned out that the officer had been killed in action. Back in August, September, and October of 1950 the casualty rate was horribly high.

After three weeks of this process, I made a preliminary report to General MacArthur and General Hickey, his chief of staff. This was at a conference in the Dai Ichi building at night. I told them what had been found so far in my investigation, what I believed to be the cause of these courts-martial trials, and who, in my opinion, was to blame.

WENT TO KOREA

Then I told General MacArthur I wanted to go to Korea, and they made arrangements for the same complete cooperation that had been given to me in Tokyo.

All through my inquiry in Korea I was allowed to see anybody I needed to see. From the beginning to the end of that part of my trip a Deputy Inspector General, Colonel D. D. Martin, accompanied me. With his authority and with my published orders from MacArthur, we could open any door. And we did. Whenever I could more easily get what was needed by myself, I would arrange to go alone. This was wholly satisfactory to Colonel Martin.

Since the 24th Infantry Regiment is part of the 25th Division, which is a part of the 8th Army, we first flew to the 8th Army headquarters in Korea. There I talked with officers at the top level and men in the lower echelons to get some further idea of what was going on.

Next we went to the 25th Division, where we had talks with General Keane and the men attached to Division headquarters. A whole day was spent getting the stories of the officers who served as defense counsel in the courts-martial cases. Although it is obvious to any lawyer that the cases were prepared in extreme haste, not a single one of these men would admit he did not have sufficient time to prepare his cases properly.

Their legal abilities cannot be questioned. The letter of the military law was observed in nearly every instance.

WHAT HAPPENED

What actually happened in virtually every case was that a defendant would be confronted by two officers, who told him they were assigned to serve as his counsel.

Then, observing the letter of military law, they would tell the prisoner, *"You are allowed to choose your own counsel if there is anyone you prefer."*

"Then I want Captain A," the accused man would say.

They'd be sorry, but Captain A was busy right now in a fire fight with North Korean forces on the Main Line of Resistance. His company needed him.

"What about Lieutenant B?" the prisoner would ask.

It was regrettable, but Lieutenant B was up on a ridge with his platoon and could not possibly be disturbed because the enemy was threatening to engulf the whole situation. While the accused man was assured of counsel of his choice, the court-assigned counsel advised him to choose them. The trial was going to begin very shortly. He's been charged with a serious offense, and he needed counsel. Captain A and Lieutenant B were away, and they—the two assigned-counsel—were right there. So was the trial.

In numerous instances the counsel spent no more than fifteen or twenty minutes with the men about to be tried. There were cases when a man was pulled out of a foxhole—told to get his blanket, get dressed and ride to Pusan. He'd arrive in Pusan in the middle of the night, be allowed to go to sleep for a while on the court-room floor, only to wake up for his trial to be held then and there.

Since these officers had no wish to endanger their careers, they certainly were not going to concede that there had been insufficient time to prepare the cases properly.

MAIN QUESTION

The following day we rode by jeep to the rear headquarters of the 24th Infantry Regiment. Although this area was called "in the rear" you could hear our artillery firing way behind you. Later we went up to the forward headquarters, where you use a jeep without any springs so as not to mar the accuracy of the 35 and 50 caliber machine guns mounted on them. We were all issued weapons, since an estimated one thousand guerillas were still at large in the country we went through. The cold air was raw and biting, but we used an uncovered jeep, because the officers with us preferred to be in the open, where they were more likely to see what they ran into on all sides.

It became apparent that we would have to consult the official records to prove what had actually happened to the regiment during those three months last summer and fall. The files we needed were kept at the 25th Division's rear. We hitch-hiked a ride back to Pusan, far behind the lines, then took another jeep to—(place withheld, by military request). There we found the Division Judge Advocate's office.

In a single room were the investigating reports, military order, and complete files of courts-martial records. Anything connected with any case was available for scrutiny. Here was the precise information, available nowhere else on earth, affecting the condemned soldiers.

The 24th Infantry had been up in the front lines for 93 straight days. Two white regiments were also fighting as long, one of them for 95 days. During that time the ratio of troops of the entire 25th Division serving in Korea, by race, was one Negro to 3.6 white men.

OFFICERS WHITE

The 24th Regiment was the same kind of Negro regiment the Army has maintained since 1865. All enlisted men were Negroes, but for the most part the officers above the level of lieutenant were white. As was apparent from my visits to the Locator File in Tokyo, the casualty rate for these officers and their replacements were extremely high. Although many of these officers were dead, they and many of their successors were responsible for the facts revealed by a comparative table drawn up to show how differently Negro and white defendants were treated by courts-martial proceedings.

A court martial begins with a complaint—usually made by an officer. The commanding officer either arrests the man or allows him to go free. An investigation, by another designated officer, ascertains whether the official charges are well founded.

In the 25th Division, between the time of Lt. Gilbert's conviction on September 6 and my visit in late February, there was a total of 118 complaints filed for all types of offenses. Of these, 82 resulted in trials, the rest being either withdrawn or dropped.

Out of the 82 cases which resulted in general court-martial trials 54 were Negroes, 27 were white, and one was Japanese. In these 82 cases, 66 were investigated by white officers and 16 were investigated by Negro officers.

Most of the charges filed against Negroes—60 of them—were for violation of the 75th Article of War, misbehavior in the presence of the enemy. This means cowardice. In Army life there is no more serious charge.

In the files were complaints against white soldiers for sleeping on their posts during guard duty, up on the front lines within spitting distance of the enemy. But they were not charged with any violation of the 75th Article of War. They were charged with sleeping on their posts. White boys were charged with leaving a sentry post and sleeping on duty who did not even put up a defense, and they were acquitted. One man was found wrapped up in a blanket sound asleep. In this case, his commanding officer testified, *"I saw him there and he was sleeping."* One witness testified he didn't *think* the man was asleep. Other witnesses took the stand all saying the boy was asleep. One sergeant testified, *"I was right there. I not only saw him, but I heard him. If he wasn't sleeping, he was snoring while wide awake."*

This accused soldier was acquitted, found not guilty.

100 PERCENT WHITE

Was it a coincidence that all the commanding officers who approved charges were white, that the entire staffs of the Inspector General's office, and of the trial Judge Advocate's office were 100 percent white? Was it also purely coincidental that one week before my visit to Korea a Negro was added to each of these two staffs?

Here is a summary of the actual results of courts-martial in Korea for alleged violation of the 75th Article of War:

	Negro	**White**
Charges withdrawn	23	2
Charges reduced to AWOL	1	0
Acquittals	4	4
Sentenced	32	2
	60	8

These are the sentences given to the defendants:

	Negro	**White**
Death	1	0
Natural life	15	0
50 years	1	0
25 years	2	0
20 years	3	0
15 years	1	0
10 years	7	0
5 years	2	1
3 years	0	1
	32	2

The white defendant who got the worst sentence (five years) offered as his defense that he was a chronic drunkard, but this sentence has been since reduced to one year.

The investigation reports, all kept as official records by the Army, revealed that no credence was ever given to the story each individual accused man would tell. The investigating officers totally ignored the statements of the men about to be charged with the worst offenses in the Army code. Scant effort was made to find out what was true and what was not. I had not only talked to these men, but had the benefit of the investigations made by the Judge Advocate's office to check what stories could be proved.

THE MEN

And what actually had happened? Who were the individuals condemned to serve out their lives in army prisons, or endure terms of 10, 15, 20, 25 and 50 years at hard labor for being cowards?

One boy convicted of cowardice had enlisted when he was fifteen. He remained in that bloody, frozen Korean fighting without telling anybody he was under age, knowing full well that he could at any time be returned to the United States as a hero. This coward remained in the front lines of his own free choice until he was confronted with court-martial charges. We checked, and found he told the truth. His 18th birthday occurred 11 days after his court martial convicted him of being a coward.

One unit of the 159th Field Artillery consisting of Negro enlisted men and white officers was in a river bed, where it was very peaceful and quiet. It was so quiet that the officers went back to town that evening. At fifteen minutes after midnight, enemy mortar shells dropped down on that unit in rapid succession. There was considerable confusion.

The captain in charge of the unit gave the command to Close Station and March Order. Artillerymen do not expect to have enough time to spell out every word in such a situation. The specific order is given by the letters, CSMO. When an officer says CSMO, he means *Get Ready to Get Out*.

They coupled the guns to vehicles called prime movers, a kind of big truck. None of the court-martial testimony is disputed except the application of the CSMO order. The captain admitted he gave it, but says it was for only one gun crew to move out and not the other batteries. He further admitted that his commanding officer had instructed him over the field telephone, "*Don't issue any order. You stay there and fight.*"

Even though the batteries were all coupled up to leave, the word was given to uncouple and get back to firing shells. One gun crew of fourteen Negroes, however, had heard the order CSMO and had moved out too fast to get the new order. Twelve men were back the very next morning, even though the battery had moved to a new position that night. The other two men reported to duty shortly afterward. Even with the emergency CSMO order they had all taken the trouble to learn the location of their new firing position.

CONFUSION COMPOUNDED

The commanding officer told them that there had been so much confusion and misunderstanding that nobody knew what was going on. They were to forget about the incident, to go back to work and fight the war. And so the fourteen men forgot about it and were back on duty as before. Nevertheless, even though every one of the fourteen men had returned, charges of misbehavior were made subsequently.

Two of the men were court martialed. Three others, who testified for the two soldiers on trial, were also court martialed. At the two trials the captain gave three distinctly different stories under oath as to what had happened.

It is safe to say that this captain did not know what had happened. He was confused. I talked with him and he still does not know what happened. But he has been promoted to Major, while five Negroes are in prison. Three of them are serving twenty years at hard labor and two of them received life sentences for "misconduct in the presence of the enemy."

As General MacArthur indicated in his cable to Walter White, when he first vetoed my visit overseas, under any decent system a man is treated as an individual. The terrible thing about these trials was the hopeless feeling common to every individual defendant. They felt they had no chance. The files showed these trials were held without any respect for the rights of individuals. The courts-martial were carried out with efficient haste, almost as on an assembly line. As many as four cases in a single day were tried, running on through the night, with all concerned anxious to get them over with.

QUICK JUSTICE

In four cases the trials which sentenced men to life imprisonment ran 42 minutes, 44 minutes, and the other two for 50 minutes each. This included the entire process of hearing the charges read, swearing in witnesses, examining all the evidence presented, hearing arguments (if any), explaining to the men their rights under the manual of courts-martial, the recess periods, discussion by the court and pronouncing sentence. Other trials ran an hour or an hour and ten minutes. I have seen many miscarriages of justice in the my capacity as head of the NAACP legal department. But even in Mississippi a Negro will get a trial longer than 42 minutes, if he is fortunate enough to be brought to trial.

The men in the stockade had a common feeling of hopelessness. Some men with air-tight defenses had not presented evidence clearly demonstrating their innocence of the charges. Time and again I would ask them, *"Why didn't you tell your lawyer what really happened? Why didn't you tell the court? Why didn't you tell somebody?"*

Even though each man is an individual in the eyes of God and under our Constitution, these individuals gave me the same answer. *"It wasn't worth trying. We knew when we went in there we were all going to come out the same way. Each one of us hoped and prayed we would only get life. They gave that officer, Lt. Gilbert, death, only because he is a Negro. What did you expect them to give a Negro enlisted man? We know what the score is."*

Such a spirit of hopelessness will strip away from any man the ability to defend himself adequately. One particular sergeant imprisoned in the stockade outside Tokyo was representative of the devotion we have come to associate with our armed forces. Under fire in Korea three of his commanding officers were killed in a period of two days. This man had kept his company together. He did not lose a single wounded man in ninety days. He brought every injured man out, sometimes on his own back. He saw to it that his men received hot food, regularly, which he took up to them at the remoter points along the firing line. One after another he saw his friends killed, but refused to be relieved. Day in and day out, he kept on fighting, several times in command of the entire company because there weren't officers around.

BATTLE FATIGUE

This sergeant is charged with wilful disobedience of an order. When he was charged, when he talked to his lawyer, when he went into the courtroom, during the trial, and even after the sentence he never told any of them that right in his pocket was a slip from a doctor, a medical corps captain, certifying that this man was suffering from battle fatigue and should be returned to the rear for treatment. He never told anyone about this slip until he talked to me. I called the captain of the guard immediately and asked to have the sergeant's belongings searched. In the condemned man's wallet, taken away from him with the rest of his personal effects upon his reception at the stockade, was the slip of paper.

"Why didn't you tell them? I asked.

"It wasn't worth it," he said. *"It wouldn't help me. You saw what happened to Sergeant B —, didn't you, when you talked with him? Sergeant B—put in as evidence the official record book kept by the Army hospital showing he was there on the days they charged him with being away from duty. The court didn't pay any attention to it. They are not paying attention to anything we say."*

There were men who were punished more than once for the same alleged offense. Four Negro soldiers were attached to a mess hall miles behind the front lines. When they finished work one day, their sergeant told them they could go off and do what they liked. They told me it was customary to drive a jeep to a place where showers had been set up. When they returned from their shower the sentry told them there was supposed to be no movement in that section, but they could drive around by the road to the back part of the mess-hall area.

These men were picked up on the road going to Pusan. They said they were lost. When these men were brought in by the M.P.'s, their commanding officer said, *"You fellows have had easy jobs behind the lines, but you haven't appreciated it. For your punishment, I am going to put you in the front lines."*

Perhaps this captain was right. He put two of these men in a heavy mortar outfit and two others with a machine-gun unit. They were in fierce front-line fighting for twenty-one days and twenty-one nights. Perhaps they deserved this, since other men had been on prolonged duty in battle without mess-hall duty behind the lines or shower baths after work.

Their record in battle was never questioned. But these four men were pulled out, brought back and court martialed for violation of the 75th Article of War because of the incident that had happened three weeks before, miles behind the lines. They were sentenced to twenty years each for misbehavior before the enemy. The only crime which they could conceivably be charged with involved the use of a jeep, without permission, which has not yet been charged against them.

OFFICER BEHAVIOR

How could officers of our Army behave in such a way? The official records proved that they did, but the explanation for their behavior was still lacking. My last Sunday in Korea was spent at a very forward position of the 24th Infantry Regiment, where I talked to the key man in every company of the regiment and of the 159th Field Artillery battery. These men knew what was behind these courts-martial operations.

The Regiment's forward positions were then moved north of Seoul. They had just taken an airstrip six hours before we got there.

These soldiers were survivors of the action occurring prior to and during the three months of courts-martial. There was one man whose father had been in the regiment for twenty years, and he's been in it for nine. I talked to about seventy of these veterans, asking them to tell me what had been going on last summer and fall.

One after another, they all said the same thing. The regiment's morale had been at a disastrously low ebb. Their white officers were in many instances Southerners who had brought their prejudices with them when assigned to duty with the 24th Infantry.

Time and again these officers told the men whom they were going to order into battle, *"I despise nigger troops. I don't want to command you or any other niggers. This Division is no good, and you are lousy. You don't know how to fight."*

I cannot imagine a worse situation in combat, where a man does not care what happens to those serving under him. There is no way to make the soldiers care less what is going to happen to the outcome of the fighting, or to their officers.

CASUALTIES HIGH

The casualty rates among the enlisted men and officers was disproportionately high. And how could it not help but be high, when you are following such leaders? This wasn't told about one officer, but about several, by fighting men who were not court martialed and certainly had no reason to tell anything but the truth.

This explained these courts-martial proceedings to me. I think the high rate of casualties among officers made it necessary to assign the blame. The answer was a wholesale conviction of Negro soldiers who had survived this prejudiced leadership.

When I talked to the men that Sunday, morale in the 24th Infantry was certainly high. They had a new commanding officer, Colonel John T. Corley. They were proud of his having earned more battlefield decorations than any officer in the active Army. He respects them, and every man with whom I talked admired him. They repeatedly told me how, instead of ordering them forward into action, Colonel Corley goes out himself and commands, "Come!"

There are still some other officers in the regiment whom the men do not respect, and have little reason to respect. So long as that sort of officer is in command of jim-crow troops, we may expect the same pattern of injustice in the future. These soldiers are fighting and dying for us, who should see to it that they are not subjected to the kind of leadership which despises them.

MADE REPORT

I now had the information for a complete report to General MacArthur, with recommendations. According to Army procedure, MacArthur did not have official responsibility for the disposition of the individual courts-martial cases. After the trials were approved by the major general in command of the 25th Division, the records were forwarded for review to the Judge Advocate General's office in the Pentagon in Washington. There the NAACP has been representing the condemned men, and has already arranged for a number of the sentences to be reversed or reduced.

But in my report it was necessary to place the ultimate responsibility for these courts-martial squarely upon General Douglas MacArthur. He had both the authority and the responsibility for maintaining or ending racial segregation in the Army's Far East Command.

In the large headquarters staff of MacArthur's Far East Command at the time, in the Dai Ichi building, there were no Negroes except for three civilian clerks. This is but one of several buildings with thousands of army personnel; nowhere were there more than one out of four men fighting with the 25th Division in Korea [who] is a Negro American. There was a handsome, elite honor guard of crack riflemen which used to guard the headquarters and the person of MacArthur, but there was not a Negro among them. Headquarters had a football team, all white. There wasn't even a Negro in the headquarters band.

MACARTHUR RESPONSIBLE

This was General MacArthur's responsibility. He was at the time the Supreme Commander of American and United Nations troops then engaged in battle with a Communist enemy which seeks to divide us from the rest of the world. The Communists preach and propagandize how Americans abuse colored people, and MacArthur had allowed discrimination in his own headquarters. Negro troops in Korea are not succumbing to the Communist propaganda any more than they believed the Germans in the last war. They see how the Communists are killing Negroes as thoroughly as they are killing others.

Major General Doyle O. Hickey, who was MacArthur's chief of staff, told me that the General was aware of these things and that a study was being made to find ways and means for correcting them. I told him that the United States Air Force took just one day to end segregation. They gave a single order, and the Air Force is now an integrated, American body of men using the best efficiency and skill each man can provide in his country's service.

Three blocks down Avenue A from the Dai Ichi building is the Far East Air Force headquarters. Negroes work alongside white soldiers there in the guard, in the offices, wherever they are capable of doing good work. The first time I went by the Air Force building there were two guards of the Air Police standing at attention. One happened to be white; the other was colored. And after the Dai Ichi building, it was a very pleasant experience to see the guard being checked by the Sergeant of the Guard, who on that day happened to be a Negro. The same policy is now in force in the U.S. Navy.

I told General MacArthur that if the Air Force and the Navy, both drawing men from the same forces as the Army, frequently from the same families, have done this without any disadvantageous results, there was no reason why the Army couldn't do it. The Army is eliminating segregation in other places, and the Far East Command has no special problems which would place it at an extra disadvantage. It is disgraceful to have the Japanese clerks in the canteens told to discriminate against Negro service men during their five day recreation rotation from Korea.

In every war in which this country has participated, Negro Americans have had to fight for the right to fight. At the start of each war, military leaders have questioned the Negro's abilities and finally accepted Negro participation under the pressure of necessity.

Although 920,000 Negroes served in the Army during the Second World War, the Army didn't take most of them until manpower shortages impelled their acceptance, using them for menial jobs wherever possible. These men were treated as inferiors in southern training camps. The great majority were used for arduous, dirty work overseas, but they covered themselves with glory just the same.

To date, the Cold War has erupted into violent action in one area, the Far East. There we face the potential enmity of hundreds of millions of men whose skins are not white, who look with extreme care to see how white men feel about colored peoples.

The NAACP believes that the men and women in our Armed Services shall have first preference on our time and efforts. But we are not only a group of Americans seeking *correction* of vicious practices and for the survival of this country, we also work to prevent injustice. The best way to accomplish this in our Armed Services is to work to bring about complete abolition of segregation now.

To date the legal department of the NAACP has secured reduction of sentence for twenty of these soldiers, but we have just begun. The NAACP is working to secure the appropriate exoneration or abbreviation of sentence for every man treated unjustly because of his race or color.

12. Remarks at a Testimonial Dinner Honoring Raymond Pace Alexander, November 25, 1951

Raymond Pace Alexander was a prominent African American lawyer in Philadelphia, who practiced law with his wife Sadie Tanner Mossell Alexander. Their law practice combined representation of African Americans (and some whites) in typical civil cases with a substantial amount of civil rights work, including the Berwyn case to which Marshall refers, which involved a challenge by African American parents to the creation of a segregated school in a Philadelphia suburb. Marshall mentions Alexander's work defending the Trenton Six, initially convicted of murder and sentenced to death. The convictions were reversed in 1949, and at the retrial four were acquitted and two convicted. The latter convictions were reversed again in 1952, and eventually only one of the initial defendants was convicted. During the course of the litigation, the NAACP and its lawyers repeatedly clashed with representatives of the Civil Rights Congress, a left-wing group which the NAACP regarded as a Communist front, over the use of publicity as a way of preventing the executions. Marshall also refers to the Groveland case, involving several African Americans charged with raping a white woman. The defendants were nearly lynched before their trial. The Supreme Court reversed their convictions in 1951. The day before a new trial was to begin, Willis McCall, the local sheriff, shot and killed one defendant, and seriously injured another. The survivor was convicted and sentenced to death; his sentence was commuted by governor Leroy Collins in 1955.

Looking at this program, I am in a spot I have always wanted to be in since I first entered law school. And now I admit I am afraid I am a coward. I always wanted to have the last say after a whole bunch of judges.

You know, I have so much on my mind and all, as I said before, I don't think I will take the chance. I am pretty glad to be here tonight. I was afraid one time I wouldn't make it. I went way down south to Louisiana where it is nice and warm, after leaving Florida where it is nice and warm. It was forty in Florida and thirty in Louisiana. I came up north to Chicago on Thursday. It is ten up there today.

So I am in the land of sunshine at last. The reason I am very glad to be here tonight is because I have already noticed friends of the Alexanders from Washington, Baltimore, New York, New Jersey. We have been talking about it as I have been getting around the country since this affair was first thought of. It is awful good to get together on an occasion like this one.

It is of particular importance to me, because I feel it is my job to say publicly what the practicing lawyers think about the Alexanders. When I started out batting my head up against the wall, I had been hearing a lot about Alexander. I heard he was a great lawyer. Very early I heard about the Berwyn School case and all of the later school cases with all of the publicity carried around with them. I'll bet a lot of people here in this audience have forgotten about that case.

Now I want to say this, and I want to say it at the very beginning, the same as a very powerful man in Trenton, New Jersey, said about Alexander after the case, the Trenton Six case. He asked me what kind of a lawyer he was, and I told him. I told him I thought he was at least one of the greatest trial lawyers in this country today. He was at least one of the greatest. And after about a month of the trial of that case, I talked to the same man—and he knew what had been going on, incidentally—and he told me I was at best only half right, because Alexander was the best trial lawyer he knew about.

It is very much my position here tonight. I thought he was one of the best, but I am convinced that, for actually trying a case, you can't beat the fellow. Now the reason I said that is because while those of you in this audience who are not lawyers, there are some here who have had brushes with lawyers. And the reason I said, when I was in law school and in my early practice, that Raymond was one of the best was because when you are fresh out of law school, there is nobody, but nobody, as good as you are. You are definitely the smartest and the best.

However, even at that, we considered in school Alexander standing out for something. That has meant a lot to the lawyers in this country. I want to be perfectly frank about one other thing. The thing that has made me feel so good tonight, and I don't know about the others of us, but not one person has referred to Raymond Pace Alexander as a great Negro lawyer, and I am very happy to see that progress. He has been talked about as a lawyer, standing on his merits just as any other lawyer, and being measured just like any other lawyer.

Negro lawyers, as a group, have had a tough time. My good friend, Judge Brown, has been telling you the jokes and the stories they tell about lawyers characterizing all in the group in the same level. That is bad for a lawyer. That is bad for any lawyer, but it is doubly bad for a Negro lawyer because he also suffers from the other one, that all Negroes are thieves and cannot be trusted. And so Negro lawyers, and I can see some out in the audience that have been fighting in this field a long time, they know exactly what I am talking about.

In this Trenton Six case—I am going to talk about it—the main reason I came here tonight is I wanted to talk about it. The reason I want to talk about it is because of the result of high-powered efforts of some people, not enough has been said about the part that Raymond Pace Alexander had in this case. He was one of the lawyers. He has a pretty good batting average on that case. He represented two men and got two men off. And I say publicly, and I will repeat it, that because of his efforts, partly at least, two of the others got off.

He didn't do it selfishly. He fought for all of them at the same time. And whenever I talk about the Trenton Six case tonight, I want you to know, and I know Raymond wants it to be known because he said so too often, that he had with him the help of two other lawyers—Clifford Moore of Trenton, New Jersey, and Mercer Burrell of Newark—who assisted him throughout the trial.

I also want you to know that when the NAACP Executive Committee of the Board picked Alexander for this case and decided to ask him if he would take it, because they believed he was the only man that could handle that case, I remember a "friend" of our association called and said that "you should have some other lawyer to represent the NAACP."

I said, "Well, we have already decided to ask him. I don't know whether he will take it or not."

He said, "That will be all right, Alexander can work under him."

I said, "I don't quite understand that. This lawyer you mentioned might be acceptable to Alexander to work under him, but Alexander is not the working-under type."

From the reputation that I get, from what I know about Alexander, after he has been working on a case for a week or so the judge is usually working under him, too. I don't mean your Philadelphia judges.

I mean judges outside the state. I don't want you to come running back to me on this, Raymond.

I called Mrs. Alexander and talked to both of them. The question was what would happen to the office while he was over there. The two of them together decided that it would and could be done because it had to be done.

And then I think this is another step in civil rights cases of this type. There have been some outfits operating in this country that believe the way to handle these cases was to go into the local community, spit on the door of the courthouse, cuss at the judge and raise holy cain—and, incidentally, get the men electrocuted—but as I understand it, the best way to try a case of this type is to try to get the men out in the first instance.

That is good for two reasons: number one, the defendants would prefer it that way.

That is one point. And they would prefer to get out, and "b", they would prefer to get out as soon as they can. The other point is that you educate the local community. You'd be surprised about the education a local community gets out of the trial of a case that is tried properly with courage, and yet in the good tradition of the legal profession, not where a bunch of lawyers or one lawyer takes it upon themselves to see just how hard they can whip on the judge and how hard they can whip on the jury.

There are some groups that would put their clients in jail or the electric chair in order to ease or build up their own ego or to be able to give foreign governments something they can yell about. That is what we have been up against.

In the Trenton Six case, the Civil Rights Congress collected all the money they could find to collect every place they could find to collect it, and they paid on everything but the case. And I give you as witnesses to that the three lawyers who tried the cases, who said they didn't get a red nickel out of it. But the community had been well gone over financially.

So when the NAACP came into the case, and the Princeton Committee came into the case, it was a question of getting blood out of the turnip. We got together, the two organizations, and we agreed to let them have our fund raiser, and we raised as much money as we could raise under the circumstances. All of that money has been spent on the case. That money hasn't been spent on billboards advertising the NAACP. It hasn't been spent on shipping members of the organization all over the world on high-powered leaflets. It hasn't been spent on high-powered petitions that the jury will never read nor the court. It hasn't been spent on anything but the case.

The branch in New Jersey raised all the money they could raise. That money went on the case, and all of that money has been put on the case, and there are a couple hundred bucks left, somewhere between three and four hundred dollars, if I remember correctly. And as soon as the certified public accountants complete the audit of the books on that case, the rest of that money will be put on the appeal for the two boys, and the public audit will be released to the newspapers.

Now I say all of that for this reason; these civil rights cases are not cases of the lawyer alone. Alexander, as much as he wants to do it, could not leave his office that long for absolutely nothing. Even with what he got, he made a sacrifice. I know he did. I know the whole office made a sacrifice. Because as the top man of the law firm, his time is supposed to be worth enough money so as to keep things moving. We couldn't pay him what he was worth, but we had to get together enough money, as much as we could, and make an honest break about it.

That is where the people come in. These civil rights cases now need the support of everyone. We are getting the support. I remember way back when these cases first started we couldn't get support from anybody. We couldn't get support from the other lawyers, if you please. Now we can get that support.

I want to tell you something about the future of the case. It wasn't a question of Alexander just trying a law suit. One of the judges mentioned that a minute ago. He lived that case. I am not just saying it because he is a fellow lawyer. You can't appreciate it unless you are a lawyer. That man's got energy that I don't know where it comes from. I mean day in and day out, work, work, work, never giving it up, matching wits with the best of the State of New Jersey, the best they could produce, and licking them every step of the way. They had the whole State of New Jersey with all their experts at their beck and call—anything they wanted. They'd just call up and get it.

If Alexander wanted something, and if Burrell and Moore couldn't get it, the three of them had to go find some way to get it; and operating on peanuts with that. So when you talk about honoring a great lawyer, I just have to get down to the details about it.

So many of us read about the Trenton Six case and said, "Wasn't that fine, Alexander got the two men off yesterday" or "Alexander got the two men off this morning."

How many of you in this audience thought about the six months it took to get them off? How many of you thought about it? You thought he got them off yesterday. It is not that simple. By the time that case was over, he didn't know hardly where he was going. Because with this matching wits, you match wits backwards and forwards day in and day out, you'll be surprised what it takes out of you. But he did it. That's not the only case he has handled. He is an old hand at this civil rights— yes, old—hand at this business.

You were out of law school before I was. Old man. But he is young enough for us to talk about the future. Just for a minute I would like to talk about the future. Civil rights: what lawyers are going to do about it; what lawyers like Alexander are going to do about it.

In the first place, the more cases that are won, the tougher the opposition will get. Simple and true. And the boys are getting rough again. I know that Alexander felt kind of funny, and I know every lawyer in this audience interested in civil rights felt kind of funny when in that Cicero case the grand jury of Cook County indicted George Layton, a lawyer, for the simple reason that George Layton advised his clients, a Negro family, advised them to move into the property that they had leased. He was indicted for that. I know you must have shuddered. I know a whole lot of people shuddered, because any lawyer worth his salt has had to do that over and over again, to advise people to exercise their rights. And the Cook County grand jury thought that that was a crime.

Fortunately, a lot of pressure and other things, well, the district attorney decided not to prosecute. He thought it would be much easier to leave it lay where it happened to be.

Or take down in Groveland, Florida, where, like the Trenton Six case, it started out as four and is now two. The Groveland, Florida, case started out as four. It is now two. Rather it is now one. One boy is in jail serving a life sentence, but there is only one left to be tried, because the sheriff down there thought he would do a little executing on the side, Willis McCall.

That was a call that came in about three o'clock one morning. A local lawyer called up and said, "Well, we don't have anymore case, because you don't have anymore defendants. They were killed tonight by the sheriff."

Fortunately one of the boys lived. Nobody understands why. Nobody understands how. The sheriff pulls them both out of the car, and they are both handcuffed, and the sheriff says that they attacked him, two men handcuffed together with no weapon. He is standing back there with a thirty-eight, and they attacked him. And in self-defense he had to shoot each of them three times. He shot Shepherd twice in the chest and once in the head. He died immediately. Walter Irvin was shot twice in the chest and once in the neck and laid there bleeding for over an hour in the ditch and lived and will live despite the fact that he still has one shot in him they can't even take out yet. But he is going to live.

The interesting thing on that case is I talked to the two families. The Shepherd family is as cool as anybody. They actually appeared to be relieved. The Irvin family is most jittery, very worried. The Shepherd family has no more worry. Their son is dead. The Irvin family, because of the fact that this boy, their boy, happened to live, still will have to go on trial, and under the perfectly normal circumstances, will have to go to the electric chair because a white woman said he raped her.

So as we talk about civil rights, things like that, let's not think that the job is anywhere over. I left Groveland and went over to Louisiana to a teacher's meeting and found that, the night before, the deputy sheriff in Opelousas had shot and killed a Negro who had filed a suit to register in that county to vote. You know, there are places in this country where it is not a means of protecting your civil rights, you just don't have any.

So that tonight it seems to me that we have two very important jobs to do. We honor Raymond Pace Alexander. We honor Sadie Alexander, and we honor them because of what they have represented so long in this fight for civil rights. And in doing so, we pause to pay honor where honor is due, and at the same time we look ahead at the job that we have yet to do.

In all seriousness, I say to my friends that he has just started. We have that much more to do. I hope we won't listen at any time to what I heard in New York this summer. I heard a big New York official, who happened to be a Negro, stand on a platform and tell some visiting delegates to a convention that the Negroes in New York no longer had any problems concerning civil rights or segregation. That always worries me as to whether at times we have a feeling that well, it is not so bad. But take it from me, I can guarantee one thing about this area. There won't be another Trenton Six case, as such, for quite a while. Before they lay charges against six Negroes like they did in that case with nothing to stand up on, and as long as they know that there is a certain lawyer hanging around someplace loose who might be over, they won't try them that way again.

The people in New Jersey will tell you what that case means to them. Oh, it didn't clean the situation up. No one case will ever clean the situation up. But it slows them down. That is the thing one lawyer recognizes in another lawyer.

Alexander, when he tries a case, has an ability to so ingratiate himself with the entire court, so that apparently without effort, the court and the jury are convinced that Alexander is their very great friend—which is not exactly true. This is not for the judges of Philadelphia. This is when Alexander is practicing outside of Philadelphia. Although Alexander gives the impression that he is helping the court and the jury, never you fear, Alexander is protecting the rights of his client.

That, my friends, is a job of a true advocate, to put your client up above everything else, and to do it in such as fashion as to get the respect of everyone else.

We could stay here tonight and hear talk after talk. We could hear them say word after word. You will never be able to get anyone to adequately express the appreciation of the people who believe in civil rights, and especially the lawyers who believe in civil rights, for the man who has meant so much to so many people. I, for one, on behalf of the NAACP, on behalf of the members of the bar throughout this country, those who I happen to know, and I am certain that I can speak for that group, the lawyers who are seriously interested in civil rights, I say to Raymond Pace Alexander, and I say to his wife, another lawyer in her own right, and I say to all of you that you are an honor to our profession. We are proud of you, but boy, you've got a lot more work still to do.

13. An Evaluation of Recent Efforts to Achieve Racial Integration in Education Through Resort to the Courts
Journal of Negro Education, vol. 21 (1952)

This article provides a fairly comprehensive survey of the NAACP's efforts to eliminate segregation in education. It includes a description of the lower court decisions in the cases brought to the Court as *Brown v. Board of Education.*

In order to evaluate recent efforts to achieve racial integration in education through legal action, it is necessary first to consider the legal background of these cases. There are three distinct periods to be considered. The period between 1896 and 1930; the period between 1930 and 1945; and the period from 1945 to date.

1896–1930 PERIOD

The Supreme Court in 1896 in the case of *Plessy v. Ferguson* involving the validity of a statute of Louisiana requiring segregation in intrastate transportation used certain state cases upholding segregation in public education as the basis for its decision upholding the statute. This decision started the "separate but equal" doctrine. During the period between 1896 and 1930, this separate-but-equal doctrine became ingrained in our case law through a lack of carefully planned legal action. Many cases were decided in state and Federal courts during that period; and almost without exception these courts cited with approval the separate-but-equal doctrine. The important point to be considered during this period is that no effort was made in any of these cases to present to the court testimony and other evidence aimed at challenging the validity of these segregation statues in these states. A good example of this is the case of *Gong Lum v. Rice* in which the Supreme Court followed the separate-but-equal doctrine. An examination of the record and briefs in this case demonstrates that the Chinese complainant did not object to the segregation statutes of the State of Mississippi but objected to being assigned to the Negro school.

This period can be summed up for our purposes by recognizing that the separate-but-equal doctrine of *Plessy v. Ferguson* was set forth without critical analysis on the part of the Supreme Court and with a record which did not give them an opportunity to consider the question adequately. This doctrine established in a case involving intrastate transportation was seized upon and used by state and Federal courts in school cases again and again without any effort being made to analyze the legality of the segregation statutes involved. This separate-but-equal doctrine thus became a rule of law sacred and apparently beyond legal attack.

1930–1945 PERIOD

The N.A.A.C.P. in 1930 started the attack on the inequalities in public education. A special fund was set up to begin the campaign. A careful study was made by the late Nathan Margold. This study formed the groundwork for the first attack which was aimed at the professional school level. The late Charles H. Houston, armed with the Margold report, amplified this report and began the blueprint for the extended legal attack against the inequalities in public education. Many of Houston's associates and students at Howard University Law School worked closely with him on this new project.

The first case in this campaign was the *Hocutt* case against the law school of the University of North Carolina in 1933. This case was handled by William H. Hastie and Conrad O. Pearson. The case was lost on a technicality when the President of the Negro college in North Carolina refused to certify the scholastic record of the plaintiff in the case. Thus, the plaintiff was ineligible for admission to the law school.

This case was followed by the *Donald Murray* case which opened the law school of the University of Maryland in 1935 and the Gaines case against the law school of the University of Missouri in 1938. At that time the best overall strategy seemed to be an attack against the segregation system by law suits seeking absolute and complete equalization of curricula, faculty and physical equipment of the white and Negro schools on the theory that the extreme cost of maintaining two "equal" school systems would eventually destroy segregation.

It did not take long to discover that this approach would not produce the necessary results. Because of the unaccounted disappearance of Lloyd Gaines, the plaintiff in the Gaines case, that case could not be followed through and ended with the establishment of a Jim Crow law school at the University of Missouri. The *Bluford* case in Missouri which followed the *Gaines* case did not open the University of Missouri but ended with the establishment of a school of journalism at the Negro college. The cases against the University of Tennessee were lost on the highly technical point of failing to exhaust administrative remedies. The case against the University of Kentucky resulted in the establishment of a makeshift engineering course at the Negro college. So that, insofar as the university level was concerned, the only graduate or professional school opened to Negroes was the law school of the University of Maryland.

This campaign moved along slowly for three reasons: (1) There was a lack of full support from the Negro community in general; (2) few Negroes were interested enough to ask to be plaintiffs and; (3) there was a lack of sufficient money to finance the cases.

An evaluation of this period would be that it marked the beginning of the period of planned legal strategy against racial segregation. It was the beginning of the period of the closing of doors used by the courts in disregarding the fundamental principles of equality of law. The greatest gains from this period was the public education of school officials, the courts and the general public in the lawlessness of school officials in depriving Negroes of their constitutional rights. It is the period whereby all of us found by experience that the tangential approach to this legal problem did not produce results in keeping with time, effort and money expended.

This period is also noted for the cases to equalize the salaries of white and Negro public school teachers. The theory behind these cases was two-fold—one, it was hoped that these cases would add to the cost of the segregated school system and be an additional burden making segregation too costly to survive. At the same time, these cases were establishing the basic principle of equal pay for equal work without regard to race and color in the hope that these principles established in public school education would filter down into other phases of life and employment.

1945–1952 PERIOD

During the period between 1930 and 1945, this legal program was being checked and rechecked and was constantly being evaluated. It shortly became obvious that the only solution to the problem was an all out attack against segregation in public education so that by 1945 plans were ready for a direct attack on the validity of segregation statutes insofar as they applied to public education on the graduate and professional school level.

It appeared that the university level was the best place to begin a campaign that had as its ultimate objective the total elimination of segregation in public educational institutions in the United States. In the first place, at the university level no provision for Negro education was a rule rather than the exception. Then, too, the difficulties incident to providing equal educational opportunities even within the concept of the "separate-but-equal" doctrine were insurmountable. To provide separate medical schools, law schools, engineering schools and graduate schools with all the variety of offerings available at most state universities would be an almost financial impossibility. Even if feasible, it would be impractical to undertake such expenditures for the few Negroes who desired such training. It was felt, therefore, that if effort at this level was pressed with sufficient vigor many states would capitulate without extended litigation. Here also it was easy to demonstrate to the courts that separate facilities for Negroes could not provide equal training to that available in the state universities which for many years had been expanding and improving their facilities in an effort to compete with the great educational centers of the North and West.

The first case filed in this program was the Sweatt case against the law school of the University of Texas in 1946. When the case was first filed, the State of Texas assumed that it was a case seeking a separate-but-equal law school. Consequently, the Legislature met and merely changed the name of the Negro state college from Prairie View to "Prairie View University" without doing anything in the line of increased appropriations or building funds. After preliminary hearings on the case and after an amendment to the pleadings, it became evident that this case was actually making a direct attack on the segregation laws as they applied to the University of Texas. Upon discovering this, the same Texas Legislature reconvened and appropriated $2,600,000 plus $500,000 per annum to establish a brand new university for Negroes.

These two moves in and of themselves demonstrated that a direct attack on segregation would produce more in dollars and cents than the other method of seeking equal facilities. It was, therefore, clear, at least in Texas, that the new approach not only produced more education for Negroes than the other approach but also presented the opportunity to break down segregation itself at the same time.

As all of you know, the University of Texas set up a Jim Crow law school and made every effort to show that if it was not equal to the University of Texas law school insofar as physical facilities were concerned, it would be made equal in short order. During the trial of the *Sweatt* case, the first efforts were made to give to the court the necessary expert testimony to make a competent judgment of the validity of segregation statutes as applied to law schools. To do this, it was necessary to demonstrate that segregation of students on the basis of race was an unreasonable classification within the accepted rules for measuring classification statutes by the states. Experts in anthropology were produced and testified that given a similar learning situation a Negro student tended to react the same as any other student, and that there were no racial characteristics which had any bearing whatsoever to the subject of public education. Experts in the field of legal education testified that it was impossible for a Negro student to get an equal education in a Jim Crow law school because of the lack of opportunity to meet with and discuss their problems with other students of varying strata of society. These witnesses also testified that even if two law schools could be made absolutely equal insofar as physical facilities, equipment, curricula and faculties, the Jim Crow law school would nevertheless not offer an education equal to that offered at the other school for the reasons set forth above. Although the Texas courts refused to follow this testimony, the United States Supreme Court reversed these decisions and ordered Sweatt admitted to the law school of the University of Texas.

You also remember the *McLaurin* decision which was in many respects an even more clear-cut decision on the question of segregation. For in the *McLaurin* case, the plaintiff had the same teacher, the same curricula, was in the same building, and, as a matter of fact, was in the same classroom, although set apart from the other students.

It is significant that the decisions in both the *McLaurin* and *Sweatt* cases were unanimous. In the *Sweatt* case the court held: ". . . petitioner may claim his full constitutional right: legal education equivalent to that offered by the State to students of other races. Such education is not available to him in a separate law school as offered by the State. . . . We hold that the Equal Protection Clause of the Fourteenth Amendment required that petitioner be admitted to the University of Texas Law School." The *McLaurin* decision asserted:

> But they signify that the State, in administering the facilities it affords for professional and graduate study, sets McLaurin apart from the other students. The result is that appellant is handicapped in his pursuit of effective graduate instruction. Such restrictions impair and inhibit his ability to study, to engage in discussions and exchange views with other students, and, in general, to learn his profession. . . .

> We conclude that the conditions under which this appellant is required to receive his education deprive him of his personal and present right to the equal protection of the laws. See *Sweatt v. Painter*. We hold that under these circumstances the Fourteenth Amendment precludes differences in treatment by the state based upon race. Appellant, having been admitted to a state-supported graduate school, must receive the same treatment at the hands of the state as students of other races. The judgment is REVERSED.

What effect have these university cases had upon the general public? In the first place, it is significant that in each university case the local white student bodies have openly shown their willingness to accept Negro students. Despite dire predictions of horrible catastrophes by die-hard state officials, the admission of qualified Negroes has been smooth and without incident. For example, when the appeal of the University of Maryland case was pending the Attorney General of Maryland told the Maryland Court of Appeals that if Murray was admitted many white students would withdraw and there would be much trouble. Donald Murray was admitted and later testified in another case as follows:

> My experience, briefly, was that I attended the University of Maryland Law School for three years, during which time I took all of the classes with the rest of the students, and participated and at no time whatever did I meet any attempted segregation or unfavorable treatment on the part of any student in the school, or any professor or assistant professor.

When the *Sweatt* and *McLaurin* cases were pending in the Supreme Court the attorneys-general for the Southern States filed a joint brief alleging that: "The Southern States trust that this Court will not strike down their power to keep peace, order and support of their public schools by maintaining equal separate facilities. If the states are shorn of this police power and physical conflict takes place . . . the states are left with no alternative but to close their schools to prevent violence." What happened to this dire prediction? No schools have been closed. More than a thousand Negroes are now attending graduate and professional schools in the

South. Benjamin Fine recently reported in the New York *Times* that a survey made by him showed:

> This situation would have been considered impossible ten years ago. Responsible educators had warned that any breaching of the segregation line would prove dangerous and might even lead to campus or community riots. Today, these same officials report that the Negroes have not disturbed normal collegiate life in any manner.

In the recent case against the University of Tennessee, application was made for a special three-judge court to hear the attack against the validity of an order of the Trustees of the University of Tennessee excluding Negroes from admission. The three-judge court decided that the attack could not be made on the validity of the order of the University of Tennessee, or the statues of the State of Tennessee requiring segregation. The court therefore referred the case to a single judge for decision. The single judge held that the statutes and order were not in question and wrote an opinion upholding the right of Negroes to attend the University of Tennessee on the grounds that no other school had been furnished them. The original order of the three-judge court was appealed to the Supreme Court where during argument, the lawyers for the University of Tennessee stated in open court that the University had at last agreed to admit the Negro students. The Supreme Court stopped argument at this point and refused to hear any further argument from the petitioners. The Supreme Court subsequently issued an order vacating the judgment of the lower court and ordering the case dismissed as moot.[1] Although the action of the Supreme Court is far from clear, by vacating the order of the lower court the Supreme Court nullified a bad precedent of a decision denying the right to challenge the constitutionality of such orders and statutes.

While the right of Negroes to attend state graduate and professional schools has now been established, most Negroes who have received their early education in segregated schools are handicapped because their early training was inadequate and inferior. It became increasingly apparent that the supreme test would have to be made—an attack on segregation at the elementary and high school levels. Acceptance of segregation under the "separate but equal" doctrine had become so ingrained that overwhelming proof was sorely needed to demonstrate that equal educational opportunities for Negroes could not be provided in a segregated system.

It is relatively easy to show that a Negro graduate student offered training in a separate school, thrown up overnight, could not get an education equal to that available at the state universities. Public elementary and high schools, however, pres-

---

[1] A case is moot when a court's decision could have no effect on the parties' legal rights in the future. The Supreme Court therefore does not decide such cases because it has no opportunity to assess the legal correctness of the lower courts' decisions. The Court ordinarily directs that those decisions be vacated, or nullified, so that they will have no weight as precedent.

ent a more difficult basis for comparison. They are normally not specialized institutions with national or even statewide reputations. Public school teachers at these levels are not likely to gain eminence in the profession comparable to that of teachers in colleges and universities. For years, however, exposure of the evils of segregation and discrimination has come from social scientists, and their help was elicited for this phase of the campaign. Social scientists are almost in universal agreement that segregated education produces inequality. Studies have been made of the personality problems caused by discrimination and segregation and most social scientists have reached the conclusion that artificial and arbitrary barriers, such as race and color bars, are likely to have an adverse effect on the personality development of the individual. The energy and strength which the individual might otherwise use in the development of his mental resources is dissipated in adjustment to the problems of segregation.

Unfortunately, the effects of segregation in education have not been isolated for study by social scientists. They have dealt with the whole problem of segregation, discrimination and prejudice, and although no social scientist can say that segregated schools alone give the Negro feelings of insecurity, self-hate, undermine his ego, make him feel inferior and warp his outlook on life, yet for the child the school provides the most important contact with organized society. What he learns, feels, and how he is affected there is apt to determine the type of adult he will become. Social scientists have found that children at a very early age are affected by and react to discrimination and prejudices. Thus they have agreed that it is sound to conclude that segregated schools, perhaps more than any other single factor, are of major concern to the individual of public school age and contributes greatly to the unwholesomeness and unhappy development of the personality of Negroes which the color caste system in the United States has produced.

The elimination of segregation in public schools may not remove all of the causes of insecurity, self-hate, etc., among Negroes, but since this is a state-sponsored program, certainly the state, consistent with the requirements of the Fourteenth Amendment, should not be a party to a system which does help produce these results. This is the thesis which is now being used to demonstrate the unconstitutionality of segregation at the public elementary and high school levels.

Preliminary test cases in Virginia and Texas demonstrated the ineffectiveness of the failure to push for a clear-cut determination of the validity of the segregation statutes. I believe that an appraisal of these cases will show that their success was limited by the same difficulties as were encountered in the earlier university cases. After considerable and costly litigation and appeals, these cases ended in court orders limited to the equalization of physical facilities. These facilities in each instance were not equalized so that it was necessary to file motions for further relief to reopen the cases for a new determination of whether or not the Fourteenth Amendment was being complied with. It is significant that in these latter proceedings it was found necessary to make a frontal attack on the validity of segregated statutes.

The *Clarendon County School* case was the first test case to make a direct attack against segregation on the elementary and high school level. That case, which was tried in Charleston, South Carolina in May of last year, was based upon the theory that the *Sweatt* and *McLaurin* decisions have pointed the way toward consideration of the validity of segregation on all levels of education. In order to extend this principle it was necessary to produce equally competent testimony to show the unreasonableness of segregation and the impossibility of equality of Jim Crow education on the lower levels.

Therefore, in the *Clarendon County* case competent expert testimony was produced to show that segregation on the elementary and high school levels was just as unequal as segregated education on the graduate and professional school level when measured by the criteria set forth in the *Sweatt* and *McLaurin* decisions. In other words, competent expert testimony was produced to show in detail the injury to the Negro pupil attending the segregated schools in Clarendon County and to show that this injury was a permanent and continuing one which prevented the Negro child from obtaining an education equal to that obtained by other students. Of course, testimony was also produced to show that there was no reasonable basis for racial segregation in public education. Two of the three judges deciding this case held that despite this testimony the separate-but-equal doctrine was still a valid doctrine supported by decisions of the Supreme Court and that although the schools were not equal in physical facilities, the Negroes were entitled to equal facilities and they should be given equal physical facilities. The majority of the court therefore refused to enjoin enforcement of the segregation statutes of South Carolina but ordered that the physical facilities be equalized and ordered the school board to report within six months on this equalization of physical facilities. Judge J. Waties Waring, however, in a most vigorous dissenting opinion held that the segregation laws were unconstitutional and stated that segregation was per se unconstitutional. A direct appeal from the majority judgment was made to the United States Supreme Court where, on January 26, 1952, the United States Supreme Court issued an order vacating the judgment of the lower court and remanding the case to that court for a consideration of the report made by the school officials and any other additional facts in order that the district court "be afforded the opportunity to take whatever action it may deem appropriate in light of that report."

A hearing was promptly held in the district court with Judge Dobie of Virginia replacing Judge Waring, who had previously retired from the Bench. After argument, the new three-judge court issued a unanimous decree again refusing to declare the statutes unconstitutional but again ordering the school board to furnish equal facilities. An appeal is now being prepared to the Supreme Court from this latest decision.

The second case in this line of cases is the *Topeka, Kansas* case which was tried in June of last year. Again similar testimony from other expert witnesses in larger number was produced and in this case the three judges unanimously found as a fact that:

Segregation of white and colored children in public schools has a detrimental effect upon the colored children. The impact is greater when it has the sanction of the law; for the policy of separating the races is usually interpreted as denoting inferiority of the Negro group. A sense of inferiority affects the motivation of a child to learn. Segregation with the sanction of law, therefore, has a tendency to retard the education and mental development of Negro children and to deprive them of some of the benefits they would receive in a racial integrated school system.

The same court, however, felt obliged not to follow this finding but to follow the antiquated decisions of the Supreme Court which seem to uphold the validity of segregation in elementary education. That case is now pending before the United States Supreme Court.

The third case was the *Wilmington, Delaware* case which was tried on October 22, 1951 and which was decided week before last in an exhaustive twenty-six page opinion by Chancellor Collins J. Seitz ordering the admission of the Negroes in the previously all white schools.

The fourth case was the *Prince Edward, Virginia* case tried before a three-judge court in Richmond, Virginia last month. In this case which was tried for a full week more expert testimony was produced than in any other of the cases. For the first time the other side produced expert testimony which while opposing the immediate removal of segregation nevertheless admitted the inequality inherent in a segregated school system in addition to the regular inequalities in physical equipment. This court in unanimous opinion refused to enjoin the segregation statutes but ordered the equalization of physical facilities. This case is also being prepared for appeal to the United States Supreme Court.

It should be pointed out that in the second hearing in the *Clarendon County* case the court was urged to abolish segregation in public schools on either of two grounds: (1) that the testimony showed that segregation laws were invalid or (2) that the absence of equality in the segregated facilities required the application of the Sipuel doctrine. The court rejected both arguments and accepted the school board's assurances that the physical facilities would be equalized by September.

On the other hand, Chancellor Seitz in the *Wilmington, Delaware* case while refusing to hold segregation invalid as such did extend the Sipuel doctrine to give effective relief. He held:

> It seems to me that when a plaintiff shows to the satisfaction of a court that there is an existing and continuing violation of the 'separate but equal' doctrine, he is entitled to have made available to him the State facilities which have been shown to be superior. To do otherwise is to say to such a plaintiff: 'Yes, your Constitutional rights are being invaded, but be patient, we will see whether in time they are still being violated.' If, as the Supreme Court has said, this right is personal, such a plaintiff is entitled to relief

immediately, in the only way it is available, namely by admission to the school with the superior facilities. To postpone such relief is to deny relief, in whole or in part, and to say that the protective provisions of the Constitution offer no immediate protection.

The school officials have decided to appeal this decision. The Supreme Court will, therefore, have an opportunity to pass upon this question presented in varying forms in these four cases.

I will, of course, not speculate as to either the outcome of the individual cases or the general decision of the Supreme Court on this point. Getting back to an appraisal of the recent cases in the line of the objective sought, we can appraise these cases in the light of their immediate effect. In South Carolina, Governor Byrnes in an effort to circumvent these cases, last year succeeded in getting through the legislature approval for a seventy-five million dollar school fund based upon a sales tax. This seventy-five million dollars will be used in both Negro and white schools. It is admitted that this fund is for the purpose of equalizing physical facilities, a large proportion of the fund will no doubt go to white schools. At any rate, if nothing more is done in the legal field, the schools of South Carolina both Negro and white will be seventy-five million dollars better off. On the other hand, Governor Byrnes followed by Governor Talmadge of Georgia had put through a plan whereby they hope to turn over the public schools to private institutions such as churches in the event that the Supreme Court declares the segregation statutes invalid. Many of us are convinced that this move to turn over the public schools to private institutions will be declared invalid by the Supreme Court. There are even more people who are convinced that the white citizens in these states are not insane enough on the segregation issue to be willing to turn over millions of dollars of their tax money invested in schools to private institutions where they will have little, if any, control over the education of their children.

Many of the people who believe that segregation is invalid and should be declared unconstitutional are moved by this threat of a few Southern governors. It seems to me that the best answer to this threat is that the same threat was made by the attorneys-general of the Southern states while the *Sweatt* and *McLaurin* cases were pending in the Supreme Court. The specific threat was that if segregation was destroyed on the graduate and professional level "the states are left with no alternative but to close their schools to prevent violence." The record shows that no state universities were closed and nothing happened except that Negroes were admitted just as if they had been attending the schools for years back. In the face of these facts, the argument is now made that elementary and high school education is different and that the South will not stand for it. There is an answer to this argument also. Many junior colleges in Texas have recently opened their doors to Negroes and nothing happened. This brings us to another phase of the objective of this litigation and that is the education of the general public to the evils of segregation, its harmful effects and the reasons why this segregation should be abolished.

The pendency of the *Sipuel, Sweatt,* and *McLaurin* cases over a period of some five years brought about wide newspaper coverage and discussion in daily press, the weekly magazine, the professional magazines and college newspapers. This education of the general public played a large part in making it possible for the Negro students to be admitted without incident, to have no trouble while in school, and to encourage other public and private colleges and universities to open their doors to qualified Negroes.

The pending cases have likewise received wide and broad coverage in the same channels. In addition, articles are now appearing in scientific journals on the validity of the scientific testimony in this field. It is doubtful that this issue will be resolved over night but the pendency of these cases will continue to educate the general public along the lines suggested above.

It has been most encouraging to find that whereas the earlier cases on the university level failed to attract the attention and support of most of the Negro communities, the present litigation has had 100 per cent cooperation in each area where these cases have been pending. For example, the courage of the Negroes in Clarendon County, South Carolina, and the support of the Negroes in other areas in South Carolina; the courage of the Negroes in Farmville, Virginia and the support from the other areas in Virginia will stand as a landmark in the struggle for full citizenship. Any appraisal of the actual cases in these fields must include an appraisal of the community support commanded by the cases.

Neither the *Sipuel* nor the *McLaurin* decisions struck down the separate-but-equal doctrine. There are many who hoped that this would happen. However, all legal minds will agree that the Supreme Court is not obliged to make far sweeping decisions but rather tends to limits its decision to the matter before it in the pending cases. So it is apparent that the whole segregation problem cannot be solved in one law suit. It would, of course, be easier and cheaper to do it that way. If we view the problem from a realistic standpoint, it means that the best possible course is a step-by-step approach on each level of education to be followed by a step by step approach at each other area of segregation.

In addition, it is necessary to implement the precedents on each level and this will require additional law suits on each level. The present cases on the elementary and high school level show the varied approach to this problem, varied as to area, and varied as to testimony.

The university cases not only opened the state universities in twelve Southern states but many private institutions in states like Kentucky and Maryland have opened their doors to qualified Negroes. There are other private colleges willing to open their doors to Negroes but are prevented from doing so by state statutes. It is expected that in the near future there will be cases filed to enjoin the enforcement of these statutes as applied to the private colleges anxious to admit qualified Negroes. There has also been some discussion as to the eventual possibility in the future of requiring a private college to admit Negro students despite its ban upon the admission of

Negro students. I imagine that this suggestion when and if made will split the legal profession in half.

In states like Alabama, Florida, South Carolina and Mississippi, the time when the universities in these states will be opened to Negroes depend solely upon when qualified Negroes apply to those universities, and are refused admission and bring suit against these universities. As soon as that is done they will be opened up. Such a case is now ready for filing in Georgia and it is expected that additional cases will be filed in Florida in order to open up the University of Florida.

The primary objective of this recent litigation has been to obtain full and complete integration of all students on all levels of public education without regard to race or color. The stumbling block in the path toward this objective is the separate-but-equal doctrine. In the beginning the Courts prevented litigants from either attacking the doctrine head on or circumventing the doctrine. In the next phase of this program the courts eventually permitted the tangential approach by ordering equality of physical facilities while upholding segregation.

Finally in the *Sweatt* and *McLaurin* decisions the tangential approach was discarded and segregation on the graduate and professional school levels was removed. Even there the Supreme Court refused to strike down the separate-but-equal doctrine as such. The elementary and high school cases are the next steps in this campaign toward the objective and complete integration of all students.

The earlier legal approach to this problem failed to bring about either integration or equality of physical facilities. The direct attack on segregation even if successful in its all-out attack on segregation nevertheless produces immediate serious efforts toward physical equality.

In evaluating these recent cases we must always bear in mind that we are dealing with a brand new field of law both as to substantive law and procedural law. Although the separate-but-equal doctrine still stands in the road blocking full equality or opportunity, recent cases have been closing the doors of escape from a clear-cut determination of the validity or invalidity of this doctrine. While evaluating the recent decisions we must constantly look to the future.

14. The Meaning and Significance of the Supreme Court Decree

Robert Carter and Thurgood Marshall

Journal of Negro Education, vol. 24 (Summer 1955)

Written for educators, this article is Marshall's first reaction to the Supreme Court's decision on remedy in *Brown*. Carefully summarizing the decision, the article expresses disappointment that the Court did not take the course Marshall had urged and order that desegregation occur forthwith, but also optimism that desegregation will proceed relatively peacefully. The article does, however, note the impediments to full compliance with the Court's decision.

I

On May 31st, 1955, the long-awaited decision of the Supreme Court, on how to implement its opinion declaring segregation in public education unconstitutional, was handed down. Like the decision of May 17, 1954, it was read by the Chief Justice of the United States for a unanimous Court, and its language was simple, direct and non-technical. After the 1954 opinion, it seemed anti-climatic, but nothing world shaking should have been expected. Utterance of a practical formula pursuant to which a great constitutional and moral abstraction may become a part of our daily lives sometimes seems to have far less impact than the initial statement of the principle itself. And that seemed to be the situation in this case.

While the Court's solution differed from that proposed by counsel for the Negro litigants, chiefly in regard to the fixing of a deadline for compliance, the formula devised is about as effective as one could have expected. The net result should be to unite the country behind a nationwide desegregation program, and if this takes place, the Court must be credited with having performed its job brilliantly.

The opinion is a very short one. The Court begins with the statement that the opinions of May 17, 1954, "declaring the fundamental principle that racial discrimination in public education is unconstitutional, are incorporated herein by reference. All provisions of federal or state or local law requiring or permitting such discrimination must yield to this principle." With this sweeping declaration, all state requirements that segregation obtain in any phase of the educational process are placed beyond the pale.

In accord with the wishes of all the parties, the decisions are remanded to the courts from which they came—the special statutory United States District Courts of three judges in the Kansas, South Carolina and Virginia cases, an ordinary United States District Court of one judge in the District of Columbia case, and the State

Supreme Court in the Delaware case. These courts are instructed and empowered to supervise and control desegregation of the schools in each of the cases involved. They are advised that each school board must begin to desegregate promptly, and are authorized to consider and determine whether "good faith implementation of the governing constitutional principles" exists. These are essentially administrative functions. Since the role assigned these five lower courts will be assumed by all lower federal and state courts faced with the problem in the future, the net result will be that the lower courts, and particularly the federal courts, will become super school boards until desegregation has been accomplished throughout the United States. The courts are told that as administrators they have wide discretion but are given a general blueprint so that exercise of that discretion will be kept within reasonable limitations. Instructions to the lower courts on how they should approach their role as administrators of the school desegregation mandate are compressed into these relatively short paragraphs. They follow:

> In fashioning and effectuating the decrees, the courts will be guided by equitable principles. Traditionally, equity has been characterized by a practical flexibility in shaping its remedies and by a facility for adjusting and reconciling public and private needs. These cases call for the exercise of these traditional attributes of equity power. At stake is the personal interest of the plaintiffs in admission to public schools as soon as practicable on a non-discriminatory basis. To effectuate this interest may call for elimination of a variety of obstacles in making the transition to school systems operated in accordance with the constitutional principles set forth in our May 17, 1954, decision. Courts of equity may properly take into account the public interest in the elimination of such obstacles in a systematic and effective manner. But it should go without saying that the vitality of these constitutional principles cannot be allowed to yield simply because of disagreement with them.
>
> While giving weight to these public and private considerations, the courts will require that the defendants make a prompt and reasonable start toward full compliance with our May 17, 1954, ruling. Once such a start has been made, the courts may find that additional time is necessary to carry out the ruling in an effective manner. The burden rests upon the defendants to establish that such time is necessary in the public interest and is consistent with good faith compliance at the earliest practicable date. To that end, the courts may consider problems related to administration, arising from the physical condition of the school plant, the school transportation system, personnel, revision of school districts and attendance areas into compact units to achieve a system of determining admission to the public schools on a nonracial basis, and revision of local laws and regulations which may be necessary in solving the foregoing problems. They

will also consider the adequacy of any plans the defendants may propose to meet these problems and to effectuate a transition to a racially nondiscriminatory school system. During this period of transition, the courts will retain jurisdiction of these cases.

You will note that the lower courts are not given a blank check. They are told to exercise their discretion in accommodating the public interest in an orderly and systematic removal of racial barriers, but are reminded of the plaintiffs' great personal interest in being afforded the benefits of non-discriminatory education without undue delay. Lower courts are advised that while the elimination of a variety of obstacles may be a necessary prerequisite to desegregation, disagreement with the principle cannot be allowed to hinder its full implementation.

Defendant school boards are under obligation to make a prompt and reasonable start toward full compliance with the May 17, 1954, ruling. Time to fully accomplish desegregation may be allowed various school boards, but theirs is the burden of establishing that "such time is necessary in the public interest and is consistent with good faith compliance at the earliest practicable date."

In effect, the Court seems to be telling the lower courts that while they may give time for necessary administrative changes and the removal of other practical obstacles, they must always be certain that a good faith effort to comply with the law is being made, and remember that their primary responsibility is to see to it that the job is accomplished as speedily as possible.

This is a temperate opinion, couched in mild terms. Its mild and temperate tone is deceiving, however, for beneath the velvet there is steel. It concedes nothing to the segregationists but an opportunity to abide by the law without loss of face. And one cannot help but be impressed with the fact, newspaper headlines to the contrary notwithstanding, that the Court is resolute in its conviction that segregation is unconstitutional and determined that the courts shall be an effective forum to speed its elimination.

II

Although on May 17, 1954, and on May 31, 1955, the Supreme Court spoke to the nation, because of the nature of the legal process, only the litigants before the Court were immediately and directly affected by these pronouncements. Here the respective school boards in Kansas, the District of Columbia, Delaware, South Carolina and Virginia are now under a direct injunction to make a reasonable and prompt start to get the desegregation process under way and are under obligation to keep as their primary objective "good faith compliance at the earliest practicable date."

The Court's mandate—that is, its order to the lower courts to act in accordance with its May 31st opinion—will not go down until June 25. After that date the respective courts will be under orders from the Supreme Court to carry out its May 31st judgment. On the motion of the parties, or on the motion of the courts themselves, hearings undoubtedly will be held in each of the five courts to determine what needs to be done to implement the Court's decision.

Both Topeka, Kansas, and the District of Columbia say that they have fully complied with the May 17, 1954, ruling and that their public schools are now completely desegregated or, at least, will be as of September, 1955. With respect to those cases, therefore, the question which the courts will have to determine is whether the desegregation plan adopted and in force constitutes full and effective desegregation in accord with the May 17, 1954, decree.

Objections have been raised concerning both plans on the ground that they do not accomplish full desegregation; that the bulk of Negro children are still attending 100 per cent Negro schools. If this point is pressed by plaintiffs, and one would think it would have to be, the district courts will probably take testimony and hear argument relative thereto. Here we think the burden now would be on the school boards to prove to the courts' satisfaction that their programs have eliminated, open or covert, enforced segregation, and not upon plaintiffs to prove that some form of segregation remains. This is an important shifting of roles and eases somewhat the plaintiffs' task. Until May 17, 1954, a Negro litigant had to affirmatively establish that segregation was illegal and that he was harmed thereby. Now the defendants must show that they have mended their ways and are operating their schools in accordance with the law.

The courts could uphold the plans, and give each school board a clean bill of health. In this event, an appeal could be taken to the Supreme Court once again. On the other hand, of course, they could uphold the contention that the plans have serious shortcomings. In this case the boards would probably be required to make the necessary changes, effective at once or at some fixed date in the future.

In Delaware, the children are integrated into the school system, but they are in school on the ground that the "separate but equal" doctrine is the law of the land and that Delaware's segregation law is valid. The State Supreme Court will have to modify its decision and strike down the Delaware law. It could also use this occasion to tell other Delaware communities how they should proceed with their desegregation programs.

Needless to say, the big tests will come with respect to Clarendon County, South Carolina, and Prince Edward County, Virginia. No desegregation steps have been taken by either school board, and both communities seem intent on defiance. Public officials, charged with such responsibility, have refused in each case to make the appropriations necessary for maintenance of public schools for 1955–1956. One can but speculate as to each school board's attitude at the anticipated hearings.

At present there seems to be little likelihood that either board will present the court with plans to desegregate their systems. It is doubtful that they would openly defy the May 31st decree at the court hearing, since they would make themselves amenable to punishment for contempt. In all probability these defendants will make every effort to obtain a delay of a showdown for as long as possible. Undoubtedly tactics of evasion will be employed. One, which immediately comes to mind, is the excuse that since no appropriations were made to operate the schools for the 1955–1956 school year, the defendants are unable to keep the schools open. Hence they see no need to make any plans to desegregate until they know whether there will be any schools in which these plans are to operate. One should not be overly alarmed at the prospect that these schools will be closed come September. In Prince Edward County a group of citizens have already made it clear that they intend to operate the schools for white children next year. One can be reasonably confident that this none too artful dodge will not work. There are many other possibilities, but we think one must anticipate that the defendants will engage in a series of delaying tactics designed to keep from being faced with the ultimate—to either obey the Court's order or go to jail. There are a number of delaying tactics which can be, and probably will be, employed in these cases, but eventually the two communities have to come to grips with the facts of life—the law must be obeyed. On the other hand, these defendants may spring a big surprise on the country and bring forth a good faith desegregation program.

Of course, all this is in the area of the wildest speculation, and since the event itself is not too far off, it is best perhaps to let it give its own answers. Certainly the hearings in these cases will be of major significance because these courts may be the first to give definite and specific content to "a prompt and reasonable start" and "good faith compliance at the earliest practicable date." The actual steps a school board must take to comply with the May 31st decision could be spelled out in these proceedings. It is almost a certainty that whatever the outcome, these proceedings will have an important bearing on the course the "resisting" states take.

III

In the states not before the Supreme Court, i.e., Kentucky, Tennessee, Texas, Mississippi, etc., the maintenance of segregated schools is unconstitutional, and state laws to the contrary are invalid. These states, however, may continue to operate their schools in accordance with their now invalid state policy of segregation and will not be compelled to conform to the May 17, 1954, and May 31, 1955, rulings until litigation is instituted by Negroes to end the discriminatory practices. Missouri and West Virginia have already begun the desegregation process on a wide scale. Maryland and Kentucky have announced that they will comply with the law. In North Carolina, a few local school boards have promised good faith compliance. Georgia and Mississippi have announced an intention to resist to the bitter end. How many areas will move on their own will not be known until well into the fall of this year. All are under obligation to comply, and the Department of Justice could prosecute all school boards that continue to maintain segregated schools as violators of the laws of the United States. But this is unlikely. Where school boards fail or refuse to act, nothing probably will be done unless Negroes demand and insist upon their constitutional right to non-discriminatory education.

The National Association for the Advancement of Colored People has directed its branches to file petitions with school boards this summer, asking for desegregation, and to commence law suits if nothing has been done by the opening of school, September 1955. Where the school board refuses to act, the Negro parents and their children will have to become plaintiffs in law suits in federal courts in which they will ask the courts to order the school board to comply with the Supreme Court ruling.

At this stage, the school boards involved will be placed in the same position as the school boards in the decided cases, i.e., under obligation to show that they have made a prompt and reasonable start towards compliance with the desegregation mandate. If they need time to complete the process, they must demonstrate its necessity and its consistency with "good faith compliance at the earliest practicable date."

Undoubtedly, there will be a flood of litigation commencing this fall. It is doubtful that gerrymandering or other plans of desegregation which cleverly maintain segregation will present problems at the outset. One can anticipate that initially resistance will come in the nature of requests for long delays to enable the school board to study the problem carefully or to enable it to eliminate community hostility, etc. Or it may be necessary, as it was in the voting cases, to litigate the constitutionality of some schemes designed to evade the law. In the light of the primary cases, these schemes may get short shrift in the lower courts.

IV

The decision has opened the door for Negroes to secure unsegregated educational facilities if they so desire. There has been some disappointment among anti-segregationists that no time limit was set. Certainly, on the surface at least, a time limit would have afforded a sense of security that segregation would end within a specific number of years. We fear, however, that such security would have been fed on false hopes.

Some states—Missouri, Maryland, West Virginia and Kentucky seem to fall in this category—would have taken official steps to comply with whatever formula the Court devised. Pressure skillfully applied in a few other states would have resulted in the adoption of a similar policy. While desegregation could be successfully undertaken in many areas of the deep South tomorrow, little will be done for the most part unless Negroes demand and insist upon desegregation. In states such as Georgia and Mississippi, it looks as if desegregation will be accomplished only after a long and bitter fight, the brunt of which will have to be borne by Negroes. In short, we must face the fact that in the deep South, with rare exceptions, desegregation will become a reality only if Negroes exhibit real militancy and press unrelentlessly [*sic*] for their rights. And this would have been the situation no matter what kind of decision the Court had handed down.

If a deadline had been fixed, it would have been open to attack as being arbitrary, unrealistic and unfair to the South, and this would have given the demagogues a great opportunity to secure support for an attitude of open defiance. Perhaps with this in mind, and with the realization that deadline or not Negroes would have to make desegregation a reality, the Court avoided setting a time limit. Now with no deadline set, and local judges with an understanding of local problems empowered to administer and supervise the desegregation process, what more could the South realistically ask for except repudiation of the May 17th decision? As a result, it is likely that the attitude will be one of resignation to living within the law, once Negroes make it clear that they will insist that their community desegregate its schools. Now deadlines will be fixed by local federal courts. The cry that the local judge is unfamiliar with local problems cannot be sustained, and the possibility of defying the authority of the respected and on the scene symbol of law and order, even aside from the power to punish for contempt, is remote indeed. Great responsibility has been placed at the local level where it belongs, and where it would have been exercised in any event.

There will be, of course, federal judges whose views on the wisdom of segregation are so deep-seated that they will seek to use their equitable discretion to frustrate and delay litigation aimed at forcing compliance. In these instances, lawyers will have to use their knowledge of legal procedure to make the judge render justice. By and large, however, events will disclose that the local federal judges will not be disposed to wink at efforts to avoid full compliance with the Supreme Court's ruling. All in all, the net result should be that more widespread voluntary desegregation is now possible than might have occurred had a more stringent order been issued.

The decision was a good one. The Court has reaffirmed its pronouncement that segregation is unconstitutional and throughout the opinion stress is placed upon the necessity for full compliance at the earliest practicable date. Delays may be occasioned by various devices. This would result in any case. We can be sure that desegregation will take place throughout the United States—tomorrow in some places, the day after in others and many, many moons hence in some, but it will come eventually to all. We look upon the May 31st decision as a ticket to desegregation which is now available to every parent and child who needs it and wants to use it.

V

As for the next steps, at present the most important thing to do is get a copy of the opinion, read it and explain its implications to others. Segregationists were at first jubilant, but much of the jubilation has died. Anti-segregationists have no cause for disappointment. Rather, theirs should be an attitude of quiet confidence.

Efforts should be made to secure the support for voluntary desegregation from among individuals and organizations, and with that support, pressure should be brought on school boards to get them to voluntarily desegregate their schools. Each local NAACP Branch will be engaged in an effort to secure voluntary compliance in many areas in the South and will need and welcome all the assistance it can get.

While the immediate problem is to secure desegregation in the public schools in the Southern and border states, it should be remembered that segregation and other forms of racial prejudices present a national, not a regional problem. Northerners need to take a long look at their school systems and bend their efforts to eliminating segregation in their own public schools. One recognizes that here the defense is residential segregation, but that is really no answer. Surely we must have the ingenuity and skill to alleviate racial segregation in our schools without being required to await the long range levelling of racial barriers with respect to housing occupancy. If segregation in public schools is bad for our children in Atlanta, Georgia, it ought to be equally bad for them in New York City, Chicago, Philadelphia or Boston.

Finally, it is important that the strongest pressures against the continuation of segregation, North or South, be continually and constantly manifested. Probably, as much as anything else, this is the key in the elimination of discrimination in the United States.

15. The Rise and Collapse of the "White Democratic Primary"

Journal of Negro Education, vol. 26 (Summer 1957)

This article presents a more detailed survey of voting rights cases described more briefly in earlier articles.

Of all the so-called "legal" devices for checking Negro participation in Southern politics perhaps the most effective, and on the surface the most legal, was the white Democratic Party primary—the most effective because it disfranchised the Negro by excluding him from participating in the preelections which for all practical purposes were the elections in the one-party South, and the most "legal" because the Democratic Party, according to contemporary legal theory, was considered as being a voluntary association of citizens which could discriminate on the basis of race and color or along any other line in the conduct of its private affairs without offending the Fourteenth and Fifteenth Amendments.

For these reasons, solely, the rise and collapse of the white Democratic primary is an important and distinct chapter in the story of the Negro's struggle for political equality. But an equally important reason for writing this chapter is its rough analogy to the chapter now being developed with respect to educational authority.

The origins of the white Democratic primary are obscure and not easily traced. Lewinson in his *Race, Class and Party*, however, suggests that its beginnings go back to the color line drawn during Reconstruction days by self-labelled "white man's parties"—first called Conservative and, subsequently, simply Democratic—which opposed Black Republicanism. V. O. Key's authoritative *Southern Politics*, on the other hand, concludes only that this device originated about as early as the direct primary method of nomination appeared on the Southern scene.

In any event, it can hardly be gainsaid that Negroes rarely were admitted to Democratic or Conservative councils, caucuses or conventions during Reconstruction and the policy of excluding Negroes from the Democratic Party's nominating process was born during that time.

Use of the primary election method of nomination did not enter Southern politics until after the end of Reconstruction. The earliest primaries were local, informal and unregulated by law. Statutory recognition and regulation first appeared in the mid-1880's when Alabama and South Carolina passed acts providing for mandatory primary elections. Thereafter, the legally-regulated primary slowly spread throughout the South and by the turn of the century every Southern state required or permitted its use. During these twenty years, roughly speaking, and, for another twenty years thereafter, exclusion of Negroes from these pre-elections was not written on the law books.

Nevertheless the white primary system flourished. First, by tacit understandings or gentlemen's agreements between competing factions within state and local Democratic organizations and, later, with formal rules passed pursuant to statutory delegations of the power to prescribe qualifications for voting in primaries, the Democratic Party limited participation in them to white voters only, although there were many localities where the formal rule was never adopted and others where it was waived in closely contested elections. But, overall, the system had become so effective that a Southern legislator who opposed another disfranchisement device, in a letter published by the Atlanta *Constitution* in 1907, was able to exclaim: "We already had the Negro eliminated from politics by the white primary."

It is one of those little ironies of which Southern politics is full, that the primary movement which was motivated, at least in part, by democratic motives and a desire for wider participation in the representative process was turned into a device for eliminating millions of Negroes from participation in government.

It is even more ironical that a petty squabble between the candidates for a minor political office in Texas ended in the enactment of a statute which declared Negroes ineligible to vote in a Democratic primary and touched off the series of law suits which brought about the collapse of the white primary system.

This chain of events was set off in 1918 by two candidates for the district attorneyship of Bexar County, Texas. Both sought the support of Negro voters and both had previously had such support in other local primaries. The unsuccessful candidate this time, however, set out upon a campaign for legislation which would require exclusion of Negro voters from the Democratic primary and thus undermine the victor's political strength in the county. The campaign attracted little support in the legislature at the outset save from those legislators who were professed Negrophobes. By 1923, however, a number of conservative legislators, who were undoubtedly encouraged by the Supreme Court's ruling in the Newberry case that primaries were not elections within the meaning of the Constitution, furnished sufficient votes to pass the law which prohibited Negroes from voting in Democratic primaries.

Four years after its enactment this statute was held unconstitutional by the Supreme court in the *First Texas White Primary Case*. The suit had been filed in 1924 on behalf of Dr. L. A. Nixon, an El Paso physician, well-known Negro Democrat, who sought to recover damages from the election officials who denied him the right to vote in the primary which nominated the Democratic candidates for seats in the Federal Congress and various state offices. Specifically, the complaint alleged that the law which the defendants had enforced against the plaintiff was violative of the Fourteenth and Fifteenth Amendments. The Federal District Court sitting in El Paso granted defendants' motion to dismiss on the merits and the case then came direct to the Supreme Court. Speaking for a unanimous Court, Justice Holmes declared: "It seems to us hard to imagine a more direct and obvious infringement of the Fourteenth Amendment." Having disposed of the case under the Fourteenth Amendment, the Court declined to consider the validity of the statute under the Fifteenth Amendment.

Most people, including Justice Holmes, felt that this decision laid the white primary to rest; but succeeding events showed them up as far too optimistic. For the Texas legislature promptly tried again. In 1928 it repealed the 1924 law and enacted another which empowered the state executive committees of political parties to determine the qualifications of voters in primary elections. And, pursuant thereto, the State Executive Committee of the Democratic Party passed a resolution limiting participation in primaries to white persons. This combination of statutory delegation and formal party rule, as we previously noted, was the means by which Negroes were excluded from Democratic primaries throughout most of the South; and it was also the one which many legal scholars deemed immune from the reach of the Federal Constitution.

This system did not long remain unchallenged. Following the exclusion of Negroes from the 1928 Democratic primaries, suits challenging it were filed in Arkansas, Florida, Texas and Virginia. Only one, the *Second Texas White Primary Case* was brought up to the Supreme Court. Dr. Nixon was again the plaintiff in an action for damages against the election officials who refused to permit him to vote. He contended that the state was a party to the discrimination against him since it had delegated control over the primary to the State Executive Committee of the Democratic Party. Both the Federal District Court and Circuit Court of Appeals upheld the challenged device. But the Supreme Court pricked open the private association fiction and reversed in a 5 to 4 decision. The majority, however, gratuitously pointed out a way in which Negroes could be excluded from primaries by remarking that the power to do this lay with the State Democratic Convention and not the State Executive Committee, if any such power existed.

Although most were apprehensive about the Court's gratuitous suggestion, Negroes and their friends generally regarded the decision as the final step in their effort to throw open the white primary. Supporters of the white primary system were also confused, not so much with respect to the course to take but how to navigate it. Within three weeks of decision day, however, the confusion was dissipated when the Democratic Party called a State Convention and it adopted a resolution restricting membership in the Party plus participation in party primaries to white citizens of Texas.

Since 1932 was an election year and the resolution was rigorously enforced, a number of cases testing the constitutionality of the Convention Resolution were filed and lost in lower Federal courts. One of them was carried up to the Supreme Court and became the *Third Texas White Primary Case*. R. R. Grovey, a Negro citizen of Houston, was the plaintiff in the case. The pleadings admitted that candidates for Federal office were to be nominated at the primary and that nomination in the primary was equivalent to election. Nevertheless, the members of the Court "blinded themselves as judges to what they knew as men" and unanimously held that the Democratic primary was a private matter and that Grovey had not been discriminated against pursuant to any state law nor had he been denied any right guaranteed under the Fourteenth and Fifteenth Amendments.

Thus on April Fools Day, 1935, the same day on which the second Scottsboro case was handed down, almost a decade of litigation was brought to naught. Dean William Pickens, in an article which appeared in the Norfolk *Journal and Guide* on April 13 could not resist commenting upon the coincidence. "If one were suspicious of the Court's motives," he said, "it would look as if they made a trade." Undoubtedly, from a purely racial perspective and in view of the Court's disposition of the earlier Texas Primary cases, the decision was a rude jolt to the political aspirations of Negroes. But hope did not die out. P. B. Young, writing for the same issue of the *Journal and Guide* as the one in which Dean Pickens' comment appeared, sensed the hope and boldly predicted that this "barrier will not be effective long. The Court in 1935 did not ferret out the trickery behind the statutes. Later, it will go behind the law."

As predicted, *Grovey* did not long remain an effective barrier. In *United States v. Classic*, the Court pierced the facade of legality which had shielded primaries from the reach of Federal laws regulating the conduct of elections. The Court, although it split 5/3 on other questions presented for decision, unanimously agreed that Congress had the right to regulate primary elections and that the criminal sections of the Civil Rights law could be invoked to penalize infractions thereof in the course of primary elections involving nominations for Federal office. The Court's opinion followed and adopted the very arguments which had been rejected in the *Third Texas White Primary Case*; and the Court, without a single reference to *Grovey*, practically overruled it.

Because it was not a white primary case, Classic, of course, did not go behind the law and ferret out the trickery. However, it paved the way to the next milestone on the long road toward political equality—the *Fourth Texas White Primary Case*.

This will be seen in proper perspective by turning back to 1940. It was the first general election year after *Grovey v. Townsend* and the assault upon the white primary began anew. Most of the cases arose in Texas. None met with any success in the trial courts and few were appealed. Indeed, in one of them, an appeal had been noted just about the time the *Classic* decision came down. That appeal, however, was withdrawn and a new suit based upon the *rationale* of the *Classic* case was filed. This was the *Fourth Texas White Primary Case*.

It was brought on behalf of Lonnie E. Smith, a Negro citizen of Houston, on behalf of himself and all other Negroes similarly qualified to vote yet denied the right to do so by the election judges. Their action, it was alleged, violated rights secured under the Constitution and laws of the United States and for this alleged illegal conduct a declaratory judgment, injunctive relief and monetary damages were sought. Needless to say, the lower courts refused to overrule *Grovey*.

The Supreme Court, however, looked behind the law and ferreted out the trickery. It concluded that the Democratic Party, after "the fusing by the *Classic* case of the primary and general elections into a single instrumentality for the choice of officers," had become, under elaborate statutory regulations, "an agency of the state" in determining the participants in primary elections. "The party takes its character as a state agency from the duties imposed upon it by state statute; the duties do not become matters of private law because they were performed by a political party." Thus the Court held that the Democratic Party as such, under the statutes, through whatever agency it acted, can no more discriminate against voters in primary elections than the state itself in general elections without violating the Fifteenth Amendment and the "privileges and immunities" clause of the Fourteenth Amendment.

This decision, one of the landmarks in constitutional history, leveled the greater barrier to Negro voting in the South. But Southern ingenuity was not spent and clever stratagems were conceived in a desperate effort to circumvent *Smith v. Allwright* and restore the white democratic primary. In South Carolina, for example, a special session of the legislature was called for the purpose of repealing all laws on its statute books which dealt with political parties and primaries. By doing this, according to the thinking of the Governor and the legislators, the tie-up between the party and the state would be severed and then like a "private club" the Democratic Party could exclude Negroes from its primaries. In Alabama and Georgia different props to avoid the *Fourth Texas Primary Case* were thrown up. All were either struck down by lower Federal courts or were not enforced.

Texas, however, was destined to be the scene of the last chapter. There, instead of an attempt to preserve the white Democratic primary, the device involved an all-white "club"—the Jaybird Party or Jaybird Democratic Association—which held its own preelection some weeks in advance of the Democratic primary regulated by the State. The winners of the Jaybird primary would then enter the Democratic primary, which was open to Negroes as well as whites, and won without opposition in the Democratic primary and the general election that followed. A suit challenging the exclusion of Negroes from the Jaybird primaries was filed after the 1948 elections by John Terry and a group of Negro citizens of Fort Bend County. Like *Smith v. Allwright*, it was a class suit and the same broad relief was sought. The case eventually came up to the Supreme Court and it held that the discriminatory practices described above were unconstitutional.

The collapse of the white Democratic primary, despite fond hopes, has not resulted in full participation by all in the political life of the South. But the story of the struggle to overcome this barrier is particularly meaningful today. For, if nothing else, it indicates the fate which awaits the "legal means" which some of the Southern states have drafted to preserve segregated schools.

PART III

WRITINGS AS A JUDGE

This Part has two sections. The first contains most of the talks Marshall gave to the annual gathering of judges and lawyers in the federal Court of Appeals for the Second Circuit. Marshall's first judicial appointment had been as a judge on that court, which sits in New York and is one of the two most important lower federal courts, and he retained a deep affection for its judges and the lawyers who regularly appeared before it (see selection 16, included here as a preface to Marshall's annual comments on the Supreme Court's work). After becoming the "Circuit Justice" for the Second Circuit—the Supreme Court justice responsible for dealing with emergency appeals from the circuit and similar matters—Marshall gave an annual talk commenting on the Court's work in the preceding year. Some of the talks were transcribed, and the transcriptions (selections 17, 22, and 24 through 27) capture some of Marshall's informality and his celebrated abilities as a storyteller. Marshall always spoke from a prepared text, and the transition between his informal remarks and his prepared text is usually apparent in the transcriptions. The remainder of the "Remarks" are the prepared texts alone. Selection 39 was initially presented at the Second Circuit Conference but is presented later in this Part because of its thematic connection with Marshall's article on the death penalty (selection 40) and his tribute to Justice Brennan (selection 41).

Grouping these remarks together allows the reader to see the Supreme Court as Marshall saw it on a yearly basis. The most notable feature of these talks is their candor, as Marshall did not hesitate in using the talks as a vehicle for expressing his deep disagreement with the direction the Court was taking. To assist the reader, I have added subtitles, not given by Marshall himself, indicating the remarks' general topics.

The second section contains other speeches and articles presented by Marshall, on topics ranging from legal services to the poor, to the death penalty, to the celebration of the Constitution's bicentennial. Selection 28 was given while Marshall was solicitor general, the others while he was on the Supreme Court. The speeches and articles dealing with the legal profession and the rule of law gave Marshall an opportunity to present his views on matters not regularly dealt with in his Supreme Court opinions. Selections 29 through 33 present Marshall's views on the proper role of the bar—both individual lawyers and the organized bar as a whole—in the promotion of social justice, and offer general reflections on law and justice, with descriptions of particular programs that he believed might advance social justice by providing representation for those who need but cannot afford it. Marshall also endorsed programs in which the organized bar supported the provision of legal services to the poor (selection 31), and criticized efforts aimed at restricting bar admission in ways that might limit the number of lawyers who could serve the poor (selection 32). Selections 34 and 35 provide more detailed criticisms of proposals to alter the existing system of administering justice, whether by changing the way judges are chosen or by changing the Supreme Court's role. Many of these proposals are no longer being actively pursued, but their discussion is of more than historical interest because what Marshall said illuminates the cast of mind he brought to his judicial work.

Selection 37 is a widely noted speech Marshall made during the Constitution's bicentennial year, offering a skeptical alternative interpretation to the celebrations of the original Constitution's wisdom. The final selections focus on the Supreme Court's death penalty jurisprudence, and include Marshall's tribute to his friend and colleague William J. Brennan.

16. Celebrating the Second Circuit Centennial
St. John's University Law Review, 1991

I am delighted to offer a few words in commemoration of the Second Circuit's one hundredth anniversary. As some readers may be aware, I have served the Second Circuit in several capacities. From 1961 to 1965, I was a judge on the Second Circuit; since 1972, I have served as its Circuit Justice. Throughout these years, my admiration of this great court has not abated. To me, the Second Circuit stands out among all other courts of appeals for the quality of its contributions to the American legal system.

Any discussion of the Second Circuit must start with its brilliant judges. The Second Circuit has been home to such legendary figures as Learned Hand, Augustus Hand, Charles Clark, Jerome Frank, and Henry Friendly. Through these men and their capable successors, the Second Circuit has acquired an unrivaled reputation for judicial craftsmanship and scholarship. It is no surprise that Second Circuit jurisprudence has achieved prominence in so many fields, including commercial law, criminal procedure, admiralty, securities law, civil rights, copyright, and the first amendment.

Yet it is a mistake to characterize the Second Circuit merely as a court of great judges and great cases. In its everyday life, the Second Circuit provides uniquely personal and prompt justice to all of its litigants. Notwithstanding the regrettable trend among our courts of appeals of limiting oral argument to "worthy cases," the Second Circuit does not screen its cases and continues to encourage parties to partake in oral argument. Solicitude for the right of each litigant to his or her "day in court" has not compromised the Second Circuit's efficiency. The Second Circuit ranks among the quickest of our courts of appeals in disposing of its docket.

I will always remember my tenure on the Second Circuit for the kindness and respect my colleagues displayed towards one another. When I visit the Second Circuit's Judicial Conference each year, I am heartened to discover that collegiality remains one of the court's hallmarks. Such collegiality not only makes a judge's work more pleasant, but in the end, it also fosters a higher quality of judging. The Second Circuit's performance in its first century confirms this. I congratulate the Second Circuit on its one hundredth anniversary and extend my sincere wishes that it will enjoy a second century as distinguished as its first.

17. Remarks at the Second Circuit Judicial Conference
[Civil Rights Enforcement and the Supreme Court's Docket]
(September 8, 1978)

It is good to be here. May I just comment that on my African trip I encountered what they call jet lag. When you go eighteen hours each way on a plane without windows—it was a freight plane—well, I think the President is quite right in saving money, but I am with him up to a point, and that was the point.

Fortunately, however, on the way over I ran across some people who wanted some lessons in poker, so the windowless plane was not an entire loss. Unfortunately, they couldn't afford but one lesson, so coming back we didn't have any game.

As I said before, the trips to Africa are important, because so many people don't understand Africa. The dedication of most Africans to what we would consider democracy is just unbelievable.

For example, let me tell you a very interesting story I was told about Jomo Kenyatta, whose funeral we went to, I as chief of the delegation representing our President, on Friday after the funeral by the now President Moi. A few weeks previously Kenyatta was getting a little sick and a little old, and he called one of his stalwart cabinet members over, with his fly whisk in his hand. That's a long stick of very hard wood, sometimes lead inside of it, on the tail of which is the tail of a giraffe. You wave flies off with it. It is also a nice little club.

He called this fellow over and he said, "What do they call you?"

The man said, "You know who I am. I am So-and-So."

He said, "That is not the question. What do they call you?"

And the fellow gave his name. Kenyatta whacked him right across his face with this stick. He said, "You know better than that. Tell me the truth. Not what your name is, but what do they call you?"

And the man said, "They are now calling me Ten Percent Jones," or whatever his last name was.

He whacked him real good and knocked him out, and said, "I'll have none of that."

When you hear a lot of stories about Africa and you get to a place like Kenya and other countries like that, where they think the same way we do, I was happy to find that the Schedule of Rights that I drew for the Kenyan Government was working very well. In some instances they have a little bit more due process than we have over here. The difference is that where we have one phrase, "due process of law," they have about three and a half pages of what is due process in their Schedule of Rights.

For instance, if somebody takes your land and you don't like it, you go to the highest court. You don't go to all the other courts. You go straight in and say, "I don't like it," and you do it without cost.

I finish on this Schedule of Rights with this story. I remember back in 1960 when we were drafting it that this Oxford professor was telling me about a "shedule," and I said, "Shedule, hell. You are talking about schedule." He said that was their English. I said it was wrong. He said, "The word is still 'shedule.'" And I said, "How are your people doing in shul?" That ended that argument. But they still say "shedule," as you know.

Well, I had to leave Africa and get back in what looked like a good cabinet for a cigar, that is, a long tubular plane, and to find a lot of things that have been going on around here.

I would like to point out that this year, in the last term, our Second Circuit's won-lost record was just about average. I guess we are settling down. Of the twelve cases from the Second Circuit and local three-judge courts that were decided on the merits, four were affirmed and eight were reversed. That two-thirds reversal rate is virtually identical to the overall reversal rate for that time. And this Circuit did actually do much better in that respect than some of the other circuits. The Ninth Circuit, for example, true to its record, lost thirteen out of fourteen cases, and the Seventh Circuit tried to catch up by losing ten out of eleven. As long as they go that way, we will be ahead.

I do not, of course, believe that these reversal rates mean very much. As you know, my own views have not always prevailed among my brethren. Interestingly enough, however, Bill Brennan and I did not find ourselves in dissent nearly as often last Term as we had in the recent past. The Term's number one dissenter was Bill Rehnquist. I don't know if that is indicative of some sort of trend on the Court that in the future Rehnquist will be the dissenter, but it's obviously not a statistic that I am unhappy about. As I told you, though, I don't like figures.

The Term was dominated, at least in the view of the news media, by the Bakke case. I have seen so many interpretations of our decision now that it's hard for me to distinguish between what we actually wrote and what the press says we wrote. This much, at least, is clear: We left a great many questions unanswered and thus plenty of work for our colleagues in what Thomas Reed Powell used to call the "inferior courts in the technical sense only."

But since Bakke has already received so much attention, and now is suing to try to get money to go to school—I don't know what else he is going to sue for next—and since most of you have probably abandoned any serious thought of applying to medical school yourselves, I'll turn to some other cases that made fewer headlines.

One that I am sure received some scrutiny from all of you was our *Monell* decision, written by Brennan, in which we overruled *Monroe v. Pape* insofar as it held that cities could not be sued under 42 U.S.C. section 1983.[1] Just the day before our *Monell* ruling, this Second Circuit held *en banc* in the *Turpin* case that cities could be sued directly under the fourteenth amendment. Obviously, no one had tipped you off as to what we were going to do, or you could have saved yourself a

---

[1] A federal statute creating a right to sue in federal court for violations of constitutional rights.

fair amount of work. Of course, I don't suppose you would have been much happier if the *Monell* decision had come down a day or two sooner, since you still would have gone to all that trouble writing, but you wouldn't have been able to publish all of it.

Monell was not the only decision last Term that went after cities. Municipalities may also be sued now for antitrust damages under the Sherman Act. In the *City of Lafayette* case, we held that the state action exemption from the antitrust laws does not apply to municipalities. On the other hand, city budgets fared a little better in the area of landmark preservation when New York's attempt to save Grand Central Station was held not to constitute a taking.

The shape of the law in another area also looks very different after last Term. In a whole series of decisions involving the double jeopardy clause, the Court overruled the *Jenkins* case—which I had thought settled double jeopardy, but it didn't even begin to settle it—which was decided only a few years ago, and left somewhat uncertain the types of trial terminations that will bar subsequent prosecutions under the clause in the future. It is clear now that a true acquittal—that is, an acquittal for insufficient evidence—or an appellate reversal of a conviction for insufficient evidence is a bar to a second trial, but not much else is clear.

In one small corner of double jeopardy law, however, we did establish a bright-line rule, and that is that the moment in a jury trial when double jeopardy attaches is now firmly fixed, as of this year, as a matter of federal constitutional law, at the time when the jury is sworn. Big deal.

One group that did not fare too well, and that has not been shy about letting the rest of us know about it, is the mass media. The case that received the most attention involved a police raid on Stanford University's student newspaper. The paper contended that the police should have employed a subpoena, but the Court held that it was appropriate to proceed by search warrant when seeking evidence in the hands of an innocent third party, including a news media party. The Court also held that the press is not entitled to any special access to prisons and that the FCC could at least threaten sanctions when a broadcaster played a monologue containing "seven dirty words." I could repeat those words for you, but you never can tell where the FCC may be lurking. If you want to read the monologue, you can find it appended to John Stevens' opinion; that is, unless some law students fired with intellectual curiosity and equipped with scissors get there first. I might say in defense that I was not in the California newspaper case involving the student newspaper. I was disqualified.

As lawyers, I am sure you were as interested as I in the Court's efforts to grapple with the question of attorney solicitation. In the 1976 Term we had held that bar associations could not ban advertising by lawyers; last Term we were faced with other forms of solicitation by the second oldest profession. One of the two cases on this subject involved classic ambulance-chasing. When I was practicing I had always been impressed with that ambulance-chasing business, because in negligence cases I was always a plaintiff's lawyer and did not find any necessity to chase ambulances, because the insurance company representing the defendant lawyers didn't chase the ambulances, they waited at the hospital for the ambulances, so I didn't see any sense in trying to catch up with them.

But in one of the ambulance-chasing cases the lawyer foisted his services on two young victims of a car accident out in Ohio, one of whom was still in the hospital when the attorney approached her. We allowed the bar to prohibit such intrusion.

The other case involved an ACLU lawyer who, acting without fee, sought to advise an indigent person that the ACLU was available to provide her certain legal services. The services were very simple. They were to prevent the state from interfering with the woman's reproductive system. This solicitation, the Court held, was constitutionally protected under the first amendment.

There is a large middle ground of solicitation between the two extremes of ambulance-chasing and the ACLU, of course, and I anticipate much bar association concern about what may and what may not be proscribed. As I suggested in a concurring opinion in these cases, the time may be ripe for reexamination of our traditional rules against all forms of solicitation by lawyers.

I am reminded of Clarence Darrow's statement some years ago that the Code of Ethics was a body of rules gotten up by those who couldn't make it to keep those who were making it from continuing to make it. But I don't know that I agree with him on that, I think there are some differences, but I still think we have to take another look at it.

I could continue with this summary of what we held last Term, but I think you may be more interested in hearing a description of two fascinating cases from the Second Circuit where we did not hold anything. What makes these cases especially intriguing to me is that it was such a struggle on our part to decide not to decide. Deciding not to decide is, of course, among the most important things done by the Supreme Court. It takes a lot of doing, but it can be done. In the overwhelming majority of cases what appears in the public record is a short, simple order denying certiorari.

There was nothing short or simple about our decisions in the two Second Circuit cases I am about to discuss. In both of them the writs of certiorari were dismissed as improvidently granted, known by some as a DIG. It was brought about by Mr. Justice Felix Frankfurter in his time, and it has survived. It is itself fairly unusual, since my brethren share the common human characteristic of not liking to admit that they have been improvident. These particular DIGs, moreover, were among the most unusual I have seen, that is, the two I am talking about.

The first DIG came in a case written by Bill Timbers called *Mallis v. Federal Deposit Insurance Corp.* We granted certiorari to consider the question of whether a pledge of stock qualified as a "purchase or sale" for purposes of a suit under Rule

10b-5. In a footnote to his opinion, Bill had written about his unsuccessful search for a separate document embodying the District Court's judgment. He had not been able to find such a document, and he ultimately concluded that a separate judgment was not really necessary.

Our Court ended up agreeing with the Second Circuit on this point, but in the process we decided that our initial grant of certiorari had been improvident. Hence, the U.S. Reports contain a seven-page per curiam discussing the highly significant issue of whether a separate District Court judgment is necessary, followed by a brief paragraph explaining that we had decided to DIG the case. It is surely one of the more unusual opinions to be found in last Term's collection.

Another gripe I had with the Second Circuit, and I still have with the Supreme Court, is a per curiam with a dissenting opinion.[2] I have great trouble with five-to-four per curiam. I don't know much Latin, practically none, but I have to find the word for "Some of the" in Latin, because it wouldn't be a per curiam, it would be per some of the curiam. But my Court still does it. The Court of Appeals does too. I am scared to death one of these days to read a single judge's District Court opinion per curiam. At least he won't have a dissent.

The second case that I want to mention involves a lady named Estelle Jacobs, also known as Mrs. Kramer. Poor Ms. Jacobs was thought by the Government to be involved with what we used to call "unsavory characters," and she was eventually called before a grand jury about these characters. She was not told, however, that she was a subject of the grand jury's investigation, she was a target. Because she had not been warned she was a target, the Second Circuit upheld the dismissal of a perjury count that was based on her grand jury testimony. Murray Gurfein's opinion made clear that the decision rested on the court's "supervisory power." He said so.

After the Supreme Court decided, two Terms ago, that the Constitution did not require a warning to grand jury targets, the Court remanded Ms. Jacobs' case for further consideration. I dissented from the remand order, joined by Bill Brennan and Potter Stewart, largely on the ground that Murray knew what he was talking about and had not based his decision on the Constitution. If Murray said supervisory power, then he meant supervisory power. Sure enough, on remand Murray wrote another opinion in which he told us just that.

The Government again sought certiorari in the Supreme Court. Certiorari was granted, and argument was held. Then a few weeks later the Court issued an order restoring the case to the calendar for reargument, which is re-re-reargument. After this second set of arguments, you might have anticipated a careful, scholarly opinion on the issues presented, else why all these arguments? But instead, as you probably know, we issued a one-sentence Dismissal as Improvidently Granted. A case that had received an extraordinary amount of attention, that had been bounced back and

---

[2] The Supreme Court's *per curiam* (literally, "by the Court") opinions do not indicate who the opinion's author is.

forth between Supreme Court and Court of Appeals twice and that had prompted a second oral argument, ended in a DIG. Murray had the last laugh.

We might perhaps look forward to a similar display of indecision next term if the Court grants certiorari in *United States v. Smith*. That was the case in which Bill Mulligan wrote that "Although his IQ score was admittedly low, Judge Brieant . . . found [the defendant] to be of average intelligence." The accuracy of that description of Charlie Brieant could become an important and divisive issue if the case comes up for argument. I shudder at what might happen.

I cannot step down without adding a comment on the Second Circuit's remarkable achievement in clearing its docket for five consecutive years. I am not only proud of it, but I don't mind, without any provocation, bragging about it in conference and unofficial meetings with the Supreme Court. I want you all to know, especially Irving [Kaufman] and everybody concerned, that I don't in the least resent your delaying this burst of productivity and this working around the clock for the past five years until after I left for Washington.

18. Remarks at the Second Circuit Judicial Conference [The Dangers of Judicial Restraint] (May 1979)

Normally, I begin these talks each year with a report on how well the Second Circuit has done in the Supreme Court. As things now stand, the Second Circuit has been reversed in 6 cases and affirmed in 3. Since all the returns are not yet in and George Gallup has not volunteered his assistance in forecasting the results, I hesitate to predict the final tally. Of the cases that have been decided this term, however, the Second Circuit has provided two of the most important: *Herbert v. Lando*, and *Bell v. Wolfish*. In my view, your performance was far better than that of my Brethren.

I reported to you last year that "Freedom of the Press" had not fared too well in our recent decisions. Unfortunately, but as expected this trend has continued. With the considerable media attention that *Herbert v. Lando* has received, both last year when the panel rendered its decision and this year, thanks to an industrious ABC reporter, even before the Supreme Court has spoken, I am sure that you are all familiar with the case.[1] My personal views on editorial autonomy can be succinctly stated: it must be afforded the utmost protection, to ensure that the public is exposed to the widest possible range of information and insights. Given that libel plaintiffs' pretrial maneuvers may be fashioned more with an eye to deterrence or retaliation than to unearthing germane material, I believe that special safeguards are needed to protect the press from abuse of the discovery process. Without such safeguards, the press may be forced to make editorial judgments that reflect less the risk of liability than the expense of vindication.

Even close supervision of pretrial procedures by trial courts, however, does not suffice to protect journalistic endeavor. Preserving a climate of free interchange among journalists is essential to sound editorial decision making. And as Jim Oakes [of the Second Circuit] recognized, such collegial discussion will likely be stifled unless confidentiality is guaranteed. Therefore, I believe that discovery in defamation cases should not be allowed as to the substance of editorial conversations. Particularly because there are so many other means of proving deliberate or reckless disregard for the truth, this privilege, in my view, would be unlikely to preclude recovery by plaintiffs with valid defamation claims.

---

[1] *Herbert v. Lando* held that the ordinary rules of pretrial discovery were applicable in cases in which a plaintiff in a libel case sought to determine how editorial decisions were made. According to the Court, libel plaintiffs can recover only if defamatory statements were published with reckless disregard of their truth or falsity, and examining the editorial process can be one way of finding out whether the publisher acted with such reckless disregard.

The second important case from this Circuit where my colleagues afforded insufficient protection to constitutional rights is *Bell v. Wolfish*. The Court ruled there that the Government could place almost any restriction on pretrial detainees, provided it did not proclaim a punitive intent or impose conditions that were arbitrary or purposeless. As if this standard afforded detainees any protection at all, the Court weakened it further by according virtually unlimited deference to detention officials' justifications for particular impositions. The fact that my Brethren essentially disregarded is the one which is truly relevant in this context—the impact of the restrictions on the detainees.

Of course, courts should not substitute their judgment for that of jail administrators. Nor should they rubber stamp their actions. As those of you with experience in complex civil rights litigation involving schools, prisons, or mental institutions appreciate, it is sometimes difficult for a federal court to know the difference between administrative convenience and institutional necessity. But we have long since abandoned the notion that the king can do no wrong. Certainly, wardens should not be treated better than royalty.

Moreover, the posture of crippling judicial restraint which the Court assumed in *Bell* is particularly inappropriate in the context of *jail* administration. To begin with, pretrial detainees are confined for the limited purpose of securing their presence at trial. They have not been convicted of a crime, and indeed, are clothed with a presumption of innocence. Detainees' rights are therefore more extensive than those of convicted criminals, and thus more active judicial review of conditions of their confinement is warranted. Second, as we are all aware, few federal offenses are non-bailable. Most individuals in pretrial detention are incarcerated simply because they are too poor to afford a bond. I think that courts have a special obligation to scrutinize impositions that have a disproportionate impact on the poor. My colleagues, however, displayed no such sensitivity, preferring instead to provide us with such enduring legal homilies as, "There is no one man, one cell principle lurking in the Due Process Clause." At least, the Court did not carry its rhetoric further, and proclaim that due process does not mandate a one man, one bed principle.

This insensitivity to the realities of pretrial detention, it seems to me, colored even the basic mode of analysis in *Bell*. The Court set out to determine whether the pretrial impositions at issue could be characterized as "punishment." Had my Brethren even considered the impact of the restrictions on the detainees, I think they would have realized that this exercise was entirely semantical. Pretrial incarceration, although frequently necessary to assure defendants' presence at trial, is essentially indistinguishable from other punishment. The detainee is involuntarily confined; he is placed in a locked cell, just as a convicted criminal. To argue over whether this form of confinement can be characterized as punishment skirts the critical constitutional inquiry: whether the state's interests in maintaining the restrictions outweigh the individual interests at stake.

It is the application of this approach, however, that most forcefully illustrates its deficiencies. In particular, the Court upheld a rule subjecting inmates to body cavity searches after every contact visit with someone from outside the jail, including defense attorneys. Although the visits were continuously monitored, the visitors were thoroughly searched, and the likelihood of smuggling was remote to say the least, the Court nonetheless, by a 5–4 vote, simply accepted the detention officials' security justifications without any meaningful inquiry. It did so, moreover, despite the conclusions of the judges of this circuit, that such searches, conducted in the absence of any suspicion of wrongdoing, were so offensive to common decency that they shocked the conscience. I can think of no more degrading experience than being subjected to one of these searches in the presence of guards and fellow inmates. It is simply an outrage that these unwarranted intrusions on personal privacy should be allowed to continue.

In sum, I find *Bell v. Wolfish* to be one of the most troubling opinions to come from the Supreme Court in quite some time. I can only hope that district and appellate judges will read the decision narrowly. To read it otherwise would afford pretrial detainees virtually no constitutional protection. Since the Court has consistently disavowed a judicial hands-off attitude even with respect to convicted criminals, this cannot be what was intended in *Bell*.

On a more positive note, the Second Circuit had the best record this term when it disagreed with other circuits. By an 8 to 1 vote, the Court resolved a conflict between this Circuit and the Fifth, and affirmed Walter Mansfield's opinion in *Parklane Hosiery v. Shore*. We held there that in a private action for damages under the Securities Acts, the Seventh Amendment did not bar application of collateral estoppel to issues previously litigated in an SEC injunctive suit. This represents a victory for the SEC's enforcement effort, a result that has not been common over the past few terms. In addition, the Second Circuit's view regarding the tax-exempt status of franchisee associations prevailed over a contrary view of the Eighth Circuit. And in *United California Bank v. United States*, the Supreme Court reversed the 9th Circuit and adopted Henry Friendly's approach to the treatment of capital gains earned by an estate and set aside for charitable purposes.

This Circuit has done well and must continue to do so. Ill conceived reversals should be considered as no more than temporary interruptions. We must stand fast for the fullest protection of individual rights.

19. Remarks at the Second Circuit Judicial Conference [The Judiciary and Fundamental Human Liberties] (May 1980)

It is customary for me to begin these talks each year with a brief report on how the Second Circuit fared in the Supreme Court for the Term. As things presently stand, with several cases not yet decided, I am pleased to report that the Second Circuit is doing quite well. Although the Circuit got off to a bad start with two summary reversals,[1] both over my dissent, the record in argued cases is much better this year than in the past. So far the Second Circuit, including a three-judge district court, has been affirmed six times and reversed only once in argued cases. There have been two summary affirmances as well, to counterbalance the summary reversals. All things considered, the Circuit can be proud of its record so far.

At last year's conference I was fairly critical of my Brethren for their performances in *Herbert v. Lando* and *Bell v. Wolfish*. I could be equally critical this year of *City of Mobile v. Bolden*, in which four of my Brethren attempted to read a requirement of *intentional* racial discrimination into the Fourteenth and Fifteenth Amendments and a fifth Justice suggested that racial discrimination through vote dilution could be permissible if it was part of politics as usual. I discussed at some length in my dissent in that case my strong disagreement with the Court's result and will not dwell on it here.

Instead, I will address a more general issue: the role of the judiciary in protecting fundamental human liberties. This topic is all the more fitting in light of the recent death of Bill Douglas, who directed every ounce of his boundless energy to the protection of personal rights. It is vitally important that we as lawyers and judges never lose sight of our basic place in the Constitutional scheme.

The Constitution embodies the very spirit of democratic government. When the Founding Fathers sat down to draft the instrument that would form the framework for this country, they did far more than establish a series of legal precepts, although of course those legal precepts are vital rights of all Americans. The Constitution also sets forth basic principles which are the very essence of the United States. The primary principle is equality. The Fifth Amendment provides that "*no person*" shall be deprived of life, liberty or property without due process of law. This was reaffirmed in the Fourteenth Amendment, which bans the denial of equal protection of the laws "to *any* person." The very first truth which we declared self-evident in the Declaration of Independence was that "all men are created equal." Every person has

---

[1] See selection 21 for a longer discussion of summary reversals.

the same "unalienable rights" of liberty, liberty and the pursuit of happiness, and all persons are to be treated with the respect and decency which those inalienable rights demand.

A related principle is participation in the governing process. It was "we the people," not some smaller or more elite group, who established the Constitution "in order to form a more perfect union." As was stated in the Declaration of Independence, "Governments are instituted among men, deriving their just powers from the consent of the governed." Participation recognizes the moral worth of each individual, and in this way shows again that all persons are equal.

From the very beginning of this Nation, therefore, we have recognized that in order to achieve the good society, there must be equality, there must be participation in the governing process, and accordingly there must be a government of laws rather than of men. Such a society will be just, for every member will be treated with equal respect and dignity.

It is the responsibility of the judiciary to make sure that we remain a government of laws and that all persons are equal under those laws. This is the essence of justice. It is a weighty responsibility, but we are uniquely qualified for the task under our Constitutional scheme.

There are three major differences between the judiciary and the other branches of government. First, the executive and legislature of necessity must be preoccupied with the needs of the moment. The economy desperately needs attention, and international crises occur almost daily. Prompt action is required. Day-to-day decisions must be made through a process of accommodation among diverse political groups in order to reach acceptable results which may be put into operation quickly. Compromise is an essential element of the political process. Second, the political branches are designed to function through the clash of partisan interests. The members of the executive and legislature are supposed to be representative of the interests of their electorate, to make sure that in the compromises which are made their groups are fairly treated. Third, the other branches in large measure deal in abstractions. The legislature passes laws of general application based on composites and projections. The executive has the responsibility to enforce those laws on a broad scale.

In the courts, by contrast, the emphasis is on the individual, impartiality is required, and political compromise has no role at all. Judges are supposed to be reflective, considering the controversy before them in light of the broader legal schemes, Constitutional and otherwise, which guide the country. Decisions traditionally are justified by opinions announcing reasoning derived from earlier cases and established principles; raw political power is never a sufficient justification for any judicial decision. Constitutional rights should never be compromised by the courts in the name of expediency.

The judiciary operates under a premise of neutrality rather than partisanship. Federal judges are insulated, as much as possible, from political pressure which might interfere with principled decision making. Article III judges have life tenure and are free from threats of economic retaliation for unpopular decisions. In addition, we cannot have a personal stake in the outcome of any case before us, and the Code of Judicial Conduct cautions us to avoid even the appearance of impropriety.

The reason for this strict requirement of impartiality is that the judiciary stands as the referee whenever the individual citizen and his government conflict. Such an arbiter must be independent and neutral. The whole purpose of the separation of powers is to establish an equal branch of the government which can check the other branches when their political compromises and generalized focus result in unfairness to the individual. If the government acts unfairly, the court stands as a guardian, forcing the other branches to recognize that basic principles have been violated and that certain persons have been denied their fundamental right to equal treatment under law. It can never be the greatest good for the greatest number to deny the equal moral worth of a fellow human being. Similarly, when the interests of individuals clash, there cannot be any danger of predisposition by the court if each litigant is to be confident that he has received equal treatment. Before the bar, all men and women must stand equal, with their claims resolved solely on the strength of legal principles.

Judges are also in a better position to be a check on the encroachment of basic human liberties because they deal with people on an individual basis. The specific facts of a case are never unimportant to the result. The litigant receives particularized attention because general principles must be applied to individual needs and concerns. There are no nameless litigants. District judges in particular see the very individuals who feel that they have been singled out for unequal treatment.

One of the great strengths of the judiciary is that it is the one branch of government which is accessible to every person. The courts do not choose what problems they will deal with each day. Instead, the litigants bring the issues, and the courts must decide each case. The trend in recent times has been toward even fuller access to the courts, through permission to proceed in forma pauperis,[2] permission to proceed pro se, appointment of counsel, and the growth of free legal services programs. And once inside the courtroom, each person has an opportunity to be heard, to participate in the legal process and to speak his mind about his fundamental rights.

This participation serves to recognize, every day in every court, the moral worth of each individual. Each person should have the sense that through the courts the avenues of government are open to him, that he can state his viewpoint and be fairly heard by a neutral decisionmaker. There has been a growing recognition that it is vitally important that people have a sense of participation in the decisionmaking process. It is not enough that the decision be correct; someone must have listened to the claimant and by that listening acknowledged the importance of the individual. Our country prides itself on the fact that every person gets his "day in court," and that ideal must never be forgotten.

---

[2] *In forma pauperis* means as a poor person.

To the extent that judges fail to accord equal treatment under law in a specific case, they lose their ability to protect basic human liberties in general. Courts derive their power in our system of government from moral suasion. Our mandates are obeyed solely because it is recognized that they are the product of individualized attention, equal treatment, and neutral decisionmaking. The losing party may well be disappointed, but he will be unlikely to disobey if he knows that someone has listened to him and dealt with him fairly on an equal level with all others. Justice Frankfurter recognized the need to maintain "the feeling, so important to popular government, that justice has been done." It is for this reason that we must justify our rulings—to demonstrate that in each individual case, we have given our attention and thought to the needs and concerns of a fellow human being, and that we have not favored one party over another solely because of who he is.

It is essential to the social fabric of this country that every person be accorded his full and equal worth. Accordingly, the judiciary must be vigilant to preserve its role in the Constitutional scheme as protector of human liberties. To the extent we fulfill our role, it becomes all the easier to command acceptance of our decision in the next case, even though the needs of the moment may make a principled decision unpopular. If we do not fulfill that role, we undermine our ability to do so in the future. If the courts fail to focus on the individual, or fail to give equal treatment to every person, or fail to apply principles and reason, then we will have lost our goal of equal justice under law. And without equal justice under law, without the recognition of the equal worth of every person, all of our "unalienable rights" will be in jeopardy. I am confident that the judges of this Circuit will never permit that to occur.

20. Remarks at the Second Circuit Judicial Conference [The Importance of Judicial Neutrality] (May 8, 1981)

It is customary for me to begin these talks with a brief review of how the Second Circuit has fared in the Supreme Court. The returns are running a little late this year, but so far you have broken even. Two reversals and two affirmances from the four cases that have been argued and decided. I felt a little bad being the Justice assigned to write *Firestone Tire & Rubber*, which led to summary vacation of a Second Circuit *en banc* opinion. And as you are probably aware, I would rather than you had not been summarily reversed in *Schweiker v. Hansen*.

Well, you win a few and you lose a few. It's in the nature of the process that you can't always be on the winning side. This term the Court has faced a number of difficult questions, and unfortunately, we have been sharply divided over many of them. Of course, we have it a little easier than you do. When you face a tough issue, you might struggle with it, then finally say, "Well, that's our decision. Let the Supreme Court reverse us if we are wrong." We've found a better method for dealing with the tough ones. We can say, "That's our decision. Let the lower courts figure it out. After all, isn't that what they're for?"

And it's true. Much of the work of any federal judge involves trying to decipher and to apply the sometimes conflicting messages contained in the cases we decide. Often our opinions seem unclear. I can only assure you that we do the best we can. If our opinions sometimes seem to offer little guidance, bear in mind that we try to decide only the case before us. The structure of the law is built that way, case by case, and all of us as judges are constrained to work within that framework. Sudden and sweeping changes in the law must come from other branches of government. We as judges are not in a position to dictate policy; we can only interpret the Constitution and the laws of the land, determining what they permit, what they require, and what they forbid.

This task of interpretation is the cornerstone of the judicial process. As we undertake it, we must strive for neutrality. None of us is perfect, and I recognize that neutrality is more ideal than real. Each of us brings along to the judicial role certain preconceived biases. It is, I suppose, impossible to make a decision totally uninfluenced by them. But we as judges must try to do so to the extent we possibly can.

This ideal of neutrality is particularly hard to maintain in times, such as this, when our society faces major unsolved problems. Indeed, we judges are frequently criticized these days for our neutrality. For example, it is argued by some members of our society that the judiciary had not taken an active enough role in combating crime. It is urged that we, as judges, should take sides, that we should stand shoulder to shoulder with the police and prosecutors. Convictions should be easier, appellate review more rapid, and resort to habeas corpus—what the Founders of this Republic called the Great Writ—drastically curtailed. All of this frightens me because when I was in law school, I was taught not that judges were there to see the defendant convicted and punished in every case, but that they were there to see justice done in every case. *Of course* the state had to carry a heavy burden to obtain a conviction. *Of course* appellate judges would weigh each case carefully. *Of course* an individual, once convicted, could attack his sentence later. This, so I was taught, was not to coddle the guilty, but to protect the innocent. I was raised in the days when the prevailing maxim was: "It is better that a thousand guilty people go free than that one innocent person suffer unjustly."

Well, that's just what I was taught, and maybe I was taught wrong. But the suggestion that we as judges take sides frightens me for another, more fundamental reason as well. As I have said, judges are required in our system to be as neutral as they possibly can, to stand above the political questions in which the other branches of government are necessarily entangled. The Constitution established a legislative branch to make the laws and an executive branch to enforce them. Both branches are elected and are designed to respond to ever changing public concerns and problems. Indeed, as we were reminded just last November, the failure of either branch to respond to the will of the majority can quickly be remedied at the polls.

But the Framers of the Constitution recognized that responsiveness to the will of the majority may, if unchecked, become a tyranny of the majority. They therefore created a third branch—the judiciary—to check the actions of the legislature and the executive. In order to fulfill this function, the judiciary was intentionally isolated from the political process and purposely spared the task of dealing with changing public concerns and problems. Article III judges are guaranteed life tenure. Similarly, their compensation cannot be decreased during their term in office—a provision, as we have recently seen, that certainly has its tangible benefits. Finally, the constitutional task we are assigned as judges is a very narrow one. We cannot make the laws, and it is not our duty to see that they are enforced. We merely interpret them, through the painstaking process of adjudicating actual "cases or controversies" that come before us.

We have seen what happens when the courts have permitted themselves to be moved by prevailing political pressures, and have deferred to the mob rather than interpret the Constitution. *Dred Scott, Plessy, Korematsu* and the trial proceedings in *Moore v. Dempsey* come readily to mind as unfortunate examples. They are decisions of which the entire judicial community, even after all these years, should be ashamed. There have also been times when the courts have stood proudly as a bulwark against what was politically expedient but also unconstitutional. One need only recall the school desegregation cases to understand why this ability to stand above the fray is so important.

Our central function is to act as neutral arbiters of disputes that arise under the law. To this end, we bind ourselves through our own code of ethics or avoid even the appearance of impropriety or partiality. We must handle the cases that come before us without regard for what result might meet with public approval. We must decide each case in accordance with the law. We must not reach for a result that we, in our arrogance, believe will further some goal not related to the concrete case before us. And we must treat the litigants in every case in an even-handed manner. It would be as wrong to favor the prosecution in every criminal case as it would be to favor the plaintiff in every tort suit.

We must never forget that the only real source of power that we, as judges, can tap is the respect of the people. We will command that respect only as long as we strive for neutrality. If we are perceived as campaigning for particular policies, as joining with other branches of government in resolving questions not committed to us by the Constitution, we may gain some public acclaim in the short run. In the long run, however, we will cease to be perceived as neutral arbiters, and we will lose that public respect so vital to our function.

I do not suggest that we as judges should not be concerned about the problem of crime. Every thinking American is worried about it. And just about all of us have, lurking somewhere in the back of our minds, what we consider the ideal solution. But when we accepted the judicial mantle, we yielded our right to advocate publicly our favored solutions for society's problems. The tools for solving these problems are in the hands of the other branches of government because that is where the Constitution has placed them. That is also where we should leave them. I therefore urge that you politely disregard any suggestion that you give up the robe for the sword.

Before I conclude, I should add that everyone seems to agree that an efficient judicial system is an essential element of any overall solution to the crime problem. The Second Circuit is by far the most efficient Circuit in the federal system, so I don't think you need to worry about whether you might be contributing to the problem. You are, I think, part of the solution. You are doing your part by being the best collection of judges in the world, and by disposing of the cases that come before you in a fair, honest, and efficient manner. I don't think that anybody could ask you do to more than that.

21. Remarks at the Second Circuit Judicial Conference
[The Problem of Summary Disposition in the Supreme Court]
(September 9, 1982)

Traditionally, I have begun my remarks at these gatherings with a report on how the Second Circuit has fared in the Supreme Court. During the last Term, this Circuit's won-lost record was better than average. Of the 15 cases from the Second Circuit decided on the merits, the Circuit was affirmed in 8 cases and reversed in 7. An 8-and-7 record is pretty good when you consider that, as in past years, the Supreme Court reversed in more than 60% of the cases argued and decided during the 1981 Term.

The eight affirmances included one of the more important decisions of the Term, *North Haven Board of Education v. Bell*. I had the good fortune of winding up in the majority. That case involved Title IX of the Education Amendments of 1972, which provides that "no person" shall be subject to sex discrimination in any educational program receiving federal assistance. In 1975 the Department of Health, Education & Welfare issued regulations forbidding employment discrimination in programs receiving Title IX aid. The issue in the *North Haven* case was the validity of these regulations. The Court reached the same conclusion that Jim Oakes had in his opinion for a unanimous panel: the regulations are valid because Title IX protects not only students enrolled in education programs receiving federal assistance but also employees who work in such programs.

The *North Haven* case was one of several this past Term concerning education. Another that received a great deal of attention was the book-banning case, *Board of Education v. Pico*, in which the Second Circuit was also affirmed.[1] However, there were seven separate opinions in the Supreme Court, so it may be pretty difficult for the lower courts, or anyone else, to figure out what exactly what the decision stands for. Even in the Second Circuit, the 3 judges on the panel produced 3 separate opinions. I know we've been criticized in recent years for decisions in which no opinion has commanded a majority. I can only say that I was one of only 2 Justices who didn't write a separate opinion in the *Pico* case.

In *Merrill Lynch v. Curran*, the Supreme Court affirmed the Second Circuit's decision recognizing an implied cause of action under the Commodity Exchange Act. In practical terms the decision was a significant one, since hundreds of suits

---

[1] In *Pico* the Court's holding was that a school board could not remove books from school libraries solely because the board's members disagreed with the books' political messages.

in which plaintiffs had asserted such a cause of action were pending. In light of some recent Supreme Court decisions (from which I dissented) taking a restrictive view of implied private rights of action, the outcome in the case was far from clear. As Henry Friendly noted in his majority opinion, prior to the amendments of the Act in 1974, all the courts that had considered the matter had recognized the existence of an implied cause of action, and the legislative history of the 1974 amendments showed that Congress was familiar with those decisions. The dissent in the Supreme Court emphasized that all of the pre-1974 cases had been decided by the lower courts and that the Supreme Court had not spoken. But a majority of the Court agreed with Henry that where the lower courts have uniformly reached the same result in applying a statute, and Congress then re-enacts the statute without modifying that result, it may be reasonable to infer that Congress intended to approve what the lower courts have done. Of course, inferring approval from re-enactment is always a tricky business, but it shouldn't depend solely on whether the Supreme Court has spoken.

One case where the Second Circuit did not fare so well involved the *Central Trust Company*. In that case, the Supreme Court summarily reversed the court of appeals in a per curiam opinion. I found the result lamentable, and I therefore joined Justice Stevens' dissent. But equally disturbing was the way in which the Court reached the result. The case exemplifies a growing and inexplicable readiness on the part of the current Court to dispose of cases summarily. When the Court issues a per curiam opinion deciding a case summarily, it does so without full briefing and any oral argument. Instead, the Court has before it only the petitions and responses on the limited issue of certiorari, in which parties are not supposed to debate the merits. Our rules specifically prohibit discussion of the merits. Rule 21.3 states: ". . . No separate brief in support of a petition for a writ of certiorari will be received, and the Clerk will refuse to file any petition for a writ of certiorari to which is annexed or appended any supporting brief."

These summary dispositions pose very real problems. First, significant issues can receive cursory treatment, creating a potential for error and confusion. One example is *United States v. Hollywood Motor Car Company*, another case decided last Term. The Court held that, when a defendant moves to dismiss an indictment because of prosecutorial vindictiveness and the district court denies the motion, no appeal can be taken before trial. This important issue of appellate jurisdiction had divided the circuits, and prior case law in the Supreme Court pointed in various directions. The issue had not been briefed or argued in either the district court or the court of appeals, and was not raised until the government filed its petition for rehearing in the Ninth Circuit. Nonetheless, the Court found summary disposition appropriate. Another example from this year was *Hutto v. Davis*. Six Justices held that the Eighth Amendment permits a sentence of 40 years and a fine of $20,000 for possession and distribution of less than 9 ounces of marijuana. The case involved a significant extension of *Rummel v. Estelle*, which upheld the validity of a life sentence for a three-time felon. Yet the Court summarily reversed the Fourth Circuit's *en banc* decision and even suggested that the lower court's approach would foster anarchy within the federal judicial system.

The Court has not only used summary dispositions to give short shrift to important issues. It has also used the device to decide cases that do not meet the traditional criteria for Supreme Court review. The nadir was reached at the end of the Term in *Board of Education v. McCluskey*, where the Court exercised its mighty power in order to enforce a school board's suspension of a 10th grade student who consumed too much alcohol on a fall day.

In addition, the Court appears to be using summary dispositions in a result-oriented fashion. In a disproportionate number of cases, the Court has employed the device to aid prosecutors, wardens, and school board officials. Last Term, for example, the Court issued 16 per curiam opinions summarily reversing lower courts. Of these 13 involved prosecutors, wardens, or school board officials. In all but one of these cases, the state prevailed. In *McCluskey*, Justice Stevens was forced to wonder whether, if the student had been unjustly suspended, the Court would still have considered the matter of such national importance to require summary reversal.

I am disturbed by the all-too-often cavalier treatment of the rights and interests of the parties involved in such cases. Instead of giving them a full opportunity to be heard on the merits, the Court's rules restrict the parties to a skeletal presentation of the issues. Rule 21.4 provides that: "The petition for writ of certiorari shall be as short as possible, but may not exceed 30 pages, excluding the subject index, table of authorities, any verbatim quotations required by subparagraph 1(f) of this Rule, and the appendix." Rule 22.2 restricts briefs in opposition in the same manner.

If these summary dispositions are to continue at all, the Court should undertake one major change in its procedures. Whenever the Court concludes that summary reversal or affirmance may be appropriate, it should notify the parties that summary disposition is under consideration and allow them time to file briefs on the merits. This would give the litigants an opportunity to be heard before their cases are decided, and give the Court the benefit of an adversarial presentation of the issues. An opportunity to brief the merits is the least we should demand before a decision is rendered by the court of last resort.

22. Remarks at the Second Circuit Judicial Conference
[Division on the Court and the "Need" for a New Appellate Court]
(October 1, 1983)

It's always good to be here. I have a couple of things on my mind that I want to talk about. Looking back at the 1982 term, I wonder whether it makes much sense to begin my remarks, as I traditionally have, by commenting on the Second Circuit's won and lost record.

Let me explain why I think we have to look behind the statistics, the cold statistics of five affirmances and six reversals on the merits. I guess that's the way you put it.

In one of the significant Fourth Amendment cases of the term, *United States v. Place*, the Supreme Court affirmed the Second Circuit. Walter Mansfield wrote the opinion holding that the removal to another location and the detention for one and a half or two hours of Place's airport baggage to determine whether the bags contained narcotics simply could not be classified as just a reasonable warrantless investigatory stop.

I love these "stops" and these adjectives, "investigatory holding," all the different words that make stopping people legal.

So, this was in the absence of any probable cause under the Terry line of cases.

Now, our Court agreed that under these circumstances a ninety-minute detention, failure of the agents to inform Place where they were taking his luggage, how long it might be held, or what arrangements would be made for its return, that this seizure of Place's bags violated the Fourth Amendment.

But did our Court truly "affirm"? I don't think so.

Of particular concern to Justices Brennan, Blackmun, and myself was the majority's gratuitous holding that a "sniff search" by a dog trained to detect narcotics is so minimally intrusive, so limited both in the manner in which the information is obtained and in the content of the information that is revealed by that procedure, that exposure of luggage in a public place to a trained canine just does not constitute a search within the meaning of the Fourth Amendment.

As we pointed out, Place in this case had not raised the canine search issue. That issue was not raised in the District Court. The canine search issue was not raised in the Court of Appeals. The Court of Appeals certainly did not reach it. It was not briefed or argued in the Supreme Court of the United States—but it was decided by the Supreme Court of the United States.

Now, how do I count such a holding in my statistical report of affirmances and reversals?

It's someplace in the middle. I think I will have to give a typical State Department report; like when you ask the State Department to determine, once and for all, what is the difference between black and white, and you get back a State Department report which says that "We sent this out after we got it two years ago. We took it over to 18 of our Embassies, 30 of our departments, 128 people that worked on it, and now, at last, we have come to a definitive answer to your question: Black is definitely black; white is definitely white; but there is a gray ground."

Well, I think that's where my statistics are going to end up this year.

The standards that ought to control the use of an investigatory technique that enhances human perception raise [such] a complex issue that I think we should all regret that the majority of my Court barreled ahead instead of waiting for a case that properly raised that precise issue.

Well, that was affirmance number one.

Now, there were other significant cases of last year: *The Guardians Association versus the Civil Service Commission*, which raised a number of important questions in areas of employment discrimination law.

Now, here again, congratulating the Second Circuit on an affirmance doesn't tell us much; but here the problem is the scourge of the contemporary Supreme Court—multiple opinions.

It must be very scant comfort to Tom Meskill, who began his opinion noting that "The authorities do not speak with one voice," and, when the authorities got through with this one, to read an affirmance which takes a box score to decipher is almost impossible.

My brother Justice White's opinion is in six parts. My brother Justice Rehnquist joins in Parts I, III, IV, and Part II of Justice Powell's separate opinion.

Justice O'Connor concurred separately and joined in some of the points in Justice Stevens' dissent; and four of us had great unanimity; we had two separate opinions.

Is that affirmance?

I guess it is. Well, we will call it that anyhow.

Now, *Guardians* is an important case, no question about it. We granted certiorari to consider whether proof of discriminatory intent is required to establish a violation of Title VI of the Civil Rights Act.

This circuit said yes; the Appeals Court said no. An affirmance?

The *Guardians* case was brought by Negro and Hispanic police officers who, although appointed to the force, found themselves the first to be laid off when the times got hard in New York City. They were in the "last hired-first fired" category because their appointments were made in order of test scores. They challenged the tests as not job-related yet having a discriminatory impact on their scores.

The District Court awarded various forms of relief under Title VI for this unintentional discrimination—"constructive seniority" they call it, and back pay, the right to sit for promotion exams, and to participate in planning future, non-discriminatory exams.

Well, the majority of the Supreme Court held that where a violation of Title VI is "unintentional"—you know, you just had your head chopped off, but it was unintentional; you just were deprived of food, but it was unintentional; you just find yourself without a job, but it was unintentional. The Court held that only limited injunctive relief is available as a remedy and so affirmed the Second Circuit's denial of relief to the class on that alternative ground.

Again, I had the misfortune to be in the minority and, as I pointed out in the opinion, every Cabinet department and about forty federal agencies have adopted standards interpreting Title VI to bar programs with any discriminatory impact, and where the legal right is so clear, I can see no limitations on the remedies available to the federal courts to make good the wrong that has been done.

Now, just to reassure you that sometimes when we affirm we are really affirming in a straight-forward manner, let me point to an important bankruptcy case last term. We drafted a decision in *Whiting Pools* that split with the Fourth Circuit. No doubt the IRS wishes that Henry Friendly, Jim Oakes, and Larry Pierce had never put their minds to the problem of whether the Bankruptcy Act authorizes a Bankruptcy Judge to order the IRS to turn over seized property on which the IRS has levied.

The Second Circuit held that a Bankruptcy Judge has the authority, and our Court for once unanimously agreed. The District Courts in the Second Circuit in turn have given the Supreme Court articulate opinions. I stress here "opinions" because I want to say a word about the encouraging emphasis that the Second Circuit has placed this past year on reducing the number of Appellate cases brought up by order.

Our evaluation of a particular case is immensely aided by the analysis and explication in a concise per curiam or more deeply analytical signed opinion.

And let me offer a wholly unscientific, unvalidated observation: Issuing an Appellate decision as an opinion rather than an order may reduce the number of petitions for certiorari filed in Supreme Court, for which my colleagues and I would be deeply grateful.

I have just reviewed, completed—all of us, each have reviewed 989 petitions for certiorari, appeals, and motions. That's just the summer workload—you know, while we were on vacation. I love that word, "vacation."

I am struck by the number of petitions filed from summary dispositions in the Courts of Appeals throughout the country, and I cannot help but sense that many times parties approach the Supreme Court because that unpublished order just didn't reassure them that their case got the careful review that it almost certainly in fact did.

We on the bench must not sacrifice the articulation of facts and law in our response to the need to administer our case law, our case loads efficiently. The legitimacy of our decision-making remains, in significant part, a function of the appearance of justice.

In the same vein, you will remember the concern I expressed in last year's Conference at my own Court's unhealthy readiness to dispose of cases summarily, without either full—or indeed any—briefing on the merits or oral argument.

I have dissented repeatedly from this practice, which to my mind creates a real potential for error and confusion. So, when I heartily endorse the Circuit's commitment to deciding cases by opinion rather than by order, I just want you to know that I am not endorsing any more hard work for you than I myself am willing to undertake with my own case load.

And speaking of "case load"—usually a noun coupled with adjectives like "crippling" or "crushing" or "crisis"—I can't resist taking a pot shot at one of the worst solutions yet devised to deal with that "problem." I am just flat against creating a third tier of review by creating a temporary experiment called the "Intercircuit Tribunal." They tell me it's for my own good. They tell me that the "crushing case load" will be helped.

Just to give you one example of how that isn't going to work: How would it have helped me review those 989 cases on our July and August lists I just told you about if I still had to read them all but then had to decide not only whether to grant or deny certiorari but also had to decide whether some of those cases ought to go to this new Tribunal?

And then, of course, I would still have to tell the Tribunal what I wanted it to do with the case, decide whether the Supreme Court should hear it.

Thanks—I would rather decide that myself; I have been doing it for sixteen years.

Or tell the Tribunal to resolve that circuit conflict for the nation?

Or say to that new Tribunal, "Create a precedent binding on all the federal courts?"

Well, there is a purely pragmatic problem with that, as Chief Justice Feinberg pointed out in his testimony to Congress last week. That problem is that the loser is probably still going to come marching back to the Supreme Court with that petition for certiorari.

So, if that happens, gee, I get to read all nine hundred over again, and the ultimate resolution of the problem is again delayed—and delayed—and delayed.

This kind of a routing is not a timesaver; it's a waste of time.

But more than that, it just doesn't match up with my reading of the Constitution. I am certainly not a great Constitutional scholar, but doesn't Article III of the Constitution say to us, "The Judicial Branch: The judicial powers of the United States shall be vested in one Supreme Court"?

Now, where I got my schooling—and I have always had a lot of trouble with English. I was over in London writing the constitution for Kenya. They asked me to write the "shedule of rights." I said, "You mean 'schedule,'" and the gentleman from Oxford said, "No, no; we mean 'shedule.'"

I said, "Oh, you are out of your mind, schedule."

He said, "Look, it's our language. We are the British."

I said, "Is it 'shedule'?"

He said, "Yes."

I said, "How are your children doing in 'shool'?"

Sometimes I am not sure; I think "one Supreme Court" does not mean one or two. I don't know.

You don't need me on the soapbox on that issue, when all of the active judges in this circuit are doing very well, telling Congress exactly what their views are on this proposed legislation.

And finally, keep up the good work here, my friends, judges, attorneys, professors, et cetera. We of the Second Circuit are, in the very best sense, all here together on these and other issues. Maybe sometime in the future the rest of the judiciary will catch up.

23. Remarks at the Second Circuit Judicial Conference
[The Need for Effective Remedies When Constitutional Rights Are Violated]
(September 14, 1984)

I usually begin my comments by giving the "box score" of the Second Circuit's cases argued and decided in the Supreme Court's last Term. Last Term there were 9 cases: 4 decisions were affirmed; 3 were reversed or vacated; and 2 were affirmed in part and reversed in part. Since these raw scores show a better than 50-50 "won and lost" record, one might think the Circuit fared pretty well. The more important question is what these cases say for the Second Circuit, and on that question, 2 of your "losses" give me grave concern.

The cases are *Schall v. Martin* and *Heckler v. Day*. Together with a number of other cases from last Term, they illustrate a very disturbing pattern. And it's a pattern that has become more and more common. The Court seems to concede in each case that important federal rights are at issue and that they may have been violated. It then denies the victims the only effective remedies to those violations. Almost as an afterthought, it sometimes suggests that the victims pursue other remedies, and it then offers ones that will have little or no effect.

Before I go on let me state a general principle that I thought was firmly entrenched in our legal culture and central to our system of protection of individual liberties. The principle is that when rights are violated, courts should normally craft remedies that attempt to make the victims "whole" and deter future violations. Decisions that do not conform to that principle will erode the faith in the law of those who rely on the law's protections. Where no remedies are offered, or where the only ones offered can accomplish little, those who need protection will have reason to turn away from the legal system. They will be convinced that their rights are being trivialized more than they are being protected.

Schall v. Martin serves as a good starting point. It was a class action challenge to New York's preventive detention scheme for juveniles. Let me describe the scheme briefly. It allows a family court judge the discretion to order that a child be "detained" for up to 17 days between that child's arrest and the adjudication of his or her guilt. The judge simply has to make a conclusory finding that there is a "serious risk" that if released the child will commit a crime. That's about it. The decision is made in a proceeding that lasts about 10 minutes, and the law gives no explicit guidance to the judge's discretion. And let me make one thing very clear: "detention" may mean something very close to imprisonment.

Now let's turn to the challenge to this scheme. All would seem to agree that arbitrary or punitive detention prior to an adjudication of guilt is a very serious violation of the Constitution. I would think that we would also agree that where a person's very liberty is made to rest on someone's unbridled discretion, we must guard against abuse. Here the discretion was *very* broad, and the plaintiffs showed that the results seemed *very* arbitrary.

Judge Robert Carter declared the law unconstitutional in an opinion that included extensive findings concerning how the system actually operated. The Second Circuit affirmed without dissent. Opinions by Ralph Winter and Jon Newman separately and persuasively bolstered the district court's conclusions. The Supreme Court reversed, but clearly it did not have the better case.

The Court upheld the system as a whole with the extraordinary conclusion that preventive detention made sense *as a benefit for the children*. Like a parent, the state is seeking to protect its children from their own propensity to stray. That's some case to make in the face of a record that showed prison-like conditions, commingling of those awaiting trial and those in long-term custody, and violence—even sexual assault. But at least the Court did concede that arbitrary or punitive detention would be unconstitutional. Given that concession I find it shocking that rather than make an assessment of how likely those evils were under the New York system, it instead validated the scheme as a whole and offered a hollow remedy for any individual abuses. In the Court's view, case by case adjudication would be a sufficient remedy.

Such reasoning illustrates the point of this talk. Individual actions under this scheme would be almost meaningless. The first problem is practical: Any child's detention would be over prior to the adjudication of his claim. Leaving aside such issues as mootness, I would note that an unconstitutional detention is hardly a minimal violation of rights, even if short in duration. The second problem is at least as bad. The statute allows detention to be imposed at a very short hearing, prior to any factfinding, and to be based on a vague and purely subjective assessment of the child's probable future behavior. Now, imagine the burden of arguing that you were improperly detained under that statute. Just as the difficulty of making such an argument is frightening, so is the prospect of evaluating it as a judge. All in all, this was a sad decision.

But it was not the only one last Term. Nor the only one from this Circuit. *Heckler v. Day* also showed the Court's growing unwillingness to provide the remedies needed to protect important rights. By statute, the Social Security Administration, after a decision to terminate disability benefits, must, within a reasonable amount of time, provide a hearing to reconsider the decision. You all know the importance of this. To someone who is truly disabled, those benefits may be their only possible means of support. Well, in Vermont, a class of recipients whose benefits were cut filed suit. Not only did everyone agree that the state-wide program had significant and unjustifiable delays; they also agreed that in more than half of the cases the long delayed hearings found that the recipients had in fact been truly disabled.

After extensive proceedings Judge James Holden carefully crafted an order that required the agency to end needless delays. He set up a timetable for proceedings that was designed to account for all the identified needs of the agency, and to make sure that only unjustifiable delays would be affected. Again, a unanimous Second Circuit panel affirmed. And again, the Supreme Court recognized the right while it destroyed the remedy.

It seems that Congress, years after it had created the right to reasonably timed hearings, had rejected proposals to bind the agency with a nation-wide, rigid timetable. Well we all know how disfavored reliance on subsequent legislative history is, especially when it involves Congress's failure to amend a statute. Nevertheless, almost entirely from this the Court inferred that the judiciary was barred from using its normal equity powers to place time limits on the agency. Although expressing an overarching concern for the need to allow the agency to function properly, the Court ignored the fact that Judge Holden's order seemed to be working fine. It was two years old and there had been no evidence of any adverse impact on the agency's operations. Of course this was precisely because of the fact that the order had little in common with the rigid proposals that Congress rejected.

What the Court did remember, however, was to pay lip-service to the need to keep some remedies available. As it did in *Schall*, it said that individual actions might be appropriate. Of course such actions would likely prove more costly and less accessible to the victims. And I would guess that the chief benefit to the agency, would be derived from people's failure to assert their rights. Somehow, I don't see much potential for deterrence in the Court's remedy, either.

Tragically, this same pattern of analyses went well beyond these Second Circuit cases. For example, in *Hobby v. United States*, the Court deplored the possibility that a federal judge might discriminate on the basis of race or sex in selecting grand jury foremen. But the Court essentially said that should this occur no convictions need be disturbed. The alternative remedy? The Court said that it trusted district judges to guard against the evil. On many issues, maybe. But that seems a quite nonsensical way of guarding against the evil of a discriminatory district court judge. In effect, the Court simply said that there will be no effective remedy.

The patter continued in *Immigration and Naturalization Service v. Lopez-Mendoza*. The Court declared that INS agents, like all law enforcement officers, had to obey the 4th Amendment. But if they do not, the exclusionary rule will not apply. And in *United States v. Leon*, the exclusionary rule was even more seriously eroded.[1]

Although in these cases the Court saw itself as evaluating the appropriateness of particular remedies, the real issue in each case was the very survival of certain human rights as meaningful. In the real world the existence of rights has no mean-

---

[1] *Leon* held that the Constitution did not require courts to exclude from evidence material seized by police officers relying in good faith on a warrant.

ing unless their violation can be effectively remedied. The *Leon* decision prompted my Brother Justice Stevens to question how we can "so easily concede the existence of a constitutional violation for which there is no remedy." He properly declared: "To do so is to convert a Bill of *Rights* into an unenforced honor code. . . . The Constitution requires more; it requires a *remedy*." If the Court's approach continues, in his words, "the Bill of Rights should be renamed."

24. Remarks at the Second Circuit Judicial Conference
[Affirmative Action]
(September 5, 1986)

As you know, it is wonderful to come up here and, I am one of the Justices on this Court who appreciates the circuit, because I don't have much trouble with it. I sit there at times and listen to the bandying back and forth about all the problems they have in this Circuit and that Circuit, and every now and then somebody asks me "What about your circuit?" I say, "It runs itself."

What I have to say this morning is, I hope, of interest. And for the record, I would like to say that before the formal remarks let me give the record of the Supreme Court of cases from this Circuit in the last term. As with the 1984 term, the results are extremely close. Fourteen cases from this Circuit came before our Court last year; seven were affirmed, seven were reversed or vacated and remanded. So far as dispositions having precedential weight is concerned, the Second Circuit batted .500 for the second consecutive season. This record is good so I thought. However, I noted of the seven cases set for oral argument and plenary consideration, one was reversed and one was remanded with instructions to dismiss as moot. Very little you can do about that one.

So the average accorded full consideration is over .700. So that's not bad as a batting average. Well, that's over and gone. What we can do is hope for the future.

I would like to speak today about an issue much discussed in recent months, in part because of cases which came to our Court from this Circuit last year. I refer to the *Sheet Metal Workers* case in which our Court affirmed the excellent decision by Judge Pratt, and to the question of affirmative action. Much has been said lately about the scope of permissible remedies, both voluntary and mandatory, in cases of employment discrimination. The decisions of our Court in this past Term suggest to me that there is still a basic agreement among a majority of the Justices that the commands of Title VII and the Equal Protection Clause should be implemented, where necessary, through broad-based relief including the imposition of affirmative duties to eradicate the effects of past discrimination. But because statements in sharp opposition to the use of affirmative remedies have recently been heard with increasing frequency, I think it is appropriate to share with you some general thoughts about why affirmative action is necessary, and on the role which it plays in our law despite many people in high offices trying to explain away our decision. We will explain it.

I believe all of the participants in the current debate about affirmative action agree that the ultimate goal is the creation of a color-blind society. From this common premise, however, two very different conclusions have apparently been drawn: The first is that race-conscious remedies may not be used to eliminate the effects of past discrimination against Negroes and other minority groups in American society. This conclusion has been expanded into the proposition that courts and parties entering into consent degrees are limited to remedies which provide relief to identified individual victims of discrimination only. But the second conclusion which may be drawn from our common preference for a color-blind society is that the vestiges of racial bias in American are so pernicious, and so difficult to remove, that we must take advantage of all the remedial measures at our disposal. The difference between these views may be accounted for, at least in part, by difference of opinion as to how close we presently are to the "colorblind society" about which everybody talks. I believe that, given the position from which America began, we still have a very long way to go. The Framers of our Constitution labored "In order to form a more perfect union, establish justice . . . and secure the blessings of liberty." These were beautiful words, but at the same time a Negro slave was but three-fifths of a man in the same Constitution. Negroes who, finding themselves purportedly the property of white men, attempted to secure the blessings of liberty by voting with their feet and running away, were to be captured and returned to slavery pursuant to that same document.

The decisions of the Supreme Court in *Prigg v. Pennsylvania* and *Ableman v. Booth* demonstrated just how strong the assertion of federal power on behalf of the slaveholder could be. There was undeniable historical truth in Chief Justice Taney's statement in *Dred Scott* that at the time of adoption of the Constitution Negroes "had for more than a century before been regarded as being of an inferior order, and altogether unfit to associate with the white race, either in social or political relations," et cetera, et cetera, et cetera.

Our constitutional jurisprudence at that time rested upon this premise and it continued for a century. So many have forgotten.

Justice Harlan, as you remember, dissenting in *Plessy v. Ferguson*, gave the first expression to the judicial principle that "our constitution is colorblind and neither knows nor tolerates classes among citizens." If Justice Harlan's views had prevailed, and *Plessy* been decided upon the principle of race neutrality, our situation now, ninety years later, would be far different than it is. Affirmative action is an issue today precisely needed because our constitution was not colorblind in the sixty years which intervened between *Plessy* and *Brown*.

Obviously, I too believe in a colorblind society; but it has been and remains an aspiration. It is a goal toward which our society has progressed uncertainly, bearing as it does the enormous burden of incalculable injuries inflicted by race prejudice and other bigotries which the law once sanctioned, and even encouraged. Not having attained our goal, we must face the simple fact that there are groups in every community which are daily paying the cost of the history of American injustice. The argument against affirmative action is but an argument in favor of leaving that cost to lie where it falls. Our fundamental sense of fairness, particularly as it is embodied in the guarantee of equal protection under the law, requires us to make an effort to see that those costs are shared equitably while we continue to work for the eradication of the consequences of discrimination. Otherwise, we must admit to ourselves that so long as the lingering effects of inequality are with us, the burden will be borne by those who are least able to pay.

For this reason, the argument that equitable remedies should be restricted to redressing the grievances of individual victims of discrimination completely misses the point. The point is that our government has a compelling interest in dealing with all the harm caused by discrimination against racial and other minorities, not merely with the harm immediately occasioned when somebody is denied a job, or a promotion, by reason of the color of his skin.

It has been argued that the use of affirmative race-conscious remedies inflicts an immediate harm on some, in the hope of ameliorating the more remote harm done to others. This, it is said, is as abhorrent as the original discrimination itself. Some have compared the use of such race conscious remedies to using alcohol to get beyond alcoholism or drugs to overcome a drug addiction, or a few more cigarettes a day to break the smoking habit. I think the comparison is inappropriate and abhorrent. Affirmative action is not, as the analogies often imply, a symptom of lack of social willpower; when judiciously employed, it is instead an instrument for sharing the burdens which our history imposes upon all of us.

This is not to say, of course, that affirmative remedies such as the establishment of goals, time tables, and all of that, in hiring, in promotion, or for protection of recently hired minority workers from the disproportionate effects of layoffs, are always necessary or appropriate. Where there is no admission or proof of past discriminatory conduct, or where those individuals whose existing interests may be adversely affected by the remedy have not had an opportunity to participate, serious questions arise which must be carefully scrutinized in the courts. Like all classifications which condition governmental behavior upon considerations of race, affirmative remedies for employment discrimination must overcome the stringent presumption in favor of neutrality which the Equal Protection Clause embodies. To undertake such remedies except in furtherance of the most important of governmental purposes, and without substantial assurance that narrower alternatives would not achieve the goal, is wrong. But what the recent statements in opposition to affirmative action do not consider, in my judgment, is the fundamental importance of eradicating the consequences of discrimination which are so visible throughout our society, and the basic injustice which is done by imposing all the costs of those lingering consequences upon those who have traditionally been the victims.

In this connection, it is especially important to reflect upon the role which affirmative relief plays when embodied in consent judgments. Last term, in *Local 93, International Association of Firefighters v. City of Cleveland*, the Court held that

Title VII does not preclude the ordering of affirmative race-conscious relief in a consent decree entered in settlement of litigation brought under the Act. Six justices agreed that the scope of remedy available in a consent decree under Title VII is at least as broad as that available in judgment after trial on the merits, and may include provisions for race-conscious relief. In my view, this holding is of great significance. We are all aware of the burden and expense which litigation, of whatever size and complexity, imposes on the litigant. Chief Judge Learned Hand surely did not exaggerate in saying that the citizen may do well to fear litigation beyond almost anything short of sickness and death. Where large scale employment discrimination litigation is concerned, the effects are many times greater. The availability of broad voluntary remedies affords parties the opportunity to settle their differences without the expense and disruption necessitated by trial on the merits, and allows employers, public and private, to correct injustices without being compelled publicly to defend the indefensible. By encouraging parties to enter into such voluntary relief, the Court's decision ensures greater flexibility in the search for workable solutions to the problem of inequality in America.

And this, finally, I believe will be the most important function of affirmative action. The problem of discrimination and prejudice in America is too deep-rooted and too widespread to be solved only in the courts, or only through the intervention of federal authority to convince the recalcitrant that justice cannot be indefinitely delayed.

Securing equality requires the attention, the energy, and the sense of justice possessed by all the well-intentioned citizens of this society. They need to be assured that the government, the law, and the courts stand behind their efforts to overcome the harm bequeathed to them by the past. They need to know that encouragement and support, not criticism and prohibition, are available from those who are sworn to uphold the law. Courts must offer guidance, to the best of our ability, to the attempts by individuals and institutions to rectify the injustices of the past. We must labor to provide examples of solutions that may work, and approaches that may be tried. If we fail, then we delay or postpone altogether the era in which, for the first time, we may say with firm conviction that we have built a society in keeping with our fundamental belief that all people are created equal.

If any one of you is worried about what I mean by the goal of a democracy such as ours, I have often said, and I repeat here, that the goal of a true democracy such as ours, explained simply, is that any baby born in these United States, even if he is born to the blackest, most illiterate, most unprivileged Negro in Mississippi, is, merely by being born and drawing his first breath in this democracy, endowed with the exact same rights as a child born to a Rockefeller.

Of course it's not true. Of course it never will be true. But I challenge anybody to tell me that it isn't the type of goal we should try to get to as fast as we can.

25. Remarks at the Second Circuit Judicial Conference
[Pretrial Detention]
(October 17, 1987)

In modest seriousness, I do confess that Ralph [Winter] was my first law clerk and we learned a lot of things together. I remember one time we got an opinion assigned to us and it involved the SEC, and I told him, "Now, Ralph, go back to the original SEC, the original act et cetera, and make yourself thoroughly familiar with all of that business and then we will talk about it."

He said, "Well, on division of work, what are you going to do?

And I remember I told him quite honestly, "I am going to look up and find out what a security is."

So that's how we started off.

He mentioned my work before I went on the Court and I just have to, every time it is mentioned, mention the name of a guy by the name of Charlie Houston who started all of this, and I doubt anybody in this room remembers him. He has been dead quite a while, but he started it all. He raised his students in the 1930's, he trained them not to be lawyers but to be "social engineers," and there is not a movement that I have come across in civil rights or civil liberties that Charlie Houston didn't have a hand in back in those days when it was rough.

When we had to travel in the south in his car—he had a big, old Grand Paige—there was no place to eat, no place to sleep. We slept in the car and we ate fruit. And one place in Mississippi we were eating, talking to people, and a little kid, I guess twelve, fourteen, a little bright-eyed boy—I was eating an orange, and he was looking at me. I said, "You want one of these?" He said, "Yes." So I gave him one, and he just bit into it, didn't peel it.

You know why? That was the first time he had ever seen an orange. And that would give you what we had in those days.

Well, enough of that. The sun didn't move and now this is my twentieth year and I just hope that each one of you here is fortunate enough to be with me on my next twentieth year.

That's if you're lucky, because my wife is going to kill me for language problems, but one old politician years ago, and I can't remember who it was, that they tried to burn off over and over again and he made the statement that I repeat for myself: For all those people who wish very dearly for me to give up and quit and what-have-you, and all these beautiful letters I get, including one that I thought was very good, the last line was, "And another thing, you suffer from complete constipation of the brain."

I thought that was original and good.

But this statement, I hope you will pardon me for saying it, but it's, "Don't worry, I'm going to outlive those bastards."

It is customary for me to preface my formal remarks with a review of the Second Circuit's record and what happened before my Court this past term. Unfortunately, the results from the most recent term are not quite as impressive as those I reported to you last year. There were eleven cases from the Second Circuit. They all came before the Court during the last term. One case was summarily reversed. Of the ten cases that were set for oral argument and plenary consideration, including one consolidated case, six were reversed, two were affirmed, one was affirmed in part and reversed in part, and in one case the writ of certiorari was dismissed as improvidently granted.

Well, you win some and you lose some, and believe me, I know exactly what that is because I had the pleasure of sharing one of this Circuit's victories when I authored the Court affirmance in the *Tashjian* case where we held that Connecticut could not prohibit a political party from permitting independent voters to participate in certain primary elections.

But I would like to focus my remarks today on a case in which I joined this Circuit in my dissent on the losing side when the Court reversed the panel opinion in the *Salerno* case and upheld the constitutionality of the 1984 Bail Reform Act. Where they got that phrase, I don't know. It had nothing to do with bail.

My dissenting opinion in the *Salerno* case expresses my views on preventive pretrial detention and the subject bears some continued discussion. Federal judges now must decide how often and in what manner to invoke the powerful provisions of that Act and the State Legislatures must decide whether to emulate Congress and enact similar bail provisions if they have not done so already.

The 1984 Act authorizes the pretrial incarceration of those accused of certain crimes upon a showing by the Government that the accused is likely to commit crimes, unrelated to the pending charges, at some time in the future, any time in the future.

The problem with this provision is simple and overwhelming. Preventive detention severely undermines our long established and much vaunted principle that a person accused of a crime is presumed innocent until proven guilty.

The Court has traced this principle back to the great civilizations of ancient Greece and Rome. An anecdote from the Roman Empire illustrates the importance of the presumption of innocence in Roman Law. A Roman prosecutor was publicly trying a case before the Emperor Julian. Midway through the proceedings, the prosecutor realized that the case was in trouble and that the defendant was likely to carry the day and so, unable to contain himself, the prosecutor passionately appealed to the Emperor, "Oh, Illustrious Caesar, if it is sufficient to deny, what will happen to the guilty?" To which Julian replied, "If it suffices to accuse, what will become of the innocent?"

The principle so eloquently defended by Julian has been recognized by our own Courts as "the undoubted law, axiomatic and elementary," whose enforcement "lies at the foundation of the administration of our criminal law." Indeed, Congress itself firmly planted the principle in the federal criminal law. Title 18 asserts that "Nothing in this section shall be construed as modifying or limiting the presumption of innocence."

That's in the same law, and yet the majority of our Court, in *Salerno*, found constitutionally permissible the jailing of people presumed to be innocent under the law.

Naturally, the majority did not see itself as advancing or even limiting the presumption of innocence. It concluded that the preventive detention of those awaiting trial is not impermissible punishment before trial, but rather permissible regulation.

The majority reasoned that detention is not meant to be punitive. Rather, they say it serves the legitimate regulatory goal of protecting the public from crime. This argument, however, proves far too much. The same reasoning would constitutionally validate measures that we all would agree have no place in a free society.

For example, imagine that Congress determines, not unrealistically, that a large proportion of violent crime is perpetuated by people who are unemployed. Congress then also determines, equally realistically, that much violent crime is committed at night. Therefore, Congress could pass a law which permits the imposition of a dusk-to-dawn curfew on anyone who is unemployed. Because the law does not have the purpose of punishing the unemployed and because preventing danger to the public is a legitimate regulatory goal, the curfew would, according to the majority's analysis, constitute permissible regulation.

Other examples are many. The majority, of course, did not approve such obnoxious measures. Rather, it defended preventive pretrial detention on the ground that in the past we have approved of at least some emergency detention measures.

The majority particularly stressed that Federal bail provisions, prior to 1984, often were used to detain those likely to flee the court's jurisdiction or those who had threatened witnesses or participants in the judicial process. Well, this argument overstates the implications of the pendency of such charges. The finding of probable cause to believe that an individual has committed the crime conveys to the government the power to try those individuals, nothing else.

The power to try necessarily includes the power to ensure that the processes of justice will not be evaded or obstructed, of course. Indictment of a crime, therefore, curtails the accused's liberty insofar as—but no further than—the conduct of his trial requires.

To conclude, as the majority seems to, that those indicted may have their liberty curtailed whenever general social welfare so demands is to convert the indictment into substantive evidence of wrongdoing, a result clearly at odds with the presumption that one is innocent in the case of accusation.

These fundamental concerns about evidence and preventive detention unfortunately did not carry the day. What yet remains to be established is the scope of that defeat. Those more sanguine than I attempt to minimize the import of the 1984 Act and portray it as an exceptional measure whose provisions apply only to a very narrow act of circumstances and curtail liberty to the smallest possible degree. I am not so optimistic.

For example, the majority confidently asserted that the Act "operates only on individuals who have been arrested for a special category of extremely serious offenses," citing Section 3142(f) of the Act. Now, this section does permit pretrial detention without bond in cases involving crimes of violence, crimes punishable by life imprisonment or death, a major drug offense, or felonies committed by a person convicted of two of the above crimes. But the majority fails to refer to other sections of the statute which defines a "crime of violence" to include "an offense that has as an element of the offense the use, attempted use, or threatened use of physical force against the person or property of another."

The attempted or threatened use of physical force against a person could take place in any ordinary street altercation resulting in a charge of misdemeanor assault. More disturbing, the use of physical force against property arguably occurs during the offenses of window breaking, trash can tipping, or graffiti writing. Indeed, one commentator has reasoned that, because the statute does not differentiate between force against persons and force against property, larceny—the seizing of property—might be a crime of violence under the Act, just as the seizure of a person would constitute a crime of violence. I am therefore unconvinced that the Act by its terms unequivocally limits its application to a narrow range of cases. To give you an example of how broadly the Act has been applied, a federal judge in Pennsylvania ordered the preventive detention of a defendant charged with the possession of child pornography. Now, it is hard to see how any possessory crime could constitute a "crime of violence" even under the broad language of the Act, but this example demonstrates that it is up to judges in interpreting the Act to limit its reach appropriately.

The majority also minimized the effect of the Act by reasoning that "the conditions of confinement envisioned by the Act 'appear to reflect the regulatory purposes relied upon by the' Government." The majority noted that the Act requires detainees to be confined in a "facility separate, to the extent practicable, from persons awaiting or serving sentences or being held in custody pending appeal." But I find nothing reassuring about the current conditions of pretrial confinement in this country. Our jails are often crowded and the conditions squalid. Commentators who have studied our jails have concluded that conditions there may well be inferior to those in penitentiaries. Moreover, pretrial detainees are cut off not only from their jobs and their families, but also from the means of preparing their defense. Their detention makes it harder for them to locate witnesses and consult with counsel. In addition, the government may use an accused's confinement as an opportunity to gather information to use against him at trial. The Supreme Court recently upheld the use of the testimony of a cellmate informant against a detainee when the informant played the role of the Government's "listening post." The Court also has concluded that pretrial detainees have almost no rights that prevail over "reasonable" institutional objectives. The Court has upheld double-bunking, room searches, body-cavity searches, and strict limitations on the receipt of reading materials by detainees. Whether we call it punishment or regulation, we must be realistic.

The majority's final sanguine note is its observation that detention under the Act is limited in duration by the provisions of the federal Speedy Trial Act. This is an upbeat way of saying that the Act itself contains no limitation on the duration of the confinement it authorizes. And the limits are the Speedy Trial Act are not much better than no limit at all. Judges are free to continue cases far beyond the Act's seventy-day limits whenever they conclude that "the ends of justice" would be served thereby. This power is used so frequently that approximately one out of every ten federal criminal cases requires almost a full year of processing time. Of course, the Salerno majority left open the possibility that excessively prolonged pretrial detention may become punitive and violate due process. This circuit has had some experience with precisely that question. Over the summer, Judge Motley in the Southern District of New York held that detention for more than twenty-four hours between arrest and arraignment violates due process. Just a week earlier, however, a circuit court panel held that a defendant's post-indictment, pretrial detention of six months did not violate the due process clause, although it raised "grave due process concerns." Determining when ostensibly regulatory detention becomes punitive in violation of the due process clause is undoubtedly a difficult and amorphous inquiry, but it is one that the Court must undertake with the utmost seriousness in order to limit the Bail Reform Act to the narrow, non-punitive function that ostensibly justifies its curtailment of the liberty of an accused.

As you can see, even putting aside my central constitutional concern, I am not as convinced as the *Salerno* majority that the Bail Reform Act is sufficiently circumscribed. It is therefore incumbent upon federal judges to consider the range, effect, and duration of pretrial confinement in applying the powerful provisions of the Act. In addition, state legislators who are considering fashioning similar legislation must bear in mind both the constitutional concern and the need for the limits on preventive detention described above. In making these important decisions, neither judges nor legislators can afford to forget that the measure of our commitment to individual liberty is our willingness to secure it for the least favored among us. The Bail Reform Act and the *Salerno* decision powerfully illustrate that the first things that society seems willing to jettison in its search for security are the rights of the accused, particularly those accused of violent or otherwise despicable crimes. I worry that we might not realize until too late the value of what we have cast aside.

26. Remarks at the Annual Judicial Conference of the Second Circuit

[The Right to Effective Assistance of Counsel]

(September 9, 1988)

Chief Judge and my friends, I am always glad to come to this Circuit's meetings. I have been coming to many of them. I remember way back when I wasn't on the Court of Appeals, I remember Chief Judge Learned Hand. He conducted these meetings in the right way. He would call a meeting on the seventeenth floor of Foley Square in the Court of Appeals room. Everybody was there. He would open the meeting by reading the statute and say, "I am commanded to hold this meeting, I have called it, I now adjourn it, goodbye." Well, if you want to really appreciate what we have now, you have to compare it to what we had in those days.

I am glad to be here. While some people panic and wonder what's going on in our courts, I for one think we are doing all right. I would like to say a lot of things about my own Court, but, boy, I am not going to say them.

Before starting out I would like briefly, as I usually do, to review the Circuit's recent record before the Supreme Court. Five cases from the Second Circuit were argued and decided last term. Three were affirmed, one was reversed and one was affirmed in part and reversed in part. In the one reversal, *United States Catholic Conference v. Abortion Rights Mobilization*, I am proud to have been the only dissenter, and I still say we were right.

Today I would like to talk about the right to counsel, which I think is still important. I can remember way back in the good old days when people used to say every man is entitled to his day in court, and they left off the rest of that sentence— if he had the money. We have come a long way from that. But I still don't feel we have come far enough. Although the text of the Sixth Amendment merely refers to the "assistance of counsel," it seems to me that for over fifty years our Supreme Court has recognized that the Constitution guarantees effective assistance. It will not do, then, for the accused's counsel simply to sit idly by. Rather, "an accused is entitled to be assisted by an attorney, whether retained or appointed, who plays the role necessary to insure that the trial is fair."

Defining the different attributes for counsel's necessary role in a particular case is difficult, especially for appellate courts, which are typically called on to address the question on a cold record by a convicted defendant who claims he received ineffective assistance at trial. And most defendants who end up convicted say they had ineffective counsel, not that they were guilty.

The prevailing wisdom from our Supreme Court as to what constitutes ineffective assistance of counsel is contained in the 1984 case of *Strickland v. Washington*. The *Strickland* case holds that a convicted defendant is entitled to a reversal if he can show, first, "that counsel's performance was deficient" and, second, "that the deficient performance prejudiced the defense." Well, how under the sun can a deficient performance not register in the defense. The Court deliberately declined to say what it meant by "deficient," because, it said, any specific guidelines would restrict the wide latitude counsel must have in making "tactical decisions." Beautiful words.

The majority's standard, therefore, was intentionally and infinitely malleable. In a lone dissent I set forth that that standard told lawyers and the lower courts "almost nothing," nothing about how to evaluate the effectiveness of counsel, or what guidelines should we have. I believed then, and I believe now, that many basic aspects of criminal defense lend themselves to uniform standards whose infringement cannot qualify as a "tactical decision," or maybe I should say excused by those two words. By "refusing to address the merits of [proposals for particularized standards], and indeed [by] suggesting that no such effort [wa]s worthwhile, the opinion of the court, I fear[ed would] stunt the development of constitutional doctrine in the area of counsel representation."

My fears when I wrote that dissent in *Strickland* appear today, if anything, to have underestimated the mischief that has resulted from that decision. The development of constitutional doctrine in the area of effective assistance since *Strickland* has not been very good. Indeed it has not been stunted, but completely ignored. Not once, in the more than four years since that case was decided has the Court found that a petitioner had received ineffective counsel. Not once. And I think everybody in this courtroom can point to at least one case where counsel was ineffective. I know the case here, when I was on the Second Circuit, where the lawyer never heard of the Jencks Act.[1] And that still happens. The district courts and courts of appeal have routinely denied *Strickland* claims, almost automatically, excusing the most inexcusable lawyering under the all-purpose banner of "strategic decisions."

I can say with confidence that the explanation for this lassitude is not that *Strickland* ushered in a golden new age of uniformly competent assistance. Hardly a week goes by that we aren't required to review a case of a colorable ineffective assistance claim. And the Supreme Court still has "never identified an instance of attorney dereliction that meets the stringent standard."

Consider just a few cases which have come up recently.

Number one, a capital case, the petitioner's lawyer called no witnesses and presented no mitigating evidence at the trial and the proceedings. He made no inquiries into the client's educational, medical, or psychological history. He made no attempt to

---

[1] A statute that requires federal prosecutors to disclose certain evidence to the defendant.

interview any of the many potential mitigating witnesses. His sole effort was to advance a far-fetched, unfounded and unsuccessful technical objection to the state's evidence.

The District Court and the Court of Appeals both concluded that counsel's actions could be excused as a tactical decision to preempt rebuttal evidence.

In the second case, a very recent case, the petitioner's lawyer undertook even fewer efforts. He devoted six hours to preparing for the case, a total of six hours. This is a capital case. He presented no closing argument in the guilt phase of the trial and in the sentencing phase he offered no expanded argument, no opening argument incidentally, no evidence, and no closing argument as I mentioned. The state Court of Appeals refused petitioner's claim for ineffective assistance of counsel. If it wasn't ineffective, I wonder what it was.

In refusing it, the court said, "Defense counsel deliberately limited his participation to the sentencing stage as a matter of trial strategy."

In yet another capital case, the petitioner's lawyer made no opening statement, put on no case in chief. He performed only cursory cross-examination and did not object to anything. His brief summation emphasized the "horror of the case." In his summation during the sentencing phase he did not give the jury a single reason why they should spare the petitioner's life. He did not inform the jury that petitioner had no prior criminal history, had been steadily employed, had an honorable military record, had been a regular churchgoer and had cooperated with the police. No mention of those. The magistrate, the only fact-finder that considered the question, concluded that counsel's performance at the sentencing phase was "outside the wide range of professionally competent assistance." If you get a chance, tell me what that means. This is a magistrate. The District Court, though, concluded that petitioner had not proven any prejudice and the Court of Appeals held that counsel's performance was not "constitutionally deficient." That phrase just pops up in all of them.

Moving from nonfeasance to actual active malfeasance, the Court recently denied certiorari in a case in which the petitioner's counsel may have been petitioner's most virulent adversary. The lawyer repeatedly demeaned his own client, the petitioner, and on direct examination characterized him as, among other things, "a leech on society." That's his client. You know, in cases like this you never find any misdeeds on the part of the prosecutor because he doesn't have to do anything.

In his closing argument the counsel urged the jury to carefully go over what he considered the atrocities involved that his client had committed and "the fear and anguish visited on the victims." This is *his* counsel. He urged the jury to punish his client, saying, "he ought to be off the streets, he ought to go, he deserves to go, he deserves to do hard time working in the fields." That's his defense counsel. The jury agreed and sentenced the petitioner to a maximum of two life sentences on two counts of robbery.

The District Court found that petitioner's counsel was ineffective because "he became the second prosecutor on the case." That's what the District Court said.

But he never won. The Court of Appeals reversed, concluding that counsel "employed a strategy in a professionally reasonable manner." That was the sole basis for affirming the conviction.

Well, I could go on with these forever, but I think these cases are aberrations. Certainly the overwhelming majority of defense counsel, paid and appointed, discharge their duties with competence and integrity. Often claims of ineffective assistance focus on the efforts of public defenders who are overworked and understaffed. Too often the combination of a crushing caseload and inadequate resources requires care to be sacrificed in favor of speed. I cannot say, nor is it my purpose to say, that the conclusion of the Court of Appeals in each of these cases was wrong. Moreover, even if constitutionally deficient, this assistance was provided in each of these instances, and I recognize that our Supreme Court is not a "court of errors." We lack the resources to correct every faulty application of well-settled law. Rather, our docket is reserved for cases of broad national significance. Maybe that's the reason. I don't know.

So why do I, at this late date, vote to grant review in these cases? To help out, in some way, to guarantee effective assistance of counsel? Because, in my opinion, the near-complete stagnation of effective-assistance law in the wake of the *Strickland* case is an issue to me of broad national significance. The short shrift given to claims of ineffective assistance look closely, with an unjaundiced eye, at the many cases that present barely colorable claims of counsel.

Appellate review of *Strickland* claims is especially important in light of the significant institutional pressures that push against reversing a conviction on grounds of ineffective assistance. Such a reversal means erasing a successful verdict for the state, branding as inadequate defense counsel who probably was court-appointed and working for little money. Such a reversal means wasting the significant judicial and administrative resources that are required whenever the government gears up to prosecute an accused. All this in the service of a defendant whom the court may well believe is guilty and raising a procedural "technicality" as a last-ditch effort to forestall rather than prevent a conviction.

These considerations provide a strong inducement for courts to dispose of ineffective counsel claims by labeling as "strategic" assistance that which is truly substandard. Our Court and the appellate court's practice of not second-guessing these judgments reinforces such summary treatment.

But it is a measure of the seriousness with which we take a fundamental constitutional right that we are willing to honor it even at a significant practical cost. It is the responsibility of the state supreme courts and the courts of appeal of our federal courts to see to its enforcement even when inertia and institutional forces make it unattractive. This is a responsibility the judicial branch has largely forsaken since the *Strickland* case, permitting all manner of negligence, ineptitude and even callous disregard for the client to be brushed off as "tactical decisions," insulated from constitutional review.

The Sixth Amendment is the poorer for our inattention and, to me, it will stay in that category until we accord greater dignity to that provision of the Constitution that actually guarantees the accused the constitutional guarantee of effective assistance of counsel.

Maybe I am just crying in the wilderness, but as long as I have breath in me I am going to cry.

27. Remarks at the Annual Conference of the Second Circuit
[The Future of Civil Rights]
(September 8, 1989)

You know I have gotten to the point now where when I get letters and requests to speak, I have a nice little form letter which says I am out of the speaking business. I just burned out. But I make certain exceptions, and this is one. I think it is particularly important right now, with all of the trouble that's going on and the arguments back and forth.

But let me review this Circuit's record before the Supreme Court in the term just completed. Twelve cases from the Second Circuit came before the Court during the 1988 term; the circuit was affirmed in seven cases and reversed in five cases. So we are ahead of the game. In the thirteenth case, *United States v. Halper*, a district court in the Southern District of New York was substantially affirmed on direct appeal. On the whole, then, it was a relatively successful term.

That's not what I want to talk about today. I would like to talk about some of the other things that happened in the Supreme Court of the United States. I would like to share with you a few thoughts about the choices confronting the civil rights community in this nation. For many years, no institution of American government has been as close a friend to civil rights as the United States Supreme Court.

Make no mistake, I do not mean for a moment to denigrate the quite considerable contributions to the enhancement of civil rights by recent presidents, recent congresses, other federal courts, and the legislatures and judiciaries of many states.

It is now 1989, however, and we must recognize that the Court's approach to civil rights cases has changed markedly. The most recent Supreme Court opinions vividly illustrate this changed judicial attitude. In *Richmond v. Croson*, the Supreme Court took a broad swipe at affirmative action, making it extraordinarily hard for any state or city to fashion a race-conscious remedial program that will survive its constitutional scrutiny. Indeed, the Court went so far as to express its doubts that the effects of past racial discrimination are still felt in the city of Richmond, and in society as a whole.

And in a series of cases interpreting federal civil rights statutes, the Court imposed new and stringent procedural requirements that make it more and more difficult for civil rights plaintiffs to gain vindication.

The most striking feature of this term's opinions was the expansiveness of their holdings; they often address broad issues wholly unnecessary to the decisions. To strike down the set-aside plan in Richmond, for example, there was no need to decide anything other than that the plan was too imprecisely tailored. Instead, the Court chose to deliver a discourse on the narrow limits within which states and localities may engage in affirmative action, and on the special infirmities of plans passed by cities with minority leaders. The Court was even more aggressive in revisiting settled statutory issues under Section 1981 and Title VII.

In *Patterson v. McLean Credit Union*, the Court took the extraordinary step of calling for rebriefing on a question that no party had raised: whether the Court in the 1976 case of *Runyon v. McCrary* had wrongly held Section 1981 to apply to private acts of racial discrimination.

And in *Ward's Cove v. Atonio*, the Court implicitly overruled *Griggs v. Duke Power Co.*, another established precedent which had required employers to bear the burden of justifying employment practices with a disparate impact on groups protected by Title VII. Henceforth, the burden will be on the employees to prove that these practices are unjustified. Such a shift of burden is uncalled for.

Stare decisis has special force on questions of statutory interpretation and Congress had expressed no dissatisfaction with either the Runyon or Griggs decisions. Thus it is difficult to characterize last term's decisions as a product of anything other than a deliberate retrenching of the civil rights agenda. In the past thirty-five years or more we have truly come full circle. We are back where we started.

Regardless of my disappointment with last term's civil rights decisions, we must do more than dwell on past battles. The important question now is where the civil rights struggle should go from here.

One answer, I suppose, is nowhere at all—to stay put. With the school desegregation and voting rights cases and with the passage of federal anti-discrimination statutes, the argument goes, the principal civil rights battles have already been won, and the structural protections necessary to assure racial equality over the long run are already in place, and we can trust the Supreme Court to ensure that they remain so.

This argument is unpersuasive for several reasons. Affirmative action, no less than the active effort to alleviate concrete economic hardship, hastens relief efforts while the victims are still around to be helped. And to those who claim that present statutes already afford enough relief to victims of ongoing discrimination, I say look to the case of Brenda Patterson. She alleged that she had been victimized by a pattern of systematic racial harassment at work—but she was told by the Supreme Court that, even accepting her allegations as true, federal statutory relief was unavailable.

We must avoid complacency for another reason. The Court's decisions last term put at risk not only the civil rights of minorities, but of all citizens.

History teaches that when the Supreme Court has been willing to shortchange the equality rights of minority groups, other basic personal civil liberties like the rights of free speech and to personal security against unreasonable searches and seizures are also threatened.

We forget at our peril that less than a generation after the Supreme Court held separate to be equal in *Plessy v. Ferguson*, it held in the *Schenck* and *Debs* decisions that the First Amendment allowed the United States to convict under the Espionage Act persons who distributed antiwar pamphlets and delivered antiwar speeches. It was less than a decade after the Supreme Court upheld the internment of Japanese citizens that, in *Dennis v. United States*, it affirmed the conviction of Communist Party agitators under the Smith Act.

On the other side of the ledger it is no coincidence that during the three decades beginning with *Brown v. Board of Education* the Court was taking its most expansive view not only of the equal protection clause, but also the liberties safeguarded by the Bill of Rights.

That the fates of equal rights and liberty rights are inexorably intertwined was never more apparent than in the opinions handed down last term. The right to be free from searches which are not justified by probable cause was dealt yet another heavy blow in the drug testing cases. The scope of the right to reproductive liberty was called into considerable question by the *Webster* decision. Although the right to free expression was preserved in several celebrated cases, it lost ground, too, most particularly in *Ward v. Rock Against Racism*, which greatly broadened the government's power to impose time, place and manner restrictions on speech.

Looming on the horizon are attacks on the right to be free from the state establishment of religion: in a separate opinion in the creche-and-menorah case, four members of the Court served notice that they are ready to replace today's establishment clause inquiry with a test that those who seek to break down the wall between church and state will find far easier to satisfy. We dare not forget that these, too, are civil rights and they apparently are in grave danger.

The response to the Court's decision is not inaction; the Supreme Court remains the institution charged with protecting constitutionally guaranteed rights and liberties. Those seeking to vindicate civil rights and equal rights must continue to press this Court for the enforcement of the constitutional and statutory mandates. Moreover, the recent decisions suggest alternate methods to further the goals of equality in contexts other than judicial forums.

For example, state legislatures can act to strengthen the hands of those seeking judicial redress. A lesson of the *Richmond* case is that detailed legislative fact-finding is critical. Civil rights lawyers will stand a far better chance in federal constitutional litigation over affirmative action if they are armed with a state legislature's documented findings of past discrimination in a particular area. Thus persons interested in the cause of racial equality can ensure that legislators have access to empirical studies and historical facts that will form the bedrock of acceptable factual findings.

Most importantly, there is Congress. With the mere passage of corrective legislation, Congress can in an instant regain the ground which was lost last term in the realm of statutory civil rights. And by prevailing upon Congress to do so, we can send a message to the Court—that the hypertechnical language games played by the Court last term in its interpretations of civil rights enactment are simply not accurate ways to read Congress's broad intent in the civil rights area.

In closing, let me emphasize that while we need not and should not give up on the Supreme Court, and while federal litigation on civil rights issues still can succeed, in the 1990s we must broaden our perspective and target other governmental bodies as well as the traditional protector of our liberties.

Paraphrasing President Kennedy, those who wish to assure the continued protection of important civil rights should "ask not what the Supreme Court alone can do for civil rights; ask what you can do to help the cause of civil rights."

Today, the answer to that question lies in bringing pressure to bear on all branches of federal and state governmental units, including the Court, and to urge each of them to undertake the battle for civil liberties that remain to be won. With that goal as our guide, let us go forward together to advance civil rights and liberty rights with the fervor we have shown in the past.

Thank you very much.

28. Law and the Quest for Equality
(*Washington University Law Quarterly*, 1967)

This address, given to an audience of law students and faculty while Marshall was solicitor general, summarizes the history of antidiscrimination law to the mid-1960s and, more important, expresses Marshall's optimistic vision of law and lawyers as instruments for progressive social change.

I have defined my subject as "Law and the Quest for Equality." Actually the subject involves several themes: the synergy of law and social patterns; the promotion of reform through, and by means of, existing legal means and doctrine; and the changing role of a lawyer in society. I hope these themes become apparent as I proceed.

I shall begin by giving a brief exegesis of the *School Segregation Cases*. I do not propose to tell of every legal recognition of equality or of every lapse or legitimization of inequality from *Dred Scott* to the school cases; the story has been told elsewhere and quite well. But it is necessary for the development of my subject and themes to discuss some of these cases.

Dred Scott sued Sandford, the executor of the estate of his former master, for damages for an assault and battery that probably never occurred; the suit was filed in a Missouri federal court in 1853. Sandford was a citizen of New York; Scott alleged that he was a citizen of Missouri, having been taken to the free state of Illinois and to territory in which slavery had been prohibited by the Missouri Compromise. The jurisdiction of the court was thus asserted to exist under the diversity clause. When the case was finally decided by the Supreme Court, however, Scott—probably the person least affected by the decision—found that he could not be a "citizen" of a state within Article III of the Federal Constitution, and that, in any event, he was not free by his having lived in free territory because Congress had no power to deprive slave owners of "property" rights by prohibiting slavery in certain territory. It had been hoped—indeed expected—that the Supreme Court's ruling would settle much controversy, including that of the status of the vast territory, and the states to arise out of it, west of the Mississippi not covered by the Northwest Ordinance of 1787, which had prohibited slavery and had been passed prior to the adoption of the Constitution. As we now know, and as was realized shortly after the decision, *Dred Scott*, rather than settling controversy, added to it.

After much travail and a costly war, the thirteenth, fourteenth, and fifteenth amendments were adopted, each of which contained an innovative provision giving Congress the power to enforce them "by appropriate legislation." And the

Reconstruction Congresses exercised that power in various civil rights legislation. The Supreme Court, however, struck down some of those provisions in the *Civil Rights Cases* in 1883, which tolled the death-knell for such legislation; and, as it turned out, Congress did not use the power specifically granted to it for the next eighty-odd years. Of course, one can hardly place all the responsibility for the *Civil Rights Cases* on the Court. By the time the Court had declared the Civil Rights Act of 1876 unconstitutional, the Act had already fallen into desuetude. Thereafter, and perhaps partially as a result of the reasoning of Chief Justice Taney in *Dred Scott*, the fourteenth amendment became not an effective shield for human rights, as it had been intended, but rather a mechanism by which corporations took on human traits and enjoyed the protections of what became known as substantive due process.

The last of this unfortunate trilogy is *Plessy v. Ferguson*, which, like *Dred Scott*, was largely a trumped-up case. The Supreme Court upheld a state statute prescribing the racial separation of railroad passengers within the state; it reasoned that establishing "separate but equal" facilities did not violate the fourteenth amendment. In so upholding the enforced separation of those who were declared by that amendment, as "citizens of the United States and the State wherein they reside," to be entitled to the "equal protection of the laws," the Court legitimized and gave impetus to the myriad laws and customs described as–

> . . . a pervasive, official system of segregation which carries from cradle to grave. . . . requir[ing] the Negro to begin life in a segregated neighborhood, attending separate schools, using segregated parks, playgrounds, swimming pools, which later kept him apart at work, at play, at worship, even at court and while going from one place to another, which confined him in segregated hospitals, and prisons, and finally relegated him to a separate burial place.

Thus, as Dean [Louis] Pollak said, the Court in *Plessy* "gave constitutional momentum to the growth of an entire way of life: the racially divided pattern known as Jim Crow."

Justice Harlan correctly prophesied in his dissent in *Plessy* that the decision would, "in time, prove to be quite as pernicious as the decision . . . in the *Dred Scott* case." But *Plessy* marks the nadir of constitutional protection for minorities.

From this point, the story changes. To be sure, there had been some earlier indication of hope for the quest for equality through the courts, most notably the decisions in the *Strauder* case in 1880, which in effect held unconstitutional a state statute prescribing that only white males could serve on a jury, and in *Yick Wo v. Hopkins* in 1886, which condemned administrative discrimination against Chinese as a class. Nevertheless, the story, despite the numerous legal victories from this point onward, does not follow an undeviating plot. Like any interesting story, it has its ups and downs.

One of the first cases in which a then fledgling organization, the National Association for the Advancement of Colored People, participated was *Guinn v. United States* in 1915, in which the "grandfather" restrictions on voting were struck down. Thereafter, the NAACP helped to have declared unconstitutional racially restrictive zoning ordinances, state laws barring Negroes from primary elections, and the mob-dominated trial of a Negro. In these and other cases in which the NAACP participated no over-all litigation strategy was developed or followed.

In the early 1930's, however, there was a change. Gratified by the ad hoc victories but dissatisfied in its quest for equality, the organization decided that it would press on every possible front for the elimination of inequality and discrimination. The means selected was through use of the courts, partially because other avenues of redress appeared to be closed, and partially because of the deep and abiding faith the planners had in the rule of law, and the efficacy and feasibility of instigating social reform through reliance upon the Constitution—which after all was designed to insure the protection of the basic values of our society. I should not, however, stress too greatly any over-all plan other than the decision to proceed through the courts, for that would be misleading.

In any event, realization of the quest proceeded, not without occasional setbacks to be sure, but it proceeded. The Supreme Court continued to rule against discrimination in the selection of grand and petit jurors and, in various ways, to insure the fairness of criminal proceedings against Negroes. It struck down abhorrent police practices, such as the beating of Negroes suspected of crime in order to obtain confessions. As Chief Justice Hughes said in the first of the coerced confession cases, *Brown v. Mississippi*: "The rack and torture chamber may not be substituted for the witness stand." That case, incidentally, was argued for the petitioners on behalf of the NAACP by a former governor of the state of Mississippi.

In the famous *Scottsboro* cases—in which a group of Negro boys were charged with raping a white woman—the Court first ruled that the trials were unfair because the defendants did not have the effective assistance of counsel, and later, after several of the boys had been retried, that the trials were unfair because of discrimination against Negroes in the selection of juries: no witness could recall when a Negro sat on a jury; in the old common law phrase, man's mind runneth not to the contrary.

Thereafter, rulings against discriminatory practices were reached in wide aspects of life. In a series of decisions the Court helped to eliminate discriminatory disenfranchisement of Negroes by looking through the ingenious white primary, gerrymandering, and other such schemes. As Justice Frankfurter said: the Constitution "nullifies sophisticated as well as simpleminded modes of discrimination." Similarly, the Court struck down peonage laws, and, under the aegis of the federal labor laws, discriminatory union practices, while at the same time protecting the right to protest and demonstrate against discrimination in employment.

In the area of discrimination in public accommodations, the Court ruled against the maintenance of separate dining cars under the Interstate Commerce Act, in a case in which the United States through the Solicitor General, though nominally a defendant, supported the petitioner against the ICC. And the Court upheld state laws proscribing discrimination in transportation.

The enforcement of racially restrictive covenants was declared to be violative of the fourteenth amendment. And in a series of rulings involving discrimination in higher education, the Court seriously undermined the rationale of the *Plessy* case, at least with respect to public education. In one of the cases the Court said *not* that the Negro student having been admitted to the state school might receive separate but equal treatment, but rather that he "must receive the *same* treatment at the hands of the state as students of other races."

I should note also that by this time, the early 1950s, many states had undertaken to eliminate racial discrimination, and that the executive branch of the federal government had not only supported the petitioners in several of the cases, but had affirmatively sought to eliminate the discrimination in the services, in governmental employment, and in the insurability of homes in mixed neighborhoods through the FHA. I mention this because it is important to realize the impetus for change stimulated by, among other things, the Court decisions I have mentioned.

Finally in 1954, *Brown v. Board of Education*, the school segregation cases, was decided. I had the privilege of arguing the cases in the Supreme Court—actually of arguing them twice, since they had been set for reargument from the previous term. Because of my participation, I might perhaps overestimate *Brown*'s importance, though I doubt it.

My friend Loren Miller prefaces the chapter on the Brown case in his recent book with an excerpt from a spiritual:

> There's a better day a' comin'
> Fare thee well, fare thee well,
> In that great gettin' up morning
> Fare thee well, fare thee well.

and refers to May 17, 1954—opinion day in *Brown*—as "That Great Gettin' Up Morning." Similarly, Dean Pollak of the Yale Law School has said that the decision in the *School Segregation Cases* was, with the exception of the wars, "the single most important governmental act of any kind since the Emancipation Proclamation." It doesn't matter for my purposes here if you do not fully share that view; surely, though, all will acknowledge the importance of the decision. In holding segregated public education unconstitutional, the Court eliminated one of the two primary pillars of the caste system (the other being disenfranchisement). The decision was not an easy one to reach, nor did it prove easy to enforce. Several states and many communities were quite recalcitrant and are only now coming to accept the decision.

Of course, the story of the quest for equality does not end with the *School Segregation Cases*. Indeed, it branches out in several directions, most notably to legislation: the Civil Rights Acts of 1957, 1960, and 1964, and the Voting Rights Act of 1965. Since it is a quest, the quest for equality is always an ongoing search, as our ideas and hopes are transmuted into reality. As President Johnson said recently at Howard University's centennial celebration:

> For the work that lies ahead is demanding, and involves far too many lives in urgent need of help, to be parceled out by race. Tomorrow's problems . . . will not be divided into "Negro problems" and "white problems." There will be only human problems, and more than enough to go around.

I should also mention at this point that for many the civil liberties problems today are not so much of active discrimination, but rather of lack of certain opportunities. Hence, the emphasis has shifted toward the seeking of affirmative action, the exhortation to legislatures to act. I am sure that all recognize that if a statute is patently unconstitutional, it can be challenged in the courts. But what if the claim relates to some lack of opportunity, a denial not of access to facilities, but rather of the refusal to take needed affirmative action? As we have seen, much of this kind of protest cannot effectively be channeled. Indeed, some of the protest cannot even be said to be directed at particular goals. Of course, civil disobedience, which is the theoretical underpinning of protest movements, is also a force for social change and progress. It is often necessary, in order to establish the need for action, to obtain and use what Professor Harry Kalven has called, in his interesting analysis of the sit-in cases, the "public forum." But he who advocates civil disobedience must be aware of its import:

> [I]t goes counter to the general obligation to obey the law and almost always there are serious dangers of undesirable consequences for others. There is, therefore, a particular obligation to act conscientiously. . . .

The NAACP participated in most of the decisions I have discussed. Indeed, it was so successful that several states began to attack it through legislation, discriminatory application of old laws, or legislative investigation—seeking directly and indirectly to prevent or curtail its operation. The attacks on each occasion were rebuffed only by action of the Supreme Court.

As I have mentioned, the quest for equality by litigation in the courts, up to the Supreme Court, and by the favorable decisions obtained is, I think, testimony to support my themes: that law cannot only respond to social change but can initiate it, and that lawyers, through their everyday work in the courts, may become social reformers.

All of the cases I have discussed involved infringements upon the rights of Negroes. Of course they involved more than the race of the particular litigant, for as President Kennedy said, echoing the thoughts of others, in a nationwide address on June 11, 1963, occasioned by the opposition of a governor of a state to the court-ordered enrollment of two students in a graduate school:

This nation . . . was founded on the principle that all men are created equal, and that the rights of every man are diminished when the rights of one man are threatened.

Moreover, these cases do not appear in *Shepard's Citations* with an asterisk to limit their precedential value to race relations.[1] They concern us as lawyers, law professors, citizens, and government officials because the principles they announce quite transcend the immediate controversy which occasioned them. Thus, *Powell v. Alabama*, the first Scottsboro case, gave rise to an important principle in the administration of justice announced finally in *Gideon v. Wainwright*: the due process right to a fair trial includes representation by counsel and the appointment thereof for the defendant who cannot afford to retain counsel. The same is true, of course, of the early coerced confession cases; they too have spawned many offspring. In short, these decisions go far to prove the truth of [former Harvard Law School] Dean [Roscoe] Pound's statement that what he called "justice according to law"—

. . . insures that the more valuable ultimate interests, social and individual, will not be sacrificed to immediate interests which are more obvious and pressing but of less real weight.

And the social reform inherent in the decisions was achieved by the efforts of men, largely lawyers, who believed that through the rule of law change could indeed be wrought. The Negro who was once enslaved by law became emancipated by it, and is achieving equality through it. To be sure law is often a response to social change; but as I think *Brown v. Board of Education* demonstrates, it also can change social patterns. Provided it is adequately enforced, law can change things for the better; moreover, it can change the hearts of men, for law has an educational function also.

Of what relevance is all of this to my second theme: the role of lawyers in society? The lawyer has often been seen by minorities, including the poor, as part of the oppressors in society. Landlords, loan sharks, businessmen specializing in shady installment credit schemes—all are represented by counsel on a fairly permanent basis. But who represents and speaks for tenants, borrowers, and consumers? Many special interest groups have permanent associations with retained counsel who seek and sponsor advantageous legislation. But who represents and speaks for the substantial segment of the populace that such legislation might disadvantage? Outside of the political processes, I think the answer is clear. Lawyers have a duty in addition to that of representing their clients; they have a duty to present the public, to be social reformers in however small a way.

---

[1] *Shepard's* is a legal research tool showing when a particular case has been cited in another decision; an asterisk indicates that the later case raised questions about the cited one.

The cases I have mentioned show what can be done by private lawyers through the courts. And the possibilities of social change and reform today are far greater. The lawyer's image as solely the protector of vested interests is changing.

For years the bar responded to the need for legal services for the poor through legal aid, but even the most ardent supporters of the legal aid movement never claimed that the needs of the poor were fully met. Now, we have at hand the tools with which to provide those services in an organized and more complete way. Of course I am referring to the Neighborhood Legal Services concept within the Office of Economic Opportunity, ninety per cent federally funded, organized legal services for the poor. Like any reform scheme, however, the success of that program is directly related to the quality of the people, especially the lawyers, who become active in it. And like one of my themes, it involves the quest for equality, no longer racial, but rather equality in access to justice.

Some may undoubtedly disagree with some of the recent changes in social patterns and in the law. Well-considered dissent is, of course, an intimate part of the process of society. But I am sure all agree that the force of law—its capacity to initiate change and its flexibility to accept and mold change—is a major force in society, a force which lawyers are most often called upon to shape. From the early days in this country's history, it has been the traditional task of lawyers to mediate between principle and practice, between man's heritage and his hopes—that is the message of Law and the Quest for Equality—and that task and message we must never forget.

29. Group Action in Pursuit of Justice
(*New York University Law Review*, 1969)

I am deeply honored to have the privilege of delivering this tenth annual lecture in the James Madison series. I am particularly pleased to have been invited to participate in the third cycle of these lectures, which is devoted to the broad, and yet vital, theme of "justice." The previous two cycles of lectures dealt with the great rights guaranteed by our Constitution. Justice Black spoke on the Bill of Rights and the Federal Government; Justice Brennan spoke of the application of these rights to the states; Chief Justice Warren dealt with the relationship of the Bill of Rights to the military; and Justice Douglas concluded the first series of lectures with a plea for a judiciary committed to the goal of maintaining the guarantees of the Bill of Rights. The second cycle of lectures, delivered by Justices Goldberg and Fortas and Circuit Justices Tuttle and Wright, was devoted to the concept of equality. Justice Clark, who preceded me both on the Supreme Court and in this forum, began the third cycle with a call for improvements in the administration of justice in our courts. I propose to deal with the topic of "Group Action in the Pursuit of Justice." I hope to explain to you tonight why I believe that organized groups are becoming increasingly necessary in the pursuit of justice. I will also explore the implications that this new development has for the legal profession.

This theme would seem to call, first, for a definition of those rights and liberties which are encompassed by the term "justice." I do not intend to dwell on this point, however, for those who have preceded me in this forum have covered the subject well. They have eloquently expounded upon these rights and liberties guaranteed by our great Bill of Rights, and reaffirmed and expanded by the thirteenth, fourteenth, and fifteenth amendments. These great constitutional declarations remain as expressions of the ideals of our society, ideals that unfortunately have only infrequently been realized throughout the history of our nation. Of course, even these grand words fail to tell the whole story. For me at least, justice means more than the traditional concepts embodied in the amendments to our Constitution. True justice requires that the ideals expressed in those amendments be translated into economic and social progress for all of our people.

But we must not let definitional problems detain us here. For there can be no justice—justice in the true sense of the word—until the Bill of Rights and the Civil War amendments, together with the broader ideals they embody, become more than mere abstract expressions. From the perspective of history, we can see that the crucial task is not so much to define our rights and liberties, but to establish institutions which can make the principles embodied in our Constitution meaningful in the lives of ordinary citizens. Only in this way can the solemn declarations embodied in that

227

document be translated into justice. Justice Douglas spoke to the point in the title of his address in this forum—"The Bill of Rights is Not Enough."

In last year's address, Justice Clark spoke to you of one of the most basic institutions for the attainment of justice—the courts. I speak to you tonight of another "institution" essential to the attainment of justice, an institution perhaps even more basic. No matter how solemn and profound the declarations of principle contained in our charter of government, no matter how dedicated and independent our judiciary, true justice can only be obtained through the actions of committed individuals, individuals acting both independently and through organized groups.

In the past several decades, committed members of the bar have played a decisive role in reviving the concepts of justice embodied in the Bill of Rights and in our other constitutional guarantees. We shall have occasion to refer to some of their efforts in a moment. Although their efforts were a significant factor in promoting the cause of justice, my message tonight is that committed action on the part of individual members of the bar will not be enough to consolidate the gains of the past or to accomplish the goals of the future. As we move into the future, the role formerly filled for the most part by individuals will have to be filled to an increasingly large degree by organized group practice. If we are to move from a declaration of rights to their implementation, especially with regard to the politically and economically underprivileged, large numbers of lawyers are needed at the working level. This need for lawyers and supporting personnel cannot be met by individual effort; the task is simply too great. The need can be met only in an organized way.

My message can be aptly illustrated by the history of the Civil War amendments, a history in which I was in recent years fortunate enough to have played a small part. That history demonstrates that mere declarations of rights have not been sufficient to secure justice. It further illustrates that true progress can only be made by organized effort. The rights guaranteed by our Constitution are not self-enforcing; they can be made meaningful only by legislative or judicial action. As we shall see, legislation does not pass itself and the courts cannot act in the absence of a controversy. Organized, committed effort is necessary to promote legislation and institute legal action on any significant scale.

The fourteenth amendment, like the Bill of Rights, was a declaration of principle. It enshrined into national law the principles of freedom and equality which an earlier generation had announced in more abstract form in the Declaration of Independence. The framers of the fourteenth amendment set their sights high. They spoke during the ratification debates in broad, general terms. The nation was to be given the power to make certain that the fundamental rights of all individuals were respected. It was not a time for defining those rights with any precision; it was a time for creating institutions which would guarantee their maintenance. Without the power to enforce basic human rights, they would become mere paper promises. But the terms of the amendment, however powerful they may seem, could mean little without activism in the pursuit of justice. Each of the two most important sections of the amendment shared the same deceptive positivism; both seemed to solve problems, while they actually only provided tools for the proper solutions.

Section one sets for the basic ideals of 1868 in positive form. It is self-executing on its face and declaratory in language. Various phrases were used to describe, in their different and overlapping aspects, the fundamental rights which were to be guaranteed to all men—privileges and immunities of citizens of the United States; life, liberty and property; equal protection of the law. As Senator Howard of Michigan put it during the ratification debates, the language of the amendment "establishes equality before the law, and it gives to the humblest, the poorest, the most despised of the race the same rights and the same protection before the law as it gives to the most powerful, the most wealthy, or the most haughty."

This self-executing language is, however, deceiving. Its positive form does not guarantee automatic enforcement. The courts, naturally enough, exercise the power in cases brought before them to decree when the rights guaranteed by the amendment have been infringed. But these rights cannot be enforced unless those who possess them know they exist and are given the legal means to vindicate them. Without the commitment of the bar, those protected by the amendment will ordinarily possess neither the knowledge nor the skills needed to make the promises of the amendment meaningful. Without the commitment of large numbers of lawyers, of "private attorneys-general" if you will, the amendment will mean nothing.

Section five of the fourteenth amendment is even more dependent for its enforcement upon the active, dedicated work of committed individuals and groups. All it does is grant legislative power. The grant is broad, and the power potentially of great importance. Although the courts were left as the last resort for individuals who felt their individual rights were being infringed, only the legislature could act more generally. The final protection of the basic rights granted by the amendment was, in effect, to be democracy itself; through participation in democracy, those formerly deprived of their rights would help insure their own future equality.

But the hopes of the framers were soon dashed. From the 1870's to the 1950's not a single civil rights measure was placed on the statute books. Without active support for the promises of 1868, the rights granted by the amendment fell from sight and became historical anachronisms. Section five, its promises and its power for good, was forgotten.

A quick glance through the history of the century which separates us from 1868 confirms this view. Although three constitutional amendments and four important civil rights bills were passed in the decade following the Civil War, the post-war radical fervor soon died. The judicial decisions of the era only reflected social attitudes as they evidenced the rapid decline of the fourteenth amendment as a declaration of justice and equality.

In the *Slaughterhouse Cases*, decided in 1873, the Court echoed the framers and read the amendment as a declaration of "the freedom of the slave race, the security and firm establishment of that freedom, and the protection of the newly-made freeman and citizen from the oppressions of those who had formerly exercised unlimited dominion over him." So sure was the Court of the great purposes for which the amendment was enacted that it explicitly doubted whether the amendment spoke to any problem but racial discrimination. Only the dissents foreshadowed what was too soon to come—the incorporation of laissez-faire economics into the fourteenth amendment.

For a while, it seemed that the Court meant what it had said in the *Slaughterhouse Cases*. In 1880, a series of state jury laws were found in conflict with the Civil Rights Act of 1875. The language of the Court in these decisions was broad enough to encompass any kind of racial discrimination.

But Reconstruction, already moribund, died with the Compromise of 1877. The attention of both Republicans and Democrats turned to the dominant themes of the day—economic expansion and the nation's surge westward. Negroes could no longer seek help through the political process—all eyes were turned elsewhere. It was thus no surprise in 1883 when the Supreme Court voided the public accommodations sections of the Civil Rights Act of 1875 in an opinion which spelled an end to the great promises of the fourteenth amendment. Only the first Justice Harlan foresaw the future, as he wanted that "the recent amendments [will become] splendid baubles, thrown out to delude those who deserved fair and generous treatment at the hands of the nation." But the nation was not listening.

While the attention of the nation was directed elsewhere, the South was undergoing a minor revolution of its own. The political structure, thrown into disarray by Reconstruction and its rather abrupt end, was stabilizing in favor of white supremacy. The Southern states were seemingly unaware of the Civil War amendments and sought to ensure the perpetuation of that supremacy through legislation—the infamous "Jim Crow laws." The laws seemed blatant violations of the fourteenth amendment, and they called out for a challenge—a challenge that was not long in coming. But the result of that challenge dealt the basic principles of the fourteenth amendment a staggering blow—a blow from which it took sixty years to recover fully.

The state legislature which enacted the segregation statute challenged in 1896 in *Plessy v. Ferguson* ironically included a number of Negroes. In addition, the challenge was at least partially motivated by economic reasons—the railroad found the cost of separate "Jim Crow" cars unduly high. The challenge was in vain. The Court was simply not interested—equal meant equal—it did not mean together. Again, only Justice Harlan called for an application of the spirit of the fourteenth amendment.

The states took their cue from *Plessy*. Separation of the races soon became firmly entrenched in the South, and elsewhere for that matter. "Jim Crow" pervaded every aspect of life—even homes for the blind were segregated. Challenges were few and sporadic; and when they succeeded, the states reenacted the same scheme in different forms. Their ingenuity was certainly not taxed. Again, through the first two and a half decades of the century, the minds of the nation and nation's lawyers and legislators were largely elsewhere, although the next two decades did see a weak but steady legal attack on racial discrimination. The situation was such that in the 1940's one commentator said:

> There is no power in the world—not even in all the mechanized armies of the earth . . . which could not force Southern white people to the abandonment of the principle of social segregation.

And yet, segregation and its incidents, while still with us, are rapidly becoming a thing of the past. What happened? The change was not imposed by mechanized armies. It was not even prompted by the states or by federal legislation. It came from the private citizen, the citizen who believed that equal protection meant just that—the citizen who, with the assistance of those lawyers who still believed in the promise of justice and equality, never gave up the fight against the relics of slavery. The fight has been long, and the targets many. The turning point was of course *Brown v. Board of Education*, whose story is familiar. During the period since 1954, law after law has been struck down and the tactics of delay are being met head-on. New life has been breathed into the Civil War Amendments and enactments. The fight to reestablish the self-executing sections of the fourteenth amendment reawakened the legislatures to their powers, under both the Civil War Amendments and other parts of the Constitution as well, to establish racial justice in the land. The acts are familiar, from the Civil Rights Acts in 1957 through the Open-Housing Act of 1968.

The spirit of justice was not limited to racial discrimination. The germ planted was infectious and has spread. It is certainly not an exaggeration to say that the concern for the rights of the criminally accused and for the economically disadvantaged has come in part from the lessons learned in the fight against discrimination. Today, the legislatures, the courts, the bar, and the people of this country are demonstrating a concern for fairness and justice unparalleled in the history of our nation.

The history of the Civil War amendments demonstrates quite clearly, I think, the necessity for committed action. It also demonstrates the second, and more important aspect of my message—that individual effort is not enough to secure justice. Today, even more than in the past, only organized action can hope to insure that the concept of justice remains meaningful to all of our people.

Until only a few decades ago, the efforts to enforce the guarantees of the fourteenth amendment and the other post-Civil War enactments were sporadic and largely defensive in nature. It was not until the rudiments of organization were applied to the problem that significant progress was made. Much of that progress was made by the NAACP, an organization I had the honor of being associated with for many years. Its example can be instructive.

During the early period of its existence, the NAACP participated in several cases that resulted in striking down discriminatory legislation. However, it was not until the 1930's that the seeds of significant progress were sown. At that time, the organization developed a conscious program of legal action designed to eliminate discrimination and inequality. The financial and human resources that were funneled into this program were in large part responsible for recent successes in striking down discriminatory laws and practices. Similar examples could be multiplied. But whichever group you examine, one thing becomes evident: the organized and committed effort of groups of this sort has been of immeasurable importance in making our constitutional guarantees meaningful.

The concept of justice is, however, not a static one. Our tactics must be revised to suit the times. The needs are many and obvious. In traditional terms, there are of course the continuing problems of criminal and racial justice. Perhaps more significant, however, are the problems peculiar to the economically and socially disadvantaged. Lawyers have long spoken for the other segments of our society, both in court and in the legislatures. But now who is to speak for the poor, the disadvantaged, and these days, for the ordinary consumer?

I think the thrust of my remarks thus far makes the answer clear. The goals of economic and social justice, like the goal of racial justice, can only be achieved through committed effort. All segments of society are, of course, essential to this effort, but one of the most effective contributions will be that made by lawyers. The brief history I have outlined for you makes another thing clear. Effective response to the problems facing our society today requires that the contribution of the bar be in terms of organized and focused effort. Individual action was, as we have seen, not sufficient to meet the more simple and identifiable problems of the past. Racial discrimination was effectively attacked only through organized effort. Certainly no less is necessary to meet the complex and pervading problems of today, particularly those problems that do not admit of solutions wholly legal. The role of the individual lawyer remains a necessary ingredient, but he simply cannot do enough to make more than a dent in the complex set of problems facing segments of today's society. The individual lawyer could, and did, secure justice for the criminally accused. But can one man, no matter how dedicated or talented, protect the consumer from the predatory commercial practices so common in many of our cities? Can he secure meaningful compliance with the Supreme Court desegregation decisions? Clearly, he cannot. Solutions to these problems demand human and financial resources that can be focused on a problem only through organization.

We come, then, as always, to the inevitable problem of remedies. If, as I have attempted to show, there are grave inadequacies in the traditional system of individual attorneys protecting particular individual rights, what is to take its place? Of course the traditional system remains perfectly adequate in many traditional contexts. But in the new problem areas, where a new institutional framework is necessary, what approach should we take? What complications will such an approach have for the legal profession?

Although in the final analysis this difficult policy question must be resolved by bar associations and legislative bodies, there are vital constitutional considerations lurking in the background. As a series of recent Supreme Court decisions has made clear, the first and fourteenth amendments forbid state interference with certain forms of group legal practice. These decisions rest on a basic assumption about the nature of litigation. As the Court said in *NAACP v. Button*, litigation is often

> a form of political expression. Groups which find themselves unable to achieve their objectives through the ballot frequently turn to the courts. . . . And under the conditions of modern government, litigation may well be the sole practicable avenue open to a minority to petition for redress of grievances.

Litigation, the Court has thus held, is a protected mode of group expression. Persons may join together to pursue joint ends through the courts, just as they do through the legislature. And this first amendment right extends beyond traditional "political" contexts. As we held just last term in the *United Mine Workers* case, "the First Amendment does not protect speech and assembly only to the extent it can be characterized as political." We therefore held that union members have a constitutional right to join together and hire attorneys to represent them in workmen's compensation cases. The union members, although actually seeking only money damages, were engaged in a group activity entitled to first amendment protection.

These cases make it clear that the states are not free to prohibit all forms of group practice. Of course, as the Court has continually stressed, the states do have vital interests in regulating the practice of law. But the Constitution protects certain kinds of group activities, and to the extent it does, the states must satisfy their legitimate concerns in other ways. The old concept that each lawyer must be an individual practitioner, hired and paid only by individual clients, and associated with other attorneys only through partnership arrangements, must yield to modern realities.

It is obvious, therefore, that the bar must face up to some basic structural questions. Changes must be made, partially because there are severe constitutional problems associated with many of the old rules of champerty[1] and maintenance and the old prohibitions against group practice, but more importantly because the old structure is no longer completely responsive to present needs. The needs of the poor, of minorities, of indigent criminal defendants—these needs can only be met through forms of group practice. If the bar is to live up to its social responsibilities, it cannot let the narrow interests of a few practitioners stand in the way.

---

[1] *Champerty*, one of the longest recognized violations of legal ethics, involves stirring up litigation, generating lawsuits that would not be brought without the lawyer's stimulus.

We have seen a number of important developments already. The Federal Government has financed a legal services program for the poor. Some privately financed endeavors have also made important contributions. Legal aid and public defender organizations have grown, often with the support of the large reservoir of talent which can be provided by law schools. The law schools themselves have recognized the changed scope of their responsibilities to society and have instituted programs and curriculum changes more responsive to the needs of today. Thus, we have seen active participation in legal aid and similar programs and more emphasis on courses in criminal law and procedure, social welfare, and the like.

But the basic decisions have not yet been made. The bar has not yet acted definitively to bring its structure into line with current needs. In the process, certain important values must be kept in mind. On one side, we have the clear need for that kind of group practice which brings legal representations to those persons who have previously been left entirely outside the system. On the other, we have the traditional values of professional responsibility which must not be impaired. We have assumed in the past that the fidelity of the lawyer to his client's interest can be strengthened by the financial bond between them. The client pays the bill, and he ultimately will call the tune. The lawyer, while maintaining proper ethical standards, represents only the interests of the person supplying the retainer. In group practice, the old financial tie is broken. The client no longer pays the bill. And yet, the lawyer's ultimate responsibility must still be to his client. The financial link with an intermediary must not be allowed to warp his responsibility.

This is the problem. The solution, however, is not to fall back on the old theory that only the financial tie between lawyer and client can guarantee professional fidelity. Group legal services must be organized in ways which insulate the lawyer–client relationship, which protect it from extraneous influences. Our ingenuity may be challenged in this endeavor. But we must never forget the ultimate goal—making the law a reality for those to whom it is now largely meaningless.

The American Bar Association has taken the first steps toward bringing its Canons of Ethics into line with current day realities. The Special Committee on Evaluation of Ethical Standards has proposed a new Code of Professional Responsibility. This August, it will be presented to the House of Delegates for action. The preliminary draft recently circulated contains some promising steps forward. It would allow lawyers to be furnished and paid by approved legal aid offices, professional or trade associations, or labor unions. More importantly, similar rights are extended to all bona fide, non-profit organizations which, as an incident to their primary activities, pay for legal services furnished to members or beneficiaries. Under this provision all sorts of community organizations presumably could be established and provided with counsel; lawyers employed by these groups could then represent their members, or others who would benefit from organization programs. Moreover, the definition of legal aid offices includes programs operated by "bona fide, non-profit community organization[s]."

These provisions of the new code would certainly be a great step forward. Of course other changes would still have to be made; state statutes regulating the practice of law also have to be updated, and even federal procedure—especially administrative procedure—could warrant some reform. But the goal is clear. The structure of the bar must be redesigned to meet the responsibilities faced by a new generation.

I need not dwell here on the mechanical details. What is important is the commitment of men dedicated to the ideals of justice. Change will not be easy. The narrow interests of the few often carry disproportionate weight. But without both structural reform and the commitment of large numbers of men, our grand ideals will speak nothing more than paper promises. The lesson of the past century is clear. The battle will not win itself. If the bar does not move forward decisively, the nation that looks to it for leadership will soon forget the lessons of the past one hundred years. Elihu Root spoke to the point in 1904. His words still hold true:

> "[The] lawyer's profession demands of him something more than the ordinary public service of citizenship. He has a duty to the law. In the cause of peace and order and human rights against all injustice and wrong, he is the advocate of all men, present and to come."

30. Remarks of the Honorable Thurgood Marshall
Upon the occasion of his acceptance of Honorary Membership in the Association of the Bar
(November 20, 1973)

(*The Record of the Association of the Bar of the City of New York*, 1974)

It is a great honor to be here this evening. It is also an opportunity for the kind of informal communication between bench and bar which is so important and all too rare. We are, after all, lawyers and judges alike, bound together in a common endeavor with a common purpose. Our common mission is nothing less than doing justice; our common charge, the responsibility for the legal system which binds together the social fabric of our troubled Nation.

Together we daily strive towards our common goals in courtrooms across the Nation as we deal with people and their individual problems on a case by case basis. Our daily encounters are, without doubt, the very heart of our system of justice. They are what gives uniqueness and strength to the judicial branch of government. And whether in the chambers of a judge on the city's Family Court or in the marbled courtroom of the Supreme Court of the United States, we who serve the law serve a common master, and in so doing sit astride the nexus between the people and their government.

Our legislatures pass laws in the abstract; they deal in a world of statistics and projections, of compromises and conjecture. The executive enforces the law on a broad scale; his concern is also with the greatest good for the greatest number.

We, however, deal in a world of individuals, whether they be the clients we serve or the litigants who appear before us. In our courtrooms, the statistics come alive, as the general rule must be applied to the specific case. The legislature's carefully prescribed criteria for release on bail must be applied to a flesh and blood man, with real problems and responsibilities. Landlord tenant laws must be applied to a real dispute between a landlord trying to maintain a crumbling ghetto building with far too little income and the tenant with little money and no place else to go. Our job is at once the most difficult and, in many ways, the most important in the process of government. And our courtrooms are perhaps the most accurate barometers of the extent to which we have succeeded in building a just society.

We are today being overwhelmed with cries for greater efficiency in our courts and for more rapid disposition of cases. But in our hurrying to erect a more efficient system of justice, we must not forget that our system derives its strength from the fact that it deals with individuals. To mechanize the system, to make it lose its human element, to forget that in every case we are dealing with a human being who, before the law, deserves to be treated as an equal of any other man, is to lose that which gives any judicial system its very life.

But while the courtroom is and will ever remain in the heart of our system of justice, it is sometimes an inadequate forum for the bench and bar to engage in the crucial exchange of ideas and insights into what can be done to make further progress in building a better legal system and a better society. I have sometimes wondered how many lawyers have left the Supreme Court after participating in oral argument with the uneasy, queasy feeling that somehow, they never really got a chance to say what they wanted to say.

As frustrating as the courtroom must be for some lawyers, it is positively incomprehensible to the laymen who come before the court seeking justice. The formalism, the ritual, the arcane attributes of the law no doubt make those few feet between the judge's bench and the counsel's table seem an inestimable chasm to the uneducated laymen whom the system serves. The law exists for the people; the courts to dispense to their needs, and the lawyer to plead their cases. The people are the consumers of the law, and I believe we owe it to them to make that law understandable to them.

That particular task is one we all too often fail to achieve. We are accused, and often rightfully, of having a narrow and technical view of justice. Criminal law is a prime example. Ask any criminal lawyer what are the prerequisites of a fair criminal justice system and he will most likely give you a laundry list of constitutionally guaranteed rights—trial by jury, assistance of counsel, cross-examination of witnesses, privilege against self-incrimination, and so forth down the line.

Now these constitutionally guaranteed rights are a mainstay of our system, and we have come a long way towards construing them liberally and enforcing them carefully so as to provide a rough measure of justice. But we sometimes tend to forget that the Constitution is more than a legal document—it should mean more to us than a list of rights.

In my opinion, our fellow citizens may have an understanding of the Constitution at once less technical, but deeper and more profound than what we were all taught in law school. The Constitution embodies not just a series of legal precepts, but the very spirit of democratic government. And that notion of our constitution might well teach us a little about our own profession.

What kind of government does the Constitution require? What is the spirit of the Constitution as understood by the people of this Nation? It is, first, that our government is a government of laws, and not of men. The Constitution does not say so, in so many words, but that principle is inherent in its system of checks and balances. It is rooted in the very history of our Nation—a history of revolution against the rule of one man. It is reflected in the words carved into the marble over the front of the Supreme Court building in Washington: Equal Justice *Under Law*. In the final analysis, it is grounded in the very fact that we, the people, have established a written Constitution which sets down rules that no men can ignore, no matter how powerful, no matter how great in number.

I submit that we will not achieve true justice in our society simply by ensuring the observance of enumerated constitutional rights. It is not enough that we provide due process in our courtrooms. We cannot stop there. Our system of justice must not only live up to the letter of the Constitution, but also to its spirit—the spirit of a government of laws, not of men; a government which provides equal justice, *under law*.

How close are we today toward achieving that goal? Do we have a system of law, rather than of men? Two aspects of our criminal justice system immediately come to mind as falling far short of that goal.

Let us look first at the way in which our system of justice initiates criminal cases. It is a process, I submit, of virtually unbridled discretion, the discretion of the prosecutor. For the most part, he alone decides whether to charge an offense or to let a given matter drop. He must decide whether the State will grant immunity from prosecution in return for cooperation in achieving the conviction of another. If a decision is made to proceed with criminal charges, he alone must choose which of several possible offenses to charge. And after a charge is filed and a case commenced, he alone must decide whether or not the state will accept a guilty plea to a lesser offense in return for dropping the more serious charges.

Whether a suspected shoplifter will be prosecuted or sent home with a warning; whether an alleged drunk driver should only be prosecuted for speeding; whether an alleged armed robber should be permitted to plead to unlawful possession of a firearm; all of the above are typical decisions relying on the decision of the prosecutor.

We must not forget that for a vast majority of our criminal defendants, plea bargaining is the only trial of their case they receive. To my mind, that imposes on the prosecutor and the defense attorney a grave responsibility. It is to them that the defendant must look for fair treatment and the sometimes ephemeral quality of justice we call due process. But, too often, I fear, copping a plea is bargain basement justice, looked upon by prosecutor and defense attorney alike as a sale more than as a determination of a human being's future. In our headlong rush for efficiency and rapid processing of criminal court case loads we must not forget that we are dealing with people's lives and futures. The individual orientation and humane character of the judicial system are its greatest strengths. To lose those qualities for the sake of efficiency is to strike a very bad bargain indeed. I do not condemn plea bargaining, but I think it must be rationalized and humanized as a system. A plea bargain should be premised not on expediency but on genuine concerns for the rights and the needs of the defendant. We settle civil cases only after careful thought and thorough research; cases in which a man's life and liberty are at stake certainly deserve no less.

Let us examine another part of our criminal system: the sentencing process. Here too we confront a system of unbridled discretion. Although virtually all of a judge's ruling at trial are controlled by elaborate codes of procedure and evidence, and are subject to review by an appellate court for failure to comply with those rules, ironically, perhaps the most important decision a judge makes in a given case is left for the most part to his unregulated and unreviewable discretion.

The problems of our present sentencing system have already received the careful, and characteristically thoughtful, consideration of a distinguished member of the bench here in the Southern District. And I will not pretend to have given the matter more thought than he has. Judge [Marvin] Frankel has expressed what to some may seem a harsh, but what I deem totally apt, characterization of the present system. If I may be permitted to crib part of my speech from his excellent book on the subject: "The almost wholly unchecked and sweeping powers we give to judges in the fashioning of sentences are terrifying and intolerable to a society that professes devotion to the rule of law."

The people of this country must find it very peculiar that our legal system would reverse a conviction for possession of marijuana because of a minor imperfection in a jury instruction relating to whether or not the defendant knew the marijuana was illegally imported, yet the very same system provides no remedy whatsoever for the lawfully convicted defendant who receives a 25-year sentence for possession of an ounce of marijuana when his best friend was let off by the D.A.'s office with a warning not to get caught again, and when most other offenders receive a small fine and a short jail sentence. And should we in the legal profession be any less disturbed?

By picking our these two areas of our criminal justice system, I do not in any sense mean to condemn our prosecutors or our judges. Indeed, the fact that our system operates on the whole as fairly as it does is a tribute to their concerned professionalism. That professionalism goes a long way in building equity into a system characterized by discretion.

Nor do I wish to suggest that we should substitute for our traditional prosecutorial and sentencing procedures a system which provides no room at all for discretion. In law, as in life, people and cases come in all shapes and sizes. Only a nation of robots could be content with a system of justice that provides no room for adjustments to meet the particular needs of individual cases and individual defendants.

Some degree of discretion is no doubt inevitable and in fact desirable in any system of justice. But discretion is subject to abuse. Powers given for certain proper purposes all too often can be perverted towards illegitimate ends. In my view we must attempt to strike a new balance between the competing goals of individualized justice and the rule of law. Discretion, where it exists and where it is necessary to ensure that justice retain its human element, should be rationalized and controlled.

Reform in this area may not easily come within the traditional case-by-case judicial process. As Judge Frankel has pointed out in his lecture on sentencing discretion, for example, review of sentences by appellate courts on a case-by-case basis is only one of several possible approaches to the problem of limiting discretion and channeling it toward proper purposes. And appellate review of sentences would be a solution fraught with great problems of its own. Other, in my view, more promising solutions would entail more innovative reforms—sentencing councils, better statutory definition of sentencing ranges, and better education of judges in sentencing matters—all are promising avenues of reform.

In the area of prosecutorial discretion as well, the future is cloudy for hoping to solve abuses of discretion through the ordinary judicial process. Discretionary prosecutorial decisions are virtually unreviewable by the courts, and for good reason. For such review would ultimately entwine the judicial and executive functions, and would be inconsistent with the neutrality of the courts vis-a-vis the executive branch of government. Solutions to the problems of unchecked discretion must come, if they are to come at all, in advances in administrative techniques for ensuring equity within a given prosecutorial system, or in better training of prosecutors as to the proper and improper uses of discretion.

But simply because problems cannot be solved within the traditional case-by-case judicial process does not mean that they are not deserving of our attention. Just the opposite is true. Our common mission of providing a fair system of justice requires that each of us be willing to step outside our traditional courtroom roles on occasion and work together in other forums for developing and implementing solutions to these problems.

The systemic problems of our judicial system are not confined to the area of criminal justice. Perhaps the most unsettling area of our law today is the problem of access to the courts by the vast majority of our citizenry. The judicial system does not exist as an end in itself. It does not exist to serve lawyers and judges, but to serve the public, our own constituency. Access to the courts, and access to the legal profession, must be preserved not only for our great corporations, not only for the victims of accidents, but for our entire citizenry, whose daily lives more today than ever before are touched by the law in its myriad forms.

One critic has labeled the judiciary the least dangerous branch of our government. In many ways, it is true, we are the least powerful branch. The judiciary cannot by the stroke of a pen conscript a million men, nor can we tax and appropriate the billions of dollars that makes our government move. The only tool at our command is moral suasion. But that doesn't mean that we are without influence at all. We have a rough bargain with our own constituency. As recent events have shown, although we lack power in our own right, we gain strength by virtue of the power of the constituency we serve, the people of our Nation. But that power will exist only so long as each person in this country can continue to believe that the courts and the law are available to him on an equal basis. That power will exist only if each person can trust that he will stand before the court, as an individual and as an equal in the eyes of the law to any other litigant.

We whose profession it is to ensure that the game is played according to the rules, have an overriding professional responsibility of ensuring that the game itself is fair for all. Our citizenry expect a system of justice that not only lives up to the letter of the Constitution, but one that also abides by its spirit. They deserve the best efforts of all of us towards meeting that need.

In our day-to-day work we must continue to realize that we are dealing with individuals—not statistics. Sure, we might be overworked. At the same time, while we are looking for more efficient ways to deal with growing backlogs of cases and appeals, we must not allow ourselves to lose our perspective of full justice in order to alleviate the pressure on us.

31. Advancing Public Interest Law Practice: The Role of the Organized Bar

(*American Bar Association Journal*, 1975)

One of the most important ideals of the legal profession is that all persons and groups should be able to receive competent representation in the legal process. The time has come for the organized bar to direct more of its energy and resources in this direction. I have some suggestions about the steps that bar assocations might consider taking.

My views have developed from basic perceptions about our legal system, which, whether in courts, legislatures, or administrative agencies, is largely an adversary process. Decision makers generally rely on facts and arguments presented to them by outside parties whose interests often conflict. The presentation of these contending viewpoints makes it possible, in theory at least, for the decision maker to arrive at a good decision and for wise law to develop.

The theory is flawed in practice. There is often an imbalance in the legal process. Not all viewpoints are equally represented before most decision makers. For obvious reasons, lawyers generally represent clients who can afford to pay them. As a result, many persons and groups fail to receive adequate legal representation. The effect is that the decision-making process itself is skewed, and the premises of the adversary system and of the lawyer's role in the legal process are questioned.

Neither the problem nor the calls for their solution are new. What is new is that over the last decade or so more and more lawyers have sought to dedicate their professional lives to providing representation to underrepresented interests in all facets of the legal process.

For want of a better term, I use the phrase "public interest law" to refer to the diffuse efforts aimed at providing legal resources for the unrepresented. As the recent report of the American Assembly on Law and a Changing Society II, cosponsored by the American Bar Association and held this year, noted: "While there may be ambiguity of definition and scope, a serious void in our legal institutions is being filled by the activities of lawyers who engage in representation of groups and interests that would otherwise be unrepresented or underrepresented." The cohesive element in this movement is recognition of the need to equalize representation and to revitalize the adversary system by assuring diversity of input.

The new wave of public interest law is built on the successes of civil rights and civil liberties lawyers who for decades have been working through private nonprofit organizations. It was given further impetus by the legal services program of the Office of Economic Opportunity. The development of the newer public interest law firms was a natural outgrowth of the expansion of public interest law into new areas. Public interest lawyers today provide representation to a broad range of relatively powerless minorities—for example, the mentally ill, children, and the poor of all races. They also represent neglected but widely diffuse interests that most of us share as consumers and as individuals in need of privacy and a healthy environment.

Public interest law practice is necessary to create a balance in the legal system, to assure that all interests get a fair chance to be heard with the help of a lawyer. The basic point was perfectly put by Justice Black in *Gideon v. Wainwright* (1963): "That government hires lawyers to prosecute and defendants who have the money hire lawyers to defend are the strongest indications of the widespread belief that lawyers . . . are necessities, not luxuries." To paraphrase Justice Black, if government and industry need high-quality lawyers to represent their interests in our complex society, less well-organized or less powerful interests also need to have access to high-quality legal representation.

ADVERSARY SYSTEM NEEDS DIVERSITY OF VIEWPOINT

We condemn the adversary system to one-sided justice if we deprive the legal process of the benefit of differing viewpoints and perspectives on a given problem. This is not to say that the viewpoint of the underrepresented must or should always prevail. I mean no such implication. Rather, I strongly contend that the decision maker should have the opportunity to assess the impact of any given administrative, legislative, or judicial decision in terms of all the people it will affect. This cannot be accomplished without a public interest presence whose function is to advocate, in the true sense, the needs and desires of the underrepresented and unrepresented segments of society.

As the *New York Times* has noted, the public interest practice has attracted some of the best legal minds—"the brightest graduates of the best law schools, the editors of law reviews, the law clerks to Supreme Court justices, [and] the disillusioned refugees from the more prestigious law firms." With a force of barely 250 lawyers, a tiny fraction of the 355,000 members of the nation's legal profession, public interest lawyers have attacked formidable foes and scored some extraordinary victories. Many of these victories have occurred in court litigation. But public interest law has increasingly turned to other forums. For example, as the *Wall Street Journal* has reported, the Nader organization has at least one lawyer who spends all of his time monitoring the activities of the Civil Aeronautics Board, attempting to supplement the presentations of the airline industry with some input from the perspective of customers who use the airlines.

Less activity has taken place on the legislative front, largely because private nonprofit organizations and their lawyers may not lobby if they wish to keep their tax-exempt status. This may be one reason that courts are asked to deal with so many large social policy issues. Perhaps the time has come to permit greater lobbying by public interest lawyers.

Public interest lawyers also have played a significant educational and research role, with direct and indirect effects on all of us.

In spite of these successes, public interest law practice has had one major problem: funding. Almost by definition, public interest lawyers represent persons or groups who cannot compete in the ordinary market for legal services. Often the cost of public interest lawyering exceeds the *economic* benefit to the *individual* client. In these circumstances, the funding of public interest law is a problem without an easy solution.

In analyzing the dimensions of this problem, Chesterfield Smith, an illustrious past president of the American Bar Association, stated: "[T]he gap between the need for legal services and the availability of those services . . . will never be closed without . . . institutionalized support by the organized bar. . . ." To foster integrity and public confidence in the government, the public interest bar must be kept financially afloat. It is not realistic to expect that busy lawyers with paying clients will be generally inclined to give scarce hours to a demanding public interest practice. But they might consider contributing the value of a few hours a month to a fund or foundation established by a state bar for the support of independent, public interest lawyers.

In view of the obligations of lawyers for the proper functioning of the adversary system and their monopolistic hold over the role of representation, each member of the profession, in my opinion, must assume a special responsibility to assure fairness in the adversary process. Toward this end several bar associations have initiated pilot funding programs to support the local public interest practice. I salute these efforts and concur in the recommendation of the recent American Assembly that called for an "increase of funding of public interest legal services by lawyers, bar associations and individuals and organizations concerned with social justice."

SEVERAL SOURCES PROVIDE HELP

At present several sources are helping to provide legal resources to those who cannot afford to pay for them, but each suffers from one or more liabilities. First, the federal government supports legal services through the newly created Legal Services Corporation. While the work of the corporation will be built on the O.E.O. legal services model, the statute proscribes federally funded lawyers from handling certain controversial matters, such as school desegregation, abortion, selective service, and postconviction procedures. Moreover, the test cases and affirmative class action cases require prior approval of the project director. These restrictions on the activities of legal services lawyers seriously limit their opportunity meaningfully and independently to represent the needs of their clients. This politicizing of legal representation may be an inevitable consequence of government funding.

On another front, Congress is considering creation of an Agency for Consumer Advocacy. The legislation has passed the Senate and has overwhelming support in the House. As drafted, the bill calls for the A.C.A. to intervene in administrative and court proceedings whenever the interest of the consumer may be affected. In my view the agency could be a major public interest law resource and deserves the endorsement of all friends of equal justice. But it cannot completely replace the need for independent lawyers representing specific consumer interests before the agencies.

Second, the judiciary has awarded attorney's fees to lawyers acting for the substantial benefit of the public in civil rights and other cases of public importance. I do not fear, as do many members of the public interest bar, that the Supreme Court's decision in *Alyeska Pipeline Service Company v. Wilderness Society* (1975) sounded the death knell for public interest law. In my opinion the majority of the Court recognized the pressing need for compensation of attorneys who act in the public interest. In the words of my Brother White: "It is also apparent from our national experience that the encouragement of private action to implement public policy has been viewed as desirable in a variety of circumstances."

While the Court declined to endorse the power of a court to identify those circumstances, it acknowledged the power of a court to redistribute litigation costs with legislative authorization. With more than thirty statutes now on the books containing provisions for awards of attorneys' fees and more on the drafting board, I envision this particular problem as temporary in nature.

BALL NOW IN CONGRESS'S COURT

It is now the responsibility of Congress to provide for the award of attorneys' fees by courts and agencies if it wishes to make it possible for private parties to enforce certain federal laws. But while the availability of attorneys' fees awards is important, it is shortsighted to place complete reliance on this particular source. Court-awarded fees are not an elixir for the funding problem. The scope of public interest law extends to activities in which fee awards are not possible, and, in any case, fee awards will always be an uncertain and delayed source of funding. Thus support for this broadened range of activities must come from a permanent, more comprehensive source.

Third, foundations and many individuals contribute generously to civil rights and public interest law firms. Some membership organizations such as the Sierra Club and the Wilderness Society rely on dues to support their legal activities, but this funding is unpredictable and permits no long-range planning capability. Foundation support has supplemented such groups and wholly supported public interest firms on a year-to-year basis. But no sustaining financial support has evolved from this source. Moreover, a tight economy has reduced the amount of grants and threatens their continued availability. While the *pro bono publico* activities of some individual lawyers and private firms have been exemplary, the activities of most private practitioners are sporadic and devoid of an ongoing commitment to public interest law.

When one reviews the current situation, it is clear that institutionalization of the public interest bar is necessary to establish a constant presence for the points of view of underrepresented persons in society and in administrative, judicial, and other legal proceedings. In my view it is incumbent on the legal profession to eliminate the tendency to one-sided justice and to assure a true adversary system by funding public interest practice on a permanent basis.

While the organized bar has philosophically accepted the idea of its responsibilities in securing adequate representation for all persons, it has yet to come to grips with its responsibility for enforcing this obligation. The American Bar Association and some local bar associations have taken initial steps in exploring new avenues for funding public interest law. The creation of the Council for Public Interest Law is an exciting new development. Through the joint efforts of the American Bar Endowment, the Ford Foundation, and others, it seeks to harness new methods of financing public interest law on a more permanent basis. The first steps by the American Bar Association at a national level are worthy of emulation, but they represent only a beginning.

More in the way of grass-roots action is necessary. In Beverly Hills, Philadelphia, and the District of Columbia there is direct evidence that the bar associations are working to obtain the institutional support required to bridge the gap between the need and availability of legal services.

In 1971 the Beverly Hills Bar Association established the Beverly Hills Bar Association Foundation with a one-time seed money grant of $15,000. The foundation has fifteen directors—seven appointed by the president of the association and the other eight elected by the members. The board of directors represents a cross-section of the legal community and includes several corporate lawyers, three law professors, a director of the local legal aid society, civil rights, environmental, and consumer lawyers, and minority group lawyers.

Financial support for the foundation comes from the private bar. Law firms are solicited to contribute at the rate of $100 a firm lawyer a year. In its first year of operation it raised more than $20,000 from these contributions. Additional staff and financial support comes from foundations, public interest organizations, and individuals.

The private bar also contributes legal staff to the foundation through a voluntary pool of about two hundred attorneys. The matters handled by the foundation include significant reform work in the problem areas of voting, broadcasting, consumer protection, and state bar examinations.

The creation of a public interest law firm bearing the name of a bar association is the most important statement any association can make regarding its commitment to providing equal justice to all. Throughout both the legal community and the poor and minority communities, the foundation is fast gaining the reputation of providing legal representation in many significant cases. But this view is not universal. Early criticism arose from members of the state legislature who were angered by the foundation's representation of Mexican-Americans on reapportionment issues, members of the bar who were upset about challenges to the bar examination, and other controversial cases. I find none of the objections valid.

CONTROVERSY REQUIRES REPRESENTATION

Controversy is an integral part of a lawyer's business. Controversy accompanies most efforts to correct social wrongs. Persons raising controversial issues are surely entitled to representation. With all lawyers arrayed on the side of justice, as they are, it is certainly appropriate to provide some opportunity for reformers to have the benefit of legal assistances. The reformers may prove to be wrong, but they deserve to be heard before we hastily decide that they are wrong.

However, it does seem to me that there is one real problem with the Beverly Hills scheme—that it places exclusive reliance on a voluntary pool of attorneys for staff power. Public interest law is a speciality like any other and requires full-time effort. Time demands and possible conflicts of interest with paying clients make it difficult, if not impossible, for volunteers to give singular focus and attention to the needs of their public interest clients.

In most respects the Philadelphia experience follows a pattern similar to that in California, but it does have certain innovative aspects that are worthy of note. At the urging of public-minded leaders of the Philadelphia Bar Association, the former Lawyers Committee for Civil Rights under Law was expanded into the Public Interest Law Center of Philadelphia. The board of directors is drawn from a cross-section of the legal profession and the community. With a seed grant of $10,000 plus an equal commitment for two additional years from the Philadelphia Bar Association—which makes charitable contributions to legally related projects from the commissions on its life insurance and disability insurance policies (as is the case with the American Bar Endowment)—the P.I.L.C.O.P. steering committee solicited three-year commitments from large law firms at $50 a lawyer, from individual practitioners, and from foundations. From one third to one half of the lawyers in a metropolitan area like Philadelphia are employed by the larger firms. These are also the locations where the need for legal services for minorities, consumers, and taxpayers will be the greatest. If Philadelphia has raised more than $50,000 annually from this source, smaller cities should be able to match this commitment on a proportional basis. Several of the local family foundations became interested in the project and agreed to substantial commitments for a three-year period.

Perhaps the most exciting source of funding for the center was the state government which, with the governor's strong endorsement, has agreed to fund Legal Services for People Who Are Different at $275,000 a year for a three-year period. Focusing on problems of the mentally ill, the elderly and the gifted, a task force will work as a special unit within the center to improve the quality of representation for these groups. The center staff of six lawyers handles other cases that have the potential of major redress or significant precedent in areas such as housing, consumer protection, education, and the environment.

I find two aspects of the Philadelphia proposal most instructive. First, the use of a pre-existing organization as the foundation of the bar-sponsored public interest law firm represents an efficient use of legal resources. The Boston Bar Association has followed this same path in making a similar professional and financial commitment in the development of its public interest law firm. Second, the presence of staff lawyers avoids the dispersion of energies that accompanies operation solely with a volunteer pool, while the co-operation of the bar in general allows the staff to draw on specific *expertise* from lawyers at large firms, if necessary.

ACTIVITY IN DISTRICT OF COLUMBIA

The District of Columbia Bar Association is also exploring avenues for funding the public interest practice. The District bar has recently conducted a symposium on *pro bono publico* needs and services in the Washington community. From this symposium issued a lengthy final report which led to the formation of a special committee to determine how much potential support there is within the bar association for funding public interest activities.

The alternatives that will surface from the committee's work will undoubtedly reflect the large number of public interest law firms in the District. With this proliferation of public interest lawyers, the development of a foundation to distribute funds to pre-existing law firms might be more advisable than the creation of another public interest firm. Perhaps the funds could be derived from an increase in membership dues or a special assessment to improve the decision-making process and the adversary system. The board of directors of the foundation then would be responsible for distribution of the funds to public interest firms regularly, thereby creating a permanent funding source for those organizations. While some objections have been raised to this approach, it seem to me as a matter of policy that lawyers are obliged to make good their moral commitments to equal justice.

Although these projects are at varying stages of development, they all reflect a common commitment to moving bar associations beyond their traditional support of legal aid and public defender projects into support of law reform programs concerned about social issues.

As our society moves toward realization of full representation for all citizens, the permanent funding of public interest law practice by the organized bar offers an administratively feasible and financially reasonable means of demonstrating in tangible form a commitment to equal justice under law. While I recognize that some difficult problems of implementation remain, I see no reason to delay making a special commitment to the public interest practice by offering direct support from the bar associations. With this in mind, I challenge lawyers and leaders of the state and local bar associations to work toward this end and to encourage the bar to take bold and effective steps in this direction.

32. Remarks, New York State Bar Association
On Receiving the Gold Medal Award for
Distinguished Service in Law
(January 30, 1976)

Thank you. I am delighted to be with you tonight. I am deeply honored and privileged to accept your Gold Medal Award for Distinguished Service in the Law—particularly in light of the stature of the award's previous recipients. Your organization has itself consistently rendered distinguished service to our profession in the past and I am confident that it will continue to do so in the future.

My remarks tonight are directed to the concern that all of us share that the performance of members of the legal profession be—and continue to be—if not always distinguished, at least uniformly competent. During the past several months the rules proposed by the Special Committee appointed by my good friend Chief Judge Irving Kaufman have focused our attention on one aspect of the problem of inadequate representation. Seeking to insure that lawyers admitted to practice before the Second Circuit have been properly trained, this well-balanced Committee, chaired by the very distinguished Robert Clare, proposed among other things a requirement that all applicants for admission have successfully completed courses in five specific subjects prior to admission.

I am, of course, in total agreement with the Clare Committee's general aim to promote a more competent bar and, indeed, with its more specific objective of insuring that young lawyers receive adequate training during their law school educations. However, I do confess to a certain skepticism about the desirability of requiring applicants for admission to the federal bar to have taken a given range of specified courses. This skepticism stems from my conviction that the imposition of such conditions is far from a costless proposition. The creativity and independence of our law schools are precious commodities that should be nurtured and not restricted. The law schools have a wealth of experience and expertise in issues of legal education that is simply not possessed either by practicing lawyers or by judges.

Requiring bar applicants to have taken certain courses runs the risk of serving as a not-so-indirect pressure on law schools to reallocate their teaching and financial resources more heavily into the areas required under the Rules. Of course, the Clare Committee requirements are nowhere near as extensive as those for being admitted to some bars. All applicants to the Indiana bar, for instance, must have taken all of a specified list of fourteen courses. The more limited nature of the Clare Committee requirements limits the risk of law school intrusion that they present, but every additional course required for bar admission is an additional restriction on the independence of our law schools. Such restrictions should only be imposed if we have very substantial reason to believe that there is a strong relationship between competency in the courtroom and successful completion of a set of specified courses.

Whatever the final fate of the Clare Committee proposals might be—however many courts adopt some variant of them—it is critical that we remain keenly alert to the fact that the proposals treat but one aspect of the problem of inadequate legal representation. To the extent that inadequate legal training of bar applicants contributes to inadequate courtroom performance, implementation of the Clare Committee proposals might help to mitigate the problem. But surely there are other causes of inadequate representation. In my own experience in practice and on the bench I have seen many lawyers who have graduated near the top of their classes at what are said to be top flight law schools and who have taken all the "right" courses but who, after many years of practice, still cannot properly try a case. Much more importantly, it is obvious that the Clare Committee proposals do not treat and are indeed not meant to treat the problem of incompetent performance on the part of lawyers *already* admitted to practice before the district courts. And it may well be that because of the extraordinarily and increasingly high academic abilities of the new entrants into our profession, the major part of the inadequate representation problem is rooted in those already practicing law rather than in those not yet admitted to the bar.

The inadequacy in performance of lawyers already in practice is a dilemma whose solution must come directly and exclusively from the practicing bar and bench. There is no turning to the law schools to improve the quality of the lawyers who are already practicing. It is to this aspect of the problem that I would like to turn my attention now.

At the outset we should face the fact that today there are relatively few factors at work either in the judiciary or in the organized bar to control or deter inadequate representation. While trial judges on occasion reprimand lawyers for instances of professional misconduct as that term is narrowly understood, the instances are few and far between in which judges take a lawyer to task simply for being unprepared or for otherwise providing inadequate representation for his client.

And in all but a few circuits only the grossest kind of inadequacy will warrant reversal of a criminal conviction on ineffective assistance of counsel grounds. With standards allowing reversal only when the representation is so bad as to make the proceedings "a farce and mockery of justice," we certainly cannot expect that the ineffective assistance of counsel doctrine will be of any substantial assistance in insuring the quality of legal representation. Moreover, the doctrine is of no help at all in civil proceedings, where litigants may be deprived of important property rights because of incompetent counsel, but where there is no judicial corrective mechanism at all.

The prevalent notion seems to be that whether the lawyer is retained or appointed the litigant must make do with him. Perhaps we judges, in a failure of humility, also fall prey to the thought that given our own skills, we are perfectly able to decide cases—and to decide them correctly—even when the positions of one or indeed both of the litigants are inadequately presented. By this analysis, the adequacy or inadequacy or representation in most contexts becomes irrelevant to the dispensing of justice. But, to my mind, competent representation is essential to considered and correct judicial decision-making, especially given the heavy case loads borne by many of our judges. And, more fundamentally, inadequate representation is every bit as basic an affront to our judicial system as are more traditionally recognized forms of professional misconduct such as champerty or corruption. In short, inadequate representation, to the extent that it is tolerated, deals a severe blow to the very integrity of the judicial process.

Nor has the practicing bar compensated for the failure of the judiciary in providing solutions to control or deter inadequate representation. After a lawyer has been admitted to practice there is little done by the bar to insure that his representation of his client is adequate. Bar organization disciplinary proceedings typically deal with such matters as conflicts of interest or improper solicitation of clients. Only in the rarest of instances—if ever—is a lawyer disciplined simply for inadequate representation of a client.

In the absence of vigorous efforts by either the judiciary or the bar, the control of inadequate representation is left largely to the free marketplace and the laws of supply and demand and, I fear, of caveat emptor. I suppose that in a perfect market the inadequate lawyers might simply be forced out of the profession. But we all realize that the market for legal assistance is far from perfect. Many, if not most, consumers of legal services—particularly those who are of low income and uneducated and for whom representation is most likely to be inadequate—are extremely unlikely to realize when they are being inadequately served.

In light of the apparent absence of any substantial control mechanisms on inadequate legal representation, we should perhaps be happily surprised that the general level of representation is so good rather than dismayed that there are a significant number of instances of inadequate representation. Indeed the level of competence that does exist in the legal profession due to the personal sense of commitment and devotion of the major portion of its members is remarkably high. But efforts are needed to control and limit the instances of incompetent representation.

What kinds of efforts are appropriate? There are a wide range of possible complementary alternatives, some more experimental than others. Let me briefly mention just a few.

As I implied earlier, judges have a special obligation to play an active role in taking lawyers to task for instances of inadequate representation. Since the ultimate responsibility for the conduct of any trial proceedings is that of the presiding judge it is he who bears the ultimate burden of controlling inadequate representation. And, it seems to me that in his role as presiding officer he has a unique opportunity to help insure competent representation. Adequacy of representation is, I suspect, far more likely to appear in courtrooms in which the judge is known to be one who expects and demands the lawyers who appear before him to be fully prepared and who will not hesitate to indicate when he is dissatisfied. Particularly to the extent that inadequate representation is due to factors within the immediate control of the lawyer—his own negligence or laziness, for instance—the bar's sensitivity to the fact that a given judge is very demanding will increase the adequacy of representation in cases tried before him, to the benefit of everyone. Conversely, tolerance by judges of inadequate representation will tend to increase its occurrence. Put simply, the more judges expect and demand of lawyers appearing before them, the better will be the quality of the lawyers' product.

Within the area of appointed counsel, in particular, judges have a substantial opportunity and responsibility to insure that the level of representation is adequate. By the appointment process itself, the court lends a special stamp of approval to the competency of a lawyer. That stamp of court approval is, of course, a valuable one to those who make a substantial portion of their living as appointed counsel. Only those lawyers whose performance is regarded as consistently reaching at least a minimum level of competence should be allowed to continue to receive appointments. Repeated instances of inadequate representation by a given lawyer should trigger a response from the trial judge. Depending on the severity of the lapse, the response should vary from a reprimand to a forced reduction in the number of appointments to, ultimately, a flat ban on the lawyer's receiving any further appointments at all.

Looking to the bar itself, there is a substantial amount that can and should be done to insure the continued competence of its members—both those who practice in court and those who do not. I shall note just a few of the possibilities.

If it is admitted that applicants to the bar may be undertrained in areas of trial advocacy, then one would expect that a fair number of practicing lawyers are also undertrained in these and other areas. And even those who were properly trained during their law school years may have forgotten what they learned and may be unaware of new developments in their field. Of course the voluminous amounts of legal literature published each year help many lawyers avoid this situation. But it is programs of continuing legal education for members of the bar that are designed most directly to meet these problems. The variety of offerings in continuing legal education programs is indeed broad; a lawyer looking for a program in any given area can generally find it. But regrettably too few lawyers take advantage of these courses. My sense is that the competency of a substantial number of lawyers would improve through exposure to some formal source of continuing legal education. The trick, then, is to devise a means for encouraging participation in such programs.

The potential methods of encouragement are many. One method, adopted by the Minnesota Supreme Court, is simply to make continuing education programs a requirement for all members of the bar.

Another approach—one that uses the carrot rather than the stick—is to give some sort of examination at the end of each program or set of programs and award a certificate to those who pass, allowing them to indicate their certification in their letterhead and telephone listing. This approach is designed to stimulate those who see no "payoff" in the programs to begin to take advantage of them. There are substantial drawbacks to such a scheme. Like the required attendance plan, it suffers from overinclusiveness. Why do we wish to encourage those who are already perfectly qualified to take these programs? And the programs themselves would have to undergo substantial change. A three-day series of lectures—as the current programs tend to be—can hardly be the source of a meaningful examination and subsequent certification. Moreover, a certification scheme would tilt the bar toward formal specialization with all the costs and risks that might incur. Nevertheless, the certification scheme is an intriguing one.

Another less innovative but perhaps just as useful method of encouraging participation in continuing legal education programs is simply to do everything possible to increase their availability. This means, first of all, keeping their prices low. Moreover, the number of places in which programs are offered should be broadly expanded. Lawyers unwilling or unable to spend the time and money necessary to take a legal education program in a far-away city might be willing and indeed anxious, to take precisely the same program were it offered in his own community through use of videotape or tape recordings.

Two other suggestions through which the bar might help insure its own competence, suggestions more wide-ranging and novel than those relating to continuing legal education, have been increasingly widely discussed, most recently in a series of articles by Paul Wolin of the ALI–ABA Committee on Continuing Professional Education. While not without drawbacks, both these suggestions are certainly worthy of serious study. The first would establish a system within the bar for monitoring the performance of lawyers. Under this proposal a lawyer's apparent inadequate performance could be reported by judges, clients or opposing lawyers to a specially established committee of the bar. This committee, not unlike traditional disciplinary committees, would have the power and responsibility to investigate and adjudicate charges of incompetence, determine the source of the incompetence, if any, and prescribe whatever remedies might be necessary.

Only in extreme cases would formal disciplinary action be taken. Rather, the aim of the scheme would be to help the lawyer himself to eliminate whatever might be behind the inadequacy of his representation. For instance, inadequacies due to a lack of training could be met with a suggestion or indeed a prescription that the lawyer take and complete continuing legal education courses in his field.

Among the disadvantages of a monitoring proposal include the fact that the bureaucratic burdens of establishing and administering such a scheme might be very substantial. The monitoring committee would have to devote substantial effort to determining precisely what constitutes inadequacy of representation. And there may be no sure way of preventing practicing lawyers from being harassed and the monitoring committee from being deluged by frivolous complaints of incompetency from dissatisfied litigants. Moreover, with the committee's trigger to action being an instance of demonstrated inadequacy, the scheme in a sense closes the barn door after the horse is out. Prevention of future inadequacy under the monitoring proposal can only follow instances of actual inadequacy. Nevertheless a monitoring system or some variant would have the advantage of providing a system for the identification and potential remedy of inadequate representation short of the rigorous legal standard of ineffective assistance of counsel.

Derived from the experience of the medical and accounting professions is the second innovative proposal that is making the rounds, that of peer review. Under this proposal lawyers, both single practitioners and law firms, could voluntarily submit themselves to review of the adequacy of the services that they are providing their clients. Reviewing panels would be comprised of members of the profession selected by the local bar. The basic thrust of the peer review would be to suggest methods for improving the quality of service rather than disciplining lawyers who are found wanting. Under this proposal, a lawyer or law firm that has received the approval of the peer review committee would be able to make that fact known to the public, thus providing an incentive to submit to such review.

As distinguished from the monitoring proposal that I discussed earlier, the peer review suggestion is one that perhaps more directly attempts to prevent inadequate representation before it occurs or at least before it reaches a point at which it is likely to arouse complaint from clients. On the other hand, the voluntary nature of the peer review proposal may mean that precisely those lawyers who need to be reviewed would be the ones least likely to undergo review. And making peer review mandatory for all lawyers would undoubtedly be so immense a task for the bar as to be bureaucratically unworkable. Nevertheless, the concept of peer review is to my mind a potentially valuable one.

A final potential aid in controlling inadequate representation that I would like to mention is different in kind from those I have already discussed. It requires a wider recognition of the role of the organized bar in financing public interest law and the representation of the underrepresented poor. The general problem of inadequate representation by lawyers is one only very rarely experienced by those individuals and corporations who can afford to hire prominent attorneys to spend substantial amounts of time on their case. Rather the impact of inadequate legal representation and indeed of no representation at all has its greatest impact on traditionally underrepresented minority groups and the economically disadvantaged. Many competent lawyers working in these areas are simply too overworked to be able to accord adequate representation to all their clients. In past years Legal Services and private foundation money have helped to close the gaps in representation being accorded the poor. But the gaps are still yawning. Moreover, in light of the limited scope of the new Legal Services Corporation and the relative unavailability of long term foundation money, representation for the poor is bound to become worse and not better, unless some other solution is found. In large part, I suggest the solution lies in local bar organizations taking an active role in financing the representation of the poor. Whether this sponsorship should take the form of the bar association itself hiring a group of lawyers to work full time on such representation or whether it should take some other form is a matter that can be legitimately debated. As I discussed in remarks delivered to last year's American Bar Association Convention in Montreal, experiments utilizing various approaches are being tried in various parts of the country. But whatever methods are ultimately adopted, the organized bar does have to come to grips with its responsibility for enforcing the obligation to secure adequate representation for all persons. And concern and responsibility for the financing of such representation is as much a part of this obligation as the disciplinary and educational solutions to inadequate representation that I discussed earlier. As Chesterfield Smith, the distinguished former president of the American Bar Association has noted:

> "The gap between the need for legal services and the availability of those services . . . will never be closed without . . . institutional support by the organized bar."

Adequate legal representation both inside and outside the courtroom is essential to the maintenance of the integrity of our judicial system and to the dispensing of justice. Solutions, it is true, are hard to come by; the controversy raging in the area is itself proof of the difficulty of the problem. But face the problem we must. Both the judiciary and the bar must spare no effort in insuring the realization of the guarantee of full and adequate representation to all our citizens.

33. Address at the Eighth Conference on the Law of the World (August 23, 1977)

It is truly a humbling experience to stand before hundreds of lawyers and judges from more than a hundred nations around the globe. Among us, we represent all of the great legal systems and traditions of the world. We are gathered, of course, to join in rededicating ourselves to the noble quest of our profession—the peaceful resolution of disputes through the carefully developed processes of the law.

Our task is becoming more urgent. The recent years have been turbulent ones, both internationally and within many of our nations. Grave problems continue to cry for solution. Overpopulation, starvation, poor housing and health care, unequal educational opportunity, and the threat of war and civil unrest, to name but a few, plague many millions of the world's citizens. We can rejoice that bombs no longer fall on innocent people in Indochina, and there are some hopeful signs of international cooperation in the Middle East. But new threats to peace have arisen in areas long neglected by the world community, such as Southern Africa. More and more the emphasis has been on human rights. More is needed.

Many of the most serious problems facing humanity are, of course, beyond the competence of the judicial process to solve. Indeed, courts are usually unable to address these great dilemmas in any but the most limited fashion. Lawyers are fortunate, however, that they have the unusual professional option to step into many government and private sector positions. There, as executive and legislative officers, they are often able to have a more direct impact on meeting human needs.

There are some who have criticized this trend as a "plague of lawyers" infesting many of the world's public and private institutions. They see our governments, legislatures, and corporations as overburdened with lawyers in policy-making positions. While there is perhaps some truth to these fears, it seems to me that the trend is not sinister. Rather, it reflects the special qualities imparted by legal training. With its respect for procedure, its disciplined analysis of problems, and its unremitting search for their fundamental sources, the law provides a unique background for public service.

Too often, perhaps, lawyers working in positions of public or private trust use their training as no more than a tool to ensure their own personal success. If so, the critics have good cause for complaint. I believe that those trained in the law have a higher obligation. Executive and legislative officials with legal backgrounds must seek not merely personal aggrandizement, but must strive over the long haul to improve the lives of all people whom they serve.

Those who choose to remain within the narrower traditional confines of the legal profession also have a vital task to perform. In a very real sense, the bench and bar might be called the glue that holds our societies together. We are, in many ways, the most potent social force against terror and revolution.

The bench and bar are often accused of being a reactionary element in society. There is some truth to this charge. Courts unfortunately may become instruments of repression. They may be used to prosecute minority groups, to enjoin free speech and peaceful assembly practiced by those with unpopular views, to enforce the property rights of the rich against those too poor to resist. Some lawyers, too, may often seek to preserve the status quo—in court and out—for the benefit of wealthy and powerful clients. These tendencies are, I am afraid, to some degree inevitable in any legal system.

But in the best functioning systems, they are strongly tempered by the role of bench and bar as the hands guiding and molding social and political change. A strong, active and independent legal system often is the key element making it possible for a society to weather the storms of change sweeping the world today. The ship of a state having such a legal system will survive the tempest, perhaps battered around the waterline and with sails torn, yet proceeding resolutely on course. But lacking a dynamic legal system, a state risks breaking up on the shoals of internal strife and civil conflict.

This point is illustrated by events across the world during the last four years. In my own country, the bench and bar played a key part in preserving democratic institutions that were badly shaken by repeated illegal acts committed by high government officials. The Watergate years subjected my country's Constitution to its greatest crisis in decades. Yet ultimately, public confidence was restored and I believe that the United States emerged stronger than it had been for many years.

It was shortly after our Abidjan Conference in 1973 that the Vice President of the United States was charged with serious criminal acts predating his term of office. Diligent investigation by prosecutorial forces undaunted by the power and importance of the defendant led to the charges. Through our independent judicial process, they were resolved, on the whole, I think, fairly to all concerned.

The Vice President, having admitted his guilt in Court, resigned his public office, and he was quickly replaced in accordance with the procedure laid down in our Constitution. The crisis had, however, only begun. As Americans watched in horror, it slowly became apparent that far more serious crimes had been committed at the highest levels of government, indeed, by the President himself. Numbered among those who pierced through the web of perjury and deceit were a determined judiciary and fearless prosecution staff, responsible legislative committees, and a dedicated free press. I might add that in this monumental venture, as in many others, the dedication and freedom of the press did not always insure accuracy, but I believe that the value of a free press was never more strongly felt or needed than in the years of Watergate.

While it is impossible to measure the contributions made by any one of the institutions involved in uncovering and punishing the Watergate crimes, lawyers and judges were high among those most prominent in the process. For example, all the members of the Judiciary Committee of the House of Representatives conducting the impeachment proceedings were lawyers. Regrettably, persons trained in the law, including the President, were also unduly notable among the guilty. Their presence should serve as a reminder that constant vigilance is required lest we allow our training to become a force for evil.

When the President did resign, under threat of almost certain impeachment, his successor took office under constitutional procedures, peacefully and in strict accordance with the rule of law. The great lesson of Watergate, I think, was that it served to remind us of the inestimable strength and resiliency of a democratic society operating under well defined principles of law. It was, in many ways, a triumph of law over lawless behavior; a triumph of the democratic process over those who sought to subvert it to serve their selfish hunger for power.

Some may argue that in the Watergate crisis, judges took an inappropriately active role in the political process. The order to President Nixon to release the White House tapes, for example, precipitated a major political crisis. But it seems to me that the actions of the courts were proper precisely because of their impact on the political sphere. What made them acceptable in a democratic society was the fact that the judges scrupulously respected the limits on their role. They acted in accordance with all the procedural regularities of the judicial branch. The decisions that were reached were right because they were based upon application of the principles of the law to concrete cases at hand.

While no judge deciding such a case can—or should—fail to be aware of the enormous political repercussions that it may generate, strict adherence to the principles and procedures of the law give the judge enormous moral authority in a crisis. There have been reports that President Nixon considered defying the court order to turn over his tape recordings. I submit that such a course would have been futile. In a battle for moral authority, the allegiance of the people will lie with the courts, as long as the judicial branch acts responsibly under the law. I am less sanguine about our performance of our everyday duties. For our real contribution is measured not in dramatic deeds, but in our daily dispensation of advice and justice to hundreds of thousands of individuals experiencing some sort of difficulty in their relationships with others.

When I last spoke to this Conference, I suggested that the governing principle of a humane society and a good legal system could be summed up in the simple phrase "People are people." It seems to me that the phrase not only states a universal rule of substantive law, but that it is equally apposite as a guiding principle for the way courts and lawyers should conduct their daily business—a procedural maxim, if you will. If bench and bar are to perform successfully their role in civilized society, they must recognize the worth and importance of every person coming before them.

Perhaps the most basic function performed by our legal systems is the ordering of social relationships. A legal system substitutes the rule of law for the violent self-help to which people would otherwise be forced to turn to defend their possessions, their lives, and their human dignity. Courts are an important part of this system, for they are the ultimate arbiters in a peaceful society of disagreements among citizens. But courts can only succeed in preventing violent confrontation if they perform their duties fairly and impartially.

And while equal justice for all is a goal to which all decent legal systems must aspire, it is not enough if only we judges and lawyers know that it has been reached. In order to displace the use of violence, a legal system must also be perceived by all the people as providing equal justice. If the system is not believed to be fair, it will be a failure, for its effectiveness depends almost entirely on its public appearance.

I would not presume to tell those of you engaged in the business of judging how to decide particular issues that might come before you. Different nations have different needs and traditions that may require varied solutions to similar problems. But I know that whatever the solution a court imposes, it will not be effective in convincing the parties and the society that justice has been done unless all people coming before it are treated as equally important people. I think there are a number of steps that we can take to serve this principle.

First, access to justice must never depend on the wealth or position of the litigant. Justice must be available to men and women struggling in abject poverty just as it is to the owners of great mansions.

When courts—consciously or unconsciously—make decisions that have the appearance of rewarding the wealthy and powerful and harming the unprivileged, they lose some of the credibility that makes them a viable alternative to violence. For decisions that are based on such factors have nothing to do with the merits of the dispute that is being settled. They are no more related to who owns a cow or a piece of land, or to whether a homicide was justifiable, than does the fact that one of the parties is a boxing champion or has a large family that will fight to defend him. In the courts, might—be it fiscal or physical—must never make right.

I am reminded of my early practice of law, during the Depression of the 1930's in the City of Baltimore, Maryland. The highest court of the state had an interesting rule at that time. All briefs, and the complete record, including the transcript of the trial, had to be printed for the court, or an appeal could not be brought before it. This was not a serious barrier for the banks and large businesses represented by prominent law firms in the city. But often it was an insurmountable obstacle for poor criminal defendants and struggling shopkeepers, the sort of clients that I represented. Nowadays, appellate printing costs in the United States are generally borne by the State. But that was decades away during the Depression. Once I complained to a clerk in the state's highest court that this was not fair to my impoverished Negro clients. His reply was simple: "Every man has his day in court—if he can pay." Happy we are that we have changed to equal justice for all—regardless of ability to pay.

I submit that in a just society, the clerk's attitude is intolerable. If justice is a scarce commodity, rationed like diamonds only to those who can afford to buy it, unrest and even revolution are inevitable. Only a society that is stabilized by brute force can long survive with an inequitable legal system. Courts can serve their role of holding society together only if they make justice freely available, whatever the wealth, social or political position of the litigants. As my Court said years ago, "there can be no equal justice where the kind of trial that a man gets depends on the amount of money that he has."

Perhaps the single most significant equalizing factor on the scales of justice is the lawyer. I believe that it is the duty of the legal profession to strive to provide lawyers to all persons in need of their assistance. The ever-growing body of laws affecting more and more aspects of everyday life makes this an imperative.

There are may ways to provide legal services for all. In some places, the government may provide lawyers for the poor or pay for their services. Unions and trade associations have experimented with plans to hire lawyers to help their members. The increased use of non-lawyers to perform routine services in much the same way as medical paraprofessionals has met with success. But so much more remains to be done, even in the most economically advantaged nations. It is, I think, the duty of our profession to explore every possible means of making the legal system serve all of our fellow human beings with maximum effectiveness.

In the meantime, courts should be readily accessible even to those who proceed without lawyers. Judges and opposing counsel should treat litigants who are unable or unwilling to obtain an attorney with respect, courtesy, and sympathy. The ways of the law are often mysterious, even to lawyers, and justifiable disgust with the system will quickly mount in the face of unnecessary dismissals on technical points, overly strict reliance on minor procedural rules, and similar pettiness. Judges have a particular responsibility, I think, to make sure that their clerks and other staff members do not lose sight, in piles of technical paperwork, of their primary duty to make justice available to all.

It is no less important for judges themselves to act in a way that maximizes their credibility as settlers of social disputes. There is nothing more disturbing for a litigant than to appear in court and receive the unmistakeable impression that he has already lost his case.

I am continually amazed by the number of judges who fail to realize that in their conduct on the bench, a simple acknowledgement of the seriousness of a litigant's argument will serve the cause of justice more than pages of erudite opinions. Often, no more is necessary than a little courtesy, a few minutes spent listening attentively, and the asking of several questions that demonstrate a thoughtful understanding of the litigant's claim.

Rational litigants realize that only one side can win a legal dispute. They usually understand—particularly if it is explained to them—that one's natural instincts of justice and the strictures of what the law allows may not coincide. Thus, litigants can rationalize the loss of their case with the thought that at least the system has given them a fair chance and the interests of society as a whole have been served. What they cannot accept, and I do not think that anyone should accept it, is the realization that their pleas were not even heard and acknowledged; that their arguments fell on deaf ears. For every litigant who leaves a courtroom with that feeling, a part of the elaborate structure of the law collapses. The loss hurts every one of us.

World peace through law is a magnificent goal. Perhaps it can not be achieved. At least we have at these conferences made a modest beginning. More and more lawyers and judges from around the world have joined us. When I think back on my own life, the changes I have seen, a few perhaps that I helped to cause, there is reason to hope. But there is so much more to be done if justice and peace are to become a way of life for every person on earth. That is, I think, the message of this conference. I hope it will become a call to action for every one of us.

34. Remarks at the American College of Trial Lawyers Spring Meeting (March 14, 1977)

In this selection Marshall discusses proposals to reform judicial selection by stressing "merit" as a basis for choosing judges. Implicitly drawing on his experience as a practicing lawyer and African American, Marshall expresses concern that merit-based selection will in fact exclude from consideration people whose life experiences, while different from those on the selection committees, nonetheless would enhance the quality of the bench.

I am delighted to be with you in this beautiful setting for the Spring Meeting of the American College of Trial Lawyers. (I would have been even more delighted to have been here for a winter meeting. This past winter, faced with the challenge of coping with snow, Washington proved once again that it is truly a city of Southern efficiency and Northern hospitality.) I would like to speak today about a topic of current interest to members of the bar, and the public generally: the selection of judges.

As you may know, exactly one month ago President Carter issued an executive order creating a new mechanism for selecting federal appellate judges. Under this order, each time a vacancy on a court of appeals occurs, a panel will be activated to report to the President the names of the five persons considered "best qualified" to fill the vacancy. These panels will consist of approximately equal numbers of lawyers and nonlawyers and will be drawn, in part, from the circuit in which the vacancy occurs. Presumably, the President will make every effort to select his nominees from these lists, as he did while Governor of Georgia.

The President's plan, you will note, to a large degree follows the so-called "merit plan" or "Missouri Plan" for selecting judges. This plan, first proposed by Dean Kales of Northwestern Law School in 1914, has spread rapidly in recent years; since 1970 the number of States using it has more than doubled, and almost half the States presently select some or all of their judges under the merit system. My aim, today, is to raise some questions—and express some reservations—about this system.

Of course, no one opposes selecting judges on merit; the alternative, after all, is a meritless selection system, hardly an appealing prospect. Nor can one quarrel with the goal, perhaps first voiced in this country by George Washington, of choosing "the fittest characters to expound the laws and dispense justice": again one need only consider the alternative. The crucial questions are what types of persons make "the fittest" judges, and by what process are they best elevated to the bench.

In theory, at least, the Missouri plan speaks only to the second question—the question of process. Its answer is that "the fittest"—however defined—are best selected by creating a commission of lawyers and laymen to submit a small list of names to the executive from which he must choose judges. My concern, as I shall explain, is that this process will subtly influence the definition of "fitness," by giving preeminent weight to technical or professional selection criteria.

Insofar as the merit plan is designed simply to put an end to cronyism and patronage in judicial appointments, no one can quarrel with it. I can think of no task that judges are properly called upon to perform that requires prior experience as a friend or backer of the appointing official (or his party). I might add, however, that the one major study that has been done of the first 20 years of the merit plan in Missouri gives substantial reason to question whether the plan can remove friendship with the executive as a criterion for judicial selection.

But questions of effectiveness aside, creating an elaborate set of commissions with broad powers seems unnecessary simply to eliminate cronyism; I cannot help believing that there is an easier way. Perhaps for this reason, proponents of the merit plan never rest their defense on this limited, essentially negative ground. Rather, they contend that it is affirmatively desirable to have a group of lawyers and laypersons assigned the tasks of ferreting out candidates for judgeships, developing information about the candidates, and determining who is best qualified.

I see no basis for objecting to commissions which perform the first two tasks. But I know of no one who suggests that the commissions should simply gather names and information for use by the executive. The crux of the merit system, in the eyes of its advocates, is the selection function of the commissions.

It is this crux that I find troubling. That is not just because I come from Washington, where skepticism about committees is almost as prevalent as committees; indeed in Washington it is said that "nothing is impossible—until you assign it to a committee." I am troubled by judicial selection by committee because it seems to me that two biases, or risks of biases, inhere in the process: (1) objective criteria will be given undue weight; and (2) to the extent subjective factors are considered, they will be value-free or technical ones.

The temptation for committees to rely on objective criteria is obvious. Such criteria simplify the task of paring down long lists of names to manageable numbers. Moreover, they can avoid endless debates as to which candidates have demonstrated the best knowledge of the law, for example, by providing seemingly clear measurements.

Perhaps the clearest example of the over-emphasis on objective factors is the weight nominating committees have assigned to prior judicial experience. A national study of members of such commissions found that after mental and physical health, this was the background factor the commissioners considered most important. Similarly, the twenty-year study in Missouri found that 57% of the intermediate court judges and 70% of the Supreme Court judges appointed under the merit plan had prior judicial experience. Yet I know of no evidence indicating that appellate judges with prior experience make better judges than those lacking such experience;

to the contrary, evaluations of Supreme Court Justices demonstrate as Felix Frankfurter put it, that at least with respect to my court, "the correlation between prior judicial experience and fitness . . . is zero."

Much the same may be true of two other objective criteria on which many place great weight: the requirement that nominees have (1) "at least fifteen years significant legal experience," and, (2) for trial judges, that the nominees have had "substantial experience in the adversary system." The first of these requirements effectively excludes all lawyers under the age of 40 and many lawyer-politicians; the second excludes from the trial bench the overwhelming majority of lawyers. It is clear to me, however, that at the very least some of those disqualified for lack of experience—Learned Hand, for one—should not be excluded from consideration. Persons like Judge Hand either already have acquired or could readily acquire the knowledge that experience is thought to guarantee. On the other hand, some who are included by virtue of their experience actually should be disqualified on this basis. These persons have spent too many years learning undesirable practices or approaches. In fact, I know of no empirical evidence to justify either experience requirement. The study of Supreme Court Justices to which I earlier referred found that more of those appointed at a young age (in this context, under 53) went on to greatness— including Justice Joseph Story, appointed at age 32.

But what troubles me most about the merit system is not that it precludes the appointment of some well-qualified persons who don't meet more-or-less arbitrary standards. I am more concerned that the merit plan may compel or induce the appointment of judges simply because they are technically well-qualified, without regard to their basic values, philosophy, or life experience.

It is to be expected that nominating commissions will tend to ignore value-related considerations. We live in an age in which values are viewed as subjective. Unless a nominating committee happens to be homogenous, therefore, it is unlikely to agree on the values that judges should hold. Moreover, even if the committee could agree, it would be improper for it to impose its values on the selection process. These committees typically are neither representative nor accountable bodies. The national study of state nominating committees found, for example, that 98% of the committee members are white, 90% are male, and that the lay members are largely businessmen and bankers.

Rather than looking to the values of would-be nominees, then, nominating committees may be expected to look exclusively to the nominees' professional abilities: their knowledge of the law, proficiency at writing, and ability to "think like a lawyer." As my late friend and colleague Judge Charles Clark put it with characteristic grace, such committees look "to the head exclusively and not to the heart." But as Charlie Clark also insisted, judging is more than just an exercise in technique or craft; it calls for value judgments. This is true of the trial judge required to decide, for example, whether the risk of prejudice outweighs the probative value of a piece of evidence, or whether the risk that an offender will commit more crimes outweighs the offender's interest in retaining his liberty before trial or pending appeal. It is equally true of the appellate judge, required to resolve conflicting claims between liberty and order, equality and efficiency, states rights and federal power. Indeed studies of judicial behavior have uniformly found clear voting patterns traceable to the attitudes or values of the judges. Thus, as Judge Clark concluded, "it is of truly vital importance that the inner convictions or bias of candidates for judicial appointment be appraised."

Of course, nothing in the merit system necessarily disables the appointing official—who *is* popularly selected—from considering "inner conviction or bias" in making his selections. But it is at least possible that, by excluding values from their inquiry, nominating committees inadvertently will develop lists of ideologically similar persons. It is also possible that the members of a nominating committee will all agree as to the values that judges should hold, and will make their selections accordingly. In either event, the executive could be precluded from appointing judges who share his—and presumably his constituency's—basic philosophical orientation. And even when nominating committees produce ideologically diverse lists, the thrust of merit selection may persuade some appointing officials that it is somehow illegitimate for them to consider the attitudes or experiences of potential nominees. This, I submit, would be tragic. It is not just legitimate but altogether proper for a popularly elected executive to seek to place on the bench persons who share his fundamental values.

This is not to say that the merit plan is wholly meritless or evil. As I said at the outset, I intend only to raise questions and concerns—not to pass definitive judgments. And since I earlier referred to President Carter's executive order, I should note that it may avoid many of the problems I have noted, since it first guarantees women and minority groups representation on the nominating panels; second, requires the panels to recommend only those who have demonstrated "commitment to equal justice under law;" and third, does not oblige the President to accept every panel's choices. Nevertheless, I am *not* persuaded that it is either necessary or desirable to give any nominating panel the power to choose the three or five most qualified persons; it seems to me sufficient to allow the panels to search for candidates, generate information, and perhaps make evaluations. But whatever one's ultimate views on the merit system I think it essential that the biases and risks inherent in the process be carefully exposed so that those involved in making selections can be attentive to them.

35. Remarks of Mr. Justice Marshall
Acceptance of Learned Hand Medal
(May 1, 1975)

In the mid-1970s a movement developed among politicians and academic critics of the Supreme Court to restructure the federal judicial system. Marshall describes a number of the proposals in this speech, which is quite critical of them. The reform proposals were based on claims that the Supreme Court was overworked or was overlooking important issues that ought to be decided because it could not handle as many cases as were coming to it. Marshall, along with other critics, believed that the empirical basis for such claims had not been established. (See also Selection 22.) More important, he believed that the reform proposals were actually motivated by political concerns. As he saw it, the proposals were not truly motivated by the view that the Court could not do the jobs it was taking on, but rather by the view that the Court was making too many liberal-leaning decisions. Marshall endorses some modest changes, but no major ones. In the end such modest changes were in fact adopted. The Court's composition changed, and the political impulse to restrict its power waned. By the 1990s the Supreme Court was deciding many fewer cases than it had during the 1970s; it had resolved the problem of overwork, such as it was, on its own.

A lot of ink has been spilled over the past couple of years concerning the plight of our federal courts, and particularly the Supreme Court. It has been said again and again that we are all drowning in a welling sea of cases that we are hopelessly underequipped to handle. Proposals have been forthcoming on all sides, all of them inventive and most having at least something of real value to offer. Some involve the most fundamental restructuring of our federal judicial system, while others content themselves with more interstitial proposals for reform. The universal theme of the plans is that somehow the flow of cases to the several levels of the federal judicial system must be lessened in order to permit the courts to be more attentive to the duties they are intended to perform.

After looking over various of these proposals, I have come to the conclusion that while some changes are sorely needed, the more drastic proposals offer overly strong medicine. In my view, substantial restructuring of the federal judicial system is not necessary, and in the end I think such restructuring might well do the federal courts considerable harm. I realize that when the enthusiasm for reform catches on, it often appears shortsighted and timid to recommend limited and modest forms of relief. On the other hand a few well-placed changes in the jurisdictional statutes would serve us all a lot better than wholesale revision of the federal court system.

Let me comment briefly on the several "restructuring" proposals that have been made, to try to indicate why I think such drastic relief is not necessary. I will start with what has been called the Freund Commission Report, the now well-known proposal for the creation of a National Court of Appeals.[1] According to the Freund proposal, that court would have the primary responsibility of sifting through the several thousand cases now filed each year with the Supreme Court and selecting those cases that are deemed important enough for the Court to hear and decide. Although as a sitting Justice, I suppose I have a built-in bias against any plan premised on the notion that our Court is not doing some part of its job well, I recognize that the huge increase in the filings in the Supreme Court over the last 10 to 15 years has put some strains on the institution and on the Justices as well. But so far, it is my impression that we have adapted fairly well to the problem. Although the number of cases filed is large, the great bulk of them raise claims that are plainly outside the area in which the Supreme Court can or should take an active role. The Court's proper sphere includes cases that present clear conflicts between circuits or important federal statutory or constitutional questions of the type that leap out of the papers, and after a short time on the job a Justice finds that it is not that difficult to select cases that the Court ought to be spending its time deciding. With all nine of us going through the petitions to find those that should be taken for plenary treatment, I am fairly confident that rather few worthy cases slip through the net undetected. Counsel whose petition has just been denied cannot always be expected to agree, but a somewhat longer view is needed here.

Even if a National Court of Appeals were somewhat more efficient at selecting cases than we can be, it would involve significant costs for the system as a whole. First, I can't imagine that it would be easy to get good judges to sit happily on such a court. Second, I have found that exposure to the cert lists is very helpful in getting a feeling for what sorts of issues are being litigated in the lower courts, how they are being resolved, and why. To have a sense of what is happening in federal law throughout the federal system is, it seems to me, essential to the decision-making process in cases that are taken for review in our court. To be cut off from the filings would leave us in the posture of blind, sedentary Queen Bees, being fed by messengers coming from nether regions with which we would have an increasingly diminished acquaintance.

If we are already in something of an ivory tower, separated from the battlefield of the district courts by a long appellate road, we would be far worse off if we were sealed into that tower by a screening court such as the one proposed by the Freund Commission. Finally, a factor that has recently surfaced seems to me to put the sword to the Freund proposal, at least if things continue in their current trend. Although our certiorari docket increased dramatically between 1960 and 1970, in the past two years it has experienced no increase at all—in fact, the filings for this year are running some eight percent below what they were a year ago. This is true

---

[1] The Freund Commission, appointed by the Federal Judicial Center (the research arm of the federal court system) was headed by Harvard law professor Paul Freund.

both in the regular and in the in forma pauperis dockets, so I doubt that the change is attributable solely to the recession. Unless this situation changes substantially and the take-off begins again, I think we can continue to handle our certiorari docket without outside help.

Other proposals for a radical restructuring of the appellate court system generally involve some kind of "super" courts of appeals that would be positioned between the current courts of appeals and the Supreme Court, and would either screen cases prior to their consideration by the Supreme Court, or would have final or semi-final authority in various classes of cases.

Two weeks ago, the Commission on the Revision of the Federal Court Appellate System—the Hruska Commission, as it is better known—published its preliminary report, recommending the establishment of a National Court of Appeals somewhat different from that recommended by the Freund Commission.[2] The Hruska Commission proposal would work something like this: The National Court of Appeals, a court of seven sitting in Washington, would hear cases that were either transferred to it from the courts of appeals or referred to it by the Supreme Court. The cases transferred from the courts of appeals would be of two sorts: those in which there is a conflict between the circuits and those in which it appears important to have an immediate and nationally binding determination. As for cases referred to the court from the Supreme Court, the Commission has left for later the task of cataloging just what types of cases those would include. Unlike the Freund proposal, the Hruska plan does not contemplate that the National Court would have any responsibility over the Supreme Court's docket, and its rulings would all be subject to subsequent review in the Supreme Court.

The Hruska Commission's plan may not have all the drawbacks of the Freund proposal, but I think it, too, has some. The Hruska plan would do little to relieve the current level of litigation in the federal courts. Its main thrust is to increase the number of nationally binding decisions rendered in the federal system each year. Its effect on the clutter of cases in the federal courts would probably be to make it somewhat worse, not better. I would anticipate that the process of transferring cases from the court of appeals might well turn out to be quite a mess. Litigants will be filing papers for transfer every time they think it in their interest, and it will seldom be that one or the other of the parties will not feel he will be better off in another forum.

Thus the courts of appeals might be put to screening virtually every case to determine whether the question presented is of substantial national importance and whether it presents a serious conflict between the circuits. These are questions that will generally take time, thought, and briefing. That will mean that a panel in the court of appeals will have to familiarize itself with a case, decide that a conflict is present, or perhaps that it would be present if the court were to rule on the matter,

---

[2] The Hruska Commission, created by Congress, was chaired by Nebraska Senator Roman Hruska.

and then ship it off to the National Court—with the effect that the panel's efforts go for nothing, and the National Court must start all over familiarizing itself with the case. At first glance, this looks pretty inefficient to me, and I would guess that despite its good intentions it will end up making the proceedings in the courts of appeals more cumbersome, slower, and more expensive for litigants.

The next question is whether the National Court will really add that much decisionmaking capacity to the system. The Commission's study estimates that the National Court could decide upwards of 150 cases per year by the seven-man court sitting en banc. This seems to me a bit ambitious, as our Court of nine currently decides on a few more than that per year, and the cases coming to the National Court would probably be of more uniform complexity. Beyond that, as to any cases that are subsequently reviewed in the Supreme Court, the National Court will not have saved any time or effort, and all the cases that turn out not to present such clear conflicts or such important issues will have wasted the time of the 7-man court where a three-man panel in the court of appeals would have done just as well.

Finally, I question whether the Commission is right in its underlying assumption—that the Supreme Court currently lets too many conflicts go by undecided. I'm not sure this is correct, or that it couldn't be largely corrected by less drastic means. I noticed, for example, that of the 18 examples of unresolved conflicts that the Commission listed, some six were in the federal tax area. Certainly tax is an area in which the emphasis on planning is so important that conflicts should be settled and settled quickly. But tax cases are probably better consigned in general to a specialized court that would automatically dispense national law. As to the other classes of conflicts, I do not think that we let many go by without a better reason than lack of time for them. Often we discover that a conflict is not nearly so clear as the petitioner would have us believe. Even if a true conflict exists, a particular case often has a peculiar problem in it—procedural or substantive—that would make it difficult to reach the merits and settle the conflict. And sometimes, quite simply, the conflict is not worth anybody's time—not the Supreme Court's, and not a National Court's. It may just be a conflict over a question that influences nobody's planning, or one that will never rise again because the statute to which it relates has been changed or has no continuing effect.

For these reasons, and because of the danger of adding new delays and sources of added expense to federal litigation, I am somewhat skeptical of the Hruska plan, at least about the portion of the plan that would send cases from the courts of appeals to the National Court according to some kind of necessarily vague standards.

Last November, Dean Griswold made a proposal that, it seems to me, incorporates some of the better parts of the Hruska plan without its weaker points.[3] He, too, recommends the creation of a National Court of Appeals, but his court would only take cases on reference from the Supreme Court. This, according to Dean

---

[3] Erwin Griswold had been dean of the Harvard Law School and solicitor general of the United States.

Griswold, would permit the court to supplement its current production with more nationwide decisions, particularly in certain nonconstitutional areas such as tax, patent, antitrust, and administrative law. This might be a good move, and the plan certainly deserves serious consideration, but I am still not convinced that the problem of intercircuit conflicts in these areas would not be better solved by putting some of them in specialized courts and restricting some of them—such as certain administrative appeals—to a single court of appeals for review. This is currently done in appeals from certain types of FCC decisions, which can be taken only to the Court of Appeals for the D.C. Circuit. Extending that practice might well solve the problem as effectively as creating a new court, and should be investigated before we are committed to a more wrenching course.

Again, it seems to me that most of the schemes that have been devised run afoul of the problem that the intermediate appellate court is stuck rather awkwardly in the midst of two functioning appellate systems that have very well defined roles, and that the new court would belong to neither one nor the other. The various tasks that the new or intermediate appellate courts would perform are, in my view, either being accomplished adequately by the current appellate courts, or are being done sufficiently by the Supreme Court now without unendurable costs, or could be effected by statutory changes of a much more modest sort.

For example, one single change in our appellate jurisdiction would work wonders—eliminating it altogether.[4] I can see but one reason for retaining a significant group of cases that come to the Supreme Court by right rather than by the ordinary route of certiorari—and that is to give the law reviews and law clerks interesting problems of jurisdiction to muse over. But the appellate docket in the Supreme Court is terribly costly to us and to the judicial system in several ways. First, it forces us to place far too much emphasis on a class of cases only some of which are worthy of the effort. If a case comes from a three-judge district court, as some 20 percent of the argued cases do each year, we have only two choices. We must affirm the decision of the district court or set the case for full argument. If there is something wrong with the district court's decision, but it would not be certworthy by our usual standards, we are still constrained to take the case, since an affirmance—even a summary affirmance—is often given undue weight in the lower courts, while a denial of certiorari is properly given no significance at all.

Similarly, in appellate cases coming from the state courts, we feel obliged to note probable jurisdiction in an unhappily high percentage as well. The problem there is somewhat less severe than in the cases coming to us on direct appeal from the federal courts, since in state cases we have the option of dismissing the appeal for

---

[4] As a technical matter, cases in the Supreme Court's appellate jurisdiction must be decided on the merits by the Court, which has no discretion to refuse to hear them. As Justice Marshall notes, however, the Court had developed a number of devices that allowed it to avoid hearing oral argument in all appellate jurisdiction cases.

want of a substantial federal question. But that, too, creates problems. If we are taken literally—god forbid—our dismissal for want of a substantial federal question means that the question was judged so insubstantial that it doesn't even rise to the level of federal cognizance. Yet we have construed the same words—a substantial federal question—very liberally in determining what is substantial enough to require the convening of a three-judge district court. Almost any constitutional question not precisely covered by a prior Supreme Court decision may be deemed "substantial" for this purpose. Plainly, the same words have come to mean different things. The entire three-judge court procedure deserves continuing scrutiny.

It is much more exciting to declare that the system is on its last legs and that it must be junked and replaced by a new model before the entire thing comes crashing down about our ears. But despite the temptation of these bolder cries for action, I am constrained to report from inside that the system does not need to be scrapped, and that by and large it still works reasonably well. With some adjustments, and with a little more intelligent concern from Congress, I think that the federal judiciary can survive in much its current form—a small and rather intimate branch of Government that, on the whole, has done its task well in an era when the other branches are constantly accusing one another of doing their tasks poorly or not at all.

36. Tribute to Charles H. Houston
Amherst magazine, Spring 1978

These are relatively informal remarks Marshall made at a program honoring his mentor Charles Hamilton Houston, a graduate of Amherst College. It contains Marshall's most extended recollections of Houston's role in Marshall's life, and reflections on Houston's impact on a generation of African American lawyers.

I am not one to believe in looking back. I believe in looking forward. And we have to look at Charlie Houston because he looked forward. Even today, many people interested in justice or just plain decency, in sitting down and talking equal with equal, invariably will hear someone say, "I wonder what Charlie would do?" Over against that, you have a large number of people who never heard of Charlie Houston; and I don't know if they ever want to hear about him. But you're going to hear about him, because he left for us such important items. Just one little minor item: when *Brown v. Board of Education* was being argued in the Supreme Court, the entire courtroom was allotted and assigned out—every seat taken. There were some two dozen lawyers on the side of the Negroes fighting for their schools. Some of us looked around, and of those thirty lawyers, at least, we very carefully went from one to another and there were only two who hadn't been touched by Charlie Houston.

It is little minor things like that that are so important, the fact that man was the engineer of all of it. Whatever's done ten years from now in the courts for justice and decency for American citizens, you bring it to me and I'll be able to point out what Charlie Houston said about it in the thirties.

A man of vision. A big man. Strong. He loved people. If he came to visit you, when he got back to Washington you got a letter thanking you and asking "How are you doing?"—and your wife calling her by name; and your *children*, calling *them* by name; and your *dog*, calling *him* by name. Because he loved life. And he loved people.

Charlie spoke for a whole lot of Negroes that day and for a whole lot of other people. And around 1929 he took over the Howard Law School. I think too much of my alma mater to call it the names people called it. But one of the nicest names was "Dummies' Retreat." That was one of the nicest names. It was not accredited. The entire faculty was part-time, including the dean. Charlie took it over as a vice dean, and in two years he raised it from "Dummies' Retreat" to a fully accredited law school, accredited by every accrediting agency in the country. He did it in two years, and he did it the hard way. He put in a system that didn't last but one year,

I'm glad to say. It was called the "cutback system," which gave every faculty member the right to deduct from your passing grade five points for no reason at all, just because you didn't shape up. Well, he gave that up, I'm glad to say.

But the things he put on us were just unbelievable. He started off by telling us what he learned in Harvard; that was, he took the whole freshmen class and said, "every man here look at the man on your left. Now look at the man on your right. This time next year, two of you won't be here." Well, you stopped to think. If he said *one* of you, the odds wouldn't be so bad; but two out of three, that's murder! Then he would say, "I'll never be satisfied until I go to one of the dances up on the hill on the campus and see everybody having fun with all my law school students sitting around the sides reading law books." He said, "Then I'll be happy, and not before." He said, "The only thing I love is to flunk valedictorians and smart people. It doesn't do me any good to flunk dumb people, because dumbs are dumbs and it doesn't mean anything." He rightfully earned such beautiful phrases that we lovingly called him: "Cement Drawers," "Iron Pants," and a few other nice names.

I remember distinctly one exam, and I remember the subject. It was Evidence. That's just one subject. The exam started at nine o'clock in the morning and ended at five in the afternoon, with forty-five minutes for lunch. For *one subject*! Of my original entering class, six graduated. The luck of the draw.

What did he do to bring us up? He got rid of the part-time faculty. He kept the good ones, and he dropped the others. He brought in visiting professors. Some people were from the smaller schools, like Dean Roscoe Pound of Harvard. Then he brought in practicing lawyers—like Clarence Darrow, Arthur Garfield Hayes, you name them. And they taught us how the law was practiced, not how it read. Because, you see, in those days Harvard, Yale, Columbia—you name them, the big law schools—were bragging that they didn't train lawyers, they trained clerks to start off in big Wall Street law firms. Charlie Houston was training lawyers to go out and go in the courts and fight and die for their people.

He had courses that never had been heard of before, and he trained and he went for perfection. He would tell us in class, in groups, privately down in the basement, privately in the library, publicly when he would break up a poker or crap game, he would tell us, "Men, you've got to be social engineers. We've got to turn this whole thing around. And the black man has got to do it; nobody's going to do it for you. The difference between the law and other professions, like medicine, is the doctors bury their mistakes, but the lawyers' mistakes are made public. You've got to go out and compete with the other man, and you've got to be better than he is. You might never get what you deserve, but you'll certainly *not* get what you *don't* deserve."

Things like that you remember, practicing law, as long as you practice, if you had Charlie to teach you. You remember him saying, "Lose your head and lose your case." Is there anything better than that to keep in mind when you have an argument?

Charlie told us at the beginning, "Get your law and get it straight. Get your research and dig deeper. When you plan, plan twice. When you map out your case, take not the two possibilities, but assume two others. You've got to do better than the other man. Nothing can we get from the executive side of the government, nothing can we get from the legislative side. If we're going to get our rights, we're going to get it when the court moves. The court can't do it all, but the court can move it on. Without court action in the meantime, we're dead pigeons." He reminded us of the time, for example, when Negroes were constantly crying at the doorstep of every President and got nothing. The nearest the Negro had ever gotten was during the Hoover Administration when Hoover accidentally—or, I don't know how—invited Negroes to the Rose Garden and looked at them. The Republican Negro leaders said—and it came down in history as a cry—"Speak, Mr. President, speak!" and he didn't even say "Howdy do."

We got the same nothing in Congress. We couldn't even get an anti-lynching bill through. We couldn't get anything through. Charlie said, "Let's go up into the law library. Let's dig out the books. Let's find a way in the court. And find a way out."

I only know one other man like him. He happens not to be Negro. He's a very big white lawyer in Beverly Hills, a very good friend of mine. And in his law firm whenever anybody says, "Hey, wait a minute, there's no law on our side," that guy will always say just what Charlie always said: "There's no law on our side? Let's *make* some."

And that's what Charlie set out to do. He got together Negro lawyers from one end of this country to the other. He went down into the deepest South and managed to get out.

Charlie Houston made his contribution. Indeed, Charlie fought one famous criminal case, George Crawford, Leesburg, Virginia, for four years. All the way up in Boston, Massachusetts, trying to fight his extradition. All the way down to Leesburg. He tried it down there, and he saved that man's life.

I can name others, many others. I can name the early primary cases where he got the Negroes the right to vote in Texas. Or the grandfather clause cases where he got the Negroes the right to vote in Oklahoma and Maryland, and Louisiana, and many other states. You can name all of this he did while running a law school. In '35 he left and went to New York, and went to work in the NAACP in the legal department—with a beautiful, huge budget of less than five thousand dollars, all the expenses available to the legal department including him, a secretary, travel, court costs, bread and butter, you name it.

You realize that today that same budget is three million dollars, and you can see where he started.

He said there should be a Negro lawyers' contribution because Negro lawyers had been laughed at and he didn't like it. He wanted them to make their own contribution. And he built up this cadre of lawyers all over the country, coast to coast, north and south.

I don't know. I can tell you this: you cannot yet, as I have said before, name anything he didn't get involved in. He did his job in the city, and then he left the NAACP and went back to Washington around 1940. You know why? He went back to his father's law firm because he said the way we were going—Bill Hastie, me, and the rest of us—we eventually were going to get thrown out of everything so we had better find some place we could get back to make a buck. And he said, "I'll do it." And he did. Then he worked harder than he did before. And he didn't even make the five thousand dollars then. He didn't even have that.

I would say, as this forum develops over the years, you'll find more and more. For example, right now, if you had a forum on the *Bakke* case or something like that, you could develop what Charlie thought about it. We discussed that, too. You think of asking, "What would he have done?" I'll tell you. You could ask him, I'm sure, "Have we come all the way?" And he'd answer, "No." Near? "No."

Negroes in this country, every time someone says, "Aren't you better off?" the answer is, "Better off than *what*? Compared to *what*?" Of course the poorest, illiterate Negro in Mississippi is better off than the black in South Africa. But is he better off than the white in New York? Sure, the Negroes are better off than they were in the thirties. So is everyone else. And the gap is getting larger.

I would pass on to you what he passed on to us: This government of ours, we call it a democracy. Indeed it is. I have said over and over again, and I repeat again tonight, that the government of a democracy is not the law as it's spoken. It's something to drive toward. It's something you hope to get to, and, I submit, it's a very simple idea. It is this: that the child born to the poorest, blackest, Negro sharecropper in Mississippi, merely by being born and drawing its first breath in a democracy, is—by that, and without more—endowed with the exact same rights as Rockefeller's children.

Of course, that's not true. Of course, it will never be true. But I doubt that anybody can deny that that's the goal we should get as close to as we can.

That's the type of thing Charlie was talking about. Charlie didn't ask for this. He only insisted on getting what the Negro was entitled to, what the Negro had been denied so many years. I keep hearing the stories about why shouldn't we have had this, why shouldn't we have done that. We wouldn't have been any place if Charlie hadn't laid the groundwork for it, because whatever you do, you do it legally or it won't last, and if you do it legally, Charlie Houston made it possible for you to do it legally.

That is what I think Charlie Houston means to all of us, and I am so glad that this school is recognizing that Charlie, in talking to us—those we hope were close to him—would talk about certain things with a certain feeling. One was here, one was the Army, one was Harvard, and of course the other one was Howard.

He was a great man. No, he wasn't a great Negro. He was a great American. If he had lived, we would have known more about him, but since he didn't, what more can we do than to push ahead where he told us to go. He told me, I'm telling you, and these forums one behind the other will tell those to come behind us, "Let it go forward." As he would say, "Don't look back. It ain't worth it. And there's something back there that you'd sure like to forget."

So let's look forward, and let's see. Maybe we can do it. Maybe we can make the day come. An old Pullman porter used to tell me that he'd been in every city of the country, and he'd always hoped that one day he would get someplace in the United States where he didn't have to put his hand up in front of his face to find out he was a Negro.

37. Commencement Address, University of Virginia (May 21, 1978)

This commencement address is one of the few formal addresses Marshall gave to a nonprofessional audience after he became a judge.

It is customary on giving speeches to say how honored and pleased the speaker is at being invited to stand before the invariably august body that is present. Sometimes this is a mere convention, and the speaker would rather be in any of a hundred other places. For several reasons, however, I am truly honored and pleased to be here today.

The University of Virginia is of course one of the outstanding universities of this country. It was conceived in grandeur, and has, more than most other institutions, fulfilled the ambitions and ideals of its founder, Thomas Jefferson. Jefferson started planning this great University over twenty years before it was chartered in 1819. His conception was, at the time, revolutionary—as befitted the man. He believed that a university should be an "academical village," a small democracy in action; it should consist of different schools devoted to different disciplines, with a curriculum that expressed the most modern ideas in scientific and liberal thought. He scandalized some of his contemporaries by proposing to omit instruction in "religious divinity;" in his view such instruction at a state institution was inconsistent with the great constitutional principles of religious freedom and separation of church and state. And Jefferson insisted on getting only the best in their fields as instructors, even if that meant going to European colleges and, to use a modern word, "raiding" their faculties.

Thomas Jefferson, in short, conceived and executed in the early 19th century a plan for a very modern university. This university today stands as a testament to the enduring nature of what some at the time thought was a wild vision. His road to this achievement was no easy one—it took twenty years of planning, perseverance and vision. It also took a willingness to engage in the inevitable compromises of politics, for it was quite a battle to get the state legislature of the time to authorize the funds for this suspicious experiment. But Jefferson did not disdain the hurly burly of political negotiation, compromise and argument; he thrived on it.

Jefferson believed as deeply as anything that an educated citizenry could make rational and responsible decisions on almost any matter. Indeed, this belief in the intelligence and wisdom of a well-educated people not only drove him to promote public education, at the primary as well as higher levels, but it also informs many of his most eloquent political passages.

I don't know how many of you graduating from the College of Arts and Sciences studied politics and government in your four years at this University. I do know that

277

one innovation that Jefferson favored strongly was that of "electives." A favorite grandson of his had groaned under the rigidities of a set curriculum at another college of the day, and Jefferson was convinced that permitting students to choose their areas of study would improve the quality of their educational experience. There are educators in this country who believe this trend has gone too far, that students are not trained in the core aspects of what an educated person should know. The way the world looks to me, it seems awfully difficult to say what "core" knowledge should be; and it may be that the last person in this country who could really claim to have mastered the whole of human knowledge was Jefferson himself.

But there are certain core values, embodied in Thomas Jefferson's handiwork in the Declaration of Independence and the Constitution, as well as in setting up this University, of which I hope you are all aware—those of you graduating with advanced degrees as well as the undergraduates. And these core values, tried and trite as they may appear, are in my judgment worthy of continued reflection, so that they may be better realized in this country, just as your university so well realized the values of its founder.

I can best introduce them by telling you of a brief incident. At one argument in a United States District Court, an attorney representing a City was arguing in support of an ordinance challenged as being unconstitutional. The details of the case are unimportant, but at one point in his argument, this attorney told the Court that there was "something higher than the Constitution of the United States." I asked him what he could be thinking of; and the poor man had no answer.

My first reaction, and probably that of many other listeners, was that his failure to answer illustrated that his assertion was wrong, and in a way it was; but in another, equally important way, the lawyer simply failed to come up with the right answer.

His answer is wrong because our system is perhaps uniquely characterized by adherence to the proposition that this is a government of laws, and not merely of men and women—and the United States Constitution is the Supreme law of the land. The Constitution is binding on federal judges and municipal courts, on Governors of the States and on Presidents of the United States—in short, on all governmental decisionmakers in the state and federal systems. There simply is no "higher law" in this country.

The democratizing aspects of the Constitution cannot be overstated. For me, its cardinal principle is that all persons stand in a position of equality before the law. The Constitution gives to each and every one of you an equal right to your own opinions and to participate in the process of your own governance. These are precious rights that we must continually strive to preserve, and whose promise we must seek to attain. There are still far too many persons in this country who cannot participate as equals in the processes of Government—persons too poor, too ignorant, persons discriminated against by other people for no good reason. But our ideal, the ideal of our Constitution, is to eliminate these barriers to the aspirations of all Americans to participate fully in our government and society. We have realized it far better than most countries, but we still have a long way to travel and we must continue to strive in that direction.

This brings me to my second point about my poor lawyer's assertion. As I said a moment ago, his statement was profoundly true in a way, for there *is* something "higher" than the Constitution—that is, quite simply, the people. I do not mean that "the people" are not bound to live under our system of laws—any other proposition could lead to violence and from there to anarchy. But what I do mean is what Thomas Jefferson said in the Declaration of our Independence—that just governments derive their authority from the consent of the governed. And because of this, you have not only a right but a responsibility to the government of this country.

Let me elaborate. Governments derive their *power* from many sources—the military or police are instruments of power and may in the short run enforce the government's directives against an unwilling people. But *authority* is a different question—and no government can govern long, or well, without the authority that comes from a shared consensus among the governed. They must believe that theirs is a rightful, and lawful, and just government.

But in order to preserve this power in the people—the power of defining and limiting the authority of their government—it is first and foremost essential that the people be well informed. Jefferson's commitment to this University was only part of a larger commitment to the value of public education. That vision accounts for the primacy of public schools in the American community, for it was Jefferson's guiding hand that helped draft the Northwest Ordinance, which resulted in public lands being dedicated across the new territories for public schools. Today, however, just as in Jefferson's times, we still see students of less privileged backgrounds than your own, or people who are just less lucky, being denied quality education at all levels. Voters turn down school financing referenda, legislatures oppose integration of school systems. There is appalling ignorance even among some of the supposedly well-educated youth of our country, and the extent of illiteracy remains staggering. Education towards the goal of an informed citizenry requires all of the qualities that Jefferson embodied: commitment to difficult projects, confidence in the soundness of one's own vision and perseverance in working through a problem.

As the areas of human knowledge have expanded, so have the aspirations of the American people. It is vitally important that the aspirations of our government keep pace with the knowledge and expectations of our people. With the explosion in human knowledge and expertise, it sometimes seems very difficult to understand what the government is doing, to understand what our problems are, and to keep up. Yet the duty to keep up, to be informed, to be knowledgeable in some area of human endeavor, is an essential one, not only for the continued survival of our government but in the long run for our civilization. It is hard work being self-informed; but it is essential work for the citizens of a democracy.

It is a work, moreover, for which people in your position have been specially prepared. The privilege of attending so fine a university as this one must bear with it an unceasing responsibility to use your knowledge and training for improving the lives of others. Whether you pursue this as a lawyer dedicated to the public interest; a doctor serving those in pain and sickness; a scholar adding to the store of human knowledge and sharing that knowledge with others; an engineer applying new technologies to serve human needs; an artist improving the quality of life by creative efforts; or just by seeking to be a good person who values helping others—matters not. What matters is to remember always the obligation you bear to the society that has placed you in a position where you could afford to spend four years of your lives—and for many of you, there have been and will be several more—in an institution of learning.

I said at the beginning of my talk that there were several reasons why I was truly honored to be here today. I have already mentioned the first—that this University represents something special in the American tradition. The second one is because you are young, you are a new generation just starting out. Those of us who are a bit older (like myself—and I said, just a bit), no matter how hard we may have worked to serve humanity—our time is coming to a close. I don't for a moment mean our *lives*, since I for one intend to keep on plugging at my present job for many years to come. But I recall to you now Thomas Jefferson's answer to the pleas of a friend in 1814. His friend begged Jefferson to take a stand then and there as a leader in the fight against slavery. Jefferson's answer, though hardly commendable, shows a human truth; he said, "No, I have outlived the generation with which mutual labors and perils begat mutual confidence and influence. This enterprise is for the young—for those who can follow it up, and bear it through to its consummation."

You people here today, about to use your degrees, it is for you now to undertake the projects of this age—in Jefferson's words, to follow them up and bear them through. It is not for me to tell you what these are—each generation must find its own calling. But you have the energies of youth—and while you have them, use them, that you may look back on your lives with as much of a sense of accomplishment as Jefferson no doubt did.

This is a great country, but fortunately for you it is not perfect. There is much to be done to bring about complete equality. Remove hunger. Bring reality closer to theory and democratic principles.

Each of you as an individual must pick your own goals. Listen to others but do not become a blind follower. Do not wait for others to move out—move out yourself—where you see wrong or inequality or injustice speak out, because this is your country. This is your democracy—make it—protect it—pass it on. You are ready. Go to it.

38. Reflections on the Bicentennial of the United States Constitution

(*Harvard Law Review*, 1987)

Marshall's address on the Constitution's bicentennial attracted a great deal of attention. He had devoted a great deal of thought to the address, seeking assistance from scholars like history professor John Hope Franklin in developing it.

Marshall was reacting to two developments during the 1980s. The Department of Justice under Attorney General Edwin Meese III had forcefully been urging a jurisprudence of "original intent" as a ground for interpreting the Constitution. Some critics of that jurisprudence argued that it urged an impossible and undesirable course for judges, claiming that it was impossible to truly discern what the Constitution's framers intended, and that social conditions had changed so much that it was unwise to confine the Constitution to its original understanding. Prior to Marshall's address the most prominent response to Attorney General Meese came from Marshall's colleague on the Supreme Court, William J. Brennan, who criticized the jurisprudence of original intent as "arrogance masked as humility." Marshall developed a different challenge to that jurisprudence. As his address shows, he wanted people to understand that the Constitution was "defective from the start," because of its commitment to the preservation of slavery and other forms of exclusion from full participation in American society.

Marshall was concerned, as well, with the overly celebratory tone of the Constitution's bicentennial observances. As he saw it, the Constitution was not created at a single moment, but rather through repeated struggles, as the American people tried to work out the ways they might realize the vision of human liberty that we attribute to that document. So, for Marshall, we should celebrate the struggles rather than the moment of creation, and should remember that struggles over the Constitution's meaning would continue.

The year 1987 marks the 200th anniversary of the United States Constitution. A Commission has been established to coordinate the celebration. The official meetings, essay contests, and festivities have begun.

The planned commemoration will span three years, and I am told 1987 is "dedicated to the memory of the Founders and the document they drafted in Philadelphia." We are to "recall the achievements of our Founders and the knowledge and experience that inspired them, the nature of the government they established, its origins, its character, and its ends, and the rights and privileges of citizenship, as well as its attendant responsibilities."

Like many anniversary celebrations, the plan for 1987 takes particular events and holds them up as the source of all the very best that has followed. Patriotic feelings will surely swell, prompting proud proclamations of the wisdom, foresight, and sense of justice shared by the framers and reflected in a written document now yellowed with age. This is unfortunate—not the patriotism itself, but the tendency for the celebration to oversimplify, and overlook the many other events that have been instrumental to our achievements as a nation. The focus of this celebration invites a complacent belief that the vision of those who debated and compromised in Philadelphia yielded the "more perfect Union" it is said we now enjoy.

I cannot accept this invitation, for I do not believe that the meaning of the Constitution was forever "fixed" at the Philadelphia Convention. Nor do I find the wisdom, foresight, and sense of justice exhibited by the framers particularly profound. To the contrary, the government they devised was defective from the start, requiring several amendments, a civil war, and momentous social transformation to attain the system of constitutional government, and its respect for the individual freedoms and human rights, that we hold as fundamental today. When contemporary Americans cite "The Constitution," they invoke a concept that is vastly different from what the framers barely began to construct two centuries ago.

For a sense of the evolving nature of the Constitution we need look no further than the first three words of the document's preamble: "We the People." When the Founding Fathers used this phrase in 1787, they did not have in mind the majority of America's citizens. "We the People" included, in the words of the framers, "the whole Number of free Persons." On a matter so basic as the right to vote, for example, Negro slaves were excluded, although they were counted for representational purposes—at three-fifths each. Women did not gain the right to vote for over a hundred and thirty years.

These omissions were intentional. The record of the framers' debates on the slave question is especially clear: the Southern states acceded to the demands of the New England states for giving Congress broad power to regulate commerce, in exchange for the right to continue the slave trade. The economic interests of the regions coalesced: New Englanders engaged in the "carrying trade" would profit from transporting slaves from Africa as well as goods produced in America by slave labor. The perpetuation of slavery ensured the primary source of wealth in the Southern states.

Despite this clear understanding of the role slavery would play in the new republic, use of the words "slaves" and "slavery" was carefully avoided in the original document. Political representation in the lower House of Congress was to be based on the population of "free Persons" in each state, plus three-fifths of all "other Persons." Moral principles against slavery, for those who had them, were compromised, with no explanation of the conflicting principles for which the American Revolutionary War had ostensibly been fought: the self-evident truths "that all men are created equal, that they are endowed by their Creator with certain unalienable Rights, that among these are Life, Liberty and the pursuit of Happiness."

It was not the first such compromise. Even these ringing phrases from the Declaration of Independence are filled with irony, for an early draft of what became that declaration assailed the King of England for suppressing legislative attempts to end the slave trade and for encouraging slave rebellions. The final draft adopted in 1776 did not contain this criticism. And so again at the Constitutional Convention eloquent objections to the institution of slavery went unheeded, and its opponents eventually consented to a document which laid a foundation for the tragic events that were to follow.

Pennsylvania's Gouverneur Morris provides an example. He opposed slavery and the counting of slaves in determining the basis for representation in Congress. At the Convention he objected that

> the inhabitant of Georgia [or] South Carolina who goes to the coast of Africa, and in defiance of the most sacred laws of humanity tears away his fellow creatures from their dearest connections and damns them to the most cruel bondages, shall have more votes in a Government instituted for protection of the rights of mankind, than the Citizen of Pennsylvania or New Jersey who views with a laudable horror, so nefarious a practice.

And yet Gouverneur Morris eventually accepted the three-fifths accommodation. In fact, he wrote the final draft of the Constitution, the very document the bicentennial will commemorate.

As a result of compromise, the right of the Southern states to continue importing slaves was extended, officially, at least until 1808. We know that it actually lasted a good deal longer, as the framers possessed no monopoly on the ability to trade moral principles for self-interest. But they nevertheless set an unfortunate example. Slaves could be imported, if the commercial interests of the North were protected. To make the compromise even more palatable, customs duties would be imposed at up to ten dollars per slave as a means of raising public revenues.

No doubt it will be said, when the unpleasant truth of the history of slavery in America is mentioned during this bicentennial year, that the Constitution was a product of its times, and embodied a compromise which, under other circumstances, would not have been made. But the effects of the framers' compromise have remained for generations. They arose from the contradiction between guaranteeing liberty and justice to all, and denying both to Negroes.

The original intent of the phrase, "We the People," was far too clear for any ameliorating construction. Writing for the Supreme Court in 1857, Chief Justice Taney penned the following passage in the *Dred Scott* case, on the issue of whether, in the eyes of the framers, slaves were "constituent members of the sovereignty," and were to be included among "We the People":

> We think they are not, and that they are not included, and were not intended to be included . . . .
>
> They had for more than a century before been regarded as beings of an inferior order, and altogether unfit to associate with the white race . . .;

and so far inferior, that they had no rights which the white man was bound to respect; and that the negro might justly and lawfully be reduced to slavery for his benefit. . . .

    . . . [A]ccordingly, a negro of the African race was regarded . . . as an article of property, and held, and bought and sold as such. . . . [N]o one seems to have doubted the correctness of the prevailing opinion of the time.

And so, nearly seven decades after the Constitutional Convention, the Supreme Court reaffirmed the prevailing opinion of the framers regarding the rights of Negroes in America. It took a bloody civil war before the thirteenth amendment could be adopted to abolish slavery, though not the consequences slavery would have for future Americans.

While the Union survived the civil war, the Constitution did not. In its place arose a new, more promising basis for justice and equality, the fourteenth amendment, ensuring protection of the life, liberty, and property of *all* persons against deprivations without due process, and guaranteeing equal protection of the laws. And yet almost another century would pass before any significant recognition was obtained of the rights of black Americans to share equally even in such basic opportunities as education, housing, and employment, and to have their votes counted, and counted equally. In the meantime, blacks joined America's military to fight its wars and invested untold hours working in its factories and on its farms, contributing to the development of this country's magnificent wealth and waiting to share in its prosperity.

What is striking is the role legal principles have played throughout America's history in determining the condition of Negroes. They were enslaved by law, emancipated by law, disenfranchised and segregated by law; and, finally, they have begun to win equality by law. Along the way, new constitutional principles have emerged to meet the challenges of a changing society. The progress has been dramatic, and it will continue.

The men who gathered in Philadelphia in 1787 could not have envisioned these changes. They could not have imagined, nor would they have accepted, that the document they were drafting would one day be construed by a Supreme Court to which had been appointed a woman and the descendent of an African slave. "We the People" no longer enslave, but the credit does not belong to the framers. It belongs to those who refused to acquiesce in outdated notions of "liberty," "justice," and "equality," and who strived to better them.

And so we must be careful, when focusing on the events which took place in Philadelphia two centuries ago, that we not overlook the momentous events which followed, and thereby lose our proper sense of perspective. Otherwise, the odds are that for many Americans the bicentennial celebration will be little more than a blind pilgrimage to the shrine of the original document now stored in a vault in the National Archives. If we seek, instead, a sensitive understanding of the Constitution's inherent defects, and its promising evolution through 200 years of history, the celebration of the "Miracle at Philadelphia" will, in my view, be a far more meaningful and humbling experience. We will see that the true miracle was not the birth of the Constitution, but its life, a life nurtured through two turbulent centuries of our own making, and a life embodying much good fortune that was not.

Thus, in this bicentennial year, we may not all participate in the festivities with flag-waving fervor. Some may more quietly commemorate the suffering, struggle, and sacrifice that has triumphed over much of what was wrong with the original document, and observe the anniversary with hopes not realized and promises not fulfilled. I plan to celebrate the bicentennial of the Constitution as a living document, including the Bill of Rights and the other amendments protecting individual freedoms and human rights.

39. Remarks on the Death Penalty Made at the Judicial Conference of the Second Circuit

(*Columbia Law Review*, 1986)

Marshall was committed to abolishing capital punishment. As a law student he had worked on a locally celebrated death penalty case, helping his mentor Charles Hamilton Houston prepare the defense of George Crawford, accused of killing a prominent white woman in Virginia's hunt country (see Selection 36). He continued to deal with death penalty cases at the NAACP Inc. Fund, which routinely received requests from people already sentenced to death for legal assistance in their appeals. Marshall was the only justice on the Supreme Court who had extensive experience in death penalty cases, and he relied on his experience in building his case against the death penalty.

The Supreme Court held that the death penalty was unconstitutional in 1972. Each justice wrote a separate opinion, however, and some of them suggested ways in which states might reenact their capital punishment statutes in a form that would satisfy the Constitution's demand that "no cruel and unusual punishments" be inflicted. States rapidly took up these suggestions. Challenges to the new death penalty statutes reached the Supreme Court in 1976. A new majority on the Court upheld the revised statutes.

Marshall and his colleague William J. Brennan never accepted the Court's 1976 rulings. They dissented every time the Court upheld a death sentence or refused to review a case in which a death sentence had been imposed. The speech that follows, published in 1986, gives Marshall's reasons for his continued resistance to capital punishment. It focuses on the *process* of administering the death penalty. Marshall believed that no capital punishment system could be devised that would ensure the fair administration in practice of statutes that, in the eyes of his colleagues, seemed fair as abstract statutes.

My remarks today shall focus on the death penalty—an element of our criminal justice system about which I have thought and agonized a great deal during my career as an advocate and judge. I do not want to talk about the theory of the eighth amendment, or about the intricacies of death penalty jurisprudence. Instead, I want to focus on the practicalities of the administration of the death penalty in this country.

My goal is to share with you some of the reasons for my belief that capital defendants do not have a fair opportunity to defend their lives in the courtroom. I hope that calling attention to the extraordinary unfairness that now surrounds the administration of the death penalty will spur us as lawyers, members of the judiciary, and public officials to begin to right this wrong.

I believe we all can agree on one basic proposition. The unique finality of a capital sentence obliges society to ensure that capital defendants receive a fair chance to present all available defenses, and that they have at least the same opportunities for acquittal as noncapital defendants. The system now in place, however, at times affords capital defendants a lesser opportunity to present their cases than virtually any other litigant. Recent decisions of the Supreme Court have taken their special toll on capital defendants and deny, rather than guarantee, these defendants an adequate opportunity to present their defenses.

Two aspects of capital case litigation create this problem. The first derives from changes in substantive law and procedural rules that have made collateral review an empty promise for many capital defendants, particularly those who cannot afford experienced trial counsel. The second results from the haste with which capital defendants' claims are reviewed once an execution date is set. I shall discuss each of these in turn.

First, capital defendants frequently suffer the consequences of having trial counsel who are ill-equipped to handle capital cases. Death penalty litigation has become a specialized field of practice, and even the most well intentioned attorneys often are unable to recognize, preserve, and defend their client's rights. Often trial counsel simply are unfamiliar with the special rules that apply in capital cases. Counsel—whether appointed or retained—often are handling their first criminal cases, or their first murder cases, when confronted with the prospect of a death penalty. Though acting in good faith, they inevitably make very serious mistakes. For example, I have read cases in which counsel was unaware that certain death penalty issues were pending before the appellate courts and that the claims should be preserved, or that a separate sentencing phase would follow a conviction. The federal reports are filled with stories of counsel who presented *no* evidence in mitigation of their client's sentences because they did not know what to offer or how to offer it, or had not read the state's sentencing statute.

As one commentator noted a few years ago,

> It is not enough that the inmates have been represented before trial and on the first appeal. Before the imposition of sentence, the case is not really a capital one. So many defendants theoretically face the death penalty, but relatively few are actually sentenced to death. For that reason, among others, capital trials are often defended by relatively young and inexperienced attorneys, without investigative sources and with no real expectation that the defendant may actually face execution. . . .

Trial counsel's lack of expertise takes a heavy toll. A capital defendant seeking post-conviction relief is today caught in an increasingly pernicious visegrip. Pressing against him from one side is the Supreme Court's continual restriction of what federal courts can remedy on post-conviction review. It has accomplished this by expanding the "presumption of correctness" afforded state court findings, and by imposing rigid doctrines of procedural default that often turn on technical pleading rules at the expense of fundamental fairness. The problem is even more acute for capital defendants. The Court purports to have created a host of rights that protect a capital defendant at the sentencing phase of a proceeding. But at the same time it has limited appellate and collateral review of those rights, and of the correctness of the sentencer's decision. These rules of limitation often deny capital defendants the kind of personalized inquiry to which they have an indisputable right. Thus, errors at sentencing are often irremediable.

Pressing against the capital defendant from the other side is the Supreme Court's restrictive definition of what constitutes unconstitutional ineffective assistance of counsel at trial. The severe rules the Court has adopted to assure that the trial is the "main event" have been unaccompanied by measures to ensure the fairness and accuracy of that event. The Court has not yet recognized that the right of effective assistance must encompass a right to counsel familiar with death penalty jurisprudence at the trial stage. Instead, in all but the most egregious case, a court cannot or will not make a finding of ineffective assistance of counsel because counsel has met what the Supreme Court has defined as a minimal standard of competence for criminal lawyers. As a consequence, many capital defendants find that errors by their lawyers preclude presentation of substantial constitutional claims, but that such errors—with the resulting forfeitures of rights—are not sufficient in themselves to constitute ineffective assistance.

These developments in the substantive law and procedural rules make it imperative for the death penalty bar to reconsider its priorities; it must readjust its thinking on how best to assist capital defendants in receiving a fair hearing. For years, private death penalty counsel have focused their attention on the collateral review phase of litigation. At the trial phase and on direct, nondiscretionary appeal, the Constitution requires that a state provide indigent defendants with counsel; that fact leaves most capital cases in the hands of state-appointed counsel through direct review. Only after direct review is complete, when the states no longer must supply counsel, have private counsel entered these cases.

In the changed legal environment death penalty lawyers now face, this assistance—laudable and valuable as it is—often comes too late to help a convicted defendant. Counsel on collateral review is boxed in by any mistakes or inadequacies of trial counsel. In these circumstances, entrance at the habeas corpus stage simply cannot guarantee the defendant the opportunity to vindicate his constitutional rights.

The only way out of the visegrip is for the death penalty bar to adjust decisively to the reality that many errors of constitutional magnitude at trial will be uncorrectable. In order to take advantage of collateral review, competent trial counsel is a necessity. The bar must focus on improving the quality of trial counsel in capital cases, and must find resources to establish training and assistance for local attorneys appointed to handle capital cases. Experienced counsel able to assist at the trial level should be made aware of pending trials through regional or nationwide information centers.

Resources are scant, and the time between arrest and trial is short. Nevertheless, there are things that can be done. If resources could be found, regional or national clearinghouses might gather information on capital cases and capital defendants; they also might provide advice on relevant case law, data, or issues for writing briefs. It is now difficult to determine how many capital trials are going on, or to find and match willing counsel with needy clients. Local counsel often are on their own to gain experience—at the expense of their indigent clients facing death. The lack of experience and expertise demonstrated by counsel who act in good faith but are unable to perform as they ought leaves too many defendants without adequate assistance.

Whatever your views about the death penalty, we simply cannot accept this state of affairs. We must do something to improve the quality of representation at the trial stage. Only then can we begin to ensure that persons convicted of capital crimes have a fair opportunity to present a defense. Unless there is a change in legal doctrine that would assure retrials until adequate representation is had, the burden will fall on the legal profession to do what it can.

The second problem relates closely to the first. It involves what I have called the Rush to Judgment—that is, the willingness of the courts and the state governments to expedite proceedings in order to bring about speedy executions. I would have thought that cases involving the death penalty might receive especially cautious handling and attention to minimize errors. The reality, however, is exactly the opposite. The Supreme Court has endorsed, and the states and courts have implemented, a scheme in which capital defendants receive *less* time to present their cases to the courts than noncapital defendants. As a result, courts must rule on the cases in a chaotic atmosphere. The tragic result is to turn fairness and logic on their heads, and to deprive these capital defendants of the attention and rights accorded other criminal defendants, for whom the penalty for conviction is so substantially less severe.

Contrary to popular perceptions, all capital defendants have *not* spent years filing frivolous claims in federal courts. Many of these defendants have not yet filed *any* federal claims when their execution dates are set. We simply cannot allow this inaccurate view to blind us to reality, or to accept the hasty review process on the ground that defendants already have the benefits of an untruncated review process.

The mechanics of this problem are as follows. Execution dates generally are set about one month before the execution is to occur. Indigent prisoners, who have no constitutional right to the assistance of counsel for habeas, often have had no counsel for collateral review up to this time. Until an execution date is set, and the situation becomes urgent, capital defendants simply have been unable to secure counsel. A recent committee report of the New York City Bar Association summed up the problem cogently:

[T]he post-conviction capital defendant who cannot afford a lawyer is left to the mercy of volunteer lawyers. If voluntary representation is not available, the defendant must act *pro se* or accept death without attempting habeas proceedings. The shortage of volunteer attorneys and the ever-growing death row population raises the specter of *pro se* defendants lacking adequate skill to present the issues in *habeas* proceedings, or worse, executions of defendants unable ever to marshall such an effort.

This lack of counsel should remove from these defendants any blame for the failure to file petitions prior to the scheduling of their executions. But the courts do not always view the issue in that way.

Once the execution date is set, the race is on. Prisoners who have not yet sought state or federal habeas corpus relief have roughly one month to do so. In a recent case, a capital defendant named Kevin Scott Roscoe filed a pro se petition for habeas corpus relief after his execution date was set and before he could obtain counsel. In the same week, another defendant was still seeking counsel a few weeks before his scheduled execution date. Generally by that time, though, counsel is found to represent the defendant, and indeed Kevin Roscoe's new counsel thereafter filed an amended petition. But the new attorney often has no knowledge of the record, has not met the client, and has only a few days to read hundreds of pages of transcripts and prepare a petition. This petition, hastily prepared, must include all claims that the defendant might raise, because subsequent petitions will likely be declared abusive of the process. The petition must be presented first to the state courts if they entertain collateral attacks. Only then will the federal court hear the case. All the while, the clock runs. State courts often wait until two to three days before the execution date to rule. Thereafter, if the federal court finds that the petition has possible merit, the court might stay the execution. Even then, the defendant has been injured, perhaps fatally: his most important filing has been prepared in necessary but inevitably harmful haste.

In other cases, the district court will expedite its proceedings in order to get the case through the system before the execution date. If the district court denies the writ but grants a certificate of probable cause, the court of appeals then must rule on the merits of the claim. The Supreme Court has authorized the reviewing courts to put these proceedings on fast-forward. The normal contracts claimant has the opportunity to study the district court opinion at length, to research responses to its points, to hone down arguments, and to sharpen the debate. He in effect has the chance to rebut the lower court judge. The same process of evaluation and consideration takes place in petitions for certiorari filed in the Supreme Court; civil litigants have ninety days in which to file a petition for review.

For the capital defendant whose execution looms, the story differs. When the process speeds up, the opportunity for deliberation, consideration, and rebuttal vanishes. The proceedings collapse into each other and the appellate process loses its vitality. Courts forego the input of the party most concerned with the outcome. Yet, the Supreme Court has allowed this process, which usually takes months to years, to occur in a matter of hours. It has taken from the capital defendant, whose life is on the line, the basic right granted to parties in run-of-the-mill civil litigation. Thus, the result of expedited proceedings is more than the patent indignity of rushing those claimants for whom the proceedings are of unique import. The process also takes it toll on the litigant's ability to present his claims. As examples of the result, last Term the Court allowed one defendant to die on a 4–4 vote to stay his execution, and it permitted the execution of another defendant although he had presented a substantial federal claim then pending in other cases in the lower federal courts.

It may be that successive habeas petitions that amount to abuses of the writ require a certain watchfulness to prevent dilatory tactics. But when the petition is a first one, or raises new arguments, this unnecessary haste robs the process of time for thought by all concerned, and it denies the defendant's crucial opportunity to participate.

This situation is remediable. First, other federal circuits could join the Court of Appeals for the Eleventh Circuit in establishing rules staying executions. They could then address, in a more considered and coherent fashion, all first habeas petitions in which certificates of probable cause have been or should have been granted. This rule could be extended to subsequent habeas petitions that raise substantial questions. Similarly, circuit and district court rules could place these petitions on the normal track earlier, at the district court stage. The result would be to remove from district judges the pressure to expedite proceedings, and to encourage development of a solid and complete hearing record.

Second, as long as the courts continue to rush these cases along, counsel could alter their approach. Attorneys could begin preparing for collateral review as soon as a capital defendant's sentence is affirmed in the direct state proceedings. The collateral process then could get underway before an execution date is scheduled. I note with a degree of hope the recent establishment in Florida of an Office of the Capital Collateral Representative. This state-appointed and state-financed public defender represents indigent capital defendants. Representation begins on termination of direct appellate proceedings, and state public defenders are required to notify the representative of the termination. If the legislation creating this office is implemented seriously, the result could be positive.

In those death penalty states in which such public assistance is not available, members of the private bar must attempt to fill the same role. The American Bar Association has noted that "without the active assistance of private attorneys on a volunteer basis, the effort to guarantee minimum legal representation in post-conviction proceedings could be poised for collapse." If the private bar can muster the resources to match lawyers with clients sooner in the process, petitions for collateral review need not be prepared in the haste imposed by an impending execution.

Third, states could take steps to slow the process. For example, states could set the execution period farther in advance of the execution. This would permit considered judicial proceedings—at least when the defendant is seeking collateral review for the first time. State statutes that set the maximum period an execution might be set in advance perhaps were passed to prevent a lengthy and agonizing wait for death, but the result is to deprive the prisoner of perhaps his only chance to avoid death.

I do not mean to suggest that these changes would solve the problems inherent in the death penalty. I continue to oppose that sentence under all circumstances. But as long as our nation permits executions, lawyers, judges, and public officials have a duty. They must ensure that people who face the ultimate sentence receive the same opportunity to present their best case to the courts that noncapital defendants receive. Until the Supreme Court will make that guarantee, others must work within the existing system to provide that opportunity. The task might be formidable; but the consequences of any failure to undertake it are unacceptably severe.

40. Remarks at the Annual Dinner in Honor of the Judiciary, American Bar Association (August 6, 1990)

"Death is different." That simple but weighty truth has been the touchstone of the Supreme Court's capital cases ever since the Court gave the go-ahead to capital punishment in 1976. The Court has consistently stated that the unique, irrevocable nature of the death penalty necessitates safeguards not required for the imposition of other forms of punishment.

I can only describe as saddening, then, the recent efforts by some members of Congress and others to treat death penalty cases differently by according capital defendants *fewer* protections than noncapital defendants. These efforts seem to be fueled by a desire to quicken the pace of executions, without sufficient regard to the cost to defendants' constitutional rights or the damage to our society's considered notions of decency and fairness.

The most significant changes in the terrain facing capital defendants have come in the area of federal habeas corpus. In last year's decision in *Teague v. Lane*, the Supreme Court narrowed the availability of habeas relief by holding that a "new" constitutional rule could not be announced or applied retroactively on habeas, unless it fell within one of two narrow exceptions. For all practical purposes, this means that a federal court no longer can hear a capital defendant's meritorious constitutional claim unless it is based on a rule that was "dictated" by precedent existing at the time the defendant had completed his direct appeal in the state courts. Although *Teague* was not a capital case, *Teague* will have its greatest impact in death penalty cases. Last Term alone, the Court rejected on *Teague* grounds the legitimate constitutional claims of three capital defendants.

The move to alter traditional avenues for habeas relief in the legislative arena includes the report of the Ad Hoc Committee of Federal Habeas Corpus in Capital Cases, chaired by retired Justice Powell, and the introduction in Congress of numerous bills seeking to amend the federal habeas statute. It is not my place to discuss the merits of the various proposals, but I would like to emphasize two reforms that must be included in any bill Congress enacts.

First, the single biggest problem with the implementation of the death penalty in this country is the lack of competent, experienced counsel to handle capital trials and direct and collateral appeals.

Tales of the pathetically inadequate representation many capital defendants receive are legion. In one capital case, defense counsel made no effort to contact any potential mitigating witnesses even though, as later became evident, affidavits of those willing to testify on the defendant's behalf were sufficient to fill 170 pages.

Defense counsel made no inquiries into the defendant's highly probative educational, medical, and psychological history. His lone contact with the defendant's family consisted of attempts to convince the family to hire a private attorney so that he would be relieved of his obligation to represent the defendant. He did not interview the sole witness to the crime. Defense counsel likewise failed to interview the police officer who witnessed the defendant's highly damaging confession, because, as he said of the officer, "I personally don't like the man." Defense counsel somehow believed none of this was necessary because he held an "ace in the hole"—an untried, untested, and unfounded legal theory to the effect that state law required written notice of any aggravating circumstances the prosecution wished to present, a theory the trial court readily rejected. Sadly, there are many other instances in which capital defendants with powerful arguments for avoiding the death penalty have been condemned by counsel who do little or nothing on their behalf.

Those who have studied the problem closely have even found cases in which counsel for capital defendants have displayed outright hostility toward their clients' causes. Consider some of the incidents listed by the ABA's Task Force on Death Penalty Habeas Corpus. In one case, defense counsel called his client a "nigger" in front of the jury. In a second, defense counsel stipulated to all the elements of first degree murder plus two aggravating circumstances for good measure. And in a third, while the prosecution was examining a key witness, defense counsel was outside parking his car.

My point is not to chronicle every instance in which the performance of capital counsel has not measured up to the demands of constitutional justice. Rather, I offer the above examples to drive home the message that any meaningful reform of the current habeas system must include measures to provide competent counsel at all stages of the process. This is not a matter that can be left to the goodwill and civic-mindedness of members of the bar who occasionally volunteer to handle a capital case. Moreover, left to themselves, states have not adequately ensured that capital defendants receive competent representation. States have aggravated the chronic shortage of competent capital counsel by limiting fees for appointed capital counsel. For example, a Mississippi statute limits compensation for appointed counsel in a capital case to $2000. Nor do states always provide sufficient supervision over capital trial counsel. In one instance, a third-year law student was allowed to try a death penalty case. Lawmakers must mandate that states provide a well-supported professional corps of experienced counsel to handle capital cases.

Second, the Court's decisions in *Teague* and its progeny should give legislators pause to consider how the original mission of the federal habeas statute can be retained. Because of *Teague*'s command that federal courts neither adopt nor retroactively apply new constitutional rules on federal habeas review, capital defendants whose valid constitutional claims are rejected in state court will find it exceedingly difficult to get redress in federal court. Habeas review might inconvenience state courts by necessitating retrial and resentencing of successful petitioners. Quite simply however, it is not fair to execute a man whose conviction or sentence was achieved by unconstitutional means. Habeas review remains the only viable way of ensuring that state courts apply the federal Constitution in a fair, nondiscriminatory manner.

The ABA is to be applauded for its vigorous efforts in promoting legislation to address problems that plague our system of capital punishment—including the problems I have discussed tonight of inadequate representation of counsel and excessively onerous procedural barriers to review of the merits of capital cases. I understand that many of the ABA's proposals were incorporated in a bill which has recently passed the House Judiciary Committee. Capital defendants are not a large or powerful constituency. It is therefore incumbent on lawyers and organizations like the ABA to continue exerting their influence on lawmakers to see to it that the rights of the condemned, as well as our society's core values of decency and fairness, are not trampled in the stampede toward quicker executions.

Additionally, it is absolutely imperative that courts do a better job of ensuring that capital defendants are accorded their full constitutional protections. Courts can do two things to improve the fairness and justice of their capital proceedings. First, state courts must improve the selection and supervision of appointed counsel for capital defendants. The instances offered earlier of capital counsel incompetence speak for themselves—and they are but a fraction of the abuses that have taken place nationwide. How can we tolerate placing matters of life and death in the hands of attorneys who may lack the skills, experience, or commitment to operate in one of the most complex arenas of our legal system?

Second, both the state and federal courts must resist what I have termed "the rush to judgment." This is a problem I discussed at more length five years ago before the Judicial Conference of the Second Circuit. The problem starts when states set early execution dates with little lead time, forcing the death row inmate into a wild scramble to secure counsel to challenge an execution that may be no more than a month away. Enormous time pressure on counsel, in turn, leads to hastily prepared claims and frantic appeals for stays of execution. When state courts wait until a few days before the planned execution to rule on the inmate's claim for relief, a mad rush to federal court inevitably follows. Potentially meritorious claims are drowned in the panic that sets in with the rush to judgment.

I have spoken out often to decry the gross injustices in the administration of capital punishment in our country. I air my concerns once again today with the fervent hope that they reach receptive ears. When in *Gregg v. Georgia* the Supreme Court gave its seal of approval to capital punishment, this endorsement was premised on the promise that capital punishment would be administered with fairness and justice. Instead, the promise has become a cruel and empty mockery. If not remedied, the scandalous state of our present system of capital punishment will cast a pall of shame over our society for years to come. We cannot let it continue.

41. A Tribute to Justice William J. Brennan, Jr.
(*Harvard Law Review*, 1990)

President Dwight D. Eisenhower appointed William J. Brennan to the Supreme Court in 1956, using the appointment in an election year to solidify his support among urban Catholics, and expecting that Brennan would be a moderate centrist on the Court. Brennan rapidly gravitated toward the Court's liberal wing, consisting of Chief Justice Earl Warren and Justices William O. Douglas and Hugo L. Black. The Court became fully committed to liberal activism in the early 1960s, with new appointments by John F. Kennedy and Lyndon Baines Johnson. Brennan was the intellectual and social leader of the newly activist Court, to the point where many scholars now think that the Court should be called the "Brennan Court" rather than the more widely used term, "Warren Court."

Brennan had a warm and engaging personality, and he and Marshall rapidly became friends, a relationship that only solidified as the Court became more conservative after 1968. Marshall increasingly relied on Brennan for emotional support as the Court began to reject the positions to which he was most attached. After Brennan retired in1990, Marshall found life on the Court more and more difficult, and his isolation, coupled with medical problems, led Marshall himself to retire in 1991.

The tribute that follows was published in 1990 to celebrate Brennan's retirement. It surveys Brennan's major opinions, but in its selection of cases and its emphasis the tribute also reflects Marshall's judgments about the most important issues facing the Supreme Court.

The *Harvard Law Review* paid its first tribute to Justice William J. Brennan, Jr., in its eightieth volume; the year was 1966. I had not yet become one of his Brethren, and he had not yet sat for a third of the years he would serve on the Court. But already he had made his mark: "In the entire history of the Court," declared Chief Justice Earl Warren, in his contribution to that tribute, "it would be difficult to name another Justice who wrote more important opinions in his first ten years than has [Justice Brennan]."

Nearly a quarter century has since passed, and the expectations engendered by that first decade have been richly fulfilled. "[A]ge," as Samuel Johnson observed, "will perform the promises of youth." For thirty-four Terms, Justice Brennan's constitutional vision emboldened the Supreme Court's work and enlightened its jurisprudence. It is hard to fathom what his departure may mean for the Court, beyond this stark truth: my friend and colleague Bill Brennan is irreplaceable. I welcome, then, this chance to augment the Review's tribute to a remarkable Justice and an extraordinary man.

Many have said much about Justice Brennan's warmth toward colleagues, his legal acuity, his grasp of the Court's dynamics, and his doctrinal innovations in

296

countless areas of the law. All this, of course, is true and worth noting. Indeed, I would add to the list: he had, as well, a remarkable talent for crisply summarizing his view of a case during the Court's post-argument conferences. Invariably brief and trenchant, these summaries greatly contributed, I think, to Justice Brennan's influence.

But, important as these formidable skills were, they fail to reveal the essence of the man. To my mind, what so distinguished Justice Brennan was his faithfulness to a consistent legal vision of how the Constitution should be interpreted. That vision was based on an unwavering commitment to certain core principles, especially first amendment freedoms and basic principles of civil rights and civil liberties. Justice Brennan's commitment to these interpretive principles was never in doubt. It did not depend on the peculiarly compelling facts of a case; it was never outweighed by the lesser values that sometimes compete for a judge's allegiance. On this question of fidelity to principles, the late Chief Justice's summary of Justice Brennan's first ten years held true for the next twenty-four: "He . . . interprets the Bill of Rights as the heart and life blood of [the Constitution]. His belief in the dignity of human beings—all human beings—is unbounded. . . . These beliefs are apparent in the warp and woof of all his opinions."

Perhaps nowhere has that commitment to human dignity been more palpable than in Justice Brennan's belief—which I share—that the eighth amendment proscribes the death penalty as cruel and unusual punishment. One of his early analyses of capital punishment was a sixty-five-page dissent in *McGautha v. California*, a case in which juries had been given unbounded discretion to assign the death sentence. After canvassing the circumstances in which due process required states to exercise powers according to some procedure, Justice Brennan concluded that the death penalty required no less: "life itself is an interest of such transcendent importance that a decision to take a life may require procedural regularity far beyond a decision simply to set a sentence at one or another term of years."

That the *McGautha* dissent dealt only with procedure was unavoidable, for the eighth amendment issue had not been raised. But some would see a broader significance in that emphasis, concluding with Professor [Robert] Post [of the University of California Law School] that Justice Brennan's "focus on process rather than power . . . pervade[d] his entire approach to constitutional law" and "deeply influenced both the Warren and the Burger Courts."

But, as Justice Brennan demonstrated the following year in *Furman v. Georgia*, his concern with the death penalty was *not* just about process—it was above all about power. In *Furman*, he concluded that under the eighth amendment "death stands condemned as fatally offensive to human dignity." I alone shared that view, however, and it seems that the procedural analysis was indeed more persuasive. Ultimately, the Court did restrict jury discretion in capital cases and the manner in which death sentences could be imposed. I have no doubt that Justice Brennan's opinion in *McGautha* planted the seed for this change in doctrine. It is one of those Brennan dissents that, in time, came to command a majority.

Despite Justice Brennan's success in imposing procedural limitations on capital punishment—last year, there were "only" sixteen executions in the United States—he has held firm to the view that the eighth amendment bars all death sentences. Some may infer from our repeated dissents a stubborn adherence to a personal belief. But, as those who have read his writings on this subject know, Justice Brennan's conception of the eighth amendment springs from that application of basic constitutional principles that has marked all of his work. As he said in his Holmes lecture, delivered at Harvard just four years ago:

> Mutilations and tortures . . . would not, I submit, be saved from unconstitutionality by having the convicted person sufficiently anesthetized such that no physical pain were felt; rather, they are unconstitutional because they are inconsistent with the fundamental premise of the eighth amendment that "even the vilest criminal remains a human being possessed of common human dignity." . . . The calculated killing of a human being by the state involves, by its very nature, an absolute denial of the executed person's humanity and thus violates the command of the eighth amendment.

Justice Brennan's commitment to human dignity has prevailed in more hopeful contexts, such as the fourteenth amendment's guarantee of equal protection. Though *Brown v. Board of Education* promised a new era of educational opportunity for Afro-Americans, that promise, of course, soon foundered on the famous stagnating phrase, "with all deliberate speed." In a few specific instances such as the Little Rock case, the Court did rebuff Southern resistance to integration. But it was Justice Brennan's opinion more than a decade later in *Green v. County School Board* that probably did most to restore *Brown*ian motion to the fourteenth amendment. In that decision, which unanimously rejected a "freedom of choice" plan in Virginia, Justice Brennan concluded that "the burden on a school board today is to come forward with a plan that promises realistically to work, and promises realistically to work *now*." *Green* was followed by Justice Brennan's decision in *Keyes v. School District No. 1*, in which the Court first found unconstitutional segregation in a Northern school district.

This commitment to eradicating dual school systems was matched by a recognition that other steps were needed to redress discrimination. Thus, Justice Brennan led the way in important cases upholding affirmative action—including the joint opinion in *Regents of the University of California v. Bakke*, signed by four of the five Justices who affirmed the right to consider race in university admissions. In that opinion, the theme of human dignity was again sounded: "we cannot . . . let color blindness become myopia which masks the reality that many 'created equal' have been treated within our lifetimes as inferior both by the law and by their fellow cit-

izens." This awareness of the legacy of discrimination also informed Justice
Brennan's opinions sustaining private programs of affirmative action against attack
under title VII. And it was Justice Brennan's opinion in *Katzenbach v. Morgan*, a
crucial voting rights case, that established broad boundaries for Congress' enforcement powers under the fourteenth amendment.

"Rights intended to protect all," Justice Murphy noted years ago, "must be
extended to all." Justice Brennan recognized that the Court's work in strengthening equal protection doctrine had left women behind. It was his plurality opinion
in *Frontiero v. Richardson* that, for the first time, explicitly tested the constitutionality of gender discrimination by something tougher than the "rational relationship" standard. Inveighing against "an attitude of 'romantic paternalism' which, in
practical effect, put women, not on a pedestal, but in a cage," Justice Brennan concluded that classifications based on gender were inherently suspect and that the Air
Force's payment of lower benefits to spouses of female military officers than to
those of male officers violated equal protection. With his subsequent opinion in
Craig v. Boren, the deferential "rationality" test for sex discrimination was interred
for good.

Despite his fidelity to core beliefs, there was nothing of the aloof philosopher
in Justice Brennan; he was, in Whitman's phrase, "no stander above men and
women." Rather, Bill Brennan has always been known for his ability to work with
colleagues. He, more than any other man I have known, combines a gifted understanding of the law with a rare appreciation of social relations. His canny ability to
forge a majority was most apparent in the drafting process—as he pruned a paragraph here or recast a thought there to accommodate his colleagues' concerns.

Nonetheless, Justice Brennan never compromised on what was essential, and
this meant that he was often in dissent—particularly in more recent years, as the
Court retreated from positions it had once embraced. Although he did not pride
himself on being a voice in the wilderness, neither did he falter in the dissenter's
role. Indeed, he told an interviewer a few years ago, "I have always felt that a member of this Court is duty-bound to continue stating the constitutional principles that
have governed his decisions, even if they are in dissent, against the day when they
may no longer be in dissent."

Even on statutory issues, Justice Brennan was willing—within the limits of stare
decisis—to dissent persistently if the issue was important. Nowhere is this better
illustrated than in his opinions concerning habeas corpus—dissents prompted by the
erosion of his majority opinion in *Fay v. Noia*, the high-water mark of the Great Writ.

Fay, of course, involved a collateral attack on a conviction obtained with a
coerced confession. Writing for the Court, Justice Brennan found that there was
power to review the conviction, derived from the historical role of habeas: "Its root
principle is that in a civilized society, government must always be accountable to
the judiciary for a man's imprisonment: if the imprisonment cannot be shown to

conform with the fundamental requirements of the law, the individual is entitled to his immediate release." But a disturbing series of subsequent opinions—each occasioning a distressed dissent from Justice Brennan—has since curtailed the reach of the writ.

That restrictive process culminated last year, when the Court subjugated the writ to rules governing retroactivity: in *Teague v. Lane*, a majority declined even to examine a habeas claim of constitutional violation because, if accepted, the claim would create a "new" application of the sixth amendment from which (the Court decided) the petitioner should not benefit. In dissent, Justice Brennan reaffirmed the importance of the courts' power "to grant writs . . . whenever a person's liberty is unconstitutionally restrained" and lamented the majority's willingness to foreclose "opportunit[ies] to check constitutional violations and to further the evolution of our thinking in some areas of the law."

The dissent in *Teague* is emblematic of Justice Brennan's jurisprudence. It again reflects his concern about questions of process—though, in this instance, it is the process controlling vindication of rights rather than the process by which government reaches out against its citizens. In that respect, the *Teague* dissent echoes another line of landmark Brennan opinions, beginning with *Bivens v. Six Unknown Named Agents of the Federal Bureau of Narcotics*, which for the first time permitted actions for damages when federal authorities violate certain constitutional rights. "[U]nless such rights are to become merely precatory," Justice Brennan wrote, "[litigants] must be able to invoke the existing jurisdiction of the courts for the[ir] protection."

The *Teague* dissent is also notable for valuing the "evolution of our thinking." Notwithstanding Justice Brennan's commitment to core principles, those principles did not always lead him to the same conclusions. He believed that constitutional doctrine moves forward, "as litigants and judges develop a better understanding of the world in which we live," and this was reflected in his own views—for example, his application of the first amendment. During his initial Term on the Court, Justice Brennan wrote the majority opinion in *Roth v. United States*, the bench-mark obscenity case that upheld a bookseller's conviction. He reaffirmed, in that decision, the established view that "'certain well-defined and narrowly limited classes of speech'" lay outside the first amendment's protection—including "material which deals with sex in a manner appealing to prurient interest" and "'[l]ibelous utterances.'" In time, however, he came to rethink both exceptions. The first to be revised was libel, which was placed in an altogether new light by Justice Brennan's historic opinion in *New York Times Co. v. Sullivan*. Recognizing that "erroneous statement . . . must be protected if the freedoms of expression are to be given the 'breathing space' that they 'need . . . to survive,'" Justice Brennan held for the Court that public officials must meet a higher standard of proof in winning damages from their detractors. Ten years later, he similarly reached a new understanding of obscenity doctrine, though he was unable to persuade a majority. In *Paris Adult Theater I v. Slaton*, he concluded that "the concept of 'obscenity' cannot be defined with sufficient specificity and clarity to provide fair notice to persons who create and distribute sexually oriented materials, [or] to prevent substantial erosion of protected speech."

Finally, no account of Justice Brennan's first amendment contributions could omit his decisions in the flag-burning cases. There, against a backdrop of politically charged national debate, Justice Brennan garnered a majority of the Court with his calm insistence on basic truths: a state may not "foster its own view of the flag by prohibiting expressive conduct relating to it," he wrote, for "[i]f there is a bedrock principle underlying the First Amendment, it is that the Government may not prohibit the expression of an idea simply because society finds the idea itself offensive or disagreeable."

One cannot, in so few pages, do justice to this Justice's career; scores of important opinions remain unmentioned. Indeed, these include the ones thought most significant by Chief Justice Warren and by Justice Brennan himself: *Baker v. Carr* (preparing the way for one person, one vote by surmounting the "political question" barrier) and *Goldberg v. Kelly* (precluding the termination of welfare benefits without an evidentiary hearing). Nor are his important opinions confined to the core principles I have stressed, for Justice Brennan is a man of catholic interests and ecumenical insights. His decision, for example, in *Penn Central Transportation Co. v. New York City* for the first time accommodated historic preservation laws within the Constitution's restrictions on deprivation of property. And, in his last week on the Court, Justice Brennan brought his insight to bear on the controversy over the right to die, arguing in dissent that the due process clause includes "a right to evaluate the potential benefit of [medical] treatment . . . and to make a personal decision whether to subject oneself to the intrusion."

It is customary to close a tribute of this sort by borrowing praise from an ancient scribe. But it seems equally fitting to measure this honoree by his own words. In his Holmes lecture, Justice Brennan described the vision of law that has animated his work on the bench:

> I am convinced that law can be a vital engine not merely of change but of . . . civilizing change. That is because law, when it merits the synonym justice, is based on reason and insight. . . . Sometimes, these insights appear pedestrian, such as when we recognize, for example, that a suitcase is more like a home than it is like a car. On occasion, these insights are momentous, such as when we finally understand that separate can never be equal. I believe that these steps, which are the building blocks of progress, are fashioned from a great deal more than the changing views of judges over time. I believe that problems are susceptible to rational solution if we work hard at making and understanding arguments that are based on reason and experience.

It was that credo that sustained Justice Brennan, both in his prevailing hours—
when the Court accepted new insights into the Constitution's ideal of human dignity—and in times of dissent. The Court will do well if it can adhere to that credo
and pursue that ideal in the years ahead. But regardless of whether future Justices
succeed in those tasks, I think they will look back on the contribution of William
J. Brennan, Jr., and say (as Hamlet said, awed by *his* father's spirit), "[He] was a
man, take him for all in all; [we] shall not look upon his like again."

PART IV

JUDICIAL OPINIONS

Justice Marshall wrote hundreds of opinions in the twenty-four years he served on the Supreme Court (see Appendix: Annotated List of Important Decisions to locate a comprehensive list of Marshall's opinions). Many dealt with areas of law of interest to specialists but not to general readers. His contributions in constitutional law were conditioned by the fact that he became a consistent dissenter from the Court's majority starting roughly in 1972, when Justices Lewis F. Powell and William H. Rehnquist joined Chief Justice Warren Burger and Justice Harry Blackmun, earlier appointees of President Richard Nixon, to form a group clearly uncomfortable with the liberal rulings of the Warren Court to which Marshall was drawn. Marshall was in a position to write majority opinions in constitutional cases only occasionally after 1972. He was a powerful voice in dissent, however. He brought a unique perspective to the Court, both as an African American and as a former trial lawyer. His background made him particularly sensitive to questions of race and equality, and led him to develop distinctive doctrinal positions, some of which have continued to retain analytic force.

The selections that follow are a small sample of Marshall's work. They begin with cases dealing directly with equality, and particularly with race and segregation. Selection 42 is Marshall's opinion in *Milliken v. Bradley*, the decision that began the long process of dismantling the Court's commitment to using the Constitution as a vehicle for achieving substantial integration of the nation's public schools. Doctrinally, *Milliken* involved the equal protection clause, and the next two selections present Marshall's important contributions to general equal protection

303

doctrine. Selections 45 and 46 present Marshall's position in two leading affirmative action cases. Marshall's opinions demonstrate sensitivity to the historical background against which affirmative action programs were developed, and express his indignation at the Court majority's action in depriving African Americans of hard-won victories they had achieved through political action. Marshall was concerned not only with racial equality but also with wealth inequality and poverty. Selections 47 through 49 deal with aspects of the issue of poverty in diverse doctrinal settings. In each, however, Marshall's opinions connect the realities of life for the poor with the constitutional interpretations that he believed best.

The next selections present Marshall's most important contributions to First Amendment law. *Chicago Police Department v. Mosley* shows how ideas about equality must be incorporated into free speech theory. It is the Court's first decision making equality ideas an explicit component of free speech jurisprudence, although those ideas had been implicit in many earlier decisions. *Stanley v. Georgia* explains the connection between free speech theory and ideas of personal privacy, in invalidating a conviction for possessing obscene material in the privacy of a man's home. The selections conclude with two criminal justice opinions. In *Powell v. Texas* Marshall adopted a position rejected by many progressive law reformers and allowed states to punish people for public drunkenness; but he was motivated at least in part by the same compassion that the reformers felt, arguing that, in the circumstances of the United States in the late 1960s, prosecution was frequently the most humane response to the tragedies associated with drunkenness. Finally, *Payne v. Tennessee*, Marshall's last opinion, is a heartfelt complaint both about the inhumanity of the death penalty and about the Court majority's reliance on the sheer power of numbers to overcome principled objections to the administration of capital punishment.

Citations to court decisions are for lawyers what allusions and metaphors are for authors of other works. Sometimes a citation shows that the writer believes he can find prior authority to support the position he is taking. Sometimes the citation has a different function: it indicates a connection between *themes* in the present case and the prior one. The edited versions of the cases omit most citations, including those identifying the sources of quoted phrases and sentences, but preserve the citations that provide, at least to specialists, particular insight into the way Marshall thought.

42. *Milliken v. Bradley* (1974)

Desegregation proceeded slowly in the decade after *Brown v. Board of Education* (see selection 2), and the Supreme Court decided no important cases other than *Cooper v. Aaron* (see selection 4). The pace of desegregation increased after Congress enacted the Civil Rights Act of 1964, which gave federal officials the authority to cut off funding to school districts that remained segregated. The Supreme Court reentered the field in 1968, invalidating a Virginia school system's plan that allowed "freedom of choice" for students in deciding which schools to attend. The Court required that school districts adopt a plan that "promises realistically to work, and promises realistically to work *now*." The decision's emphasis on plans that "worked" shifted the lower courts' attention from desegregation—the elimination of race as a basis for making student assignments to schools—to integration—the creation of schools attended by students of all races. The lower federal courts began to require that school districts arrange for the transportation of students from one part of the district to another to ensure that schools were integrated. Busing became politically controversial, but was upheld by the Court in 1971.

Around the same time, civil rights lawyers began to challenge segregation in Northern school districts. Often the races attended different schools because of segregated housing, creating what is known as *de facto* segregation. The Supreme Court held in 1973 that Northern districts were under a duty to desegregate when they had made deliberate decisions to maintain segregated schools in a substantial part of the district, creating a condition of *de jure* segregation. When this rule was joined with the possibility of busing as a remedy, some federal trial judges concluded that they could satisfy the command for plans that "worked" only by including suburban school districts in plans to desegregate inner-city schools. *Milliken v. Bradley* involved a plan that proposed to desegregate Detroit's schools through such an interdistrict remedy. The Supreme Court rejected the plan, saying that interdistrict remedies could be used only if the suburban school districts themselves had assisted in creating the segregation of Detroit's schools.

MR. JUSTICE MARSHALL, WITH WHOM MR. JUSTICE DOUGLAS, MR. JUSTICE BRENNAN, AND MR. JUSTICE WHITE JOIN, DISSENTING.

In *Brown v. Board of Education*, this Court held that segregation of children in public schools on the basis of race deprives minority group children of equal educational opportunities and therefore denies them the equal protection of the laws under the Fourteenth Amendment. This Court recognized then that remedying decades of segregation in public education would not be an easy task. Subsequent events, unfortunately, have seen that prediction bear bitter fruit. But however imbedded old ways, however ingrained old prejudices, this Court has not been diverted from its appointed task of making "a living truth" of our constitutional ideal of equal justice under law. *Cooper v. Aaron.*

After 20 years of small, often difficult steps toward that great end, the Court today takes a giant step backwards. Notwithstanding a record showing widespread and pervasive racial segregation in the educational system provided by the State of Michigan for children in Detroit, this Court holds that the District Court was powerless to require the State to remedy its constitutional violation in any meaningful fashion. Ironically purporting to base its result on the principle that the scope of the remedy in a desegregation case should be determined by the nature and the extent of the constitutional violation, the Court's answer is to provide no remedy at all for the violation proved in this case, thereby guaranteeing that Negro children in Detroit will receive the same separate and inherently unequal education in the future as they have been unconstitutionally afforded in the past.

I cannot subscribe to this emasculation of our constitutional guarantee of equal protection of the laws and must respectfully dissent. Our precedents, in my view, firmly establish that where, as here, state-imposed segregation has been demonstrated, it becomes the duty of the State to eliminate root and branch all vestiges of racial discrimination and to achieve the greatest possible degree of actual desegregation. I agree with both the District Court and the Court of Appeals that, under the facts of this case, this duty cannot be fulfilled unless the State of Michigan involves outlying metropolitan area school districts in its desegregation remedy. Furthermore, I perceive no basis either in law or in the practicalities of the situation justifying the State's interposition of school district boundaries as absolute barriers to the implementation of an effective desegregation remedy. Under established and frequently used Michigan procedures, school district lines are both flexible and permeable for a wide variety of purposes, and there is no reason why they must now stand in the way of meaningful desegregation relief.

The rights at issue in this case are too fundamental to be abridged on grounds as superficial as those relied on by the majority today. We deal here with the right of all of our children, whatever their race, to an equal start in life and to an equal opportunity to reach their full potential as citizens. Those children who have been denied that right in the past deserve better than to see fences thrown up to deny them that right in the future. Our Nation, I fear, will be ill served by the Court's refusal to remedy separate and unequal education, for unless our children begin to learn together, there is little hope that our people will ever learn to live together.

I

The great irony of the Court's opinion and, in my view, its most serious analytical flaw may be gleaned from its concluding sentence, in which the Court remands for "prompt formulation of a decree directed to eliminating the segregation found to exist in Detroit city schools, a remedy which has been delayed since 1970." The majority, however, seems to have forgotten the District Court's explicit finding that a Detroit-only decree, the only remedy permitted under today's decision, "would not accomplish desegregation."

Nowhere in the Court's opinion does the majority confront, let alone respond to, the District Court's conclusion that a remedy limited to the city of Detroit would not effectively desegregate the Detroit city schools. I, for one, find the District Court's conclusion well supported by the record and its analysis compelled by our prior cases. . . .

The District Court's consideration of this case began with its finding, which the majority accepts, that the State of Michigan, through its instrumentality, the Detroit Board of Education, engaged in widespread purposeful acts of racial segregation in the Detroit School District. Without belaboring the details, it is sufficient to note that the various techniques used in Detroit were typical of methods employed to segregate students by race in areas where no statutory dual system of education has existed. Exacerbating the effects of extensive residential segregation between Negroes and whites, the school board consciously drew attendance zones along lines which maximized the segregation of the races in schools as well. Optional attendance zones were created for neighborhoods undergoing racial transition so as to allow whites in these areas to escape integration. Negro students in areas with overcrowded schools were transported past or away from closer white schools with available space to more distant Negro schools. Grade structures and feeder-school patterns were created and maintained in a manner which had the foreseeable and actual effect of keeping Negro and white pupils in separate schools. Schools were also constructed in locations and in sizes which ensured that they would open with predominantly one-race student bodies. In sum, the evidence adduced below showed that Negro children had been intentionally confined to an expanding core of virtually all-Negro schools immediately surrounded by a receding band of all-white schools.

Contrary to the suggestions in the Court's opinion, the basis for affording a desegregation remedy in this case was not some perceived racial imbalance either between schools within a single school district or between independent school districts. What we confront here is "a systematic program of segregation affecting a substantial portion of the students, schools . . . and facilities within the school system . . . ." The constitutional violation found here was not some *de facto* racial imbalance, but rather the purposeful, intentional, massive, *de jure* segregation of the Detroit city schools, which under our decision in *Keyes*, forms "a predicate for a finding of the existence of a dual school system," and justifies "all-out desegregation."

Having found a *de jure* segregated public school system in operation in the city of Detroit, the District Court turned next to consider which officials and agencies should be assigned the affirmative obligation to cure the constitutional violation. The court concluded that responsibility for the segregation in the Detroit city schools rested not only with the Detroit Board of Education, but belonged to the State of Michigan itself and the state defendants in this case—that is, the Governor of Michigan, the Attorney General, the State Board of Education, and the State

Superintendent of Public Instruction. While the validity of this conclusion will merit more extensive analysis below, suffice it for now to say that it was based on three considerations. First, the evidence at trial showed that the State itself had taken actions contributing to the segregation within the Detroit schools. Second, since the Detroit Board of Education was an agency of the State of Michigan, its acts of racial discrimination were acts of the State for purposes of the Fourteenth Amendment. Finally, the District Court found that under Michigan law and practice, the system of education was in fact a *state* school system, characterized by relatively little local control and a large degree of centralized state regulation, with respect to both educational policy and the structure and operation of school districts.

Having concluded, then, that the school system in the city of Detroit was a *de jure* segregated system and that the State of Michigan had the affirmative duty to remedy that condition of segregation, the District Court then turned to the difficult task of devising an effective remedy. It bears repeating that the District Court's focus at this stage of the litigation remained what it had been at the beginning—the condition of segregation within the Detroit city schools. As the District Court stated: "From the initial ruling [on segregation] to this day, the basis of the proceedings has been and remains the violation: de jure school segregation. . . . The task before this court, therefore, is now, and . . . has always been, how to desegregate the Detroit public schools."

The District Court first considered three desegregation plans limited to the geographical boundaries of the city of Detroit. All were rejected as ineffective to desegregate the Detroit city schools. Specifically, the District Court determined that the racial composition of the Detroit student body is such that implementation of any Detroit-only plan "would clearly make the entire Detroit public school system racially identifiable as Black" and would "leave many of its schools 75 to 90 per cent Black." The District Court also found that a Detroit-only plan "would change a school system which is now Black and White to one that would be perceived as Black, thereby increasing the flight of Whites from the city and the system, thereby increasing the Black student population." Based on these findings, the District Court reasoned that "relief of segregation in the public schools of the City of Detroit cannot be accomplished within the corporate geographical limits of the city" because a Detroit-only decree "would accentuate the racial identifiability of the district as a Black school system, and would not accomplish desegregation." The District Court therefore concluded that it "must look beyond the limits of the Detroit school district for a solution to the problem of segregation in the Detroit public schools . . . ."

In seeking to define the appropriate scope of that expanded desegregation area, however, the District Court continued to maintain as its sole focus the condition shown to violate the Constitution in this case—the segregation of the Detroit school system. As it stated, the primary question "remains the determination of the area necessary and practicable effectively to eliminate 'root and branch' the effects of state-imposed and supported segregation and to desegregate the Detroit public schools."

There is simply no foundation in the record, then, for the majority's accusation that the only basis for the District Court's order was some desire to achieve a racial balance in the Detroit metropolitan area. In fact, just the contrary is the case. In considering proposed desegregation areas, the District Court had occasion to criticize one of the State's proposals specifically because it had no basis other than its "particular racial ratio" and did not focus on "relevant factors, like eliminating racially identifiable schools [and] accomplishing maximum actual desegregation of the Detroit public schools." . . .

The Court also misstates the basis for the District Court's order by suggesting that since the only segregation proved at trial was within the Detroit school system, any relief which extended beyond the jurisdiction of the Detroit Board of Education would be inappropriate because it would impose a remedy on outlying districts "not shown to have committed any constitutional violation." The essential foundation of interdistrict relief in this case was not to correct conditions within outlying districts which themselves engaged in purposeful segregation. Instead, interdistrict relief was seen as a necessary part of any meaningful effort by the State of Michigan to remedy the state-caused segregation within the city of Detroit.

Rather than consider the propriety of interdistrict relief on this basis, however, the Court has conjured up a largely fictional account of what the District Court was attempting to accomplish. With all due respect, the Court, in my view, does a great disservice to the District Judge who labored long and hard with this complex litigation by accusing him of changing horses in midstream and shifting the focus of this case from the pursuit of a remedy for the condition of segregation within the Detroit school system to some unprincipled attempt to impose his own philosophy of racial balance on the entire Detroit metropolitan area. The focus of this case has always been the segregated system of education in the city of Detroit. The District Court determined that interdistrict relief was necessary and appropriate only because it found that the condition of segregation within the Detroit school system could not be cured with a Detroit-only remedy. It is on this theory that the interdistrict relief must stand or fall. Unlike the Court, I perceive my task to be to review the District Court's order for what it is, rather than to criticize it for what it manifestly is not.

II

As the foregoing demonstrates, the District Court's decision to expand its desegregation decree beyond the geographical limits of the city of Detroit rested in large part on its conclusions (A) that the State of Michigan was ultimately responsible for curing the condition of segregation within the Detroit city schools, and (B) that a Detroit-only remedy would not accomplish this task. In my view, both of these conclusions are well supported by the facts of this case and by this Court's precedents.

A

To begin with, the record amply supports the District Court's findings that the State of Michigan, through state officers and state agencies, had engaged in purposeful acts which created or aggravated segregation in the Detroit schools. The State Board of Education, for example, prior to 1962, exercised its authority to supervise local school site selection in a manner which contributed to segregation. Furthermore, the State's continuing authority, after 1962, to approve school building construction plans had intertwined the State with site-selection decisions of the Detroit Board of Education which had the purpose and effect of maintaining segregation.

The State had also stood in the way of past efforts to desegregate the Detroit city schools. In 1970, for example, the Detroit School Board had begun implementation of its own desegregation plan for its high schools, despite considerable public and official resistance. The State Legislature intervened by enacting Act 48 of the Public Acts of 1970, specifically prohibiting implementation of the desegregation plan and thereby continuing the growing segregation of the Detroit school system. Adequate desegregation of the Detroit system was also hampered by discriminatory restrictions placed by the State on the use of transportation within Detroit. While state aid for transportation was provided by statute for suburban districts, many of which were highly urbanized, aid for intracity transportation was excepted. One of the effects of this restriction was to encourage the construction of small walk-in neighborhood schools in Detroit, thereby lending aid to the intentional policy of creating a school system which reflected, to the greatest extent feasible, extensive residential segregation. Indeed, that one of the purposes of the transportation restriction was to impede desegregation was evidenced when the Michigan Legislature amended the State Transportation Aid Act to cover intracity transportation but expressly prohibited the allocation of funds for cross-busing of students within a school district to achieve racial balance. . . .

The State's control over education is reflected in the fact that, contrary to the Court's implication, there is little or no relationship between school districts and local political units. To take the 85 outlying local school districts in the Detroit metropolitan area as examples, 17 districts lie in two counties, two in three counties. One district serves five municipalities; other suburban municipalities are fragmented into as many as six school districts. Nor is there any apparent state policy with regard to the size of school districts, as they now range from 2,000 to 285,000 students.

Centralized state control manifests itself in practice as well as in theory. The State controls the financing of education in several ways. The legislature contributes a substantial portion of most school districts' operating budgets with funds appropriated from the State's General Fund revenues raised through statewide taxation. The State's power over the purse can be and is in fact used to enforce the State's powers over local districts. In addition, although local districts obtain funds through local property taxation, the State has assumed the responsibility to ensure equalized property valuations throughout the State. The State also establishes standards for teacher certification and teacher tenure; determines part of the required curriculum; sets the minimum school term; approves bus routes, equipment, and drivers; approves textbooks; and establishes procedures for student discipline. The State Superintendent of Public Instruction and the State Board of Education have the power to remove local school board members from office for neglect of their duties.

Most significantly for present purposes, the State has wide-ranging powers to consolidate and merge school districts, even without the consent of the districts themselves or of the local citizenry. Indeed, recent years have witnessed an accelerated program of school district consolidations, mergers, and annexations, many of which were state imposed. Whereas the State had 7,362 local districts in 1912, the number had been reduced to 1,438 in 1964 and to 738 in 1968. By June 1972, only 608 school districts remained. Furthermore, the State has broad powers to transfer property from one district to another, again without the consent of the local school districts affected by the transfer.

Whatever may be the history of public education in other parts of our Nation, it simply flies in the face of reality to say, as does the majority, that in Michigan, "[no] single tradition in public education is more deeply rooted than local control over the operation of schools . . . ." As the State's Supreme Court has said: "We have repeatedly held that education in this State is not a matter of local concern, but belongs to the State at large." Indeed, a study prepared for the 1961 Michigan Constitutional Convention noted that the Michigan Constitution's articles on education had resulted in "the establishment of a state system of education in contrast to a series of local school systems."

In sum, several factors in this case coalesce to support the District Court's ruling that it was the State of Michigan itself, not simply the Detroit Board of Education, which bore the obligation of curing the condition of segregation within the Detroit city schools. The actions of the State itself directly contributed to Detroit's segregation. Under the Fourteenth Amendment, the State is ultimately responsible for the actions of its local agencies. And, finally, given the structure of Michigan's educational system, Detroit's segregation cannot be viewed as the problem of an independent and separate entity. Michigan operates a single statewide system of education, a substantial part of which was shown to be segregated in this case.

B

What action, then, could the District Court require the State to take in order to cure Detroit's condition of segregation? Our prior cases have not minced words as to what steps responsible officials and agencies must take in order to remedy segregation in the public schools. Not only must distinctions on the basis of race be terminated for the future, but school officials are also "clearly charged with the affirmative duty to take whatever steps might be necessary to convert to a unitary system in which racial discrimination would be eliminated root and branch." Negro students are not only entitled to neutral nondiscriminatory treatment in the future. They must receive "what *Brown II* promised them: a school system in which all vestiges of enforced racial segregation have been eliminated." These remedial standards are fully applicable not only to school districts where a dual system was compelled by statute, but also where, as here, a dual system was the product of purposeful and intentional state action.

After examining three plans limited to the city of Detroit, the District Court correctly concluded that none would eliminate root and branch the vestiges of unconstitutional segregation. The plans' effectiveness, of course, had to be evaluated in the context of the District Court's findings as to the extent of segregation in the Detroit city schools. As indicated earlier, the most essential finding was that Negro children in Detroit had been confined by intentional acts of segregation to a growing core of Negro schools surrounded by a receding ring of white schools. Thus, in 1960, of Detroit's 251 regular-attendance schools, 100 were 90% or more white and 71 were 90% or more Negro. In 1970, of Detroit's 282 regular-attendance schools, 69 were 90% or more white and 133 were 90% or more Negro. While in 1960, 68% of all schools were 90% or more one race, by 1970, 71.6% of the schools fell into that category. The growing core of all-Negro schools was further evidenced in total school district population figures. In 1960 the Detroit system had 46% Negro students and 54% white students, but by 1970, 64% of the students were Negro and only 36% were white. This increase in the proportion of Negro students was the highest of any major Northern city.

It was with these figures in the background that the District Court evaluated the adequacy of the three Detroit-only plans submitted by the parties. Plan A, proposed by the Detroit Board of Education, desegregated the high schools and about a fifth of the middle-level schools. It was deemed inadequate, however, because it did not desegregate elementary schools and left the middle-level schools not included in the plan more segregated than ever. Plan C, also proposed by the Detroit Board, was deemed inadequate because it too covered only some grade levels and would leave elementary schools segregated. Plan B, the plaintiffs' plan, though requiring the transportation of 82,000 pupils and the acquisition of 900 school buses, would make little headway in rooting out the vestiges of segregation. To begin with, because of practical limitations, the District Court found that the plan would leave many of the Detroit city schools 75% to 90% Negro. More significantly, the District Court recognized that in the context of a community which historically had a school system marked by rigid *de jure* segregation, the likely effect of a Detroit-only plan would be to "change a school system which is now Black and White to one that would be perceived as Black . . . ." The result of this changed perception, the District Court found, would be to increase the flight of whites from the city to the outlying suburbs, compounding the effects of the present rate of increase in the proportion of Negro students in the Detroit system. Thus, even if a plan were adopted which, at its outset, provided in every school a 65% Negro–35% white racial mix in keeping with the Negro–white proportions of the total student population, such a system would, in short order, devolve into an all-Negro system. The net result would be a continuation of the all-Negro schools which were the hallmarks of Detroit's former dual system of one-race schools.

Under our decisions, it was clearly proper for the District Court to take into account the so-called "white flight" from the city schools which would be forthcoming from any Detroit-only decree. The court's prediction of white flight was well supported by expert testimony based on past experience in other cities undergoing desegregation relief. We ourselves took the possibility of white flight into account in evaluating the effectiveness of a desegregation plan in *Wright*, where we relied on the District Court's finding that if the city of Emporia were allowed to withdraw from the existing system, leaving a system with a higher proportion of Negroes, it "'may be anticipated that the proportion of whites in county schools may drop as those who can register in private academies' . . . ." One cannot ignore the white-flight problem, for where legally imposed segregation has been established, the District Court has the responsibility to see to it not only that the dual system is terminated at once but also that future events do not serve to perpetuate or re-establish segregation.

We held in *Swann* that where *de jure* segregation is shown, school authorities must make "every effort to achieve the greatest possible degree of actual desegregation. . . ." If these words have any meaning at all, surely it is that school authorities must, to the extent possible, take all practicable steps to ensure that Negro and white children in fact go to school together. This is, in the final analysis, what desegregation of the public schools is all about.

Because of the already high and rapidly increasing percentage of Negro students in the Detroit system, as well as the prospect of white flight, a Detroit-only plan simply has no hope of achieving actual desegregation. Under such a plan white and Negro students will not go to school together. Instead, Negro children will continue to attend all-Negro schools. The very evil that *Brown I* was aimed at will not be cured, but will be perpetuated for the future.

Racially identifiable schools are one of the primary vestiges of state-imposed segregation which an effective desegregation decree must attempt to eliminate. In *Swann*, for example, we held that "[t]he district judge or school authorities . . . will thus necessarily be concerned with the elimination of one-race schools." There is "a presumption," we stated, "against schools that are substantially disproportionate in their racial composition." And in evaluating the effectiveness of desegregation plans in prior cases, we ourselves have considered the extent to which they discontinued racially identifiable schools. For a principal end of any desegregation remedy is to ensure that it is no longer "possible to identify a 'white school' or a

'Negro school.'" The evil to be remedied in the dismantling of a dual system is the "[r]acial identification of the system's schools." The goal is a system without white schools or Negro schools—a system with "just schools." A school authority's remedial plan or a district court's remedial decree is to be judged by its effectiveness in achieving this end.

We cautioned in *Swann*, of course, that the dismantling of a segregated school system does not mandate any particular racial balance. We also concluded that a remedy under which there would remain a small number of racially identifiable schools was only presumptively inadequate and might be justified. But this is a totally different case. The flaw of a Detroit-only decree is not that it does not reach some ideal degree of racial balance or mixing. It simply does not promise to achieve actual desegregation at all. It is one thing to have a system where a small number of students remain in racially identifiable schools. It is something else entirely to have a system where all students continue to attend such schools.

The continued racial identifiability of the Detroit schools under a Detroit-only remedy is not simply a reflection of their high percentage of Negro students. What is or is not a racially identifiable vestige of *de jure* segregation must necessarily depend on several factors. Foremost among these should be the relationship between the schools in question and the neighboring community. For these purposes the city of Detroit and its surrounding suburbs must be viewed as a single community. Detroit is closely connected to its suburbs in many ways, and the metropolitan area is viewed as a single cohesive unit by its residents. About 40% of the residents of the two suburban counties included in the desegregation plan work in Wayne County, in which Detroit is situated. Many residents of the city work in the suburbs. The three counties participate in a wide variety of cooperative governmental ventures on a metropolitan-wide basis, including a metropolitan transit system, park authority, water and sewer system, and council of governments. The Federal Government has classified the tri-county area as a Standard Metropolitan Statistical Area, indicating that it is an area of "economic and social integration."

Under a Detroit-only decree, Detroit's schools will clearly remain racially identifiable in comparison with neighboring schools in the metropolitan community. Schools with 65% and more Negro students will stand in sharp and obvious contrast to schools in neighboring districts with less than 2% Negro enrollment. Negro students will continue to perceive their schools as segregated educational facilities and this perception will only be increased when whites react to a Detroit-only decree by fleeing to the suburbs to avoid integration. School district lines, however innocently drawn, will surely be perceived as fences to separate the races when, under a Detroit-only decree, white parents withdraw their children from the Detroit city schools and move to the suburbs in order to continue them in all-white schools. The message of this action will not escape the Negro children in the city of Detroit. It will be of scant significance to Negro children who have for years been confined by *de jure* acts of segregation to a growing core of all-Negro schools surrounded by a ring of all-white schools that the new dividing line between the races is the school district boundary.

Nor can it be said that the State is free from any responsibility for the disparity between the racial makeup of Detroit and its surrounding suburbs. The State's creation, through *de jure* acts of segregation, of a growing core of all-Negro schools inevitably acted as a magnet to attract Negroes to the areas served by such schools and to deter them from settling either in other areas of the city or in the suburbs. By the same token, the growing core of all-Negro schools inevitably helped drive whites to other areas of the city or to the suburbs. As we recognized in *Swann*:

> "People gravitate toward school facilities, just as schools are located in response to the needs of people. The location of schools may thus influence the patterns of residential development of a metropolitan area and have important impact on composition of inner-city neighborhoods. . . . [Action taken] to maintain the separation of the races with a minimum departure from the formal principles of 'neighborhood zoning' . . . does more than simply influence the short-run composition of the student body . . . . It may well promote segregated residential patterns which, when combined with 'neighborhood zoning,' further lock the school system into the mold of separation of the races. Upon a proper showing a district court may consider this in fashioning a remedy."

The rippling effects on residential patterns caused by purposeful acts of segregation do not automatically subside at the school district border. With rare exceptions, these effects naturally spread through all the residential neighborhoods within a metropolitan area.

The State must also bear part of the blame for the white flight to the suburbs which would be forthcoming from a Detroit-only decree and would render such a remedy ineffective. Having created a system where whites and Negroes were intentionally kept apart so that they could not become accustomed to learning together, the State is responsible for the fact that many whites will react to the dismantling of that segregated system by attempting to flee to the suburbs. Indeed, by limiting the District Court to a Detroit-only remedy and allowing that flight to the suburbs to succeed, the Court today allows the State to profit from its own wrong and to perpetuate for years to come the separation of the races it achieved in the past by purposeful state action.

The majority asserts, however, that involvement of outlying districts would do violence to the accepted principle that "the nature of the violation determines the scope of the remedy." Not only is the majority's attempt to find in this single phrase the answer to the complex and difficult questions presented in this case hopelessly simplistic, but more important, the Court reads these words in a manner which perverts their obvious meaning. The nature of a violation determines the scope of the remedy simply because the function of any remedy is to cure the violation to which it is addressed. In school segregation cases, as in other equitable causes, a remedy which effectively cures the violation is what is required. No more is necessary, but we can tolerate no less. To read this principle as barring a district court from imposing the only effective remedy for past segregation and remitting the court to a patently ineffective alternative is, in my view, to turn a simple commonsense rule into a cruel and meaningless paradox. Ironically, by ruling out an interdistrict remedy, the only relief which promises to cure segregation in the Detroit public schools, the majority flouts the very principle on which it purports to rely.

Nor should it be of any significance that the suburban school districts were not shown to have themselves taken any direct action to promote segregation of the races. Given the State's broad powers over local school districts, it was well within the State's powers to require those districts surrounding the Detroit school district to participate in a metropolitan remedy. The State's duty should be no different here than in cases where it is shown that certain of a State's voting districts are malapportioned in violation of the Fourteenth Amendment. Overrepresented electoral districts are required to participate in reapportionment although their only "participation" in the violation was to do nothing about it. Similarly, electoral districts which themselves meet representation standards must frequently be redrawn as part of a remedy for other over- and under-inclusive districts. No finding of fault on the part of each electoral district and no finding of a discriminatory effect on each district is a prerequisite to its involvement in the constitutionally required remedy. By the same logic, no finding of fault on the part of the suburban school districts in this case and no finding of a discriminatory effect on each district should be a prerequisite to their involvement in the constitutionally required remedy.

It is the State, after all, which bears the responsibility under *Brown* of affording a nondiscriminatory system of education. The State, of course, is ordinarily free to choose any decentralized framework for education it wishes, so long as it fulfills that Fourteenth Amendment obligation. But the State should no more be allowed to hide behind its delegation and compartmentalization of school districts to avoid its constitutional obligations to its children than it could hide behind its political subdivisions to avoid its obligations to its voters.

It is a hollow remedy indeed where "after supposed 'desegregation' the schools remained segregated in fact." We must do better than "'substitute . . . one segregated school system for another segregated school system.'" To suggest, as does the majority, that a Detroit-only plan somehow remedies the effects of *de jure* segregation of the races is, in my view, to make a solemn mockery of *Brown I*'s holding that separate educational facilities are inherently unequal and of *Swann's* unequivocal mandate that the answer to *de jure* segregation is the greatest possible degree of actual desegregation.

III

One final set of problems remains to be considered. We recognized in *Brown II*, and have re-emphasized ever since, that in fashioning relief in desegregation cases, "the courts will be guided by equitable principles. Traditionally, equity has been characterized by a practical flexibility in shaping its remedies and by a facility for adjusting and reconciling public and private needs."

Though not resting its holding on this point, the majority suggests that various equitable considerations militate against interdistrict relief. The Court, for example, refers to financing and administrative problems, the logistical problems attending large-scale transportation of students, and the prospect of the District Court's becoming a *"de facto* 'legislative authority'" and "'school superintendent' for the entire area." The entangling web of problems woven by the Court, however, appears on further consideration to be constructed of the flimsiest of threads.

I deal first with the last of the problems posed by the Court—the specter of the District Court *qua* "school superintendent" and "legislative authority"—for analysis of this problem helps put the other issues in proper perspective. Our cases, of course, make clear that the initial responsibility for devising an adequate desegregation plan belongs with school authorities, not with the District Court. The court's primary role is to review the adequacy of the school authorities' efforts and to substitute its own plan only if and to the extent they default. Contrary to the majority's suggestions, the District Judge in this case consistently adhered to these procedures and there is every indication that he would have continued to do so. After finding *de jure* segregation the court ordered the parties to submit proposed Detroit-only plans. The state defendants were also ordered to submit a proposed metropolitan plan extending beyond Detroit's boundaries. As the District Court stated, "the State defendants . . . bear the initial burden of coming forward with a proposal that promises to work." The state defendants defaulted in this obligation, however. Rather than submit a complete plan, the State Board of Education submitted six proposals, none of which was in fact a desegregation plan. It was only upon this default that the District Court began to take steps to develop its own plan. Even then the District Court maximized school authority participation by appointing a panel representing both plaintiffs and defendants to develop a plan. Furthermore, the District Court still left the state defendants the initial responsibility for developing both interim and final financial and administrative arrangements to implement interdistrict relief. The Court of Appeals further protected the interests of local school authorities by ensuring that the outlying suburban districts could fully participate in the proceedings to develop a metropolitan remedy.

These processes have not been allowed to run their course. No final desegregation plan has been proposed by the panel of experts, let alone approved by the District Court. We do not know in any detail how many students will be transported to effect a metropolitan remedy, and we do not know how long or how far they will have to travel. No recommendations have yet been submitted by the state defendants on financial and administrative arrangements. In sum, the practicality of a final metropolitan plan is simply not before us at the present time. Since the State and the panel of experts have not yet had an opportunity to come up with a workable remedy, there is no foundation for the majority's suggestion of the impracticality of interdistrict relief. Furthermore, there is no basis whatever for assuming that the District Court will inevitably be forced to assume the role of legislature or school superintendent. Were we to hold that it was its constitutional duty to do so, there is every indication that the State of Michigan would fulfill its obligation and develop a plan which is workable, administrable, financially sound, and, most important, in the best interest of quality education for all of the children in the Detroit metropolitan area.

Since the Court chooses, however, to speculate on the feasibility of a metropolitan plan, I feel constrained to comment on the problem areas it has targeted. To begin with, the majority's questions concerning the practicality of consolidation of school districts need not give us pause. The State clearly has the power, under existing law, to effect a consolidation if it is ultimately determined that this offers the best prospect for a workable and stable desegregation plan. And given the 1,000 or so consolidations of school districts which have taken place in the past, it is hard to believe that the State has not already devised means of solving most, if not all, of the practical problems which the Court suggests consolidation would entail.

Furthermore, the majority ignores long-established Michigan procedures under which school districts may enter into contractual agreements to educate their pupils in other districts using state or local funds to finance nonresident education. Such agreements could form an easily administrable framework for interdistrict relief short of outright consolidation of the school districts. The District Court found that interdistrict procedures like these were frequently used to provide special educational services for handicapped children, and extensive statutory provision is also made for their use in vocational education. Surely if school districts are willing to engage in interdistrict programs to help those unfortunate children crippled by physical or mental handicaps, school districts can be required to participate in an interdistrict program to help those children in the city of Detroit whose educations and very futures have been crippled by purposeful state segregation.

Although the majority gives this last matter only fleeting reference, it is plain that one of the basic emotional and legal issues underlying these cases concerns the propriety of transportation of students to achieve desegregation. While others may have retreated from its standards, I continue to adhere to the guidelines set forth in *Swann* on this issue. And though no final desegregation plan is presently before us, to the extent the outline of such a plan is now visible, it is clear that the transportation it would entail will be fully consistent with these guidelines.

First of all, the metropolitan plan would not involve the busing of substantially more students than already ride buses. The District Court found that, statewide, 35%–40% of all students already arrive at school on a bus. In those school districts in the tri-county Detroit metropolitan area eligible for state reimbursement of transportation costs, 42%–52% of all students rode buses to school. In the tri-county areas as a whole, approximately 300,000 pupils arrived at school on some type of bus, with about 60,000 of these apparently using regular public transit. In comparison, the desegregation plan, according to its present rough outline, would involve the transportation of 310,000 students, about 40% of the population within the desegregation area.

With respect to distance and amount of time traveled, 17 of the outlying school districts involved in the plan are contiguous to the Detroit district. The rest are all within 8 miles of the Detroit city limits. The trial court, in defining the desegregation area, placed a ceiling of 40 minutes one way on the amount of travel time, and many students will obviously travel for far shorter periods. As to distance, the average statewide bus trip is 8½ miles one way, and in some parts of the tri-county area, students already travel for one and a quarter hours or more each way. In sum, with regard to both the number of students transported and the time and distances involved, the outlined desegregation plan "compares favorably with the transportation plan previously operated . . . ."

As far as economics are concerned, a metropolitan remedy would actually be more sensible than a Detroit-only remedy. Because of prior transportation aid restrictions, Detroit largely relied on public transport, at student expense, for those students who lived too far away to walk to school. Since no inventory of school buses existed, a Detroit-only plan was estimated to require the purchase of 900 buses to effectuate the necessary transportation. The tri-county area, in contrast, already has an inventory of 1,800 buses, many of which are now under-utilized. Since increased utilization of the existing inventory can take up much of the increase in transportation involved in the interdistrict remedy, the District Court found that only 350 additional buses would probably be needed, almost two-thirds fewer than a Detroit-only remedy. Other features of an interdistrict remedy bespeak its practicality, such as the possibility of pairing up Negro schools near Detroit's boundary with nearby white schools on the other side of the present school district line.

Some disruption, of course, is the inevitable product of any desegregation decree, whether it operates within one district or on an interdistrict basis. As we said in *Swann*, however:

"Absent a constitutional violation there would be no basis for judicially ordering assignment of students on a racial basis. All things being equal, with no history of discrimination, it might well be desirable to assign pupils to schools nearest their homes. But all things are not equal in a system that has been deliberately constructed and maintained to enforce racial segregation. The remedy for such segregation may be administratively awkward, inconvenient, and even bizarre in some situations and may impose burdens on some; but all awkwardness and inconvenience cannot be avoided. . . ."

Desegregation is not and was never expected to be an easy task. Racial attitudes ingrained in our Nation's childhood and adolescence are not quickly thrown aside in its middle years. But just as the inconvenience of some cannot be allowed to stand in the way of the rights of others, so public opposition, no matter how strident, cannot be permitted to divert this Court from the enforcement of the constitutional principles at issue in this case. Today's holding, I fear, is more a reflection of a perceived public mood that we have gone far enough in enforcing the Constitution's guarantee of equal justice than it is the product of neutral principles of law. In the short run, it may seem to be the easier course to allow our great metropolitan areas to be divided up each into two cities—one white, the other black— but it is a course, I predict, our people will ultimately regret. I dissent.

In the last years of Marshall's tenure, the Court began to allow school districts that had once been segregated to operate without further judicial supervision. Within a few years of his retirement, most districts that once were required to engage in substantial efforts to eliminate the vestiges of segregation were relieved of their obligation to do so. Most urban school districts (and many suburban ones) operated schools that were racially identifiable, and the national commitment to eliminating racial segregation in the schools had weakened substantially.

43. *Dandridge v. Williams* (1970)

The Fourteenth Amendment bars states from denying people the "equal protection of the laws." Every statute treats some people differently from others, however. Equal protection doctrine must help courts and legislatures decide when a specific form of unequal treatment is unconstitutionally discriminatory, and this doctrine developed along two lines. First, some classifications were "suspect." Laws employing them had to have a very strong justification, phrased doctrinally as a requirement that they survive "strict scrutiny" by serving a compelling governmental interest in ways that could not be equally well served by laws avoiding the use of the suspect classification. Laws relying on racial classifications were the core example of statutes in this category. Second, all other classifications were subject to "rational basis" review. They would be constitutional if they promoted some reasonable governmental goal, and the Court was quite generous in coming up with such goals.

This approach began to break down in the Warren and Burger Court years. The Court began to consider cases involving classifications that were not quite as problematic as race, but which seemed to be used inappropriately. These classifications included gender and birth out of wedlock. The Court struggled to fit the cases involving them into its two-tier framework, but few found that approach satisfactory. In addition, the Court developed another equal protection doctrine, under which classifications that affected "fundamental rights" were also scrutinized carefully. *Dandridge v. Williams* involves this branch of equal protection doctrine. Justice Marshall's dissent outlines his distinctive analysis of equal protection doctrine, which has come to be known as the "sliding scale" or balancing approach. Most academic commentators find that it describes the Court's cases more accurately than any competing doctrinal alternatives, and that it is generally more satisfying as a way of getting a handle on equal protection problems.

Dandridge was a challenge to one aspect of Maryland's public assistance program. Under the program, state administrators determined what a person receiving public assistance would need. Families were given public assistance grants according to their need, but state law placed a cap on such grants. The cap meant that large families received public assistance in amounts less than the state's own calculations showed they needed. The plaintiffs argued that the statute's distinction between small families—who, according to the state's own calculations, received all they needed—and large families was unreasonable and therefore unconstitutional. The Supreme Court rejected the challenge. Justice Stewart's majority opinion said that states had great latitude in the area of social and economic welfare, and that limiting the amounts any family could receive might be a rational way both to encourage family heads to obtain employment and to maintain a fair balance in well-being between the working poor and families receiving public assistance.

MR. JUSTICE MARSHALL, WHOM MR. JUSTICE BRENNAN JOINS, DISSENTING.
The Court holds today that regardless of the arbitrariness of a classification it must
be sustained if any state goal can be imagined that is arguably furthered by its
effects. This is so even though the classification's underinclusiveness or overinclusiveness clearly demonstrates that its actual basis is something other than that
asserted by the State, and even though the relationship between the classification
and the state interests which it purports to serve is so tenuous that it could not seriously be maintained that the classification tends to accomplish the ascribed goals.

The Court recognizes, as it must, that this case involves "the most basic economic needs of impoverished human beings," and that there is therefore a "dramatically real factual difference" between the instant case and those decisions upon
which the Court relies. The acknowledgment that these dramatic differences exist
is a candid recognition that the Court's decision today is wholly without precedent.
I cannot subscribe to the Court's sweeping refusal to accord the Equal Protection
Clause any role in this entire area of the law, and I therefore dissent from both parts
of the Court's decision. . . .

The Maryland AFDC program in its basic structure operates uniformly with
regard to all needy children by taking into account the basic subsistence needs of
all eligible individuals in the formulation of the standards of need for families of
various sizes. However, superimposed upon this uniform system is the maximum
grant regulation, the operative effect of which is to create two classes of needy
children and two classes of eligible families: those small families and their members who receive payments to cover their subsistence needs and those large families who do not.

This classification process effected by the maximum grant regulation produces a basic denial of equal treatment. Persons who are concededly similarly situated (dependent children and their families), are not afforded equal, or even
approximately equal, treatment under the maximum grant regulation. Subsistence
benefits are paid with respect to some needy dependent children; nothing is paid
with respect to others. Some needy families receive full subsistence assistance as
calculated by the State; the assistance paid to other families is grossly below their
similarly calculated needs.

Yet, as a general principle, individuals should not be afforded different treatment by the State unless there is a relevant distinction between them, and "a statutory discrimination must be based on differences that are reasonably related to the
purposes of the Act in which it is found." Consequently, the State may not, in the
provision of important services or the distribution of governmental payments, supply benefits to some individuals while denying them to others who are similarly
situated.

In the instant case, the only distinction between those children with respect to
whom assistance is granted and those children who are denied such assistance is the
size of the family into which the child permits himself to be born. The class of indi-

viduals with respect to whom payments are actually made (the first four or five eligible dependent children in a family), is grossly underinclusive in terms of the class that the AFDC program was designed to assist, namely, all needy dependent children. Such underinclusiveness manifests "a prima facie violation of the equal protection requirement of reasonable classification," compelling the State to come forward with a persuasive justification for the classification.

The Court never undertakes to inquire for such a justification; rather it avoids the task by focusing upon the abstract dichotomy between two different approaches to equal protection problems that have been utilized by this Court.

Under the so-called "traditional test," a classification is said to be permissible under the Equal Protection Clause unless it is "without any reasonable basis." On the other hand, if the classification affects a "fundamental right," then the state interest in perpetuating the classification must be "compelling" in order to be sustained.

This case simply defies easy characterization in terms of one or the other of these "tests." The cases relied on by the Court, in which a "mere rationality" test was actually used, are most accurately described as involving the application of equal protection reasoning to the regulation of business interests. The extremes to which the Court has gone in dreaming up rational bases for state regulation in that area may in many instances be ascribed to a healthy revulsion from the Court's earlier excesses in using the Constitution to protect interests that have more than enough power to protect themselves in the legislative halls. This case, involving the literally vital interests of a powerless minority—poor families without breadwinners—is far removed from the area of business regulation, as the Court concedes. Why then is the standard used in those cases imposed here? We are told no more than that this case falls in "the area of economics and social welfare," with the implication that from there the answer is obvious.

In my view, equal protection analysis of this case is not appreciably advanced by the *a priori* definition of a "right," fundamental or otherwise. Rather, concentration must be placed upon the character of the classification in question, the relative importance to individuals in the class discriminated against of the governmental benefits that they do not receive, and the asserted state interests in support of the classification. As we said only recently, "In determining whether or not a state law violates the Equal Protection Clause, we must consider the facts and circumstances behind the law, the interests which the State claims to be protecting, and the interests of those who are disadvantaged by the classification."

It is the individual interests here at stake that, as the Court concedes, most clearly distinguish this case from the "business regulation" equal protection cases. AFDC support to needy dependent children provides the stuff that sustains those children's lives: food, clothing, shelter. And this Court has already recognized several times that when a benefit, even a "gratuitous" benefit, is necessary to sustain life, stricter constitutional standards, both procedural and substantive, are applied to the deprivation of that benefit.

Nor is the distinction upon which the deprivation is here based—the distinction between large and small families—one that readily commends itself as a basis for determining which children are to have support approximating subsistence and which are not. Indeed, governmental discrimination between children on the basis of a factor over which they have no control—the number of their brothers and sisters—bears some resemblance to the classification between legitimate and illegitimate children which we condemned as a violation of the Equal Protection Clause in *Levy v. Louisiana* (1968).

The asserted state interests in the maintenance of the maximum grant regulation, on the other hand, are hardly clear. In the early stages of this litigation, the State attempted to rationalize the maximum grant regulation on the theory that it was merely a device to conserve state funds, in the language of the motion to dismiss, "a legitimate way of allocating the State's limited resources available for AFDC assistance." Indeed, the initial opinion of the District Court concluded that the sole reason for the regulation, as revealed by the record, was "to fit the total needs of the State's dependent children, as measured by the State's standards of their subsistence requirements, into an inadequate State appropriation." The District Court quite properly rejected this asserted justification, for "the saving of welfare costs cannot justify an otherwise invidious classification."

In post-trial proceedings in the District Court, and in briefs to this court, the State apparently abandoned reliance on the fiscal justification. In its place, there have now appeared several different rationales for the maximum grant regulation, prominent among them being those relied upon by the majority—the notions that imposition of the maximum serves as an incentive to welfare recipients to find and maintain employment and provides a semblance of equality with persons earning a minimum wage.

With regard to the latter, Maryland has urged that the maximum grant regulation serves to maintain a rough equality between wage earning families and AFDC families, thereby increasing the political support for—or perhaps reducing the opposition to—the AFDC program. It is questionable whether the Court really relies on this ground, especially when in many States the prescribed family maximum bears no such relation to the minimum wage. But the Court does not indicate that a different result might obtain in other cases. Indeed, whether elimination of the maximum would produce welfare incomes out of line with other incomes in Maryland is itself open to question on this record. It is true that government in the United States, unlike certain other countries, has not chosen to make public aid available to assist families generally in raising their children. Rather, in this case Maryland, with the encouragement and assistance of the Federal Government, has elected to provide assistance at a subsistence level for those in particular need—the aged, the blind, the infirm, and the unemployed and unemployable, and their children. The only question presented here is whether, having once undertaken such a program, the State may arbitrarily select from among the concededly eligible those to whom it will provide benefits. And it is too late to argue that political expediency will sustain discrimination not otherwise supportable. Cf. *Cooper v. Aaron* (1958).

Vital to the employment-incentive basis found by the Court to sustain the regulation is, of course, the supposition that an appreciable number of AFDC recipients are in fact employable. For it is perfectly obvious that limitations upon assistance cannot reasonably operate as a work incentive with regard to those who cannot work or who cannot be expected to work. In this connection, Maryland candidly notes that "only a very small percentage of the total universe of welfare recipients are employable." The State, however, urges us to ignore the "total universe" and to concentrate attention instead upon the heads of AFDC families. Yet the very purpose of the AFDC program since its inception has been to provide assistance for dependent *children*. The State's position is thus that the State may deprive certain needy children of assistance to which they would otherwise be entitled in order to provide an arguable work incentive for their parents. But the State may not wield its economic whip in this fashion when the effect is to cause a deprivation to needy dependent children in order to correct an arguable fault of their parents.

Even if the invitation of the State to focus upon the heads of AFDC families is accepted, the minimum rationality of the maximum grant regulation is hard to discern. The District Court found that of Maryland's more than 32,000 AFDC families, only about 116 could be classified as having employable members, and, of these, the number to which the maximum grant regulation was applicable is not disclosed by the record. The State objects that this figure includes only families in which the father is unemployed and fails to take account of families in which an employable mother is the head of the household. At the same time, however, the State itself has recognized that the vast proportion of these mothers are in fact unemployable because they are mentally or physically incapacitated, because they have no marketable skills, or, most prominently, because the best interests of the children dictate that the mother remain in the home. Thus, it is clear, although the record does not disclose precise figures, that the total number of "employable" mothers is but a fraction of the total number of AFDC mothers. Furthermore, the record is silent as to what proportion of large families subject to the maximum have "employable" mothers. Indeed, one must assume that the presence of the mother in the home can be less easily dispensed with in the case of large families, particularly where small children are involved and alternative provisions for their care are accordingly more difficult to arrange. In short, not only has the State failed to establish that there is a substantial or even a significant proportion of AFDC heads of households as to whom the maximum grant regulation arguably serves as a viable and logical work incentive, but it is also indisputable that the regulation at best is drastically *over-inclusive* since it applies with equal vigor to a very substantial number of persons who like appellees are completely disabled from working.

Finally, it should be noted that, to the extent there is a legitimate state interest in encouraging heads of AFDC households to find employment, application of the maximum grant regulation is also grossly *underinclusive* because it singles out and affects only large families. No reason is suggested why this particular group should be carved out for the purpose of having unusually harsh "work incentives" imposed upon them. Not only has the State selected for special treatment a small group from among similarly situated families, but it has done so on a basis—family size—that bears no relation to the evil that the State claims the regulation was designed to correct. There is simply no indication whatever that heads of large families, as opposed to heads of small families, are particularly prone to refuse to seek or to maintain employment.

The State has presented other arguments to support the regulation. However, they are not dealt with specifically by the Court, and the reason is not difficult to discern. The Court has picked the strongest available; the others suffer from similar and greater defects. Moreover, it is relevant to note that both Congress and the State have adopted other measures that deal specifically with exactly those interests the State contends are advanced by the maximum grant regulation. Thus, for example, employable AFDC recipients are required to seek employment through the congressionally established Work Incentive Program which provides an elaborate system of counseling, training, and incentive payments for heads of AFDC families. The existence of these alternatives does not, of course, conclusively establish the invalidity of the maximum grant regulation. It is certainly relevant, however, in appraising the overall interest of the State in the maintenance of the regulation.

In the final analysis, Maryland has set up an AFDC program structured to calculate and pay the minimum standard of need to dependent children. Having set up that program, however, the State denies some of those needy children the minimum subsistence standard of living, and it does so on the wholly arbitrary basis that they happen to be members of large families. One need not speculate too far on the actual reason for the regulation, for in the early stages of this litigation the State virtually conceded that it set out to limit the total cost of the program along the path of least resistance. Now, however, we are told that other rationales can be manufactured to support the regulation and to sustain it against a fundamental constitutional challenge.

However, these asserted state interests, which are not insignificant in themselves, are advanced either not at all or by complete accident by the maximum grant regulation. Clearly they could be served by measures far less destructive of the individual interests at stake. Moreover, the device assertedly chosen to further them is at one and the same time both grossly underinclusive—because it does not apply at all to a much larger class in an equal position—and grossly overinclusive—because it applies so strongly against a substantial class as to which it can rationally serve no end. Were this a case of pure business regulation, these defects would place it beyond what has heretofore seemed a borderline case, and I do not believe that the regulation can be sustained even under the Court's "reasonableness" test.

In any event, it cannot suffice merely to invoke the spectre of the past and to recite from *Lindsley v. Natural Carbonic Gas Co.* and *Williamson v. Lee Optical Co.* to decide the case. Appellees are not a gas company or an optical dispenser; they are needy dependent children and families who are discriminated against by the State. The basis of that discrimination—the classification of individuals into large and small families—is too arbitrary and too unconnected to the asserted rationale, the impact on those discriminated against—the denial of even a subsistence existence—too great, and the supposed interests served too contrived and attenuated to meet the requirements of the Constitution. In my view Maryland's maximum grant regulation is invalid under the Equal Protection Clause of the Fourteenth Amendment.

I would affirm the judgment of the District Court.

44. *San Antonio Independent School District v. Rodriguez* (1973)

Two strands of law revision converged in the following case. Doctrinally, the case ended the development of the "fundamental interest" branch of equal protection law. Justice Powell's opinion for the Court held that the Equal Protection Clause required strict scrutiny only when interests explicitly or implicitly protected by the Constitution were involved. The case also represented the temporary defeat of litigation efforts to equalize school financing. Like many states, Texas used a combination of financing based on local property taxes and financing based on state grants to support local education, although (as Justice Marshall's opinion indicates) the degree to which there really was local control over educational finances was a matter of dispute. The case was a challenge to the use of property-tax financing, on the ground that it produced substantial differences in expenditures per student, depending solely on the amount of taxable property in the district. Although here, too, the facts were controverted, the litigants relied on the proposition that suburbs with large numbers of expensive homes were able to raise large amounts for their schools without imposing high tax rates, while cities with industrial plants or vacant space were unable to impose taxes at rates high enough to match the suburban districts. The state grants reduced the disparities, but they remained substantial—the least affluent district in Texas spent $248 per pupil while the most affluent spent $558.

Justice Powell's opinion for the Court held that the system of property-tax financing did not unconstitutionally discriminate against the poor, in part because the differences resulted not from the wealth of individuals but from the amount of taxable property in the districts and in part because the system did not absolutely deprive poor people of education. The Court also held that the connection between education and the right to vote was insufficient to make education a "fundamental interest" for equal protection purposes. Justice Powell, who had served as a member of the Richmond city and Virginia state boards of education, stressed the importance of judicial restraint in an area of important educational policy. He argued that states should be allowed to choose among a variety of financing systems to promote local control of education if they so desired. And, for him, local control meant, in part, control over the amount spent on education.

Justice Marshall's dissenting opinion restated and elaborated upon his "sliding scale" approach to equal protection law, and applied it to the facts of the case.

MR. JUSTICE MARSHALL, WITH WHOM MR. JUSTICE DOUGLAS CONCURS, DISSENTING.

The Court today decides, in effect, that a State may constitutionally vary the quality of education which it offers its children in accordance with the amount of taxable wealth located in the school districts within which they reside. The majority's decision represents an abrupt departure from the mainstream of recent state and federal court decisions concerning the unconstitutionality of state educational financing schemes dependent upon taxable local wealth. More unfortunately, though, the majority's holding can only be seen as a retreat from our historic commitment to equality of educational opportunity and as unsupportable acquiescence in a system which deprives children in their earliest years of the chance to reach their full potential as citizens. The Court does this despite the absence of any substantial justification for a scheme which arbitrarily channels educational resources in accordance with the fortuity of the amount of taxable wealth within each district.

In my judgment, the right of every American to an equal start in life, so far as the provision of a state service as important as education is concerned, is far too vital to permit state discrimination on grounds as tenuous as those presented by this record. Nor can I accept the notion that it is sufficient to remit these appellees to the vagaries of the political process which, contrary to the majority's suggestion, has proved singularly unsuited to the task of providing a remedy for this discrimination. I, for one, am unsatisfied with the hope of an ultimate "political" solution sometime in the indefinite future while, in the meantime, countless children unjustifiably receive inferior educations that "may affect their hearts and minds in a way unlikely ever to be undone." *Brown v. Board of Education* (1954). I must therefore respectfully dissent.

I

The Court acknowledges that "substantial interdistrict disparities in school expenditures" exist in Texas, and that these disparities are "largely attributable to differences in the amounts of money collected through local property taxation." But instead of closely examining the seriousness of these disparities and the invidiousness of the Texas financing scheme, the Court undertakes an elaborate exploration of the efforts Texas has purportedly made to close the gaps between its districts in terms of levels of district wealth and resulting educational funding. Yet, however praiseworthy Texas' equalizing efforts, the issue in this case is not whether Texas is doing its best to ameliorate the worst features of a discriminatory scheme but, rather, whether the scheme itself is in fact unconstitutionally discriminatory in the face of the Fourteenth Amendment's guarantee of equal protection of the laws. When the Texas financing scheme is taken as a whole, I do not think it can be doubted that it produces a discriminatory impact on substantial numbers of the school age children of the State of Texas. . . .

B

The appellants do not deny the disparities in educational funding caused by variations in taxable district property wealth. They do contend, however, that whatever the differences in per-pupil spending among Texas districts, there are no discriminatory consequences for the children of the disadvantaged districts. They recognize that what is at stake in this case is the quality of the public education provided Texas children in the districts in which they live. But appellants reject the suggestion that the quality of education in any particular district is determined by money—beyond some minimal level of funding which they believe to be assured every Texas district by the Minimum Foundation School Program. In their view, there is simply no denial of equal educational opportunity to any Texas schoolchildren as a result of the widely varying per-pupil spending power provided districts under the current financing scheme.

In my view, though, even an unadorned restatement of this contention is sufficient to reveal its absurdity. Authorities concerned with educational quality no doubt disagree as to the significance of variations in per-pupil spending. Indeed, conflicting expert testimony was presented to the District Court in this case concerning the effect of spending variations on educational achievement. We sit, however, not to resolve disputes over educational theory but to enforce our Constitution. It is an inescapable fact that if one district has more funds available per pupil than another district, the former will have greater choice in educational planning than will the latter. In this regard, I believe the question of discrimination in educational quality must be deemed to be an objective one that looks to what the State provides its children, not to what the children are able to do with what they receive. That a child forced to attend an underfunded school with poorer physical facilities, less experienced teachers, larger classes, and a narrower range of courses than a school with substantially more funds—and thus with greater choice in educational planning—may nevertheless excel is to the credit of the child, not the State. Indeed, who can ever measure for such a child the opportunities lost and the talents wasted for want of a broader, more enriched education? Discrimination in the opportunity to learn that is afforded a child must be our standard.

Hence, even before this Court recognized its duty to tear down the barriers of state-enforced racial segregation in public education, it acknowledged that inequality in the educational facilities provided to students may be discriminatory state action as contemplated by the Equal Protection Clause. As a basis for striking down state-enforced segregation of a law school, the Court in *Sweatt v. Painter* stated:

> "[W]e cannot find substantial equality in the educational opportunities offered white and Negro law students by the State. In terms of number of the faculty, variety of courses and opportunity for specialization, size of the student body, scope of the library, availability of law review and similar activities, the [whites-only] Law School is superior. . . . It is difficult to believe that one who had a free choice between these law schools would consider the question close."

Likewise, it is difficult to believe that if the children of Texas had a free choice, they would choose to be educated in districts with fewer resources, and hence with more antiquated plants, less experienced teachers, and a less diversified curriculum. In fact, if financing variations are so insignificant to educational quality, it is difficult to understand why a number of our country's wealthiest school districts, which have no legal obligation to argue in support of the constitutionality of the Texas legislation, have nevertheless zealously pursued its cause before this Court.

The consequences, in terms of objective educational input, of the variations in district funding caused by the Texas financing scheme are apparent from the data introduced before the District Court. For example, in 1968–1969, 100% of the teachers in the property-rich Alamo Heights School District had college degrees. By contrast, during the same school year only 80.02% of the teachers had college degrees in the property poor Edgewood Independent School District. Also, in 1968–1969, approximately 47% of the teachers in the Edgewood District were on emergency teaching permits, whereas only 11% of the teachers in Alamo Heights were on such permits. This is undoubtedly a reflection of the fact that the top of Edgewood's teacher salary scale was approximately 80% of Alamo Heights'. And, not surprisingly, the teacher-student ratio varies significantly between the two districts. In other words, as might be expected, a difference in the funds available to districts results in a difference in educational inputs available for a child's public education in Texas. For constitutional purposes, I believe this situation, which is directly attributable to the Texas financing scheme, raises a grave question of state-created discrimination in the provision of public education.

At the very least, in view of the substantial interdistrict disparities in funding and in resulting educational inputs shown by appellees to exist under the Texas financing scheme, the burden of proving that these disparities do not in fact affect the quality of children's education must fall upon the appellants. Yet appellants made no effort in the District Court to demonstrate that educational quality is not affected by variations in funding and in resulting inputs. And, in this Court, they have argued no more than that the relationship is ambiguous. This is hardly sufficient to overcome appellees' prima facie showing of state-created discrimination between the school children of Texas with respect to objective educational opportunity. . . .

Alternatively, the appellants and the majority may believe that the Equal Protection Clause cannot be offended by substantially unequal state treatment of persons who are similarly situated so long as the State provides everyone with some unspecified amount of education which evidently is "enough." The basis for such a novel view is far from clear. It is, of course, true that the Constitution does not require precise equality in the treatment of all persons. As Mr. Justice Frankfurter explained:

> "The equality at which the 'equal protection' clause aims is not a disembodied equality. The Fourteenth Amendment enjoins 'the equal protection of the laws,' and laws are not abstract propositions. . . . The Constitution does not require things which are different in fact or opinion to be treated in law as though they were the same."

But this Court has never suggested that because some "adequate" level of benefits is provided to all, discrimination in the provision of services is therefore constitutionally excusable. The Equal Protection Clause is not addressed to the minimal sufficiency but rather to the unjustifiable inequalities of state action. It mandates nothing less than that "all persons similarly circumstanced shall be treated alike."

Even if the Equal Protection Clause encompassed some theory of constitutional adequacy, discrimination in the provision of educational opportunity would certainly seem to be a poor candidate for its application. Neither the majority nor appellants inform us how judicially manageable standards are to be derived for determining how much education is "enough" to excuse constitutional discrimination. One would think that the majority would heed its own fervent affirmation of judicial self-restraint before undertaking the complex task of determining at large what level of education is constitutionally sufficient. Indeed, the majority's apparent reliance upon the adequacy of the educational opportunity assured by the Texas Minimum Foundation School Program seems fundamentally inconsistent with its own recognition that educational authorities are unable to agree upon what makes for educational quality. If, as the majority stresses, such authorities are uncertain as to the impact of various levels of funding on educational quality, I fail to see where it finds the expertise to divine that the particular levels of funding provided by the Program assure an adequate educational opportunity—much less an education substantially equivalent in quality to that which a higher level of funding might provide. Certainly appellants' mere assertion before this Court of the adequacy of the education guaranteed by the Minimum Foundation School Program cannot obscure the constitutional implications of the discrimination in educational funding and objective educational inputs resulting from the local property tax—particularly since the appellees offered substantial uncontroverted evidence before the District Court impugning the now much touted "adequacy" of the education guaranteed by the Foundation Program.

In my view, then, it is inequality—not some notion of gross inadequacy—of educational opportunity that raises a question of denial of equal protection of the laws. I find any other approach to the issue unintelligible and without directing principle. Here, appellees have made a substantial showing of wide variations in educational funding and the resulting educational opportunity afforded to the school children of Texas. This discrimination is, in large measure, attributable to significant disparities in the taxable wealth of local Texas school districts. This is a sufficient showing to raise a substantial question of discriminatory state action in violation of the Equal Protection Clause.

C

Despite the evident discriminatory effect of the Texas financing scheme, both the appellants and the majority raise substantial questions concerning the precise character of the disadvantaged class in this case. The District Court concluded that the Texas financing scheme draws "distinction between groups of citizens depending upon the wealth of the district in which they live" and thus creates a disadvantaged class composed of persons living in property-poor districts. In light of the data introduced before the District Court, the conclusion that the schoolchildren of property-poor districts constitute a sufficient class for our purposes seems indisputable to me.

Appellants contend, however, that in constitutional terms this case involves nothing more than discrimination against local school districts, not against individuals, since on its face the state scheme is concerned only with the provision of funds to local districts. The result of the Texas financing scheme, appellants suggest, is merely that some local districts have more available revenues for education; others have less. In that respect, they point out, the States have broad discretion in drawing reasonable distinctions between their political subdivisions.

But this Court has consistently recognized that where there is in fact discrimination against individual interests, the constitutional guarantee of equal protection of the laws is not inapplicable simply because the discrimination is based upon some group characteristic such as geographic location. Texas has chosen to provide free public education for all its citizens, and it has embodied that decision in its constitution. Yet, having established public education for its citizens, the State, as a direct consequence of the variations in local property wealth endemic to Texas' financing scheme, has provided some Texas schoolchildren with substantially less resources for their education than others. Thus, while on its face the Texas scheme may merely discriminate between local districts, the impact of that discrimination falls directly upon the children whose educational opportunity is dependent upon where they happen to live. Consequently, the District Court correctly concluded that the Texas financing scheme discriminates, from a constitutional perspective, between schoolchildren on the basis of the amount of taxable property located within their local districts. . . .

I believe it is sufficient that the overarching form of discrimination in this case is between the schoolchildren of Texas on the basis of the taxable property wealth of the districts in which they happen to live. To understand both the precise nature of this discrimination and the parameters of the disadvantaged class it is sufficient to consider the constitutional principle which appellees contend is controlling in the context of educational financing. In their complaint appellees asserted that the Constitution does not permit local district wealth to be determinative of educational opportunity. This is simply another way of saying, as the District Court concluded, that consistent with the guarantee of equal protection of the laws, "the quality of public education may not be a function of wealth, other than the wealth of the state as a whole." Under such a principle, the children of a district are excessively advantaged if that district has more taxable property per pupil than the average amount of taxable property per pupil considering the State as a whole. By contrast, the children of a district are disadvantaged if that district has less taxable property per pupil than the state average. The majority attempts to disparage such a definition of the disadvantaged class as the product of an "artificially defined level" of district wealth. But such is clearly not the case, for this is the definition unmistakably dictated by the constitutional principle for which appellees have argued throughout the course of this litigation. And I do not believe that a clearer definition of either the disadvantaged class of Texas school-children or the allegedly unconstitutional discrimination suffered by the members of that class under the present Texas financing scheme could be asked for, much less need-ed. Whether this discrimination, against the schoolchildren of property-poor districts, inherent in the Texas financing scheme, is violative of the Equal Protection Clause is the question to which we must now turn.

II

To avoid having the Texas financing scheme struck down because of the inter-district variations in taxable property wealth, the District Court determined that it was insufficient for appellants to show merely that the State's scheme was rationally related to some legitimate state purpose; rather, the discrimination inherent in the scheme had to be shown necessary to promote a "compelling state interest" in order to withstand constitutional scrutiny. The basis for this determination was twofold: first, the financing scheme divides citizens on a wealth basis, a classification which the District Court viewed as highly suspect; and second, the discriminatory scheme directly affects what it considered to be a "fundamental interest," namely, education.

This Court has repeatedly held that state discrimination which either adversely affects a "fundamental interest," or is based on a distinction of a suspect character, must be carefully scrutinized to ensure that the scheme is necessary to promote a substantial, legitimate state interest. The majority today concludes, however, that the Texas scheme is not subject to such a strict standard of review under the Equal Protection Clause. Instead, in its view, the Texas scheme must be tested by noth-ing more than that lenient standard of rationality which we have traditionally applied to discriminatory state action in the context of economic and commercial matters. By so doing, the Court avoids the telling task of searching for a substantial state inter-est which the Texas financing scheme, with its variations in taxable district prop-erty wealth, is necessary to further. I cannot accept such an emasculation of the Equal Protection Clause in the context of this case.

A

To begin, I must once more voice my disagreement with the Court's rigidified approach to equal protection analysis. The Court apparently seeks to establish today that equal protection cases fall into one of two neat categories which dictate the appropriate standard of review—strict scrutiny or mere rationality. But this Court's decisions in the field of equal protection defy such easy categorization. A princi-pled reading of what this Court has done reveals that it has applied a spectrum of stan-dards in reviewing discrimination allegedly violative of the Equal Protection Clause. This spectrum clearly comprehends variations in the degree of care with which the

Court will scrutinize particular classifications, depending, I believe, on the constitutional and societal importance of the interest adversely affected and the recognized invidiousness of the basis upon which the particular classification is drawn. I find in fact that many of the Court's recent decisions embody the very sort of reasoned approach to equal protection analysis for which I previously argued—that is, an approach in which "concentration [is] placed upon the character of the classification in question, the relative importance to individuals in the class discriminated against of the governmental benefits that they do not receive, and the asserted state interests in support of the classification." *Dandridge v. Williams.*

I therefore cannot accept the majority's labored efforts to demonstrate that fundamental interests, which call for strict scrutiny of the challenged classification, encompass only established rights which we are somehow bound to recognize from the text of the Constitution itself. To be sure, some interests which the Court has deemed to be fundamental for purposes of equal protection analysis are themselves constitutionally protected rights. Thus, discrimination against the guaranteed right of freedom of speech has called for strict judicial scrutiny. See *Police Dept. of Chicago v. Mosley.* Further, every citizen's right to travel interstate, although nowhere expressly mentioned in the Constitution, has long been recognized as implicit in the premises underlying that document: the right "was conceived from the beginning to be a necessary concomitant of the stronger Union the Constitution created." Consequently, the Court has required that a state classification affecting the constitutionally protected right to travel must be "shown to be necessary to promote a *compelling* governmental interest." But it will not do to suggest that the "answer" to whether an interest is fundamental for purposes of equal protection analysis is *always* determined by whether that interest "is a right . . . explicitly or implicitly guaranteed by the Constitution."

I would like to know where the Constitution guarantees the right to procreate, *Skinner v. Oklahoma* (1942), or the right to vote in state elections, or the right to an appeal from a criminal conviction. These are instances in which, due to the importance of the interests at stake, the Court has displayed a strong concern with the existence of discriminatory state treatment. But the Court has never said or indicated that these are interests which independently enjoy full-blown constitutional protection. . . .

The majority is, of course, correct when it suggests that the process of determining which interests are fundamental is a difficult one. But I do not think the problem is insurmountable. And I certainly do not accept the view that the process need necessarily degenerate into an unprincipled, subjective "picking-and-choosing" between various interests or that it must involve this Court in creating "substantive constitutional rights in the name of guaranteeing equal protection of the laws." Although not all fundamental interests are constitutionally guaranteed, the determination of which interests are fundamental should be firmly rooted in the text of the

Constitution. The task in every case should be to determine the extent to which constitutionally guaranteed rights are dependent on interests not mentioned in the Constitution. As the nexus between the specific constitutional guarantee and the nonconstitutional interest draws closer, the nonconstitutional interest becomes more fundamental and the degree of judicial scrutiny applied when the interest is infringed on a discriminatory basis must be adjusted accordingly. Thus, it cannot be denied that interests such as procreation, the exercise of the state franchise, and access to criminal appellate processes are not fully guaranteed to the citizen by our Constitution. But these interests have nonetheless been afforded special judicial consideration in the face of discrimination because they are, to some extent, interrelated with constitutional guarantees. Procreation is now understood to be important because of its interaction with the established constitutional right of privacy . . .

A similar process of analysis with respect to the invidiousness of the basis on which a particular classification is drawn has also influenced the Court as to the appropriate degree of scrutiny to be accorded any particular case. The highly suspect character of classifications based on race, nationality, or alienage is well established. The reasons why such classifications call for close judicial scrutiny are manifold. Certain racial and ethnic groups have frequently been recognized as "discrete and insular minorities" who are relatively powerless to protect their interests in the political process. Moreover, race, nationality, or alienage is "'in most circumstances irrelevant' to any constitutionally acceptable legislative purpose." Instead, lines drawn on such bases are frequently the reflection of historic prejudices rather than legislative rationality. It may be that all of these considerations, which make for particular judicial solicitude in the face of discrimination on the basis of race, nationality, or alienage, do not coalesce—or at least not to the same degree—in other forms of discrimination. Nevertheless, these considerations have undoubtedly influenced the care with which the Court has scrutinized other forms of discrimination.

In *James v. Strange* (1972), the Court held unconstitutional a state statute which provided for recoupment from indigent convicts of legal defense fees paid by the State. The Court found that the statute impermissibly differentiated between indigent criminals in debt to the State and civil judgment debtors, since criminal debtors were denied various protective exemptions afforded civil judgment debtors. The Court suggested that in reviewing the statute under the Equal Protection Clause, it was merely applying the traditional requirement that there be "'some rationality'" in the line drawn between the different types of debtors. Yet it then proceeded to scrutinize the statute with less than traditional deference and restraint. Thus, the Court recognized "that state recoupment statutes may betoken legitimate state interests" in recovering expenses and discouraging fraud. Nevertheless, MR. JUSTICE POWELL, speaking for the Court, concluded that

> "these interests are not thwarted by requiring more even treatment of indigent criminal defendants with other classes of debtors to whom the statute

itself repeatedly makes reference. State recoupment laws, notwithstanding the state interests they may serve, need not blight in such discriminatory fashion the hopes of indigents for self-sufficiency and self-respect."

The Court, in short, clearly did not consider the problems of fraud and collection that the state legislature might have concluded were peculiar to indigent criminal defendants to be either sufficiently important or at least sufficiently substantiated to justify denial of the protective exemptions afforded to all civil judgment debtors, to a class composed exclusively of indigent criminal debtors.

Similarly, in *Reed v. Reed* (1971), the Court, in striking down a state statute which gave men preference over women when persons of equal entitlement apply for assignment as an administrator of a particular estate, resorted to a more stringent standard of equal protection review than that employed in cases involving commercial matters. The Court indicated that it was testing the claim of sex discrimination by nothing more than whether the line drawn bore "a rational relationship to a state objective," which it recognized as a legitimate effort to reduce the work of probate courts in choosing between competing applications for letters of administration. Accepting such a purpose, the Idaho Supreme Court had thought the classification to be sustainable on the basis that the legislature might have reasonably concluded that, as a rule, men have more experience than women in business matters relevant to the administration of estate. This Court, however, concluded that "[t]o give a mandatory preference to members of either sex over members of the other, merely to accomplish the elimination of hearings on the merits, is to make the very kind of arbitrary legislative choice forbidden by the Equal Protection Clause of the Fourteenth Amendment . . . " This Court, in other words, was unwilling to consider a theoretical and unsubstantiated basis for distinction—however reasonable it might appear—sufficient to sustain a statute discriminating on the basis of sex.

James and *Reed* can only be understood as instances in which the particularly invidious character of the classification caused the Court to pause and scrutinize with more than traditional care the rationality of state discrimination. Discrimination on the basis of past criminality and on the basis of sex posed for the Court the specter of forms of discrimination which it implicitly recognized to have deep social and legal roots without necessarily having any basis in actual differences. . . .

In summary, it seems to me inescapably clear that this Court has consistently adjusted the care with which it will review state discrimination in light of the constitutional significance of the interests affected and the invidiousness of the particular classification. In the context of economic interests, we find that discriminatory state action is almost always sustained, for such interests are generally far removed from constitutional guarantees. Moreover, "[t]he extremes to which the Court has gone in dreaming up rational bases for state regulation in that area may in many instances be ascribed to a healthy revulsion from the Court's earlier excesses in using the Constitution to protect interests that have more than enough power to protect themselves in the legislative halls." *Dandridge v. Williams* (dissenting opinion). But the situation differs markedly when discrimination against important individual interests with constitutional implications and against particularly disadvantaged or powerless classes is involved. The majority suggests, however, that a variable standard of review would give this Court the appearance of a "superlegislature." I cannot agree. Such an approach seems to me a part of the guarantees of our Constitution and of the historic experiences with oppression of and discrimination against discrete, powerless minorities which underlie that document. In truth, the Court itself will be open to the criticism raised by the majority so long as it continues on its present course of effectively selecting in private which cases will be afforded special consideration without acknowledging the true basis of its action. Opinions such as those in *Reed* and *James* seem drawn more as efforts to shield rather than to reveal the true basis of the Court's decisions. Such obfuscated action may be appropriate to a political body such as a legislature, but it is not appropriate to this Court. Open debate of the bases for the Court's action is essential to the rationality and consistency of our decisionmaking process. Only in this way can we avoid the label of legislature and ensure the integrity of the judicial process.

Nevertheless, the majority today attempts to force this case into the same category for purposes of equal protection analysis as decisions involving discrimination affecting commercial interests. By so doing, the majority singles this case out for analytic treatment at odds with what seems to me to be the clear trend of recent decisions in this Court, and thereby ignores the constitutional importance of the interest at stake and the invidiousness of the particular classification, factors that call for far more than the lenient scrutiny of the Texas financing scheme which the majority pursues. Yet if the discrimination inherent in the Texas scheme is scrutinized with the care demanded by the interest and classification present in this case, the unconstitutionality of that scheme is unmistakable.

B

Since the Court now suggests that only interests guaranteed by the Constitution are fundamental for purposes of equal protection analysis, and since it rejects the contention that public education is fundamental, it follows that the Court concludes that public education is not constitutionally guaranteed. It is true that this Court has never deemed the provision of free public education to be required by the Constitution. Indeed, it has on occasion suggested that state-supported education is a privilege bestowed by a State on its citizens. Nevertheless, the fundamental importance of education is amply indicated by the prior decisions of this Court, by the unique status accorded public education by our society, and by the close relationship between education and some of our most basic constitutional values.

The special concern of this Court with the educational process of our country is a matter of common knowledge. Undoubtedly, this Court's most famous statement on the subject is that contained in *Brown v. Board of Education:*

"Today, education is perhaps the most important function of state and local governments. Compulsory school attendance laws and the great expenditures for education both demonstrate our recognition of the importance of education to our democratic society. It is required in the performance of our most basic public responsibilities, even service in the armed forces. It is the very foundation of good citizenship. Today it is a principal instrument in awakening the child to cultural values, in preparing him for later professional training, and in helping him to adjust normally to his environment. . . ."

Only last Term, the Court recognized that "[p]roviding public schools ranks at the very apex of the function of a State." This is clearly borne out by the fact that in 48 of our 50 States the provision of public education is mandated by the state constitution. No other state function is so uniformly recognized as an essential element of our society's well-being. In large measure, the explanation for the special importance attached to education must rest . . . on the facts that "some degree of education is necessary to prepare citizens to participate effectively and intelligently in our open political system . . .," and that "education prepares individuals to be self-reliant and self-sufficient participants in society." Both facets of this observation are suggestive of the substantial relationship which education bears to guarantees of our Constitution.

Education directly affects the ability of a child to exercise his First Amendment rights, both as a source and as a receiver of information and ideas, whatever interests he may pursue in life. This Court's decision in *Sweezy v. New Hampshire* (1957), speaks of the right of students "to inquire, to study and to evaluate, to gain new maturity and understanding . . . " Thus, we have not casually described the classroom as the "'marketplace of ideas.'" The opportunity for formal education may not necessarily be the essential determinant of an individual's ability to enjoy throughout his life the rights of free speech and association guaranteed to him by the First Amendment. But such an opportunity may enhance the individual's enjoyment of those rights, not only during but also following school attendance. Thus, in the final analysis, "the pivotal position of education to success in American society and its essential role in opening up to the individual the central experiences of our culture lend it an importance that is undeniable."

Of particular importance is the relationship between education and the political process. "Americans regard the public schools as a most vital civic institution for the preservation of a democratic system of government." Education serves the essential function of instilling in our young an understanding of and appreciation for the principles and operation of our governmental processes. Education may instill the interest and provide the tools necessary for political discourse and debate. Indeed, it has frequently been suggested that education is the dominant factor affecting political consciousness and participation. A system of "[c]ompetition in ideas and governmental policies is at the core of our electoral process and of the First Amendment freedoms." But of most immediate and direct concern must be the demonstrated effect of education on the exercise of the franchise by the electorate. The right to vote in federal elections is conferred by Art. I, §2, and the Seventeenth Amendment of the Constitution, and access to the state franchise has been afforded special protection because it is "preservative of other basic civil and political rights." Data from the Presidential Election of 1968 clearly demonstrate a direct relationship between participation in the electoral process and level of educational attainment; and, as this Court recognized in *Gaston County v. United States* (1969), the quality of education offered may influence a child's decision to "enter or remain in school." It is this very sort of intimate relationship between a particular personal interest and specific constitutional guarantees that has heretofore caused the Court to attach special significance, for purposes of equal protection analysis, to individual interests such as procreation and the exercise of the state franchise.

While ultimately disputing little of this, the majority seeks refuge in the fact that the Court has "never presumed to possess either the ability or the authority to guarantee to the citizenry the most *effective* speech or the most *informed* electoral choice." This serves only to blur what is in fact at stake. With due respect, the issue is neither provision of the most *effective* speech nor of the most *informed* vote. Appellees do not now seek the best education Texas might provide. They do seek, however, an end to state discrimination resulting from the unequal distribution of taxable district property wealth that directly impairs the ability of some districts to provide the same educational opportunity that other districts can provide with the same or even substantially less tax effort. The issue is, in other words, one of discrimination that affects the quality of the education which Texas has chosen to provide its children; and, the precise question here is what importance should attach to education for purposes of equal protection analysis of that discrimination. As this Court held in *Brown v. Board of Education*, the opportunity of education, "where the state has undertaken to provide it, is a right which must be made available to all on equal terms." The factors just considered, including the relationship between education and the social and political interests enshrined within the Constitution, compel us to recognize the fundamentality of education and to scrutinize with appropriate care the bases for state discrimination affecting equality of educational opportunity in Texas' school districts—a conclusion which is only strengthened when we consider the character of the classification in this case.

C

The District Court found that in discriminating between Texas schoolchildren on the basis of the amount of taxable property wealth located in the district in which they live, the Texas financing scheme created a form of wealth discrimination. This Court has frequently recognized that discrimination on the basis of wealth may create a classification of a suspect character and thereby call for exacting judicial scrutiny. The majority, however, considers any wealth classification in this case to lack certain essential characteristics which it contends are common to the instances of wealth discrimination that this Court has heretofore recognized. We are told that in every prior case involving a wealth classification, the members of the disadvantaged class have "shared two distinguishing characteristics: because of their impecunity they were completely unable to pay for some desired benefit, and as a consequence, they sustained an absolute deprivation of a meaningful opportunity to enjoy that benefit." I cannot agree. . . .

This is not to say that the form of wealth classification in this case does not differ significantly from those recognized in the previous decisions of this Court. Our prior cases have dealt essentially with discrimination on the basis of personal wealth. Here, by contrast, the children of the disadvantaged Texas school districts are being discriminated against not necessarily because of their personal wealth or the wealth of their families, but because of the taxable property wealth of the residents of the district in which they happen to live. The appropriate question, then, is whether the same degree of judicial solicitude and scrutiny that has previously been afforded wealth classifications is warranted here.

As the Court points out, no previous decision has deemed the presence of just a wealth classification to be sufficient basis to call forth rigorous judicial scrutiny of allegedly discriminatory state action. That wealth classifications alone have not necessarily been considered to bear the same high degree of suspectness as have classifications based on, for instance, race or alienage may be explainable on a number of grounds. The "poor" may not be seen as politically powerless as certain discrete and insular minority groups. Personal poverty may entail much the same social stigma as historically attached to certain racial or ethnic groups. But personal poverty is not a permanent disability; its shackles may be escaped. Perhaps most importantly, though, personal wealth may not necessarily share the general irrelevance as a basis for legislative action that race or nationality is recognized to have. While the "poor" have frequently been a legally disadvantaged group, it cannot be ignored that social legislation must frequently take cognizance of the economic status of our citizens. Thus, we have generally gauged the invidiousness of wealth classifications with an awareness of the importance of the interests being affected and the relevance of personal wealth to those interests.

When evaluated with these considerations in mind, it seems to me that discrimination on the basis of group wealth in this case likewise calls for careful judicial scrutiny. First, it must be recognized that while local district wealth may serve other interests, it bears no relationship whatsoever to the interest of Texas school children in the educational opportunity afforded them by the State of Texas. Given the importance of that interest, we must be particularly sensitive to the invidious characteristics of any form of discrimination that is not clearly intended to serve it, as opposed to some other distinct state interest. Discrimination on the basis of group wealth may not, to be sure, reflect the social stigma frequently attached to personal poverty. Nevertheless, insofar as group wealth discrimination involves wealth over which the disadvantaged individual has no significant control, it represents in fact a more serious basis of discrimination than does personal wealth. For such discrimination is no reflection of the individual's characteristics or his abilities. And thus—particularly in the context of a disadvantaged class composed of children—we have previously treated discrimination on a basis which the individual cannot control as constitutionally disfavored.

The disability of the disadvantaged class in this case extends as well into the political processes upon which we ordinarily rely as adequate for the protection and promotion of all interests. Here legislative reallocation of the State's property wealth must be sought in the face of inevitable opposition from significantly advantaged districts that have a strong vested interest in the preservation of the status quo, a problem not completely dissimilar to that faced by underrepresented districts prior to the Court's intervention in the process of reapportionment.

Nor can we ignore the extent to which, in contrast to our prior decisions, the State is responsible for the wealth discrimination in this instance. . . . [Our] prior cases have dealt with discrimination on the basis of indigency which was attributable to the operation of the private sector. But we have no such simple *de facto* wealth discrimination here. The means for financing public education in Texas are selected and specified by the State. It is the State that has created local school districts, and tied educational funding to the local property tax and thereby to local district wealth. At the same time, governmentally imposed land use controls have undoubtedly encouraged and rigidified natural trends in the allocation of particular areas for residential or commercial use, and thus determined each district's amount of taxable property wealth. In short, this case, in contrast to the Court's previous wealth discrimination decisions, can only be seen as "unusual in the extent to which governmental action *is* the cause of the wealth classifications."

In the final analysis, then, the invidious characteristics of the group wealth classification present in this case merely serve to emphasize the need for careful judicial scrutiny of the State's justifications for the resulting interdistrict discrimination in the educational opportunity afforded to the schoolchildren of Texas.

D

The nature of our inquiry into the justifications for state discrimination is essentially the same in all equal protection cases: We must consider the substantiality of the state interests sought to be served, and we must scrutinize the reasonableness of the means by which the State has sought to advance its interests. Differences in the application of this test are, in my view, a function of the constitutional importance of the interests at stake and the invidiousness of the particular classification. In terms of the asserted state interests, the Court has indicated that it will require, for instance, a "compelling," or a "substantial" or "important," state interest to justify discrimination affecting individual interests of constitutional significance. Whatever the differences, if any, in these descriptions of the character of the state interest necessary to sustain such discrimination, basic to each is, I believe, a concern with the legitimacy and the reality of the asserted state interests. Thus, when interests of constitutional importance are at stake, the Court does not stand ready to credit the State's classification with any conceivable legitimate purpose, but demands a clear showing that there are legitimate state interests which the classification was in fact intended to serve. Beyond the question of the adequacy of the State's purpose for the classification, the Court traditionally has become increasingly sensitive to the means by which a State chooses to act as its action affects more directly interests of constitutional significance. Thus, by now, "less restrictive alternatives" analysis is firmly established in equal protection jurisprudence. It seems to me that the range of choice we are willing to accord the State in selecting the means by which it will act, and the care with which we scrutinize the effectiveness of the means which the State selects, also must reflect the constitutional importance of the interest affected and the invidiousness of the particular classification. Here, both the nature of the interest and the classification dictate close judicial scrutiny of the purposes which Texas seeks to serve with its present educational financing scheme and of the means it has selected to serve that purpose.

The only justification offered by appellants to sustain the discrimination in educational opportunity caused by the Texas financing scheme is local educational control. Presented with this justification, the District Court concluded that "[n]ot only are defendants unable to demonstrate compelling state interests for their classifications based upon wealth, they fail even to establish a reasonable basis for these classifications." I must agree with this conclusion.

At the outset, I do not question that local control of public education, as an abstract matter, constitutes a very substantial state interest. We observed only last Term that "[d]irect control over decisions vitally affecting the education of one's children is a need that is strongly felt in our society." The State's interest in local educational control—which certainly includes questions of educational funding—has deep roots in the inherent benefits of community support for public education. Consequently, true state dedication to local control would present, I think, a substantial justification to weigh against simply interdistrict variations in the treatment of a State's schoolchildren. But I need not now decide how I might ultimately strike the balance were we confronted with a situation where the State's sincere concern for local control inevitably produced educational inequality. For, on this record, it is apparent that the State's purported concern with local control is offered primarily as an excuse rather than as a justification for interdistrict inequality.

In Texas, statewide laws regulate in fact the most minute details of local public education. For example, the State prescribes required courses. All textbooks must be submitted for state approval, and only approved textbooks may be used. The State has established the qualifications necessary for teaching in Texas public schools and the procedures for obtaining certification. The State has even legislated on the length of the school day. Texas' own courts have said:

"As a result of the acts of the Legislature our school system is not of mere local concern but it is statewide. While a school district is local in territorial limits, it is an integral part of the vast school system which is coextensive with the confines of the State of Texas."

Moreover, even if we accept Texas' general dedication to local control in educational matters, it is difficult to find any evidence of such dedication with respect to fiscal matters. It ignores reality to suggest—as the Court does—that the local property tax element of the Texas financing scheme reflects a conscious legislative effort to provide school districts with local fiscal control. If Texas had a system truly dedicated to local fiscal control, one would expect the quality of the educational opportunity provided in each district to vary with the decision of the voters in that district as to the level of sacrifice they wish to make for public education. In fact, the Texas scheme produces precisely the opposite result. Local school districts cannot choose to have the best education in the State by imposing the highest tax rate. Instead, the quality of the educational opportunity offered by any particular district is largely determined by the amount of taxable property located in the district—a factor over which local voters can exercise no control.

The study introduced in the District Court showed a direct inverse relationship between equalized taxable district property wealth and district tax effort with the result that the property-poor districts making the highest tax effort obtained the lowest per-pupil yield. The implications of this situation for local choice are illustrated by again comparing the Edgewood and Alamo Heights School Districts. In 1967–1968, Edgewood, after contributing its share to the Local Fund Assignment, raised only $26 per pupil through its local property tax, whereas Alamo Heights was able to raise $333 per pupil. Since the funds received through the Minimum Foundation School Program are to be used only for minimum professional salaries, transportation costs, and operating expenses, it is not hard to see the lack of local choice—with respect to higher teacher salaries to attract more and better teachers, physical facilities, library books, and facilities, special courses, or participation in special state and federal matching funds programs—under which a property-poor district such as Edgewood is forced to labor. In fact, because of the difference in taxable local property wealth, Edgewood would have to tax itself almost nine times as heavily to obtain the same yield as Alamo Heights. At present, then, local control is a myth for many of the local school districts in Texas. As one district court has observed, "rather than reposing in each school district the economic power to fix its own level of per pupil expenditure, the State has so arranged the structure as to guarantee that some districts will spend low (with high taxes) while others will spend high (with low taxes)."

In my judgment, any substantial degree of scrutiny of the operation of the Texas financing scheme reveals that the State has selected means wholly inappropriate to secure its purported interest in assuring its school districts local fiscal control. At the same time, appellees have pointed out a variety of alternative financing schemes which may serve the State's purported interest in local control as well as, if not better than, the present scheme without the current impairment of the educational opportunity of vast numbers of Texas schoolchildren. I see no need, however, to explore the practical or constitutional merits of those suggested alternatives at this time for, whatever their positive or negative features, experience with the present financing scheme impugns any suggestion that it constitutes a serious effort to provide local fiscal control. If, for the sake of local education control, this Court is to sustain interdistrict discrimination in the educational opportunity afforded Texas school children, it should require that the State present something more than the mere sham now before us.

III

In conclusion, it is essential to recognize that an end to the wide variations in taxable district property wealth inherent in the Texas financing scheme would entail none of the untoward consequences suggested by the Court or by the appellants.

First, affirmance of the District Court's decisions would hardly sound the death knell for local control of education. It would mean neither centralized decision-making nor federal court intervention in the operation of public schools. Clearly, this suit has nothing to do with local decisionmaking with respect to educational policy or even educational spending. It involves only a narrow aspect of local control— namely, local control over the raising of educational funds. In fact, in striking down interdistrict disparities in taxable local wealth, the District Court took the course which is most likely to make true local control over educational decisionmaking a reality for *all* Texas school districts.

Nor does the District Court's decision even necessarily eliminate local control of educational funding. The District Court struck down nothing more than the continued interdistrict wealth discrimination inherent in the present property tax. Both centralized and decentralized plans for educational funding not involving such interdistrict discrimination have been put forward. The choice among these or other alternatives would remain with the State, not with the federal courts. In this regard, it should be evident that the degree of federal intervention in matters of local concern would be substantially less in this context than in previous decisions in which we have been asked effectively to impose a particular scheme upon the States under the guise of the Equal Protection Clause.

Still, we are told that this case requires us "to condemn the State's judgment in conferring on political subdivisions the power to tax local property to supply revenues for local interests." Yet no one in the course of this entire litigation has ever questioned the constitutionality of the local property tax as a device for raising educational funds. The District Court's decision, at most, restricts the power of the State to make educational funding dependent exclusively upon local property taxation so long as there exists interdistrict disparities in taxable property wealth. But it hardly eliminates the local property tax as a source of educational funding or as a means of providing local fiscal control.

The Court seeks solace for its action today in the possibility of legislative reform. The Court's suggestions of legislative redress and experimentation will doubtless be of great comfort to the schoolchildren of Texas' disadvantaged districts, but considering the vested interests of wealthy school districts in the preservation of the status quo, they are worth little more. The possibility of legislative action is, in all events, no answer to this Court's duty under the Constitution to eliminate unjustified state discrimination. In this case we have been presented with an instance of such discrimination, in a particularly invidious form, against an individual interest of large constitutional and practical importance. To support the demonstrated discrimination in the provision of educational opportunity the State has offered a justification which, on analysis, takes on at best an ephemeral character. Thus, I believe that the wide disparities in taxable district property wealth inherent in the local property tax element of the Texas financing scheme render that scheme violative of the Equal Protection Clause.

I would therefore affirm the judgment of the District Court.

School finance litigation continued after *Rodriguez*. A number of state supreme courts relied on state constitutional provisions to require steps in the direction of equalization. Sometimes, the state courts invoked provisions requiring the state to provide "adequate" education, rather than equality provisions. Changes in state tax systems, particularly the imposition of caps on tax increases, have had the effect of shifting fiscal responsibility for education upward, away from local school districts and toward state legislatures.

45. *Regents of the University of California v. Bakke* (1978)

The Supreme Court first addressed the constitutionality of affirmative action here, after a prior case became moot when the person challenging the University of Washington's affirmative action program graduated. The medical school of the University of California at Davis operated an affirmative action program that effectively reserved sixteen out of one hundred places in each year's entering class to members of minority groups. The Supreme Court held that this program was unconstitutional because of its rigidity, but five members of the Court indicated that universities could take race into account by treating it as a "plus" factor in evaluating applications. Four justices, including Justice Marshall, joined an opinion by Justice Brennan stating that the University's affirmative action program in its original form was constitutionally acceptable. Justice Marshall wrote a separate opinion as well.

One issue in affirmative action cases is the standard against which they are to be assessed. Traditionally, government programs that distributed goods or imposed disadvantages based on race were treated as highly suspect, and the cases in which this approach had been adopted all involved programs that imposed disadvantages on racial minorities. The doctrinal issue in Bakke, however, was whether the same "suspect classification" analysis should be applied when the program at issue purported to benefit those minorities. Justice Marshall's opinion explains why the standard for evaluating affirmative action programs should be different, relying on material from the original debates over the Fourteenth Amendment and on his own analysis of the historical background against which affirmative action programs should be assessed.

MR. JUSTICE MARSHALL.

I agree with the judgment of the Court only insofar as it permits a university to consider the race of an applicant in making admissions decisions. I do not agree that petitioner's admissions program violates the Constitution. For it must be remembered that, during most of the past 200 years, the Constitution as interpreted by this Court did not prohibit the most ingenious and pervasive forms of discrimination against the Negro. Now, when a State acts to remedy the effects of that legacy of discrimination, I cannot believe that this same Constitution stands as a barrier.

I

A

Three hundred and fifty years ago, the Negro was dragged to this country in chains to be sold into slavery. Uprooted from his homeland and thrust into bondage for forced labor, the slave was deprived of all legal rights. It was unlawful to teach him to read; he could be sold away from his family and friends at the whim of his master; and killing or maiming him was not a crime. The system of slavery brutalized and dehumanized both master and slave.

The denial of human rights was etched into the American Colonies' first attempts at establishing self-government. When the colonists determined to seek their independence from England, they drafted a unique document cataloguing their grievances against the King and proclaiming as "self-evident" that "all men are created equal" and are endowed "with certain unalienable Rights," including those to "Life, Liberty and the pursuit of Happiness." The self-evident truths and the unalienable rights were intended, however, to apply only to white men. An earlier draft of the Declaration of Independence, submitted by Thomas Jefferson to the Continental Congress, had included among the charges against the King that

> "[h]e has waged cruel war against human nature itself, violating its most sacred rights of life and liberty in the persons of a distant people who never offended him, captivating and carrying them into slavery in another hemisphere, or to incur miserable death in their transportation thither."

The Southern delegation insisted that the charge be deleted; the colonists themselves were implicated in the slave trade, and inclusion of this claim might have made it more difficult to justify the continuation of slavery once the ties to England were severed. Thus, even as the colonists embarked on a course to secure their own freedom and equality, they ensured perpetuation of the system that deprived a whole race of those rights.

The implicit protection of slavery embodied in the Declaration of Independence was made explicit in the Constitution, which treated a slave as being equivalent to three-fifths of a person for purposes of apportioning representatives and taxes among the States. The Constitution also contained a clause ensuring that the "Migration or Importation" of slaves into the existing States would be legal until at least 1808, and a fugitive slave clause requiring that when a slave escaped to another State, he must be returned on the claim of the master. In their declaration of the principles that were to provide the cornerstone of the new Nation, therefore, the Framers made it plain that "we the people," for whose protection the Constitution was designed, did not include those whose skins were the wrong color. As Professor John Hope Franklin has observed, Americans "proudly accepted the challenge and responsibility of their new political freedom by establishing the machinery and safeguards that insured the continued enslavement of blacks."

The individual States likewise established the machinery to protect the system of slavery through the promulgation of the Slave Codes, which were designed primarily to defend the property interest of the owner in his slave. The position of the Negro slave as mere property was confirmed by this Court in *Dred Scott v. Sandford* (1857), holding that the Missouri Compromise—which prohibited slavery in the portion of the Louisiana Purchase Territory north of Missouri—was unconstitutional because it deprived slave owners of their property without due process. The Court declared that under the Constitution a slave was property, and "[t]he right to traffic in it, like an ordinary article of merchandise and property, was guarantied [sic] to the citizens of the United States . . . ." The Court further concluded that Negroes were not intended to be included as citizens under the Constitution but were "regarded as beings of an inferior order . . . altogether unfit to associate with the white race, either in social or political relations; and so far inferior, that they had no rights which the white man was bound to respect . . . ."

B

The status of the Negro as property was officially erased by his emancipation at the end of the Civil War. But the long-awaited emancipation, while freeing the Negro from slavery, did not bring him citizenship or equality in any meaningful way. Slavery was replaced by a system of "laws which imposed upon the colored race onerous disabilities and burdens, and curtailed their rights in the pursuit of life, liberty, and property to such an extent that their freedom was of little value." Despite the passage of the Thirteenth, Fourteenth, and Fifteenth Amendments, the Negro was systematically denied the rights those Amendments were supposed to secure. The combined actions and inactions of the State and Federal Governments maintained Negroes in a position of legal inferiority for another century after the Civil War.

The Southern States took the first steps to re-enslave the Negroes. Immediately following the end of the Civil War, many of the provisional legislatures passed Black Codes, similar to the Slave Codes, which, among other things, limited the rights of Negroes to own or rent property and permitted imprisonment for breach of employment contracts. Over the next several decades, the South managed to disenfranchise the Negroes in spite of the Fifteenth Amendment by various techniques, including poll taxes, deliberately complicated balloting processes, property and literacy qualifications, and finally the white primary.

Congress responded to the legal disabilities being imposed in the Southern States by passing the Reconstruction Acts and the Civil Rights Acts. Congress also responded to the needs of the Negroes at the end of the Civil War by establishing the Bureau of Refugees, Freedmen, and Abandoned Lands, better known as the Freedmen's Bureau, to supply food, hospitals, land, and education to the newly freed slaves. Thus, for a time it seemed as if the Negro might be protected from the continued denial of his civil rights and might be relieved of the disabilities that prevented him from taking his place as a free and equal citizen.

That time, however, was short-lived. Reconstruction came to a close, and, with the assistance of this Court, the Negro was rapidly stripped of his new civil rights. In the words of C. Vann Woodward: "By narrow and ingenious interpretation [the Supreme Court's] decisions over a period of years had whittled away a great part of the authority presumably given the government for protection of civil rights."

The Court began by interpreting the Civil War Amendments in a manner that sharply curtailed their substantive protections. Then in the notorious *Civil Rights*

Cases, the Court strangled Congress' efforts to use its power to promote racial equality. In those cases the Court invalidated sections of the Civil Rights Act of 1875 that made it a crime to deny equal access to "inns, public conveyances, theatres and other places of public amusement." According to the Court, the Fourteenth Amendment gave Congress the power to proscribe only discriminatory action by the State. The Court ruled that the Negroes who were excluded from public places suffered only an invasion of their social rights at the hands of private individuals, and Congress had no power to remedy that. "When a man has emerged from slavery, and by the aid of beneficent legislation has shaken off the inseparable concomitants of that state," the Court concluded, "there must be some stage in the progress of his elevation when he takes the rank of a mere citizen, and ceases to be the special favorite of the laws . . . ." As Mr. Justice Harlan noted in dissent, however, the Civil War Amendments and Civil Rights Acts did not make the Negroes the "special favorite" of the laws but instead "sought to accomplish in reference to that race . . .—what had already been done in every State of the Union for the white race—to secure and protect rights belonging to them as freemen and citizens; nothing more."

The Court's ultimate blow to the Civil War Amendments and to the equality of Negroes came in *Plessy v. Ferguson*. In upholding a Louisiana law that required railway companies to provide "equal but separate" accommodations for whites and Negroes, the Court held that the Fourteenth Amendment was not intended "to abolish distinctions based upon color, or to enforce social, as distinguished from political equality, or a commingling of the two races upon terms unsatisfactory to either." Ignoring totally the realities of the positions of the two races, the Court remarked:

> "We consider the underlying fallacy of the plaintiff's argument to consist in the assumption that the enforced separation of the two races stamps the colored race with a badge of inferiority. If this be so, it is not by reason of anything found in the act, but solely because the colored race chooses to put that construction upon it."

Mr. Justice Harlan's dissenting opinion recognized the bankruptcy of the Court's reasoning. He noted that the "real meaning" of the legislation was "that colored citizens are so inferior and degraded that they cannot be allowed to sit in public coaches occupied by white citizens." He expressed his fear that if like laws were enacted in other States, "the effect would be in the highest degree mischievous." Although slavery would have disappeared, the States would retain the power "to interfere with the full enjoyment of the blessings of freedom; to regulate civil rights, common to all citizens, upon the basis of race; and to place in a condition of legal inferiority a large body of American citizens . . . ."

The fears of Mr. Justice Harlan were soon to be realized. In the wake of *Plessy*, many States expanded their Jim Crow laws, which had up until that time been limited primarily to passenger trains and schools. The segregation of the races was extended to residential areas, parks, hospitals, theaters, waiting rooms, and bathrooms. There were even statutes and ordinances which authorized separate phone booths for Negroes and whites, which required that textbooks used by children of one race be kept separate from those used by the other, and which required that Negro and white prostitutes be kept in separate districts. In 1898, after *Plessy*, the Charlestown News and Courier printed a parody of Jim Crow laws:

> "'If there must be Jim Crow cars on the railroads, there should be Jim Crow cars on the street railways. Also on all passenger boats. . . . If there are to be Jim Crow cars, moreover, there should be Jim Crow waiting saloons at all stations, and Jim Crow eating houses. . . . There should be Jim Crow sections of the jury box, and a separate Jim Crow dock and witness stand in every court—and a Jim Crow Bible for colored witnesses to kiss.'"

The irony is that before many years had passed, with the exception of the Jim Crow witness stand, "all the improbable applications of the principle suggested by the editor in derision had been put into practice—down to and including the Jim Crow Bible."

Nor were the laws restricting the rights of Negroes limited solely to the Southern States. In many of the Northern States, the Negro was denied the right to vote, prevented from serving on juries, and excluded from theaters, restaurants, hotels, and inns. Under President Wilson, the Federal Government began to require segregation in Government buildings; desks of Negro employees were curtained off; separate bathrooms and separate tables in the cafeterias were provided; and even the galleries of the Congress were segregated. When his segregationist policies were attacked, President Wilson responded that segregation was "'not humiliating but a benefit'" and that he was "'rendering [the Negroes] more safe in their possession of office and less likely to be discriminated against.'"

The enforced segregation of the races continued into the middle of the 20th century. In both World Wars, Negroes were for the most part confined to separate military units; it was not until 1948 that an end to segregation in the military was ordered by President Truman. And the history of the exclusion of Negro children from white public schools is too well known and recent to require repeating here. That Negroes were deliberately excluded from public graduate and professional schools—and thereby denied the opportunity to become doctors, lawyers, engineers, and the like—is also well established. It is of course true that some of the Jim Crow laws (which the decisions of this Court had helped to foster) were struck down by this Court in a series of decisions leading up to *Brown v. Board of Education*. Those decisions, however, did not automatically end segregation, nor did they move Negroes from a position of legal inferiority to one of equality. The legacy of years of slavery and of years of second-class citizenship in the wake of emancipation could not be so easily eliminated.

II

The position of the Negro today in America is the tragic but inevitable consequence of centuries of unequal treatment. Measured by any benchmark of comfort or achievement, meaningful equality remains a distant dream for the Negro.

A Negro child today has a life expectancy which is shorter by more than five years than that of a white child. The Negro child's mother is over three times more likely to die of complications in childbirth, and the infant mortality rate for Negroes is nearly twice that for whites. The median income of the Negro family is only 60% that of the median of a white family, and the percentage of Negroes who live in families with incomes below the poverty line is nearly four times greater than that of whites.

When the Negro child reaches working age, he finds that America offers him significantly less than it offers his white counterpart. For Negro adults, the unemployment rate is twice that of whites, and the unemployment rate for Negro teenagers is nearly three times that of white teenagers. A Negro male who completes four years of college can expect a median annual income of merely $110 more than a white male who has only a high school diploma. Although Negroes represent 11.5% of the population, they are only 1.2% of the lawyers and judges, 2% of the physicians, 2.3% of the dentists, 1.1% of the engineers and 2.6% of the college and university professors.

The relationship between those figures and the history of unequal treatment afforded to the Negro cannot be denied. At every point from birth to death the impact of the past is reflected in the still disfavored position of the Negro.

In light of the sorry history of discrimination and its devastating impact on the lives of Negroes, bringing the Negro into the mainstream of American life should be a state interest of the highest order. To fail to do so is to ensure that America will forever remain a divided society.

III

I do not believe that the Fourteenth Amendment requires us to accept that fate. Neither its history nor our past cases lend any support to the conclusion that a university may not remedy the cumulative effects of society's discrimination by giving consideration to race in an effort to increase the number and percentage of Negro doctors.

A

This Court long ago remarked that

"in any fair and just construction of any section or phrase of these [Civil War] amendments, it is necessary to look to the purpose which we have said was the pervading spirit of them all, the evil which they were designed to remedy . . . ."

It is plain that the Fourteenth Amendment was not intended to prohibit measures designed to remedy the effects of the Nation's past treatment of Negroes. The

Congress that passed the Fourteenth Amendment is the same Congress that passed the 1866 Freedmen's Bureau Act, an Act that provided many of its benefits only to Negroes. Although the Freedmen's Bureau legislation provided aid for refugees, thereby including white persons within some of the relief measures, the bill was regarded, to the dismay of many Congressmen, as "solely and entirely for the freedmen, and to the exclusion of all other persons . . . ." Indeed, the bill was bitterly opposed on the ground that it "undertakes to make the negro in some respects . . . superior . . . and gives them favors that the poor white boy in the North cannot get." The bill's supporters defended it—not by rebutting the claim of special treatment—but by pointing to the need for such treatment:

> "The very discrimination it makes between 'destitute and suffering' negroes, and destitute and suffering white paupers, proceeds upon the distinction that, in the omitted case, civil rights and immunities are already sufficiently protected by the possession of political power, the absence of which in the case provided for necessitates governmental protection."

Despite the objection to the special treatment the bill would provide for Negroes, it was passed by Congress. President Johnson vetoed this bill and also a subsequent bill that contained some modifications; one of his principal objections to both bills was that they gave special benefits to Negroes. Rejecting the concerns of the President and the bill's opponents, Congress overrode the President's second veto.

Since the Congress that considered and rejected the objections to the 1866 Freedmen's Bureau Act concerning special relief to Negroes also proposed the Fourteenth Amendment, it is inconceivable that the Fourteenth Amendment was intended to prohibit all race-conscious relief measures. It "would be a distortion of the policy manifested in that amendment, which was adopted to prevent state legislation designed to perpetuate discrimination on the basis of race or color," to hold that it barred state action to remedy the effects of that discrimination. Such a result would pervert the intent of the Framers by substituting abstract equality for the genuine equality the Amendment was intended to achieve. . . .

IV

While I applaud the judgment of the Court that a university may consider race in its admissions process, it is more than a little ironic that, after several hundred years of class-based discrimination against Negroes, the Court is unwilling to hold that a class-based remedy for that discrimination is permissible. In declining to so hold, today's judgment ignores the fact that for several hundred years Negroes have been discriminated against, not as individuals, but rather solely because of the color of their skins. It is unnecessary in 20th-century America to have individual Negroes demonstrate that they have been victims of racial discrimination; the racism of our society has been so pervasive that none, regardless of wealth or position, has managed to escape its impact. The experience of Negroes in America has been different in kind, not just in degree, from that of other ethnic groups. It is not merely the history of slavery alone but also that a whole people were marked as inferior by the law. And that mark has endured. The dream of America as the great melting pot has not been realized for the Negro; because of his skin color he never even made it into the pot.

These differences in the experience of the Negro make it difficult for me to accept that Negroes cannot be afforded greater protection under the Fourteenth Amendment where it is necessary to remedy the effects of past discrimination. In the *Civil Rights Cases*, the Court wrote that the Negro emerging from slavery must cease "to be the special favorite of the laws." We cannot in light of the history of the last century yield to that view. Had the Court in that decision and others been willing to "do for human liberty and the fundamental rights of American citizenship, what it did . . . for the protection of slavery and the rights of the masters of fugitive slaves," we would not need now to permit the recognition of any "special wards."

Most importantly, had the Court been willing in 1896, in *Plessy v. Ferguson*, to hold that the Equal Protection Clause forbids differences in treatment based on race, we would not be faced with this dilemma in 1978. We must remember, however, that the principle that the "Constitution is colorblind" appeared only in the opinion of the lone dissenter. The majority of the Court rejected the principle of color blindness, and for the next 60 years, from *Plessy* to *Brown v. Board of Education*, ours was a Nation where, *by law*, an individual could be given "special" treatment based on the color of his skin.

It is because of a legacy of unequal treatment that we now must permit the institutions of this society to give consideration to race in making decisions about who will hold the positions of influence, affluence, and prestige in America. For far too long, the doors to those positions have been shut to Negroes. If we are ever to become a fully integrated society, one in which the color of a person's skin will not determine the opportunities available to him or her, we must be willing to take steps to open those doors. I do not believe that anyone can truly look into America's past and still find that a remedy for the effects of that past is impermissible.

It has been said that this case involves only the individual, Bakke, and this University. I doubt, however, that there is a computer capable of determining the number of persons and institutions that may be affected by the decision in this case. For example, we are told by the Attorney General of the United States that at least 27 federal agencies have adopted regulations requiring recipients of federal funds to take "'*affirmative action* to overcome the effects of conditions which resulted in limiting participation . . . by persons of a particular race, color, or national origin.'" I cannot even guess the number of state and local governments that have set up affirmative-action programs, which may be affected by today's decision.

I fear that we have come full circle. After the Civil War our Government started several "affirmative action" programs. This Court in the *Civil Rights Cases* and

Plessy v. Ferguson destroyed the movement toward complete equality. For almost a century no action was taken, and this nonaction was with the tacit approval of the courts. Then we had *Brown v. Board of Education* and the Civil Rights Acts of Congress, followed by numerous affirmative-action programs. *Now*, we have this Court again stepping in, this time to stop affirmative-action programs of the type used by the University of California.

46. *City of Richmond v. J. A. Croson Co.* (1989)

The Court's divisions in *Bakke* meant that the constitutionality of affirmative action remained unsettled. A majority was clearly uncomfortable with affirmative action, but had not coalesced around a single standard by which its constitutionality was to be determined. The Court's next affirmative action case, the *Fullilove* decision discussed in this excerpt, involved a federal program that set aside 10% of the funds in a program to finance transportation improvements for minority business enterprises. Again the Court was sharply divided. Although the Court upheld the program, no opinion gained a majority.

 J. A. Croson gave the Court an opportunity to revisit the constitutional question, in a context—government contracting—in which some of the reasons that might justify affirmative action, such as the interest in promoting a diversity of views within a university, had little force. Evaluating Richmond's affirmative action program for building contracts, Justice O'Connor for the majority required that affirmative action programs satisfy the same standard—"strict scrutiny"—that laws adversely affecting the interests of racial minorities did. Justice O'Connor said that the *Fullilove* decision did not control the outcome in *J. A. Croson* because the standards for evaluating *federal* programs were different from, and less restrictive of affirmative action than, the standards for evaluating *state* and local programs. (Six years later, after Marshall had retired, the Court, again in an opinion by Justice O'Connor, rejected that proposition and held that the standards for evaluating federal and state affirmative action programs were the same.) The Richmond program, the Court further held, did not satisfy the "strict scrutiny" requirement and was therefore unconstitutional. Justice Marshall's dissent focuses on the history of racial discrimination in the South and in Richmond in particular. It may be worth noting that Oliver Hill, one of his Howard Law School classmates, was a prominent civil rights lawyer in Richmond and had served on the Richmond City Council in the late 1940s, and that Henry Marsh III, Hill's law partner, was a member of the City Council when it adopted the program in question in *J. A. Croson.*

JUSTICE MARSHALL, WITH WHOM JUSTICE BRENNAN AND JUSTICE BLACKMUN JOIN, DISSENTING.

It is a welcome symbol of racial progress when the former capital of the Confederacy acts forthrightly to confront the effects of racial discrimination in its midst. In my view, nothing in the Constitution can be construed to prevent Richmond, Virginia, from allocating a portion of its contracting dollars for businesses owned or controlled by members of minority groups. Indeed, Richmond's set-aside program is indistinguishable in all meaningful respects from—and in fact was patterned upon—the federal set-aside plan which this Court upheld in *Fullilove v. Klutznick* (1980).

 A majority of this Court holds today, however, that the Equal Protection Clause of the Fourteenth Amendment blocks Richmond's initiative. The essence of the majority's position is that Richmond has failed to catalog adequate findings to prove that past discrimination has impeded minorities from joining or participating fully in Richmond's construction contracting industry. I find deep irony in second-guessing Richmond's judgment on this point. As much as any municipality in the United States, Richmond knows what racial discrimination is; a century of decisions by this and other federal courts has richly documented the city's disgraceful history of public and private racial discrimination. In any event, the Richmond City Council *has* supported its determination that minorities have been wrongly excluded from local construction contracting. Its proof includes statistics showing that minority-owned businesses have received virtually no city contracting dollars and rarely if ever belonged to area trade associations; testimony by municipal officials that discrimination has been widespread in the local construction industry; and the same exhaustive and widely publicized federal studies relied on in *Fullilove*, studies which showed that pervasive discrimination in the Nation's tight-knit construction industry had operated to exclude minorities from public contracting. These are precisely the types of statistical and testimonial evidence which, until today, this Court had credited in cases approving of race-conscious measures designed to remedy past discrimination.

More fundamentally, today's decision marks a deliberate and giant step backward in this Court's affirmative-action jurisprudence. Cynical of one municipality's attempt to redress the effects of past racial discrimination in a particular industry, the majority launches a grapeshot attack on race-conscious remedies in general. The majority's unnecessary pronouncements will inevitably discourage or prevent governmental entities, particularly States and localities, from acting to rectify the scourge of past discrimination. This is the harsh reality of the majority's decision, but it is not the Constitution's command.

I

As an initial matter, the majority takes an exceedingly myopic view of the factual predicate on which the Richmond City Council relied when it passed the Minority Business Utilization Plan. The majority analyzes Richmond's initiative as if it were based solely upon the facts about local construction and contracting practices adduced during the city council session at which the measure was enacted. In so doing, the majority downplays the fact that the city council had before it a rich trove of evidence that discrimination in the Nation's construction industry had seriously impaired the competitive position of businesses owned or controlled by members of minority groups. It is only against this backdrop of documented national discrimination, however, that the local evidence adduced by Richmond can be properly understood. The majority's refusal to recognize that Richmond has proved itself no exception to the dismaying pattern of national exclusion which Congress so painstakingly identified infects its entire analysis of this case.

Six years before Richmond acted, Congress passed, and the President signed, the Public Works Employment Act of 1977, a measure which appropriated $4 billion in federal grants to state and local governments for use in public works projects.

Section 103(f)(2) of the Act was a minority business set-aside provision. It required state or local grantees to use 10% of their federal grants to procure services or supplies from businesses owned or controlled by members of statutorily identified minority groups, absent an administrative waiver. In 1980, in *Fullilove*, this Court upheld the validity of this federal set-aside. Chief Justice Burger's principal opinion noted the importance of overcoming those "criteria, methods, or practices thought by Congress to have the effect of defeating, or substantially impairing, access by the minority business community to public funds made available by congressional appropriations." Finding the set-aside provision properly tailored to this goal, the Chief Justice concluded that the program was valid under either strict or intermediate scrutiny.

The congressional program upheld in *Fullilove* was based upon an array of congressional and agency studies which documented the powerful influence of racially exclusionary practices in the business world. A 1975 Report by the House Committee on Small Business concluded:

> "The effects of past inequities stemming from racial prejudice have not remained in the past. The Congress has recognized the reality that past discriminatory practices have, to some degree, adversely affected our present economic system.
>
> "While minority persons comprise about 16 percent of the Nation's population, of the 13 million businesses in the United States, only 382,000, or approximately 3.0 percent, are owned by minority individuals. The most recent data from the Department of Commerce also indicates that the gross receipts of all businesses in this country totals about $2,540.8 billion, and of this amount only $16.6 billion, or about 0.65 percent was realized by minority business concerns.
>
> "These statistics are not the result of random chance. *The presumption must be made that past discriminatory systems have resulted in present economic inequities.*"

A 1977 Report by the same Committee concluded:

> "[O]ver the years, there has developed a business system which has traditionally excluded measurable minority participation. In the past more than the present, this system of conducting business transactions overtly precluded minority input. Currently, we more often encounter a business system which is racially neutral on its face, but because of past overt social and economic discrimination is presently operating, in effect, to perpetuate these past inequities. Minorities, until recently, have not participated to any measurable extent, in our total business system generally, or in the construction industry in particular."

Congress further found that minorities seeking initial public contracting assignments often faced immense entry barriers which did not confront experienced non-minority contractors. A report submitted to Congress in 1975 by the United States Commission on Civil Rights, for example, described the way in which fledgling minority-owned businesses were hampered by "deficiencies in working capital, inability to meet bonding requirements, disabilities caused by an inadequate 'track record,' lack of awareness of bidding opportunities, unfamiliarity with bidding procedures, preselection before the formal advertising process, and the exercise of discretion by government procurement officers to disfavor minority businesses."

Thus, as of 1977, there was "abundant evidence" in the public domain "that minority businesses ha[d] been denied effective participation in public contracting opportunities by procurement practices that perpetuated the effects of prior discrimination." Significantly, this evidence demonstrated that discrimination had prevented existing or nascent minority-owned businesses from obtaining not only federal contracting assignments, but state and local ones as well.

The members of the Richmond City Council were well aware of these exhaustive congressional findings, a point the majority, tellingly, elides. The transcript of the session at which the council enacted the local set-aside initiative contains numerous references to the 6-year-old congressional set-aside program, to the evidence of nationwide discrimination barriers described above, and to the *Fullilove* decision itself.

The city council's members also heard testimony that, although minority groups made up half of the city's population, only 0.67% of the $24.6 million which Richmond had dispensed in construction contracts during the five years ending in March 1983 had gone to minority-owned prime contractors. They heard testimony that the major Richmond area construction trade associations had virtually no minorities among their hundreds of members. Finally, they heard testimony from city officials as to the exclusionary history of the local construction industry. As the District Court noted, not a single person who testified before the city council denied that discrimination in Richmond's construction industry had been widespread. So long as one views Richmond's local evidence of discrimination against the backdrop of systematic nationwide racial discrimination which Congress had so painstakingly identified in this very industry, this case is readily resolved.

II

"Agreement upon a means for applying the Equal Protection Clause to an affirmative-action program has eluded this Court every time the issue has come before us." My view has long been that race-conscious classifications designed to further remedial goals "must serve important governmental objectives and must be substantially related to achievement of those objectives" in order to withstand constitutional scrutiny. Analyzed in terms of this two-pronged standard, Richmond's set-aside, like the federal program on which it was modeled, is "plainly constitutional."

A

1

Turning first to the governmental interest inquiry, Richmond has two powerful interests in setting aside a portion of public contracting funds for minority-
owned enterprises. The first is the city's interest in eradicating the effects of past
racial discrimination. It is far too late in the day to doubt that remedying such discrimination is a compelling, let alone an important, interest. In *Fullilove*, six
Members of this Court deemed this interest sufficient to support a race-conscious
set-aside program governing federal contract procurement. The decision, in holding that the federal set-aside provision satisfied the equal protection principles
under any level of scrutiny, recognized that the measure sought to remove "barriers to competitive access which had their roots in racial and ethnic discrimination,
and which continue today, even absent any intentional discrimination or unlawful
conduct." Indeed, we have repeatedly reaffirmed the government's interest in breaking down barriers erected by past racial discrimination in cases involving access to
public education, employment, and valuable government contracts.

Richmond has a second compelling interest in setting aside, where possible, a
portion of its contracting dollars. That interest is the prospective one of preventing
the city's own spending decisions from reinforcing and perpetuating the exclusionary effects of past discrimination.

The majority pays only lipservice to this additional governmental interest. But
our decisions have often emphasized the danger of the government tacitly adopting, encouraging, or furthering racial discrimination even by its own routine operations. In *Shelley v. Kraemer* (1948), this Court recognized this interest as a constitutional command, holding unanimously that the Equal Protection Clause forbids
courts to enforce racially restrictive covenants even where such covenants satisfied
all requirements of state law and where the State harbored no discriminatory intent.
Similarly, in *Norwood v. Harrison* (1973), we invalidated a program in which a
State purchased textbooks and loaned them to students in public and private schools,
including private schools with racially discriminatory policies. We stated that the
Constitution requires a State "to steer clear, not only of operating the old dual system of racially segregated schools, but also of giving significant aid to institutions
that practice racial or other invidious discrimination."

The majority is wrong to trivialize the continuing impact of government acceptance or use of private institutions or structures once wrought by discrimination.
When government channels all its contracting funds to a white-dominated community of established contractors whose racial homogeneity is the product of private discrimination, it does more than place its *imprimatur* on the practices which
forged and which continue to define that community. It also provides a measura-
ble boost to those economic entities that have thrived within it, while denying
important economic benefits to those entities which, but for prior discrimination,

might well be better qualified to receive valuable government contracts. In my view, the interest in ensuring that the government does not reflect and reinforce prior private discrimination in dispensing public contracts is every bit as strong as the interest in eliminating private discrimination—an interest which this Court has repeatedly deemed compelling. The more government bestows its rewards on those persons or businesses that were positioned to thrive during a period of private racial discrimination, the tighter the deadhand grip of prior discrimination becomes on the present and future. Cities like Richmond may not be constitutionally required to adopt set-aside plans. But there can be no doubt that when Richmond acted affirmatively to stem the perpetuation of patterns of discrimination through its own decision-making, it served an interest of the highest order.

2

The remaining question with respect to the "governmental interest" prong of equal protection analysis is whether Richmond has proffered satisfactory proof of past racial discrimination to support its twin interests in remediation and in governmental nonperpetuation. Although the Members of this Court have differed on the appropriate standard of review for race-conscious remedial measures, we have always regarded this factual inquiry as a practical one. Thus, the Court has eschewed rigid tests which require the provision of particular species of evidence, statistical or otherwise. At the same time we have required that government adduce evidence that, taken as a whole, is sufficient to support its claimed interest and to dispel the natural concern that it acted out of mere "paternalistic stereotyping, not on a careful consideration of modern social conditions." . . .

The varied body of evidence on which Richmond relied provides a "strong," "firm," and "unquestionably legitimate" basis upon which the city council could determine that the effects of past racial discrimination warranted a remedial and prophylactic governmental response. As I have noted, Richmond acted against a backdrop of congressional and Executive Branch studies which demonstrated with such force the nationwide pervasiveness of prior discrimination that Congress presumed that "'present economic inequities'" in construction contracting resulted from "'past discriminatory systems.'" The city's local evidence confirmed that Richmond's construction industry did not deviate from this pernicious national pattern. The fact that just 0.67% of public construction expenditures over the previous five years had gone to minority-owned prime contractors, despite the city's racially mixed population, strongly suggests that construction contracting in the area was rife with "present economic inequities." To the extent this enormous disparity did not itself demonstrate that discrimination had occurred, the descriptive testimony of Richmond's elected and appointed leaders drew the necessary link between the pitifully small presence of minorities in construction contracting and past exclusionary practices. That *no one* who testified challenged this depiction of widespread racial discrimination in area construction contracting lent significant weight to these accounts. The fact that area trade associations had virtually no minority members dramatized the extent of present inequities and suggested the lasting power of past discriminatory systems. In sum, to suggest that the facts on which Richmond has relied do not provide a sound basis for its finding of past racial discrimination simply blinks credibility.

Richmond's reliance on localized, industry-specific findings is a far cry from the reliance on generalized "societal discrimination" which the majority decries as a basis for remedial action. But characterizing the plight of Richmond's minority contractors as mere "societal discrimination" is not the only respect in which the majority's critique shows an unwillingness to come to grips with why construction-contracting in Richmond is essentially a whites-only enterprise. The majority also takes the disingenuous approach of disaggregating Richmond's local evidence, attacking it piecemeal, and thereby concluding that no *single* piece of evidence adduced by the city, "standing alone," suffices to prove past discrimination. But items of evidence do not, of course, "stan[d] alone" or exist in alien juxtaposition; they necessarily work together, reinforcing or contradicting each other.

In any event, the majority's criticisms of individual items of Richmond's evidence rest on flimsy foundations. The majority states, for example, that reliance on the disparity between the share of city contracts awarded to minority firms (0.67%) and the minority population of Richmond (approximately 50%) is "misplaced." It is true that, when the factual predicate needed to be proved is one of *present* discrimination, we have generally credited statistical contrasts between the racial composition of a work force and the general population as proving discrimination only where this contrast revealed "gross statistical disparities." But this principle does not impugn Richmond's statistical contrast, for two reasons. First, considering how minuscule the share of Richmond public construction contracting dollars received by minority-owned businesses is, it is hardly unreasonable to conclude that this case involves a "gross statistical disparit[y]." There are roughly equal numbers of minorities and nonminorities in Richmond—yet minority-owned businesses receive *one-seventy-fifth* of the public contracting funds that other businesses receive.

Second, and more fundamentally, where the issue is not present discrimination but rather whether *past* discrimination has resulted in the *continuing exclusion* of minorities from a historically tight-knit industry, a contrast between population and work force is entirely appropriate to help gauge the degree of the exclusion. In *Johnson v. Transportation Agency, Santa Clara County*, JUSTICE O'CONNOR specifically observed that, when it is alleged that discrimination has prevented blacks from "obtaining th[e] experience" needed to qualify for a position, the "relevant comparison" is not to the percentage of blacks in the pool of qualified candidates, but to "the total percentage of blacks in the labor force." This contrast is especially illuminating in cases like this, where a main avenue of introduction into the work force—here, membership in the trade associations whose members presumably train apprentices and help them procure subcontracting assignments—is itself grossly dominated by nonminorities. The majority's assertion that the city "does not even know how many MBE's in the relevant market are qualified," is thus entirely beside the point. If Richmond indeed has a monochromatic contracting community—a conclusion reached by the District Court—this most likely reflects the lingering power of past exclusionary practices. Certainly this is the explanation Congress has found persuasive at the national level. The city's requirement that prime public contractors set aside 30% of their subcontracting assignments for minority-owned enterprises, subject to the ordinance's provision for waivers where minority-owned enterprises are unavailable or unwilling to participate, is designed precisely to ease minority contractors into the industry.

The majority's perfunctory dismissal of the testimony of Richmond's appointed and elected leaders is also deeply disturbing. These officials—including councilmembers, a former mayor, and the present city manager—asserted that race discrimination in area contracting had been widespread, and that the set-aside ordinance was a sincere and necessary attempt to eradicate the effects of this discrimination. The majority, however, states that where racial classifications are concerned, "simple legislative assurances of good intention cannot suffice." It similarly discounts as minimally probative the city council's designation of its set-aside plan as remedial. "[B]lind judicial deference to legislative or executive pronouncements," the majority explains, "has no place in equal protection analysis."

No one, of course, advocates "blind judicial deference" to the findings of the city council or the testimony of city leaders. The majority's suggestion that wholesale deference is what Richmond seeks is a classic straw-man argument. But the majority's trivialization of the testimony of Richmond's leaders is dismaying in a far more serious respect. By disregarding the testimony of local leaders and the judgment of local government, the majority does violence to the very principles of comity within our federal system which this Court has long championed. Local officials, by virtue of their proximity to, and their expertise with, local affairs, are exceptionally well qualified to make determinations of public good "within their respective spheres of authority." The majority, however, leaves any traces of comity behind in its headlong rush to strike down Richmond's race-conscious measure.

Had the majority paused for a moment on the facts of the Richmond experience, it would have discovered that the city's leadership is deeply familiar with what racial discrimination is. The members of the Richmond City Council have spent long years witnessing multifarious acts of discrimination, including, but not limited to, the deliberate diminution of black residents' voting rights, resistance to school desegregation, and publicly sanctioned housing discrimination. Numerous decisions of federal courts chronicle this disgraceful recent history. In *Richmond v. United States* (1975), for example, this Court denounced Richmond's decision to annex part of an adjacent county at a time when the city's black population was nearing 50% because it was "infected by the impermissible purpose of denying the right to vote based on race through perpetuating white majority power to exclude Negroes from office." . . .

When the legislatures and leaders of cities with histories of pervasive discrimination testify that past discrimination has infected one of their industries, armchair cynicism like that exercised by the majority has no place. It may well be that "the autonomy of a State is an essential component of federalism," and that "each State is sovereign within its own domain, governing its citizens and providing for their general welfare," but apparently this is not the case when federal judges, with nothing but their impressions to go on, choose to disbelieve the explanations of these local governments and officials. Disbelief is particularly inappropriate here in light of the fact that appellee Croson, which had the burden of proving unconstitutionality at trial, has *at no point* come forward with *any* direct evidence that the city council's motives were anything other than sincere.

Finally, I vehemently disagree with the majority's dismissal of the congressional and Executive Branch findings noted in *Fullilove* as having "extremely limited" probative value in this case. The majority concedes that Congress established nothing less than a "presumption" that minority contracting firms have been disadvantaged by prior discrimination. The majority, inexplicably, would forbid Richmond to "share" in this information, and permit only Congress to take note of these ample findings. In thus requiring that Richmond's local evidence be severed from the context in which it was prepared, the majority would require cities seeking to eradicate the effects of past discrimination within their borders to reinvent the evidentiary wheel and engage in unnecessarily duplicative, costly, and time-consuming factfinding.

No principle of federalism or of federal power, however, forbids a state or local government to draw upon a nationally relevant historical record prepared by the Federal Government. Of course, Richmond could have built an even more compendious record of past discrimination, one including additional stark statistics and additional individual accounts of past discrimination. But nothing in the Fourteenth Amendment imposes such onerous documentary obligations upon States and localities once the reality of past discrimination is apparent.

B

In my judgment, Richmond's set-aside plan also comports with the second prong of the equal protection inquiry, for it is substantially related to the interests it seeks to serve in remedying past discrimination and in ensuring that municipal contract procurement does not perpetuate that discrimination. The most striking aspect of the city's ordinance is the similarity it bears to the "appropriately limited" federal set-aside provision upheld in *Fullilove*. Like the federal provision, Richmond's is limited to five years in duration, and was not renewed when it came up for reconsideration in 1988. Like the federal provision, Richmond's contains a waiver provision freeing from its subcontracting requirements those nonminority firms that demonstrate that they cannot comply with its provisions. Like the federal provision, Richmond's has a minimal impact on innocent third parties. While the measure affects 30% of *public* contracting dollars, that translates to only 3% of overall Richmond area contracting.

Finally, like the federal provision, Richmond's does not interfere with any vested right of a contractor to a particular contract; instead it operates entirely prospectively. Richmond's initiative affects only future economic arrangements and imposes only a diffuse burden on nonminority competitors—here, businesses owned or controlled by nonminorities which seek subcontracting work on public construction projects. The plurality in *Wygant* emphasized the importance of not disrupting the settled and legitimate expectations of innocent parties. "While hiring goals impose a diffuse burden, often foreclosing only one of several opportunities, layoffs impose the entire burden of achieving racial equality on particular individuals, often resulting in serious disruption of their lives. That burden is too intrusive."

These factors, far from "justify[ing] a preference of any size or duration," are precisely the factors to which this Court looked in *Fullilove*. The majority takes issue, however, with two aspects of Richmond's tailoring: the city's refusal to explore the use of race-neutral measures to increase minority business participation in contracting, and the selection of a 30% set-aside figure. The majority's first criticism is flawed in two respects. First, the majority overlooks the fact that since 1975, Richmond has barred both discrimination by the city in awarding public contracts and discrimination by public contractors. The virtual absence of minority businesses from the city's contracting rolls, indicated by the fact that such businesses have received less than 1% of public contracting dollars, strongly suggests that this ban has not succeeded in redressing the impact of past discrimination or in preventing city contract procurement from reinforcing racial homogeneity. Second, the majority's suggestion that Richmond should have first undertaken such race-neutral measures as a program of city financing for small firms, ignores the fact that such measures, while theoretically appealing, have been discredited by Congress as ineffectual in eradicating the effects of past discrimination in this very industry. For this reason, this Court in *Fullilove* refused to fault Congress for not undertaking race-neutral measures as precursors to its race-conscious set-aside. The Equal Protection Clause does not require Richmond to retrace Congress' steps when Congress has found that those steps lead nowhere. Given the well-exposed limitations of race-neutral measures, it was thus appropriate for a municipality like Richmond to conclude that, in the words of JUSTICE BLACKMUN, "[i]n order to get beyond racism, we must first take account of race. There is no other way." *Bakke*.

As for Richmond's 30% target, the majority states that this figure "cannot be said to be narrowly tailored to any goal, except perhaps outright racial balancing." The majority ignores two important facts. First, the set-aside measure affects only 3% of overall city contracting; thus, any imprecision in tailoring has far less impact than the majority suggests. But more important, the majority ignores the fact that Richmond's 30% figure was patterned directly on the *Fullilove* precedent. Congress' 10% figure fell "roughly halfway between the present percentage of minority contractors and the percentage of minority group members in the Nation." The Richmond City Council's 30% figure similarly falls roughly halfway between the present percentage of Richmond-based minority contractors (almost zero) and the percentage of minorities in Richmond (50%). In faulting Richmond for not presenting a different explanation for its choice of a set-aside figure, the majority honors *Fullilove* only in the breach.

III

I would ordinarily end my analysis at this point and conclude that Richmond's ordinance satisfies both the governmental interest and substantial relationship prongs of our Equal Protection Clause analysis. However, I am compelled to add more, for the majority has gone beyond the facts of this case to announce a set of principles which unnecessarily restricts the power of governmental entities to take race-conscious measures to redress the effects of prior discrimination.

A

Today, for the first time, a majority of this Court has adopted strict scrutiny as its standard of Equal Protection Clause review of race-conscious remedial measures. This is an unwelcome development. A profound difference separates governmental actions that themselves are racist, and governmental actions that seek to remedy the effects of prior racism or to prevent neutral governmental activity from perpetuating the effects of such racism.

Racial classifications "drawn on the presumption that one race is inferior to another or because they put the weight of government behind racial hatred and separatism" warrant the strictest judicial scrutiny because of the very irrelevance of these rationales. By contrast, racial classifications drawn for the purpose of remedying the effects of discrimination that itself was race based have a highly pertinent basis: the tragic and indelible fact that discrimination against blacks and other racial minorities in this Nation has pervaded our Nation's history and continues to scar our society. As I stated in *Fullilove*: "Because the consideration of race is relevant to remedying the continuing effects of past racial discrimination, and because governmental programs employing racial classifications for remedial purposes can be crafted to avoid stigmatization, . . . such programs should not be subjected to conventional 'strict scrutiny'—scrutiny that is strict in theory, but fatal in fact."

In concluding that remedial classifications warrant no different standard of review under the Constitution than the most brutal and repugnant forms of state-sponsored racism, a majority of this Court signals that it regards racial discrimination as largely a phenomenon of the past, and that government bodies need no longer preoccupy themselves with rectifying racial injustice. I, however, do not believe this

Nation is anywhere close to eradicating racial discrimination or its vestiges. In constitutionalizing its wishful thinking, the majority today does a grave disservice not only to those victims of past and present racial discrimination in this Nation whom government has sought to assist, but also to this Court's long tradition of approaching issues of race with the utmost sensitivity.

B

I am also troubled by the majority's assertion that, even if it did not believe generally in strict scrutiny of race-based remedial measures, "the circumstances of this case" require this Court to look upon the Richmond City Council's measure with the strictest scrutiny. The sole such circumstance which the majority cites, however, is the fact that blacks in Richmond are a "dominant racial grou[p]" in the city. In support of this characterization of dominance, the majority observes that "blacks constitute approximately 50% of the population of the city of Richmond" and that "[f]ive of the nine seats on the City Council are held by blacks."

While I agree that the numerical and political supremacy of a given racial group is a factor bearing upon the level of scrutiny to be applied, this Court has never held that numerical inferiority, standing alone, makes a racial group "suspect" and thus entitled to strict scrutiny review. Rather, we have identified *other* "traditional indicia of suspectness": whether a group has been "saddled with such disabilities, or subjected to such a history of purposeful unequal treatment, or relegated to such a position of political powerlessness as to command extraordinary protection from the majoritarian political process."

It cannot seriously be suggested that nonminorities in Richmond have any "history of purposeful unequal treatment." Nor is there any indication that they have any of the disabilities that have characteristically afflicted those groups this Court has deemed suspect. Indeed, the numerical and political dominance of nonminorities within the State of Virginia and the Nation as a whole provides an enormous political check against the "simple racial politics" at the municipal level which the majority fears. If the majority really believes that groups like Richmond's nonminorities, which constitute approximately half the population but which are outnumbered even marginally in political fora, are deserving of suspect class status for these reasons alone, this Court's decisions denying suspect status to women, and to persons with below-average incomes, stand on extremely shaky ground.

In my view, the "circumstances of this case" underscore the importance of not subjecting to a strict scrutiny straitjacket the increasing number of cities which have recently come under minority leadership and are eager to rectify, or at least prevent the perpetuation of, past racial discrimination. In many cases, these cities will be the ones with the most in the way of prior discrimination to rectify. Richmond's leaders had just witnessed decades of publicly sanctioned racial discrimination in virtually all walks of life—discrimination amply documented in the decisions of the federal judiciary. This history of "purposefully unequal treatment" forced upon minorities, not imposed by them, should raise an inference that minorities in Richmond had much to remedy—and that the 1983 set-aside was undertaken with sincere remedial goals in mind, not "simple racial politics."

Richmond's own recent political history underscores the facile nature of the majority's assumption that elected officials' voting decisions are based on the color of their skins. In recent years, white and black councilmembers in Richmond have increasingly joined hands on controversial matters. When the Richmond City Council elected a black man mayor in 1982, for example, his victory was won with the support of the city council's four white members. The vote on the set-aside plan a year later also was not purely along racial lines. Of the four white councilmembers, one voted for the measure and another abstained. The majority's view that remedial measures undertaken by municipalities with black leadership must face a stiffer test of Equal Protection Clause scrutiny than remedial measures undertaken by municipalities with white leadership implies a lack of political maturity on the part of this Nation's elected minority officials that is totally unwarranted. Such insulting judgments have no place in constitutional jurisprudence.

C

Today's decision, finally, is particularly noteworthy for the daunting standard it imposes upon States and localities contemplating the use of race-conscious measures to eradicate the present effects of prior discrimination and prevent its perpetuation. The majority restricts the use of such measures to situations in which a State or locality can put forth "a prima facie case of a constitutional or statutory violation." In so doing, the majority calls into question the validity of the business set-asides which dozens of municipalities across this Nation have adopted on the authority of *Fullilove*.

Nothing in the Constitution or in the prior decisions of this Court supports limiting state authority to confront the effects of past discrimination to those situations in which a prima facie case of a constitutional or statutory violation can be made out. By its very terms, the majority's standard effectively cedes control of a large component of the content of that constitutional provision to Congress and to state legislatures. If an antecedent Virginia or Richmond law had defined as unlawful the award to nonminorities of an overwhelming share of a city's contracting dollars, for example, Richmond's subsequent set-aside initiative would then satisfy the majority's standard. But without such a law, the initiative might not withstand constitutional scrutiny. The meaning of "equal protection of the laws" thus turns on the happenstance of whether a state or local body has previously defined illegal discrimination. Indeed, given that racially discriminatory cities may be the ones least likely to have tough antidiscrimination laws on their books, the majority's constitutional incorporation of state and local statutes has the perverse effect of inhibiting those States or localities with the worst records of official racism from taking remedial action. . . .

In adopting its prima facie standard for States and localities, the majority closes its eyes to this constitutional history and social reality. So, too, does JUSTICE SCALIA. He would further limit consideration of race to those cases in which States find it "necessary to eliminate their own maintenance of a system of unlawful racial classification"—a "distinction" which, he states, "explains our school desegregation cases." But this Court's remedy-stage school desegregation decisions cannot so conveniently be cordoned off. These decisions (like those involving voting rights and affirmative action) stand for the same broad principles of equal protection which Richmond seeks to vindicate in this case: all persons have equal worth, and it is permissible, given a sufficient factual predicate and appropriate tailoring, for government to take account of race to eradicate the present effects of race-based subjugation denying that basic equality. JUSTICE SCALIA's artful distinction allows him to avoid having to repudiate "our school desegregation cases," but, like the arbitrary limitation on race-conscious relief adopted by the majority, his approach "would freeze the status quo that is the very target" of the remedial actions of States and localities.

The fact is that Congress' concern in passing the Reconstruction Amendments, and particularly their congressional authorization provisions, was that States would not adequately respond to racial violence or discrimination against newly freed slaves. To interpret any aspect of these Amendments as proscribing state remedial responses to these very problems turns the Amendments on their heads. As four Justices, of whom I was one, stated in *University of California Regents v. Bakke*:

> "[There is] no reason to conclude that the States cannot voluntarily accomplish under § 1 of the Fourteenth Amendment what Congress under § 5 of the Fourteenth Amendment validly may authorize or compel either the States or private persons to do. A contrary position would conflict with the traditional understanding recognizing the competence of the States to initiate measures consistent with federal policy in the absence of congressional pre-emption of the subject matter. *Nothing whatever in the legislative history of either the Fourteenth Amendment or the Civil Rights Acts even remotely suggests that the States are foreclosed from furthering the fundamental purpose of equal opportunity to which the Amendment and those Acts are addressed.* Indeed, voluntary initiatives by the States to achieve the national goal of equal opportunity have been recognized to be essential to its attainment. 'To use the Fourteenth Amendment as a sword against such State power would stultify that Amendment.'

In short, there is simply no credible evidence that the Framers of the Fourteenth Amendment sought "to transfer the security and protection of all the civil rights . . . from the States to the Federal government." The three Reconstruction Amendments undeniably "worked a dramatic change in the balance between congressional and state power": they forbade state-sanctioned slavery, forbade the state-sanctioned denial of the right to vote, and (until the content of the Equal Protection Clause was substantially applied to the Federal Government through the Due Process Clause of the Fifth Amendment) uniquely forbade States to deny equal protection. The Amendments also specifically empowered the Federal Government to combat discrimination at a time when the breadth of federal power under the Constitution was less apparent than it is today. But nothing in the Amendments themselves, or in our long history of interpreting or applying those momentous charters, suggests that States, exercising their police power, are in any way constitutionally inhibited from working alongside the Federal Government in the fight against discrimination and its effects.

IV

The majority today sounds a full-scale retreat from the Court's longstanding solicitude to race-conscious remedial efforts "directed toward deliverance of the century-old promise of equality of economic opportunity." The new and restrictive tests it applies scuttle one city's effort to surmount its discriminatory past, and imperil those of dozens more localities. I, however, profoundly disagree with the cramped vision of the Equal Protection Clause which the majority offers today and with its application of that vision to Richmond, Virginia's, laudable set-aside plan. The battle against pernicious racial discrimination or its effects is nowhere near won. I must dissent.

47. *United States v. Kras* (1973)

This case was part of the challenge brought by poverty lawyers against statutes that served to increase the normal burdens of the poor. Here the statute required a filing fee of $50 of people seeking to get free of their debts by going into bankruptcy. The fee could be paid in installments; but Kras, an unemployed father living in a small apartment with his family, including a child with cystic fibrosis, was unable to save anything from his public assistance grants, all of which went to paying his rent and day-to-day living expenses. Kras's lawyers relied on a 1971 decision finding it unconstitutional for a state to require indigent people seeking a divorce to pay a filing fee. Justice Harry Blackmun, writing the majority opinion for five members of the Court, held that the filing fee was constitutional. Obtaining a discharge of debts in bankruptcy was not, to the Court, a fundamental interest, as was the interest in obtaining a divorce, an interest the Court described as arising out of freedom of association. People in financial trouble might be able to work out their problems with their creditors without going into bankruptcy, which meant that the government did not have a monopoly over debt relief, as it did over divorce. Justice Blackmun's opinion observed that the weekly installments might, under some circumstances, be about $1.28, "less than the price of a movie and little more than the cost of a pack or two of cigarettes." The principal dissent, by Justice Potter Stewart, summarized the majority opinion: "The Court today holds that Congress may say that some of the poor are too poor even to go bankrupt." Justice Marshall wrote a separate dissent, severely criticizing the majority for its view of the life led by people in poverty.

MR. JUSTICE MARSHALL, DISSENTING.

The dissent of MR. JUSTICE STEWART, in which I have joined, makes clear the majority's failure to distinguish this case from *Boddie v. Connecticut* (1971). I add only some comments on the extraordinary route by which the majority reaches its conclusion.

The majority notes that the minimum amount that appellee Kras must pay each week if he is permitted to pay the filing fees in installments is only $1.28. It says that "this much available revenue should be within his able-bodied reach." . . .

I cannot agree with the majority that it is so easy for the desperately poor to save $1.92 *each week* over the course of six months. The 1970 Census found that over 800,000 families in the Nation had annual incomes of less than $1,000 or $19.23 a week. I see no reason to require that families in such straits sacrifice over 5% of their annual income as a prerequisite to getting a discharge in bankruptcy.[1]

---

[1] The majority, in citing the "record of achievement" of the bankruptcy system in terminating 107,481 no-asset cases in the fiscal year 1969, relies on spectral evidence. Because the filing fees bar relief through the bankruptcy system, statistics showing how many people got relief through that system are unenlightening on the question of how many people could not use the system because they were too poor. I do not know how many people cannot afford to pay a $50 fee in installments. But I find nothing in the majority's opinion to convince me that due process is afforded a person who cannot receive a discharge in bankruptcy because he is too poor. Even if only one person is affected by the filing fees, *he* is denied due process. [footnote in original]

It may be easy for some people to think that weekly savings of less than $2 are no burden. But no one who has had close contact with poor people can fail to understand how close to the margin of survival many of them are. A sudden illness, for example, may destroy whatever savings they may have accumulated, and by eliminating a sense of security may destroy the incentive to save in the future. A pack or two of cigarettes may be, for them, not a routine purchase but a luxury indulged in only rarely. The desperately poor almost never go to see a movie, which the majority seems to believe is an almost weekly activity. They have more important things to do with what little money they have—like attempting to provide some comforts for a gravely ill child, as Kras must do.

It is perfectly proper for judges to disagree about what the Constitution requires. But it is disgraceful for an interpretation of the Constitution to be premised upon unfounded assumptions about how people live. . . .

48. *Ake v. Oklahoma* (1985)

JUSTICE MARSHALL DELIVERED THE OPINION OF THE COURT.

The issue in this case is whether the Constitution requires that an indigent defendant have access to the psychiatric examination and assistance necessary to prepare an effective defense based on his mental condition, when his sanity at the time of the offense is seriously in question.

I

Late in 1979, Glen Burton Ake was arrested and charged with murdering a couple and wounding their two children. He was arraigned in the District Court for Canadian County, Okla., in February 1980. His behavior at arraignment, and in other prearraignment incidents at the jail, was so bizarre that the trial judge, *sua sponte*, ordered him to be examined by a psychiatrist "for the purpose of advising with the Court as to his impressions of whether the Defendant may need an extended period of mental observation." The examining psychiatrist reported: "At times [Ake] appears to be frankly delusional. . . . He claims to be the 'sword of vengeance' of the Lord and that he will sit at the left hand of God in heaven." He diagnosed Ake as a probable paranoid schizophrenic and recommended a prolonged psychiatric evaluation to determine whether Ake was competent to stand trial.

In March, Ake was committed to a state hospital to be examined with respect to his "present sanity," *i.e.,* his competency to stand trial. On April 10, less than six months after the incidents for which Ake was indicted, the chief forensic psychiatrist at the state hospital informed the court that Ake was not competent to stand trial. The court then held a competency hearing, at which a psychiatrist testified:

> "[Ake] is a psychotic . . . his psychiatric diagnosis was that of paranoid schizophrenia—chronic, with exacerbation, that is with current upset, and that in addition . . . he is dangerous. . . . [B]ecause of the severity of his mental illness and because of the intensities of his rage, his poor control, his delusions, he requires a maximum security facility within—I believe—the State Psychiatric Hospital system."

The court found Ake to be a "mentally ill person in need of care and treatment" and incompetent to stand trial, and ordered him committed to the state mental hospital.

Six weeks later, the chief forensic psychiatrist informed the court that Ake had become competent to stand trial. At the time, Ake was receiving 200 milligrams of Thorazine, an antipsychotic drug, three times daily, and the psychiatrist indicated that, if Ake continued to receive that dosage, his condition would remain stable. The State then resumed proceedings against Ake.

At a pretrial conference in June, Ake's attorney informed the court that his client would raise an insanity defense. To enable him to prepare and present such a defense adequately, the attorney stated, a psychiatrist would have to examine Ake with respect to his mental condition at the time of the offense. During Ake's 3-month stay at the state hospital, no inquiry had been made into his sanity at the time of the offense, and, as an indigent, Ake could not afford to pay for a psychiatrist. Counsel asked the court either to arrange to have a psychiatrist perform the examination, or to provide funds to allow the defense to arrange one. The trial judge rejected counsel's argument that the Federal Constitution requires that an indigent defendant receive the assistance of a psychiatrist when that assistance is necessary to the defense, and he denied the motion for a psychiatric evaluation at state expense on the basis of this Court's decision in *United States ex rel. Smith v. Baldi* (1953).

Ake was tried for two counts of murder in the first degree, a crime punishable by death in Oklahoma, and for two counts of shooting with intent to kill. At the guilt phase of trial, his sole defense was insanity. Although defense counsel called to the stand and questioned each of the psychiatrists who had examined Ake at the state hospital, none testified about his mental state at the time of the offense because none had examined him on that point. The prosecution, in turn, asked each of these psychiatrists whether he had performed or seen the results of any examination diagnosing Ake's mental state at the time of the offense, and each doctor replied that he had not. *As a result, there was no expert testimony for either side on Ake's sanity at the time of the offense.* The jurors were then instructed that Ake could be found not guilty by reason of insanity if he did not have the ability to distinguish right from wrong at the time of the alleged offense. They were further told that Ake was to be presumed sane at the time of the crime unless *he* presented evidence sufficient to raise a reasonable doubt about his sanity at that time. If he raised such a doubt in their minds, the jurors were informed, the burden of proof shifted to the State to prove sanity beyond a reasonable doubt. The jury rejected Ake's insanity defense and returned a verdict of guilty on all counts.

At the sentencing proceeding, the State asked for the death penalty. No new evidence was presented. The prosecutor relied significantly on the testimony of the state psychiatrists who had examined Ake, and who had testified at the guilt phase that Ake was dangerous to society, to establish the likelihood of his future dangerous behavior. Ake had no expert witness to rebut this testimony or to introduce on his behalf evidence in mitigation of his punishment. The jury sentenced Ake to death on each of the two murder counts, and to 500 years' imprisonment on each of the two counts of shooting with intent to kill. . . .

We hold that when a defendant has made a preliminary showing that his sanity at the time of the offense is likely to be a significant factor at trial, the Constitution requires that a State provide access to a psychiatrist's assistance on this issue if the defendant cannot otherwise afford one. Accordingly, we reverse. . . .

III

This Court has long recognized that when a State brings its judicial power to bear on an indigent defendant in a criminal proceeding, it must take steps to assure that the defendant has a fair opportunity to present his defense. This elementary principle, grounded in significant part on the Fourteenth Amendment's due process guarantee of fundamental fairness, derives from the belief that justice cannot be equal where, simply as a result of his poverty, a defendant is denied the opportunity to participate meaningfully in a judicial proceeding in which his liberty is at stake. In recognition of this right, this Court held almost 30 years ago that once a State offers to criminal defendants the opportunity to appeal their cases, it must provide a trial transcript to an indigent defendant if the transcript is necessary to a decision on the merits of the appeal. Since then, this Court has held that an indigent defendant may not be required to pay a fee before filing a notice of appeal of his conviction, that an indigent defendant is entitled to the assistance of counsel at trial, and on his first direct appeal as of right, and that such assistance must be effective. Indeed, in *Little v. Streater*, we extended this principle of meaningful participation to a "quasi-criminal" proceeding and held that, in a paternity action, the State cannot deny the putative father blood grouping tests, if he cannot otherwise afford them.

Meaningful access to justice has been the consistent theme of these cases. We recognized long ago that mere access to the courthouse doors does not by itself assure a proper functioning of the adversary process, and that a criminal trial is fundamentally unfair if the State proceeds against an indigent defendant without making certain that he has access to the raw materials integral to the building of an effective defense. Thus, while the Court has not held that a State must purchase for the indigent defendant all the assistance that his wealthier counterpart might buy, it has often reaffirmed that fundamental fairness entitles indigent defendants to "an adequate opportunity to present their claims fairly within the adversary system." To implement this principle, we have focused on identifying the "basic tools of an adequate defense or appeal," and we have required that such tools be provided to those defendants who cannot afford to pay for them.

To say that these basic tools must be provided is, of course, merely to begin our inquiry. In this case we must decide whether, and under what conditions, the participation of a psychiatrist is important enough to preparation of a defense to require the State to provide an indigent defendant with access to competent psychiatric assistance in preparing the defense. Three factors are relevant to this determination. The first is the private interest that will be affected by the action of the State. The second is the governmental interest that will be affected if the safeguard is to be provided. The third is the probable value of the additional or substitute procedural safeguards that are sought, and the risk of an erroneous deprivation of the affected interest if those safeguards are not provided. We turn, then, to apply this standard to the issue before us.

A

The private interest in the accuracy of a criminal proceeding that places an individual's life or liberty at risk is almost uniquely compelling. Indeed, the host of safeguards fashioned by this Court over the years to diminish the risk of erroneous conviction stands as a testament to that concern. The interest of the individual in the outcome of the State's effort to overcome the presumption of innocence is obvious and weighs heavily in our analysis.

We consider, next, the interest of the State. Oklahoma asserts that to provide Ake with psychiatric assistance on the record before us would result in a staggering burden to the State. We are unpersuaded by this assertion. Many States, as well as the Federal Government, currently make psychiatric assistance available to indigent defendants, and they have not found the financial burden so great as to preclude this assistance. This is especially so when the obligation of the State is limited to provision of one competent psychiatrist, as it is in many States, and as we limit the right we recognize today. At the same time, it is difficult to identify any interest of the State, other than that in its economy, that weighs against recognition of this right. The State's interest in prevailing at trial—unlike that of a private litigant—is necessarily tempered by its interest in the fair and accurate adjudication of criminal cases. Thus, also unlike a private litigant, a State may not legitimately assert an interest in maintenance of a strategic advantage over the defense, if the result of that advantage is to cast a pall on the accuracy of the verdict obtained. We therefore conclude that the governmental interest in denying Ake the assistance of a psychiatrist is not substantial, in light of the compelling interest of both the State and the individual in accurate dispositions.

Last, we inquire into the probable value of the psychiatric assistance sought, and the risk of error in the proceeding if such assistance is not offered. We begin by considering the pivotal role that psychiatry has come to play in criminal proceedings. More than 40 States, as well as the Federal Government, have decided either through legislation or judicial decision that indigent defendants are entitled, under certain circumstances, to the assistance of a psychiatrist's expertise. For example, in subsection (e) of the Criminal Justice Act, 18 U.S.C. §3006A, Congress has provided that indigent defendants shall receive the assistance of all experts "necessary for an adequate defense." Numerous state statutes guarantee reimbursement for expert services under a like standard. And in many States that have not assured access to psychiatrists through the legislative process, state courts have interpreted the State or Federal Constitution to require that psychiatric assistance be provided to indigent defendants when necessary for an adequate defense, or when insanity is at issue.

These statutes and court decisions reflect a reality that we recognize today, namely, that when the State has made the defendant's mental condition relevant to his criminal culpability and to the punishment he might suffer, the assistance of a psychiatrist may well be crucial to the defendant's ability to marshal his defense. In this role, psychiatrists gather facts, through professional examination, interviews, and elsewhere, that they will share with the judge or jury; they analyze the information gathered and from it draw plausible conclusions about the defendant's mental condition, and about the effects of any disorder on behavior; and they offer opinions about how the defendant's mental condition might have affected his behavior at the time in question. They know the probative questions to ask of the opposing party's psychiatrists and how to interpret their answers. Unlike lay witnesses, who can merely describe symptoms they believe might be relevant to the defendant's mental state, psychiatrists can identify the "elusive and often deceptive" symptoms of insanity, and tell the jury why their observations are relevant. Further, where permitted by evidentiary rules, psychiatrists can translate a medical diagnosis into language that will assist the trier of fact, and therefore offer evidence in a form that has meaning for the task at hand. Through this process of investigation, interpretation, and testimony, psychiatrists ideally assist lay jurors, who generally have no training in psychiatric matters, to make a sensible and educated determination about the mental condition of the defendant at the time of the offense.

Psychiatry is not, however, an exact science, and psychiatrists disagree widely and frequently on what constitutes mental illness, on the appropriate diagnosis to be attached to given behavior and symptoms, on cure and treatment, and on likelihood of future dangerousness. Perhaps because there often is no single, accurate psychiatric conclusion on legal insanity in a given case, juries remain the primary factfinders on this issue, and they must resolve differences in opinion within the psychiatric profession on the basis of the evidence offered by each party. When jurors make this determination about issues that inevitably are complex and foreign, the testimony of psychiatrists can be crucial and "a virtual necessity if an insanity plea is to have any chance of success." By organizing a defendant's mental history, examination results and behavior, and other information, interpreting it in light of their expertise, and then laying out their investigative and analytic process to the jury, the psychiatrists for each party enable the jury to make its most accurate determination of the truth on the issue before them. It is for this reason that States rely on psychiatrists as examiners, consultants, and witnesses, and that private individuals do as well, when they can afford to do so. In so saying, we neither approve nor disapprove the widespread reliance on psychiatrists but instead recognize the unfairness of a contrary holding in light of the evolving practice.

The foregoing leads inexorably to the conclusion that, without the assistance of a psychiatrist to conduct a professional examination on issues relevant to the defense, to help determine whether the insanity defense is viable, to present testimony, and to assist in preparing the cross-examination of a State's psychiatric witnesses, the risk of an inaccurate resolution of sanity issues is extremely high. With such assistance, the defendant is fairly able to present at least enough information to the jury, in a meaningful manner, as to permit it to make a sensible determination.

A defendant's mental condition is not necessarily at issue in every criminal proceeding, however, and it is unlikely that psychiatric assistance of the kind we have described would be of probable value in cases where it is not. The risk of error from denial of such assistance, as well as its probable value, is most predictably at its height when the defendant's mental condition is seriously in question. When the defendant is able to make an *ex parte* threshold showing to the trial court that his sanity is likely to be a significant factor in his defense, the need for the assistance of a psychiatrist is readily apparent. It is in such cases that a defense may be devastated by the absence of a psychiatric examination and testimony; with such assistance, the defendant might have a reasonable chance of success. In such a circumstance, where the potential accuracy of the jury's determination is so dramatically enhanced, and where the interests of the individual and the State in an accurate proceeding are substantial, the State's interest in its fisc must yield.

We therefore hold that when a defendant demonstrates to the trial judge that his sanity at the time of the offense is to be a significant factor at trial, the State must, at a minimum, assure the defendant access to a competent psychiatrist who will conduct an appropriate examination and assist in evaluation, preparation, and presentation of the defense. This is not to say, of course, that the indigent defendant has a constitutional right to choose a psychiatrist of his personal liking or to receive funds to hire his own. Our concern is that the indigent defendant have access to a competent psychiatrist for the purpose we have discussed, and as in the case of the provision of counsel we leave to the States the decision on how to implement this right.

B

Ake also was denied the means of presenting evidence to rebut the State's evidence of his future dangerousness. The foregoing discussion compels a similar conclusion in the context of a capital sentencing proceeding, when the State presents psychiatric evidence of the defendant's future dangerousness. We have repeatedly recognized the defendant's compelling interest in fair adjudication at the sentencing phase of a capital case. The State, too, has a profound interest in assuring that its ultimate sanction is not erroneously imposed, and we do not see why monetary considerations should be more persuasive in this context than at trial. The variable on which we must focus is, therefore, the probable value that the assistance of a psychiatrist will have in this area, and the risk attendant on its absence.

This Court has upheld the practice in many States of placing before the jury psychiatric testimony on the question of future dangerousness, at least where the defendant has had access to an expert of his own. In so holding, the Court relied, in part, on the assumption that the factfinder would have before it both the views of the prosecutor's psychiatrists and the "opposing views of the defendant's doctors" and would therefore be competent to "uncover, recognize, and take due account of . . . shortcomings" in predictions on this point. Without a psychiatrist's assistance, the defendant cannot offer a well-informed expert's opposing view, and thereby loses a significant opportunity to raise in the jurors' minds questions about the State's proof of an aggravating factor. In such a circumstance, where the consequence of error is so great, the relevance of responsive psychiatric testimony so evident, and the burden on the State so slim, due process requires access to a psychiatric examination on relevant issues, to the testimony of the psychiatrist, and to assistance in preparation at the sentencing phase.

C

The trial court in this case believed that our decision in *United States ex rel. Smith v. Baldi* absolved it completely of the obligation to provide access to a psychiatrist. . . . [We] disagree. . . . [*Smith*] was decided at a time when indigent defendants in state courts had no constitutional right to even the presence of counsel. Our recognition since then of elemental constitutional rights, each of which has enhanced the ability of an indigent defendant to attain a fair hearing, has signaled our increased commitment to assuring meaningful access to the judicial process. Also, neither trial practice nor legislative treatment of the role of insanity in the criminal process sits paralyzed simply because this Court has once addressed them, and we would surely be remiss to ignore the extraordinarily enhanced role of psychiatry in criminal law today. Shifts in all these areas since the time of *Smith* convince us that the opinion in that case was addressed to altogether different variables, and that we are not limited by it in considering whether fundamental fairness today requires a different result.

IV

We turn now to apply these standards to the facts of this case. On the record before us, it is clear that Ake's mental state at the time of the offense was a substantial factor in his defense, and that the trial court was on notice of that fact when the request for a court-appointed psychiatrist was made. For one, Ake's sole defense was that of insanity. Second, Ake's behavior at arraignment, just four months after the offense, was so bizarre as to prompt the trial judge, *sua sponte*, to have him examined for competency. Third, a state psychiatrist shortly thereafter found Ake to be incompetent to stand trial, and suggested that he be committed. Fourth, when he was found to be competent six weeks later, it was only on the condition that he be sedated with large doses of Thorazine three times a day, during trial. Fifth, the psychiatrists who examined Ake for competency described to the trial court the severity of Ake's mental illness less than six months after the offense in question, and suggested that this mental illness might have begun many years earlier. Finally, Oklahoma recognizes a defense of insanity, under which the initial burden of producing evidence falls on the defendant. Taken together, these factors make clear that the question of Ake's sanity was likely to be a significant factor in his defense.

In addition, Ake's future dangerousness was a significant factor at the sentencing phase. The state psychiatrist who treated Ake at the state mental hospital testified at the guilt phase that, because of his mental illness, Ake posed a threat of continuing criminal violence. This testimony raised the issue of Ake's future dangerousness, which is an aggravating factor under Oklahoma's capital sentencing scheme, and on which the prosecutor relied at sentencing. We therefore conclude that Ake also was entitled to the assistance of a psychiatrist on this issue and that the denial of that assistance deprived him of due process.

Accordingly, we reverse and remand for a new trial.

Chief Justice Burger concurred in the judgment; he would have restricted the decision to capital cases. Justice Rehnquist dissented.

49. *Bounds v. Smith* (1977)

In 1971 the Court held that prisoners had a constitutional right of access to the courts, which the state could satisfy by giving prisoners adequate law libraries or other ways of obtaining "legal knowledge." In this case, North Carolina's prison officials asked the Court to reconsider its earlier ruling. The trial court had found the only prison library in the state to be "severely inadequate." It asked the state to prepare a plan for legal assistance, which might include improving the library or making lawyers and law students available to prisoners. The state proposed a plan to improve the law libraries at several of the state's prisons, but not at all of them. The plan would stock the libraries with law books approved as the minimum for prison law libraries by the American Bar Association, and would allow prisoners at other institutions to travel to the ones with the improved libraries. The state would also train inmates as legal assistants. It estimated that about 350 prisoners a week would be able to use the libraries, although it acknowledged that prisoners who did not face court deadlines would have to wait three or four weeks for their turn at a library. The trial court approved the plan, and the state appealed.

MR. JUSTICE MARSHALL DELIVERED THE OPINION OF THE COURT.

II

A. It is now established beyond doubt that prisoners have a constitutional right of access to the courts. This Court recognized that right more than 35 years ago when it struck down a regulation prohibiting state prisoners from filing petitions for habeas corpus unless they were found "'properly drawn'" by the "'legal investigator'" for the parole board. We held this violated the principle that "the state and its officers may not abridge or impair petitioner's right to apply to a federal court for a writ of habeas corpus."

More recent decisions have struck down restrictions and required remedial measures to insure that inmate access to the courts is adequate, effective, and meaningful. Thus, in order to prevent "effectively foreclosed access," indigent prisoners must be allowed to file appeals and habeas corpus petitions without payment of docket fees. Because we recognized that "adequate and effective appellate review" is impossible without a trial transcript or adequate substitute, we held that States must provide trial records to inmates unable to buy them. Similarly, counsel must be appointed to give indigent inmates "a meaningful appeal" from their convictions.

Essentially the same standards of access were applied in *Johnson v. Avery* (1969), which struck down a regulation prohibiting prisoners from assisting each other with habeas corpus applications and other legal matters. Since inmates had no alternative form of legal assistance available to them, we reasoned that this ban on jailhouse lawyers effectively prevented prisoners who were "unable themselves, with reasonable adequacy, to prepare their petitions," from challenging the legality of their confinements. *Johnson* was unanimously extended to cover assistance in civil rights actions in *Wolff v. McDonnell* (1974). And even as it rejected a claim that indigent defendants have a constitutional right to appointed counsel for discretionary appeals, the Court reaffirmed that States must "assure the indigent defendant an adequate opportunity to present his claims fairly." "[M]eaningful access" to the courts is the touchstone.

Petitioners contend, however, that this constitutional duty merely obliges States to allow inmate "writ writers" to function. They argue that under *Johnson v. Avery,* as long as inmate communications on legal problems are not restricted, there is no further obligation to expend state funds to implement affirmatively the right of access. This argument misreads the cases. . . .

Moreover, our decisions have consistently required States to shoulder affirmative obligations to assure all prisoners meaningful access to the courts. It is indisputable that indigent inmates must be provided at state expense with paper and pen to draft legal documents, with notarial services to authenticate them, and with stamps to mail them. States must forgo collection of docket fees otherwise payable to the treasury and expend funds for transcripts. State expenditures are necessary to pay lawyers for indigent defendants at trial, and in appeals as of right. This is not to say that economic factors may not be considered, for example, in choosing the methods used to provide meaningful access. But the cost of protecting a constitutional right cannot justify its total denial. Thus, neither the availability of jailhouse lawyers nor the necessity for affirmative state action is dispositive of respondents' claims. The inquiry is rather whether law libraries or other forms of legal assistance are needed to give prisoners a reasonably adequate opportunity to present claimed violations of fundamental constitutional rights to the courts.

B. Although it is essentially true, as petitioners argue, that a habeas corpus petition or civil rights complaint need only set forth facts giving rise to the cause of action, it hardly follows that a law library or other legal assistance is not essential to frame such documents. It would verge on incompetence for a lawyer to file an initial pleading without researching such issues as jurisdiction, venue, standing, exhaustion of remedies, proper parties plaintiff and defendant, and types of relief available. Most importantly, of course, a lawyer must know what the law is in order to determine whether a colorable claim exists, and if so, what facts are necessary to state a cause of action.

If a lawyer must perform such preliminary research, it is no less vital for a *pro se* prisoner. Indeed, despite the "less stringent standards" by which a *pro se* pleading is judged, it is often more important that a prisoner complaint set forth a nonfrivolous claim meeting all procedural prerequisites, since the court may pass on the complaint's sufficiency before allowing filing *in forma pauperis* and may dismiss the case if it is deemed frivolous. Moreover, if the State files a response to a *pro se* pleading, it will undoubtedly contain seemingly authoritative citations.

Without a library, an inmate will be unable to rebut the State's argument. It is not enough to answer that the court will evaluate the facts pleaded in light of the relevant law. Even the most dedicated trial judges are bound to overlook meritorious cases without the benefit of an adversary presentation. . . .

We reject the State's claim that inmates are "ill-equipped to use" "the tools of the trade of the legal profession," making libraries useless in assuring meaningful access. In the first place, the claim is inconsistent with the State's representations on its LEAA grant application, and with its argument that access is adequately protected by allowing inmates to help each other with legal problems. More importantly, this Court's experience indicates that *pro se* petitioners are capable of using lawbooks to file cases raising claims that are serious and legitimate even if ultimately unsuccessful. Finally, we note that if petitioners had any doubts about the efficacy of libraries, the District Court's initial decision left them free to choose another means of assuring access. . . .

[I]n this case, we are concerned in large part with original actions seeking new trials, release from confinement, or vindication of fundamental civil rights. Rather than presenting claims that have been passed on by two courts, they frequently raise heretofore unlitigated issues. As this Court has "constantly emphasized," habeas corpus and civil rights actions are of "fundamental importance . . . in our constitutional scheme" because they directly protect our most valued rights. While applications for discretionary review need only apprise an appellate court of a case's possible relevance to the development of the law, the prisoner petitions here are the first line of defense against constitutional violations. The need for new legal research or advice to make a meaningful initial presentation to a trial court in such a case is far greater than is required to file an adequate petition for discretionary review.

We hold, therefore, that the fundamental constitutional right of access to the courts requires prison authorities to assist inmates in the preparation and filing of meaningful legal papers by providing prisoners with adequate law libraries or adequate assistance from persons trained in the law. . . .

C. . . . It should be noted that while adequate law libraries are one constitutionally acceptable method to assure meaningful access to the courts, our decision here does not foreclose alternative means to achieve that goal. Nearly half the States and the District of Columbia provide some degree of professional or quasi-professional legal assistance to prisoners. Such programs take many imaginative forms and may have a number of advantages over libraries alone. Among the alternatives are the training of inmates as paralegal assistants to work under lawyers' supervision, the use of paraprofessionals and law students, either as volunteers or in formal clinical programs, the organization of volunteer attorneys through bar associations or other groups, the hiring of lawyers on a part-time consultant basis, and the use of full-time staff attorneys, working either in new prison legal assistance organizations or as part of public defender or legal services offices. Legal services plans not only result in more efficient and skillful handling of prisoner cases, but also avoid the disciplinary problems associated with writ writers. Independent legal advisors can mediate or resolve administratively many prisoner complaints that would otherwise burden the courts, and can convince inmates that other grievances against the prison or the legal system are ill-founded, thereby facilitating rehabilitation by assuring the inmate that he has not been treated unfairly. It has been estimated that as few as 500 full-time lawyers would be needed to serve the legal needs of the entire national prison population. Nevertheless, a legal access program need not include any particular element we have discussed, and we encourage local experimentation. Any plan, however, must be evaluated as a whole to ascertain its compliance with constitutional standards.

III

Finally, petitioners urge us to reverse the decision below because federal courts should not "sit as co-administrators of state prisons," and because the District Court "exceeded its powers when it puts [*sic*] itself in the place of the [prison] administrators." While we have recognized that judicial restraint is often appropriate in prisoners' rights cases, we have also repeatedly held that this policy "cannot encompass any failure to take cognizance of valid constitutional claims."

Petitioners' hyperbolic claim is particularly inappropriate in this case, for the courts below scrupulously respected the limits on their role. The District Court initially held only that petitioners had violated the "fundamental constitutional guarantee" of access to the courts. It did not thereupon thrust itself into prison administration. Rather, it ordered petitioners themselves to devise a remedy for the violation, strongly suggesting that it would prefer a plan providing trained legal advisors. Petitioners chose to establish law libraries, however, and their plan was approved with only minimal changes over the strong objections of respondents. Prison administrators thus exercised wide discretion within the bounds of constitutional requirements in this case.

The judgment is
Affirmed.

Justice Powell concurred and Chief Justice Burger, Justice Stewart, and Justice Rehnquist dissented. The substantive rule in *Bounds* largely remains good law, but its practical implementation has been substantially limited by the Court's decision in *Lewis v. Casey* (1996), which allowed challenges to inadequate prison libraries to be brought only by those prisoners who could show that they had non-frivolous claims relating to their convictions or the conditions under which they were confined, which they were unable to pursue because the institution failed to provide adequate assistance to them as they sought access to the courts.

50. *Stanley v. Georgia* (1969)

MR. JUSTICE MARSHALL DELIVERED THE OPINION OF THE COURT.

An investigation of appellant's alleged bookmaking activities led to the issuance of a search warrant for appellant's home. Under authority of this warrant, federal and state agents secured entrance. They found very little evidence of bookmaking activity, but while looking through a desk drawer in an upstairs bedroom, one of the federal agents, accompanied by a state officer, found three reels of eight-millimeter film. Using a projector and screen found in an upstairs living room, they viewed the films. The state officer concluded that they were obscene and seized them. Since a further examination of the bedroom indicated that appellant occupied it, he was charged with possession of obscene matter and placed under arrest. He was later indicted for "knowingly hav[ing] possession of . . . obscene matter" in violation of Georgia law. Appellant was tried before a jury and convicted. The Supreme Court of Georgia affirmed. . . .

Appellant raises several challenges to the validity of his conviction. We find it necessary to consider only one. Appellant argues here, and argued below, that the Georgia obscenity statute, insofar as it punishes mere private possession of obscene matter, violates the First Amendment, as made applicable to the States by the Fourteenth Amendment. For reasons set forth below, we agree that the mere private possession of obscene matter cannot constitutionally be made a crime.

The court below saw no valid constitutional objection to the Georgia statute, even though it extends further than the typical statute forbidding commercial sales of obscene material. It held that "it is not essential to an indictment charging one with possession of obscene matter that it be alleged that such possession was 'with intent to sell, expose or circulate the same.'" The State and appellant both agree that the question here before us is whether "a statute imposing criminal sanctions upon the mere [knowing] possession of obscene matter" is constitutional. In this context, Georgia concedes that the present case appears to be one of "first impression . . . on this exact point," but contends that since "obscenity is not within the area of constitutionally protected speech or press," *Roth v. United States* (1957), the States are free, subject to the limits of other provisions of the Constitution to deal with it any way deemed necessary, just as they may deal with possession of other things thought to be detrimental to the welfare of their citizens. If the State can protect the body of a citizen, may it not, argues Georgia, protect his mind? . . .

In this context, we do not believe that this case can be decided simply by citing *Roth*. *Roth* and its progeny certainly do mean that the First and Fourteenth Amendments recognize a valid governmental interest in dealing with the problem of obscenity. But the assertion of that interest cannot, in every context, be insulated from all constitutional protections. Neither *Roth* nor any other decision of this Court reaches that far. As the Court said in *Roth* itself, "ceaseless vigilance is the watchword to prevent . . . erosion [of First Amendment rights] by Congress or by the States. The door barring federal and state intrusion into this area cannot be left ajar; it must be kept tightly closed and opened only the slightest crack necessary to prevent encroachment upon more important interests." *Roth* and the cases following it discerned such an "important interest" in the regulation of commercial distribution of obscene material. That holding cannot foreclose an examination of the constitutional implications of a statute forbidding mere private possession of such material.

It is now well established that the Constitution protects the right to receive information and ideas. "This freedom [of speech and press] . . . necessarily protects the right to receive . . . ." This right to receive information and ideas, regardless of their social worth, is fundamental to our free society. Moreover, in the context of this case—a prosecution for mere possession of printed or filmed matter in the privacy of a person's own home—that right takes on an added dimension. For also fundamental is the right to be free, except in very limited circumstances, from unwanted governmental intrusions into one's privacy.

> "The makers of our Constitution undertook to secure conditions favorable to the pursuit of happiness. They recognized the significance of man's spiritual nature, of his feelings and of his intellect. They knew that only a part of the pain, pleasure and satisfactions of life are to be found in material things. They sought to protect Americans in their beliefs, their thoughts, their emotions and their sensations. They conferred, as against the Government, the right to be let alone—the most comprehensive of rights and the right most valued by civilized man." *Olmstead v. United States* (1928) (Brandeis, J., dissenting).

These are the rights that appellant is asserting in the case before us. He is asserting the right to read or observe what he pleases—the right to satisfy his intellectual and emotional needs in the privacy of his own home. He is asserting the right to be free from state inquiry into the contents of his library. Georgia contends that appellant does not have these rights, that there are certain types of materials that the individual may not read or even possess. Georgia justifies this assertion by arguing that the films in the present case are obscene. But we think that mere categorization of these films as "obscene" is insufficient justification for such a drastic invasion of personal liberties guaranteed by the First and Fourteenth Amendments. Whatever may be the justifications for other statutes regulating obscenity, we do not think they reach into the privacy of one's own home. If the First Amendment means anything, it means that a State has no business telling a man, sitting alone in his own house, what books he may read or what films he may watch. Our whole constitutional heritage rebels at the thought of giving government the power to control men's minds.

And yet, in the face of these traditional notions of individual liberty, Georgia asserts the right to protect the individual's mind from the effects of obscenity. We are not certain that this argument amounts to anything more than the assertion that the State has the right to control the moral content of a person's thoughts.[1] To some, this may be a noble purpose, but it is wholly inconsistent with the philosophy of the First Amendment. As the Court said in *Kingsley International Pictures Corp. v. Regents*, "this argument misconceives what it is that the Constitution protects. Its guarantee is not confined to the expression of ideas that are conventional or shared by a majority. . . . And in the realm of ideas it protects expression which is eloquent no less than that which is unconvincing." Nor is it relevant that obscene materials in general, or the particular films before the Court, are arguably devoid of any ideological content. The line between the transmission of ideas and mere entertainment is much too elusive for this Court to draw, if indeed such a line can be drawn at all. Whatever the power of the state to control public dissemination of ideas inimical to the public morality, it cannot constitutionally premise legislation on the desirability of controlling a person's private thoughts.

Perhaps recognizing this, Georgia asserts that exposure to obscene materials may lead to deviant sexual behavior or crimes of sexual violence. There appears to be little empirical basis for that assertion. But more important, if the State is only concerned about printed or filmed materials inducing antisocial conduct, we believe that in the context of private consumption of ideas and information we should adhere to the view that "among free men, the deterrents ordinarily to be applied to prevent crime are education and punishment for violations of the law. . . ." *Whitney v. California* (1927) (Brandeis, J., concurring). Given the present state of knowledge, the State may no more prohibit mere possession of obscene matter on the ground that it may lead to antisocial conduct than it may prohibit possession of chemistry books on the ground that they may lead to the manufacture of homemade spirits.

It is true that in *Roth* this Court rejected the necessity of proving that exposure to obscene material would create a clear and present danger of antisocial conduct or would probably induce its recipients to such conduct. But that case dealt with public distribution of obscene materials and such distribution is subject to different objections. For example, there is always the danger that obscene material might

---

[1] "Communities believe, and act on the belief, that obscenity is immoral, is wrong for the individual, and has no place in a decent society. They believe, too, that adults as well as children are corruptible in morals and character, and that obscenity is a source of corruption that should be eliminated. Obscenity is not suppressed primarily for the protection of others. Much of it is suppressed for the purity of the community and for the salvation and welfare of the 'consumer.' Obscenity, at bottom, is not crime. Obscenity is sin." Henkin, *Morals and the Constitution: The Sin of Obscenity*. 63 Col. L. Rev. 391, 395 (1963). [footnote in original]

fall into the hands of children, or that it might intrude upon the sensibilities or privacy of the general public. No such dangers are present in this case.

Finally, we are faced with the argument that prohibition of possession of obscene materials is a necessary incident to statutory schemes prohibiting distribution. That argument is based on alleged difficulties of proving an intent to distribute or in producing evidence of actual distribution. We are not convinced that such difficulties exist, but even if they did we do not think that they would justify infringement of the individual's right to read or observe what he pleases. Because that right is so fundamental to our scheme of individual liberty, its restriction may not be justified by the need to ease the administration of otherwise valid criminal laws.

We hold that the First and Fourteenth Amendments prohibit making mere private possession of obscene material a crime. *Roth* and the cases following that decision are not impaired by today's holding. As we have said, the States retain broad power to regulate obscenity; that power simply does not extend to mere possession by the individual in the privacy of his own home. Accordingly, the judgment of the court below is reversed and the case is remanded for proceedings not inconsistent with this opinion.

It is so ordered.

Justice Black concurred, and Justice Stewart, joined by Justices Brennan and White, concurred in the result. Justice Stewart argued that Stanley's rights under the Fourth Amendment were violated by the search that resulted in the film's discovery. The Court has adhered to *Stanley*, but later cases held that Congress and the states could make it unlawful for people to sell obscene materials. If a person obtains such materials and manages to transport them to his home, *Stanley* bars prosecution, but the First Amendment does not stop governments from trying to make it difficult for people to get the material in the first place.

51. *Police Department of the City of Chicago v. Mosley* (1972)

MR. JUSTICE MARSHALL DELIVERED THE OPINION OF THE COURT.

At issue in this case is the constitutionality of the following Chicago ordinance:

"A person commits disorderly conduct when he knowingly:

. . . .

"(i) Pickets or demonstrates on a public way within 150 feet of any primary or secondary school building while the school is in session and one-half hour before the school is in session and one-half hour after the school session has been concluded, provided that this subsection does not prohibit the peaceful picketing of any school involved in a labor dispute . . . ."

The suit was brought by Earl Mosley, a federal postal employee, who for seven months prior to the enactment of the ordinance had frequently picketed Jones Commercial High School in Chicago. During school hours and usually by himself, Mosley would walk the public sidewalk adjoining the school, carrying a sign that read: "Jones High School practices black discrimination. Jones High School has a black quota." His lonely crusade was always peaceful, orderly, and quiet, and was conceded to be so by the city of Chicago. . . .

I

The city of Chicago exempts peaceful labor picketing from its general prohibition on picketing next to a school. The question we consider here is whether this selective exclusion from a public place is permitted. Our answer is "No."

Because Chicago treats some picketing differently from others, we analyze this ordinance in terms of the Equal Protection Clause of the Fourteenth Amendment. Of course, the equal protection claim in this case is closely intertwined with First Amendment interests; the Chicago ordinance affects picketing, which is expressive conduct; moreover, it does so by classifications formulated in terms of the subject of the picketing. As in all equal protection cases, however, the crucial question is whether there is an appropriate governmental interest suitably furthered by the differential treatment.

The central problem with Chicago's ordinance is that it describes permissible picketing in terms of its subject matter. Peaceful picketing on the subject of a school's labor-management dispute is permitted, but all other peaceful picketing is prohibited. The operative distinction is the message on a picket sign. But, above all else, the First Amendment means that government has no power to restrict expression because of its message, its ideas, its subject matter, or its content. To permit

389

the continued building of our politics and culture, and to assure self-fulfillment for each individual, our people are guaranteed the right to express any thought, free from government censorship. The essence of this forbidden censorship is content control. Any restriction on expressive activity because of its content would completely undercut the "profound national commitment to the principle that debate on public issues should be uninhibited, robust, and wide-open."

Necessarily, then, under the Equal Protection Clause, not to mention the First Amendment itself, government may not grant the use of a forum to people whose views it finds acceptable, but deny use to those wishing to express less favored or more controversial views. And it may not select which issues are worth discussing or debating in public facilities. There is an "equality of status in the field of ideas," and government must afford all points of view an equal opportunity to be heard. Once a forum is opened up to assembly or speaking by some groups, government may not prohibit others from assembling or speaking on the basis of what they intend to say. Selective exclusions from a public forum may not be based on content alone, and may not be justified by reference to content alone. . . .

The late Mr. Justice Black, who thought that picketing was not only a method of expressing an idea but also conduct subject to broad state regulation, nevertheless recognized the deficiencies of laws like Chicago's ordinance. This was the thrust of his opinion concurring in *Cox v. Louisiana* (1965):

> "By specifically permitting picketing for the publication of labor union views [but prohibiting other sorts of picketing], Louisiana is attempting to pick and choose among the views it is willing to have discussed on its streets. It thus is trying to prescribe by law what matters of public interest people whom it allows to assemble on its streets may and may not discuss. This seems to me to be censorship in a most odious form, unconstitutional under the First and Fourteenth Amendments. And to deny this appellant and his group use of the streets because of their views against racial discrimination, while allowing other groups to use the streets to voice opinions on other subjects, also amounts, I think, to an invidious discrimination forbidden by the Equal Protection Clause of the Fourteenth Amendment."

We accept Mr. Justice Black's quoted views.

II

This is not to say that all picketing must always be allowed. We have continually recognized that reasonable "time, place and manner" regulations of picketing may be necessary to further significant governmental interests. Similarly, under an equal protection analysis, there may be sufficient regulatory interests justifying selective exclusions or distinctions among pickets. Conflicting demands on the same place may compel the State to make choices among potential users and uses.

And the State may have a legitimate interest in prohibiting some picketing to protect public order. But these justifications for selective exclusions from a public forum must be carefully scrutinized. Because picketing plainly involves expressive conduct within the protection of the First Amendment, discriminations among pickets must be tailored to serve a substantial governmental interest.

III

In this case, the ordinance itself describes impermissible picketing not in terms of time, place, and manner, but in terms of subject matter. The regulation "thus slip[s] from the neutrality of time, place, and circumstance into a concern about content." This is never permitted. In spite of this, Chicago urges that the ordinance is not improper content censorship, but rather a device for preventing disruption of the school. Cities certainly have a substantial interest in stopping picketing which disrupts a school. "The crucial question, however, is whether [Chicago's ordinance] advances that objective in a manner consistent with the command of the Equal Protection Clause." It does not.

Although preventing school disruption is a city's legitimate concern, Chicago itself has determined that peaceful labor picketing during school hours is not an undue interference with school. Therefore, under the Equal Protection Clause, Chicago may not maintain that other picketing disrupts the school unless that picketing is clearly more disruptive than the picketing Chicago already permits. If peaceful labor picketing is permitted, there is no justification for prohibiting all nonlabor picketing, both peaceful and nonpeaceful. "Peaceful" nonlabor picketing, however the term "peaceful" is defined, is obviously no more disruptive than "peaceful" labor picketing. But Chicago's ordinance permits the latter and prohibits the former. . . .

Similarly, we reject the city's argument that, although it permits peaceful labor picketing, it may prohibit all nonlabor picketing because, as a class, nonlabor picketing is more prone to produce violence than labor picketing. Predictions about imminent disruption from picketing involve judgments appropriately made on an individualized basis, not by means of broad classifications, especially those based on subject matter. Freedom of expression, and its intersection with the guarantee of equal protection, would rest on a soft foundation indeed if government could distinguish among picketers on such a wholesale and categorical basis. "In our system, undifferentiated fear or apprehension of disturbance is not enough to overcome the right to freedom of expression." Some labor picketing is peaceful, some disorderly; the same is true of picketing on other themes. No labor picketing could be more peaceful or less prone to violence than Mosley's solitary vigil. In seeking to restrict nonlabor picketing that is clearly more disruptive than peaceful labor picketing, Chicago may not prohibit all nonlabor picketing at the school forum.

The Equal Protection Clause requires that statutes affecting First Amendment interests be narrowly tailored to their legitimate objectives. Chicago may not vindicate its interest in preventing disruption by the wholesale exclusion of picketing on all but one preferred subject. Given what Chicago tolerates from labor picketing, the excesses of some nonlabor picketing may not be controlled by a broad ordinance prohibiting both peaceful and violent picketing. Such excesses "can be controlled by narrowly drawn statutes," focusing on the abuses and dealing evenhandedly with picketing regardless of subject matter. Chicago's ordinance imposes a selective restriction on expressive conduct far "greater than is essential to the furtherance of [a substantial governmental] interest." Far from being tailored to a substantial governmental interest, the discrimination among pickets is based on the content of their expression. Therefore, under the Equal Protection Clause, it may not stand.

The judgment is

Affirmed.

The Court has adhered to the basic rule articulated in *Mosley*, requiring very strong justifications for regulations that discriminate among types of speech based on their content. It has retreated, however, from Justice Marshall's statement that discrimination based on subject matter is equally suspect. Drawing the line between content-based regulations and subject-matter regulations is not always an easy task.

52. *Powell v. Texas* (1968)

In 1962 the Supreme Court decided *Robinson v. California*, holding that the Constitution's prohibition on cruel and unusual punishments made it unconstitutional for a state to make it a crime to *be* a drug addict. Penalizing someone for status rather than conduct, the Court said, was unconstitutional. *Robinson* opened up the possibility that the Constitution might impose limits on a large range of state substantive criminal law. (The Court had already placed substantial limits on state criminal *procedure*, but it had done little to regulate the states' ability to designate what sorts of activity or behavior might be criminal.) *Powell* was the first case testing the meaning of *Robinson* that reached the Supreme Court. The justices initially voted to strike down Texas's public drunkenness law, with Marshall voting tentatively with that majority. He changed his mind, however, and ultimately wrote the opinion for four justices upholding the law. His opinion incorporated large segments that had initially been written by Chief Justice Warren, and contains two themes of interest in connection with Marshall's career. First, the opinion is quite disdainful of the thin record regarding the facts about drunkenness, perhaps because Marshall understood the contrast between the record in *Powell* and the care with which he and his colleagues had developed the attack on segregation. The opinion's tone suggests that Marshall did not think that such a substantial revision of public policy should take place until the lawyers developed a more substantial record. Second, the opinion stresses the seriousness of the social problem of public drunkenness and, more important, the lack of alternatives to arrest as a means of dealing with it. Perhaps Marshall the social engineer needed to be assured that something sensible was available to replace the system under challenge.

MR. JUSTICE MARSHALL ANNOUNCED THE JUDGMENT OF THE COURT AND DELIVERED AN OPINION IN WHICH THE CHIEF JUSTICE, MR. JUSTICE BLACK, AND MR. JUSTICE HARLAN JOIN.

In late December 1966, appellant was arrested and charged with being found in a state of intoxication in a public place, in violation of Texas Penal Code, Art. 477 (1952), which reads as follows:

> "Whoever shall get drunk or be found in a state of intoxication in any public place, or at any private house except his own, shall be fined not exceeding one hundred dollars."

Appellant was tried in the Corporation Court of Austin, Texas, found guilty, and fined $20. He appealed to the County Court at Law No. 1 of Travis County, Texas, where a trial *de novo* was held. His counsel urged that appellant was "afflicted with the disease of chronic alcoholism," that "his appearance in public [while drunk was] . . . not of his own volition," and therefore that to punish him criminally for

393

that conduct would be cruel and unusual, in violation of the Eighth and Fourteenth Amendments to the United States Constitution.

The trial judge in the county court, sitting without a jury, made certain findings of fact, but ruled as a matter of law that chronic alcoholism was not a defense to the charge. He found appellant guilty, and fined him $50. There being no further right to appeal within the Texas judicial system, appellant appealed to this Court; we noted probable jurisdiction.

I

The principal testimony was that of Dr. David Wade, a Fellow of the American Medical Association, duly certificated in psychiatry. His testimony consumed a total of 17 pages in the trial transcript. Five of those pages were taken up with a recitation of Dr. Wade's qualifications. In the next 12 pages Dr. Wade was examined by appellant's counsel, cross-examined by the State, and re-examined by the defense, and those 12 pages contain virtually all the material developed at trial which is relevant to the constitutional issue we face here. Dr. Wade sketched the outlines of the "disease" concept of alcoholism; noted that there is no generally accepted definition of "alcoholism"; alluded to the ongoing debate within the medical profession over whether alcohol is actually physically "addicting" or merely psychologically "habituating"; and concluded that in either case a "chronic alcoholic" is an "involuntary drinker," who is "powerless not to drink," and who "loses his self-control over his drinking." He testified that he had examined appellant, and that appellant is a "chronic alcoholic," who "by the time he has reached [the state of intoxication] . . . is not able to control his behavior, and [who] . . . has reached this point because he has an uncontrollable compulsion to drink." Dr. Wade also responded in the negative to the question whether appellant has "the willpower to resist the constant excessive consumption of alcohol." He added that in his opinion jailing appellant without medical attention would operate neither to rehabilitate him nor to lessen his desire for alcohol.

On cross-examination, Dr. Wade admitted that when appellant was sober he knew the difference between right and wrong, and he responded affirmatively to the question whether appellant's act of taking the first drink in any given instance when he was sober was a "voluntary exercise of his will." Qualifying his answer, Dr. Wade stated that "these individuals have a compulsion, and this compulsion, while not completely overpowering, is a very strong influence, an exceedingly strong influence, and this compulsion coupled with the firm belief in their mind that they are going to be able to handle it from now on causes their judgment to be somewhat clouded."

Appellant testified concerning the history of his drinking problem. He reviewed his many arrests for drunkenness; testified that he was unable to stop drinking; stated that when he was intoxicated he had no control over his actions and could not remember them later, but that he did not become violent; and admitted that he did not remember his arrest on the occasion for which he was being tried. On cross-examination, appellant admitted that he had had one drink on the morning of the trial and had been able to discontinue drinking. In relevant part, the cross-examination went as follows:

"Q. You took that one at eight o'clock because you wanted to drink?

"A. Yes, sir.

"Q. And you knew that if you drank it, you could keep on drinking and get drunk?

"A. Well, I was supposed to be here on trial, and I didn't take but that one drink.

"Q. You knew you had to be here this afternoon, but this morning you took one drink and then you knew that you couldn't afford to drink any more and come to court; is that right?

"A. Yes, sir, that's right.

"Q. So you exercised your will power and kept from drinking anything today except that one drink?

"A. Yes, sir, that's right.

"Q. Because you knew what you would do if you kept drinking, that you would finally pass out or be picked up?

"A. Yes, sir.

"Q. And you didn't want that to happen to you today?

"A. No, sir.

"Q. Not today?

"A. No, sir.

"Q. So you only had one drink today?

"A. Yes, sir."

On redirect examination, appellant's lawyer elicited the following:

"Q. Leroy, isn't the real reason why you just had one drink today because you just had enough money to buy one drink?

"A. Well, that was just give to me.

"Q. In other words, you didn't have any money with which you could buy any drinks yourself?

"A. No, sir, that was give to me.

"Q. And that's really what controlled the amount you drank this morning, isn't it?

"A. Yes, sir.

"Q. Leroy, when you start drinking, do you have any control over how many drinks you can take?

"A. No, sir."

Evidence in the case then closed. The State made no effort to obtain expert psychiatric testimony of its own, or even to explore with appellant's witness the question of appellant's power to control the frequency, timing, and location of his drinking bouts, or the substantial disagreement within the medical profession concerning the nature of the disease, the efficacy of treatment and the prerequisites for effective treatment. It did nothing to examine or illuminate what Dr. Wade might have meant by his reference to a "compulsion" which was "not completely overpowering," but which was "an exceedingly strong influence," or to inquire into the question of the proper role of such a "compulsion" in constitutional adjudication. Instead, the State contented itself with a brief argument that appellant had no defense to the charge because he "is legally sane and knows the difference between right and wrong."

Following this abbreviated exposition of the problem before it, the trial court indicated its intention to disallow appellant's claimed defense of "chronic alcoholism." Thereupon defense counsel submitted, and the trial court entered, the following "findings of fact":

"(1) That chronic alcoholism is a disease which destroys the afflicted person's will power to resist the constant, excessive consumption of alcohol.

"(2) That a chronic alcoholic does not appear in public by his own volition but under a compulsion symptomatic of the disease of chronic alcoholism.

"(3) That Leroy Powell, defendant herein, is a chronic alcoholic who is afflicted with the disease of chronic alcoholism."

Whatever else may be said of them, those are not "findings of fact" in any recognizable, traditional sense in which that term has been used in a court of law; they are the premises of a syllogism transparently designed to bring this case within the scope of this Court's opinion in *Robinson v. California*. Nonetheless, the dissent would have us adopt these "findings" without critical examination; it would use them as the basis for a constitutional holding that "a person may not be punished if the condition essential to constitute the defined crime is part of the pattern of his disease and is occasioned by a compulsion symptomatic of the disease."

The difficulty with that position, as we shall show, is that it goes much too far on the basis of too little knowledge. In the first place, the record in this case is utterly inadequate to permit the sort of informed and responsible adjudication which alone can support the announcement of an important and wide-ranging new constitutional principle. We know very little about the circumstances surrounding the drinking bout which resulted in this conviction, or about Leroy Powell's drinking problem, or indeed about alcoholism itself. The trial hardly reflects the sharp legal and evidentiary clash between fully prepared adversary litigants which is traditionally expected in major constitutional cases. The State put on only one witness, the arresting officer. The defense put on three—a policeman who testified to appellant's long history of arrests for public drunkenness, the psychiatrist, and appellant himself.

Furthermore, the inescapable fact is that there is no agreement among members of the medical profession about what it means to say that "alcoholism" is a "disease." One of the principal works in this field states that the major difficulty in articulating a "disease concept of alcoholism" is that "alcoholism has too many definitions and disease has practically none." This same author concludes that "*a disease is what the medical profession recognizes as such.*" In other words, there is widespread agreement today that "alcoholism" is a "disease," for the simple reason that the medical profession has concluded that it should attempt to treat those who have drinking problems. There the agreement stops. Debate rages within the medical profession as to whether "alcoholism" is a separate "disease" in any meaningful biochemical, physiological or psychological sense, or whether it represents one peculiar manifestation in some individuals of underlying psychiatric disorders.

Nor is there any substantial consensus as to the "manifestations of alcoholism." E. M. Jellinek, one of the outstanding authorities on the subject, identifies five different types of alcoholics which predominate in the United States, and these types display a broad range of different and occasionally inconsistent symptoms. Moreover, wholly distinct types, relatively rare in this country, predominate in nations with different cultural attitudes regarding the consumption of alcohol. Even if we limit our consideration to the range of alcoholic symptoms more typically found in this country, there is substantial disagreement as to the manifestations of the "disease" called "alcoholism." Jellinek, for example, considers that only two of his five alcoholic types can truly be said to be suffering from "alcoholism" as a "disease," because only these two types attain what he believes to be the requisite degree of physiological dependence on alcohol. He applies the label "gamma alcoholism" to "that species of alcoholism in which (1) acquired increased tissue tolerance to alcohol, (2) adaptive cell metabolism . . . , (3) withdrawal symptoms and 'craving,' i.e., physical dependence, and (4) loss of control are involved." A "delta" alcoholic, on the other hand, "shows the first three characteristics of gamma alcoholism as well as a less marked form of the fourth characteristic—that is, instead of loss of control there is inability to abstain." Other authorities approach the problems of classification in an entirely different manner and, taking account of the large role which psycho-social factors seem to play in "problem drinking," define the "disease" in terms of the earliest identifiable manifestations of any sort of abnormality in drinking patterns.

Dr. Wade appears to have testified about appellant's "chronic alcoholism" in terms similar to Jellinek's "gamma" and "delta" types, for these types are largely defined, in their later stages, in terms of a strong compulsion to drink, physiological dependence and an inability to abstain from drinking. No attempt was made in the court below, of course, to determine whether Leroy Powell could in fact properly be diagnosed as a "gamma" or "delta" alcoholic in Jellinek's terms. The focus at the trial, and in the dissent here, has been exclusively upon the factors of loss of control and inability to abstain. Assuming that it makes sense to compartmentalize in this manner the diagnosis of such a formless "disease," tremendous gaps in our knowledge remain, which the record in this case does nothing to fill.

The trial court's "finding" that Powell "is afflicted with the disease of chronic alcoholism," which "destroys the afflicted person's will power to resist the constant, excessive consumption of alcohol" covers a multitude of sins. Dr. Wade's testimony that appellant suffered from a compulsion which was an "exceedingly strong influence," but which was "not completely overpowering" is at least more carefully stated, if no less mystifying. Jellinek insists that conceptual clarity can only be achieved by distinguishing carefully between "loss of control" once an individual has commenced to drink and "inability to abstain" from drinking in the first place. Presumably a person would have to display both characteristics in order to make out a constitutional defense, should one be recognized. Yet the "findings" of the trial court utterly fail to make this crucial distinction, and there is serious question whether the record can be read to support a finding of either loss of control or inability to abstain.

Dr. Wade did testify that once appellant began drinking he appeared to have no control over the amount of alcohol he finally ingested. Appellant's own testimony concerning his drinking on the day of the trial would certainly appear, however, to cast doubt upon the conclusion that he was without control over his consumption of alcohol when he had sufficiently important reasons to exercise such control. However that may be, there are more serious factual and conceptual difficulties with reading this record to show that appellant was unable to abstain from drinking. Dr. Wade testified that when appellant was sober, the act of taking the first drink was a "voluntary exercise of his will," but that this exercise of will was undertaken under the "exceedingly strong influence" of a "compulsion" which was "not completely overpowering." Such concepts, when juxtaposed in this fashion, have little meaning.

Moreover, Jellinek asserts that it cannot accurately be said that a person is truly unable to abstain from drinking unless he is suffering the physical symptoms of withdrawal. There is no testimony in this record that Leroy Powell underwent withdrawal symptoms either before he began the drinking spree which resulted in the conviction under review here, or at any other time. In attempting to deal with the alcoholic's desire for drink in the absence of withdrawal symptoms, Jellinek is reduced to unintelligible distinctions between a "compulsion" (a "psychopathological phenomenon" which can apparently serve in some instances as the functional equivalent of a "craving" or symptom of withdrawal) and an "impulse" (something which differs from a loss of control, a craving or a compulsion, and to which Jellinek attributes the start of a new drinking bout for a "gamma" alcoholic). Other scholars are equally unhelpful in articulating the nature of a "compulsion."

It is one thing to say that if a man is deprived of alcohol his hands will begin to shake, he will suffer agonizing pains and ultimately he will have hallucinations; it is quite another to say that a man has a "compulsion" to take a drink, but that he also retains a certain amount of "free will" with which to resist. It is simply impossible, in the present state of our knowledge, to ascribe a useful meaning to the latter statement. This definitional confusion reflects, of course, not merely the undeveloped state of the psychiatric art but also the conceptual difficulties inevitably attendant upon the importation of scientific and medical models into a legal system generally predicated upon a different set of assumptions.

II

Despite the comparatively primitive state of our knowledge on the subject, it cannot be denied that the destructive use of alcoholic beverages is one of our principal social and public health problems. The lowest current informed estimate places the number of "alcoholics" in America (definitional problems aside) at 4,000,000, and most authorities are inclined to put the figure considerably higher. The problem is compounded by the fact that a very large percentage of the alcoholics in this country are "invisible"— they possess the means to keep their drinking problems secret, and the traditionally uncharitable attitude of our society toward alcoholics causes many of them to refrain from seeking treatment from any source. Nor can it be gainsaid that the legislative response to this enormous problem has in general been inadequate.

There is as yet no known generally effective method for treating the vast number of alcoholics in our society. Some individual alcoholics have responded to particular forms of therapy with remissions of their symptomatic dependence upon the drug. But just as there is no agreement among doctors and social workers with respect to the causes of alcoholism, there is no consensus as to why particular treatments have been effective in particular cases and there is no generally agreed-upon approach to the problem of treatment on a large scale. Most psychiatrists are apparently of the opinion that alcoholism is far more difficult to treat than other forms of behavioral disorders, and some believe it is impossible to cure by means of psychotherapy; indeed, the medical profession as a whole, and psychiatrists in particular, have been severely criticized for the prevailing reluctance to undertake the treatment of drinking problems. Thus it is entirely possible that, even were the manpower and facilities available for a full-scale attack upon chronic alcoholism, we would find ourselves unable to help the vast bulk of our "visible"—let alone our "invisible"—alcoholic population.

However, facilities for the attempted treatment of indigent alcoholics are woefully lacking throughout the country. It would be tragic to return large numbers of helpless, sometimes dangerous and frequently unsanitary inebriates to the streets of our cities without even the opportunity to sober up adequately which a brief jail term provides. Presumably no State or city will tolerate such a state of affairs. Yet the medical profession cannot, and does not, tell us with any assurance that, even if the buildings, equipment and trained personnel were made available, it could provide anything more than slightly higher-class jails for our indigent habitual inebriates. Thus we run the grave risk that nothing will be accomplished beyond the hanging of a new sign—reading "hospital"—over one wing of the jailhouse.

One virtue of the criminal process is, at least, that the duration of penal incarceration typically has some outside statutory limit; this is universally true in the case of petty offenses, such as public drunkenness, where jail terms are quite short on the whole. "Therapeutic civil commitment" lacks this feature; one is typically committed until one is "cured." Thus, to do otherwise than affirm might subject indigent alcoholics to the risk that they may be locked up for an indefinite period of time under the same conditions as before, with no more hope than before of receiving effective treatment and no prospect of periodic "freedom."

Faced with this unpleasant reality, we are unable to assert that the use of the criminal process as a means of dealing with the public aspects of problem drinking can never be defended as rational. The picture of the penniless drunk propelled aimlessly and endlessly through the law's "revolving door" of arrest, incarceration, release and re-arrest is not a pretty one. But before we condemn the present practice across-the-board, perhaps we ought to be able to point to some clear promise of a better world for these unfortunate people. Unfortunately, no such promise has yet been forthcoming. If, in addition to the absence of a coherent approach to the problem of treatment, we consider the almost complete absence of facilities and manpower for the implementation of a rehabilitation program, it is difficult to say in the present context that the criminal process is utterly lacking in social value. This Court has never held that anything in the Constitution requires that penal sanctions be designed solely to achieve therapeutic or rehabilitative effects, and it can hardly be said with assurance that incarceration serves such purposes any better for the general run of criminals than it does for public drunks.

Ignorance likewise impedes our assessment of the deterrent effect of criminal sanctions for public drunkenness. The fact that a high percentage of American alcoholics conceal their drinking problems, not merely by avoiding public displays of intoxication but also by shunning all forms of treatment, is indicative that some powerful deterrent operates to inhibit the public revelation of the existence of alcoholism. Quite probably this deterrent effect can be largely attributed to the harsh moral attitude which our society has traditionally taken toward intoxication and the shame which we have associated with alcoholism. Criminal conviction represents the degrading public revelation of what Anglo-American society has long condemned as a moral defect, and the existence of criminal sanctions may serve to reinforce this cultural taboo, just as we presume it serves to reinforce other, stronger feelings against murder, rape, theft, and other forms of antisocial conduct.

Obviously, chronic alcoholics have not been deterred from drinking to excess by the existence of criminal sanctions against public drunkenness. But all those who violate penal laws of any kind are by definition undeterred. The long-standing and still raging debate over the validity of the deterrence justification for penal sanctions has not reached any sufficiently clear conclusions to permit it to be said that such sanctions are ineffective in any particular context or for any particular group of people who are able to appreciate the consequences of their acts. Certainly no effort was made at the trial of this case, beyond a monosyllabic answer to a perfunctory one-line question, to determine the effectiveness of penal sanctions in deterring Leroy Powell in particular or chronic alcoholics in general from drinking at all or from getting drunk in particular places or at particular times.

III

Appellant claims that his conviction on the facts of this case would violate the Cruel and Unusual Punishment Clause of the Eighth Amendment as applied to the States through the Fourteenth Amendment. The primary purpose of that clause has always been considered, and properly so, to be directed at the method or kind of punishment imposed for the violation of criminal statutes; the nature of the conduct made criminal is ordinarily relevant only to the fitness of the punishment imposed.

Appellant, however, seeks to come within the application of the Cruel and Unusual Punishment Clause announced in *Robinson v. California*, which involved a state statute making it a crime to "be addicted to the use of narcotics." This Court held there that "a state law which imprisons a person thus afflicted [with narcotic addiction] as a criminal, even though he has never touched any narcotic drug within the State or been guilty of any irregular behavior there, inflicts a cruel and unusual punishment. . . ."

On its face the present case does not fall within that holding, since appellant was convicted, not for being a chronic alcoholic, but for being in public while drunk on a particular occasion. The State of Texas thus has not sought to punish a mere status, as California did in *Robinson*; nor has it attempted to regulate appellant's behavior in the privacy of his own home. Rather, it has imposed upon appellant a criminal sanction for public behavior which may create substantial health and safety hazards, both for appellant and for members of the general public, and which offends the moral and esthetic sensibilities of a large segment of the community. This seems a far cry from convicting one for being an addict, being a chronic alcoholic, being "mentally ill, or a leper. . . ."

Robinson so viewed brings this Court but a very small way into the substantive criminal law. And unless *Robinson* is so viewed it is difficult to see any limiting principle that would serve to prevent this Court from becoming, under the aegis of the Cruel and Unusual Punishment Clause, the ultimate arbiter of the standards of criminal responsibility, in diverse areas of the criminal law, throughout the country.

It is suggested in dissent that *Robinson* stands for the "simple" but "subtle" principle that "[c]riminal penalties may not be inflicted upon a person for being in a condition he is powerless to change." In that view, appellant's "condition" of public intoxication was "occasioned by a compulsion symptomatic of the disease" of chronic alcoholism, and thus, apparently, his behavior lacked the critical element of *mens rea*. Whatever may be the merits of such a doctrine of criminal responsibility, it surely cannot be said to follow from *Robinson*. The entire thrust of *Robinson*'s interpretation of the Cruel and Unusual Punishment Clause is that criminal penalties may be inflicted only if the accused has committed some act, has engaged in some behavior, which society has an interest in preventing, or perhaps in historical common law terms, has committed some *actus reus*. It thus does not deal with the question of whether certain conduct cannot constitutionally be punished because it is, in some sense, "involuntary" or "occasioned by a compulsion."

Likewise, as the dissent acknowledges, there is a substantial definitional distinction between a "status," as in *Robinson*, and a "condition," which is said to be involved in this case. Whatever may be the merits of an attempt to distinguish between behavior and a condition, it is perfectly clear that the crucial element in this case, so far as the dissent is concerned, is whether or not appellant can legally be held responsible for his appearance in public in a state of intoxication. The only relevance of *Robinson* to this issue is that because the Court interpreted the statute there involved as making a "status" criminal, it was able to suggest that the statute would cover even a situation in which addiction had been acquired involuntarily. That this factor was not determinative in the case is shown by the fact that there was no indication of how Robinson himself had become an addict.

Ultimately, then, the most troubling aspects of this case, were *Robinson* to be extended to meet it, would be the scope and content of what could only be a constitutional doctrine of criminal responsibility. In dissent it is urged that the decision could be limited to conduct which is "a characteristic and involuntary part of the pattern of the disease as it afflicts" the particular individual, and that "[i]t is not foreseeable" that it would be applied "in the case of offenses such as driving a car while intoxicated, assault, theft, or robbery." That is limitation by fiat. In the first place, nothing in the logic of the dissent would limit its application to chronic alcoholics. If Leroy Powell cannot be convicted of public intoxication, it is difficult to see how a State can convict an individual for murder, if that individual, while exhibiting normal behavior in all other respects, suffers from a "compulsion" to kill, which is an "exceedingly strong influence," but "not completely overpowering." Even if we limit our consideration to chronic alcoholics, it would seem impossible to confine the principle within the arbitrary bounds which the dissent seems to envision.

It is not difficult to imagine a case involving psychiatric testimony to the effect that an individual suffers from some aggressive neurosis which he is able to control when sober; that very little alcohol suffices to remove the inhibitions which normally contain these aggressions, with the result that the individual engages in assaultive behavior without becoming actually intoxicated; and that the individual suffers from a very strong desire to drink, which is an "exceedingly strong influence" but "not completely overpowering." Without being untrue to the rationale of this case, should the principles advanced in dissent be accepted here, the Court could not avoid holding such an individual constitutionally unaccountable for his assaultive behavior.

Traditional common-law concepts of personal accountability and essential considerations of federalism lead us to disagree with appellant. We are unable to conclude, on the state of this record or on the current state of medical knowledge, that chronic alcoholics in general, and Leroy Powell in particular, suffer from such an irresistible compulsion to drink and to get drunk in public that they are utterly unable to control their performance of either or both of these acts and thus cannot be deterred at all from public intoxication. And in any event this Court has never articulated a general constitutional doctrine of *mens rea*.

We cannot cast aside the centuries-long evolution of the collection of interlocking and overlapping concepts which the common law has utilized to assess the moral accountability of an individual for his antisocial deeds. The doctrines of *actus reus, mens rea*, insanity, mistake, justification, and duress have historically provided the tools for a constantly shifting adjustment of the tension between the evolving aims of the criminal law and changing religious, moral, philosophical, and medical views of the nature of man. This process of adjustment has always been thought to be the province of the States.

Nothing could be less fruitful than for this Court to be impelled into defining some sort of insanity test in constitutional terms. Yet, that task would seem to follow inexorably from an extension of *Robinson* to this case. If a person in the "condition" of being a chronic alcoholic cannot be criminally punished as a constitutional matter for being drunk in public, it would seem to follow that a person who contends that, in terms of one test, "his unlawful act was the product of mental disease or mental defect," would state an issue of constitutional dimension with regard to his criminal responsibility had he been tried under some different and perhaps lesser standard, *e.g.*, the right-wrong test of *M'Naghten's Case*. The experimentation of one jurisdiction in that field alone indicates the magnitude of the problem. But formulating a constitutional rule would reduce, if not eliminate, that fruitful experimentation, and freeze the developing productive dialogue between law and psychiatry into a rigid constitutional mold. It is simply not yet the time to write into the Constitution formulas cast in terms whose meaning, let alone relevance, is not yet clear either to doctors or to lawyers.

Affirmed.

Justices Black, Harlan, and White concurred. Justice Fortas wrote the long dissent, originally the majority opinion, which was joined by Justices Douglas, Brennan, and Stewart.

53. *Payne v. Tennessee* (1991)

The opinion in *Payne v. Tennessee* was delivered on June 27, 1991, the day Marshall announced his retirement from the Court. His dissent, sharply criticizing the majority for exercising power rather than reason, was his last public act as a justice.

The issue in *Payne* was whether "victim-impact statements" could be admitted for juries to consider when they were deciding whether to impose the death penalty on a defendant whom they had already convicted. In *Booth v. Maryland* (1987) a sharply divided Supreme Court held that victim-impact statements could not be admitted. Justice Powell, generally regarded as a law-and-order conservative, wrote the Court's opinion in *Booth*. Victim-impact statements should not be admitted, he wrote, because they made it possible for juries to vote for a death sentence when the victim was "sympathetic" or left family members able to testify in strong emotional terms about the loss the defendant had imposed on them, but to vote against a death sentence when the victim was unsympathetic or happened to have few friends or family to present a powerful view of the killing's effects on them and their community. The death penalty would then become a measure of the victim's standing in the community rather than a punishment based on the nature of the crime the defendant committed. In short, victim-impact statements raised the possibility that the death penalty would become a form of class justice.

Two years after *Booth*, and after Justice Powell's retirement, the Court revisited the issue in *South Carolina v. Gathers* (1989). Again, a five-to-four majority voted against victim-impact statements. This time, however, the majority included Justice Byron White, who had dissented in *Booth*. Justice White clearly was willing to overrule *Booth*, but was annoyed that his colleagues tried to distinguish the case rather than forthrightly overrule it. *Payne v. Tennessee* gave the Court another chance to reconsider *Booth*, this time after Justice David Souter had replaced Justice Brennan on the Court.

The defendant, Pervis Tyrone Payne, killed a woman and one of her two children after the woman had rejected Payne's sexual advances. The victims bled to death after Payne stabbed them each over thirty times. (Payne also stabbed the woman's three-year-old son, who survived after seven hours of surgery and after transfusions of more blood than he ordinarily had in his body.) Although there was no serious doubt of his guilt, Payne denied committing the crimes. After the jury found him guilty, Payne presented evidence from his girlfriend, who said that Payne devoted a lot of time to her and her children and was a very caring person, and from his parents. The state presented victim-impact testimony from the victim's mother. She testified that the surviving son "cries for his mom" and did not understand why his mother did not come home.

The jury voted for the death penalty, and the state supreme court affirmed the conviction and sentence. Payne sought Supreme Court review. According to the majority opinion, the Court granted review to reconsider *Booth* and *Gathers*. Six members of the Court joined Chief Justice Rehnquist's opinion overruling those cases. Justice Marshall wrote a dissent that Justice Blackmun joined. (Justice John Paul Stevens wrote a separate dissent.)

JUSTICE MARSHALL, WITH WHOM JUSTICE BLACKMUN JOINS, DISSENTING.

Power, not reason, is the new currency of this Court's decisionmaking. Four Terms ago, a five-Justice majority of this Court held that "victim impact" evidence of the type at issue in this case could not constitutionally be introduced during the penalty phase of a capital trial. By another 5–4 vote, a majority of this Court rebuffed an attack upon this ruling just two Terms ago. Nevertheless, having expressly invited respondent to renew the attack, today's majority overrules *Booth* and *Gathers* and credits the dissenting views expressed in those cases. Neither the law nor the facts supporting *Booth* and *Gathers* underwent any change in the last four years. Only the personnel of this Court did.

In dispatching *Booth* and *Gathers* to their graves, today's majority ominously suggests that an even more extensive upheaval of this Court's precedents may be in store. Renouncing this Court's historical commitment to a conception of "the judiciary as a source of impersonal and reasoned judgments," the majority declares itself free to discard any principle of constitutional liberty which was recognized or reaffirmed over the dissenting votes of four Justices and with which five or more Justices *now* disagree. The implications of this radical new exception to the doctrine of *stare decisis* are staggering. The majority today sends a clear signal that scores of established constitutional liberties are now ripe for reconsideration, thereby inviting the very type of open defiance of our precedents that the majority rewards in this case. Because I believe that this Court owes more to its constitutional precedents in general and to *Booth* and *Gathers* in particular, I dissent.

I

Speaking for the Court as then constituted, Justice Powell and Justice Brennan set out the rationale for excluding victim-impact evidence from the sentencing proceedings in a capital case. As the majorities in *Booth* and *Gathers* recognized, the core principle of this Court's capital jurisprudence is that the sentence of death must reflect an "'*individualized* determination'" of the defendant's "'personal responsibility and moral guilt'" and must be based upon factors that channel the jury's discretion "'so as to minimize the risk of wholly arbitrary and capricious action.'" The State's introduction of victim-impact evidence, Justice Powell and Justice Brennan explained, violates this fundamental principle. Where, as is ordinarily the case, the defendant was unaware of the personal circumstances of his victim, admitting evidence of the victim's character and the impact of the murder upon the victim's family predicates the sentencing determination on "factors . . . wholly unrelated to the blameworthiness of [the] particular defendant." And even where the defendant *was* in a position to foresee the likely impact of his conduct, admission of victim-impact evidence creates an unacceptable risk of sentencing arbitrariness. As Justice Powell explained in *Booth*, the probative value of such evidence is always outweighed by its prejudicial effect because of its inherent capacity to draw the jury's attention away from the character of the defendant and the circumstances of the crime to such illicit considerations as the eloquence with which family members express their grief and the status of the victim in the community. I continue to find these considerations wholly persuasive, and I see no purpose in trying to improve upon Justice Powell's and Justice Brennan's exposition of them.

There is nothing new in the majority's discussion of the supposed deficiencies in *Booth* and *Gathers*. Every one of the arguments made by the majority can be found in the dissenting opinions filed in those two cases, and . . . each argument was convincingly answered by Justice Powell and Justice Brennan.

But contrary to the impression that one might receive from reading the majority's lengthy rehearsing of the issues addressed in *Booth* and *Gathers*, the outcome of this case does not turn simply on who—the *Booth* and *Gathers* majorities or the *Booth* and *Gathers* dissenters—had the better of the argument. Justice Powell and Justice Brennan's position carried the day in those cases and became the law of the land. The real question, then, is whether today's majority has come forward with the type of extraordinary showing that this Court has historically demanded before overruling one of its precedents. In my view, the majority clearly has not made any such showing. Indeed, the striking feature of the majority's opinion is its radical assertion that it need not even try.

II

The overruling of one of this Court's precedents ought to be a matter of great moment and consequence. Although the doctrine of *stare decisis* is not an "inexorable command," this Court has repeatedly stressed that fidelity to precedent is fundamental to "a society governed by the rule of law."

Consequently, this Court has never departed from precedent without "special justification." Such justifications include the advent of "subsequent changes or development in the law" that undermine a decision's rationale, the need "to bring [a decision] into agreement with experience and with facts newly ascertained" and a showing that a particular precedent has become a "detriment to coherence and consistency in the law."

The majority cannot seriously claim that *any* of these traditional bases for overruling a precedent applies to *Booth* or *Gathers*. The majority does not suggest that the legal rationale of these decisions has been undercut by changes or developments in doctrine during the last two years. Nor does the majority claim that experience over that period of time has discredited the principle that "any decision to impose the death sentence be, and appear to be, based on reason rather than caprice or emotion," the larger postulate of political morality on which *Booth* and *Gathers* rest.

The majority does assert that *Booth* and *Gathers* "have defied consistent application by the lower courts," but the evidence that the majority proffers is so feeble that the majority cannot sincerely expect anyone to believe this claim. To support its contention, the majority points to JUSTICE O'CONNOR's dissent in *Gathers*, which noted a division among lower courts over whether *Booth* prohibited prosecutorial arguments relating to the victim's personal characteristics. That, of course, was the issue expressly considered and resolved in *Gathers*. The majority also cites THE CHIEF JUSTICE's dissent in *Mills v. Maryland* (1988). That opinion does not contain *a single word* about any supposed "[in]consistent application" of *Booth* in the lower courts. Finally, the majority refers to a divided Ohio Supreme Court decision disposing of an issue concerning victim-impact evidence. Obviously, if a division among the members of a single lower court in a single case were sufficient to demonstrate that a particular precedent was a "detriment to coherence and consistency in the law," there would hardly be a decision in United States Reports that we would not be obliged to reconsider.

It takes little real detective work to discern just what *has* changed since this Court decided *Booth* and *Gathers*: this Court's own personnel. Indeed, the majority candidly explains why this particular contingency, which until now has been almost universally understood *not* to be sufficient to warrant overruling a precedent *is* sufficient to justify overruling *Booth* and *Gathers*. "Considerations in favor of *stare decisis* are at their acme," the majority explains, "in cases involving property and contract rights, where reliance interests are involved[;] the opposite is true in cases such as the present one involving procedural and evidentiary rules." In addition, the majority points out, "*Booth* and *Gathers* were decided by the narrowest of margins, over spirited dissents" and thereafter were "questioned by Members of the Court." Taken together, these considerations make it legitimate, in the majority's view, to elevate the position of the *Booth* and *Gathers* dissenters into the law of the land.

This truncation of the Court's duty to stand by its own precedents is astonishing. By limiting full protection of the doctrine of *stare decisis* to "cases involving property and contract rights," the majority sends a clear signal that essentially *all* decisions implementing the personal liberties protected by the Bill of Rights and the Fourteenth Amendment are open to reexamination. Taking into account the majority's additional criterion for overruling—that a case either was decided or reaffirmed by a 5–4 margin "over spirited dissen[t]"—the continued vitality of literally scores of decisions must be understood to depend on nothing more than the proclivities of the individuals who *now* comprise a majority of this Court.

In my view, this impoverished conception of *stare decisis* cannot possibly be reconciled with the values that inform the proper judicial function. Contrary to what the majority suggests, *stare decisis* is important not merely because individuals rely on precedent to structure their commercial activity but because fidelity to precedent is part and parcel of a conception of "the judiciary as a source of impersonal and reasoned judgments." Indeed, this function of *stare decisis* is in many respects even *more* critical in adjudication involving constitutional liberties than in adjudication involving commercial entitlements. Because enforcement of the Bill of Rights and the Fourteenth Amendment frequently requires this Court to rein in the forces of democratic politics, this Court can legitimately lay claim to compliance with its directives only if the public understands the Court to be implementing "principles . . . founded in the law rather than in the proclivities of individuals."[1] Thus, as JUSTICE STEVENS has explained, the "stron[g] presumption of validity" to which "recently decided cases" are entitled "is an essential thread in the mantle of protection that the law affords the individual . . . . It is the unpopular or beleaguered individual—not the man in power—who has the greatest stake in the integrity of the law."

Carried to its logical conclusion, the majority's debilitated conception of *stare decisis* would destroy the Court's very capacity to resolve authoritatively the abiding conflicts between those with power and those without. If this Court shows so little respect for its own precedents, it can hardly expect them to be treated more respectfully by the state actors whom these decisions are supposed to bind. By signaling its willingness to give fresh consideration to any constitutional liberty recognized by a 5–4 vote "over spirited dissen[t]," the majority invites state actors to renew the very policies deemed unconstitutional in the hope that this Court may now reverse course, even if it has only recently reaffirmed the constitutional liberty in question.

Indeed, the majority's disposition of this case nicely illustrates the rewards of such a strategy of defiance. The Tennessee Supreme Court did nothing in this case to disguise its contempt for this Court's decisions in *Booth* and *Gathers*. Summing up its reaction to those cases, it concluded:

> "It is an affront to the civilized members of the human race to say that at sentencing in a capital case, a parade of witnesses may praise the background, character and good deeds of Defendant (as was done in this case), without limitation as to relevancy, but nothing may be said that bears upon the character of, or harm imposed, upon the victims."

Offering no explanation for how this case could possibly be distinguished from *Booth* and *Gathers*—for obviously, there is none to offer—the court perfunctorily declared that the victim-impact evidence and the prosecutor's argument based on this evidence "did not violate either [of those decisions]." It cannot be clearer that the court simply declined to be bound by this Court's precedents.

---

[1] It does not answer this concern to suggest that Justices owe fidelity to the text of the Constitution rather than to the case law of this Court interpreting the Constitution. The text of the Constitution is rarely so plain as to be self-executing; invariably, this Court must develop mediating principles and doctrines in order to bring the text of constitutional provisions to bear on particular facts. Thus, to rebut the charge of personal lawmaking, Justices who would discard the mediating principles embodied in precedent must do more than state that they are following the "text" of the Constitution; they must explain why they are entitled to substitute *their* mediating principles for those that are already settled in the law. And such an explanation will be sufficient to legitimize the departure from precedent only if it measures up to the extraordinary standard necessary to justify overruling one of this Court's precedents. [footnote in original]

Far from condemning this blatant disregard for the rule of law, the majority applauds it. In the Tennessee Supreme Court's denigration of *Booth* and *Gathers* as "'an affront to the civilized members of the human race,'" the majority finds only confirmation of "the unfairness of the rule pronounced by" the majorities in those cases. It is hard to imagine a more complete abdication of this Court's historic commitment to defending the supremacy of its own pronouncements on issues of constitutional liberty. See *Cooper v. Aaron* (1958). In light of the cost that such abdication exacts on the authoritativeness of all of this Court's pronouncements, it is also hard to imagine a more short-sighted strategy for effecting change in our constitutional order.

III

Today's decision charts an unmistakable course. If the majority's radical reconstruction of the rules for overturning this Court's decisions is to be taken at face value—and the majority offers us no reason why it should not—then the overruling of *Booth* and *Gathers* is but a preview of an even broader and more far-reaching assault upon this Court's precedents. Cast aside today are those condemned to face society's ultimate penalty. Tomorrow's victims may be minorities, women, or the indigent. Inevitably, this campaign to resurrect yesterday's "spirited dissents" will squander the authority and the legitimacy of this Court as a protector of the powerless.

I dissent.

The Supreme Court has continued to invoke the criteria for overruling precedents that Marshall criticized as inadequate in *Payne*; however, the ideological coloration of the Court has not changed as dramatically as it did in the late 1980s, and decisions overruling precedents have usually been easier to defend on traditional grounds. The Court's adherence in 1992 and again in 2000 to what some justices called the "core holding" of its 1973 abortion decisions, when coupled with its willingness to overrule other decisions, does provide more evidence to support Marshall's charge in *Payne* that the Court's adherence to *stare decisis* turned more on politics than on principle.

PART V

REMINISCENCES

T his section contains the transcript of an oral history interview given by Justice Marshall in 1977. The interview
(conducted by Ed Erwin for the Columbia Oral History
Research Office) occurred in four sessions, but the transcript has
been edited to omit indications of when one session ended and
another began. It captures Marshall's voice extremely well, and has
been edited only lightly, primarily to correct errors in transcription
and repetition of questions rather than to ensure that the spoken
words read as if they had been written in the first instance. Several
anecdotes Marshall told twice remain in the transcript, as he
recounts his perspective on many incidents discussed in earlier
selections.

54. "The Reminiscences of Thurgood Marshall" (Columbia Oral History Research Office, 1977)

Q: First of all, Justice Marshall, when and where were you born, and then could you recall your early life influences that led you in professional directions, and in the civic activism directions that you went—family, school, peers, events?

Marshall: Well, I was born in Baltimore, Maryland, which I have considered to be "way up South," July 2, 1908, in the middle of the Negro area of northwest Baltimore. Negroes were concentrated in three areas—northwest Baltimore, east Baltimore, and south Baltimore.

I went to [an] elementary school that was known as Division Street, a short walk from where I was born, and of course, it was an all-Negro elementary school, small, full eight grades—what I considered to be better-than-average teachers, and one very interesting thing is that my second year teacher is still alive, and was in Washington last year.

In the elementary school, contact with white people would fall in two categories. There was a white Catholic elementary school two blocks from Division Street, and for some reason, we didn't get along very well. They were practically all Italians, and we used to have periodic fights—not too bad. Maybe a rock here and there. It was fists, and eventually they let them out fifteen minutes before we got out, so that they could get home.

I would like to tie that in, because when I began practicing law, I came up against an assistant state's attorney with an Italian name, and in a discussion one morning, he mentioned the fact that I should remember him. And I said I was sorry, I didn't. And it developed that he belonged to that group in that school.

He said, "Well, if you don't remember me, I remember you." He showed a little scar, up here on his forehead, which I then remembered that I gave him, in a little fight we had.

But getting back to the relations at that time, the only relations would be with the corner grocery store, nothing with people downtown, and that went through the whole time I was in Baltimore.

A study was made by the Urban League around 1930 which showed that segregation in Baltimore was more rigid than any other city in the country, including Jackson, Mississippi. I know this is almost unbelievable, but it's true. In the department stores downtown, a Negro was not allowed to buy anything off the counters. As you went in the store, you were told to get the hell out.

Another thing I remember very well was that there were no toilet facilities available to Negroes in the downtown area, and I remember one day, I had to go, and the only thing I could do was get on a trolley car and try to get home. And I did get almost in the house, when I ruined the front doorsteps. That gives you an idea what we went through.

But I never had any hatred of white people as such, because there were some that touched my life, whom I considered to be very good. I knew, for example, a man by the name of Mr. Schoen. I worked for him during my high school period, as a delivery boy. Mr. Schoen had a very elite dress shop on Charles Street, the biggest street, and some of his customers, for example—well, one of his customers was President [Inaudible]—

There are two stories I remember about him. One was that he promised my brother and me, who were two of the four delivery boys—that he would put both of us through college, and I'm sure he would have, had he not died before we went to college, and had his son [not] thought more of a chorus girl than he did of helping people out.

The other thing I remember was: one day in the afternoon, when I had a whole lot of hats in boxes to be delivered, I was getting on a trolley car, and joined the people getting on; a man grabbed me and pulled me back and said, "Nigger, don't you push in front of white people!"

And my dad had always taught me that when anybody called me a nigger, to have business with them then and there, so I did. I was arrested, and Mr. Schoen came around to the police station, and I apologized to him, because the five hats were wrecks and it was a complete loss to him, and he said, "Forget about them, what about you?"

I told him. And he asked the man, how much was the bail money, or what have you, and the man said, "Well, Mr. Schoen, it's up to you." Mr. Schoen got his lawyer, and that was the end of that.

I had some other experiences like that with white people in my high school days—but things didn't get better in Baltimore, so far as Negroes were concerned, until, I guess, the late thirties or forties. When I finished high school, I remember another interesting experience: they had built a new high school which would be opened the year after I graduated. I guess they didn't want us to break it up. And I remember the superintendent of schools—his name was something like Wigline, I don't remember how to spell it—but he was so prejudiced that when he found there was to be a swimming pool in the one Negro high school, he halted construction of it, merely because, as he said, "Niggers didn't deserve swimming pools."

I went through college in Lincoln University, in Pennsylvania. It's about sixty miles above Baltimore, Route 1; it was practically an all-Negro college, about three hundred-and-some students—with one or two white students who were from the local community. I spent my four years there, starting out to major in the sciences, so as to become a dentist. But I had great trouble with the professor—he and I had a mutual dislike for each other—so I gave that up, and went into the social sciences under Professor Labaree, and I did take chemistry, and as much math as they would give, which ended up with integral calculus.

I graduated, managing to be on the honor list, even though I was the last one on there—but I made it. During that time, I worked in the summer on the railroad, the B and O Railroad, as a dining car waiter. As I remember, we got the munificent salary of fifty-five dollars a month, and that did not include overtime. So the only money you made was tips, and it was not a good living.

In the summertime of my last year in college, I went to work at Gibson Island Club, where my father was the steward.

I also remember at Lincoln—When you look at the cost of educating youngsters today, and I have two boys in college; but when I went to college, it cost three hundred dollars and some a year, with room and board, and you worked off half of that, so I guess they were the "good old days."

Now, you want to know how I got involved in law? I don't know. The nearest I can get is that my dad, my brother, and I had the most violent arguments you ever heard about anything. I guess we argued five out of seven nights at the dinner table. When we were away at college, and we would come back, the first dinner we'd have—I remember a neighbor of ours, Mrs. Hall, would tell her husband, "Ah, the boys are home."

The reason was, she could hear the arguments through the walls.

So maybe that got me interested in law. I had, of course, given up dentistry because I didn't have the qualifications to enter dental school. The only possible way I could get an education, financially, was at Howard. Of course, I couldn't go to the University of Maryland because they wouldn't take Negroes. So I went over to Howard in 1930, and began law school, and for the first time in my life, I studied. The rest of the time, I just eased along—you know, do good enough to pass. But in the law school, I realized, that was it. And in my first year, I really studied, and the best example of it is that I lost fifty-five pounds in one year.

I had to commute from Baltimore to Washington, which meant I got up around five o'clock in the morning and got home around eight o'clock, and then worked after I got home. As a result of that, I came out top man in my class, and that pushed me up to the position of being the student librarian. That took care of half of my tuition payments. I, of course, finished at the top of my class.

During that time, Dean Charles H. Houston was the vice-dean. He was a graduate of Amherst and Harvard, and had a SJD degree, which is a graduate degree in law. Very brilliant, very decent person, but a very hard man. Prior to his taking over, Howard was not a good law school, and he wanted it to be accredited and managed to do it in about two or three years. He used to tell us, in our first year, to look at the man on your right and look at the man on your left, and bear in mind that two of you won't be here next year. Well, that sort of kept your feet to the fire.

Then he put in another rule called the cutback, which was that regardless of the mark you made in your examination, the professor could take five points off for no reason at all, which meant, you had to get five in order to get along.

In the library, as student librarian, I didn't have anything to do but watch over the law books, so in my spare time, I read them. And that didn't hurt.

Then we started sitting around with Charles Houston and William H. Hastie, who just died a year or so ago, and Andrew Ransom—people like that—and we began to work out this attack on the segregated school system.[1] We talked about it. We did research on it. We studied it. And in my last year, I worked with Houston on criminal cases, including the Crawford case in upper Virginia and the University of North Carolina case, which was filed by William Hastie.

But we were trained, and were part of the program which Houston called the program of making lawyers social engineers, instead of just somebody going out to make a dollar practicing law. And I have watched in years since, and most of the Negro lawyers who have been in this struggle have at some time been touched by Houston, who died back in the fifties, I've forgotten just when it was.

Q: Justice Marshall, to backtrack a little bit, what were these arguments over the family dinner table about?

Marshall: Oh, anything. Anything. Like, one day—today it would be, what's happening in Iran? World problems —
And of course, the race problem too.

Q: Then they were serious questions?

Marshall: Oh yes. Oh yes. My father had a lot of sayings about—you see, for example, he knew the, what would I say? The real problem in race, as race. For example, it would be nothing for him to say—say I would do something good, my father would say, "Well, that's right black of you." You've always heard, "that's very white of you." You understand what he was saying.

And another favorite statement of my father's was, "Ah, that's the white man in the wood pile."

He would tell jokes, too. But he felt it. He felt it doubly because he was blond and blue-eyed and he could have passed for white, and a lot of times, he would get in a big fight because somebody would think he was white.

But those were the arguments we'd have. Race and everything in general. Very loud.

Q: When he did this reversal of the code words, did he explain what he was doing?

---

[1] Leon Andrew Ransom began teaching at Howard Law School in 1930 and served as acting dean between 1941 and 1943, while William Hastie was on leave serving as civilian aide to the secretary of war. He also worked on numerous NAACP cases.

Marshall: Oh, sure. Oh, he'd explain it, and from then on you would do the same thing. You'd do the same thing.

Q: How did your mother feel about this?

Marshall: Well, my mother—believe it or not, my father was the noisiest and loudest, but my mother was by far the strongest. My mother was a school teacher. She worked like just all get out. And her only fault was that she was with you, if you were in the family, she was with you, right or wrong. I mean, she would just defend you. And I know some people are with you if you're right, but my mother was—

And I know of one time when we had a little rough time in college, and everybody was out of money; and I remember two interesting things. One, we wanted to go to a football game, with Howard University, and my mother and father said, "We just don't have the money for either one of you."

Then the morning of the game, my mother called and said, "Go on, we'll have the money."

Well, we found out afterwards that the night before, my dad says, "Norma, how much money do we have, total?"

She said, "Six dollars."

He said, "Give it to me."

He said, "Just give it to me." And he went down to a gambling joint, and ran that six dollars up into about $150.

That was a good one.

Then the other one, I've forgotten what it was, but we wanted some money for something, and it wasn't there, and later on my mother says, "Here's the money."

And we never found out until years later, she pawned her wedding ring and her engagement ring. Well, you can't ask for more than that. And incidentally, by the time she got the money to get them back, they'd been gone. You know, they'd been sold.

So you can't ask for better than that. But she was strong.

My grandmother, her mother, was also a very strong person. I would talk to her for hours on end, and her life went all the way back to the early days of the Negro, right after Reconstruction, and her husband knew all of the prominent Negroes in those days. I would just listen to her for hours on end, and I think she had a great influence too. I don't know who had the greater influence. I think my mother and father and—it's between the three of those. No, I would not weight them, for any one.

But once I got into the law side, it was the Houston influence, wholeheartedly. I don't know anything I did in the practice of law that wasn't the result of what Charlie Houston banged into my head.

Q: How do you recall your feelings generally toward the segregated life that you had to lead down in the streets of Baltimore?

Marshall: Well, I was struck with one thing, that in my third year or so in college, I was talking to another student about Baltimore. He was from some place, I've forgotten where, and I was telling him all these things that Negroes couldn't do.

He says, "How do you know it?"

I said, "Everybody knows it."

He said, "Well, did you ever try?"

That sort of stuck in my craw, as to, why not do something about it? I got into law school and got into this segregated legal business—my first idea was to get even with Maryland for not letting me go to its law school. And I did. I don't know how long after I started practicing I filed a case against the University of Maryland. It was within a year. And it was merely to—they had given a scholarship fund, so that Negroes could go outside the state and get money, get tuition paid, and I took the position that that wasn't good enough. I went after that with hammer and tongs. Charlie Houston was the lead counsel. I was under him, of course.

I remember, when I moved its admission to the federal court, Judge Morris Soper, the chief judge, said, "Well, this is interesting, here's a student moving admission of a dean."

I said, "Well, that's how things go."

Judge O'Dunne ruled with us, that they had to let Negroes into law school. It was an extremely interesting case, for a lot of reasons.

In the meantime, I wasn't making any money. I don't know whether I made a big mistake or not, because in law school, Dean [Roscoe Pound] who was then Dean of Harvard, used to teach us periodically—when he would come in town—and he got to know me, and at the end when I graduated, he offered me a scholarship to go to Harvard and take the graduate degree of Doctor of Laws. It was a full scholarship, enough for my wife and I to live on, and some money left over. And I refused it because I couldn't wait to get out and practice.

As I look back on it, I never studied economics, because I would have had a year of training, the best legal training in the world, for free, and instead I went out and practiced, and ended up three thousand dollars in debt. So it looks to me like I should have known more about economics. But in the meantime, I was trying this case.

In this case, Herbert O'Connor was the attorney general, and his assistant was a man by the name of Leviness, and they kept getting postponements. And one day I came into court, and they had moved for an adjournment, and Judge O'Dunne sent for me and said, "Look, do you want to try this case or not?"

I said, "Yes, sir, of course I do."

He said, "Well, act like it."

I said, "What do you mean by that?"

He said, "When the attorney general asks for adjournment, object."

I said, "Is that —?"

He said, "Sure, that's all you have to do."

So Leviness came in and said he wanted it, expecting me to jump up and say "No objection." I said, "I object." Judge O'Dunne said, "We'll start trying this tomorrow morning."

And we did. We put on our evidence, and they put on theirs, and much to my surprise, Judge O'Dunne—typical Baltimore blue-blooded aristocrat judge, very nice man and very intelligent, ruled with us, that Murray—his name was Donald G. Murray—should be admitted to the law school. He was admitted, and when he graduated, he was given a job by the same man, Leviness, in the attorney general's office.

So that was the breakthrough, I think, in Baltimore, and the state of Maryland. Then I was stuck. One time an old colored lady came to my office at 4 East Redwood Street, Baltimore, and said she had a property case and she needed a lawyer.

I said, "Well, have you got any money?"

She said, "No, I don't have a nickel."

I said, "What are you doing coming to me for?"

She said, "Well, down in North Carolina in my little town, when we have a legal problem, we go to the judge and he helps us out, so I asked for the court house and I went down there and I walked into the judges' chambers and told him. And he said he was sorry, but they didn't do things that way in Baltimore." She had to get a lawyer.

She said, "But I don't have any money."

He said, "Well, that's a problem. But I tell you what—you go down to this lawyer Thurgood Marshall, at 4 East Redwood Street."

She said, "What 'bout that?"

He says, "Well, he's a freebie lawyer, he'll do it for you for nothing."

Well, then I realized that that wasn't a good way to make a living. Indeed, during that time, my secretary and I would bring lunch. She would bring lunch for two one day and I'd bring lunch for two the next day, and that's the way we lived.

Then after two or three years, I got a couple of paying clients who paid well, and I did a little better. And in the fall of '36, I went to New York with the NAACP.

Q: Well, before we get into the NAACP, I want to go back to what you said about your grandmother. Did you know anything about these Negro leaders from way back, the postreconstructionist period, before she told you?

Marshall: No. No. But I guess it was high school, or it might have been early college—From what she told me, I'd go and pull out books. The first one was

Frederick Douglass, which incidentally I still read every once in a while—because I don't know of a Negro today, or later than Douglass, who had the courage he had, in the things he said. I mean, the things he would tell the President of the United States, I don't—

He was great. But these others, like Bruce of Mississippi, and couple of others—

You see, the reason they knew them was that—This is almost unbelievable, but during the 1890s, I think it was, or around that time, there were two big grocery stores in Baltimore, and each of them was owned by one of my grandfathers. If they had had any business acumen, or the children had had any, they would have been very wealthy people.

Now, my grandfather on my mother's side—I also remember that the door was left open to the basement of his home and his store, and the poor Negroes that lived in back had access to go down there and get wood, coal and vegetables and stuff. And he would tell them, "Now, don't take more than you need." Nobody ever did. On the other side, my other grandfather did the exact same thing. But both of them did all right, and when they died, the children just went through the money—instead of carrying on the business.

So that's how he happened to know them, because he was then one of the wealthiest Negroes in Baltimore. When these guys would come to Baltimore, they would go by his place, and he always had great food and great liquor, et cetera.

But she could tell all those stories. And I think that got me interested. And then my aunt did a study, like this thing on *Roots* that just came out; she made a pretty good study and found that we came from the Congo.

Incidentally, that never was—She got mad one day and tore it up. She got mad at us, the whole family. . . .

But I can remember, because my great-great-great-grandfather, whoever it was—There was a family of Marylanders who went over to hunt in Africa and this teenage youngster followed them and worked for them, and when they got back to the boat, he was still following them. So they wondered, did he want to go? He said, "Yes," so they brought him to the United States. They got themselves a slave for nothing. They didn't even pay for him.

But in due time—I don't remember—he was in his early twenties, his master said, "Now, look—you are so ornery and mean to white people that you'll never be a good servant, you'll never be a slave, and I in good conscience can't sell you to another white person. So I'm telling you this—if you agree to leave the county and the state, I'll turn you loose and give you your freedom."

He said, "I'm not going any place." And he gave him his freedom.

Well, I'm proud of a guy like that. He doesn't worry me at all.

And incidentally, I don't know the name of the white family. I don't know anything. I don't know whether I'm too interested in details like that. I know about him. That's all I need to know.

Q: When you went to look up more history of the Negro leaders that your grandmother told you about, were you satisfied that you could find enough, or did you find a paucity of materials?

Marshall: Oh, there was nothing. Practically nothing. I didn't know about the Schomberg Collection in New York, for example, until I went to New York in '36. I didn't know about Arthur Spingarn's collection until then, because that's when I met him.[2] And he had a terrific—you see, Spingarn had every book published by a Negro; up until he died—within the last ten years, he was ninety some—he just automatically bought every book published by a Negro. It's a terrific collection. But I didn't know about those, then.

Q: Incidentally, during this period, were you aware of the Marcus Garvey movement?

Marshall: Yes, when I used to visit New York. I knew his lawyer very well, a guy named Matthews, at least my parents did. That was a terrific swindle. To give you an idea, I'm not a great admirer of Garvey, because I think he had great ideas but he didn't have the right people around him, and as a result—what he could have done with that money—

To give you an idea how much money, Matthews told us that when they were closing out the movement in the state and all—after Garvey went down to the West Indies—they found four desk drawers, that when you pulled them open, money orders which hadn't even been cashed just bulged out.

But he just wasn't a businessman. He just was, you know, straight up, and I think that—Yes, it gave us consciousness, but it gave us the wrong kind of consciousness. The emphasis was on "Black." For example, when they would parade up Seventh Avenue, if my brother and I were out there in the street, we had to get off the street. Right in the middle of Harlem. I mean, no lightskinned Negro was allowed around. And that I thought was a great mistake. But—yes, he was great.

And then too, you had this other movement going along—[William E. B.] Du Bois and those people had the intellectual group, Countee Cullen, Du Bois and those; some I knew very well.

So I don't think we paid too much attention the Garvey thing. As I remember, I didn't like it. I didn't like people calling me names.

Q: Let's go back to when you were studying the law. Did Houston and the others—to what extent did they instruct you in the meaning of independence in the practice of law?

---

[2] Arthur Spingarn was one of the NAACP's founding members, and was president of the organization when Marshall became a staff member.

Marshall: Well, number one, they were hell-bent on establishing a cadre of Negro lawyers dedicated to fighting for equal rights under the Constitution, in the courts. This was done for a twofold purpose. One was to do something for Negroes as such, and the other was to raise the image of the Negro lawyer. In those days, it wasn't high. There were no more than about ten prominent Negro lawyers as late as the thirties, in the whole country. I can name them, pretty much. Let me just think—the guy in—well, one was Bill [William] Lewis, in Boston, who was former assistant attorney general of the United States under Teddy Roosevelt. There were two in West Virginia, T. G. Nutter, in Charleston, and Harry J. Capehart in Welsh, West Virginia, who represented the coal mines, not the coal miners. They represented the mines. This man in Chicago whose name slips me represented either Armour or one of those big packing companies in Chicago. There was one prominent man named [William J., Jr.] Carter in Harrisburg, but the run-of-the-mill Negro lawyers were not known, and had not made what Charlie thought was a contribution, and that was his aim.

I was glad to be a part of it. And that's what we did.

Q: After you started practicing law, how did you feel about the preparation you had for it in the school?

Marshall: We were told two things that I can remember very well. There was a clerk of the court here in Washington—I don't remember his name—who lectured to us once a year, and he did it deliberately, and I've always been deeply in debt to him for doing it. He would say that, with very few exceptions, he could look at a pleading filed by a lawyer and tell from looking at it whether it was done by a white or a Negro lawyer.

Later on, talking to him, he admitted that that was not true. But it stuck; from that day until I stopped practicing law, I never filed a paper in any court with an erasure on it. If I changed a word, it had to be typed all over, because I didn't want that on it. Well, it helped some.

I also remember trying a case in Baton Rouge, Louisiana, before a judge—and I know you can't spell his name, Calouette—who ruled against me almost every time, but on one occasion, when a motion was being argued, and the lawyer on the other side said, "Well, Judge, I would like some more time to file another memorandum brief," he said, "Why?"

He said, "Well, Mr. Marshall has just filed one, two days ago, and I haven't had time to check as to whether his citations are accurate nor not, and I'd like that time to check them."

And in open court this judge, who was no friend, said, "You don't have to worry about that. If Mr. Marshall puts his signature on it, you don't have to check it."

Well, that's good enough for me. That's good enough for me.

And Charlie insisted on that. He himself was a perfectionist, and he insisted that we each be, and if we did a slipshod job, boy, he would lay it on you. I recall one time that we nicknamed him Ironpants, and Cement Shoes. We named him everything. But he insisted on perfection.

I guess he'd spend as much time on that as he would on the research itself. But you had to go the extra mile on any case that you tried with him. So, if you got in the habit of doing it with him, you sort of—you know, you'd do it afterwards. But he was great. Hastie was just like him, too.

But during all of this time with the NAACP, there was no—we had a Margold Report prepared by a lawyer by the name of Nathan Margold, who was then assistant secretary of the interior. He later became a judge in the District [of Columbia] and died at an early age. But it was not a blueprint. We tried our cases one by one. We had no plan, because you couldn't make a plan. You were limited by money, and you were also limited by people who wanted you to file the suits. Under the canon of ethics, you can't solicit clients. So that's what determined how you went from step to step.

Everybody tries to find a plan. There is none. And I see people try to write one up. But we took them as they came.

Q: I mean, in determining your strategy, then, it was case by case?

Marshall: Case by case. We first started off to make the schools equal on the theory—and this was Margold's theory—that if you made them so expensive they couldn't maintain them, then segregation would die of its own weight.

Well, eventually we found it wasn't working, so then we shifted to hitting it straight on.

Like, for example, the Maryland case, that first one, was strictly separate but equal, and the last one, the [Heman M.] Sweatt case, was straight out segregation [*Sweatt vs. Painter*].

Q: To go back to your legal training again, aside from your possible regrets that you did not take the graduate course at Harvard, what additional preparation do you wish that you might have had before you started practicing law?

Marshall: Personally, I don't think any. I might have been contaminated. Well, I mean, suppose I'd started right out making a whole lot of money. That would have been dangerous, I think. I might have liked it. I know, for example, when I was at the NAACP a member of our board, Charlie Studen, a very, very prosperous lawyer in New York, very wonderful guy—we were walking out of a board meeting one day and Charlie said, "You know something, Thurgood? When you gave your report like you always do, you seemed to have so much fun."

I said, "Yes, I *do* have fun in my work."

He said, "Well, let me tell you something." He said, "I know how much you make, because I'm on the board."

I said, "That's right."

And he said, "You can imagine how much I make. You don't know, but you can imagine."

I said, "Yep, I can."

He said, "I don't begin to have the fun you do."

I said, "Well, it's your problem, boy, it's your problem. Let's switch around—[if you want]."

But you take money, when I went with the NAACP in '36, I made $2,400 a year, and as I look back, my first wife and I—we lived. We had an apartment. We had a car. On $2,400. And after a couple of years, the board of directors had a great big meeting, and raised my salary, with a whole lot of hoopla, you know. I was really carried away with it. And they raised me from $2,400 to $2,600. And when I got home, my wife was not a complaining woman, she was very—she put up with me—and I remember, after I told her about it, she said, "Oh, that's fine."

Then after a half hour or so, she said, "By the way, how much is that a week?" Two hundred dollars—it suddenly dawned on me—dawned on me—-

But when I left in 1961, 1 think I was only making around $15,000. They just didn't pay, in those days. They pay well now. No retirement money, no nothing. But it was fun.

Q: Then would I be correct in drawing the inference that you never felt really deprived, although you weren't making as much money as you could have in law practice?

Marshall: Not at all. I was fortunate that both of my wives were willing to go along. You see, the trouble is, if you've got a wife that won't—and another thing is, a lot of people have left the NAACP because of the travel. I would do a hundred thousand miles a year in travel, and be home—one year, the first year I kept track of it, I was away three-fourths of the time, and was in town one-fourth. Well, some wives will say they won't take that. Or, "Why can't I have more money?" Neither one of my wives ever asked for more money. They could have used it.

Q: In your feeling about public service, which developed while you were still in law school—was that really rooted primarily in your outrage against segregation?

Marshall: Oh, sure. Sure. Well, you see, everybody that I mentioned, everybody in my family was mad about it. They went along with it, but they weren't for it. And I think I did what all of them would have done, if they'd had legal training. I know my father would have. I know my mother would have. No question about it.

I mean, for example, my father had a flat rule. He believed that every man's house was his castle. He had a flat rule, no man could come in his house without his permission. And he used to say, if anybody ever did, he'd kill him.

I can't—well, I'll tell you how true it was: the captain of our precinct was a very good friend of my father's, Captain Cook. (I don't know whether it's Cooke with an *e* on it or not.) And Captain Cook, I can remember, would come to the door and ring the doorbell, and I'd go to the door, and he'd say, "Hey, young man, is your father in?"

I'd say, "Yes, come on in."

He'd say, "Oh no. No." Then he'd holler in, "Can I come in, Willie?"

Father would say, "Yes, come on in, Captain." But he didn't—he believed, that was his castle.

Q: Let's come back to your move over to the NAACP. How did that come about?

Marshall: Well, I've forgotten which case I was working on. And Charlie Houston was going to take a leave of absence for six months, I think, and he said, "Will you come up and hold the job down for six months?"

And I said, "Sure." That's when I went up for six months.

I never had a contract for more than a year. It was all just step by step. Then he eventually in about '38, said, "Well, the way things are going," and money was awful close— "I think I'd better go back to Washington"—in his father's office— "and rebuild it, so that you and Hastie and the others will have some place to come, when the money runs out."

"And that means, you'll have to stay here." That's how he went. And he did, he built it up very well.

His father was William H. Houston. Charlie's father was a wonderful man, very good lawyer, but not like we were. He used to say, "You know, I agree with you and Charlie, you are all doing the right thing. You're saving all of the colored people, and you're fighting for that." He said, "I'm for it, too. There's only one difference. You want to save them all, I want to save them all. You want to save all of them at one time. And I want to save them one at a time. Soon as I get enough money for myself, I'll go work for some of the others."

But yet he would give us his house and his office. He would go along with us. But he wouldn't admit it. He wouldn't. He didn't do so bad. He ended up assistant attorney general under Roosevelt.

Q: Of course, in those days, an assistant attorney general didn't make an awful lot of money either, did he? He wouldn't make nearly as much as he would in private practice.

Marshall: Oh, no, nowhere near it. Hell, judges were only getting ten thousand dollars. They couldn't have been getting more than that. Judges were getting ten or fifteen, back in those days.

Q: Now, was your title at the NAACP "Assistant Special Counsel," to start with?

Marshall: It started, it was "Assistant First Counsel."

Q: When you decided to stay on, you were—

Marshall: It was "Special Counsel." And then I went over to the Legal Defense Fund, and that was as director. We set up the Legal Defense Fund in order to get tax-exempt money. When they wouldn't let us have tax exemption, Arthur Spingarn—who was then the head of the legal committee—and I got this idea, of getting tax exemption for the new one, and all of a sudden we realized that there wasn't any real problem, because Arthur Spingarn was the closest friend of a man by the name of Henry Morgenthau, who was then secretary of the treasury. So we didn't have too much trouble.

Q: As you look back on those years as special counsel and director of the Legal Defense Fund, what were the cases that you became involved in, that you feel have meant the most?

Marshall: Oh boy. Well, the primary case in Texas, *Smith vs. Allwright* was, I think, the first real big one I had. There had been four previous cases, and Negroes still weren't voting in the primary, and we started that one, *Smith vs. Allwright*, and the Negroes who contributed to it in Texas told me, they said, "We want you to know, this is the last go-round; we've contributed four times before, if you lose this one, forget about it."

So that put a little weight on me, too, and at the trial, before a Republican judge—I've forgotten his name—in Houston, it was delayed several times. Wasn't his fault, wasn't anybody else's fault, and eventually we tried it, and we lost it. And then we went to the Court of Appeals, the Fifth Circuit, in Fort Worth, Texas, and you usually have a half hour to an hour of argument. And when I walked in that morning, Chief Judge [Joseph C.] Hutcheson [Jr.] very, very capable judge, one of the best—but he drafted the first white primary law to keep Negroes out, so I mean, I knew where his heart was. When we started the argument, I said, "I think I'm running out of time."

And Judge Hutcheson said, "Oh, no. We've got the whole day. Feel at ease." And he started in on his questioning, and he questioned me about qualifications for voters, step by step, back, back, back, and I kept giving him the answers.

Eventually he asked me a question, and I said, "Now, Judge Hutcheson, with all due respect, I don't know anything better than the truth, and I have to tell you what the truth is."

He says, "What's that?"

I said, "You're talking about the Justinian Code, aren't you?"

He said, "Yes. Of course."

I said, "Well, I just want to warn you that I can answer that, but that's as far as I go."

He said, "Join the club. That's as far as I go."

He had me on my feet for three hours, and he ruled against me. Then I said, "Well, I'm going to the Supreme Court."

He said, "Of course." And I know, I saw him a couple of months later, in the Court of Appeals of New Orleans, and he said, "Have you filed your petition for certiorari yet?"

I said, "No, sir."

He said, "Well, why don't you hurry up? You know you're going to win."

I remember thinking then, I'd go ahead, and we brought it up here, and we did; we won it.

That case that started the whole voting of the Negroes in the South. And after that, thanks to former Justice Tom Clark, who was then attorney general—he told the other states that they'd better fall in line or he'd whack them one. And they all fell in line except Georgia and South Carolina, and we had to file two more cases.

The South Carolina case was very interesting. It was a three-judge court. The senior judge—no, it was not a three-judge court. Judge [Julius Waties] Waring tried it, a single judge, and ruled with us, and that case went to the court of appeals, Judge [John J.] Parker, Judge [Morris] Soper, and Judge [Armistead M.] Dobie, and they affirmed Judge Waring.

Then we had one or two more small ones, but I think that was important because it changed the whole complexion in the South.

Another sideline on that—you talk about bloc voting, Negro bloc voting. By the time the Texas case, *Smith v. Allwright*, was decided—April 7, 1 think it was, 1944—I guarantee you that every Negro in Texas was thinking in one mind, as solid a bloc as you could find. We raised all that money—and it was around two hundred thousand dollars altogether—for expenses, and the primary was in June, July, or August. Between April and the primary, those Negroes had divided into three blocs. So where do you get your Negro bloc voting? There is no such thing. It's a myth.

I know, in South Carolina, when we won the right to vote there—to register—and if I remember correctly, we put something like eighty thousand Negroes on the books in a ten-day period. And they don't have that many now. I remember, in Charleston, a story a newspaper boy told me,—the Negroes all dressed up to register, to vote in the primary. They put on their Sunday clothes. It was a big day.

And they were in this line, which this newspaper reporter saw, and there were a couple of white people pushing, you know, who wanted to get ahead. And these Negroes, of course, they'd been there waiting. And so when these white people kept pushing, this Negro woman turned around to the man behind her and she said, "You seem to be in a hurry. So you just go right ahead. You know, we been waiting a long time. We don't mind waiting a little longer."

She said, "We don't mind waiting a little longer."

But I think that was important. The school cases, of course, were going along, and I don't know, I guess the school cases would be next.

Meantime, we were having about one a year: good criminal cases, on confessions, jury trial, and things like that; and then we had riots. I investigated every race riot from 1940 until I left. Right in the middle of them. And some of them were rough.

The one in Columbia, South Carolina,—was about '45, as I remember. And there, there was an altercation when a radio repairman struck a Negro woman, who called him a liar. And as a result, her son, a teenager, knocked the white man down and beat him up. The mob came down to the Negro section of town to work it over, and the Negroes fired back. That night the National Guard came in and surrounded the Negro neighborhood, which was called Mink Slide, and set up fifty-calibre machine guns and just—I mean, it was horrible. These wood houses, they just went right through them like that. I don't know how many people got killed.

But as it ended up, one white man was killed, and a whole gang of Negroes were charged with murder.

We went down to try that case, and I got ill. I had Virus X, and I was in the hospital for about three months. And when I went back afterwards, the mob got me one night, and they were taking me down to the river, where all of the white people were waiting to do a little bit of lynching. And I managed to get away. But I switched cars and got in another car, and they caught the guy who was driving the car that I was in, they caught him, and they beat him up. He was in the hospital for a couple of months, busted legs—Well, that was the—one of the closest ones I ever was into.

Q: When you say they were taking you down to the river, what were they doing? Escorting your car?

Marshall: No, they pulled the car over, and behind me, I could see there were three or four state highway patrol cars and two city cars, and they wanted to see my— They said they had a warrant to search the car. It was a dry county, and they knew that lawyers are gonna drink liquor. Well, believe it or not, we didn't have any whiskey in the car. They looked around, they said, "We'll go in the trunk."

I told the other two cars, "Look, wherever they go, you go. Don't let them put something in there, on us."

So I could hear a guy behind, but I could never see him, and they said, "Well, maybe they'll let us search them."

I said, "You got a warrant to search us?"

He said, "No."

I said, "Well, the answer is, *no.*"

And "So, well, I guess you have to let them go."

So I told a local lawyer, [Z. A.] Looby, I said, "You'd better drive," since it was his car, "because I've got a New York license," and he said, "Okay," and we drove off.

The sirens went off again, and the guy came back with the others—I was in the back seat—and they said, "You were driving this car, weren't you?"

I said, "I'm not answering any questions."

They said, "Well, let's see your driver's license." So I gave it to him, and he carried it back, and again—I never found out who this voice was—so then the guy says, "Get out."

I say, "What's up?"

He says, "Put your hands up."

I said, "What is it?"

He said, "Drunken driving."

I said, "Drunken driving? I haven't had a drink in twenty-four hours."

"You're a drunken driver," he says, "get in the car."

And then they told Looby and the others to keep going up the road, and they wouldn't go. They stayed following this police car, and when they couldn't shake Looby, they turned around and went back in to town, and when they got into town— big, wide street, nobody there hardly, about two or three people, middle of the afternoon, they're all down at the river.

So then we realized what was up. And he said, "There's a magistrate over there, on the second floor—you see him, right over there?"

I said, "Yes, what about it?"

He said, "You go over there. We'll be over."

I said, "No you won't." I said, "If we go over, I'm going with you."

He said, "Why?"

I said, "You're not going to shoot me in the back while I'm 'escaping'. I mean, let's make this legal."

So he said, "Smart-ass nigger," and things like that, and so we went over, and there was a little gentleman, the magistrate; a little man, he couldn't have been much over five-foot-one at the most, and he said, "What's up?"

The officer said, "It's drunken driving."

The magistrate said, "He doesn't look drunk to me."

I said, "I'm not drunk."

He said, "You want to take my test?"

I said, "Well, what's your test?"

He said, "I'm a teetotaller. I've never had a drink in my life. I can smell liquor a mile off. You blow your breath on me."

I said, "Sure," and I blew my breath. I almost rocked this man, I blew so hard.

He said, "Hell, this man hasn't had a drink. What are you talking about?"

And I turned around and looked, they're gone. So I said, "What else is there?"

He said, "You're free to go." So I went out and ran as fast as I could, down to this Mink Slide. It was about three blocks down. And when I got down there, I told what had happened, and they said, "Boy, they'll be down here in a minute."

So they put me in this other car, and we went down, and we forked out like that, and I went around like this, and came back to Nashville.

The other funny thing, I remember, I called Tom Clark, who was attorney general, and I told him what happened, and he said, "Drunken driving?"

I said, "Yes."

He said, "Were you drunk?"

I said, "Well, Mr. Attorney General, about five minutes after I hang up this phone, I'm going to be drunk. I'm going to be drunk!"

The other interesting thing about that—the leader of the mob I didn't know; but the next man was the constable of the town of Columbia, whose name was Lynch. I thought that was a beautiful name.

We got all those people off, all but one. All but one.

Q: And that was the one they beat up and put in the hospital?

Marshall: No. No, the other one. I mean, the one guy went to jail. The guy they beat up, they didn't put him in jail. He just went to the hospital.

Oh, another thing about that case—when I was in the hospital, with this Virus X, a great big package came home, and the man who delivered it, the Railway Express man, told my wife, "You know, I'm from Tennessee, and from the smell I know what's in here, and I would sure like to have some of it."

And it was a great big, twenty-pound, country-cured ham. And the note, I thought, was priceless:

"Dear lawyer," et cetera, "we decided we'd get you something. We didn't know what to get you. The wives all wanted to send you flowers, but we knew what you'd rather have."

They sent the ham.

Q: When you worked on these riots, did you go in while they were actually in progress in some other places?

Marshall: Well, the best one was the Detroit riot. They started one night, and I got there the next morning. And it was rough. I got on the phone, talking to the department of justice in the morning. They sent troops out there—well, then it sort of simmered down, after they sent the troops out there.

But as a result, I headed up a study by Governor [Harry F.] Kelly, who appointed me a special attorney general, and made an investigation. The FBI made an investigation, and Wayne University. We, all three, ran independent investigations for a couple of months.

Mine was kind of boggled, because—whoever was behind this—we never did find out just who—hired some Negroes to sort of work me over. Decided to get a private detective. And I did have two or three scrapes, but nothing serious, because he was good, and he had a good-sized .38.

The interesting thing was that we were all sure that it was the Klan or some organized body that started it, and it was not true. That night, in hot summer—all the riots are usually always when it's hot—but two stories started at approximately the same time. One went through the Negro section, that a white Marine had raped a seven-year-old colored girl, at this park. And the other one was that a Negro had raped a white seven-year-old girl. And they started around the same time.

That made us think. But we never could pin it on anybody. And both sides just went out like that. It was rough, I'm telling you.

I know, I was going up one of the main Negro streets—this was about a day or so after it happened—and a white fellow drove by in his car. He said something. I said something back to him. And he pulled out a great big shotgun, and I was so glad there was this trooper standing there with a machine gun. And he said, "Now, who is going to drop what?"

So this guy drops his shotgun.

The one thing you get out of race riots is that no guilty person ever gets hurt. The innocent people get hurt. And the best example was, in the Detroit riot, a colored lady, businesswoman, upper middle class—she didn't want any part of the riot. She stayed at her country home in Canada until it had quieted down, and she was sure it was safe and quieted down.

So she came by to see how her store was doing. She had two stores. And she's driving down, what they call the Valley, where the Negroes were, and there were two colored teen-age kids standing on the side—two or three, I don't know how many—and they didn't recognize her, thought she was white. I mean, from her skin she looked just like a white person. And they said something about that white so-and-so, and they threw a small rock, I guess about two inches in diameter or something like that, aiming at the windshield, and it went in at a soft place on the right side of her skull, and killed her.

Now, there's a woman that wanted no part of it. She stayed out as long as she could. And you can get examples like that all the way through. It's the innocent people who get hurt in the riot. I don't know anything that will sober you down like a riot will. Especially if you get out in it.

Q: Even though you could never find evidence that some group like the Klan had come into start these riots, did you find evidence that professional agitator-types came in after the riots?

Marshall: Oh yes. Oh yes. The Blue Shirt, Black Shirt, something they were called—Brown Shirts—a Michigan group—they came up. But the FBI moved in on them right nicely. Right nicely.

But that's something. And the other footnote to that riot was, I went out two or three years later, to find out what the city had learned. And I went to the then chief of police, and he said, "Oh, yes, if you're interested, I'll be glad to show you. Come with me."

Very proud of it. And he took me to this huge warehouse. Do you know what they had in there? Half-tracks, machine guns, all kinds of military equipment. That was the lesson he learned.

I said, "Well, buddy, what about the cause? What have you done about the cause?"

He didn't know what I was talking about. He didn't know what I was talking about.

I guess the stuff's still out there.

The Harlem riots were much better controlled. We learned in the LaGuardia administration about defusing it, and when a riot would break in Harlem, a code number would go out. I don't know what it was. And all policemen, except those who were flat on their back in bed, sick, reported to the 123rd Street precinct. That's right in the middle of Harlem.

In the meantime, all of the white policemen in Harlem, in the area where the riot's going on, just stand perfectly still, and don't use a weapon, don't use a gun— you just stand there until you're replaced. And the guys looting and everything, they just stand there.

And then these guys go out, and these other guys—the colored fellow taps the white fellow on the shoulder, he gets in the car, and in less than an hour, you have all black cops there. So where's the "race riot"? The race riot's gone. The race riot's gone. Then, Walter White, Roy Wilkins and I would get in radio cars and ride around with loudspeakers, telling them, "Cool it, cool it," you know. And we managed to keep them down pretty well.

At times, in the latter years, when the Muslims started going real bad, they were rough. I got into trouble with one. The then-police commissioner Stephen Kennedy was a very good friend of mine. I liked him because he was a good guy, and we were pretty close. He called me one night. He said, "Have you been listening?"

I said, "Yes. It's right down the street here, I can see them."

He said, "Well, it's calmed down now, would you mind going along?"

The story was that [a] white policeman had beaten up this Negro woman, and that was the story, and it was going all around. And Willie Mays, Jackie Robinson, and somebody else went down and quieted the mob down. They were pretty quiet after that.

I first went to see this colored woman who had been beaten up. Number one, she wasn't colored, she was a Puerto Rican. Spoke practically no English, and drunk as anybody you'd ever run across. And then I went to Harlem Hospital to see the white policeman. And both of his legs, when they took the bandages off, there was no skin at all on his shins. She'd kicked it all off. He's the one that was guilty of "police brutality."'

So I said, this is a dirty damned story, and I started with the police commissioner—oh boy, then the Negroes want[ed] me then, you know. But I told him, that's right, and Kennedy said, "Well, you'd better get some protection."

I said, "I don't need any protection."

The second night he called up and he said, "How about buying me a drink?"

I said, "Okay," and he came on up, and he came in, he had this box all tied up with ribbons, and I said, "What's that?"

He said, "It's a present for you."

So I opened up, and it was a .32, with the license and all in there.

I said, "I told you, I'm not going to take a gun."

He said, "You'd better." I wouldn't. So he put a cop on me. I saw no sense in walking around with a gun.

But riots—any time you hear about one, you go the other way. I wouldn't go. The last one I was in was the one here. You remember the one, after the Martin Luther King thing? But I wasn't out in the street. I was in Ramsey Clark's—the attorney general's—command post. That was a rough night.

That was the second experience my boys had. They had one up in New York. But they know.

Well, what else you got now?

Q: You made a fleeting reference to the Muslims in this context—aware of the Black Muslim organization, and —

(Crosstalk—may have mentioned Elijah Muhammad)

Marshall: I knew him. Oh, the old one was—in World War II; it was a very violent one. It's not the same one. It's a different group. They were violent. That's where I knew them. I worked with the government on some of them. They were really bad.

Then this one started in—I guess it was around about the end of World War II. Then, Malcolm X and I never got along, because I just don't believe that everything that's black is right, and everything that's white is wrong. I think anybody in their right mind knows it. And that's what they were preaching. They were rough about it. They used to hold meetings up in the middle of Harlem, on 125th and Seventh Avenue, and the police department would tape them, and boy, they were rough.

What really had me worried was one day, they gave my address out. Anybody want to know where I live. That's not playing fair. That's not playing fair!

But the average Muslim person—I know, because a cousin of mine was on the squad in New York that rode herd on them—they were the nicest, sweetest, most decent people you will ever run across. He was shocked. He gave me one particular story. They had a meeting at that place where the old prizefights were, St. Nicholas Arena, which is a big place, and the Honorable Elijah Muhammad was coming there, and about an hour before he was there, this audience was completely—these people are all in their seats, the women all dressed in immaculate white, the men all dressed in black. This is thousands of people—and about fifteen or more minutes before Elijah Muhammad came in, the presiding officer said, "Now, look, Elijah Muhammad will be here in so many minutes, and I don't want anyone to move while he's here. Now, any of you who gotta go to the toilet or anything else, you do it now."

And they did, and Elijah Muhammad came in and spoke for two hours and a half, and not a soul moved.

Now, where do you get discipline like that?

But there was another police report, on them training with wooden rifles, on 155th Street in another big arena, and that's what got me worried. That went to pot. It seems as though that wasn't him, that was some offshoot of his. It wasn't him.

So all I think about Elijah Muhammad is—I do not pass any judgement on him or them, but I know those people—they're like Father Divine's[3] people, they are inherently decent people. I'm telling you. No, nothing phony. They bring their children up beautifully. The same thing is true of Elijah—I don't know.

Look at Father Divine, not a single one on home relief. Not a single one on welfare. Not one.

And if you want work done, we had a big valance in our living room that my wife wanted, and somebody told her about this carpenter. He was one of them. And he came up and measured it, and told her how much it would cost. It was about—oh, almost a tenth of what anybody else was charging. And he brought it up and he said, "Oh, there are things here I didn't measure properly." He said, "If you don't mind, it's going to take a little time."

She says, "Go right ahead." And he got a knife out, and he had cut this all around so it would fit in there just right. It only took him a little over three hours, in addition to the regular time. And when he got through, she said, "Well, how much is it?"

---

[3] Father Divine (born George Baker) founded the nonsectarian and interracial Peace Mission Movement. The movement faltered after his death in 1965.

He said, "Oh, no—"

She said, "Well, what about all that extra work?"

He said, "The agreement was this, and that's all I will take."

You don't find New Yorkers like that.

And another thing about Father Divine, the bank up there in Harlem, I forget the name—the Rockefeller's bank—the cashier was a friend of mine from Baltimore, and he told me about a woman who came in there, from Oklahoma, a young woman, in her twenties, to open an account.

He said, "Well, fine. You want to make a deposit?"

She said, "Yes, it's this," and she had a bank draft for forty-some thousand dollars. It was oil property out in Oklahoma. And that built up to way over a hundred thousand dollars, and one night he called me up, he said, "Man, I'm in trouble, come on around—"

She had come in, and she first wanted to change her name on the book. It was, say, Mary Jones, or something—she wanted to change to "Holier Than Thou," one of those Father Divine names, and he said, "Oh, no" and she said, "Peace, Father's truly wonderful."

She wanted to draw the money out. This is in the middle of Harlem. He said, "Well, you want a check?"

She said, "Oh no. Cash."

He said, "Well, I've got three days before I have to give it to you, so you come back in three days." So she did come back. And I talked to her. He talked to her. Nothing to it.

So we arranged for two friends of ours who were New York detectives—imagine walking through Harlem with that much money in her pocketbook! They went with her, and she went down to 126th Street, and that money went right in there. Just like that.

But the people themselves are devoted people, and I think a lot of these Muslims, as with Father Divine—I don't know. I don't know.

Q: Any reference—in your reference to this police report, of men drilling with wooden guns, apparently it was not the Muslims but an offshoot—but if I recall correctly, when Malcolm was with Elijah Muhammad, didn't he take the position that there was no point in arming simply because you were outweaponed?

Marshall: Maybe. I don't know. But his boys were not unarmed.

Q: You're talking now about the Fruit of Islam, the guards? They have permits?

Marshall: I don't know. I don't know. I doubt it. But I don't know. I saw one of them on 125th Street who had a shoulder holster. The one who came after me. That's why I was so peaceful with him.

But no, Malcolm—well, Malcolm's background—how many convictions did he have?

Q: Several.

Marshall: Yes. But they weren't violent. They were pimping and stuff like that, but I don't think they were violent.

In the end, he kept wanting to talk to me, and I kept telling him to go to hell. He changed. When he went over to Islam and those places over there, he really changed.

Q: You never did sit down and talk with him, then.

Marshall: Not lately. I mean, not when he came back. I talked to him, in the early days, and then we had this—something he did I didn't like, or something I did he didn't like. But then, when I became friendly with the chief of police, that was the worst thing I could do.

Old Kennedy was a great guy. I got a Christmas card from him. He's out in California.

Q: To go back to the NAACP days, when did you first meet Roy Wilkins?

Marshall: When the convention came to Baltimore. That would be '34 or '35.

Q: This was shortly after you began practicing law.

Marshall: Yes. Well, I represented the [NAACP] branch from the day I started practicing law.

Q: In Baltimore?

Marshall: Yep. And I met Roy, Walter White, Arthur Spingarn, Daisy Lampkin—I met them all.

Roy's the salt of the earth. I know there's no more dedicated person. I know him, World War II-ish. The owner of this paper I was just talking to, *The Amsterdam News*, a man by the name of Dr. [C. B.] Powell, called me and said he'd like to talk to me; and as it ended up, he said, "Have you talked to Roy about working for me?"

I said, "Nope."

He said, "Well, I've tried to hire him."

I said, "So?"

He said, "I want you to help me."

I said, "Why would I do that?"

He said, "Well, it's to his best interests."

I said, "What are you offering him?"

He said, "Here's the contract. And everything's in it but two things—his duties and responsibilities, and his salary, and I told him to fill that in himself."

I said, "Well, C. B., just between you and me, you know there's a no such thing as a—what are the limits for that?"

He said, "Oh, you want to be cute."

I said, "Nope. If you want me to get involved in it, I gotta know the facts."

And this is back in the forties. He says, "Well, I'll go—the minimum would be twenty-five, the maximum would be forty."

I said, "You're not kidding?"

He said, "Nope."

Well, then Roy was making less than fifteen, ten or twelve.

I went to Roy, and Roy said, "What are you getting in my business for?" I said, "Well, what will I tell him?"

"Tell him to go to hell."

Would you think that's a devoted man? And that's his field. See, he was a newspaper editor before he came there. That was his field. But no, he's a devoted guy. And now he's going to leave, in—what, July, or whatever it is. But my connection with the NAACP ended when I went on the Court of Appeals in '61. I've had no connection since that time, deliberately, because I don't think it would be proper. The only thing I did do—on his seventieth birthday, I went to a private party, and that's all. But I have had nothing to do with the NAACP, the Legal Defense Fund, nothing except reading the paper.

Q: What about some of the other key members of NAACP, particularly in the early days?

Marshall: Well, those were the best days, the early days, because we didn't have anything to fight about except the enemy. We didn't have to fight among ourselves. And when I went there in '36, the whole budget was about seventy or eighty thousand dollars. My whole legal department's budget was seven thousand dollars. That included Houston, Marshall and a secretary, plus calls and everything else. And we got along very well. I think when we got larger and larger, problems grew and grew and grew. But I don't know. I didn't have any trouble with them. Of course, we had our discussions, and we had our fights, and we had our disagreements, but we always ended up pretty much together. Sometimes, between Walter White and Roy Wilkins and myself, we would really get at each other. And sometimes we would get some board member to come in and arbitrate. It always worked out with everybody having a good solid laugh about it.

Those were the good days. I don't know how it is now. Now they've got six million here and three million there—maybe they've got too much money, I don't know.

Q: Can you recall anything more about what these disagreements were about? Were they over tactics, or strategy even?

Marshall: Strictly tactics. Strictly tactics. You see, Walter White was the front man. He went out. He met with the president. He did this, he made that public statement and all—we went along.

Roy was the one that actually ran the organization, the day-by-day nuts and bolts—Roy ran that. And I had the legal side. But at times the real problem would come up because Walter White always thought he was a lawyer, and he would interfere with my legal business, and he'd get his head chopped off because I didn't believe in letting laymen tell me what I had to do. So that's what the usual fights would be.

He would come into the Supreme Court and sit in the lawyers' section. Everybody thought he was a lawyer. And one time I told him, I said, "Now, look— you're not supposed to be in there, and they know you're connected with me, and one of these days, they're going to find out you're not a lawyer, and I'm going to get blamed for it. And it's going to affect my standing, and I don't believe in letting anything affect my standing in the Supreme Court. So I'm telling you, don't let me catch you sitting in there again. If you do, I'm going to tell the guard."

He said, "You wouldn't!"

I said, "Try me."

And the next case that I was arguing, I kept looking around, and I didn't see Walter sitting there, so I thought I won. And I had to look over [at] the judge's box—he was over there. He had gone to Hugo Black and gotten Hugo Black to put him in the box. So he won anyhow.

Well, it was nothing serious.

Q: Were there any particularly significant officials under Roy Wilkins that were coming up during that early period? Was that before field organizers like Gloster Current?

Marshall: Goddamn, we didn't have that many. Current didn't come until— oh, it was in the forties before he came there. When we first went there, we had an old gentleman, Dean Pickens, and he died on a world cruise. And then I think they put Gloster in. Gloster had been there a long time, but he wasn't there when I went there. Gloster came, I'll tell you, it was after the big UAW (United Auto Workers) fight with the Ford people, and the UAW won. It was that period of time. I think that would be around '40.

But when I was there, all we had was Walter White, Charlie Houston, Roy, and Pickens, that's all.

Q: Actually, wasn't the NAACP at that time the only real civil rights organization, as far as Negroes or blacks were concerned?

Marshall: No. The National Negro Congress cropped up, and they were charged with being fellow travelers, et cetera, and sort of went by the boards. And the Urban League, of course, handled the employment. That would be about all that we had. I just can't remember. There were other outfits with funny kind of names that would come up, and drop dead. The only one that really moved a little was the National Negro Congress, I think it was called, run by a guy named John A. Davis.

That's all I remember.

Q: Did he run on the national ticket, splinter party, some time?

Marshall: No. Ben Davis did. Ben Davis.[4]

Q: Did you know anything more about this National Negro Congress—for example, whether it really was left-controlled or not?

Marshall: No. I don't think it was ever proved. I don't think it ever was. There were a lot of suspect people in there, but as I remember, we knew pretty well who was a Commie and who wasn't, and I don't think there were more than two or three in there. We knew them pretty well. We can shut them up.

Q: You feel, in the thirties, that you probably knew just about every black person who was in the Communist Party.

Marshall: No. No, but I knew most of them. I knew most of them. Ben Davis used to come to our conventions. We were very friendly. We knew what he was up to, and he knew what we were up to. And we didn't pay any attention. They had no control, and they were nice guys.

Around World War II, we decided to get rid of them. We wouldn't even allow them to come to a meeting. We ran them out.

We had a funny one in California. The Commies had a resolution they wanted to put through, to stop the Marshall Plan, you know, General Marshall's plan? And all of a sudden, we wondered, would they have any chance? Out in the sunshine and all around the church where the meeting was, the people were all lollygagging

---

[4] Benjamin Davis was the Communist party's most prominent African American member; he ran for national and local office several times in the 1940s.

around, all of a sudden one guy said, "Come on, we gotta get in there quick, come on, everybody get in there, everybody's gotta get in there—"

Somebody says, "What for?"

He says, "They're in there, the Commies are fighting, they're trying to get rid of our lawyer!"

They said, "What?"

"They're voting against the Marshall Plan!"

And we won. They thought they were going to fire their lawyer.

And then, in Boston, we really, we socked them good. We defeated everything they put up, and did it so wholeheartedly about at the end—I mean, for example, they had a word around there about how much money we were making, and I was going into the church one day, and some of them were standing there, and they said, "Hey, there goes that lawyer."

And I said, "What's on your mind?"

And one of them said, "All this money that you and Walter and Roy make."

I said, "Well what's wrong with that? We earn it."

And they said, "By the way, how much do you make? Are you willing to tell?"

I said, "The hell I won't, of course I'll tell you. If you're a member of the NAACP, you're entitled to know."

He said, "Well, how much do you make?"

I said, "$55,000 plus expenses."

"How much does Walter make?"

I said, "I don't know, I think it's around eighty."

Well, at that I was making less than ten and Walter was making ten.

One guy said, "Why did you say that?"

I said, "If they got in there on the floor and say that, they're gonna be hooted off the floor."

Sure enough, the damn fools did.

And then, after we killed them on every resolution they had, I had an old lady friend of mine from Houston, Texas, and I told the presiding officer, Bishop [Stephen Gill] Spottswood, I said, "Now, you be sure and recognize that lady."

He said, "Okay." And when we got all the way through and they lost the last resolution, she got up, and she says "Mr. Chairman?"

Bishop Spottswood said, "Yes, Ma'am?"

She said, "I hope you'll all join me," and she started singing, "We Shall Not Be Moved."

And they walked out, and they never came back. They never came back.

I was very happy about that. I got a verbal recommendation from, guess who? Mr. [J. Edgar] Hoover. He evidently had the meeting monitored.

But I don't think they'll ever come back in there.

Q: Incidentally, did you have the feeling in those days that the FBI had agents watching you?

Marshall: I, for one—and all of us would say, if we saw somebody in the audience that we didn't know—we'd say, "Why don't you move up front? You can hear better."

Sure. I don't care what they hear. I'll tell 'em.

There was military intelligence, that was more than the FBI. We'd catch them every once in a while, when we'd travel. Because what I would do, in places like Boston— I caught two of them up in Boston, because I had some guys, lawyers up there who were good friends of mine, and I said, "Will you go to your Red Squad in the police department to find out who's here?"

Those fools would tell the police. And the police would tell the lawyer, and the lawyer would tell me.

In the Little Rock case, which we'll talk about later, the man out there from the FBI was sitting right in the audience. So that's a mixed bag there.

Q: Justice Marshall, you were mentioning your travels, to Korea, Kenya, and there have been others, I believe. Do you want to talk about Korea first?

Marshall: Well, in the Korea situation—as I remember—it was the latter part of 1950. A newspaper reporter, a Negro from the *Afro-American* in Baltimore called me, on his return from Tokyo, and reported that there was something going on which brought about the arrest of fifty or more Negro soldiers in Korea. The NAACP decided that I should look into it. I found enough substance to warrant going over, but in applying for a passport, a Mrs. [Ruth B.] Shipley of the state department— who had a built-in dislike for Negroes and the NAACP—would not give me a passport. She even had the FBI to check me out, and they gave me a clean bill of health, but she still wouldn't grant it. And then she got General [Douglas] MacArthur to refuse me an entry permit, and that blocked it, and I decided the best thing to do would be to go to President Truman, and I did. He ordered that the passport be issued.

But it was delivered to me as I was getting on the plane, and when I got on the plane, I opened up the passport and looked at it, and it said, "Not good for travel in Korea."

I figured I might have some trouble, and I did. But when I got to Tokyo, after trouble of getting located, I began meeting with Inspector General Zondell, the inspector general of the Far East Command, and the Assistant Inspector D. D. Martin. They were extremely cooperative, decent, well-trained investigators, and of course lawyers. They arranged for me to interview all of the Negroes who were then in the Tokyo stockade, and the procedure was that I would go by the Dai-Ichi building, which [was] the headquarters for the Army, each morning, discuss the day's work with General Zondell and [Colonel] Martin. From there, I would go to the stockade and interview the prisoners, one at a time. Come back in the afternoon, work up my work sheets, and then be ready to report back to the solicitor general in the morning.

The reason for this was that many leads that were gotten from the prisoners had to be run down by the inspector general's office. This went on for several weeks, I've forgotten now how many, until I talked to some sixty or eighty people involved.

I found enough to warrant a trip to Korea, and then I had to go to MacArthur's chief of staff, the name slips me for the moment, who was also very cooperative; and he arranged for me to go to Korea, and Colonel Martin went along with me.

Just prior to that, I was given an audience with General MacArthur, and I found it very interesting. I questioned him about the continuation of segregation in the Army, and he said he was working on it. And I asked him how many years he'd been working on it, and he didn't really remember how many.

I reminded him that at the very time we were talking, the Air Force was completely integrated, and the Navy was quite integrated, and the only group not integrated was the Army. He said that he didn't find the Negroes qualified, and when he found them qualified, they would be integrated.

Well, we didn't part very friendly. I guess I told him what I thought, and he told me what he thought. And he being the boss, he cancelled, and I left.

Well, getting back to the trip—when I got to Korea, we went all the way up from Tejon to just below Seoul, where the enemy was. We were in the area where there was great movement, and at times you'd go into one place, and the next time you'd get there, they'd tell you, you can't go in because the enemy was there.

This was for the purpose of interviewing people, Negroes, in these service units. The stories were almost unbelievable. On the big hill, I believe it was Pork Chop Hill, the casualties were between eighty-five and ninety-five percent, which is high for anybody, and they were constantly being pushed around. The Negroes were just getting it in the neck.

Then I was investigating these court-martials, and eventually I got on the track, and I found where they were stored, down near Tejon. Colonel Martin, the deputy inspector general who I said was willing to cooperate, arranged for me to get to the warehouse where these records were kept. I got there just as they were about to be shipped away, I don't know where.

But once the inspector general clamped down on them, we got them, and I spent days going through them, and they were unbelievable. There were records of trials, so-called trials, in the middle of the night where the men were sentenced to life imprisonment in hearings that lasted less than ten minutes. They were the old, well-known drumhead court-martials, done in the heat of passion and in the heat of war. There were fifty or sixty involved. One death penalty case. I remember in particular: the record showed that this man was charged with being absent in the presence of the enemy. Instead of being charged with AWOL, he was charged with cowardice in the presence of the enemy. And fortunately for him, he produced two witnesses: a major in the Medical Corps and a lieutenant in the Nurse Corps, both of whom testified that he was in a base hospital the very day that he was supposed to be AWOL.

And despite their testimony, he was convicted and given life imprisonment.

You could go through them like that. I took my notes. I worked on these records. And I came back to Tokyo, and back to the United States, and fortunately in the judge advocate general's office of the Army, we were able to bust every one of the convictions. Although we didn't get them all out scot-free, we got most of them out scot-free, and the others [with] a very short term.

To me, that was very important. It was good experience, to be with the military and to be up in actual warfare. It wasn't what I relished, but I learned a whole lot.

Now, the next experience with the military—no, this was before. This was in World War II. Outside of San Francisco, at the naval establishment of Yerba Buena Island, fifty Negro seamen were charged with mutiny because they refused to load ammunition during the time of war.

The reason they refused was that the day before they were given the orders, directly across from where they were working, there was another group of Negroes loading ammunition, and being rushed by the lieutenants who were over them, and it was also in the record that they, the lieutenants, had bet between the two of them as to which gang would do it the fastest. And so they were actually not just moving cases of live ammunition, they were throwing it, from one to the other, to speed up the loading. And, as should have been expected, one of the cases dropped, and the whole thing just took off, and everybody was killed.

And these men right across, a few hundred yards away, saw this. The next day when they were ordered to load their ship the same way, rather than be killed, they said "No" and they were charged with mutiny.

Well, I went out to defend them at the court-martial, and it ran quite a while, and it ended up with a conviction, and they were all convicted. The, same as with the Army, we had to work them up through the judge advocate general's office, and eventually to the Secretary of the Navy [James] Forrestal. The conclusion of that case was extremely interesting, because there was no official notice of what happened in that case. The records of the final disposition were never entered, but I happen to know, from Secretary Forrestal himself, that all of the men were released and put back onto active duty in the Pacific. But there's no record in the Navy Department about it.

Now, the African trips were interesting. I went to the inauguration of President [William V. S.] Tubman in Liberia, the latter part of '60. From there I went to

Kenya, Nairobi, to meet with the Kenya nationals, the native Kenyan people, whom I would later represent.

When I got to Nairobi, they were under detention orders. Jomo Kenyatta was way out in the country, couldn't be reached. Tom Mboya and Dr. [Hastings] Banda met me, and I met with the delegations. I listened to them and took their instructions, and I left Kenya after a week or so under great handicap. While you were there the restrictions were almost unbelievable. Africans could not hold a meeting in a building. So as a result, the only meetings they had were outside. And when I got there, the second day, I went out to a place outside of Nairobi, Keambu or something—I don't know the name of it—and there were two thousand Africans standing out in the field, perfectly quiet, and the leaders were meeting in the building but they couldn't go in. The leaders were in one building. They were out. They were standing out in that hot sun, all day, waiting for the leaders to come out and report to them.

Well, when I got there, I started to go in to the meeting, and the district officer came up to me and introduced himself, very politely, like the British always are, and he said, "What do you propose to do?" I said, "I'm going in there. That's what I came over here for, was to talk to these people."

He said, "Well, you can't go in there."

I said, "Why?"

He said, "You don't have a permit."

And Tom Mboya spoke up and he said, "Why, of course he has a permit. We got one last week."

He said, "Yes, and it was revoked yesterday."

So I started to be loud and boisterous and get arrested, and suddenly it dawned on me that if I was arrested, I'd be searched. I had money and paraphernalia and stuff for Mboya and others in my pockets, and if I was caught with that, I would really spend the rest of my life in jail.

So I decided to be very polite, and I told the district officer, "Of course. I understand. But before I leave, I wonder if I could just say a word to all those people out there?"

They said, "Nope. No speeches."

I said, "I'm not going to make a speech. Just let me say one word of greeting."

He said, "All right, all right, just one word."

I said, "Okay," and I jumped up on top of this station wagon that Mboya was driving, and I looked over the crowd, and they all recognized Tom Mboya, and I guess they knew who I was, I don't know.

Well, as I looked at them, I just shouted out real loud one word, "Uhuru!" and pandemonium broke out. They all crowded, cheered, and everything, and the district officer was really mad as all get out.

The reason was, the word "Uhuru" means "Freedom Now," Not tomorrow, but freedom right now.

And he said, "I told you not to—"

I said, "But I didn't say but one word."

So he told me where I'd better go right quick, so I did.

Well, I went from there to London and spent seven weeks, drawing up the constitution for the freedom of Kenya. The meeting was held by Ian McCleod, who was the colonial secretary, a Scotchman, very strong, intelligent, and a capable official, and at the opening session, McCleod told the gathering that the question of whether Kenya would get its freedom was not subject to debate. Her Majesty's government had decided that Kenya would be free. So the only thing to be decided was when and how.

Well, there were four delegations present. The first one I represented, [and] was made up of all native African men born in Kenya. Across from us was a group by Captain Blondell, as I remember, which was mixed up. It had Africans, it had white British, it had Indians, all mixed together.

To our right was Group Captain Briggs' group, all white, and the best way I can explain them is that if you compared them to the Ku Klux Klan in its heyday in this country, the Ku Klux Klan would look like a Sunday School picnic. These were real rabid, awful. And the fourth group were the East Indians.

Well, everybody was at everybody's throat. We would meet together, and then go upstairs on the top floor, and each had separate meeting rooms, so we'd meet together and then separately. And the meetings were held in a building called Lancaster House, a huge mansion belonging to the government, right next to the home of Princess Margaret.

One sidelight during all of this was a young boy was born to the queen, and the interesting thing was that when it was announced that the baby was born, the meeting was of course suspended, and we all went into the big lounge and got cocktails and toasted the young prince.

Well, I was drinking my cocktail, of course, and Ian McCleod came over to me, either he or somebody else, and said, "I notice you're drinking, but you're not 'pip-pippin,' you're not cheering."

I said, "Well, why should I cheer? I don't see anything to cheer about."

He said, "What do you mean by that?"

I said, "All you're cheering is, is another mouth to feed, and a damned expensive mouth at that. What are you cheering about?"

Well, it seemed like that wasn't the right thing to say, in Great Britain and in Lancaster House, but I said it and I got away with it.

We ended up drawing this constitution. I wrote the whole "schedule" of rights, as they call it in Britain. I said it was a schedule. The Britishers said, it's their language, they knew what they were talking about, and the correct pronunciation was "shedule." I said, "Well, if that's true, how are your children doing in shul today?"— but it still came down as a shedule.

The Schedule of Rights gave the white citizen living in Kenya absolute protection, the strongest, I maintained, of any constitution in the world, spelled out in detail. For example, the important thing was to protect land, because land is about all you have in Kenya. Marvelous land, but that's all. And the Schedule of Rights provides that if the government takes your land, and you don't like it, you can go directly to the highest court in Kenya and go there without payment of costs, and find out whether or not you were cheated.

When we got back and got it all straightened out, we had to make one change. There were no Africans capable of being judges. And that was pretty tough. There was only one, Charles Adjonjo, and Jomo Kenyatta wanted him for his attorney general, so he wasn't available to be a judge.

So we had to keep all of the judges there. When I went back a few years later, they had trained several, so that by now I'm sure that they're all there.

That, to my mind, is really working toward democracy, when you can give to the white man in Africa what you couldn't give the black man in Mississippi. It's good.

The white people who remained in Kenya, for the most part, were beautiful. For example, when the panic started, Ian McCleod said, "Well, I don't see why everybody's panicking. My mother lives here, and I wouldn't leave my mother here if I were afraid of something."

Now, the interesting thing to me is that the white people who stayed there took part in the government—I remember when the leadership was turned over to Kenyatta. My wife and I were over there as his guests, the independence was declared at midnight. The next morning in Parliament, Jomo Kenyatta said, "We will now attend to the first order of business of the new government. Governor so and so," whatever the whole governor's name was, "stand up," and this man stood up.

He said, "The first order of business is, we're going to reappoint you as governor."

And that gave to everybody the meaning of the world, "harrambee," which means, "pull together," and the whole government was like that, and it's like that to this day.

Well, I'm glad I had a part in it.

Q: Justice, how did this assignment come about in the first place, that you would help draft the constitution?

Marshall: Ha ha! Two friends of mine, one from the Urban League, and one from the UAW, came to me with this idea. And along with there was a man, Lansdale Christie, a very wealthy Wall Street guy, who owned the iron mine in Liberia. And they said they had gotten together the money for this trip, from a man whose name I've forgotten—a very wealthy businessman in New Jersey, a millionaire—and he did show up in London twice, three times. He not only took care of all of my expenses, but all of this whole delegation's expenses, and we did run short one time. And I came back to my friends in New York and got a few thousand dollars and went back.

But the basic money came from this guy, I don't remember his name, a multi-millionaire, and I found out later that he had less money than I did.

Then, I got two and two—and I still suspect it was CIA money, that's all I could—I know it wasn't Commie money, so what else could it be? I don't know.

But they took care of most of the expense. The other part of the expenses, the NAACP took care of.

We had one fellow who was very interesting. Talit was his name. Masai tribe, a very violent tribe, but he was the sweetest person in the world, and he was a philosopher. He loved philosophy, and we had an awful time with him, because we'd give him money for his meals and held go out and buy a philosophy book with it. And he couldn't eat the book. So he was always a problem for us.

But it was a very good bunch. I was impressed most effectively with the ability of those Africans to sense and act politically. Their timing was perfect. They knew just when to walk out. They knew just when to walk back in. They didn't lose a single point in that seven weeks. And I was very proud of them.

The East Indians were unbelievably stupid. They fought to the bitter end, and what they had to gain I don't know. It was all settled, because Kenyatta told them if they didn't take out citizenship, they could get out of the country. So they then took out citizenship.

That's about all I can do on that one.

Q: Did you sense at any time that the new government would try to expel the East Indians?

Marshall: Sure. In their own self-defense. They didn't want to be Africans.

Q: Did they control more of the economy?

Marshall: Yes. Yes. They'd have to get out. But they controlled the retail business, that's all. They didn't, they couldn't control the coffee, tea, and the big stuff. They didn't control that. They just controlled the little shops on the street, and stuff like that.

But they joined up in the end. They said that India wouldn't allow them to have dual citizenship. And we went over to India, and Nehru said, "Of course they can have dual citizenship," then they had no other thing to do, so they joined up.

Q: What further was your impression of Kenyatta?

Marshall: Well, start with my wife. My wife adored him. He has a very piercing set of eyes—you know, looks straight through you. And he is a warm—just unbelievably human person. But no middle ground. You're right or you're wrong. And he's strong. He's not now, he's weak, physically, not mentally, but physically he's very weak.

I just had the greatest respect for him. And had it not been for him, it would have been one of the damnedest bloodbaths you ever saw in your life. He was the one thing that stood in the way of that.

He also is the controlling spirit over there, yet. And all of us are worried to death about what happens at his death. I think the Commies are going to take over, after an awful bloodbath.

One guy's name is Adjonjo or something—he's the same tribe as Tom Mboya's, and he collects from both the Communists and the Chinese Communists. He's a bad one.

Q: What was your impression of Tom Mboya?

Marshall: He was great. Tom played it cool, but I think he was as strong as Jomo, in his way. He would not be—he was maybe better educated. You know exactly where you stand with him. A marvelous politician, but if you were on his side, you knew where he was. If you were on the other side, you didn't know.

But I found him with great strength. He and Jonjo and a couple of others were awfully close to Jomo. I would say he was just like Jomo's son. He was great.

Q: There was quite an age difference between them.

Marshall: Yes. Oh, yes. Tom is—I guess he was in his forties when he died. He was very young. Very.

Q: Didn't Tom Mboya make frequent trips over here?

Marshall: Oh, yes. The UAW used to bring him over here. With that foreign fund they have, they used to bring him over here regularly, and he'd raise money for the movement over there. I'd go around with him making speeches and all. Yes. I guess he'd come over at least twice a year.

Q: Had you known him before you went over there?

Marshall: Oh yes. Sure. Sure. I knew him very well.

Q: Did he, as a matter of fact, make a practice of calling you on each trip?

Marshall: No, not every trip. Most of them.

Q: Or, when you knew that he was here, did you seek him out?

Marshall: Of course I would. Any other African. Any other African.

I was not interested in Africa, as long as they weren't interested in fighting. When they got interested in fighting, then I got interested in them. And I went over there, and I participated in a lot of stuff. I got people out of South Africa, got them all the way over to the States.

Once, I went to one of their camps, in Tanganyika.

Q: Did you personally go to South Africa?

Marshall: I never went to South Africa. No. If they'd invite me, I wouldn't go.

But on the other hand, the South African Air Force, in the army, were the best friends the Negro had. Nobody can explain it to me.

When I was in Korea, as I mentioned earlier, one night, I don't know where we were, we were in some camp, and at dusk, then D. D. Martin, Colonel Martin, came in and said, "Hey, you want to go to a party, drink a little liquor?"

I said, "Sure. Of course." I said, "Where?"

He said, "This outfit next to us."

I said, "You mean that damned South African Air Force? I wouldn't be caught dead with the so-and-so and so-and-so's, et cetera."

He said, "You're wrong. They're the best friends that the Negro has, in the Air Force, and what have you."

I said, "Do you mind if I check on what you said?"

"Go ahead."

So I went out and talked to a couple of Negro captains. And a lieutenant. They said, "Of course. As a matter of fact, the party there that's given is for the Negro anti-aircraft outfit."

I said, "You're kidding!"

They said, "No." So I went over. And I had a delightful time. It was real two-fisted drinking, real rough. They're extremely wealthy, all of them. They buy their own aircraft. They draw no salaries. And they are, I think, just interested in fighting. They just like to fight.

I talked to the lead guy, and we got good and drunk around midnight or so, and he said: it wasn't racial, it was economic. Solely economics. That he owned half of a diamond mine and half of a coal mine, and if the blacks took over, he'd lose it.

Then he used that old statement, "I'm not worried about it for myself, but for my children"—you know, that lot of stuff—

But that's it. He said he had no objection to associating with blacks or Negroes any place *except* South Africa. He said, "Now, I'm coming to New York in about three months, when I get out and retire, and I would like to see you."

I said, "You mean, me?"

He said, "Yes."

I said, "Well, suppose I come over to Johannesburg?"

He said, "No."

I said, "Why?"

He said, "It's different there." And how they rationalize that, to me—I still don't understand.

Sure enough, we were kidding, he said, "I've never been to the States, and they tell me that they want me to stay in a hotel called the Waldorf-Astoria or something. What about that?"

We all told him, "Well—it's a pretty good third-rate fleabag, it'll do pretty good."

Three or four months later, sure enough, the phone rang, and he called. He said, "I'm at that fleabag you were talking about."

I went over there to lunch with him, and—in one of those tower apartments, huge things—and we had a good time.

But I don't understand it. It's when they get away from home. He says he goes to London once a year, he has no feeling about seeing blacks on the street, in the restaurant, any place. He says, once he gets on a South African airplane, even before he gets to South Africa, he gets that feeling. Well—

Q: Wouldn't this be contradistinctive to the older traditional American's attitude, where he considers black inferior—

Marshall: Right. But his, it's inferior, but it's inferior because of economics. When I pinned him right down to it, he couldn't spell out his "inferior," he couldn't spell it out. He started off, they were inferior. Then he starts on his economics, and the two don't go together. And I think he—I don't remember now, but I think he just about admitted that that's what it was.

He told me that if it were a group of white Frenchmen or white Englishmen, who had that many there and were about to take over his property, he would have the same response.

Well, I still am not going down there. No way.

Q: Did the NAACP actively contribute then also to this drafting of the constitution of Kenya, and perhaps others, or how was that arranged, with the NAACP?

Marshall: They didn't put anything in it except my salary. I mean, the money that I got, I raised on my own.

Q: Did you help draft any other constitutions?

Marshall: No. I helped a little on the Nigerian one. That was before. But that was through somebody else.

Q: Whom did you work with on the Nigerian constitution?

Marshall: I can't—in the State Department—I can't. They don't let you say anything, you know. I guess they won't let me admit that I did.

Q: To go back to your trip to Korea, how about a little passport detail? Do you think that was deliberate that they stamped your passport, "Not good for Korea"? Or was it just a bureaucratic oversight, after Truman had ordered it granted?

Marshall: I don't know. I don't know.
When I got over there, the chief of staff, General Doyle Hickey, he said, "Would you mind going back and telling Miss Shipley who's running this thing over here?"
With that he just did like this [crossed out the restriction] with his pen.

Q: Did you have more detailed knowledge than you've already indicated of what was going on in the court-martial of black soldiers over there, or was this just a general—?

Marshall: Oh, I'd been in many court-martials, before that, and most of them were bad. The trouble with court-martials is that historically, the sentence is cut either by command at that level or the level up, so the tendency is to give more than you would give. The catch is, if it doesn't go up, you're stuck with that heavy sentence.

Anybody will tell you that in those days, the court-martial of anyone was horrible. It's not true today. If a commanding officer wanted to get somebody, he would deliberately pick officers of the court-martial in the following way. He would find everyone that's up for promotion, and put them on his court-martial. Well, if they wanted to go against him, they're just giving up their promotions.

You throw rank and all. I've been in many of them. But none as bad as those. Those were just horrible.

They had one fellow named Lieutenant Gilbert. He was supposed to go up a hill, and he started with the company, and he got shot up; and half a dozen came back and they never even got up the hill. And he went up three or four times. And then when they came back, and they would tell him to go again.

He said, "Well, look, if I can't get up there with a company of thirty men, how am I going to get up there with four?"

They said, either-or. He said: Well, he'd or.

That's it, he was guilty of disobeying a command. He didn't get all the way out. He was the one who was sentenced to death. He ended up, I think, with five years. Something like that.

But court-martials are bad. Court-martials today are better. And I've been in stockades. At Camp Maxie, Texas, I tried a case against Leon Jaworski, who was in the Nixon thing. I've been in big ones, small ones. I'm agin' em.

Q: When I was in the Army in World War II, our indoctrination was that you would not be court-martialed unless they were pretty sure you were guilty, and therefore, it really presumed that you would be convicted if you ever got court-martialed.

Marshall: Well, that's because of the CIA—no, they call it the CID.

Q: CID, the Corps of Investigation–

Marshall: Well, that is an overrated thing. In some outfits it's marvelous. In others it's not. Some are good and some are bad. We had one island, I've forgotten which one it was, where they sequestered the guys for two days in a tent in the hot sun. That's not my idea of the way to do business. And you'd find others that were—I know on this trip to Tokyo that ended up with MacArthur guards on me. I had a different one every two days, and it worked out beautifully because the first one let me know and then he told each one of the others that I knew as much as MacArthur about it.

I did get caught one night in a nightclub I wasn't supposed to be, but they didn't do anything.

Q: Do you have any further impressions of General MacArthur? Do you feel he was definitely biased or just opinionated?

Marshall: He was as biased as any person I've run across.

Q: In other words, he felt basically that blacks were inferior?

Marshall: Inferior. No question about it. No question about it. I told him about all these instances. I said, "Well, General, look—you've got all those guards out there with all this spit and polish and there's not one Negro in the whole group."
He said, "There's none qualified."
I said, "Well, what's qualification?"
"In field of battle, et cetera."
I said, "Well, I just talked to a Negro yesterday, a sergeant, who has killed more people with a rifle than anybody in history. And he's not qualified?"
And he said, "No."
I said, "Well, now, General, remember yesterday you had the big band playing at the ceremony over there?"
He said, "Yes, wasn't it wonderful?"
I said, "Yes. The Headquarters Band, it's beautiful." I said, "Now General, just between you and me, goddamn it, don't you tell me that there's no Negro that can play a horn?"

That's when he said for me to go.

There's gotta be prejudice.

Best proof of it was, General Matthew Ridgway took over after him, and desegregated in about three weeks. Desegregated the whole thing. And the only opposition he found was among the Negroes. They didn't want to be integrated.

No, that man was something.

Q: Were you involved with the Ridgway move at all?

Marshall: I only saw Ridgway once. When I was over in Korea itself, it took me about a week to catch up with him. Every time I would make a date with him, he was gone by the time I got there. But I know, one time, it was called something like, "right up on the line"—and I got up there, and a guy said, "If you want to see something, come on."

So I went on up there, and Ridgway was sitting on the top of a fox hole—the lead one, his enemy was right over there—and he was sitting with his back to the enemy, talking to his men.

Now it takes something to do that. It takes something. Boy, that guy was something!

Q: Did you have the impression, when you were in Korea, that the Negro soldiers tended to be given the riskiest missions?

Marshall: Well, we had proof of it, but we lost it. What happened over there is that they had this big withdrawal, and the records show that that was just damnedest retreat you've ever seen. They were running, ducking—I mean, it was awful. And they had to stop it. And the only way to stop it was to pick a unit, and court-martial them and make examples of them, and here was this Negro unit. So that's the one they grabbed.

Q: You're talking about retreat after the Chinese came in.

Marshall: Yes.

Q: What did you find about treatment of Negro soldiers in stockades here in this country?

Marshall: It depended on whose. The one I know most about was this Camp Maxie, and that was absolutely perfect. They got along swell. You know something? I don't even know whether they were segregated or not. I mean, I never even noticed. So they may have been integrated. I know they had Negro officers there, in the guards.

There you see the evil of court-martial in general. So one afternoon, there was a white fellow, little kid about nineteen, who was in there on another charge, very minor charge, and he was told to lay grass sod. And he said, "No," and he cussed out the sergeant. The sergeant brought him in. I was sitting [r]ight there, and told the lieutenant what happened and the lieutenant said, "Well, bring him in."

So he brought him in. And he said, "You disobeyed the order of a noncommissioned officer. Do you realize the penalty for that?"

And he said, "Yes."

He said, "Well, you know [what] this bar is on my shoulder?"

He said, "Yes, you're a first louie."

He said, "First lieutenant to you." He said, "Well, I'm going to give you an order."

He said, "You go for a general court." So he went out. I said, "Lieutenant, what the hell you mean, general court?"

He said, "Yes. He'll go next week."

I said, "What will he get?"

He said, "Five years."

I said, "What? Why would you do that to a young kid like that?"

He said, "If I'd done that, I'd go."

That's how the military works. Five years. Now, if that was in a civilian jail, and he refused to work, what could they do to him? They couldn't increase his sentence. But there you are.

Maybe I don't love the military. I don't know.

Q: Was this visit in Texas in World War II, or after?

Marshall: That was World War II. There were three Negroes charged with rape. I got all of them out. All three of them. A fourth went up.

They got off with the time they served. They were in jail about three years, while the case was going. That's what it was.

Q: Had they committed rape?

Marshall: No. Well, the only proof that I had that they didn't was against their own testimony. For some reason, they testified that they had intercourse with this woman for pay. And they testified to that three times. Yet the records showed: one, that this woman had the most violent case of gonorrhea that Major McGuffern had ever seen in his life. And that there was no way that she could have had intercourse without infecting them. And yet not a one of them was infected. So they lied in one place. They've got to be lying. I don't know why they would tell a lie like that. But they did. And twice they got sentenced to die.

I don't know.

Q: You mentioned the disappearance or destruction of records of that one case. Did you find that frequently, that records trial of Negro soldiers were missing?

Marshall: No. Very seldom. Usually, if you know where to go, you could find them.

These, I think, were deliberate. I think when they found out that I was over there—because they were nailing these—and we got them.

But the power of the inspector general is just unbelievable.

Q: Coming back to some of the civil rights cases that you worked on after the war in this country, you selected a handful of them for your Who's Who profile. Do you consider those the major ones that you worked on, or are there other benchmark cases that you feel are equally important?

Marshall: I don't know. I think the voting ones were probably the most important. That goes into the Texas primary, the Oklahoma case, cases like that. The criminal cases, of course, did the most immediate good, because they saved people's lives. So I don't know, how do you measure—whether you save people's lives, or put a piece of bread in their mouths? I don't know which is the more important.

I once had a letter from a guy in prison in California that said, one of these days he should write and tell me how it felt to be in the electric chair and then be taken out.

Incidentally, he never wrote another letter, but at least I got one from him.

But those give me the most important feeling, because you can see and talk to the people.

I had one in Florida, Walter Irwin, where his mother—oh, boy, she had a strong face. And I was doing pretty well with that case, until she came to me and looked me straight in the face. She said, "Lawyer, don't let my boy die, you understand that?"

I could hardly go to sleep. I could see this face, and boy, it really—.

He was a great guy, though.

I don't know. I can't add them up. If anybody asked me to say which cases are most important, I would always say, "The one I'm going to handle next." I think that's it.

Q: In reference to President Truman, were you initially surprised when he took such a strong position on civil rights?

Marshall: Yes. I had no reason to believe it, because I was for everybody but him, to be vice president. I don't know when I first got notice of it. But it wasn't long. It wasn't long. I think I got it through Tom Clark first.

Q: Now was Tom Clark initially—

Marshall: Yes always. I knew him when he first came to Washington. I knew his mother. And his brother in Dallas. I knew him way back. His mother, way back—this will go back to the late thirties—her housekeeper, a Negro, ate dinner with her. They ate right at the same table together. Now, back in the thirties, you didn't do that in Texas.

No, he's always been great.

Q: Did the Truman position, especially after the 1948 election, make it easier for you, as you were pleading the cases through the courts?

Marshall: Well, you knew you had somebody to rely on. Who would go the whole hog, and one you—I almost said, it's a spiritual feeling. It's a warm feeling, you just can't put your hands on. But you know he's there when you need him. Like on this trip to Korea—all I had to do was get in touch with him, and you know he's going to do it. And you know he will do it.

Oh, yes. I think his greatest influence, in my book—he and Johnson, can't leave out [Lyndon B.] Johnson—

Q: Did you find that Johnson felt this way when he was vice president, or did that come after Kennedy's death and his accession?

Marshall: It came after about Sam Rayburn died. Sam Rayburn was the influence that held him down the road. When Rayburn died, early in the last term, early in the last term, that's when he moved. That would be about 1964, 1965, around in there. That's when he moved. Rayburn had a great influence on him, and Rayburn was not for rocking the boat. He wanted the good old status quo, and that's it. He would do anything, except get rid of segregation. He would do anything also. But he wasn't for that. He liked good old segregation.

Q: Did you find, during that time, to paraphrase that question, that the attitudes in the lower court began changing, that the judges began changing because of higher sentiment in the land?

Marshall: Never thought about it. Never thought of it. Might have. No, no. There were judges down South—that's the great benefit of lifetime appointments—who would go absolutely straight, I know.

Well, let me give you one in particular, and this would be in the forties. There was a judge, Louis Strom, in the district court in Jacksonville, Florida. It was the early forties and we had a teachers' salary case: to get Negro teachers the same salary as white teachers. The white teachers sought to intervene in the case, and they chose as their lawyer, a man named [Robert] Shackleford of Tampa, Florida—who, incidentally, was Judge Strom's former law partner, so they didn't pick him accidentally.

When he filled his petition to intervene, I looked the law up, and found that if Judge Strom ruled with me, there could be an appeal by Shackleford; but if he ruled against me, I couldn't appeal. That's the way this intervention law works.

So I said, "Well, that's the end of the case. That's one I just lost."

Briefs were done, and we went down for a hearing, and the hearing was in the judge's chambers, and the conversation between them was, "Now, Louis, this" and "Now, Bob, this" and I thought: oh God, there goes the ball again.

Then he says, "Well, by the way, Mr. Marshall, I noticed that you have not filed a reply to Mr. Shackleford's last brief."

I said, "That's right, sir."

He said, "Why?"

I said, "Well, Judge, I went over it, and I went over the cases he cited, and everything he cites is accurate. There's nothing wrong with it. It's just off the point. So why answer it? It's just not on the point," feeling, of course, that this is the end of the road.

Whereupon Judge Strom turned and said, "Bob, I agree with him fully. I'm going to keep your memorandum to use with some other case. But it does you no good in this case, and I'm going to rule against you."

Now, what more can you ask a judge than that?

Now, that's the type of federal judge we had. There were others that were on the other side, but there were many just like Judge Strom—that, when you gave them the law, they went with it. And I think that's the blessing in the federal judiciary. I can give you a dozen just like him. Or, I can give you some other ones, too.

Q: Did you have a pretty good idea of where the judges stood, when you—?

Marshall: Oh, yes.

Q: Before you went into the court? Did you ever try to get the judge changed, as a result?

Marshall: Oh, yes. We had one in Norfolk, a school case, Judge Way, I think his name was. This was another case to equalize teachers' salaries, and when we went into the courtroom, we waited and waited, and the judge wasn't there. The judge was out meeting with people about the case. And then when he came in, I said, "Well, Judge, I noticed your case is set for Lincoln's Birthday. And this is a federal court."

He said, "Well, you follow Lincoln's Birthday up your way—down here, we follow Jeff Davis day down here."

So I knew where I stood then. Then, he just ripped at everything I said. He'd rip into me, and ripped into me, et cetera—and it was rough. And he ruled against me. And we carried the case to [the] Court of Appeals of the Fourth Circuit, with Judge Soper and Judge John J. Parker and Judge Dobie, and they reversed him, and said that he was wrong, and that the Negro teachers have to get the same salary as the white teachers.

When we went back and filed our papers, the superintendent of schools said, "I will not be a party to paying a nigger the same money I pay a white person. And I refuse to do it."

So we filed contempt proceedings before this same judge, and we had a hearing in his chambers, and he said, "Mr. Marshall," this is the same judge who really tore into me before and ruled against me. He said, "You have asked in very broad language for contempt, and I don't know whether you want civil or criminal. Which do you want?"

I said, "Well, Judge, I thought I drew it that way so that you could take your choice."

He said, "Then I'm asking you, which do you want?"

I said, "I see nothing to be gained by putting a man in jail. Furthermore, his age is against that." The guy was way up in his sixties. "So I'm perfectly willing to go with civil, if it's all right with you."

He said, "Let me ask you a question."

I said, "Yes, sir."

He said, "Did you know that that's my best friend?"

I said, "No, sir. I did not."

He said, "Well, despite that, I'm going to go with you. I'm not going to put him in jail."

That's the same man. He was getting ready to put his best friend in jail. Because, you see, in his mind, the law had changed. He thought the law was one way. When the court of appeals tells him the law is the other way, that's the way he went. Yes, I can find plenty like that, too. I'm for federal judges.

Q: You mentioned last time that you wanted to talk about Little Rock. Would you like to talk about Little Rock this morning?

Marshall: Well, Little Rock was rough. It was rough in all kinds of ways. Governor [Orval] Faubus, for some unknown reason, decided to take the tack he took despite the fact that the records shows that when he came out for absolute segregation in Little Rock his own son was going to an integrated school in upstate Arkansas. So, it wasn't personally so with him.

Another thing along the same lines is that Mr. Henry Luce, owner of *Time* magazine, spent thousands of dollars to try to find out who was behind Faubus. And he did. And he told me, but on condition I wouldn't tell anybody else. So they did find out who it was. But that doesn't help the story.

The story is that Faubus just set himself up against everybody, and the court case was one thing. He had good lawyers. We went down there to try the case, and you never knew what would happen the next day, or indeed the next hour. Everybody was arming. The police were bad. The attorney general [of Arkansas] was stupid.

And then, the attorney general of the United States got involved, and indeed, they tried to take over the lawsuit, and I wouldn't let them. But the important thing, I think, to the case was the people involved. Those children were unbelievable. And once you met their families, you knew. If you'd gone out with psychiatrists, sociologists to pick people, there's no way you could have done a better job.

I know of one night, we had gotten together some money, and we were hiring bodyguards for the families. One man spoke up, one father, and said, "Not me."

I said, "Why not you?"

He said, "I just don't want it."

I said, "Well, it's not going to cost you anything."

He said, "I'm against violence."

I said, "You mean you've got your own?"

He said, "Nope." He said, "When I left the Army, I said I wouldn't touch a gun again, and I'm not going to."

I said, "Well, why is it?" and he said, "I am just not afraid." End of quote.

And once I took a good look at him, he was telling the truth. He wasn't. He wasn't.

So, we couldn't quite go along with him, we put a guard across the street—but that's the type of people we were dealing with. The children were marvelous. I would say that that was one of the toughest ones we had. We had to come up here to the Supreme Court, I don't know how many times. Back and forth.

Eventually, we persuaded Eisenhower to send those troops down. I didn't think he would, but he did. And they did it. They cleaned it up. They did a very good job.

Just during that same period, the chief of police changed, and the new chief of police was a good guy. He went to town. So those two things, I think, broke it up. And when the last opinion of this court, *Cooper vs Aaron*, came down very rapidly, during the summer, that just about cleared it up.

One interesting sideline was that in the courtroom, during each session, there would be a whole lot of the most horrible-looking women, with Confederate flags and all that. Boy, they were tough looking. And a man with them, a great big guy with a stubble beard, who looked real rough too.

And one day, I was out at the Coca Cola fountain, and he came out, and when I looked at him, I started to decide where I was going to run. And he came up beside me and he said out of the corner of his mouth, "You know something? I think I knew your father."

I said, "You what?"

He said, "I think I knew your father."

I said, "Where? B and O Railroad?"

He said, "No."

"Southern Railroad? New York Central?"

"No." "Gibson Island Club?" "No." "Maryland Club?" "No." "Engineers Club?"
He said, "No."

I said, "Where did you know my father?"

He said, "The school."

I said, "You are kidding!"

He said, "See you later."

Well, the last job my father had was at a school on Charles Street, in two buildings down there, where the FBI was training military intelligence people. This guy
was right in the middle of them. I said, "Woo woo!"

That made me feel a little better, too.

But I don't know how Little Rock frames up with all of the others, except that
Little Rock brought about the prompt action of the president of the United States,
who wasn't for it, originally. That was very important.

Q: What was the main thrust of your argument vis-à-vis the president himself?

Marshall: Well, you just don't have a government; you just have chaos, and it's
not going to get any better. I explained to him what I'd seen out there. I saw an old
colored gentleman sitting on a box with an old squirrel rifle, one of those real long
barreled rifles—on Fourth Street, the main Negro street—and I went up to him. I
said, "What are you doing sitting there for?"

He said, "Get out of my way. Get out of my way. Just let a white son of a gun
come by here."

Now, here's a sixty, seventy-year-old man, going to shoot somebody. That's the
end of the road.

And it would have. That violence there, but for the good chief of police—all
hell would have broken loose.

And Jim [James E.] Haggerty, who was not a liberal by any stretch of the word,
he had had a similar experience as a Catholic in a Protestant area, and he worked
on the president too.

Q: You're talking about Jim Haggerty while he was press secretary.

Marshall: Yes. You wouldn't think he'd do anything like that, would you?
Cold-blooded as he was. He was a cold-blooded guy.

Q: Did I understand you met with the president personally?

Marshall: No. No, over the phone. And I wasn't—no, as I remember, it might have been Haggerty. I'm not sure. It must have been Haggerty. Somebody else was in there. There was somebody in there, somebody in the White House. It was not the president. The reason I say that is, I don't believe I talked to him more than two or three times, and it was before then. I believe it was Haggerty. Haggerty didn't tell me, but I was told that Haggerty was the one that did the job. And he just went in and spent one whole night with the president. Now, I don't have the slightest idea who told me that.

Q: As you went along arguing these cases, especially the educational cases I'm thinking of now, do I understand correctly that you're broadening your briefs to include sociological and medical or health factors, rather gradually?

Marshall: We first did it in a California case, way back in the forties, involving Mexicans. We had a brief in this court—I don't remember the name of the case—and then it sort of simmered along, and it didn't really come out until the university cases, *Sweatt, McLaurin* in Oklahoma, the North Carolina case, and ones like that. That would be in the late forties, I'd venture. It would be around the late forties or early fifties, when we started talking to people like Kenneth B. Clark and—who's the woman? Helen Traeger, people like that. The timing is not clear. But it would have to be around '50, it would have to be.
Then, it seems to me, we had a meeting in Atlanta, where we decided to go whole hog on this. Now, when that was—I don't know. It would have to be around '50. If you go back from '54, it would be about '50. That's the best I can do.

Q: When did you first meet Professor Kenneth B. Clark, or become aware of his writings?

Marshall: Oh, I knew him way back. I knew both of them [Kenneth and Mamie Clark] way back. But I didn't get to know him on these terms, about this, until that period, about the early fifties. I guess. Late forties. I knew him socially, and I knew they were child psychiatrists, but I didn't know this was what they were doing till Bob [Robert L.] Carter told me. And that would have to be in the late forties.

Q: Did this strike you as being an unusual or perhaps even innovative approach to these briefs?

Marshall: No, because I went to the basic principle that if you had an automobile accident, and you are "injured," you have to prove your injuries—you had to put on a doctor, and the doctor will explain what your injuries are and how you are damaged. So I said that these Negro kids are damaged, we will have to prove it.

Everybody said, "You're crazy." I said, "How can you prove it?"

Then we were talking around. As I remember, Bob Carter said, "Believe it or not, I believe we can do it." And he got to Kenneth and we all sat down together. Kenneth had been proving it all along. But I mean, it was just a plain lawsuit, just the way you have a lawsuit.

Q: Incidentally, roughly, during this period, was there a group of you—perhaps a group of twelve or a group of a hundred—that used to meet to discuss strategy in the future?

Marshall: No, sir. There never was any strategy in this business. We took them case by case. The only thing was Margold's report, that's all, and that's way back in '32, or '33. We were getting—

Let me correct myself: we would get together, but not officially. We would get tighter, like we talk about a case, and we would talk about other things like that. But to sit down and say, "We are going to plan to do this," I don't think we ever did, except at the annual conferences when we would get together. But there was no committee. Strictly informal, as I remember.

Q: I have Richard Kluger's *Simple Justice* here, has he correctly reported your activities, where he mentions them in here?

Marshall: Some of them. And they moved around. What happened was, each person he talked to gave their version of it or vision of it. And some of them don't quite agree with mine, nor mine doesn't quite agrees with theirs, but I don't see anything in there worth arguing about.

Q: I think you—I think he mentions there that you said that you still have a copy of the Margold report.

Marshall: I don't. Nobody does. Honestly. We looked for it in the late fifties, and we couldn't find it. Really couldn't find it. I haven't got it. I haven't got it. I think Jack Greenberg has, because Jack Greenberg never satisfactorily explained to me a quote that he had in a book he wrote. He has a quote from the Margold Report, and he says that he got that from another thing he wrote. I think he's got it. But no, I haven't.

I had it for years, and then, I assumed it was still there, and I've forgotten now where it was that we looked for it. And we checked our files—well, our files are very thick.

I'll tell you what kind of files we had: you pull out the file and you look in it like this, and you'll find "Joe Doakes against Sam Brown," and the next page will be "Jim Jones against somebody else," in and the next section you'll see the lunch menu and the order that you had for lunch two weeks ago.

Q: Are there any points in Kluger's *Simple Justice* that you think of now, where you think the version as presented, from whatever source, is wrong from your standpoint?

Marshall: Oh, no. Nothing is quite wrong. Nothing is quite wrong. A little detail here is wrong, a little detail there. But I don't—I just ran through it, but I didn't see anything that was completely wrong. And I told him so, not too long ago. It has to come out in a play, and he said, "If there's anything in there you want changed, you let me know."

I told him, let it go the way it was. If the book doesn't sell, I don't see how the play is going to sell.

Q: These various approaches which you made in education, do you weigh them about the same, or differently, depending on whether you're trying to get an admission into graduate school, whether you're trying to get equal teachers' salaries, whether you're trying to get equal facilities? Is any one of those thrusts more significant?

Marshall: No. You're whittling it away. You're cutting it down. I had thought, we'd all thought, that once we got the Brown case, the thing was going to be over. You see, we were always looking for that one case to end all of it. And that case hasn't come up yet. So I think, what we were doing was whittling away.

The teachers' salaries, the reason for that was, we had bogged down. We didn't have any money. We didn't have anything to operate with. So I came up with the idea that the teachers could pay for those cases, because it's their money. They'll get an increase. Like, you take the first ones I did were in Maryland, and those teachers ended up with three and a half million dollars a year—which incidentally, if they'd paid me a fee on that three and a half million, I'd have been doing pretty good. But in the meantime, we were waiting for a good case to come up.

I just can't say what did it. I don't know. When did we get the feeling? I was never sure we were going to win those school cases. I wasn't sure. I certainly didn't expect it to be unanimous. But I know, other people said they knew everything, so I don't know.

I think I was just methodically going down the road, going past bridge by bridge by bridge. That's the way I look at it. Winning some and losing some. Best I can do with it.

Q: Well, did I understand you correctly, that at one point you thought the Brown case was going to solve your legal problems, and it did not?

Marshall: Well, it did not, because we all shouted and sat down. That was when we should have sat down and planned. That was when we should have all sat down and said, "Look, what are we going to do?"

The other side did. The other side planned all the delaying tactics they could think of. And so they took the initiative, and we ended up blocking their blocking passes. By that time, we'd lost all of our initiative. And I think that's where we made a mistake, and I'm just as responsible for that as anybody else.

Q: As you went along trying these cases, pleading these cases, when did you feel that you might like to be a judge, if ever?

Marshall: Well, now, let's go all the way back. People tell me I'm a liar when I tell them that when I was a young lawyer in Baltimore, my highest aim was to be a magistrate. Everybody says, "You must have had a higher goal than that."

Well, there were only two Negro magistrates in the country then. So, when the goal changed, I don't know. I don't know. But I do know this, that when I went on the court of appeals, I thought that I was ready to go there, for two reasons: I thought I'd kind of outlived my usefulness, in original ideas, in the NAACP hierarchy, what have you. And I had been shopping around, thinking of going in some law firm, making myself a good hunk of money, and then this judgeship came through.

Well, once you get to become a judge, you want to get on the Supreme Court, after that.

But I never had any ambitions for it. When I left the NAACP, I was going to make myself a whole lot of money.

Q: How did this appointment to the court of appeals come about?

Marshall: The one to the court of appeals was, first, that I would be a district judge, and I told Bobby Kennedy that I was not district judge material, because my fuse was too short. I lose my temper. And that wasn't good. But I would like to be on the court of appeals.

He said, "Well, you can't."

I said, "There's an opening."

He said, "No, but that one's been filled."

So he said, "Well, that's it. It's that or nothing."

I said, "Well, I've been dealing with nothing all my life, there's nothing new on that."

And about two or three days later, Louis Martin from Chicago, who was an assistant head of the Democratic Party, saw me at LaGuardia Field, and said, "Are you still thinking about that court of appeals job?"

I said, "Sure, I've been thinking." (Or, "Sure, I would take it.")

And the next day, the appointment went through. That's how that one came through.

Q: How did Louis Martin hear about your interest?

Marshall: Oh, he and the president were awful close. And any time you talked to Louis, he was talking for the president. You knew that. You knew that. He was way up there. He was way up there with Johnson, too. Yes, sir.

Q: He's back with his publishing house now, isn't that right? In Chicago?

Marshall: In Chicago. Well, he was then. He was with the Sengstacke Newspapers. He's a wonderful guy. He was there when Johnson announced my appointment. He was in the next room.

Q: Now, are you talking about the judgeship?

Marshall: The appointment to the Supreme Court. He was there. And Clifford Alexander was there.

Q: Was Clifford Alexander with the Democratic Committee at that time?[5]

Marshall: Yes.

Q: As far as serious thought went, did you think that probably the court of appeals would be where you would continue?

Marshall: Oh, sure. I'd settle for that. That was it. That was it. And I was very happy. I had a marvelous buy on an apartment. We were having a good time. I had a place up in the country that Arthur Spingarn let me have. Very nice place, about an hour from New York, in Amenia.

Unfortunately after about three years or four years, it burnt down.

Yes, I'd settled for that, till that telephone call came. Had no idea of anything else.

Just that day I was sitting upstairs in the judges' dining room up on—I think it's the twentieth floor of the Foley Square building, and my bailiff came up and said, "Judge, Judge . . .

---

[5] Clifford Alexander, a lawyer and Democratic Party activist, served as secretary of the Army during the administration of Jimmy Carter.

I said, "I told you, don't bother me when I'm eating."

He said, "The president wants to see you."

I said, "The president of what?" I thought it was the president of some company.

He said, "The president of the United States."

The president said, after a very few words, he says, "I want to make you my solicitor general."

I said, "Wait a minute! I'd never thought of such a thing."

He said, "Well, you think of it."

I said, "Mr. President, I'll be glad to think about it, but there are a lot of things I have to think about."

He said, "Take your time. But don't talk to a living soul about it."

I said, "Well, I assume that doesn't include my wife."

He said, "Of course you can talk to her, but nobody else. Take as much time as you want."

I said, "Okay, sir." Hung up. That afternoon I went home and I talked to my wife, and I explained to her the options, and then we talked to the boys, and we all agreed that: well, it was worth considering. I went back to work the next day, and that morning—it is the next day now, I guess it's about eleven o'clock, the phone rang. President Johnson.

I said, "Yes, sir, Mr. President."

He said, "Have you made up your mind?"

I said, "Well, Mr. President, you said take as much time as you want, is that right?"

He said, "Yes, and you've had that much time."

I said, "Yes, sir."

He said, "Now, you come on down here, and we'll talk it over."

I said, "All right." So I went down the next day or the day after, I've forgotten what it was, and I told him, I said, "Mr. President, number one, it's a salary loss of $4,500."

He said, "I know that."

I said, "Number two, I'm giving up a lifetime job."

He said, "I know that."

I said, "And finally, I haven't got any money."

He said, "I know that, too. You want to see your income tax report? And your bank account?"

I said, "No. I know what's in them."

So he kept talking, and I said, "Okay."

He said, "Now, one thing you've got to keep in mind: this is not a stepping-stone to anything else, do you understand that?"

I said, "Yes sir."

"Anything, including the Supreme Court."

I said, "Yes sir. That's all right with me."

So he said, "Okay."

The announcement was made. The hearing was not bad, and I came down for the swearing-in, and my wife and I had arranged that I would commute on weekends, and get a little efficiency apartment down here. We had it all worked out, because the boys were in school and all, and I had this good buy on an apartment up there in New York.

And as he walked in the cabinet room to swear me in, he passed by me and he said out of the corner of his mouth, "What the hell is this about your commuting?"

I said, "But—"

He said, "But nothing, move down."

I was moving them down. And getting back to that point about giving up a lifetime job, at one time I was over in the Oval Room on something with some other people, and the president said, "I've got an idea about doing this, what do you think of it, so-and-so?" and they said, "Fine, okay."

He got around to me and said, "What does my lawyer think about it?"

I said, "I think it's a lousy idea, and it won't do any good, and I think it's wrong."

He looked me straight in the face and said, "How did you like having *been* my solicitor general?"

So, that's how you get those jobs.

Q: Did you think that President Johnson was serious when he said solicitor general would be the end of the line?

Marshall: Yes, he said it at least two out of every three times I talked to him. At least that many times. And he convinced me, at least.

As a matter of fact, I was at a party with him the night before he gave me the job, and he said it, again. He had completely disarmed me, completely. And the morning when the appointment came through, Ramsey Clark, the attorney general, called my secretary and said, "Is the Judge in?"

She said, "Yes."

"Is anybody with him?"

She said, "No."

He said, "Well, don't let anybody in there. I'm coming down to see him."

She said, "Fine." So he came down the hall, came in, and we had pleasantries and all, and I said, "Well, what're you up to, Ramsey?"

He said, "What are you doing this morning?"

I said, "Well, at eleven o'clock" or whatever time it was "I've got to go up to the White House, the executive side, to talk to some students or something, some people."

He said, "Do you have a car?"

I said, "Look, Mrs. Avery knows what she's doing, if I've got an appointment she's going to have a car ready for me."

He said, "Well, you go up there at ten forty-five instead of eleven o'clock. Instead of going there, you go to the Oval Room."

I said, "What for, Ramsey?"

He said, "I don't know." It still ended up, "I don't know."

I said, "Okay." I said, "Well, what do I do, walk on in there?"

Then he said, "No, no, no."

Well, there were several ways, three ways at least, you could get in there without being seen. And he told me, he said, "You'd better take that number one way."

I said, "Okeydokey."

So I went down and got in the car and went that way, and this is a very nice route, because what you do at a certain spot, you just get out of the car, and you walk over and there's a guard standing there watching the line of people going in that morning session, you know, visitors, visitors. And he puts you in line, and you go in with all the other people, looking, saying, "Oh! Ah!" you are all excited, it's the first time you've ever seen the building.

And then, when you get in the building, when you get to a certain door, there's a Secret Service man that will beckon to you, and you go in there. As a matter of fact, I went in, two people came behind and the guard said, "Oh, no, no, not you, you stay out."

Then you go the cabinet room, and Marv Watson [Marvin Watson] said, "The president will see you in a couple of minutes."

I said, "What's up, Marv?"

He said, "I dunno. I dunno."

So, next he said, "Go on in."

I went in, and he was over there at the ticker tape machine, and I waited a little while, and I coughed, and he said, "Oh, hi, Thurgood. Sit down, sit down."

So we chatted just a few minutes, and I didn't ask him what was on his mind, I let him speak. And all of a sudden, he just looked at me and said, "You know something, Thurgood?"

I said, "No, sir, what's that?"

He said, "I'm going to put you on the Supreme Court."

I said, "Oh, yipe! What did you say?"

He said, "That's it."

I said, "Okay, sir."

He had the press out there waiting in the Rose Garden, and he carried me out and announced it, and then we came back in the Oval Room. And I said, "Mr. President, look, they're going to get that on the wire in about a minute. Now, can I call my wife so she won't hear it on the air?"

He said, "You mean, you haven't told Cissie yet?"

I said, "No. How could I? I've been with you all the time." So we called her, and I said, got her on the phone, I said, "Cissie, are you sitting down?"

She said, "No."

I said, "Well, you better sit down."

And she did, and then I beckoned to the president. The president said, "Cissie, this is Lyndon Johnson."

She said, "Yes, Mr. President?"

He said, "I just put your husband on the Supreme Court."

And Cissie said, "I sure am glad I'm sitting down."

That's as honest as I can be. I had no idea about it.

Then he said, very interesting, he said, "I guess this is the end of our friendship."

I said, "Yep. Just about. Be no more of that." I said, "Well, I'll tell you this, Mr. President. You know, Tom Clark and Harry Truman were close as anybody, but when that steel case came up, Tom had to sock it to him."

He said, "Well, you wouldn't do like that to me?"

I said, "No sooner than!!"

He said, "Well, that's the way I want it." And that's the way it was.

Q: Had there been any rumors that you might fill that vacancy?

Marshall: It was, up until I—funny. When I got the solicitor job, there was a rumor then. And I think the getting of the solicitor job cut that rumor off, I think, because it stopped right there.

When I walked in the press conference to be announced as solicitor general, the word went all the way through: who's off the Supreme Court? They thought that's what that announcement was going to be.

And then, this other thing, I think it knocked me off.

You know, he always loved to do that. He always loved to do something that nobody expected him to do. That's all right with me. But I'll betcha I don't give up *this* lifetime job!

Q: There is one viewpoint, apparently, which is brought out in the Kluger book, and that was that William Hastie—

Marshall: Oh yes—

Q: —was going to go to the Supreme Court, but—

Marshall: We had agreed on it. All of the Negroes with any—what have you— had agreed that whenever any of us were asked about it, we would immediately all converge on Hastie. So that it wouldn't be split, all around. That's what I heard. And I also heard, and I could not get it confirmed by either Hastie or Johnson, that Hastie was offered the solicitor general's job and wouldn't take it. And neither one of them will affirm or deny it. I don't know why, but they didn't.

Oh, Hastie was far—Hastie should have been on this court way back. He's a great man. Much better than I am. Much better than I ever will be. Honest.

But we agreed on it. And I raised the point, the time he told me he was going to put me on there. He said, "Well, you let me mind my own business," that's what the president said.

I said, "Yes sir."

His opinions are among the best I've ever read, Hastie's. Just great.

Q: To your knowledge, did President Kennedy decide against Hastie at one point because he felt it would be premature, at least from his standpoint?

Marshall: Everything was, politically. Bobby convinced him that he shouldn't rock the boat until the second term. On everything. That's the way it worked. And he didn't. He wasn't getting any appointments on this Court. How many did he have? He never had them.

Q: I think Arthur Goldberg was one of his appointments. Wasn't he?

Marshall: Goldberg, yes. Goldberg. . . .

Q: What do you consider your major achievements, major missions you had as solicitor general?

Marshall: All run-of-the-mill. There were no major things at all. You had no time for it. You see, you were constantly handling just hundreds of cases every day. You didn't have any time for any particular one.

The Penn Central merger was a lot of trouble, and one case called the High Mountain Sheep, which involved a dam out on the Colorado River. There were cases like that that were a lot of trouble. But they were also run-of-the-mill cases, and all of them tough. You see, every case on appeal—where the federal government's involved—the solicitor's got to handle it. I know that, because when I was there, I had nine people, including myself, to run that department, and now they've have eighteen. They have just doubled.

Q: Did you find that work somewhat frustrating because there was so much to do?

Marshall: Oh. Stanley Reed, on this Court, who used to be solicitor general, said it was the greatest job he ever had. I think I agree with him. You're on the top of everything all the time. You know what I mean? You stay on the top of every-thing. And as soon as you get through with that, there is another right there. The sec-retary just comes in and picks up one and hands you another. It just goes like that.

All of a sudden, somebody will come in, and say, "Do you realize what you did an hour ago? You did—"

No, it's awfully good, I liked it. No rest for the weary. But it was—

Q: To backtrack a little bit here, we've gone through this period when some other Negro, black leaders were emerging. How did Martin Luther King first come to your attention?

Marshall: The Montgomery boycott had started, and a man by the name of [E. D.] Nixon, a former Pullman porter, president of our branch in Montgomery, called me about it. And we were advising them of the legal steps to be made, and I referred the case to Bob Carter on my staff and he was handling it. We were pro-ceeding, and all of a sudden, this preacher started jumping out of there. We'd never even heard of him before. I had known his father in Atlanta, but I never heard of him until then.

Q: What was your initial reaction, as you recall, to his organizing the Southern Christian Leadership Conference?

Marshall: Oh, I had no quarrel with it. And as a matter of fact, I told the young people of that group there—they met with me in New York—and I told them they could do whatever they pleased. We'd back them up. We'd get them bail money, anything. They could do whatever they wanted.

I didn't agree with them. I used to have a lot of fights with Martin about his the-ory about disobeying the law. I didn't believe in that. I thought you did have a right to disobey a law, and you also had a right to go to jail for it. He kept talking about Thoreau, and I told him, I said, "If I understand it, Thoreau wrote his book in jail. If you want to write a book, you go to jail and write it."

He changed it eventually. He did stay there.

I think he had a great influence. He came at the right time. It's very interest-ing how people pop up at the right time. Very interesting.

Q: What did you think of him as a leader?

Marshall: I think he was great, as a leader. As an organizer, he wasn't worth diddley-squat. But very few leaders are.

You take Walter White at the NAACP. He couldn't. You need a second guy to run the show. And you get out there. But for convincing people, I don't think anybody comes close to King, except that fellow at the Urban League, way back, what's his name? The cat who just died.

Q: Whitney Young?

Marshall: Whitney Young. He could do it.

Q: How well did you know him?

Marshall: Oh, very well. I knew him in Atlanta. Anybody that could go from the meeting with David Rockefeller and his group, and an hour later meet with a bunch of Negroes over a chitling feast in Harlem, you gotta be something!
And he was at home in both places.

Q: Did you know Lester Granger before him?

Marshall: Very well. Very well. Lester was a take-it-easy guy, he and [Eugene] Kinkley Jones, you know, don't rock the boat.[6] But Whitney took over the job deliberately to rock the boat. And that's where he had his success—in rocking the boat.
Before that time, the Urban League wouldn't do anything to anybody who was a big contributor or what have you. And Whitney would make them spend, give him the money to fight them. Yes, I liked Whitney.

Q: Now, when you were telling the young people that you had no objections to what they were doing, were you still talking about the Southern Christian Leadership Conference, or were you talking about SNCC? [Student Nonviolent Coordinating Committee].

Marshall: It was an offshoot of SNCC. This guy, John Lewis, who is running for Andy Young's seat, that was the guy I talked to. It was John and a girl from Fisk. I don't remember her name. But that was the group. And I got Grenville Clark and a couple of other people.[7] They put up, oh, close to two hundred thousand dollars in bail money.

Q: What about CORE [Congress for Racial Equality], James Farmer?

Marshall: The only thing I know good about CORE is James Farmer. He is good. But I don't know anything else.

---

[6] Lester Granger and Eugene K. Jones were early chief executives of the National Urban League.

[7] Grenville Clark was a prominent New York lawyer and philanthropist, whose primary interests were in world peace and human rights.

When they first started, they were beautiful. That was way back. They would go in a restaurant in Detroit, New York, some place, where Negroes weren't welcome, and go in—just walk up to a table and ask, "Do you mind Negroes eating here?"

And they'd eat, pay off, and all. They had plenty of guts and savvy and all.

Then when Farmer left it, it really went to—when Farmer left, then who took over first? [Floyd] McKissick, I think it was. Well, anyhow, when they took it over, if I had one, I had half a dozen people; several big contributors to the Legal Defense Fund also contributed to CORE, and these people were good friends of mine. They would call me and say, "Should we still contribute to that?" They lost all their support. They've got a guy there now that just don't know what he's doing.

Q: During this period, did you continue to stay in touch with Carl Murphy at the *Afro*?[8]

Marshall: Always, until he died. I was at his funeral.

He gave us maximum support. I know, when I was practicing and handled the University of Maryland case, he had Clarence Mitchell, who was then a reporter, and each edition of the *Afro-American*, Clarence could use the whole back page or a half of the front page on our cases. You can't get no better support than that.

And then, when we started arguing cases in the Supreme Court, every time we had an argument, he would have a big party for us afterwards, after, and the sky was the limit. You could buy all the whiskey you wanted, all the food you wanted. He didn't drink, himself. Oh, he was great. I liked him. I liked the whole family.

Q: Were those parties in Baltimore or in Washington?

Marshall: No, in Washington. We used to get a whole floor of the Sheraton Park Hotel. That's where we prepared arguments for them. And then, after that, we'd have this party.

Q: What were your views of the Negro press or all the news media over this period?

Marshall: Oh, very good. I didn't like some of the things they published. I thought they went way off base. I'd fuss with them about it. But I know this, I met with them twice a year, the whole time I was with NAACP, and at the board meetings, I was right in there. I think they did a terrific job. Without exception. I think

---

[8] Carl Murphy was the publisher of the Baltimore *Afro-American* and one of Marshall's most important early clients after Marshall opened his law practice in Baltimore.

a lot of the success we had came through that. Matter of fact, I'm going to meet with them on the eighteenth, the day before the Gridiron thing.

I'm going to the Gridiron again this year. I go once every four years.

Q: Do you feel somewhat that the Negro media in earlier years concentrated too much on sensational-type news?

Marshall: They had to. You had to meet with them to understand. On the sensational news, there was a guy named Bill Walker of the Cleveland Negro paper—I think it's the *Call Post*—and he told us at one of the meetings (this would be twenty years ago) that things were happening; there was a record out called "Caldonia," that the Negroes were buying this record like mad, and there was a violent murder of a Negro man and his girlfriend. One of his cameramen was in a corner store having a sandwich when the word came out, and he got in there before the police and got all these gory pictures of this voodoo murder, and the woman's name was Caldonia.

He not only carried these pictures on the front page, but it was horrible journalism, and he got all kinds of letters and telephone calls about that. And for seven—yes, seven months on the front page of the paper, he carried the pro and con of whether you should do this—for seven months! And just sold newspapers like mad.

So when they don't have any money except from sensationalism then, of course—

Now, where would we get the whole copy of our pleadings printed, except in the Negro newspaper?

I know one case, the Norfolk *Journal*, another Negro paper in which the editor of that paper, Mr. [Plummer B.] Young was a very good friend of the owner of the Norfolk *Pilot*, the white paper. And Mr. Young said, "Let me see if we can't really do something to this guy. If you'll cooperate, I can really hook him."

I said, "Sure, I'll cooperate."

So I got all the pleadings ready for the case I was going to file, and I gave it to the newspaper night before. They set up all the type, with the whole complaint and everything, verbatim, and the story, and the feature story, and the editorial. So by ten o'clock the next morning, the stuff was rolling. And I filed the case, it went out in the hall, they called it. They said, "Let it go."

And ten minutes after that, there's an "Extra" out on the street, of a case that had been filed ten minutes before.

The guy that filed it called up Young and wanted to know, was I there? He said, "Yes, he's right here." "Well we called that, let's have lunch."

They laughed. They had a ball. I said, "Well, I realize I violated the code of ethics and everything else, but we had some fun."

So I think the criticism was just, but they—I guess you realize that the other papers were in the same category.

Do you know when the white newspapers became solvent? In the forties. They were all families. Look at them, they were all families. They only became big corporations—

It's the same way with the Negroes: they were always families. I don't see any difference between the two. Oh, I wouldn't print what they printed, and they wouldn't print what I'd probably run, during those times.

Q: Let me just mention a couple of other leaders, if I could. How do you evaluate A. Philip Randolph?

Marshall: Oh, solid. I know this, I know that during the efforts to organize the Pullman porters, the Pullman company offered him, back in those days, close to a quarter of a million dollars, in cash—which he turned down.

I think that is typical of his whole life. I think he's the greatest thing in the movement. Sure. I don't know a single thing wrong with him. And he's still alive.

Q: Were you involved when he set up the American Negro Labor Council, Negro-American Labor Council?

Marshall: No. Just on the fringes.

Q: And from the standpoint of the civil rights struggle, how would you evaluate the role of Adam Clayton Powell?

Marshall: Ha! The greatest showman in the business. He could raise any amount of money, and his influence with his people was just unbelievable. I don't know how many of us were sitting down one night. There must have been six or eight of us. And we decided that, at that time, in his heyday, if you had a mass meeting in Harlem with Ralph Bunche, Walter White, Roy Wilkins, Thurgood Marshall, Phil Randolph, you name them—and at the same time, had one with Adam Powell—he'd have everybody, and you'd have nobody.

I mean, his influence was just unbelievable. His effectiveness was not anywhere near as much as it should be. But I think the final word is what Lyndon Johnson said—that with all of that carrying-on he did, he was the most effective committee chairman in Congress. And you'll never see that in writing any place, but it's true.

Oh, I criticized him more. I criticized him for what he didn't do. But he did enough.

Q: Justice Marshall, since 1954, perhaps since a little later really, there have been a lot more blacks elected to public office, offices at many levels. Do you believe that this can be attributed largely to the Brown decision, or would this have come about anyway?

Marshall: Yes and no. The Brown decision, I feel, was an important step. But you have to bear in mind that when Chief Justice [Earl] Warren, the late Chief Justice Warren, a few years ago, was asked which decision he considered to be the most important in his term, he said it was *Baker v. Carr*, the "one man-one vote" decision. And to me, that is significant, because while *Brown* set the background for the whole racial struggle, it was understood years before that that the voting arm of the fight was also important, in the Texas primary and other cases.

I do, however, think that the focus was the movement of Martin Luther King and people in that category, the protest movement that seized upon the right to vote. Following that, the NAACP, headed by Clarence Mitchell, often called the 101st senator because of his influence in the Congress of the United States, really spearheaded the drive for the Civil Rights Act passed in the 1960s. It was those acts that got the right to vote. It was those acts that were used to increase the enrollment of Negroes throughout the South, and that was important.

I realize that there was a change from the legal movement in the courts, to the protest movement in the streets, to the legislative halls, that brought about—to my mind—the registration and voting. To put your handle on exactly what was important, I think it's a conglomeration of all of them.

I also would mention that the leadership of President Johnson in that period was most important, and his speech at Howard University, which ended with the phrase, "We shall overcome," laid the groundwork.

I have maintained all along that whatever movement we really get comes from the person I call "the doorkeeper." I use that because it might be the president of the United States, it might be the governor of a state, it might be the mayor of a city, it might be a sheriff. But the person with the authority, speaking out, usually moves the balance of the community.

I was over in London in '61, drawing the constitution for Kenya, in January and February of that year, when word came over of the movement of Martin Luther King and the others, and after several telephone calls with the office in New York, I decided I'd better come home and take care of home, instead of trying to take care of Kenya. However, we did finish our work on the constitution, and the next day I came over and got in touch with the students who were picketing, the young people and the old people. We had two or three meetings, and I pledged the entire support of the Legal Defense Fund to protect their legal rights. We even set up a huge bail fund, from large contributors, in order to assure that they would not go to jail.

I think that was the movement that led up to the voting. And as I say as of now, that that was the important thing that occurred during that period.

Q: Now, you mentioned in the last interview that a number of you felt, after the Brown decision, that this had really accomplished your purpose, and that you did not prepare for the counterthrusts that subsequently came. You might elaborate on that a little bit.

Marshall: I guess, as you look back, you might get the idea that we put some trust in the decency of man, maybe. Or, bear in mind that after the primary fight, in the one state of Texas, the other states immediately gave in—with the exception of Georgia and South Carolina—and I'm afraid we assumed that after a short period of time of one to five years, the states would give in. We did not, however, give enough credence to the two Richmond papers, the Richmond *Times Dispatch*, and the other one whose name I don't remember [Richmond *News Leader*], and people like that, who were determined that they would build up the type of opposition that would prevent the states from voluntarily going along.

Secondly, it became apparent too late, to me at least, the Supreme Court was not going to move. And we were sort of caught in a bind. We did, however, manage to work in states like Kentucky, West Virginia, Arkansas—if you please, Oklahoma—and parts of Texas, where we were able to convince them that it could be done without further court action.

So I say, I think the major blame was on us, in not pushing, not planning, and letting it go by default, I guess, during that period of time. I'll take my share of the blame.

Q: Was there any event that marked kind of the crest of the opposition, or the countermovement, such as when the southern congressmen passed the Southern Manifesto?

Marshall: Oh, that was a waste of time. The movements on the surface had no effect. It was the movements below the surface that had the effect. If President Eisenhower had used his good offices to say that "This is the law and it should be obeyed," that would have accomplished much. We hoped for it. And we found out too late that indeed, President Eisenhower was opposed to it, and was working against it, and even went so far as to try to convince Chief Justice Warren to vote the other way.

That, to my mind, is the most despicable job that any president has done in my life. I think that was bad. No governor spoke out. Nobody in authority spoke out on our side. And the church did very little. So I said, it was just inaction that allowed it to happen. I don't think the big movements—

For example, with that act of Congress that you mentioned, bear in mind, at the same time, there was a secret meeting held in Virginia, with the governors of some ten or twelve states, where they actually laid plans as to what they would do to undercut the whole thing. And I know exactly what happened at that meeting, because the governor of Georgia, Governor [Eugene] Talmadge, told me. And it was almost unbelievable. By the time we heard about it, it was too late to move.

Q: Now, do you mean all the southern governors participated, or were there some not so active?

Marshall: No, there were some who didn't show up, but it wasn't that they weren't interested. They just didn't show.

It was not just governors. One of the key figures was a man from Louisiana who wasn't a governor, Leander Perez. He was the most vicious of the segregationists in the country. Indeed, he put five or ten thousand dollars up for my head. I mean, I can remember him. There were people like that who were at the meeting.

Q: Now, are you talking seriously, that he had let out a contract on you?

Marshall: Oh, that was the rumor all over Louisiana. And on several occasions, I had pretty close—jobs, down there. But it never materialized. He was vicious.

Q: Can you recall either the names of the governors who did not attend, or of states that were not represented?

Marshall: No.

Q: Now, you mentioned this was a secret meeting. How did you find out about it?

Marshall: It leaked to the press. And next, one time on the telephone about something else, some case I had in Georgia, I mentioned it to Governor Talmadge, and he told me about it. And he said it was too rough for him. He left.

Q: As I recall it, Governor Talmadge was quite racist.

Marshall: Oh yes. Oh yes. But we understood each other.

I always found, despite the fact that he was a racist of the—as much as anybody I know of—he never lied. At least, he never lied to me. He would tell me in front what he was going to do, and then go ahead and do it.

But I don't know just what went wrong there. I do think we were to blame. And then we got so wrapped up with supporting Martin Luther King. I guess maybe that was a part of it. The major part of our work, in the sixties, after I left—I say mine, I mean the work of the Legal Defense Fund, was in protecting them. And filing suits for them and all. Maybe that was the cause of it.

But the emphasis shifted entirely from lawsuits to obtain equality, and non-segregation, to political pressure and what have you.

Q: Do you feel these various protests had the main effect of dramatizing the cause, rather than actually achieving anything in the immediate quick term?

Marshall: Oh, they achieved much. If you put them in the scale, they would weigh very heavy, because it reached people's consciousness. To see a man go to jail was one thing. And while Dr. King was all for this civil disobedience, I kept telling him that, under our government, you had two rights. You had the right to disobey a law, and you also had the right to go to jail for it. And he couldn't see the second part, but eventually he did.

I think that reached the conscience of the people. I know a very conservative group in New York, the Association of the Bar of the City of New York—King spoke to them in the early sixties, and he moved every one of them. There was not a dry eye in the joint when he got through. He was a great speaker, of all sorts, but as for getting the work done, he was not too good at that.

Q: Incidentally, speaking of the Association of the Bar of New York, to interject a question—how active were you in various bar associations?

Marshall: None. None.

Q: The New York Bar Association?

Marshall: No. Never was a member. I became an honorary member. As a matter of fact, I was given an honorary membership about two years ago. It was quite a sizeable group of about twenty, Chief Justice Warren, people like that.

No, because the Bar Association of New York and the American Bar Association, I consider too little and too late. They wouldn't let Negroes in for so many years. Then when they let them in, I just said, "Well, too little and too late." They did support me, when I was up for the court of appeals and this Court. They did support me. And I appreciated that, of course.

Q: Did you decide that as far as the civil rights movement went, that it indeed regained the initiative once the protests and demonstration achieved their momentum?

Marshall: Yes. Yes, I think it saved it. I think it might have died on the vine.

We knew in the beginning that the courts could not solve the problem, because the courts just don't have that authority. It's the public, the minds, the souls of the people that have to do it, and you do that with protest.

But bear in mind that the protests in the sixties weren't the first protests. I know, way back, and I think it was the twenties, back in that time, the NAACP had a huge parade down Fifth Avenue against lynching. That was way back, around the twenties.

I mean, protest is not new. But it sort of—I guess it hit at the right time.

Q: Didn't the NAACP in those earlier years, twenties or into thirties, stage picketing also?

Marshall: Oh, sure. We had, when I was in law school, 1932 I think it was, the Anti-Crime Conference or something by the then-attorney general, Homer Cummings; and they would not put lynching on their calendar or their agenda. And we protested, and my law school, Howard University Law School, set up a picket line, headed by our dean, Charlie Houston, and about twenty of us went out on the picket line, in front of the meeting which was held here in Washington in the Pan-American build-ing. The captain of police said it was an illegal picket line, and we told him, so what? He was very nice. He asked us to stop and we wouldn't. And the second day he got instructions, and he said, "Well, look—you either stop or you're under arrest."

And we said, "Well, what are you waiting for? What do you think we picketed for? That's what we picketed for. Go ahead." And he called up the patrol, and put the guys in, and there were three of us for whom there wasn't room in the two wag-ons. So we said, "What about us?"

They said, "You have to get your own way."

We got a taxi and followed the patrol to the precinct, and got back into line.

He said, quote, "This is the damndest bunch of criminals I've ever run across." End of quote.

They got a book out, and made all of us sign up, and he said, "Well, now you're booked, and you're released on your own recognizance, and we'll let you know when the hearing's coming up."

Nothing happened, and after a month or so Charlie Houston and I went to see the captain and said, "When is our trial coming up?"

He said, "You're not going to be tried."

We said, "Well, you arrested us."

He said, "No, we didn't."

We said, "We signed the book."

He said, "That's just an ordinary book we keep around here."

We were quite angry, I mean, that we weren't arrested.

I've been on the picket lines for the drug stores that wouldn't serve Negroes. That was back in the thirties. I was counsel to the Baltimore group that picketed the A and P stores, and the five-and-ten-cent store on Pennsylvania Avenue, and that would be 1934-ish, and as a result, we got Negro employees in all of the stores. There's nothing new about that.

I guess I'm an old rebel anyhow. In college, I participated in four strikes, and I led two of them. So I mean, I don't know—

Q: I think you mentioned one of those in the first interview. What were the others?

Marshall: Oh, that was at Lincoln University in Pennsylvania. It's in the country. All boys, no girls, you had to do something to let out your steam. So when spring would come around we would find some reason, and the last one was about the food in the dining room. That's always bad, so it was always a good reason. And we would stay out of school, and walk around and picket and things like that, and after a reasonable time, we'd find some ground where we could save face and the school could save face, and we'd go back.

One time, we had a strike early, when school first opened. I've forgotten what it was about. And Prof [Walter] Wright, who was president, was a very lovely gentleman—we all loved him and he was always reasonable—and he called the leaders in and said, "Look, you guys haven't studied your books."

We said, "That's what we're striking about."

He said, "No, on picketing. Striking." He said, "Never strike at the beginning of the year. Always strike at the end."

We said, "Why?"

He said, "We can always replace you, because we've got people that applied and weren't let in. So I would suggest you call it off."

We said, "Well, you have to give us something," so he gave us something, I've forgotten what it was. We were put out, once. We were expelled, for about two weeks. I've forgotten what that one was. But I enjoyed it.

Q: Going back to *Brown* again, did you share the feeling of some others that the Court after that was quite, quite cautious in many ways? It was concerned about domestic tranquility after it had made that decision.

Marshall: Since I've been on this Court, I've tried to find out. And I've been able to find out everything about the past, but the Brown case. Nobody will talk. So I don't know.

I assume that they said, "Now, look, we're going to let this—we've got a unanimous opinion, and let's let this ride itself out, on the local level. I think that's what it was. And they had hoped that it would work better than it did. And then you remember, when the Little Rock case came up, they really came down hard. And I think that's the only opinion I know of where this Court had each justice sign. Most of the opinions, start off, "Mr. Justice Marshall, speaking for the Court, said," Or, "Mr. Justice Jones, speaking for the Court, said—." This had named each one, which meant that it was the unanimous opinion of all nine, and they figured that was it. That was the way to handle it.

I don't think it's over yet. This busing business. I don't know.

Q: Going back to your reference to President Eisenhower's intervention, do you recall any more details, on how he approached—

Marshall: Yes. It's coming out, I think, in Chief Justice Warren's book. I understand it's in there. But we got the report from Ralph Bunche, and anybody who either knew him or knew of him knew of his integrity. He was not a man to lie and he was not a man to use hyperbole. He told me, and Bill Hastie, that at one of the regular businessmen's dinners that Eisenhower held at the White House regularly, Bunche was there and Chief Justice Warren was there, and he was going over to say something to Warren, when Eisenhower went to Warren. So Bunche stayed, a reasonable distance away, and he overheard Eisenhower use the words "school cases" or "segregated schools" or something like that, and he didn't hear any more. But he distinctly heard Chief Justice Warren say to President Eisenhower, "I thought I would never have to say this to you, but I now find it necessary to say to you specifically, you mind your business and I'll mind mine."

Now, Ralph said, he was shocked when he heard that. And I understand it's coming out in Chief Justice Warren's book.

Q: Do you see anything improper in a president approaching any Supreme Court justice in that fashion?

Marshall: Well, if the president had said anything me, I would have told him in no uncertain terms to go to hell, because of the separation of powers. He has no right to do it.

I know when President Johnson named me to the Supreme Court, that very day, he said, "Well, I guess our friendship is about busted up now. I won't be seeing you too much."

And I said, "I don't know what you're talking about, but I think I do."

He said, "What do you think I mean?"

I said, "I think you can get what I think by Mr. Justice Clark. You remember, he was the very best friend, outside of Chief Justice Vinson, that Truman had."

He said, "That's right."

And I said, "You remember what he did to Truman in the Steel case?"

He really socked it to him—his very best friend.

I said, "I would have no hesitancy in socking it to you. Do we understand each other?"

He said, "I'm glad we do understand each other."

I think they have to be separate. Now, history will tell you that in the administration of the Chief Justice [Morrison] Waite, as I remember it, back in the 1880s—there's a long section in his biography pointing out that not only the chief justice, but every justice of the Court had a cabinet member that he was friendly to, and they would discuss the Court opinions with them, before they were rendered.

That was shocking to me. I would hate to see that happen again, and I would not be a party to it. Under any circumstances. I don't care who he is. If the president were my brother, it would be the same thing.

I think that's a black mark on President Eisenhower, and there's nothing in his record that would correct it, in my book.

Q: Yes, I believe you've already gone into his attitudes, at the time of Little Rock, that it was almost a last-resort action on his part, to restore order, before he would intervene.

Marshall: That's right. He wasn't going to do it. He was persuaded to do it.

Q: Did you find that President [John F.] Kennedy, prior to proposing the Voting Rights Act, was pretty wary?

Marshall: Well, no. That's an easy story. I talked with Senator Kennedy, before he decided to run. Indeed, I had lunch with him, just the two of us, in his office. And I told him he shouldn't run, because I remembered what happened to Al [Alfred E.] Smith, and I wouldn't want that to happen to any friend of mine. He listened, as he always did. Didn't say anything, didn't commit himself. But then he did run. And indeed, I was right, because the Masons in this country are in two groups, one white and one Negro. I'm in the Negro group, and I happen to be as high as you can get. I am a past active, which—the active thirty-three degree Masons, on both sides have exactly the same machinery. There are only thirty-three, and they are on top. When I was made active, I was only about fifty-ish, and I wrecked the average age because the average age, before I went in there, was sixty-eight. So I pulled it down a long ways. And the white group, of the South—I am part of the South—they despise the Negroes no end, Negro Masons. They are very nasty.

On one occasion, I was grand minister of the state and part of my job was to do a new constitution, and I thought I would get all the material I could, and I wrote a letter, but had the grand commander, who was the head of the outfit, sign it, to the southern jurisdiction of the white Masons, saying, "Would you let us have a copy of your constitutions? It's not secret. I'm drawing one."

And they wrote a very nasty letter back and said, one, "We don't have any extra copies. And if we did we wouldn't give them to you."

So we said, okay. And a few months later, the commander and I were in Chicago, on that big street, I've forgotten the name of it. There's a huge Masonic library and store. They sell all Masonic materials and books. And whenever we'd get there, we'd rummage through, to see something we wanted for our own library.

And there we saw twelve or thirteen copies of the Southern Jurisdiction lying on a shelf there.

So John Lewis, the commander—he's not a pauper—said, "Well, here's . . ." then he said, "Well, wait a minute, let's have some fun." So he bought the whole batch of them, a piece of money, and he wrote a letter back to the same guy and told him that this great secret document of his was not on the public shelves out there, so we wanted him to know we both now had a copy of it. And, "Since you don't have any extra copies, we bought twelve more and we're going to share them with you." And he sent them back.

Well, to get back to the Kennedy story—one of the Masonic laws, those things called landmarks, which are just absolute, like commandments—you just can't violate them—and one is, you shall not engage in politics of any kind under any circumstances, as an outfit, as a unit. You can personally, but not—

And I was shocked to get a letter—all thirty-three of us got the same letter—saying that Kennedy was a Catholic and was no good and should be opposed, and urging us to join them in the opposition to Kennedy—which is just what I thought would happen, and it did.

Well, we had a very good time writing back to them, quoting the landmark and telling them that they were violating it, and that they were no good, et cetera, et cetera.

But Kennedy had a very extensive civil rights program, on paper, and verbal, with dates to go along. Bobby was primarily interested in getting the president re-elected, and I think it's great, but he constantly pushed Kennedy to push the dates back on when he would make these moves, and it slowed things down considerably. It would have gone much faster but for that. It was not the president. That was Bobby. And that's why we didn't go as fast as we were scheduled to go, during that period. It was very interesting.

See, I got out of all of that, because in '61 the president put me on the court of appeals, so that took me out of it. But he'd already started moving then. And Bobby was awfully ruthless. He was ruthless. Kennedy, the president, was a very sweet man. As a matter of fact, Bobby wanted me to go on the trial court in New York and I told him no, and he says, "Well, why?"

I said, "My boiling point is too low for the trial court. I'd blow my stack and then get reversed. But I would go on the court of appeals."

He said, "Well, you can't go on the court of appeals."

I said, "There's an opening."

He said, "But that's already been filled."

I said, "So?"

He said, "You don't seem to understand, it's this or nothing."

I said, "Well, I *do* understand. The trouble is that you are different from me. You don't know what it means, but all I've had in my life is nothing. It's not new to me, so, good-bye." And walked out.

That was about the second time I had a good run-in with him. And about—I don't know, days later or maybe a week later, a fellow ran into me, what's his name now? He was a Negro who was the vice-chairman of the Democratic Party, Louis Martin, and he asked me, would I take the court of appeals job?

I told him, "Sure." And the next day I was appointed. But Bobby is the one who slowed the roll on—

Q: Doesn't this rather contrast with the later political image which he seemed to project?

Marshall: Yes. He took credit for all the civil rights stuff. He took credit for all of it. I don't know, you see, because I was out of it then. I don't know. I don't know what happened afterwards, after '61.

Q: Did you sense, in the earlier period, that Bobby was motivated solely by political considerations?

Marshall: Bobby was like his father. He was a cold, calculating character. "What's in it for me?" I mean, not like his brother. He had no warm feelings. None at all. With that big old dog of his, walking around, cocking his leg up on your leg.

Q: So does that mean that you don't think that Bobby Kennedy was seriously interested in civil rights? That he went with it when it was necessary politically?

Marshall: And John believed in it. He believed in it. He believed in it. I could be wrong. You see, they were so close that I don't think you could separate them too much. Because once my appointment was made by the president, I mean, Bobby was arranging for my hearings and all. You'd think he was the nicest guy in the world. Taking all the credit for it. All the credit for it. Well, to show you the type of operator he is, at one of my hearings, we were going down the hall, and he said, "Oh, we have to stop here. We have to pay our respects."
I said, "Who?" And I looked there and it was Eastland's door. [Senator James Eastland] I said, "What do you want me to do? I'm not going to go in there and genuflect to that man."
He said, "Well, you ought to."
I said, "Well, I'm not," and I didn't.

Q: Did I recall correctly that he was chairman of the Judiciary Committee at that time?

Marshall: For the last twenty years, I think. Oh, he gave me a hard time. He gave me a hard time. It was under Olin Johnston from South Carolina, and I understand Olin Johnston held me up for eleven months. And at the—by the eleventh month, I was sitting as a judge on an interim appointment. And then, it suddenly dawned on me, and I checked on it—at the end of a year, I could continue to sit but I wouldn't be paid. And I can't live with nothing.
I remember distinctly that President Kennedy telephoned me and said, "Look, do you understand this problem?"
I said, "Yes."

He said, "Well, what are you going to do?"

I said, "Well, I understand the Negro Masons in the South are going to take up the slack from the salary point, but I don't want that done because it's a private outfit."

He said, "Don't worry, it's been taken care of." So I gathered from that, that maybe his father or somebody, I don't know—it would have been a real problem.

And then my good friend Henry Luce of *Time* magazine got in touch with Eastland, and some words were had, and Eastland told Johnson to let me out right away, so I got out the next week. He held it as long as he could.

Q: When you made reference to "bad time," what other details are there, other than the one that you've just gone over?

Marshall: Oh, they brought up everything—about the Lawyers' Guild. He thought he had something there. He said, "Were you ever interested in the Lawyers' Guild?" This is Olin Johnston. I said, "Interested? I was in the group that organized it. I was a member. I was a member of the board of directors. If you call that interested, yes."

And he said, "Well, how can you explain that?"

I said, "With a little letter."

He said, "What do you mean, a little letter?"

I said, "This, if you wouldn't mind putting it on the record." Which is my resignation [from the Lawyer's Guild], and explaining why. That took a little bit off of it.

But oh, they had the FBI to do three field investigations on me—three. That meant they went to every place in the country where I'd ever been, and talked to people. And where I lived then at Morningside Gardens in New York, there are eleven hundred apartments, and they went to every single apartment. I remember, they went to the janitor in my building where I lived, and I came home one day and he said, "Hey, Mr. Marshall—"

"Yes?"

He said, "The FBI been checking on you."

I said, "Yes, I know. What they do with you?"

He said, "Well, they kept giving your business, about how many people visited you, and how many liquor bottles came out, and all like that."

I said, "Well, what did you tell them?"

He said, "I don't know, I told them if they wanted to know about you, to ask you."

I said, "Well, that's a good answer."

But that eleven months of hanging is tough. I survived.

Q: You said Henry Luce and Senator Eastland had words. What kind of words are you talking about?

Marshall: Luce just said if he didn't think it was fair. And that if they had something on me, bring it out. And if they didn't, every week he would put something favorable in *Time* magazine.

Q: Would this be a veiled hint that he would put something unfavorable in it about Eastland?

Marshall: Now, I don't think so. No, he didn't—Luce didn't make any veiled threats. If he threatened you, boy, you got it. I liked him. I liked him very much. We got along swell.

Q: Incidentally, what was the genesis of your friendship with Henry Luce?

Marshall: Strictly business. I don't know how it came about. We were on a board, the first thing was the board—that thing New York University has, great Americans with all the busts up there, I've forgotten the name of it now. That's where we first got together. Then we were on a couple of commissions in the state, appointed by [Nelson] Rockefeller. I remember one occasion that Rockefeller sent his plane down to take us to Albany, and three of us went up on the plane—[David] Sarnoff of RCA, and Luce, and me. And when we got on this plane, it was so lush. It was real lush, with three pilots—not two—three and we were all saying, "Ooh, ah," you know, looking at the furnishings in the plane and all and all of a sudden I turned to them. I said, "Look, I can afford to say, ooh, ah, and all like that, but you guys can't."
They said, "What do you mean?"
I said, "You know, you're not exactly paupers." And I never will forget that Luce said to Sarnoff, "Well, look, by the way, what kind of plane does your company have?"
And he said, "We got an old broken-down DC-3."
He said, "Well, *Time* magazine doesn't even have one."
And then they both turned to me and said, "Thurgood," I've forgotten which one said it, "Now, let me tell you the facts of life. There are wealthy people. There are very wealthy people. There are exceptionally wealthy people. And then, there are the Rockefellers."
But now and then I would call him for advice, and now and then he would call and check things with me. But I liked him very much.

Q: Were these calls for advice dealing with some story that might be in the works?

Marshall: From him? No. No. No. He wouldn't call anybody on that. That was his final authority. It would be about in general, sometimes politics. I know, during the latter part of the [Richard M.] Nixon election, we talked a lot about it because

I didn't want—I never wanted all the Negroes to be in the Democratic Party. I wanted them to be in the Republican Party. And we used to discuss how they could get them to come over to the Republican Party. That's what we would talk about mostly. He was for it. He really was.

Q: Did you ever sense that he felt frustrated not being able to get more blacks into the Republican Party?

Marshall: Yes. I know he was. I know he was. He was very mad at [Thomas E.] Dewey, because Dewey just wouldn't move. And Dewey was not anti-Negro. Not at all. But he was just bullheaded. When the bill to set up the State Committee Against Discrimination in New York was up, we got together a committee—about seven, eight, nine of us, headed by Charlie [Charles Evans, Jr.] Hughes, Charles Evans Hughes's son—to go up and talk to Dewey. And on the way up, on the train that morning, we got in the drawing room and we worked out about five or six things that we were going to ask Dewey to do. And everybody put their input in, and when they got up there and we went in, Dewey spent a considerable amount of time talking to Hughes about when his father was governor, and now about the building changes, and all kinds of small talk. And then we all sat down and he says, "Well, now, I know what you're here for, and I might be able to save a little time, but let me tell you what I propose to do."

And he proposed, whatever it was, six or eight, he proposed two more things than we were asking him for. So we said, "What are we up here for?" So then we went on and we had a nice talk about it, and he said, "Well, I know you guys, and organizations and all," and I said, "Well, what do we do now?"

He said, "It's up to you. You can check me as to what I'm going to do. I'm going to do these things."

Charlie [Charles D.] Breitel, his counsel, was sitting right there, and somebody said, "Well, what will we tell the press? The press knows we're up here."

He said, "Whatever you want to." He turned to me and he said, "As for you and your organization, you always like a whole lot of publicity. I don't object to you saying that you persuaded me to do this."

I said, "You must be kidding."

He said, "No. I don't care one way or the other. It doesn't matter to me, because I'm going to pass the bill. And there's nothing you can do that will hurt it." So, we were satisfied with that, and the bill was about to pass, and I got a call from Breitel. And he says, "Any way you can come up here tomorrow and see the governor?"

I said, "If the train's running, I can come up there."

So I went up there, and I got up there about ten o'clock, I think it was, and the bill was passing. And during that time, from ten until about five, there was Governor Dewey and me and nobody else in that room. And he took two telephone calls, that's all, and they were from [John] Foster Dulles. They were good buddies. We were talking about what was to be done, and about halfway through I realized what he was up to. He was not going to do what I wanted done, and he was trying to find out a middle ground. Like for example, he said, "How would you like to head up the commission?"

I said, "Are you offering me a job?"

He said, "Nope. I'm asking you a question."

I said, "I wouldn't take it."

He said, "Why not? You've been around here fighting for it, and all like that."

I said, "Well, the reason is very simple. You would put a commission in there that I couldn't handle. And I would be sitting up there as the target, with the commission not backing me up."

He burst out laughing. He said, "That's an idea. That's an idea."

Then he kept putting up names. You know, "would you go for this guy?"

Then I got the very bad feeling that I might name somebody that he might appoint. So we had a good understanding that that wasn't really what he was up to. He really wanted to know somebody who—if he wanted him, and it was all right with me, then obviously it's a good guy. Then he said, "Well, now, if you were going to run the commission, what would you do?"

I said, "Well, what I would do—I would take Metropolitan Life Insurance Company, the worst violator in the state—that big tall skyscraper building—and they don't have a Negro in that building, not even in the subbasement sweeping out a toilet."

He said, "Well, what would you do with Metropolitan?"

I said I would, number one, find them guilty, issue an injunction against them, put them in jail, and let them find a way of getting out."

He said, "What about due process?"

I said, "They don't get a due process." And he laughed. He said, "You know, that's just about what you would do."

I said, "Yep. That's what I would do."

Metropolitan came up to him the next week—no, it was the week before, that's right—and threatened him something awful. They really did. And he told them in direct quote to "go to hell."

Now, with a guy like that, then running for president—and never made one speech on civil rights. Not one. Not one. He just got bad advice from somebody.

Now, that's when I pleaded with Luce, and Luce pleaded with him, but he wouldn't do it. They had three speeches that Frank [Francis] Rivers, a judge, Negro, prepared for him, and the last one was one of these kind of speeches that "all people are people"—you know, nothing rough in it. But he wouldn't do it.

Incidentally, I think that's why he lost the election. Oh, another thing during that time I said, "You know, Governor, not that it matters, but I've always voted for you for governor, because I thought you were a great governor and I still do. But I'd never vote for you for president."

And I thought his answer was classic. The governor said to them, "You know, as I think about it, I believe I can get elected without that great big one vote of yours."

He had a marvelous sense of humor. But he would suppress it, unless he was in a room. I saw him, you know, at the Gridiron Dinner, the night before he died.

Q: Yes, he certainly didn't in public appearances seem to be a man of humor or warmth.

Marshall: How he did it, I don't know. They say his wife was that way. I didn't know her at all. But they say she was very cold. I don't know. But I mean, in his office—you would notice anybody who would come into his office, including the staff—they'd stop outside the door and arrange the tie and, do the hair, before they go in before him. Which is typical of what was wrong with the guy.

Q: What about the other governors that you dealt with in Albany?

Marshall: The only other one was [Herbert] Lehman. We usually dealt through Charlie [Charles] Polletti, his lieutenant governor. For that, the door was wide open. We could go there any time to see Charlie.

Q: Going back to the Kennedy time table, you mentioned that Bobby's focus was getting his brother reelected. Was it your impression then, until at least the [Eugene R.] Bull Connor episode, that President Kennedy would not have proposed that Voting Rights Act until after his reelection?

Marshall: I don't think so. I don't know. The one thing I do know about was the housing thing, HUD, Housing and Urban Development, and the decision to make Bob [Robert C.] Weaver a cabinet member. That was supposed to have been done. That was agreed on, in December before he was inaugurated, and it wasn't done. It was just pushed back, back, back. That I know. Wasn't it the last thing he did, just about the last thing?

Q: Now, actually, that act actually was not passed until after Johnson had succeeded him.

Marshall: That's right. As I remember it, Johnson just bullied it right straight through. But you see, as soon as Sam Rayburn died, Johnson just went.

Q: You feel that he would have felt restrained if Sam Rayburn had lived, that he might not have pushed that bill through as he did?

Marshall: I don't know. Nobody knows the influence that Sam Rayburn had. It was unbelievable. It was unbelievable, familywise and all. Sam was just the— I guess he was like old man Kennedy, he just was the boss of the show. That's what it looked like to me. Because when I was named solicitor general, somebody asked him about it, and he said he had just changed, and can't a man change? He said that publicly. And this was after Rayburn died. I don't know what influenced him. I know Rayburn was an awfully tough guy. I know, Judge J. Waties Waring of South Carolina, who ruled with me in the primary cases down there, and Congressman [Mendel] Rivers introduced a bill to impeach him, and Judge Waring called me up, and I went down to see him, and he said, "What are you going to do about that bill?"

I said, "You don't have to worry about that. Those things just sit there and die."

He said, "That's not good enough for me. I want it taken care of."

I said, "If you want it taken care of, I'll get it taken care of." So I came back to Washington, and Tom Clark was attorney general, as I remember, and he said, "you go down to Peyton Ford, the deputy attorney general," and Peyton and I were good friends, and I went down. They said, "Nothing's going to happen."

I said, "The judge wants assurances."

He said, "Well, let me see. You know Mr. Sam?"

I said, "Yes, I know him well."

He said, "Well, lemme call him." So he called Rayburn and Rayburn told him, "Don't worry about it, et cetera, and he said, "But—"

"Is Thurgood there?"

"Yes."

"Well, let me talk to him." And he said, "What is he worried about?" Then he said, "Well, you give him my word, personally, that nothing will happen to that bill."

I said, "Mr. Sam, does that mean it's not going to get out of committee?"

He said, "Get out of committee? It's not *in* committee, it's in my safe."

That's the kind of guy he was. He said, "It's in my safe. It's not even in committee."

He was rough. And his influence was just unbelievable.

Q: Well, did this come as a surprise to you, considering particularly the personality of Lyndon Johnson, and the fact that he had been majority leader in the Senate?

Marshall: I don't know when I first realized it. I did realize that when he was majority leader, a couple of things he got through that the NAACP wanted. I know that. And Clarence Mitchell thought the world and all of him. So evidently he was doing the best he could.

Q: Do you think he was any more deeply committed to equal rights than John Kennedy?

Marshall: His favorite statement, to people like me, and I don't know whether he told anybody else that, but in his sessions that I would have with him when I was solicitor general, he would say—this I think is a direct quote—"I am going to make Abraham Lincoln look like a piker." End of quote.

And if he had been reelected, he would have. The things he was going to do were just terrific. He had a schedule too. But it was all on that second term.

Q: Do you think that that might have been one of his motivations for moving you up to the Supreme Court?

Marshall: Well, he thought that moving me here was what killed him off.

Q: You mean that, that was more critical than the Vietnam War?

Marshall: That they used the Vietnam War as the excuse. He told me that as late as—about a week before he died. Because every time we'd talk on the phone, he would say—once he got out of the presidency, then he would call me up, and that time he told me. I said, "Have you changed your mind?"

He said, "Nope. More and more I'm sure I'm right, and I'm going to write about it." I said, "I'll help you, best I can do." I know because the day I was confirmed was on a Thursday, and that's the day that Ramsey Clark, attorney general, would spend the afternoon with the president. And the phone rang and it was Ramsey, saying, "Congratulations." "Thank you, thank you," et cetera.

Then he said, "Somebody else wants to talk to you," and the president got on the phone and said, "Well, congratulations, but the hell you caused me, goddamnit, I never went through so much hell to get that—and all that you caused me—"

I said, "Who caused what? It was your idea, it wasn't mine."

And he just held at it. He said, "I guess that's right."

But he knew more about it than you or I would ever know. And that note he had, saying that he wasn't going to run—I found out that that was about three months since, he had that written out, and the only person who knew it was Mrs. Johnson. And I remembered, when I heard it, that at two sessions of Congress, when he spoke, he always would look up at the gallery toward her and wink at her, like that. And my wife was always so impressed because she maintained that Johnson was winking at her.

And then I remembered that both times, he did like this, he patted his pocket. And then the last time, the third time, he took it out and read it.

But I don't know. I think if he'd been reelected, he'd have been still alive today. He died of a broken heart, man. What a lovely guy.

Q: Okay. Did he say anything further to you, to corroborate your statement?

Marshall: No, no facts. No facts, no. He very seldom gave you facts. Very seldom. Very seldom.

Q: In your conversations with him after he had left office, did he ever get into a lamenting mood?

Marshall: He would call me for the express purpose of getting out of it. He would say, "no moaning at the bar," or something like that. And then he'd say, "Okay now, go have a drink." I'd say, "Providing you do."

Q: You've mentioned how much difficulty there was in your confirmation for Supreme Court—

Marshall: No, Supreme Court wasn't too bad. The only guy I had against me then was Strom Thurmond. The rest of them just made, you know, little statements for the record.

Q: In other words, it was much worse when you went to the court of appeals?

Marshall: See, Strom Thurmond had a whole lot of questions about what happened when the Fourteenth Amendment was adopted, and said, "Well, Senator, I'm not a memory expert. I do research. And if you give me the question and let me get to my library, tomorrow morning I'll give you the answer."

He said, "I want the answer now."

I said, "I don't know." Then he asked another question. I said, "I don't have the slightest idea what the answer is." And one of his questions was, "Who were the members of the committee that drafted the Fourteenth Amendment?"

I said, "I don't have the slightest idea. I can find it out in the Congressional Library."

"You don't know?" I said, "No."

"You don't know?"

I said, "Nope, I don't know a one of them."

And I remember, at the confirmation hearing on the Senate floor, he raised up and said, "And this stupid guy didn't even know the members of the committee that drafted the Fourteenth Amendment."

And when he did, Ted [Edward M.] Kennedy, Senator Kennedy, said, "Will he yield for a question?" He said he'd yield.

He said, "You know, Senator, I too am interested—who were the members of the committee?"

You know what he said? "I'll let you know." He didn't know himself. But everybody knew that that was just a—we took that in stride, I guess.

Q: Well, to your knowledge, what were the difficulties caused President Johnson after announcing your appointment?

Marshall: I don't know. But he got the votes. I got something like ten votes against me, something like that—a very small number. He must have. He had to make a deal of some kind with Eastland, I should think.

Q: Now, with the suddenness with which you were appointed—and you mentioned Ramsey Clark and one other person claimed they did not know you were being called to the Oval Room—

Marshall: Oh, they knew.

Q: They did. Do you think he had done any kind of missionary work in the Congress before?

Marshall: He must have. He must have. He didn't do things like that without knowing what he was doing.

Q: In other words, no bombshell approach.

Marshall: I don't think so. I couldn't say who, but I know he called about six people when I was sitting there, senators and congressmen. And told him, "I've done this." The first one was [Hubert J.] Humphrey, and I will not name the senators. And he called Earl Warren. But the guys he called, they were no minor people.

Q: You mentioned, you wanted at least to be an appeals judge—you mentioned your quick fuse, and you also mentioned that you're sort of a natural rebel. Did you find it difficult, moving from the state of activist that you had been, sitting on the court of appeals?

Marshall: No, because Chief Justice Warren asked me to come down and talk to him, and I did. He said he just wanted to give me some advice, and his advice was very simple: that the same books are on both sides of the bench. You use the same books, as lawyers or judges, and it's not any different. He said, "Your real trouble is going to be lack of talking to people. You'll wander around the hall and say, 'Will somebody please talk to me?'"

It never happened. I got so tied up writing opinions and doing memoranda and working that I didn't have time to worry about people. So nothing happened.

There are some judges whom it did happen to. There are some judges who have left the bench because they couldn't stand it.

I know a judge right now who gets in trouble every week or so. It's just—he's too active. I guess that's what I ought to have been doing. You take, from over a hundred thousand miles a year to practically no miles of travel—I've gotten so now that I love to travel, but I didn't always. I went out to Arizona, to a moot court, two weeks ago. Now, that's a good racket. They said, "You can stay out here a week if you want, and we won't bother you, but the sun's so beautiful—" So I did stay three days in a beautiful hotel, cottages, all individual cottages, beautiful sun, swimming pool, tennis court. I loafed for two days. I worked one day. So I had a piece of the racket, in Tucson. Boy, that's beautiful country!

Q: Justice Marshall, first of all, to go back to what you mentioned about your appointment to the Supreme Court . . . and also some references you made to Louis Martin when I believe you were appointed an appellate judge, when you learned that President Johnson wanted to make you solicitor general, and when you related that you emphasized how he told you not once but repeatedly not to expect anything higher, presumably in reference to the Supreme Court appointment. Was there any informal discussion with you, at any time, prior or as you were deciding to accept that appointment, with anyone else who may have told you that if there ever should be a possibility of a higher appointment, that would be only if you took the appointment of solicitor general?

Marshall: Oh, no. At no time did anybody tie the two together. And the president kept them separate, but I don't know that anybody's ever discussed it with me. Maybe it was because I wouldn't talk about it. Newspaper people would ask me one way or the other, and I'd just tell them, "I don't know what you're talking about."

But there's never been any connection. If there was any plan, I don't know about it until this day. The only thing I have to say is that Lyndon Johnson very seldom did things off the top of his head. And the way he usually planned his moves: looking at it from hindsight, he might have had that in his mind. But if he did, he kept it to himself.

Q: Was there any discussion, in any context at all, with Louis Martin, relative to the Supreme Court appointment?

Marshall: No. No. He was there, the morning that the president notified me of the appointment. When I went in with Marv Watson, and Marv left us, and the President told me about it, and then he talked it over by telephone with Vice President

Humphrey, and two or three senators—I forget now the other senators. And after that, it seems to me that Louis Martin and Clifford Alexander were in another room, and they were brought in. I think I'm correct on that, as best I can remember. But there was nothing before that.

Q: Going back to the solicitor general appointment, was there any discussion in any context whatsoever about your accepting that appointment, with Louis Martin or Clifford Alexander?

Marshall: No. And I'm sure they didn't know about it. I'm as sure as I'm sitting here, they didn't know about it.

Q: Was it your impression, over those particular years, that Louis Martin was probably the most influential black politically, as far as the White House went, at least?

Marshall: Yes. He was the vice chairman of something. He was the number two man. He really had power, and he deserved it. He was a great guy. He knew his way around. I doubt that any meaningful Negro in this country would exist without Louis knowing about it. He knew them, from coast to coast. And he had their respect. Oh yes.

Q: Now, was it your impression that he was actually brought into that high Democratic post by the Kennedys?

Marshall: No. No. He was pretty powerful when he was in Detroit, running a Negro newspaper, the name of which slips me. He was a power in that area then. That goes way back to the forties, early forties. And from there, he changed to Chicago, so he was in the middle of Democratic politics nationally, before he even came to Washington. He was way ahead of the Kennedys.

Q: Did you have the impression, or perhaps knowledge of this, that he was influential in helping more blacks get higher appointments?

Marshall: Yes. Yes, state and federal. He had a lot of influence in state politics too—in Michigan, Illinois, New York, he had some power, I know. His job was to get the Negro represented on the political side, rather than legal or what have you, and I think that's where he stands.

Q: Did you contact him quite a bit over all of these years, especially when you were going into a place like Detroit?

Marshall: Of course, I mean, I wouldn't think of going to Detroit without letting him know, and the same in Chicago. Certainly, we'd sit down and discuss the NAACP; and he was very, very powerful in the National Negro Publishers Association, and he would support me in getting money from them and getting their support, their front page support.

Q: To go back into another area of your activism particularly with the [Legal Defense] Fund, did you find what you wanted to do more difficult in the North, where there were not the legal restrictions? There was not legal segregation, for example, but institutionalized segregation, through attitudes and practice. Most of your legal challenges took place in the South, didn't they?

Marshall: Well, one of our bigger cases in the schools was in a place in upstate New York. I've forgotten its name offhand, but they had rigid school segregation: the wooden building for Negroes, a big brick building for white children; and we had to carry it all the way to the court to get it straightened out. That would be back in the forties.

Several states. We had trouble in Kansas.

Q: But you did have one of your big cases there.

Marshall: Yes, at Topeka, yes. But we had cases before that.

Then, another thing that's interesting—I was denied the right to practice in only one court in the country, and that was way down South in Bridgeport, Connecticut!

I've forgotten the judge's name, but he said, "Now, you can't do it."

So we had our problems in the North, but the biggest trouble you had was to convince people that they had a problem. They had escaped the South, they'd come North, and they didn't realize what was happening. And that went on, I guess, all the way up to the thirties, and then after the thirties they began to realize it.

Oh, that place in New York was Hilburn. Yes, I would say, we could get more action in the South because the Negroes had a feeling that they were being oppressed. But you take New York, for example, they'd give Negroes little five-cent jobs here and there—and they thought they had something. And the same in Chicago and any of the metropolitan areas.

It wasn't until the late forties that they began to realize that they weren't getting anything, actually, compared to what they were giving.

Yes, I think that we had more trouble in the North than in the South. We never had any trouble with support in the South. Never. In Texas alone, on the Texas primary case, I raised over half a million dollars down there—right in the state of Texas.

Q: From blacks?

Marshall: Ninety-five percent, at least. We would have meetings in churches. I remember one church where we had a meeting and the speaker said, "Well, we're going to get all the money we can tonight."

After about ten collections, one lady got up and said, "Well, I'm getting kind of broke here. I only have seventy-five cents. Will anybody let me have a quarter, so I can make another dollar contribution?"

And the Reverend Lucas, who was presiding, said, "Well, I think we've about reached it. We've got it all."

Those were poor people, but they knew the importance of the vote. They knew it. The people in the North didn't realize how important it was.

Q: Did you personally find this frustrating?

Marshall: No. You couldn't afford to get frustrated. I guess the answer is, I should have been frustrated. But you couldn't, because all you could do was to push with what you had. If you give up, you're gone.

Q: To go back to the Charleston case, more specifically to Professor Kenneth B. Clark's role in it. What do you recall, of first hearing about—first his work and that of his wife Mamie?

Marshall: I had heard about it way back, about when it started, peripherally, and had forgotten it. When we got to this problem with the school case, I'd forgotten it completely. And I mentioned it in one of our staff meetings, and Bob [Robert L.] Carter was the one that remembered Kenneth. As I remember, he called him and we got together right away. But I had forgotten it. It was Bob Carter that remembered it, and gets all the credit for it.

Q: Now, when you heard about his work, had you just heard about his testing generally or had you heard about his projective techniques with the dolls?

Marshall: Yes, I'd heard about the dolls, and that was all that I'd heard, that it was a technique that was being used, but I didn't realize that it was being used for this purpose. And Bob Carter remembered it. That's why I said he deserves the credit for it.

Then there was Helen Trager in Philadelphia, who did the same thing. Who was first and who was second, I don't know.

Q: How well acquainted had you been, up to that time, with projective techniques? Psychological techniques?

Marshall: Very little. Very little.

Q: You knew about the Rorschach test, perhaps?

Marshall: Oh, sure. But very little.

Q: Were you dubious at all about the doll technique?

Marshall: No. No. Because to me, once it was explained and put down, I thought: if I could understand it, anybody could understand it. It was so clear that it just couldn't be pushed aside. And I had realized that, talking to people. In the South, I knew a man in a pool room on Ninth Street in Little Rock, Arkansas, about 1941 or so—when I'd go into these towns, I would go down where the poor Negroes were and talk to them. And I remember talking to this poor fellow in a pool room, and he said, "Lawyer, you got anything to do with this business of when you come back after you die?"
I said, "You talking about reincarnation?"
He said, "I don't know, what is it? Is that what it is?"
I said, "Yes."
He said, "Well, if you got anything to do with it, when I come back, I don't care whether it's a man, woman, or dog, or cat, let it be *white*."
That was the type of thing you'd hear throughout the South. I knew about that. But when these tests were made, to me they proved what I knew all along—that the average Negro had this complex that was built in as a result solely of segregation, and it *was* there. But Kenneth's proof was good enough for me. It was good enough for the Court.

Q: What questions did you have about bringing that kind of testimony into the Court for the first time?

Marshall: Oh, I didn't have any problem with it. The Brandeis brief, that was done way back before World War I—that type of brief had been done a long time ago. I think it was just the same kind of proof you'd make in the ordinary case for damages: you show your damages. If you show your damages, you collect. I didn't have any problem with it.

Q: A tangential question—this complex you've mentioned, to what extent, in your earlier years in this activist work, did you find that Negroes were aware of the semantic institutionalizing—such as "that's white of you," or "free, white and twenty-one" adapted from the Constitution—with which I, as a white, grew up, hearing it but not knowing what it meant. And used it not knowing what it meant.

Marshall: My Dad didn't let us do that.

Q: How widespread did you find this?

Marshall: Oh, I don't know. I still say it depends on your parents. Sometimes a parent had to explain to you that there was a problem. I think he could tell you one or he could tell you the other. But my dad and my mother both used to tell us that we had what everybody else had. And the fact that you happened to be a different color didn't mean anything. My dad would say that my mother was the prettiest brown-skinned woman in the world. And my mother say, "Brown-skinned? No, I'm the prettiest woman in the world." Well, there you are.

You get it over the dining room table. You get it in the living room when you're talking. But I think the parents had to do it, and very often, it was not done. See, most of the parents had to work. They didn't have time to sit down and talk with children at night. My parents would sit down and talk. They had trouble, but—I don't believe anybody pushed it at all. Not when I was a kid.

We used to have fights with the white kids, just on general principles. We had a group of Italians, and we used to fight. The only reason we fought once a day was that we only met each other once a day. But we never—two of them became lawyers, and we'd sit down and talk about it, try to figure out what we were fighting about. We just fought for general principles.

But I don't know how you can measure what happened in the kid's mind or what have you. I don't know.

I didn't get it good until I got to law school. That's when I got it. Up until then, I sort of knew it was there, but law school was when I decided I was going to get something down about it.

Q: When you first examined the Clark findings, did it come as any surprise to you that this feeling was in children so young, that it was already there? Or did you think that this was something they got later on in life?

Marshall: Oh, I knew it. I knew it, because I knew that Negro kids I talked to, "What are you going to be when you grow up?"

"I'm going to be a good butler."

"What are you going to be when you grow up?"

"Well, I hope I might be able to get in the post office."

I mean, we had a phrase around school that "white is right." Now, when I would say it, I was joking. Was the other guy joking? I'm not too sure he was joking. I'm not too sure.

I just don't know. I'm not a psychiatrist. I'm not a sociologist. I just don't know.

I knew where I was going. But that's all.

Q: Now, when you found out what the Clarks had done, and also Helen Trager, did you consider this a major breakthrough, as far as research for your briefs goes?

Marshall: It was all we had. When we started, it was all we had. Everything else we had grew from that. We then ran into John Hope Franklin,[9] and the other man from Hopkins—I'll think of his name in a minute.

Q: Are you thinking of Dr. [Frederick] Wertham?

Marshall: Well, anyhow, people like that. But Kenneth's study was the one that started it.

Q: Now, you mentioned that Robert Carter suggested that you bring Kenneth Clark into this. Did the other lawyers at the [Legal Defense] Fund agree with you or with him?

Marshall: I don't know and don't care. I'm sure they did, because if they hadn't, I would have remembered it. But I mean, I was going to run that case. I'd determined that from the beginning. I wasn't going to shop around. I'd take everybody's ideas and put them all in the pot, but once I'd picked everybody else's brains, I was going to do it. I'm sure we might have had some who said, "What good is this?"—who might have questioned it. But it wouldn't have been serious, because, it was that clear and that simple, in my mind. It would be to anybody else.

Q: You don't recall if any of the lawyers thought that this was getting away from the notion they may have held that this case should be based on legal facts, rather than—

Marshall: It *was* based on law. It was based on that. The old mossbacks, I mean, like Professor [Thomas R.] Powell in Harvard said it was the silliest thing he'd ever heard of. But on the other hand, when we'd have our meetings of lawyers and law professors, we'd have as high as five or six from Harvard who believed what we were doing was right. So what did we care about one man saying we were crazy?

Q: Was Carter quite a vigorous advocate, when he suggested an approach like that, the use of Clark? Did you find him some sort of spearhead on your staff?

Marshall: No. No. It was my idea that we had to get some kind of evidence. Carter says, "This is the kind of evidence that would do what you want done."

---

[9] John Hope Franklin was a young historian when he helped draft the NAACP's brief in *Brown v. Board of Education*; he later served as chair of President Clinton's advisory Initiative on Race, and as president of the Organization of American Historians.

And I agreed with him. That's how that came about.

But bear in mind that Carter was the best-trained guy we had. He had possibly one of the best legal minds I've ever run across, until this day. He just never, I guess, got all he should have gotten. But he was brilliant—and could write. Oh boy! When he'd write a brief, it was beautiful. Beautiful.

I've read some of his opinions since he's been on the Court, and I'm glad to say they are just as persuasive.

Q: Now, about this time or shortly afterward—I guess it was shortly afterward, wasn't it, when Jack Greenberg was brought in?

Marshall: Yes, shortly—no. He might have been on board, because he was handling the Delaware case, around the same time.

Q: That's right.

Marshall: Carter was handling Topeka. I was handling South Carolina. Spott [Spottswood] Robinson and Oliver Hill were handling Prince Edward County, Virginia, and Greenberg was handling Delaware. And they were about the same time—within a few years. But they all hit the Supreme Court at the same time.

So he must have been there.

Q: What were the principles that you applied, as you built up the [Legal Defense] Fund staff? How did you go about finding these younger lawyers?

Marshall: Usually by accident. Bob Carter came about by—somebody left. I believe it was Frank Reeves or somebody. And I mentioned to Bill Hastie that we had an opening, and Bill Hastie said, "This guy from Florida's terrific, Bob Carter."

I got in touch with him and hired him.

Connie [Constance Baker] Motley had worked as a volunteer, and when she graduated, we hired her. Greenberg came about when a vacancy came, and Walter Gellhorn, professor at Columbia, said he had just the man, and that's how—They all got on like that.

When they'd find a real good guy, somebody would call me up. And if I had an opening, I'd use him. If I didn't, I'd let him wait.

Q: How did you persuade them to join, especially in the light of the salaries?

Marshall: Didn't have to. Didn't have to. They all wanted to. They knew enough about it.

Q: Did you ever have any problems with internal dissension on the part of the staff?

Marshall: Only once. A guy, whose name will remain anonymous, but he thought he was great, and I did too. I didn't think he was as great as he thought he was. And it reached the point where he said he had to do something, and I said he couldn't, and he said, "I won't take it."

I said, "Well"—so he went out. At that time, Walter White was connected with the Legal Defense Fund, and he went over to Walter White. Some friends of mine over there told me that Walter told him that he didn't have to worry about Thurgood Marshall, that he'd get a job as long as he was secretary, et cetera.

And when I was told that, I merely told the telephone operator to let me know when he came back.

She says, "There's the man."

When he came back, he walked in the door and I said, "You're fired."

He went back to Walter White. Walter White said, "Why, I didn't mean that."

That's the only time I had any trouble. And I'm glad I handled it that way, so it wouldn't have grown.

Q: By the way, how did you get along with Walter White, especially in the later years?

Marshall: As long as he stayed out of my business. When he got into it, we didn't get along. He had an idea of telling a lawyer how to handle a lawsuit. You don't do that.

Q: Would you say there was a certain amount of tension, then?

Marshall: Well, once the government did us a favor by separating the two organizations; and the government ordered them to be completely separated about the first or second year of Eisenhower's administration. So after that we had no more problem.

Q: You discussed to some extent your reaction to the rise of the other organizations: CORE, Martin Luther King's Southern Christian Leadership—Do you recall during that period any discussion, high in the NAACP, about "carving up the field"—a phrase that I've heard Roy Wilkins use once.

Marshall: I think that that was tried. I was not a party to it. I wouldn't join it, because I didn't feel our work interfered with—but it seems to me that at one time, somebody had a meeting, and I don't remember—but, like with Martin Luther

King's group, all he did was to dump all his legal work on us, including the bills. And that was all right with him, so long as he didn't have to pay the bills.

They used to meet together way back, the Urban League and the NAACP. And then with CORE—there was never anything official. It was that the individuals of the two organizations would talk together, informally, with no commitment. That would happen. For example, I was on the board of the American Civil Liberties Union for about five or six years, I guess, and we would do that, move around like that.

Q: Of course, now, actually, prior to the emergence of CORE and Southern Christian Leadership, there had been a division between the Urban League and the NAACP.

Marshall: No problem. No problem. The Urban League was the State Department and the NAACP was the War Department. We used to agree on that. And in many a city, North and South, the Urban League would go in to the powers that be and say, "Now, look, Mr. Mayor—" or so-and-so, "We've got a very moderate thing here we want you to do, and if you don't do it, we're going to tell the NAACP about it."

And they would do it, get it done. We knew what was going on. It was all right with us.

The only trouble is, sometimes they wouldn't get it, and then we would have to go to court and fight it out. But it was fun. Never a real problem between the two.

CORE, there was no problem originally. But CORE was always a one-man outfit, and whereas you could work with one guy, you couldn't work with the next guy. That was the trouble with CORE.

The present guy is a nut, I think. I know him. He's over there with Amin, over there in Uganda.

Q: Was James Farmer one of those who caused some difficult situations?

Marshall: No. None. Farmer was a very cooperative guy.

I think Farmer worked for the NAACP once, in the branch department, way back, I think. But Farmer can work with anybody. He's a decent guy. He's a very decent guy.

I don't know of anybody who had any trouble with him. He was more trouble to himself than to anybody else.

Q: To go back to this question of semantics, in a different context: for Negroes, the term Negro has been used, colored, and more recently, black. What is your view of this evolution in their terms, from the standpoint of self-esteem?

Marshall: I don't think it's evolution. Because I know a time when if you called a Negro "black," he'd fight you. So it's not evolution. No, I think that a black or a white is wrong. I don't know if it's English-wise or what. A person is not a black or a white. And if so, it would have to be capitalized. Black is an adjective, in my book, and the way I use it, sometimes I'll say "black people." But if I'm talking about a person, I'm going to say a Negro, because I was taught to say that and I don't see any reason to change it. I don't think that gives pride or anything else. I don't think you get pride by calling yourself this or that. I don't think you get any pride by wearing a dashiki or an Afro haircut. I think you get pride by studying your background and finding that you have nothing to be ashamed of. That's how you become proud. I don't think you can make it—to me, it's a sort of a guilty feeling. I know, I watched when everybody was around wearing Afro haircuts, and I was invited to the White House, from the people from one of those African countries—I've forgotten which one it was now—and my wife and I noticed that there were about sixteen people there from this African country, and not a one of them had an African haircut. Not a one of them!

So why were we wearing African haircuts?

Q: To go back to the legal work that you had at the [Legal Defense] Fund, were there any notable changes in the way the courts operated during your period there, especially changes that may have influenced your strategy or tactics?

Marshall: No. We got out of the state courts into the federal courts, because we could get independent judges in the federal courts that we couldn't get in the state courts. And once we got over there, I don't think—we just took the rules as they were, and I don't know of any changes that we made in them at all. We just learned to use them—like the three-judge court system, and things like that, but that wasn't original with us. The statute had been there all along. I don't think so, no.

Q: Richard Kluger in his book *Simple Justice* said that the first legal assignment you gave Jack Greenberg was to examine the merits, or lack of merits, of using the three-man federal courts. Do you recall that particular assignment to him?

Marshall: No.

Q: Or do you recall why you might have wanted such a study made at that time?

Marshall: No. I know everybody opposed it but me. They didn't think it would work. But it did. It might be true. I just don't remember.

Q: Why did you believe it was a good idea?

Marshall: Because we had to get off the treadmill. Stop one judge from holding the case up. And with three judges, they can't hold it up. That was the reasoning for it. And a direct appeal to the Supreme Court. You don't have to go through
the court of appeals.

Q: When you say others opposed it, are you talking about your staff members, other lawyers?

Marshall: Oh, everybody. Everybody.

Q: What did they think was wrong with it?

Marshall: That it just wouldn't work. General principles.

Q: They had no reason?

Marshall: No. Or I don't remember them. But they were dead set against it. But
I was just bullheaded.

Q: The question about a certain sociopolitical period—that was when Senator
Joseph McCarthy held so much sway—how did that affect, if at all, your work?

Marshall: It didn't bother me at all. We took a position, I was one of several
Negroes who took the position that if you weren't on the McCarthy list or the Un-
American Activities [Committee] list; if you were a Negro and you were not on both
of those lists, you should blow your brains out.
    That's how much we worried about it.

Q: Did his influence impede your work, though, any place in the field?

Marshall: Not too much. I imagine, for some contributors it might have. I
don't know. Not that my attention was brought to it, no. Made me mad, that's all.
    And I felt sorry for the people that he really did clobber. I don't think he ever
got around to us. And we used to dare the Un-American Activities Committee to
investigate us. We used to dare them to do it, and they wouldn't do it.
    Then eventually we got a clean bill of health from J. Edgar Hoover. That stopped
it all.

Q: Were you able to use that clean bill, then, if you went into any locality
where you thought, they might say, "These are agitators and therefore, they're
Communists."

Marshall: Oh, in places like Kansas City, Missouri—we had a swimming pool case, and the city attorney filed a petition with the court to prevent me from trying the case out there, saying I was a former member of the National Lawyers' Guild, and that I was a fellow traveler, or something else.

The case came up on several motions, including that one. The judge ruled on the other two or three motions, and then said, "This one," he would take up in chambers and would the lawyer please come in.

The city attorney started off, and I said, "Excuse me, but are you taking the position that I am now or have ever been a Communist?"

He said, "Not as such. Why?"

I said, "Because if you say it, I'm going to punch you in the mouth."

The judge said, "Well, now, now, let's not act like that."

The judge said to the city attorney, "I would suggest that you withdraw it without me ruling on it, because I am going to rule if you don't withdraw it."

He said, "What are you going to rule?"

He said, "I noticed that Mr. Marshall has a thirty-third degree Mason's ring on, and I happen to know he is a thirty-third degree Mason, and while you might not know, I'm a Catholic but I know about Masons, and I'll take judicial notice that no thirty-third degree Mason could ever be a Communist. Now, do you want to withdraw it or not?" And he withdrew it.

We had things like that, and letters, and people. But we knew. We knew our own position. So there was nothing to it.

Q: To go back to your reference about bringing in outside advisors, professors—law professors from Harvard and others.

Marshall: Over a hundred. One hundred and twenty, one hundred and thirty of them.

Q: Building up that big network took a while?

Marshall: About two years. What we tried to do was to get the two leaders in each field who were deathly enemies of each other, on a position, and get them to sit down and fight it out. If they ever agreed on a paper, you knew it was right.

I know one man I had—gee, the name slips me—and he said, "Where did you get this idea from? I know I'm right, and this position paper says I'm wrong."

I said, "Well, that just happens to be your professor who taught you." He said, "I better go look it up again."

So that's how we got it. That was airtight stuff we had.

Q: Did you bring them together physically to do this?

Marshall: We did a lot of correspondence, but we had two meetings, I remember, in New York where we had them all together. At least—I think it was twice. I could be wrong. It was no more than twice. But most of it they would bring in papers, sometimes ten to a hundred pages, and then we would discuss those. And then we got them all together, twice at least. All for nothing. They didn't get a red nickel.

Q: You mentioned how Robert Carter went to the federal bench—of course you have, and Constance Baker Motley, I believe, did.

Marshall: Yes. Spottswood Robinson.

Q: Was the [Legal Defense] Fund at any time viewed as some sort of a mechanism for bringing lawyers, Negro lawyers especially, to the attention of the political appointive authorities?

Marshall: No. When we started in the thirties with Charlie Houston, the idea was to get Negro lawyers the respect from the general public that they deserved. That wasn't looking for jobs or anything. That was just respect. And that's what we worked on. And it just ended up that way.

Q: What were your main problems in raising money for the Fund?

Marshall: Normal problems: no money. There's so many people who had money who took the position that, "If we give you the money you need, then you'll get lazy and won't do your work." I didn't believe that, no.

We did have some very good people. Marshall Field at one time gave us the small sum of two hundred thousand dollars. Senator Lehman would give us just about whatever we asked for, but I don't know any time when we asked for more than twenty thousand dollars. A few other big people like that. The rest of it was in fives, tens. We had a mailing list that any mailing would bring in about seventy-five thousand dollars, minimum. And that's how we raised it. I don't know who's on the list, but that's how we raised it. It was an awful lot of work, going around talking to people and all. You go in to one guy and talk to him forever and come out—I know I talked to one poor man, Tom Watson of IBM, and he listened to me for a whole hour and gave us five hundred dollars, which I started to give back; but I was told, we don't do that.

But some people—I mean, the Episcopal bishop used to give us very good money, but always anonymously. We had a group of Catholic priests in New Orleans who had to give their money anonymous[ly] because they were all Jesuits and not supposed to have any money.

Q: It would signify violation of their oath of poverty?

Marshall: That's right. That's right.

Q: As you recall, how did you proportion your time between developing briefs, strategy and briefs, managerial, and fund-raising?

Marshall: I did each thing that came up, on a day-by-day basis. That's the only way you could do it. I mean, sometimes I'd have a fund-raising deal going on that I'd have to break and go try a lawsuit. It was just an emergency. There was always an emergency, in whichever branch you were going on. No set time, nothing.

Q: You can't generalize over the long haul, that half the time was spent on law work, or—

Marshall: No. I couldn't do it.

Q: You've mentioned these religious people that helped you. How did you feel over the years about the role of the churches in the civil rights struggle?

Marshall: Not anywhere close to as much as they should have done. I don't know of a single church group that did what it should have done. Areas, yes. The Catholic Church in Louisiana did a beautiful job. The Catholic bishop in Mississippi, whose name I should remember, did a beautiful job. The Episcopal churches, not any large group, did a good job. They are all individuals, but to come right out as a church, I don't think any of them did. Maybe I was wrong. I don't remember.

Q: How did you feel about the role of the Negro churches in the black community?

Marshall: Eighty percent of the branches of NAACP when I went there were run by ministers, in churches. Ninety-eight percent of the meetings were held in Negro churches. The Negro church support was beautiful, from one end of the country to the other.

Q: And you would disagree—

Marshall: Take the gentleman I mentioned a minute ago, Reverend Lucas, of one of the biggest Baptist churches in Houston, Texas. One of the finest gentlemen you'd run across. In the glove compartment of his car, he had two items—a Bible and a .45. And his answer was very simple: "I'll try the Bible first."

Q: Would you disagree with the Muslim position enunciated that many of the Negro churches have actually perpetuated problems?

Marshall: I wouldn't agree with anything any Muslim ever said, any time, any place.

But, there of course were some ministers, Negro ministers, who were against the program and against themselves. Just like there were Negro lawyers, Negro doctors, Negro businessmen. We have our share of skunks, just the same as anybody else. But I'm talking about the average Negro minister who was behind us one hundred percent. The average one. The big ones. The good ones. The bishops were all with us.

Q: You didn't find that a good many of them preferred a more gradual course, perhaps?

Marshall: Oh, sure. Oh sure! Sure. But you'd always find another one.

Incidentally, that gradual one would be in the Urban League.

You had them to speak out. I know in Little Rock, Arkansas, the Methodist church every Sunday—I've forgotten what it was, a big religious day; every year the minister of the big Methodist white church would come and preach at the Negro church. And on this year, he came over there, and when he got through the pastor of the Negro church said, "Thank you so much, Reverend so-and-so, for coming. We appreciate your coming every year. But just one mild suggestion. Your sermon was just perfect about: we're all the same, take off the skin, we're all God's children and all like that. Next year, wouldn't it be better if you preached that sermon in your church than this church?" Just a little something or other—you know. You know, a little something or other.

Oh, of course, you can criticize them. There were some bad ones. But I don't think there would have been an NAACP without the church.

Q: A question about a certain type of activist, as things became more vigorous in the sixties. I'm thinking of a person like Medgar Evers. Did some of them outlast their usefulness, because of the counteraction that their moves brought about?

Marshall: No. Not Medgar. Medgar was sweet. You wouldn't think that Medgar had any gumption at all. And that's how he got so much accomplished. People underplayed him. He had more courage than anybody I've ever run across. No, he would be a bad, not a good example. He had as many years ahead of him as he had behind him.

But there are others who jumped up and just died out; you'll find some in the NAACP. One famous one is Daisy Bates of Little Rock, who did so much on the Little Rock case, and I don't know what she's doing since.

We have some who just come up, you know, and die out. But there are others who are steady. Medgar would be one of the good ones.

Q: What you say about, had as many good years ahead of him as had behind him—

Marshall: Sure.

Q: I'm thinking here of a remark that a high NAACP official told me once. He took the position that he thought he'd done about as much as he could accomplish, and he was actually more valuable in the martyr status, to the cause, than had he lived.

Marshall: That's a disgusting thing to say. Why didn't he go shoot him? That's horrible. No. I think he was on his way up. I know he was, because the Negro Masons in Mississippi had just built a brand-new building in Jackson, and they gave him office space in that, and he would have had about five times the office space he had before, five or ten times the money he had before, and twice the staff he had before. And when he died, nobody else got it. It was for Evers. That's who it was for. Because I talked to the grand master afterwards.

You know, somebody said that about Martin Luther King—that he had come to the end of his usefulness. I think that's an awful thing to say.

Q: As a matter of fact, that relates to another question I had about that. I heard that, especially when he went in to organize Chicago, that he may have lost his touch.

Marshall: He lost in Chicago. They outfoxed him in Chicago. The Negroes who rushed to his aid in Chicago were really [Mayor Richard E.] Daley people. And every move he made, Mayor Daley knew about. But that—I mean, a man can't win 'em all. Can't win 'em all. I think that man had a great future. If he had lived, we might not have stayed in the Vietnam War as long as we did.

Q: Incidentally, at the time that he came out against the Vietnam War, did you feel that he was diluting—

Marshall: Yes, sir.

Q:—the race issue?

Marshall: Told him so. Told him so. And he said he didn't think so, and if his Lord told him to do something, he was going to do it.

"Well," I said, "no use in arguing about that."

No, I thought he was. I really did. But I told him and it didn't change him.

Q: A retrospective type of question here. You have already gone into the detail of how you built up until you got the favorable 1954 decision, and then hadn't prepared to follow that through on the basis that perhaps it was not necessary. Looking back over all the time you have been active in civil rights, and at the risk here of some repetition, what would you say were the peaks as far as accomplishments in the struggle, and what were the valleys or the low periods?

Marshall: Well, I guess the first one would be—well, leave out the criminal cases. The Texas primary case was the greatest. That was April 14, 1944. That, to me, was the greatest one.

A few years later, the Georgia and South Carolina primaries would be great. The Wilmington, Delaware bus case was great. The Irene Morgan case, on bus transportation, would be great. Restrictive covenants. And then the school cases. And with all of those, you had valleys between them when you didn't have money or anything else. But I couldn't spell them out too much. We could only move when we had the money—which is not their problem now.

Q: What about the nonlegal peaks and valleys, perhaps going prior to World War II on this?

Marshall: I don't know. I don't know. I can't—

Q: I mean, for example, did you see the Roosevelt Executive Order of 1942 as being a peak, when the war contractors were barred from discriminating? Then, after the war, the last hired were the first fired.

Marshall: With all of those executive orders, they're best exemplified by the one that [James] Forrestal issued—bless him for it—desegregating the Navy. And in the NAACP records, we have affidavits from executive officers on three battleships who had never seen the order.

What happened was, Forrestal issued the order. It got down to the operational level, and it dropped dead, right there. So all of these orders were so poorly implemented; I don't know where you get any boost out of any of them, as you look back. The follow-through is what's expensive. It's hard. And I don't think the NAACP ever had enough money to follow through on any of them. Maybe. But I don't think so.

Q: When you were at the [Legal Defense] Fund, did you lead any cases against labor unions for discriminating in hiring, or letting persons into an apprenticeship program?

Marshall: No, but I had one better than that. I had two cases against the boilermakers' union, early in World War II; one in Providence, Rhode Island, and one in the Marine shipyard in San Francisco, where the boilermakers would not let Negroes join the union. They would put them in auxiliary unions, with no rights, no anything. And in both cases, after a year of trying and everything, I got an injunction, telling the union they had the choice of two things: they could either admit Negroes into full membership in the union, or give up the closed shop. So they didn't have any trouble. They let them in the union. And that's the type of cases we filed. All of organized labor was behind us, because that was one of the worst unions. It was awful. It had no real democracy—for example, in those days, you could only have a convention upon the call of the international vice president—I mean president. None of the expense accounts of him or any vice president could be audited by anybody but him.

Also, you had to pay for life insurance, in a group life insurance policy in a company owned by the president's son. And the only way you could recover death benefits was to die while employed and a member of the union. And the record showed that in one year—that three years running, they had paid off a total of seven policies, in three years.

That's the kind of union it was. And why Negroes would want to join it, I don't know, but they wanted to.

Q: When you were in that case, were you in liaison with A. Philip Randolph?

Marshall: No. We were good friends. But no, I handled it on my own.

Q: When you say all the labor leaders and organizations supported you there, which ones are you talking about?

Marshall: Oh, the good top guys in the CIO.

Q: Walter Reuther?

Marshall: Sure, anybody who was trying to clean up that type of a union. They were ready to get rid of them. That was that old craft union in which nobody got any money but the top guys. They were drawing huge salaries and huge accounts. I only got a hold of one, but one executive vice president in a year put in a partial one for ninety thousand dollars for travel! And he covered the states of Maine, Rhode Island and Massachusetts. And you realize how much traveling there is up there. . . .

Q: One more question about the peaks, the valleys. When the Voting Rights Legislation was passed, you believe that had bigger follow-through? Was that more important than the executive orders?

Marshall: Yes. Yes. That did a beautiful job. Everybody went to work on it. I mean—see, I was out of it then, I could just see it in the papers. But when you see the number of Negroes that they've got registered—gee! I think that's the only wave of the future. That's the future. I shouldn't talk too much about it, because we have cases on it.

Q: Is there any further comment you'd like to make about changes in the way the courts have gone about their business, especially in more recent years, since you were first on as an appellate judge?

Marshall: Nope. That's got to come for the future. About a year from now or so I'm going to be forced to say something about it. But I'm not going to do it now. This is not the time.

Selected Bibliography

A comprehensive research guide, through 1993, is Ruth Johnson Hill, "Mr. Justice Thurgood Marshall, 1908–1993: A Bio-Bibliographic Research Guide," *Southern University Law Review*, Vol. 20, pp. 113–39 (1993).

Bland, Randall W. *Private Pressure on Public Law: The Legal Career of Justice Thurgood Marshall*. Lanham, MD: University Press of America, 1993.

Blasi, Vincent. *The Burger Court: The Counter-Revolution That Wasn't*. New Haven: Yale University Press, 1983.

Davis, Michael D., and Hunter R. Clark. *Thurgood Marshall: Warrior at the Bar, Rebel on the Bench*. New York: Carol Publishing Group, 1994.

Friedman, Leon, editor. *Argument: The Complete Oral Argument Before the Supreme Court in* Brown v. Board of Education of Topeka, 1952–1955. New York: Chelsea House, 1969.

Goldman, Roger, and David Gallen. *Thurgood Marshall: Justice for All*. New York: Carroll & Graf, 1992.

Greenberg, Jack. *Crusaders in the Courts: How a Dedicated Band of Lawyers Fought for the Civil Rights Revolution*. New York: Basic Books, 1994.

Kluger, Richard. *Simple Justice*. New York: Alfred A. Knopf, 1976.

Powe, Lucas A. Jr. *The Warren Court and American Politics*. Cambridge: Harvard University Press, 2000.

Rowan, Carl. T. *Dream Makers, Dream Breakers: The World of Justice Thurgood Marshall*. Boston: Little, Brown, 1993.

Simon, James T. *The Center Holds: The Power Struggle Inside the Rehnquist Court*. New York: Simon & Schuster, 1995.

Special Issue: A Tribute to Justice Thurgood Marshall. Stanford Law Review, Vol. 44, pp. 1213–99.

"Tribute to Justice Thurgood Marshall." *Harvard Law Review*, volume 105, pp. 23–76 (1991).

Tributes. *Yale Law Journal*, volume 101, pp. 1–29 (1991).

Tushnet, Mark V. *The NAACP's Legal Strategy Against Segregated Education, 1925–1950*. Chapel Hill: University of North Carolina Press, 1987.

Tushnet, Mark V. *Making Civil Rights Law: Thurgood Marshall and the Supreme Court, 1936–1961*. New York: Oxford University Press, 1994.

Tushnet, Mark V. *Making Civil Rights Law: Thurgood Marshall and the Supreme Court, 1961–1991*. New York: Oxford University Press, 1997.

Tushnet, Mark V., editor. *The Warren Court in Historical and Political Perspective*. Charlottesville: University of Virginia Press, 1993.

Williams, Juan. *Thurgood Marshall: American Revolutionary*. New York: Times Books, 1998.

Woodward, Bob, and Scott Armstrong. *The Brethren*. New York: Simon & Schuster, 1979.

The Manuscript Division of the Library of Congress holds two major collections of Marshall's papers: those from his years on the Supreme Court; and the NAACP Papers, which contain a great deal of material written by and to Marshall while he was with the NAACP Legal Defense Fund. Much of the latter material is also available, on microfilm or microform, from University Publications of America and at many libraries.

Appendix: Annotated List of Important Decisions

According to statistics compiled by the *Harvard Law Review*, Justice Marshall wrote 322 majority opinions, 83 concurrences, and 363 dissents in his years on the Court. The list below identifies the most important of these opinions, aside from the ones presented in Part Four. Unless otherwise indicated, the opinion is for a majority of the Court.

Adams v. Williams, 407 U.S. 143 (1972) (dissent): The Court upheld a police "stop" of a person based on information that the defendant was in a nearby car with a gun and narcotics, and a protective search to seize the gun. That, in turn, gave the officer probable cause to arrest the person and search him. Marshall's dissent argued that the decision "invokes the specter of a society in which innocent citizens may be stopped, searched, and arrested at the whim of police officers who have only the slightest suspicion of improper conduct."

Amalgamated Food Employees Union v. Logan Valley Plaza, 391 U.S. 308 (1968): Writing for the Court, Marshall found that a shopping mall could not use state laws against trespass to bar peaceful union picketing. Barring such demonstrations from a city's streets would violate the First Amendment, and in modern times shopping malls were the equivalent of city streets. The government could not "delegate the power . . . wholly to exclude those members of the public wishing to exercise their First Amendment rights on the premises in a manner and for a purpose generally consonant with the use to which the property is actually put."

Arkansas Writers' Project, Inc. v. Ragland, 481 U.S. 221 (1987): The Court invalidated a state sales tax that applied to many magazines but exempted religious, professional, trade, and sports magazines. Marshall's opinion found this an impermissible distinction among publications, based on their content.

Austin v. Michigan Chamber of Commerce, 494 U.S. 652 (1990): Marshall's opinion for the Court upheld a state law barring corporations from using corporate treasury funds for expenditures supporting candidates. The opinion emphasized the "unique legal and economic characteristics of corporations" that gave them "political advantage" because the money they compiled was "not an indication of popular support for the corporation's political ideas." The ban was justified to reduce "the corrosive and distorting effects of immense aggregations of wealth that are accumulated with the help of the corporate form and that have little or no correlation to the public's support for the corporation's political ideas."

Barefoot v. Estelle, 463 U.S. 880 (1983) (dissent): The Court approved the use of expedited procedures to deal with death penalty cases, and held in addition that expert testimony from a psychiatrist on the defendant's future dangerousness could be used to support a death sentence. Marshall criticized the majority for approving expedited procedures in cases where life was at stake "[i]n view of the irreversible nature of the death penalty and the extraordinary number of death sentences that have been found to suffer from some constitutional infirmity."

Batson v. Kentucky, 476 U.S. 79 (1986) (concurrence): The Court held that attorneys using their power to eliminate potential jurors from service through "peremptory" challenges for which they offer no reasons may not use that power to strike jurors on the basis of their race. Marshall's concurring opinion agreed with the result; but he also argued that racial discrimination in juror selection could be eliminated only by doing away with the entire process of allowing peremptory challenges, because of difficulties courts would have in determining whether a lawyer had in fact based such a challenge on the juror's race.

Beal v. Roe, 432 U.S. 438 (1977) (dissent): The Court upheld state statutes denying state funding under the Medicaid program for abortions. Criticizing the Court's "insensitivity to the human dimension of these decisions," Marshall described the statutes as "the most vicious attacks yet devised" on the right to obtain an abortion, because they would have "the practical effect of preventing nearly all poor women from obtaining safe and legal abortions." He applied his approach to equal protection law and found that the statutes were unconstitutional, because the funds were vital to the recipients (poor and, in many cases, minority women), and because, in light of the Court's basic abortion decisions, there was no strong state interest in protecting the life of the fetus at an early stage.

Benton v. Maryland, 395 U.S. 784 (1969): The Due Process Clause of the Fourteenth Amendment "incorporates" (that is, makes applicable to the states) the ban on placing people twice in jeopardy – the Double Jeopardy Clause of the Fifth Amendment. This opinion overruled the leading precedent on incorporation, *Palko v. Connecticut*, 302 U.S. 319 (1937), in which the Court, through Justice Benjamin Cardozo, had held that the Due Process Clause barred states from using only those procedures that violated rights "implicit in the concept of ordered liberty."

Berkemer v. McCarty, 468 U.S. 420 (1984): The Court held that drivers stopped by police officers who suspected that the drivers were intoxicated did not have to be given the *Miranda* warnings at the roadside, but warnings were required if the drivers were taken into custody. Marshall's opinion said that allowing an exception to *Miranda* for traffic offenses would introduce "Byzantine" complexities into a body of law designed to give police officers clear guidance; but simply being detained at the roadside did not create the kinds of coercive pressures with which the Court in *Miranda* was concerned.

Bethel School Dist. v. Fraser, 478 U.S. 675 (1986) (dissent): The Court upheld a school's action disciplining a student who, while nominating another student for student body office, delivered a speech filled with sexual innuendo. Marshall's dissent argued that the Court should require the school to show that the speech disrupted the educational process.

Board of Education of Oklahoma City v. Dowell, 498 U.S. 237 (1991) (dissent): The Court reversed a court of appeals decision, which itself had reversed a trial court's decision to relieve the school board of its obligations under a long-standing desegregation order. The trial court was directed to reconsider whether the order should be dissolved after determining whether the board had been acting in good faith and whether the vestiges of discrimination had been eliminated. Marshall's dissent, interpreting the majority opinion as an assertion that "13 years of desegregation was enough," objected that the purposes of the original order had not yet been fully achieved because there were still a number of one-race schools in the district, and because the board's past behavior demonstrated "nearly unflagging resistance" to desegregation.

Bolger v. Youngs Drug Products Corp., 463 U.S. 60 (1983): The Court held unconstitutional a federal statute barring the mailing of unsolicited advertisements for contraceptive products. Justice Marshall wrote that the Court would not broadly allow the government to "shut off the flow of mailings to protect those recipients who might potentially be offended." Parents, not the government, should act to ensure that children not read offensive materials mailed to the home.

Brown v. Socialist Workers '74 Campaign Committee, 459 U.S. 87 (1982): Because the Socialist Workers Party had shown that its contributors would probably be threatened or harassed if their contributions became known, Justice Marshall's opinion for the Court found that applying campaign finance laws requiring disclosure of Party contributors' names would violate the First Amendment.

Brewer v. Williams, 430 U.S. 387 (1977) (concurrence): The Court held that the *Miranda* decision required the exclusion of a statement made after police officers driving the suspect to the police station spoke in the suspect's presence of how important it was that the victim, a young girl whose body had not yet been found, receive a Christian burial. Concurring, Marshall responded to dissenters who called the "Christian burial" speech "good police work, "good police work is something far different from catching the criminal at any price. It is equally important that the police, as guardians of the law, fulfill their responsibility to obey its commands scrupulously." Here the officers deliberately decided to ignore *Miranda*, and therefore did not engage in good police work.

Buckley v. Valeo, 424 U.S. 1 (1976) (concurrence and dissent): The Court upheld parts of the federal campaign finance system and invalidated others. Marshall's separate opinion dissented from the portion that struck down limits on the amounts candidates could spend from their own resources, and emphasized the government's interest "in promoting the reality and appearance of equal access to the political arena," noting that "the perception that personal wealth wins election may . . . undermine public confidence in the integrity of the electoral process." He also noted that allowing candidates to spend as much of their money as they wanted was in tension with limits on contributions made to other candidates, because "[l]arge contributions are the less wealthy candidate's only hope of countering the wealthy candidate's immediate access to substantial sums of money."

Caldwell v. Mississippi, 472 U.S. 320 (1985): In a death penalty case, Marshall wrote for the Court that the Constitution was violated by a prosecutor's argument that the jury's decision to impose the death penalty was not as substantial as the defense had contended because the death penalty would be reviewed by higher courts. It was constitutionally impermissible, Marshall wrote, "to rest a death sentence on a determination made by a sentencer who has been led to believe that the responsibility for determining the appropriateness of the defendant's death rests elsewhere."

California Federal Savings & Loan v. Guerra, 479 U.S. 272 (1987): The federal statute barring sex discrimination in employment did not displace a state statute requiring employers to provide maternity leave. The federal statute, Marshall's opinion said, did not preclude the state from adopting a statute requiring that women be given "special treatment," when doing so would promote the goal of equal employment opportunity.

Casteneda v. Partida, 430 U.S. 482 (1977) (concurrence): The Court found sufficient evidence to establish that there had been discrimination against Mexican Americans in selecting members of a grand jury, even though the "governing majority" in the area was itself Mexican American. Marshall's concurring opinion relied on social science evidence that "members of minority groups frequently respond to discrimination and prejudice by attempting to disassociate themselves from the group, even to the point of adopting the majority's negative attitudes towards the minority."

City of Cleburne v. Cleburne Living Center, 473 U.S. 432 (1985) (concurrence and dissent): The Court overturned a city's refusal to grant a zoning variance to a group home for the mentally retarded, finding that the refusal rested on impermissible stereotypes and served no valid public purpose; but the Court refused to find that the mentally retarded were a "suspect class," discrimination against which had to be justified by the strongest reasons. Marshall's separate opinion agreed with the outcome, but argued in favor of his own approach to equal protection analysis, pointing out that the Court here (as in other cases) actually used the supposedly low standard of review in a manner inconsistent with the real meaning of that standard.

City of Mobile v. Bolden, 446 U.S. 55 (1980) (dissent): The Court held that plaintiffs, who alleged that the districts drawn for municipal elections violated their right to vote under the Fifteenth Amendment, had to establish that the district lines were drawn with the intent to discriminate on the basis of race. Marshall, dissenting, argued that this standard was too strict, forcing courts "to undertake an unguided, tortuous look into the minds of officials in the hope of guessing why certain policies were adopted and others rejected." He criticized the majority for its "indifference to the plight of minorities" and for attempting "to bury the legitimate concerns of the minority beneath the soil of a doctrine almost as impermeable as it is specious."

Clark v. Community for Creative Nonviolence, 468 U.S. 288 (1984) (dissent): The Court found that a National Park Service regulation barring people from sleeping overnight in national parks did not violate the constitutional rights of homeless people who sought to demonstrate their plight to the public by sleeping overnight in a park near the White House and on the National Mall. Marshall's dissent argued that the regulation deprived the demonstrators of their ability to make their political point in the effective way they preferred; and that the restriction on free expression was not justified by any demonstration that the homeless, simply by sleeping in the parks, would in fact cause substantial wear and tear on park property or any other impairment of the public space. His opinion emphasized the incentives public officials have in using rules that appear to be neutral—barring all sleeping in the national parks—while having the effect of limiting criticism of public policy.

Crawford v. Los Angeles Board of Education, 458 U.S. 527 (1982) (dissent): The Court upheld a California initiative that barred state courts from entering either pupil assignment or transportation orders requiring busing in desegregation cases, unless such orders were required by the federal Constitution. Relying on a companion case in which the Court struck down a Washington initiative barring *school boards* from adopting such desegregation plans, Marshall wrote that the California initiative "works an unconstitutional reallocation of state power by depriving California courts of the ability to grant meaningful relief to those seeking to vindicate the State's guarantee against de facto segregation in the public schools."

Duckworth v. Eagan, 492 U.S. 195 (1989) (dissent): The Court upheld the admission of a statement given after a defendant received *Miranda* warnings, one part of which departed from the usual version in saying that a lawyer would be appointed for the suspect "if and when you go to court." Marshall's dissent pointed out that the "recipients of police warnings are often frightened suspects unlettered in the law, not lawyers or judges or others schooled in interpreting legal or semantic nuance."

Dunn v. Blumstein, 405 U.S. 330 (1972): The Court struck down Tennessee's requirement that only those who had resided in the state for twelve months or longer could vote in its elections. Noting that such durational residency requirements "penalize those persons who have traveled from one place to another to establish a new residence during the qualifying period," Marshall's opinion for the Court held that such discrimination could be justified only if the requirement was the least restrictive method to achieve the state's goal of reducing voter fraud, and concluded that it was not.

Estelle v. Gamble, 429 U.S. 97 (1976): The Court's opinion established that "deliberate indifference" by prison officials, including prison doctors, to a prisoner's medical needs violated the Constitution's ban on cruel and unusual punishments. Prisoners "must rely on prison authorities to treat [their] medical needs," and failure to do so could result in death or pain and suffering that served no legitimate penological interest.

Fare v. Michael C., 442 U.S. 707 (1977) (dissent): The Court held that, after giving the *Miranda* warnings, the police could continue to interrogate a juvenile who had asked them to let him see his probation officer, although the juvenile had not requested an attorney. Marshall's dissent argued that questioning should cease "whenever a juvenile requests access to an adult who is obligated to represent his interests," and that only such an approach would serve the purpose of the *Miranda* requirements of protecting suspects against coercion.

Flagg Brothers v. Brooks, 436 U.S. 149 (1978) (dissent): The Court held that a commercial enterprise renting storage space to customers did not engage in "state action" when it sold the stored items for overdue rents, and therefore did not have to provide a hearing to the customers before they sold the goods. Marshall criticized the Court for "an attitude of callous indifference to the realities of life for the poor," and emphasized the role the government had historically played in supervising recovery of goods by people with whom they had been stored.

Florida v. Bostick, 501 U.S. 429 (1991) (dissent): The Court held that there was no seizure within the meaning of the Fourth Amendment when the police boarded an interstate bus, questioned passengers, and demanded identification. Marshall's dissent emphasized the adverse impact the ruling would have on poor people, who must use public transportation for their travel.

Florida Star v. B.J.F., 491 U.S. 524 (1989): The Court overturned a judgment that a newspaper had violated the privacy of a victim of the sexual assault by publishing her name, which it had obtained from a police report made available in the police press room. Punishing the newspaper for publishing material it had obtained in a lawful manner violated the First Amendment.

Foley v. Connelie, 435 U.S. 291 (1978) (dissent): The Court upheld a state law barring lawfully resident aliens from serving on the state police force, finding that police officers played an important part in regulating "the political community," and that eligibility for the force could therefore be limited to members of that community. Marshall argued in dissent that discrimination against aliens was presumptively unconstitutional, and that police officers did not fall within a narrow exception for those "actually setting government policy."

Ford v. Wainwright, 477 U.S. 399 (1986) (plurality opinion): Ford was sentenced to death. His lawyer claimed that by the time the execution was scheduled to occur, Ford had become insane and could not appreciate the meaning of the punishment. Relying on the Constitution and long-standing tradition, which reflected "the natural abhorrence civilized societies feel at killing one who has no capacity to come to grips with his own conscience or deity," Marshall's opinion argued that it was unconstitutional to execute the insane, and that states had to develop adequate procedures for determining whether a person was in fact insane at the time of the proposed execution.

Furman v. Georgia, 408 U.S. 238 (1972) (concurrence): The Court held the death penalty as administered in 1972 unconstitutional. Marshall's concurring opinion argued that the death penalty violated the Eighth Amendment's ban on cruel and unusual punishment in all circumstances because it was excessive, unnecessary, and offensive to contemporary values.

Gillette v. United States, 401 U.S. 437 (1971): Writing for the Court, Marshall held that Congress could exempt people who objected to *all* war from the draft while still drafting those who objected to a *particular* war. Religious gerrymanders, aimed at singling out a favored or disfavored religious view, were impermissible, but in this case the government had an interest in showing that the administration of the draft was conducted in a sufficiently fair and neutral manner.

Gooding v. United States, 416 U.S. 430 (1974) (dissent): The Court upheld a nighttime search of a home, based on traditional standards of probable cause. Believing that a nighttime search was so intrusive that more than the usual amount of cause should be required, Marshall dissented: "[T]here is no expectation of privacy more reasonable and more demanding of constitutional protection than our right that we will be let alone in the privacy of our homes during the night." The police conduct "smack[ed] of a 'police state.'"

Gregg v. Georgia, 428 U.S. 153 (1976) (dissent): The Court upheld death penalty statutes adopted after 1972 which were aimed at eliminating the arbitrary administration that led the Court to invalidate the death penalty in *Furman v. Georgia*. Marshall's dissent restated his opposition to the death penalty under all circumstances.

Grayned v. City of Rockford, 408 U.S. 104 (1972): Justice Marshall's opinion for the Court affirmed a conviction for violating a city ordinance against noise near school buildings. In this case, the ordinance was applied against people who had demonstrated to protest black underrepresentation in school activities. The opinion found that excessive noise was "basically incompatible with the normal activity" of the school. That standard had not been as clearly articulated in earlier cases.

Hodgson v. Minnesota, 450 U.S. 398 (1981) (concurrence and dissent): The Court invalidated a statute that required a minor to obtain the permission of both of her parents before obtaining an abortion, without providing as an alternative the possibility of obtaining permission for the abortion from a judge. Five justices indicated that a statute including such a judicial bypass would be constitutional, but Marshall's separate opinion said that this position would "force[] a young woman in an already dire situation to choose between two fundamentally unacceptable alternatives: notifying a possibly dictatorial or even abusive parent and justifying her profoundly personal decision in an intimidating judicial proceeding to a black-robed stranger."

Holland v. Illinois, 493 U.S. 474 (1990) (dissent): The Court held that, although *Batson v. Kentucky* (above) established that race-based peremptory challenges violated the Equal Protection Clause of the Constitution, they were not violations of the Sixth Amendment right to trial by an impartial jury. The defendant, who was white, did not claim that *his* Equal Protection rights had been violated. Marshall found a Sixth Amendment violation, because that amendment requires not only an impartial jury but one drawn from a fair cross-section of the community, and "the peremptory exclusion of Afro-American jurors on account of their race makes a truly impartial jury impossible to achieve." The dissent ended with the statement: "The elimination of racial discrimination in our system of criminal justice is not a constitutional goal that should lightly be set aside."

Hudgens v. NLRB, 424 U.S. 507 (1976): The Court formally overruled *Amalgamated Food Employees Union v. Logan Valley Plaza* (above), and Marshall dissented.

Illinois v. Perkins, 496 U.S. 292 (1990) (dissent): The Court upheld the admissions of statements given to a police undercover officer who, while posing as a fellow prisoner, elicited incriminating statements without giving the defendant the *Miranda* warnings. Marshall objected that the Court's "jailhouse informant" exception to the *Miranda* requirements diluted their clarity, and allowed the police "intentionally to take advantage of suspects unaware of their constitutional rights."

James v. Valtierra, 402 U.S. 137 (1971) (dissent): The Court held that a California proposition, which provided that no low-income housing could be built in any community unless the community approved the project in a referendum, did not violate the Equal Protection Clause. Marshall's dissent found a constitutional violation: "[S]ingling out the poor to bear a burden not placed on any other class of citizens tramples the values that the Fourteenth Amendment was designed to protect."

Jackson v. Metropolitan Edison Co., 419 U.S. 345 (1974) (dissent): The Court held that a heavily regulated public utility that terminated service to customers was not engaged in "state action," and therefore did not have to comply with the procedural requirements of the Due Process Clause. Marshall's dissent noted that, under the Court's holding, the utility could deny service on the basis of race without violating the Constitution, and argued for a broader notion of state action that would balance the utility's interest in autonomy against the importance of the service it provided and the fairness of the procedures it followed.

Kadrmas v. Dickinson Public Schools, 487 U.S. 450 (1988) (dissent): The Court upheld a state statute that required parents to pay fees for bus service used to transport their children in school districts that had not consolidated their systems. Marshall dissented, finding that the statute "places a special burden on poor families," and "places discriminatory barriers between indigents and the basic tools and opportunities that might enable them to rise," without sufficient justification under his approach to the Equal Protection Clause.

Kelley v. Johnson, 425 U.S. 238 (1976) (dissent): The Court upheld a police department's requirement that its officers leave their hair short. Citing both historical and contemporary evidence of governments using control over personal appearance to serve more repressive goals, Marshall argued that control over personal appearance was a "liberty" protected by the Fourteenth Amendment: "In taking control over a citizen's personal appearance, the government forces him to sacrifice substantial elements of his integrity and identity as well." The department's regulation of personal appearance was not, to Marshall, justified by sufficiently weighty reasons to offset its intrusion on personal liberty.

Leathers v. Medlock, 499 U.S. 439 (1991) (dissent): The Court upheld a sales tax system in which operators of cable systems were taxed but newspapers, magazines, and direct satellite broadcast services were not. Marshall's dissent objected to the discrimination: "[B]y imposing tax burdens that disadvantage one information medium relative to another, the State can favor those media that it likes and punish those that it dislikes."

Linmark Associates, Inc. v. Willingboro, 431 U.S. 85 (1977): The Court invalidated a town's effort to eliminate white flight and panic selling by banning the posting of "For Sale" and "Sold" signs. Justice Marshall's opinion for the Court said that the town was trying "to prevent its residents from obtaining . . . information . . . of vital interest" to them. The town had to demonstrate a compelling need, because it was limiting information out of concern for the effect of the information on those who saw the signs. It could not do so here, because the principle on which the ordinance rested would allow "every locality in the country . . . [to] suppress any facts that reflect poorly" on it, to avoid irrational responses by readers.

Lloyd Corp. v. Tanner, 407 U.S. 551 (1972) (dissent): The Court distinguished the *Logan Valley Plaza* decision and allowed a shopping mall to ban the distribution of leaflets protesting the war in Vietnam. Marshall's dissent emphasized the "tremendous need" the protestors had for access to the mall: "For many persons who do not have easy access to television, radio, the major newspapers, and the other forms of mass media, the only way they can express themselves to a broad range of citizens on issues of general public concern is to picket . . . in those areas in which most of their fellow citizens can be found."

Loretto v. Teleprompter Manhattan CATV, 458 U.S. 419 (1982): The Court held that the Takings Clause of the Fifth Amendment required the state to compensate apartment owners for requiring that they allow cable television companies to place small reception boxes on the roofs of their buildings. According to Marshall's opinion for the Court, a "permanent physical occupation" of private property is a taking even if the space occupied is quite small.

Massachusetts Board of Retirement v. Murgia, 427 U.S. 307 (1976) (dissent): The Court held that the Equal Protection Clause was not violated by a statute requiring state police officers to retire at age fifty. Discrimination based on age, the Court held, was not subject to "strict scrutiny" because, historically, discrimination based on age was much less severe than racial discrimination. Marshall's dissent objected to the Court's two-tier approach to equal protection law, and argued that under his own approach the discrimination, which affected an important interest in public employment and took a form that had historic roots, was unconstitutional. He pointed out, "While depriving any government employee of his job is a significant deprivation, it is particularly burdensome when the person deprived is an older citizen. Once terminated, the elderly cannot readily find alternative employment."

McCleskey v. Zant, 499 U.S. 467 (1991) (dissent): After the Supreme Court rejected his claim that the death penalty in Georgia was administered in a racially discriminatory manner, *McCleskey v. Kemp*, 481 U.S. 279 (1987), McCleskey filed a second challenge to his conviction using the writ of habeas corpus, arguing that the state had improperly used a fellow prisoner's testimony to incriminate him. The Court held that federal statutes did not allow McCleskey to bring this second challenge because it had not been raised in his first case. Marshall's dissent argued that the Court improperly narrowed the historically broad scope given to the writ of habeas corpus.

McCray v. New York, 461 U.S. 961 (1983) (dissent from denial of review): Marshall disagreed with the Court's refusal to review a criminal conviction in which the defendant argued that attorneys should not be allowed to use their power to eliminate jurors from service, if their reason for striking the juror was the juror's race. In his dissent, Marshall argued that "[t]he right to a jury drawn from a fair cross-section of the community is rendered meaningless if the State is permitted to utilize several peremptory challenges to exclude all Negroes from the jury," and urged that contrary precedent be overruled, as it eventually was in *Batson v. Kentucky* (above).

McDonald v. Santa Fe Trail Transportation Co., 427 U.S. 273 (1976): Relying on statutory language, legislative history, and administrative interpretations, Marshall's opinion for the Court held that federal statutes enacted in 1866 and 1964 to prohibit discrimination based on race prohibited discrimination against white as well as African American employees.

Memorial Hospital v. Maricopa County, 415 U.S. 250 (1974): Marshall held that Arizona's refusal to provide nonemergency medical services at public hospitals to indigents who had lived in the state for less than one year violated the constitutionally protected right to interstate travel by penalizing indigents for exercising that right. Quoting the Biblical admonition, "Ye shall have one manner of law, as well for the stranger, as for one of your own country," Marshall's opinion concluded, "the right of interstate travel must be seen as insuring new residents the same right to vital government benefits and privileges in the States to which they migrate as are enjoyed by other residents."

Mempa v. Rhay, 389 U.S. 128 (1967): In Marshall's first opinion as a justice, the Court held that criminal defendants had a right to counsel at sentencing when sentencing had been deferred during the defendant's period of probation. Describing the state's sentencing system as "an enlightened step forward," Marshall's opinion held that the sentencing was a critical stage of the criminal proceeding, at which some of the defendant's important rights might be lost without a lawyer present.

Memphis v. Greene, 451 U.S. 100 (1981) (dissent): The Court held that the city did not violate a statute enacted in 1866, which guaranteed all persons the "same rights" as enjoyed by whites, when it closed off the end of a street used by African American residents to gain access to a public park through a white residential area. Marshall's dissent argued that the city's justification, that closing the street would eliminate undesirable traffic, was "a code phrase[] for racial discrimination," and that the street closing was, in effect, the city's way of "carv[ing] out racial enclaves."

Mueller v. Allen, 463 U.S. 388 (1983) (dissent): The Court upheld a Minnesota tax statute giving tax deductions for expenses incurred in sending children to school. Although the deductions were available for expenses associated with both public and private education, by far the largest part of the deductions were claimed by parents for tuition at religiously affiliated schools. The Court found that this program was neutral as between religion and nonreligion, and did not have the effect of advancing religion. Marshall's dissent criticized the Court for failing adequately to distinguish an earlier case in which the Court had invalidated a New York system of giving tax *credit* (not deductions) for school expenses, and argued that the tax subsidy supported the religious mission of the schools that were the largest recipients of its benefits through parental decisions about schooling.

Munro v. Socialist Workers Party, 479 U.S. 189 (1986) (dissent): The Court upheld a Washington state statute allowing only those parties whose candidates had received 1% of the total votes cast in the primary elections to appear on the general election ballot. Marshall's dissent argued that this restriction on ballot access, which in effect excluded minority parties from the ballot, placed too heavy a burden on the rights of association of people in minor parties. His opinion described "the crucial role minor parties play in the American political arena" as "broaden[ing] political debate, expand[ing] the range of issues with which the electorate is concerned, and influenc[ing] the positions of the majority, in some instances ultimately becoming majority positions."

New York Times v. United States, 403 U.S. 713 (1971) (concurrence): The Court held that courts could not bar *The New York Times* from publishing the Pentagon Papers. Justice Marshall's opinion focused on the fact that no statute authorized the executive branch to seek, or the courts to enter, injunctions against publishing material that was said to threaten national security.

New York v. Quarles, 467 U.S. 649 (1984) (dissent): The Court held that the *Miranda* decision had a "public safety" exception, allowing police to question suspects without giving the *Miranda* warnings when they sought information (such as the location of a gun) that was urgently needed to protect the general public from further harm. Marshall's dissent criticized the Court for "abandon[ing] the clear guidelines" in *Miranda* and "endors[ing] the introduction of coerced self-incrimination confessions."

Oliver v. United States, 466 U.S. 170 (1984) (dissent): The Court upheld the admission of marijuana found in "open fields" around the defendant's house, finding that people have no reasonable expectation of privacy in their open fields, even if they post them with "No Trespassing" signs. Marshall's dissent said, "By exempting from the coverage of the [Fourth] Amendment large areas of private land, the Court opens the way to investigative activities we would all find repugnant," and concluded that the majority "opinion bespeaks and will help to promote an impoverished vision of that fundamental right."

Oregon v. Bradshaw, 462 U.S. 1039 (1983) (dissent): After receiving the *Miranda* warnings and requesting an attorney, the defendant asked, "What will happen to me now?" The police then engaged him in conversation, and eventually suggested that he take a lie detector test. The defendant agreed, and took the test after signing a waiver of his right to an attorney. The Court upheld the admission of his incriminating statements. Marshall dissented, saying that the defendant had not initiated the interchange and that the police should therefore have refrained from anything more than a brief reply before the defendant saw his attorney: "To allow the authorities to recommence an interrogation based on such a question is to permit them to capitalize on the custodial setting."

Pasadena Board of Education v. Spangler, 427 U.S. 424 (1976) (dissent): The Court directed the lower courts to reconsider whether the city should be required to make annual adjustments in student assignments to ensure that its schools would remain integrated. Marshall's dissent argued that directing annual reassignments was a proper exercise of the discretion lower courts had in administering desegregation plans.

Pennsylvania v. Muniz, 496 U.S. 582 (1990) (concurrence and dissent): The Court allowed the admission of a videotape showing a defendant being "booked" for drunk driving, even though the defendant had not been given his *Miranda* warnings;

although the Court also held that some of the information obtained during this process should be excluded. Marshall argued that all the answers obtained in the booking process were the result of an interrogation of a suspect in custody, and should be preceded by the *Miranda* warning to preserve the clarity of the *Miranda* rule. Marshall also maintained that, in light of the suspect's evident intoxication, the police should have known that asking any questions was likely to elicit incriminating responses.

Pickering v. Board of Education, 391 U.S. 563 (1968): The Court held that a public school teacher could not be fired for writing a letter to a newspaper criticizing the school board's funding policies. Although the government did have special interests as an employer, "[t]he problem in any case is to arrive at a balance between the interests of the teacher, as a citizen, in commenting upon matters of public concern and the interest of the State, as an employer, in promoting the efficiency of the public services it performs through its employees." In this case, Marshall wrote, the balance favored the employee's speech rights, in part because the letter was not shown to have impeded the teacher's daily work or interfered with the schools' operations.

Procunier v. Martinez, 416 U.S. 396 (1974) (concurrence): While agreeing with the Court's decision that California's practice of censoring mail sent to and by prisoners violated the outside correspondents' rights under the First Amendment, Marshall would have gone further and explicitly recognized that the prisoners themselves had First Amendment rights. This recognition would have meant that prison authorities lacked the power to "read inmate mail as a matter of course": "A prisoner's free and open expression will surely be restrained by the knowledge that his every word may be read by his jailors and that his message could well find its way into a disciplinary file, be the object of ridicule, or even lead to reprisals."

Rankin v. McPherson, 483 U.S. 378 (1987): The Court held that a clerical worker in a public office could not be fired for remarking, after hearing of the attempted assassination of President Reagan in 1981, "If they go for him again, I hope they get him." Justice Marshall's opinion described the remark as speech on a matter of public concern, and found that the State had not shown that the interest in effective government operations outweighed the clerk's interest in speech.

Rhode Island v. Innis, 446 U.S. 291 (1980) (dissent): The Court allowed the introduction of an statement made by a suspect in custody after the suspect invoked his right to counsel, when the police had commented in his presence that handicapped children in the area were in danger if they found the weapon used in the crime. This, the Court said, was not an impermissible "interrogation" of the suspect. Marshall's dissent agreed with the Court's test for determining whether an interrogation had occurred, but concluded that, on the facts of the case, one clearly had:

"One can scarcely imagine a stronger appeal to the conscience of a suspect—*any* suspect—than the assertion that if the weapon is not found an innocent person will be hurt or killed. And not just any innocent person, but an innocent child—a little girl—a helpless, handicapped little girl on her way to school."

Rhodes v. Chapman, 452 U.S. 337 (1981) (dissent): The Court held that the Eighth Amendment's ban on cruel and usual punishment was not violated by placing two prison inmates in a cell initially designed to hold only one. Marshall, in dissent, thought that the Constitution was violated by "imprisonment in conditions so crowded that serious harm will result," and that the evidence in this case established that such harm did in fact result from overcrowding.

Schneckloth v. Bustamonte, 412 U.S. 218 (1973) (dissent): The Court held that evidence could be introduced at trial when obtained in a search conducted with the defendant's consent, even though the prosecution did not show that the defendant knew that he had the right to refuse consent. Marshall's dissent emphasized the importance of knowledge as a basis for consent, and argued that the evidence should have been excluded unless the prosecution established that the defendant knew of his rights, and noted the possibility that police could inform suspects of their rights before they asked for consent to search.

Skinner v. Railway Labor Executives Association, 489 U.S. 602 (1989) (dissent): Marshall objected to the Court's decision allowing routine drug-testing of railroad employees, asserting that the decision resulted more from the Court's preoccupation with the war on drugs than with a principled interpretation of the Constitution, and that the drug tests were an unjustifiable intrusion on employees' privacy unless there was some reason to think that a particular employee had used drugs.

Smith v. Maryland, 442 U.S. 735 (1979) (dissent): The Court held that the police could install a "pen register" that indicated the telephone numbers called from a phone, without having probable cause or obtaining a warrant. Marshall's dissent objected to the majority's observation that people should know that the telephone company records these numbers. "Privacy is not a discrete commodity, possessed absolutely or not at all. Those who disclose certain facts to a bank or phone company for a limited business purpose need not assume that this information will be released to other persons for other purposes." Pen registers, he wrote, are "extensive intrusions."

Steagald v. United States, 451 U.S. 204 (1981): Writing for the Court, Marshall relied on historical evidence and the different interests protected by search and arrest warrants to conclude that police with an arrest warrant who did not find the suspect at home could not search the house. Any other rule, he wrote, "would create a significant potential for abuse. Armed solely with an arrest warrant for a single person, the police could search all the homes of that individual's friends and acquaintances."

Strickland v. Washington, 466 U.S. 668 (1984) (dissent): The Court upheld a death penalty over the objection that the defendant's attorney had provided ineffective assistance of counsel. The constitutional standard, according to the Court, was whether the lawyer had acted unreasonably, in a way that prejudiced the defendant's case. Marshall thought that the Court's standard was too "malleable," and proposed that the courts develop guidelines identifying the minimal requirements of competent performance. Marshall also expressed concern that the Court's standard in effect allowed discrimination against defendants unable to afford to hire their own lawyers.

Tashjian v. Republican Party of Connecticut, 479 U.S. 208 (1986): Writing for the Court, Marshall held that a state statute barring a political party from allowing nonmembers to vote in the party's primary violated the party's rights under the First Amendment "to enter into political association with individuals of its own choosing," seeing the party's effort as an "attempt to broaden the base of public participation in and support for its activities."

Tollett v. Henderson, 411 U.S. 258 (1973) (dissent): The Court held that the writ of habeas corpus was not available to a person who had pleaded guilty and not raised a challenge to the absence of African Americans on the grand jury that indicted him, even though the petitioner claimed that he and his attorney did not know of the relevant facts at the time of the plea. Marshall's dissent argued that the plea was not voluntary and the attorney's actions inadequate. The Court's approach "would let an attorney 'advance' the interests of his client without even informing himself about the facts underlying a constitutional challenge so that he might inform the client about the way in which, in the attorney's professional judgment, the course he is taking in fact advances those interests. 'Faithful representation of the interest of his client' means, I believe, that an attorney must consult with the client fully on matters of constitutional magnitude. Without such consultation, the representation of criminal defendants becomes only another method of manipulating persons in situations where their control over their lives is precisely what is at stake."

United States v. Bagley, 473 U.S. 667 (1985) (dissent): The Court found no constitutional error in the prosecution's failure to turn over evidence to the defense that would have cast doubt on the credibility of its chief witnesses, because the evidence was unlikely to change the trial's outcome. Marshall, dissenting, focused on the facts of the case, including the fact that the witnesses in question were the only ones implicating the defendant directly. He wrote that the prosecution should "disclose information in its possession that might reasonably be considered favorable to the defense," because of "the frequently considerable imbalance in resources between most criminal defendants and most prosecutors' offices."

United States v. Payner, 447 U.S. 727 (1980) (dissent): The Court upheld the admission of evidence obtained by Internal Revenue Service agents who illegally searched the briefcase of a third party, a bank officer. Marshall would have invoked the general powers of federal courts "to protect the integrity of the judicial system from such gross Government misconduct."

United States v. Robinson, 414 U.S. 218 (1973) (dissent): The Court upheld the admission of evidence seized during a full body search of a suspect who had been arrested for driving without a license, rejecting the argument that the officer could do no more than frisk the suspect to protect the officer from danger and holding that the police could always conduct a full search incident to a lawful arrest without regard to any other circumstances. Marshall criticized the Court for its "clear and marked departure from our long tradition of case-by-case adjudication of the reasonableness of searches and seizures under the Fourth Amendment."

United States v. Ross, 456 U.S. 798 (1982) (dissent): Overruling earlier decisions, the Court held that if the police had probable cause to search a lawfully stopped car, they could search anything in the car (such as a paper bag) without obtaining a warrant, even though their information was only that narcotics were in the car's trunk. Marshall's dissent described the Court as "repeal[ing] all realistic limits on automobile searches," and as disregarding the importance of an assessment of probable cause by a neutral magistrate rather than by police officers.

United States v. Salerno, 481 U.S. 739 (1987) (dissent): The Court upheld the constitutionality of a federal statute permitting the detention of indicted defendants before trial, without a showing that they might not show up for their trials. For Marshall's explanation of his dissent, see selection 25.

United States v. Sokolow, 490 U.S. 1 (1989) (dissent): The Court upheld a conviction based on evidence found during a "stop" that occurred without probable cause. Marshall's dissent criticized the Court for allowing the police to stop people based on "profiles," the practice of which led police officers to overlook the particular facts associated with each individual case. The "drug courier profile" was, in Marshall's view, a "dubious" indicator of criminal activity.

United States v. Watson, 423 U.S. 411 (1976) (dissent): Marshall dissented from the Court's opinion, which held that the police could make an arrest in a public place without a warrant if they had probable cause to believe that the defendant had committed a felony. He objected to the "broad powers" the Court's decision gave police, and would have held that the police must obtain an arrest warrant unless they lacked the time to do so.

Village of Belle Terre v. Boraas, 416 U.S. 1 (1974) (dissent): The Court upheld a town's zoning ordinance that allowed only traditional families, or two unrelated people, to live in the same house. Marshall's dissent argued that the ordinance violated the right of unrelated people to associate with each other and their right to privacy, and that it was not justified by the strong reasons of public policy needed to overcome infringements on fundamental rights.

Wardius v. Oregon, 412 U.S. 470 (1973): Marshall's opinion for the Court invalidated a statute that barred a defendant from introducing an alibi witness unless he had given the prosecution prior notice that the witness would be called. The Due Process Clause meant that defendants could be required to give a notice of an alibi defense only if they received some reciprocal discovery from the prosecution: "The State may not insist that trials be run as a 'search for truth' so far as defense witnesses are concerned, while maintaining 'poker game' secrecy for its own witnesses."

Witters v. Washington Dept. of Services for the Blind, 474 U.S. 481 (1988): Marshall wrote for the Court upholding the use by a blind student of public grants to the disabled for education, where the student, preparing for a career as a pastor, used the aid to pay his tuition at a private Christian college. Writing a narrow opinion, Marshall found a secular purpose in aiding the career preparation of the handicapped, emphasized that the case did not involve a direct government grant to a religiously affiliated college, and noted that only a small portion of the overall state budget for the handicapped flowed to religiously affiliated institutions.

Wygant v. Jackson Board of Education, 476 U.S. 267 (1986) (dissent): The Court found unconstitutional an affirmative action plan that allowed the school board to discharge more-senior white employees before less-senior African American ones when staff cuts had to be made for fiscal reasons. Although agreeing that "layoffs are unfair," Marshall's dissent argued that the school board's purpose of "preserving the integrity of a hiring policy . . . which . . . sought to achieve diversity and stability for the benefit of *all* students" was constitutional, and that the layoff provision was a permissible means of achieving this purpose because it "allocated the impact of an unavoidable burden proportionately between two racial groups," and was arrived at through the process of collective bargaining."

Wyman v. James, 400 U.S. 309 (1971) (dissent): The Court held that "home visits" by social workers to the apartments of public assistance recipients were authorized by federal statutes and were not "searches" within the meaning of the Fourth

Amendment. These visits, therefore, could be conducted without probable cause or a warrant. For Marshall, in dissent, "the welfare visit is not some sort of purely benevolent inspection. No one questions the motives of the dedicated welfare caseworker. Of course, caseworkers seek to be friends, but the point is that they are also required to be sleuths." To the concern that the visits were aimed at finding out whether children in the home were being abused, Marshall pointed out that abuse was "not confined to indigent households," and asked, "[I]s this Court prepared to hold as a matter of constitutional law that a mother, merely because she is poor, is substantially more likely to injure or exploit her children? Such a categorical approach to an entire class of citizens would be dangerously at odds with the tenets of our democracy."

Zablocki v. Redhail, 434 U.S. 374 (1978): The Court, in an opinion by Marshall, held unconstitutional a state statute barring a person under a court order to support children from marrying again without the court's permission. The statute interfered with the fundamental right to marry, without strong enough justification.

Permissions Acknowledgments

"Equal Justice Under Law." The editor wishes to thank The Crisis Publishing Co., Inc., the publisher of the magazine of the National Association for the Advancement of Colored People, for authorizing the use of this work.

"Negro Discrimination and the Need for Federal Action." Reprinted with the permission of the *Guild Practitioner.*

"The Gestapo in Detroit." The editor wishes to thank The Crisis Publishing Co., Inc., the publisher of the magazine of the National Association for the Advancement of Colored People, for authorizing the use of this work.

"The Legal Attack to Secure Civil Rights." Reprinted with the permission of Mrs. Thurgood Marshall.

"Mr. Justice Murphy and Civil Rights." Reprinted with the permission of the *Michigan Law Review.*

"The Supreme Court as Protector of Civil Rights: Equal Protection of the Laws." Reprinted with the permission of the *Annals,* American Academy of Political and Social Sciences.

"Summary Justice—The Negro GI in Korea." The editor wishes to thank The Crisis Publishing Co., Inc., the publisher of the magazine of the National Association for the Advancement of Colored People, for authorizing the use of this work.

Remarks at a Testimonial Dinner Honoring Raymond Pace Alexander, November 25, 1951. Reprinted with the permission of Mrs. Thurgood Marshall.

"An Evaluation of Recent Efforts to Achieve Racial Integration in Education Through Resort to the Courts." *Journal of Negro Education*, Vol. 21, No. 3 (1952). Copyright © 1952 Howard University. Reprinted with permission.

"The Meaning and Significance of the Supreme Court Decree." *Journal of Negro Education*, Vol. 24, No. 3 (1955). Copyright © 1955 Howard University. Reprinted with permission.

"The Rise and Collapse of the 'White Democratic Primary.'" *Journal of Negro Education*, Vol. 26, No. 2 (1957). Copyright © 1957 Howard University. Reprinted with permission.

"Celebrating the Second Circuit Centennial." Reprinted with the permission of the *St. John's University Law Review.*

"Law and the Quest for Equality." Reprinted with the permission of the *Washington University Law Quarterly.*

"Group Action in Pursuit of Justice." 44 N.Y.U. L. Rev. 661 (1969). Reprinted with the permission of the *New York University Law Review.*

Remarks of the Honorable Thurgood Marshall upon the occasion of his acceptance of Honorary Membership in the Association of the Bar (November 20, 1973). Reprinted with the permission of the Record of the Association of the Bar of the City of New York.

"Advancing Public Interest Law Practice: The Role of the Organized Bar." Reprinted by permission of the *ABA Journal*.

Tribute to Charles H. Houston. Reprinted with permission of *Amherst* magazine.

"Reflections on the Bicentennial of the United States Constitution." Copyright © 1987 by the Harvard Law Review Association. Reprinted by permission.

"Remarks on the Death Penalty Made at the Judicial Conference of the Second Circuit." This article originally appeared at 86 *Columbia Law Review* 1 (1986). Reprinted by permission.

"A Tribute to Justice William J. Brennan, Jr." Copyright © 1990 by the Harvard Law Review Association. Reprinted by permission.

"The Reminiscences of Thurgood Marshall." Reprinted with permission from the Oral History Collection of Columbia University.

Index

The Library of Black America publishes authoritative editions of important African American writing, much of it otherwise unavailable, ranging from the earliest slave narratives to the present day. Each volume includes a selection of works either by a single author or in a single genre and is introduced by an important black writer. The series makes accessible to all readers the impressive body of inventive, lucid, thoughtful, and passionate work that is the black contribution to American literature.

ALSO AVAILABLE:

I WAS BORN A SLAVE
An Anthology of Classic Slave Narratives
Edited by Yuval Taylor
Foreword by Charles Johnson

cloth, vol. I: 1-55652-334-3; vol. II: 1-55652-335-1
paper, vol. I: 1-55652-331-9; vol. II: 1-55652-332-7

FREDERICK DOUGLASS
Selected Speeches and Writings
Edited by Philip S. Foner

cloth: 1-55652-349-1
paper: 1-55652-352-1

THE FICTION OF LEROI JONES/ AMIRI BARAKA
Foreword by Greg Tate

cloth: 1-55652-346-7
paper: 1-55652-353-X